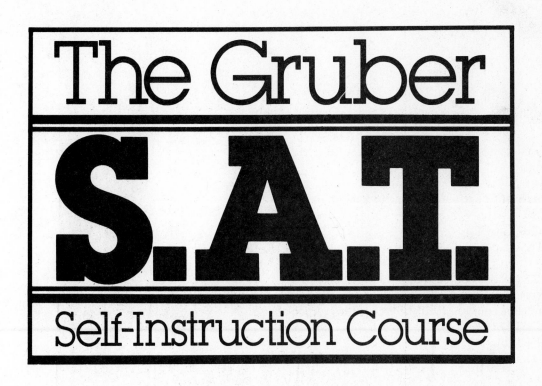

The Gruber
S.A.T.
Self-Instruction Course

Gary R. Gruber, Ph.D.

Addison-Wesley Publishing Company
Reading, Massachusetts • Menlo Park, California
Don Mills, Ontario • Wokingham, England • Amsterdam
Sydney • Singapore • Toyko • Mexico City • Bogotá
Santiago • San Juan

Library of Congress Cataloging in Publication Data

Gruber, Gary R.
  The Gruber S.A.T. self-instruction course.

  1. Scholastic aptitude test—Study guides.
I. Title.   II. Title: Gruber SAT self-instruction course.   III. Title: S.A.T. self-instruction course.   IV. Title: SAT self-instruction course.
LB2353.57.G78   1984   378′.1664   83-25777
ISBN 0-201-10865-8

Cover design by Marshall Henrichs

CDEFGHIJ-MU-865

Third Printing, January 1985

IMPORTANT NOTE TO STUDENTS AND PARENTS

The scored questions on your SAT measure your ability to critically analyze verbal and math problems, in the shortest time possible. After 20 years of research and field-testing with up-to-the minute analysis, Dr. Gary R. Gruber, the nation's leading exam prep specialist, has developed *The Gruber SAT Self-Instruction Course*.

The book is carefully constructed. If used properly, your SAT verbal and math scores can increase by 300 points, as they have for many students who have used this book. See page 11 for instructions on how to use this preparation program properly. For the most complete SAT preparation use the 15-Day Self-Instruction Course, beginning on page vii.

Everything that you need for high performance on the SAT has been included:

1. You have four complete practice SAT tests with explanatory answers. No other book has questions as close to the actual questions appearing on the current SAT.
2. You have a complete description of all the subtests of the SAT, and clear methods and strategies to use for each of the question types.
3. There is a section on developing your vocabulary skills.
4. There are seven diagnostic math tests and a complete math refresher section.
5. We also have a mini-math refresher section for those who wish to get just a "bird's eye" view of what you need to know in math for the SAT.
6. Besides a wealth of additional SAT practice questions the book contains a unique Special Math Techniques and Shortcuts section. When these shortcuts and strategies are adopted by the student it is found that he or she can answer many of the SAT questions 12 times faster!

In summation, what Dr. Gruber's SAT book does is place the student in a position where he or she sees exactly what is being tested for in each question. This enables the student to answer the question in the shortest time and with the greatest accuracy. We have also found that by using this book the student develops confidence in the test-taking experience and, in the long run, is able to develop his or her critical thinking ability. What Dr. Gruber presents is a well organized way of approaching problems and situations appearing on all tests.

Addison-Wesley Publishing Company

CONTENTS

Important Note to Students and Parents *iii*
The Gruber SAT Self-Instruction Course: The Course in a Book *vi*

Preface *1*

Structure of the SAT *3*

Typical Format of a Current SAT *3*

Getting Ready for College *5*
  What Kind of College Do You Want? 5
  How Do You Apply for Admission? 7
  What If You Need Financial Aid? 7
  What About Admissions Tests? 8

The Admissions Tests *8*
  The SAT 9
  Test Administration 9
  Taking the SAT 10

Condensed Version: A 15-Day Self-Instruction Course *11*

Part I 4 SCHOLASTIC APTITUDE TESTS CLOSELY PATTERNED AFTER THE ACTUAL SAT 13

SAT Practice Test 1 *14*
  Section 1: Mathematics Questions 15
  Section 2: Verbal Questions 22
  Section 3: Standard Written English Test 31
  Section 4: Verbal Questions 32
  Section 5: Mathematics Questions 41
  Section 6: Verbal Questions 50
  Answer Key for Practice Test 1 60
  Explanatory Answers for Practice Test 1 62
  How to Improve Your SAT Score 85
  Raw Score–Scaled Score Conversion Table 85
    Practice Test 1 86
    Practice Test 2 88
    Practice Test 3 90
    Practice Test 4 92

Self-Appraisal Table 94
  Practice Test 1 94
  Practice Test 2 94
  Practice Test 3 95
  Practice Test 4 95

SAT Practice Test 2 *96*
  Section 1: Verbal Questions 97
  Section 2: Mathematics Questions 107
  Section 3: Mathematics Questions 114
  Section 4: Standard Written English Test 123
  Section 5: Verbal Questions 124
  Section 6: Mathematics Questions 132
  Answer Key for Practice Test 2 139
  Explanatory Answers for Practice Test 2 140

SAT Practice Test 3 *163*
  Section 1: Mathematics Questions 164
  Section 2: Verbal Questions 171
  Section 3: Mathematics Questions 181
  Section 4: Verbal Questions 191
  Section 5: Mathematics Questions 199
  Section 6: Standard Written English Test 207
  Answer Key for Practice Test 3 208
  Explanatory Answers for Practice Test 3 209

SAT Practice Test 4 *233*
  Section 1: Verbal Questions 234
  Section 2: Mathematics Questions 242
  Section 3: Verbal Questions 248
  Section 4: Standard Written English Test 256
  Section 5: Mathematics Questions 257
  Section 6: Verbal Questions 267
  Answer Key for Practice Test 4 277
  Explanatory Answers for Practice Test 4 279

Part II ABOUT THE SUBTESTS OF THE SAT 299

About Antonym Tests *300*

About Analogy Tests *301*
  Typical Kinds of Analogies on the SAT 301

About Reading Comprehension Tests *306*

About Sentence Completion Tests *310*

About the Regular Mathematics Tests *315*

About Quantitative Comparison Tests *316*

Part III VERBAL ABILITY 319

Developing Your Vocabulary *320*

Common Prefixes *320*

Common Suffixes *323*

Common Roots *324*

Vocabulary Review List *331*

Part IV DIAGNOSTIC MATH TESTS 359

Diagnostic Test 1: Fraction, Decimal, Percentage, Deviation, Ratio, and Proportion Problems *360*

Diagnostic Test 2: Rate Problems: Distance and Time, Work, Mixture, and Cost *366*

Diagnostic Test 3: Area, Perimeter, and Volume Problems *375*

Diagnostic Test 4: Algebra Problems *380*

Diagnostic Test 5: Geometry Problems *385*

Diagnostic Test 6: Miscellaneous Problems *391*

Diagnostic Test 7: Graph (or Chart) and Table Problems *395*

Part V MATHEMATICAL ABILITY (MATH REFRESHER) 403

1. Arithmetic *404*
   Fractions 404
   Decimal Fractions 414
   Percentage 420
   Graphs 427
   Properties of Numbers 434
   Signed Numbers 441

2. Algebra *447*
   Algebraic Equations 447
   Evaluation of Algebraic Expressions and Formulas 451
   Solving for Two Unknowns 454
   Verbal Problems 456
   Monomials and Polynomials 469
   Factoring 475
   Solving Quadratic Equations 447
   Inequalities 481

3. Geometry *484*
   Angles 484
   Triangles 490
   Plane and Solid Figures 495

4. Additional Topics and Review Aids *505*
   Coordinate Geometry 505
   Trigonometry 508
   Binary System 511
   Logarithms 511
   Weights and Measures 511
   Table of Equivalents 512
   The Metric System 513

Part VI SPECIAL MATH TECHNIQUES AND SHORTCUTS 515

The Minimum Sets of Math Rules and Concepts with Which You Must Be Familiar *516*
  Algebra and Arithmetic 516
  Geometry 519

What the SAT Is Testing in Math and How to Be One Step Ahead *522*

Mathematical Shortcuts You Should Know *537*
  Adding Fractions 537
  Subtracting Fractions 538
  Comparing Fractions 539

Shortcuts and Techniques for Answering the Quantitative Comparison Type Question *540*
Key Method for Solving Quantitative Comparison Type Questions *541*
General Method Which Works for Many Algebraic Quantitative Comparison Questions *553*

Part VII 80 ADDITIONAL QUANTITATIVE COMPARISON PRACTICE QUESTIONS 557

80 Quantitative Comparison Questions *558*
Explanatory Answers *573*

THE GRUBER SAT SELF-INSTRUCTION COURSE: THE COURSE IN A BOOK

From the Author:

The Gruber SAT Self-Instruction Course has been carefully planned to facilitate your use of this book to prepare for the Scholastic Aptitude Test. It has been developed and tested with thousands of SAT candidates. We continue to have excellent results.

If you take this course as presented, begin your preparation at least three weeks before the test. Before beginning make sure that you obtain the booklet *Student Bulletin* from your college counselor or from the College Board. This bulletin officially describes everything you need to know to register for and take the SAT.

As outlined, the course requires 15 days to complete, although some students shorten this by doing more than a day's work at a time. This is fine. For some students who want to spend less time or who feel their skills and knowledge in some areas are fairly strong, a more condensed version of this course may be desirable. For this reason a shortened course schedule has been provided. It appears in this book on page 11.

If you take *The Gruber SAT Self-Instruction Course* as outlined here, we feel that you will be quite satisfied with the results you achieve on the actual SAT.

Gary R. Gruber, Ph.D.

A 15-DAY SELF-INSTRUCTION COURSE

Before beginning your preparation for the SAT, read through the entire 15-day course outline. This will give you an idea of the work required for each day and how much time you should allot for each day's work. If you diligently follow the outline given here, you will get excellent results. It is suggested that as you read and complete each part you should check off that section in the box provided.

DAY 1: GENERAL TEST-TAKING STRATEGIES
Suggested Time: 60 minutes

What Does the SAT Measure? The SAT measures your ability to think logically and critically, especially when dealing with new and original situations. These abilities are tested through the Math and Verbal areas.

What Does the SAT Contain? Read through the *Structure of the SAT* at the top of page 3. Then get an idea of a typical SAT by reading through the *Typical Format of the Current SAT,* on pages 3–4. On all SATs only *four sections* count toward your actual SAT score. They are *two math sections* and *two verbal sections.* The SWET (Standard Written English Test) section is only used for placement in your college English class and does not count toward your SAT score. Section 2 of the SAT shown is also experimental. It may be made up of verbal questions *or* math questions; it does not count toward your score.

How Do I Approach the SAT? Preparation is vital, and it is two-fold. You must, of course, approach the SAT knowing what to expect, knowing that your skills and knowledge have been well sharpened, and knowing what it will be like to take a standardized test such as the SAT.

The second part of preparation has to do with the attitude with which you approach the test. A certain amount of nervousness and anxiety is expected. More important, however, is developing a positive offensive to tackle the test itself. Research shows that if you get involved and become interested in what is being tested, asked, or discussed on the SAT, and if you look at the test objectively and unemotionally, you will do well. This is the *offensive* approach. You will, of course, develop that offensive approach and positive attitude as you work through this preparation course.

How Should I Time Myself on the SAT? Each section of the SAT is timed exactly 30 minutes. Suppose now that there are 60 questions in Section 1 of the test. The average time that you should spend on each question in Section 1 then would be ½ minute. Now, suppose that you are attempting a question in Section 1 and 20 seconds have already gone by and you still do not know how to answer the question. It would be better to go on to the next question. In other words, figure out approximately what amount of time you should devote to each question in a section and time yourself accordingly. Make sure that if you have a reading passage that you allot yourself time for reading the passage. The practice tests in this book will give you a good idea about how fast you have to work.

What Do I Do If I Get a Difficult Question? If you see what you believe is a difficult or tedious question and you think that you will spend a lot of time answering it, you should go right to the next question. You can go back to that difficult question after you have answered all the easier ones. Make sure that you mark your answer sheet to show that you skipped the question or questions.

When Should I Guess? This is one of the key questions that is asked. You should realize that on the SAT there is a penalty of one-quarter point for every answer you get wrong or guess wrong. This is the case for 5-choice questions. For 4-choice questions, as in the quantitative comparison type, there is a one-third point penalty. Certainly, if you can eliminate an incorrect choice, by all means GUESS! Now there are two main reasons for guessing even though you may not be able to eliminate an incorrect choice. The reasons are:

1. By putting an answer on your answer sheet, you do not run the risk of leaving a blank for an answer, and then marking the blank with an answer to a different question.
2. You have at least some chance of getting the right answer.

There is one disadvantage to guessing blindly.

You may get penalized for an incorrect guess.

Research indicates that it is usually wiser for you to guess if you cannot figure out the answer.

How Much Time Should I Spend Reading the Directions on the Actual SAT? You should spend very little time looking through the directions for the question type or doing the sample problems on the *actual* SAT. *In this course, you should familiarize yourself with the directions for each part of the exam.* The directions on your actual SAT will be exactly the same as those which you will have already encountered in this book. For example, the College Board is not going to pull a fast one like giving you questions on synonyms rather than the usual antonyms questions. You can always check to see that the directions for the question types are the same by reading through your SAT Bulletin of Information written by the College Board. The College Board is certainly going to be fair enough to use the same format on the actual test as they describe in their own bulletin.

DAY 2: MATH DIAGNOSTIC TESTS 1, 2, 3
(If you prefer to do the Verbal Sections first, go directly to Day 8)
Suggested Time: 2 hours–3 hours 45 minutes, depending on abilities

The math questions on the SAT test your background in algebra and geometry and test your ability to use the rules and concepts to solve problems dealing with standard or new situations.

Turn to page 315. Read pages 315–316, *About the Regular Mathematics Tests* and *About Quantitative Comparison Tests*. This will give you an idea of the two types of math questions on the SAT. Pay attention to the *Do's and Don'ts* for answering the two kinds of math questions. Make a handy pocket card to study the numerical information you are asked to memorize (page 315).

☐ **15 minutes**

Turn to page 359. Take each of the first three (3) diagnostic tests one after the other. These are on pages 360–377. Go over all the explanatory answers at the end of each diagnostic test. Note that all explanatory answers end with a number in parentheses, e.g., (4.21). The number refers to a specific section in *Part V, Mathematical Ability (Math Refresher)*, starting on page 403. The rules and principles involved in the question are explained there. Referring to this *Math Refresher* section is very important for strengthening any weaknesses in specific math areas. Make sure that if you got a diagnostic question wrong, or did not know or understand how to solve the problem, that you go over the explanatory answer and refer to the *Math Refesher* section keyed to that problem.

☐ **1¾– 3½ hours**

DAY 3: MATH DIAGNOSTIC TESTS 4, 5, 6, 7
Suggested Time: 2 hours 15 minutes–7 hours, depending on abilities. You may want to carry this over to another day.

Turn to page 380. Take the next four (4) diagnostic tests (4–7). These are on pages 380–398. Go over all the explanatory answers at the end of each diagnostic test. As before, refer to the *Math Refresher* section (Part V), which is keyed to each explanatory answer, for those questions you got wrong or did not know how to answer.

☐ **2¼–5 hours**

0–2 hours ☐

Turn to page 400. Follow the *Steps to Take After You Have Completed the Diagnostic Math Tests.* You are again urged in this section to make good use of the *Math Refresher.* This is easy to do after you have pinpointed your weaknesses.

DAY 4: Six Essential SAT Abilities: What the SAT Is Testing in Math and How to Be One Step Ahead
Suggested Time: 2 hours 15 minutes–3 hours 45 minutes, depending on abilities

Turn to page 516: *The Minimum Sets of Math Rules and Concepts with Which You Must Be Familiar.* Make sure that you understand and know how to use all the rules and concepts on pages 516–522. If there is any rule or concept that you are unfamiliar with or are unsure of, refer to the section in the *Math Refresher* denoted by the number in parentheses e.g., (2.52). This section, beginning on page 403, will describe the rule or concept in more detail.

30–60 minutes ☐

It is a good idea to make a set of flash cards as a way to review and memorize the math concepts shown on pages 516–522. Review them often.

5 minutes ☐

Turn to page 522: *What the SAT Is Testing in Math and How to Be One Step Ahead.* Read through each of the six abilities; they are constantly tested in the SAT math sections.

90–100 minutes ☐

Go on to page 523. Each of the six abilities is fully explained. Example problems with detailed solutions and correct answers are given for you to study. Go through each ability. First read the ability. Then look at the first example shown without looking at the answer. Do you understand the question? Now look at the answer. Would you have answered the question this way? Bear in mind that there are sometimes many ways to answer a question. The way described in these answers has been shown to be the most helpful in building your ability to use special techniques to solve SAT problems. Once you understand how to answer the first example, go on to Examples 2 and 3. Make sure you first understand the problem. Work the solution without looking. Then carefully read through the solution to learn the technique recommended for the most efficient use of your time. See if you solved the problem in the same way given in the explanatory answer. Give yourself 3 minutes to work through each example. Do all three examples of each of the six abilities listed.

0–60 minutes ☐

IMPORTANT NOTES: (1) Whenever you do not understand a concept, rule, or approach, review it in the Math Refresher (page 403). (2) Review your flash cards often.

DAY 5: Beginning Math Practice
SAT Practice Test 1: Sections 1 and 5: Mathematics Questions
Suggested Time: 2 hours

Turn to page 15: *Section 1: Mathematics Questions.* Read the directions; then do problems 1–25. Give yourself 45 minutes to ensure that you work every problem. Later you will cut your time so that you use the test time listed in the book. Check your answers using the answer key on page 60. Then carefully review the explanatory answers beginning on page 62. Try to relate the approach you used to solve the problems to the approaches described in the section *What the SAT Is Testing in Math,* pages 522–537.

□ 80 minutes

Turn to page 41: *Section 5: Mathematics Questions.* Read the directions; then do problems 1–15. Give yourself only 20 minutes. (You are only doing the first 15 problems.) Check your answers using the answer key on page 61. Then carefully review the explanatory answers beginning on page 75. Again, try to relate the approach you used to solve the problems to the approaches described in the section *What the SAT Is Testing in Math,* pages 522–537.

□ 40 minutes

DAY 6: Time Saving Shortcuts, Techniques, and Strategies
Suggested Time: 2 hours 30 minutes

Turn to page 537: *Mathematical Shortcuts You Should Know.* Read pages 537–538. Make sure that you understand these shortcuts.

□ 13 minutes

Go on to page 538. Make sure that you understand the shortcuts on this page. Did you know that you can compare fractions this way?

□ 12 minutes

Go on to page 540: *Shortcuts and Techniques for Answering the Quantitative Comparison Type Question.* Read this material. Make sure that you understand the directions for the quantitative comparison question. Read pages 541–543. Make sure you understand these pages.

□ 25 minutes

Go to page 544. Read through each of the 8 examples on pages 544–547. Study the methods of solutions for each of these examples. Pay particular attention to the techniques, shortcuts, and strategies used in the solution of each problem. If in any of the solutions, you have discovered what you believe is an approach that you feel more comfortable with, that is fine. But it would be a good idea to be aware of my approach also.

□ 60 minutes

30 minutes ☐

Turn to page 548. Do the 8 problems. Time yourself 6 minutes. Carefully read the explanatory answers for the examples that you have just done. Try to see a relation between the examples you have just done and the eight examples on pages 544–547.

10 minutes ☐

Turn to page 553. Read the *General Method Which Works for Many Algebraic Quantitative Comparison Problems*. Make sure that you understand how to use the method in the given example.

DAY 7:   Practicing Quantitative Comparison Problems
Suggested Time: 1 hour 30 minutes

25 minutes ☐

Turn to page 46. Read the directions given. Do problems 16–35. Give yourself 12 minutes. The answers appear on page 61 (Section 5). Carefully go over the explanatory answers on page 77 and make sure that you understand the method used for each example. This is a good idea even if you got most of the questions right. Try to relate the approach you used to solve the problems to the approaches described in the section *Shortcuts and Techniques for Answering the Quantitative Comparison Type Questions*, pages 540–547.

Turn to page 557: *80 Quantitative Comparison Questions.*
Do questions 1–15. Give yourself 12 minutes.
Do questions 16–30. Give yourself 10 minutes.
Do questions 31–45. Give yourself 9 minutes.

60 minutes ☐

Study the explanatory answers that begin on page 573. Make sure you understand each problem. Try to relate the approach you used to solve the problems to the approaches described in the section *Shortcuts and Techniques for Answering the Quantitative Comparison Type Questions*, pages 540–547.

DAY 8:   SAT Verbal Sections: Antonyms, Prefixes, Suffixes, and Common Roots
Suggested Time: 2 hours 15 minutes

The Verbal sections of the SAT contain questions on vocabulary, sentence completions, analogies, and reading comprehension.

5 minutes ☐

Turn to page 300: *About Antonym Tests.* Read *Study the Following Sample.* Here you will get an idea of a typical antonym question on the SAT. On any antonym question on the SAT, if you are not familiar with the word in the question (not the choices), guess and go right to the next question. Do not spend any time trying to "psych out" the test maker.

Many times, if you know the *prefix, suffix,* or *root* of the word, you can correctly guess its meaning. For example, the word "precursory" means preliminary or introductory. The *prefix* of precursory is "pre" and on page 322 we see that *pre* means *before*. So we may assume that precursory means something that goes before something else.

Turn to page 320: *Developing Your Vocabulary*. Make sure that you *learn* the Common Prefixes (pages 320–322). You may want to learn these gradually, like 20 per day. Again, it is a good idea to make a set of flash cards to review whenever possible.

☐ 30 minutes

Turn to page 323. Make sure that you *learn* these Common Suffixes (pages 323–324). Make flash cards. Study them briefly several times each day.

☐ 20 minutes

Turn to page 324. Make sure that you *learn* these Common Roots. You may want to learn these gradually. Learn 25 per day. Make flash cards and study them several times each day.

☐ 60 minutes

Turn to page 331. Here is a vocabulary list of words which frequently appear on the SAT. You may want to learn 50 of these words per day. This is optional.

☐ OPTIONAL

Turn to page 22: *Section 2: Verbal Questions*. Do questions 1–10. How many of the ten antonym questions can you answer correctly? (Answers are on page 60. Explanatory answers appear on page 67.) How many of these antonyms can you answer by knowing the *prefix, suffix,* or *root*? See if you can find the prefix, suffix, or root of each word by looking at pages 320–330.

☐ 20 minutes

DAY 9:   Analogies: Strategies and Timed Practice
Suggested Time: 1 hour 30 minutes

Turn to page 301. Read page 301 to get a good idea of what the analogy questions test for and how to answer them.

Start with the *Typical Kinds of Analogies That Appear on the SAT* beginning at the bottom of the page. Look at the first example. Concentrate on seeing relationships. You should be able to put the analogy in the form of a sentence that shows the relationships. Don't say LEG is to BODY as WHEEL is to CAR. Say: LEG is a part of the BODY as WHEEL is a part of the CAR. Look at the second example: Say: A CLOUD causes RAIN as the SUN causes HEAT. Look for relationships.

☐ 10 minutes

Go on to page 302. Look at the analogy at the top of the page. You should say: A BOY is a specific type of PERSON as a BUS is a specific type of VEHICLE. Notice that in this analogy we did·not use the order: First Word is to Second Word as Third Word is to Fourth Word. We used the order: Second Word (BOY) is to First Word (PERSON) as Fourth Word (BUS) is to Third Word (VEHICLE). Note the Analogy can be:

        1st Word : 2nd Word as 3rd Word : 4th Word

or 2nd Word : 1st Word as 4th Word : 3rd Word

It can *never* be:

        1st Word : 2nd Word as 4th Word : 3rd Word

or 2nd Word : 1st Word as 3rd Word : 4th Word.

35 minutes ☐ Now read the rest of the examples on pages 302–304. Make sure that you put the analogy in the form of a sentence as we did before.

10 minutes ☐ **Go on to page 304.** Read the *Do's and Don'ts for Answering Analogy Tests,* on pages 304–305. Next read *Study the Following Sample,* on page 305.

20 minutes ☐ **Turn to page 23.** Do analogy questions 11–20. Allow yourself 10 minutes. Study the answers on page 60 and the explanatory answers on pages 67–68. How many of the questions did you answer correctly? Do you see your mistakes? Did you put the analogies in sentence form? Did you sometimes reverse the order (instead of 1 : 2 as 3 : 4, use 2 : 1 as 4 : 3)?

Turn to page 40. Do analogies 36–45. Time yourself 7 minutes now. Study the answers on page 60 and the explanatory answers on pages 73 and 74. Do you see your mistakes? Did you put each analogy in the form of a sentence? Did you sometimes change the order? Remember the order of an analogy can be:

        1st word : 2nd word as 3rd word : 4th word

or 2nd word : 1st word as 4th word : 3rd word

It can *never* be:

15 minutes ☐   1st word : 2nd word as 4th word : 3rd word

or 2nd word : 1st word as 3rd word : 4th word

DAY 10: Sentence Completion and Reading Comprehension: Strategies and Timed Practice
Suggested Time: 2 hours

20 minutes ☐ **Turn to page 310:** *About Sentence Completion Tests.* Read pages 310–315. Make sure that you understand the section *Key Words in Sentence Completion Questions.*

Turn to page 29. Do questions 31–40 on pages 29–30. Allow yourself 10 minutes. Did you watch for Key Words? Did you note that in Question #31, the Key Word is *since,* and in Question #35, the Key Word is *defined?* Look at the answers on page 60 and the explanatory answers on pages 69–70. Make sure that you understand every explanation.

☐ **20 minutes**

Turn to page 34. Do questions 16–25 on pages 34–35. Allow yourself 8 minutes. Did you spot the Key Words? Look at the answers on page 60 and the explanatory answers on page 72. Make sure that you now understand how to do all the questions.

☐ **16 minutes**

Turn to page 306: *About Reading Comprehension Tests.* Read pages 306–310.

In the reading passages you must get involved with what the author is saying. You should immerse yourself in the passage so that you are interested and concerned with what the author is telling you even though you may not agree with it. Many students ask the question, "Should I look at the questions (not the choices) before reading the passage?" You may look at the questions first, but bear in mind that you may be wasting precious time. We have learned that if you get involved with the passage while reading it, you will start to anticipate many of the questions that will follow. For example, if you notice while reading a passage that the author is very angry or caustic in what he or she is saying, you can be pretty sure that there will be a question about the author's *mood.* So why bother to read through the questions that follow the passage *before* reading the passage? You will probably anticipate most of the questions as you read the passage.

You should also be aware that if the author discusses something in the passage which appears irrelevant to the rest of the passage and you ask yourself, "Why was this mentioned?" you can be pretty sure that there will be a question about this "irrelevant" item.

☐ **20 minutes**

Turn to page 24. Read the directions. Then read the passage on pages 24–25. Give yourself 6 minutes. Did you anticipate any of the questions? What was the mood expressed in the passage? What is the tone of the selection? Now answer questions 21–25. Time yourself 6 minutes. Look at the explanatory answers on pages 68–69. Make sure you understand any errors you make.

☐ **20 minutes**

Turn to page 26. Read the passage on the shedding of tears. Time yourself 5 minutes. Now answer questions 26–30. Time yourself 5 minutes. Look at the explanatory answers on page 69. How did you do? Do you see your errors? This is a difficult passage. Don't get discouraged.

☐ **15 minutes**

DAY 11: Taking a Complete Verbal Practice Test
Suggested Time: 1 hour 30 minutes

You are now ready to do a complete Verbal Section on the SAT.

1 hour & 30 minutes ☐   **Turn to page 50:** *Section 6: Verbal Questions.* Do questions 1–40. Time yourself 45 minutes (not 30 minutes). Afterwards, go over the explanatory answers on pages 81–84.

DAY 12: Taking a Complete SAT Practice Test:
Practice Test 2: Sections 1, 2, 3
Suggested Time: 2 hours–2 hours 30 minutes

Now you are ready to do a complete SAT practice test.

1 minute ☐   **Turn to page 96.** Read the instructions on this page for obtaining your answer sheet.

2–2½ hours ☐   **Turn to page 97.** Do sections 1, 2, and 3 of *Practice Test 2,* timing yourself 30 minutes for each section. Record your answers on your answer sheets. Check your answers on page 139. Read through the explanatory answers (pages 140–155) especially for those questions that you got wrong or didn't know how to answer.

DAY 13: More Practice: Practice Test 2: Sections 5, 6
Raw Score–Scaled Score Conversions
Suggested Time: 2 hours–4 hours, depending on abilities

1 hour & 40 minutes ☐   **Turn to page 124.** Do sections 5 and 6 and time yourself 30 minutes for each section. After you have finished, look at the correct answers on pages 139–140 and read through the explanatory answers on pages 155–162, especially for those questions that you got wrong or did not know how to answer.

5 minutes ☐   **Turn to page 85.** Read the section about *Raw Score–Scaled Score Conversion Table.*

Turn to page 88. For the complete *Practice Test 2* which you just took, count your *correct* answers for Sections 1 and 5. Deduct from this number one-quarter your total *incorrect* answers for Sections 1 and 5. This will give you what is called a *Raw Score*. You can now figure out what *Verbal Scaled Score* (SAT Score) you got by looking at the table on page 88.

5 minutes

Turn to page 89. For the *Practice Test 2* which you took, count the *correct* answers for Sections 2 and 3. Deduct from this number one-quarter of your total incorrect answers for Sections 2 and 3. This is your *Raw Score*. You can now figure out what your *Math Scaled Score* (SAT Score) is by referring to the table on page 89.

5 minutes

Turn to page 94. For a diagnosis of how you did on *Practice Test 2,* look at the *Self-Appraisal Table* for that test on page 94. For the areas in which you were weak, reread the sections that pertain to those areas, such as the math sections (Parts V and VI) and the verbal sections that we already discussed. For example, if you were weak in Analogies, read pages 302–305 again, or just go back to that part of the course where we discussed and practiced analogies.

5 minutes–
2 hours

DAY 14: Taking the SAT in One Sitting
Suggested Time: 4–5 hours (May be spread over 2 days)

Turn to page 163. Read the instructions on this page for obtaining your answer sheet for *Practice Test 3.*

1 minute

Turn to page 164. Do Sections 1, 2, and 3, timing yourself 30 minutes for each section. Record your answers on your answer sheet. Stop after Section 3 is over and take a 10-minute break.

1 hour &
40 minutes

Turn to page 191. Do Sections 4 and 5, timing yourself 30 minutes for each section. Record your answers on your answer sheet.

60 minutes

Turn to page 207. Read the instructions in the box, *After You Have Finished Practice Test 3.*

10 minutes

Turn to page 95. See how you performed on each part by referring to the *Self-Appraisal Table* for Test 3 on page 95. Make sure that you understand your errors by going over the explanatory answers on pages 209–232.

1–2 hours
(You may want to do this the next day.)

DAY 15: Practice Test 4

Suggested Time: 4–5 hours (May be spread to 2 days)

Now you may take *Practice Test 4*.

1 minute
☐

Turn to page 233. Read the instructions to obtain your answer sheet.

1 hour & 40 minutes
☐

Turn to page 234. Do Sections 1, 2, and 3, timing yourself 30 minutes for each section. Record your answers on your answer sheet. Stop after Section 3 is over and take a 10-minute break.

60 minutes
☐

Turn to page 257. Do Sections 5 and 6, timing yourself 30 minutes for each section. Record your answers on your answer sheet.

10 minutes
☐

Turn to page 276. Read the instructions in the box, *After You Have Finished Practice Test 4*.

1–2 hours (You may want to do this the next day.)
☐

Turn to page 95. See how you performed on each part of the SAT by referring to the *Self-Appraisal Table* for Test 4 on page 95. Make sure that you understand your errors by going over the explanatory answers on page 279–298.

Make sure that you look back to the Math Refresher for math review that you may need. Also, pay particular attention to Part VI, Special Math Techniques and Shortcuts, page 516. You may also want to retake some of the math diagnostic tests to further assess your weaknesses. You may also want to review some of the material (verbal and math) which we have already covered in this course.

DAY 16: A Final Way to Practice (Optional)

Make up your own examples in analogies, sentence completions, etc. Make up your own math examples. If your questions are ambiguous, try to make them better.

Good Luck!

PREFACE

This book is designed for the millions of high school students who plan to go to college.

For years, one of the most serious obstacles in the way of college admission has been the College Entrance Examination Board's three-hour Scholastic Aptitude Test (SAT). Today almost every college requires the submission of SAT scores by admissions applicants.

To aid college applicants, this book has been based on carefully tested educational principles. Many special features make this book a unique study tool for the Scholastic Aptitude Test. You are in good hands. This book was written by Gary R. Gruber, Ph.D., one of the leading authorities in the examination preparation field.

Getting Ready for College

This book gives the college applicant suggestions of things to consider as he selects the colleges to which he wishes to apply. It also tells him how to arrange to take the College Board admissions tests and what to expect when he takes them.

Step-by-Step Programming

This book closely follows the format and content of the College Board's admissions tests and is programmed with step-by-step directions, simulated tests, and explanatory answers.

Learning by Doing

First, the candidate can simulate taking the actual examination by taking the four tests in this book. He marks his answers in the margins of the book in the same way he will mark the machine-graded answer sheet when he takes the examination. Then the candidate can evaluate his own aptitude by comparing his answers to the correct answers at the end of each test.

Special Section on Field-Tested Techniques and Shortcuts

This is a unique section not found in any other SAT book or course. It describes powerful shortcuts and techniques for answering the math questions on the SAT. It is written in such a way that the student is able to realize the type of thinking approach that is required for the successful SAT candidate. By going through this section the student should be able to answer many of the SAT math questions in a much shorter time and with greater accuracy.

Diagnostic Tests in Math

Seven diagnostic tests are included to assess and correct your math weaknesses. The tests are all coded to the Math Refresher section.

Variety of Question Types

This book contains a variety of kinds of questions and problems that may appear on the SAT. As a result, the candidate will be familiar with almost any kind of question that appears on the exam.

Self-Evaluation

By using the Self-Appraisal Table developed for this book, the student can determine his areas of weakness at a glance and plan a program of intensive study to insure his success on the admissions tests.

College-Level Scholarship

The contents of the questions and problems reflect the scholarship and the academic standards required for college admission.

Test-Oriented Materials Only

Only materials that will specifically help prepare the candidate for the College Board's admissions tests have been included in this book. Extraneous materials have been rigidly excluded.

Structure of the SAT

2 Verbal Sections comprised of 85 questions	2 Math Sections comprised of
25 antonyms 15 sentence completions 25 reading comprehension questions (5 passages) 20 analogies	40 regular multiple-choice math questions + 20 quantitative comparison questions
1 Math, 1 Verbal or 1 SWET (Standard Written English Test) Section Number of questions and question types vary (This section is experimental and does not count toward any score.)	**1 SWET (Standard Written English Test) Section** This section does not count toward your score and is only used for college Freshman English Placement. 50 questions

TYPICAL FORMAT OF A CURRENT SAT*

SECTIONS OF THE SAT	NUMBER OF QUESTIONS	TIME LIMIT (Minutes)
SECTION ONE MATH QUESTIONS (Regular Math Questions)	25 altogether	30
SECTION TWO VERBAL QUESTIONS Antonyms ——→ 10 Sentence Completions ——→ 10 Reading Comprehension ——→ 10 (2 passages) Analogies ——→ 10	40 altogether	30
OR MATH QUESTIONS (Regular Math Questions)	25 altogether	30

SECTION THREE		
STANDARD WRITTEN ENGLISH TEST	**50** altogether	**30**
Grammar and Usage	30	
Sentence Correction	20	
SECTION FOUR		
VERBAL QUESTIONS		
Antonyms	15	**45** altogether
Sentence Completions	10	**30**
Reading Comprehension (2 passages)	10	
Analogies	10	
SECTION FIVE		
MATH QUESTIONS		
Regular Math Questions	15	**35** altogether
Quantitative Comparison Questions	20	**30**
SECTION SIX		
VERBAL QUESTIONS		
Antonyms	10	**40** altogether
Sentence Completions	5	**30**
Reading Comprehension (3 passages)	15	
Analogies	10	

TOTAL TIME   180 Minutes (3 Hours)

* The order in which the sections are presented on the actual SAT and the number of questions per section on the actual SAT are subject to change. This is because the SAT has many different forms.

GETTING READY FOR COLLEGE

About the time a student begins his junior year of high school, he probably begins to think about what he will do after graduation. Many students plan to get married or to go to work. Many plan to continue their education.

This book is designed to help you, the student who wants to go to college. It tells you what to look for as you select a school, how to apply, and especially how to prepare for the admissions tests that most colleges and universities require.

What Kind of College Do You Want?

Colleges and universities vary. For one thing, they vary in size. Some universities have literally thousands of students, most of whom never see or know each other. Others have only a few hundred or thousand students, most of whom at least recognize the face of everyone else on campus.

Large universities often have many excellent educational facilities and a number of excellent faculty members. They are well known and attract attention and money. Smaller schools generally have fewer facilities, although their quality may also be excellent. Many fine faculty members are also attracted to smaller schools.

The major difference between large and small schools is likely to be the degree of personal interaction among students, faculty, and administration. In a small school, students usually have smaller classes and few, if any, large lecture courses attended by hundreds of students. They are more likely to have informal contact with their professors outside the classroom.

Colleges and universities also differ in their emphasis on academics. In very academic schools, less emphasis is likely to be placed on inter-collegiate sports and extracurricular activities than at less academic schools. The emphasis will be on educational and, often, cultural activities, although most students at both kinds of schools find time for leisure, social activities, and a certain amount of campus humor.

To an extent, your high school grades will help you decide how academic a school you will choose. If you have very high grades, you probably will be able to handle work at a very difficult school with ease. If not, a highly academic school would probably not accept you even if you applied.

Another decision you must make is whether or not to go to a school that you can attend while living at home. Financial considerations often make it necessary for a student to live at home and attend a nearby institution or to attend a school to which he can travel without great expense. If you have a choice, you should consider the value of living with other students in a college community. Institutions of learning offer many advantages besides an academic education. One of these is the opportunity to meet many kinds of people with backgrounds different from your own, to gain experience in community living, and to develop as an independent person.

It is important to think about the kind of preparation your college or university will give you for your life after college. Some schools give a generalized liberal arts background; others prepare you for a specific career or for specific postgraduate study. If you have a definite career in mind or a strong interest in a particular field, consider applying to schools with strong departments in your area of interest. If you have many interests or no particular interest, consider applying to a liberal arts school.

Many students are uncertain whether they can succeed in college or whether they want to commit themselves to four full years of higher education. If this is your case, have a look at junior and community colleges that offer two-year programs. While two years of study at a four-year college is an "incomplete" education, two years at a two-year college can earn you a degree and prepare you for a career. In addition, if you choose to continue, you can follow two years at a junior or community college with two more years at a four-year institution and receive a regular diploma from the second school.

You can find out about colleges that interest you in a number of ways. The first is to look over the college catalog, which you can probably find in your guidance department or library. It tells you the size of the school and describes its programs, courses, and facilities. If you know someone who went to the school in question, ask him about it. Your guidance counselor can often provide information, too.

If you can, go and visit the school. Many colleges and universities make arrangements for prospective students to meet and talk with students already on campus. In some places, "prospectives" are invited to spend a day or two living in a dorm with students. If you notify the admissions office that you are coming to visit, you can probably talk with someone in that office and ask questions of him. Take a look at the students you see—their manner and their dress. Browse over student bulletin boards, and leaf through the college yearbook. You can find many clues to the kind of atmosphere you will find there. Ask yourself how you would fit in.

Meanwhile, be sure that your high school courses fulfill all the requirements of the schools to which you plan to apply. If they do not, perhaps you can arrange to take the required courses before you graduate.

How Do You Apply for Admission?

You should start exploring colleges in your junior year of high school. By the early part of your senior year, you should narrow down the number of schools that interest you and begin making application to them.

To get an application, write to the director of admissions at the college. Tell him where you presently attend school and when you will graduate. Describe what course or program you wish to apply for, and request an application form.

Colleges and universities usually charge a fee for processing an application. And they generally require a personal interview with the applicant before they accept him.

When you receive the application, fill it out accurately, completely, and neatly. If the college asks for a photograph or any other materials, send them with the application. Follow all instructions for forwarding records, and be sure you get documents in on time.

What If You Need Financial Aid?

Each year, a college education becomes increasingly expensive. Many families cannot afford the thousands of dollars it costs to send a son or daughter to college, particularly when there is more than one child to educate.

For this reason, scholarship aid and student loans are available to those who need them. Many colleges and universities offer their own scholarships. Many organizations do, too. There are scholarships available for people who are going to study certain subjects or who meet various other requirements. Ask your guidance counselor where you can apply.

Do not hesitate to inform the colleges to which you apply that you need aid. You will not be rejected on that basis.

When you apply to a college, the school will probably ask your parents to fill out the Parents' Confidential Statement, which will help the school decide what kind of aid you need. This form, which you can get either from your guidance counselor or from the school to which you are applying, comes from the College Scholarship Service, administered by the College Entrance Examination Board. Your parents complete the form, and the College Scholarship Service will send copies of it to the colleges or universities you request.

In addition to scholarship aid, many students work at campus jobs and summer jobs to earn money to help finance their education. If they receive aid, the college often expects them to supplement their scholarship money in this way.

What About Admissions Tests?

Many colleges and universities require or encourage prospective students to submit their scores on college admissions tests. Among the most popular of these examinations is the SAT. Some 2,000,000 students take the SAT each year.

One reason to begin your exploration of colleges early is to be sure to take the SAT at the right time. Colleges often specify a date by which they need to receive your admissions tests scores in order to accept you. In addition, if you know in your junior year that you will be taking the SAT, you may take the Preliminary Scholastic Aptitude Test/National Merit Scholarship Qualifying Test (PSAT/NMSQT) in October of your junior year for practice.

The following section gives the information you need to know about the SAT.

THE ADMISSIONS TESTS

The Scholastic Aptitude Test (SAT) is administered by the Educational Testing Service at the direction of the College Entrance Examination Board. The tests in the program are designed to provide objective measurements of the abilities considered necessary for success in college work. The test results are used by most colleges in the screening of applicants for admission.

The test scores are valuable to colleges because they allow the admissions officers to compare students whose high school backgrounds are very different. For example, a straight-A student at the top of his class in a small high school may not have as strong a background in skills necessary for college work as a B+ student from a large school with an academic emphasis. When the two students take the SAT, their work can be compared directly.

The fact that the College Board admissions tests provide this common denominator, however, does not mean that the scores on these tests are of greater importance for admission to a college than the applicant's scholastic standing, letters of recommendation, reports of committees that have interviewed him, or his personal qualities and characteristics. Colleges consider many factors when accepting students.

The SAT

The SAT is an objective examination designed to appraise the candidate's aptitude for college work by testing his verbal and mathematical skills. The verbal part of the test shows how well the student understands what he reads and grasps the ideas that are presented. The mathematics part shows how well the student understands math and solves problems. The student is given a total working time of three hours to complete the test.

Test Administration

There are several administrations of the College Board admissions tests. The SAT is given during the morning session throughout the year.

The College Board admissions tests are administered at established testing centers in every state of the United States and in many other countries.

Every candidate must file a formal Registration Form with the College Board and pay an examination fee. The fee for taking the SAT is $10.50 ($11.00 in New York). The fee for sending additional score reports to colleges after the first three is $3.75.

To obtain a Registration Form and information on the times and places for this year's College Board tests, ask at your school or write directly to the College Board. Write to:

College Board ATP
Box 592-R
Princeton, NJ 08540

After you submit your registration form, the College Board will send you an admission ticket that will admit you to the test on the date and at the test center for which you registered. In addition, this ticket contains your registration number, which you will use to identify your answer sheets and to request transcript reports.

You should arrive at the test center with your admission ticket, some positive personal identification, three or four sharpened number 2 pencils (or a soft-lead mechanical pencil), an eraser, and, if possible, a watch.

You must be prompt. You may not start the test late nor work past the time limit. No one will be admitted to the room after testing begins. You may not take books, slide rules, papers, or any other study aids into the testing room. A candidate who does so will not be allowed to continue testing. Other grounds for dismissing a candidate from the test are giving or accepting help, using notes or other aids, or taking test materials or notes from the room. When dismissed for one of these reasons, the candidate may not come back, and he will receive no scores.

After the tests have been scored, scores are released to the candidate's high school, to the colleges specified on the Registration Form, and to scholarship programs specified on the Registration Form. Scores are not available directly to candidates; students receive their examination results through their high school counselor or principal. No fee is charged for sending scores to the candidate's high school, to as many as three colleges, and to any number of scholarship programs specified on the Registration Form. The scores range from 200 to 800.

To get detailed information about the admissions tests, write to the CEEB at the address given above and ask for the latest "Bulletin of Information."

Taking the SAT

The best preparation for taking the SAT is a solid background in your high school courses and a good night's sleep the night before you take the tests.

The SAT is given at 8:30 A.M. on the test dates. Arrive on time, taking the materials you are instructed to take to the test center. You know from your own experience in test-taking that you should read and follow directions carefully and work quickly and accurately.

Part of this book will offer specific suggestions for taking tests of each kind.

All the test questions will be multiple-choice. For this reason, students usually want to know whether or not they should guess at answers they don't know. It might seem that guessing could help your score since there's a chance of getting the answer right. The College Board tests, however, are scored in such a way that there is a penalty for wrong answers. This is the way it works: If a question has five answer choices, the student scores one point if he answers correctly and no points if the answer column is left blank. If the answer is *marked incorrectly,* however, one-fourth point is *deducted* from his score. This penalty is designed to discourage wild guessing.

Probably the best rule of thumb for answering questions you aren't sure about is to try to eliminate some of the answer choices. If you can definitely eliminate one or more choices, you have a greater chance of choosing the right answer, and you should probably guess.

Many students are tempted to guess when they discover a series of questions that they cannot answer. This is no cause for worry. The test is designed so that *no* student is expected to make a perfect score.

Condensed Version:
A 15-Day Self-Instruction Course

1. Look at the structure of the SAT and typical SAT format on pages 3 and 4.
2. Get an idea of the different types of questions in the SAT by referring to pages 299–318.
3. If you wish, take the DIAGNOSTIC MATH TESTS beginning on page 359. Find your areas of weakness and improve them by referring to the Math Refresher (Part V).
4. Read THE MINIMUM SETS OF MATH RULES AND CONCEPTS WITH WHICH YOU MUST BE FAMILIAR, pages 516–522. For any rule or concept you are not familiar with or feel uncomfortable about, refer to the part in the Math Refresher section to which the rule or concept is keyed. You may want to go over the complete Math Refresher section (begins on page 403) in its entirety.
5. Read WHAT THE SAT IS TESTING IN MATH AND HOW TO BE ONE STEP AHEAD, pages 522–537.
6. Read MATHEMATICAL SHORTCUTS YOU SHOULD KNOW, pages 537–539.
7. Read SHORTCUTS AND TECHNIQUES FOR ANSWERING THE QUANTITATIVE COMPARISON TYPE QUESTION, pages 540–553.
8. Look at the section VERBAL ABILITY, beginning on page 319.
9. Take PRACTICE TEST 1. Find your correct answers and score yourself.
10. Make sure that you understand your errors by referring to the explanatory answers after the Practice Test.
11. You may want to refer again to the complete Math Refresher (Part V) and the Special Math Techniques and Shortcuts (Part VI).
12. Take PRACTICE TEST 2, score yourself, and analyze your incorrect or "guessed" answers and errors by referring to the explanatory answers at the end of the test.
13. Take PRACTICE TEST 3 and PRACTICE TEST 4, score yourself, and analyze your answers by referring to the explanatory answers at the end of each test.
14. You may want to refer once more to the refresher and shortcuts sections, etc., for material that you are still unsure of or uncomfortable with.
15. You may want to practice with the 80 ADDITIONAL QUANTITATIVE COMPARISON QUESTIONS, beginning on page 557.

part I

4 SCHOLASTIC APTITUDE TESTS CLOSELY PATTERNED AFTER THE ACTUAL SAT

Take each Practice Test as if you were taking the actual exam.

SAT PRACTICE TEST 1 ⟶

Tear out the answer sheet for this test at the end of the book.

Section 1: Mathematics Questions

Time: 30 minutes

Directions: Each question in this section is followed by five choices lettered (A) through (E). Choose the correct answer. Then mark the appropriate space in the answer column.

The following information may be useful to you in solving some of the mathematics problems in this part:

Circle, radius = r:
  Area $= \pi r^2$.
  Circumference $= 2\pi r$.
  A circle has 360 degrees of arc.

Triangle:
  The sum of the three angles in a triangle is 180 degrees.
  Area $= \frac{1}{2}$ (any side $\times$ altitude to that side).

Right Triangle:
  The sum of the squares of the legs $=$ the square of the hypotenuse.

Definitions of certain mathematical symbols:

  $>$ is greater than
  $<$ is less than
  $\geq$ is greater than or equal to
  $\leq$ is less than or equal to
  $\perp$ is perpendicular to
  $\parallel$ is parallel to

Important Note: Figures in this section are not always drawn to scale. All numbers are real numbers and all figures lie in a plane unless otherwise stated.

1. A man can run 4 mi. in 1 hr. After running for $2\frac{1}{2}$ hr., he returns to his starting place by walking in 6 hr. What is his average rate of walking?

   (A) $2\frac{1}{10}$ mph

   (B) $2\frac{1}{2}$ mph

   (C) $\frac{7}{8}$ mph

   (D) $1\frac{2}{3}$ mph

   (E) $2\frac{2}{3}$ mph

2. Angle AOB $= 60°$ and angle DOC $= 40°$. How many degrees are in angle BOC?
   (A) 100
   (B) 80
   (C) 60
   (D) 90
   (E) 120

   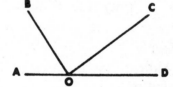

3. The equation $2x - y - 4 = 0$ is represented graphically below. Which, if any, of the following statements is false?
   (A) As x increases, y increases.
   (B) When $x = 0$, $y = -4$; when $y = 0$, $x = 2$.
   (C) The angle marked θ is greater than $45°$.
   (D) The graph, if continued, would pass through the point $x = 15$, $y = 26$.
   (E) none of these

   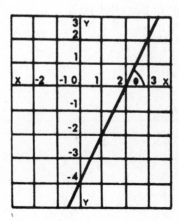

4. If *n* oranges cost *c* cents, how much do *x* oranges cost?

   (A) $\dfrac{xn}{c}$

   (B) $\dfrac{nc}{x}$

   (C) $xn + c$

   (D) $\dfrac{xc}{n}$

   (E) $nc + x$

5. Find the number of inches in the diagonal of a square inscribed in a circle whose circumference is 72π in.
   (A) 72 in.
   (B) 36 in.
   (C) 24 in.
   (D) 48 in.
   (E) 60 in.

6. The area of a rectangle is 57 sq. in. Its perimeter is 44 in. Find its length.

   (A) $6\frac{1}{3}$ in.

   (B) $8\frac{1}{7}$ in.

   (C) $7\frac{1}{8}$ in.

   (D) 19 in.

   (E) 23 in.

7. Five pounds of apples and 3 pounds of pears cost $1.10. But 3 pounds of apples and 5 pounds of pears cost $1.30. How much does 1 pound of apples cost?
   (A) $.05
   (B) $.06
   (C) $.10
   (D) $.08
   (E) $.03

8. Assume that $c = 1 + \dfrac{1}{x}$, and *x* is a positive number that increases in value. Therefore, *c*
   (A) increases in value
   (B) remains unchanged
   (C) decreases in value
   (D) fluctuates in value
   (E) none of these

9. If, in the figure shown below AB = BC, then y =
   (A) 135
   (B) 145
   (C) 155
   (D) 165
   (E) 175

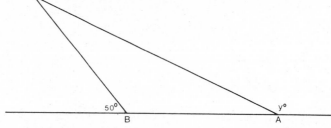

10. In the diagram, triangle ABC is isosceles, with AB equal to AC and angle A equal to 42°. If line l is parallel to BC, then what is the measure of angle x?
    (A) 75°
    (B) 69°
    (C) 42°
    (D) 138°
    (E) 88°

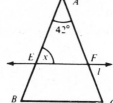

11. A room is 14 feet by 10 feet. At $.12 a square foot, how much would it cost to carpet the room?
    (A) $12.00
    (B) $14.40
    (C) $15.10
    (D) $22.20
    (E) $16.80

12. If A $= \dfrac{C}{3B}$ and B is doubled, then the original value of A is
    (A) doubled
    (B) halved
    (C) divided by four
    (D) increased by two
    (E) decreased by two

13. If each edge of a cube is increased by 2 in.,
    (A) the volume is increased by 8 cu. in.
    (B) the area of each face is increased by 4 sq. in.
    (C) the diagonal of each face is increased by 5 in.
    (D) the sum of the edges is increased by 24 in.
    (E) the sum of the edges is increased by 12 in.

14. If $a \neq b$, then $\dfrac{a - b}{a^2 - b^2} =$

(A) $\dfrac{1}{a - b}$

(B) $a - b$

(C) $a^2 - b^2$

(D) $\dfrac{1}{a + b}$

(E) $\dfrac{1}{b - a}$

15. $8y = \dfrac{6y + 2}{2x + 1}$

Express x in terms of y.

(A) $\dfrac{6y + 2}{8y}$

(B) $\dfrac{7y + 1}{8y}$

(C) $\dfrac{2y + 1}{8y}$

(D) $14y + 2$

(E) $\dfrac{1 - y}{8y}$

16. In the figure shown, line l is parallel to line m. As point C moves to the right along line l (A and B remain fixed), the area of triangle ABC

(A) increases without bound
(B) decreases without bound
(C) increases to a limit and then decreases
(D) decreases to a limit and then increases
(E) remains the same

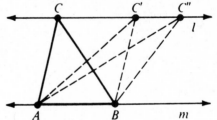

17. What is the smallest number m such that the product of m consecutive integers is always divisible by three?

(A) 2
(B) 3
(C) 4
(D) 5
(E) 6

18. According to the graphs below, what percent of the writing materials in an art class are yellow pencils?

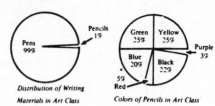

Distribution of Writing Materials in Art Class   Colors of Pencils in Art Class

(A) 2.5%
(B) 0.25%
(C) 1%
(D) 25%
(E) Cannot be determined from the given information

19. What is the correct solution to the following inequality: $-(1 - x^3) \geq 2$?

(A) $x \geq 3^{\frac{1}{3}}$

(B) $x \leq 3^{\frac{1}{3}}$

(C) $x \geq 3^{\frac{1}{2}}$

(D) $-x \geq 3^{\frac{1}{3}}$

(E) cannot be determined from the given information

20. For what numbers m is $\dfrac{6m - 2}{4m^2} = \dfrac{3 - 2m}{2m} + \dfrac{2m^2 - 1}{2m^2}$?

(A) 1 only
(B) 1 and -1 only
(C) 1 and -2 only
(D) all numbers except zero
(E) all numbers

21. Which of the points marked on the coordinate system below lie on the graph of $\dfrac{x^2}{5} + \dfrac{y^2}{5} = 5$?

(A) A and B only
(B) E and D only
(C) A only
(D) A, B, and D only
(E) A, B, C, D, and E

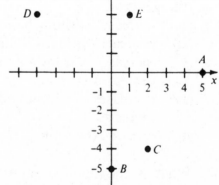

22. If $a^3b^4c^5$ is less than zero, which of the following statements implies that a is less than zero?
(A) a^2 is positive.
(B) b is positive.
(C) b is negative.
(D) c is negative.
(E) c is positive.

23. If it is true that p implies q, then which of the following could not be possible?
(A) p is true, q is true.
(B) p is false, q is false.
(C) p is false, q is true.
(D) p is true, q is false.
(E) p is equivalent to q.

24. If $\dfrac{4ab}{a+b} = a + b$, where $a + b \neq 0$, then it must be true that
(A) $ab = 1$
(B) $a + b = 1$
(C) $a = b$
(D) $\dfrac{a}{b} = 4$
(E) $\dfrac{1}{a} + \dfrac{1}{b} = 1$

25. Which of the following statements is (are) false?

I. $\sqrt{\dfrac{a}{b}} = \dfrac{\sqrt{a}}{\sqrt{b}}$

II. $\sqrt{a+b} = \sqrt{a} + \sqrt{b}$

III. $(\sqrt{c})^2 = c$

(A) I, II, and III
(B) I and II only
(C) II and III only
(D) III only
(E) II only

IF YOU FINISH THIS SECTION OF THE SAT BEFORE YOUR TIME IS UP, YOU MAY LOOK BACK AT YOUR WORK IN THIS SECTION ONLY. YOU ARE NOT PERMITTED TO LOOK AT ANY OTHER SECTION OF THE TEST. WHEN THE TIME IS UP, TURN TO THE NEXT SECTION AND START WORK ON THAT SECTION.

Section 2: Verbal Questions

Time: 30 minutes

Antonyms

Directions: Each question in this test consists of a word printed in capital letters followed by five words lettered (A) through (E). Choose the word that has most nearly the OPPOSITE meaning from the word in capital letters. Then mark the appropriate space in the answer column.

---

1. DECOROUS
   (A) appropriate
   (B) befitting
   (C) decent
   (D) unsuitable
   (E) afraid

2. RIBALD
   (A) uncouth
   (B) polished
   (C) picky
   (D) hirsute
   (E) glum

3. EDIFY
   (A) edit
   (B) elicit
   (C) instruct
   (D) not to print
   (E) confuse

4. SEDITIOUS
   (A) willful
   (B) anarchic
   (C) true
   (D) treasonous
   (E) loyal

5. MUNIFICENT
   (A) illiberal
   (B) lavish
   (C) abundant
   (D) magnificent
   (E) tiny

6. LACONIC
   (A) discursive
   (B) curt
   (C) brief
   (D) torpid
   (E) lustful

7. GUILE
   (A) disfavor
   (B) fraud
   (C) honesty
   (D) power
   (E) insight

8. ADHERENT
   (A) partisan
   (B) opponent
   (C) conformist
   (D) chemical
   (E) part

9. RECALCITRANT
   (A) amenable
   (B) realistic
   (C) disobedient
   (D) uncommon
   (E) strange

10. LITHE
    (A) clumsy
    (B) coarse
    (C) painted
    (D) heavy
    (E) graceful

Analogies

Directions: In each of the following questions choose the pair of words
that *best* completes the analogy. Then mark the appropriate space
in the answer column.

11. ART : CUBISM : :
 (A) scenery : play
 (B) setting : ring
 (C) mustache : face
 (D) poem : epic
 (E) drape : window

12. STATION : TRAIN : :
 (A) lair : fox
 (B) whistle : cab
 (C) home : parent
 (D) haven : refugee
 (E) dock : ship

13. FISH : MERMAID : :
 (A) horse : centaur
 (B) crocodile : dragon
 (C) fish : nymph
 (D) shark : whale
 (E) horse : man

14. OWNER : SLAVE : :
 (A) soldier : civilian
 (B) captain : tar
 (C) policeman : prisoner
 (D) native : alien
 (E) master : vassal

15. ORDINATION : PRIEST : :
 (A) promulgation : list
 (B) promotion : officer
 (C) matriculation : student
 (D) inauguration : president
 (E) election : candidate

16. AIR : DIRIGIBLE : :
 (A) locomotive : steam
 (B) lion : tiger
 (C) wagon : horse
 (D) gasoline : taxi
 (E) water : boat

17. IMMORTALITY : MORTALITY : :
 (A) second : minute
 (B) month : day
 (C) hour : minute
 (D) infinite : finite
 (E) era : decade

18. WEIGHT : PAPER : :
 (A) stopper : door
 (B) anchor : water
 (C) sound : whisper
 (D) cork : bottle
 (E) length : inch

19. WAIL : WHIMPER : :
 (A) lament : yell
 (B) chuckle : snicker
 (C) guffaw : laugh
 (D) smirk : simper
 (E) face : mouth

20. CONDUCT : CONSCIENCE : :
 (A) promoter : event
 (B) state : army
 (C) victory : leader
 (D) nation : patriotism
 (E) ship : navigator

Reading Comprehension

Directions: Read the following passages and answer each of the questions that come after them. Choose the *best* answer. Then mark the appropriate space in the answer column.

In 1575—over 400 years ago!—the French scholar Louis Le Roy published a learned book in which he voiced despair over the upheavals caused by the social and technological innovations of his time, what we now call the Renaissance. "All is pell-mell, confounded, nothing goes as it should." We, also, feel that our times are out of joint; we even have reason to believe that our descendants will be worse off than we are.

The earth will soon be overcrowded and its resources exhausted. Pollution will ruin the environment, upset the climate, damage human health. The gap in living standards between the rich and the poor will widen and lead the angry, hungry people of the world to acts of desperation including the use of nuclear weapons as blackmail. Such are the inevitable consequences of population and technological growth *if* present trends continue. But what a big *if* this is!

The future is never an extrapolation of the past. Animals probably have no chance to escape from the tyranny of biological evolution, but human beings are blessed with the freedom of social evolution. For us, trend is not destiny. The escape from existing trends is now facilitated by the fact that societies anticipate future dangers and take preventive steps against expected upheavals.

During the 1950s environmental degradation and population growth reached critical levels in many parts of the world. These problems are still with us, but progress is being made toward their control wherever the public realizes the dangers of present trends.

Urban agglomerations are in a state of crisis, but efforts are being made everywhere to reform urban life. Old cities are rediscovering the value of their ancient buildings and traditions; large new cities are being created, especially in Europe, each with its own economic and cultural identity; even New York City may eventually establish a sounder budgetary basis on which to build its future.

These examples are typical of our times in that they do not correspond to final solutions of problems but rather symbolize a kind of social ferment generated by public concern for the future.

Despite the widespread belief that the world has become too complex for comprehension by the human brain, modern societies have often responded effectively to critical situations.

The decrease in birth rates, the shelving of the supersonic transport, the partial banning of pesticides, the rethinking of technologies for the production and use of energy are but a few examples illustrating a sudden reversal of trends caused not by political upsets or scientific breakthroughs, but by public awareness of consequences.

Even more striking are the situations in which social attitudes concerning future difficulties undergo rapid changes before the problems have come to pass—witness the heated controversies about the ethics of behavior control and of genetic engineering even though there is as yet no proof that effective methods can be developed to manipulate behavior and genes on a population scale.

One of the characteristics of our times is thus the rapidity with which steps can be taken to change the orientation of certain trends and even to reverse them. Such changes usually emerge from grass roots movements rather than from official directives; they are less a result of conventional education than of the widespread awareness of problems generated by the news media.

There is the danger, admittedly, that such awareness is not always sufficient for rapid enough feedback to prevent critical processes from overshooting and causing catastrophes. But hope against the danger of overshooting can be found in the fact that most biological and social systems are extremely resilient. It is this resilience which leads me to reject the myth of inevitability and reaffirm that, wherever human beings are concerned, trend is not destiny.

21. In the first paragraph of the selection, the mood expressed is one of
(A) blatant despair
(B) guarded optimism
(C) poignant nostalgia
(D) muted pessimism
(E) unbridled idealism

22. According to the reading selection, if present trends continue, which one of the following situations will *not* occur?
(A) New sources of energy from vast coal deposits will be substituted for the soon-to-be-exhausted resources of oil and natural gas.
(B) The rich will become richer and the poor will become poorer.
(C) An overpopulated earth will be unable to sustain its inhabitants.
(D) Nuclear weapons will play a more prominent role in dealings among peoples.
(E) The ravages of pollution will render the earth and its atmosphere a menace to mankind.

23. Which of the following is the best illustration of the meaning of the title, "Trend Is Not Destiny"?
    (A)   Urban agglomerations are in a state of crisis.
    (B)   Human beings are blessed with the freedom of social evolution.
    (C)   The world has become too complex for comprehension by the human brain.
    (D)   Critical processes can overshoot and cause catastrophes.
    (E)   The earth will soon be overcrowded and its resources exhausted.

24. According to the selection, evidences of the insight of the public into the dangers which surround us can be found in all of the following *except*
    (A)   the activities of the news media
    (B)   a declining birth rate
    (C)   the efforts of New York City to balance its budget
    (D)   opposition to the use of pesticides
    (E)   renewed veneration of traditions and cultural identities

25. The overall tone of the reading selection is one of
    (A)   patient resignation
    (B)   cautious confidence
    (C)   thinly veiled cynicism
    (D)   carefree abandon
    (E)   tiresome remonstrance

The shedding of tears as an accompaniment of emotional distress has been attributed to other animals, but the fact is that psychic weeping is not known to occur in any animal other than man.

As is well known, human infants do not usually cry with tears until they are about 6 weeks of age. Weeping, then, would appear to be a trait acquired not with, but some time after the assumption of the hominid status.

The length of the dependency period of the human child suggests itself as a responsible factor in the appearance of weeping. During the earlier part of his dependency period the human infant's principal means of attracting the attention of others when he is in distress is by crying. Even a fairly short session of tearless crying in a young infant has a drying effect upon the mucous membranes of his naso-pharynx.

It is the mucous membrane of the nose that constitutes the most immediate contact of the respiratory system with the external world. The nasal mucous membrane must withstand the impact of respired air laden with bacteria, dust, particles, and gases. Discharges from the eye entering by the nasolacrimal ducts trickle down over it. If drying is produced in the mucous membrane, the cilia die and a gelatinous mass of mucus is formed, constituting a most hospitable culture medium for bacteria, which may then in large numbers easily pass through the permeable nasal mucosa. The consequences of this are not infrequently lethal.

The hypothesis is advanced that natural selection favored those infants who could produce tears, and that in this way the function became established in man.

26. Which of the following inferences can best be made on the basis of the statements in the paragraph?
    (A) Weeping occurs in other species possessing the necessary lacrimal and orbicular muscles.
    (B) Tearless crying in the young of early man, with an increased dependency period, would repeatedly have caused dehydration of the mucous membranes, and thus have rendered them vulnerable to the insults of the environment.
    (C) Tears are noxious as well as moistening.
    (D) Most infants cry with tears at about 3 weeks of age.
    (E) None of the other four conclusions given here can properly be inferred on the basis of the information given in the paragraph.

27. On the basis of the paragraph, which of the following statements is *most* tenable?
    (A) Nature is not homogeneous in its changes.
    (B) Suffering readily causes the secretion of tears, without being necessarily accompanied by any other action.
    (C) Infants who cried for prolonged periods of time during the years of their lives without benefit of tears would stand less chance of surviving than those who cried with tears.
    (D) Social forces, acting through sensory channels, influence the psychological mechanisms of members so as to produce parallel development.
    (E) None of the above is appropriate.

28. The selection explains crying with tears as
    I.   a defense mechanism
    II. a response to social stimuli
    III. genetically determined
    IV. a teleologically determined pattern
    (A) I only
    (B) II only
    (C) III only
    (D) IV only
    (E) all of the above

29. According to the passage
- (A) animals other than man have been found to cry because of psychological reasons
- (B) a newborn baby cries with tears because of respiratory reasons
- (C) the mucous membrane in the nose forms a defense against outside air
- (D) an infant that does not shed tears may incur disease, but in most cases the lack of tear-shedding capacity will not be of any serious consequence
- (E) none of the above is true

30. The main topic of this passage is
- (A) the psychological relation of animal and man
- (B) the infant's respiratory system
- (C) the importance of infant crying
- (D) weeping and survival in humans
- (E) the structure and function of the nasal mucous membrane

Sentence Completions

Directions: Each question in this test consists of a sentence or group of sentences in which one or two words are missing. Beneath the question are five pairs of words lettered (A) through (E). Choose the word or the pair of words that *best* completes the sentence or sentences. Then mark the appropriate space in the answer column.

31. Since she felt that the tragedy was _____, she ascribed its cause to fate.
    (A) poignant
    (B) justified
    (C) unavoidable
    (D) unnecessary
    (E) necessary

32. After _____ has been removed, the _____ is that which is left.
    (A) one—residuum
    (B) the interest—dividend
    (C) the stain—evidence
    (D) juice—fruit
    (E) the obstruction—drawbridge

33. Though he was romantic and sensual in his outlook, his life was one of _____.
    (A) profligacy
    (B) naivete
    (C) austerity
    (D) virtuosity
    (E) maturity

34. As long as learning is made continually repugnant, so long will there be a predisposition to _____ it when one is free from the authority of parents and teachers.
    (A) master
    (B) reject
    (C) minimize
    (D) inculcate
    (E) enjoy

35. In economics, scarcity is defined as _____ of amount or supply in _____ to demands or wants.
    (A) copiousness—regard
    (B) puerility—respect
    (C) plethora—respect
    (D) satiety—proportion
    (E) paucity—relation

36. Students who display a(n) _____ attitude toward their teachers cannot expect to receive _____ for their efforts.
- (A) receptive—rewards
- (B) stubborn—plaudits
- (C) deceptive—failure
- (D) intransigent—grades
- (E) abysmal—punishment

37. In accordance with the _____, the restrictions against freedom of worship were _____.
- (A) will—abrogated
- (B) morality—lifted
- (C) movement—developed
- (D) formula—aggravated
- (E) ukase—rescinded

38. The electrician put the parts of the televison set together with the skill of the master craftsman for whom this was a(n) _____ occupation.
- (A) morbid
- (B) natural
- (C) peculiar
- (D) unnatural
- (E) avocational

39. The closet _____ a reprehensible odor from _____ fumes.
- (A) enclosed—noxious
- (B) exuded—stifling
- (C) developed—aromatic
- (D) convened—herbivorous
- (E) grimaced—foul

40. International law _____ that a country _____ diplomatic representatives of countries with whom it maintains friendly relations.
- (A) suggests—emulate
- (B) states—scrutinize
- (C) includes—spurn
- (D) mandates—accredit
- (E) requires—welcome

IF YOU FINISH THIS SECTION OF THE SAT BEFORE YOUR TIME IS UP, YOU MAY LOOK BACK AT YOUR WORK IN THIS SECTION ONLY. YOU ARE NOT PERMITTED TO LOOK AT ANY OTHER SECTION OF THE TEST. WHEN THE TIME IS UP, TURN TO THE NEXT SECTION AND START WORK ON THAT SECTION.

Section 3: Standard Written English Test

Time: 30 minutes

Because the SWET (Standard Written English Test) does not count toward your score but is only used for Freshman English placement when you get into college, questions of this type are not included.

TURN TO THE NEXT SECTION AND START WORK ON THAT SECTION.

Section 4: Verbal Questions

Time: 30 minutes

Antonyms

Directions: Each question in this test consists of a word printed in capital letters followed by five words lettered (A) through (E). Choose the word that has most nearly the OPPOSITE meaning from the word in capital letters. Then mark the appropriate space in the answer column.

1. QUIXOTIC
   (A) idealistic
   (B) realistic
   (C) scheming
   (D) comical
   (E) imitable

2. EXTROVERT
   (A) boisterous person
   (B) withdrawn person
   (C) desiccation
   (D) spurn
   (E) renegade

3. ALLAY
   (A) provoke
   (B) arrange
   (C) calm
   (D) melt
   (E) rejoice

4. SNARE
   (A) entrap
   (B) free
   (C) scare
   (D) frighten
   (E) protect

5. MUNDANE
   (A) worldly
   (B) usual
   (C) spiritual
   (D) brief
   (E) exultant

6. PARSIMONIOUS
   (A) greedy
   (B) stingy
   (C) extravagant
   (D) vacant
   (E) spicy

7. DEMUR
   (A) object
   (B) consent
   (C) prance
   (D) modify
   (E) able

8. ACRIMONY
   (A) blandness
   (B) pungency
   (C) sweetness
   (D) matrimony
   (E) restraint

9. TENACIOUS
   (A) vacillating
   (B) persistent
   (C) unworthy
   (D) cowardly
   (E) tabular

10. SECESSION
    (A) joining
    (B) purge
    (C) war
    (D) withdrawal
    (E) meeting

11. REPELLENT
    (A) odious
    (B) repugnant
    (C) comic
    (D) flirtatious
    (E) inviting

12. IMPERVIOUS
    (A) in peril
    (B) strong
    (C) impenetrable
    (D) unfamiliar
    (E) vulnerable

13. GENERIC
    (A) individual
    (B) common
    (C) general
    (D) benevolent
    (E) hasty

14. INNOCUOUS
    (A) artful
    (B) deleterious
    (C) inoffensive
    (D) searching
    (E) light

15. WARY
    (A) foolhardy
    (B) cautious
    (C) fatigued
    (D) spare
    (E) diffident

Sentence Completions

Directions: Each question in this test consists of a sentence or group of sentences in which one or two words are missing. Beneath the question are five pairs of words lettered (A) through (E). Choose the word or the pair of words that *best* completes the sentence or sentences. Then mark the appropriate space in the answer column.

16. Early in the 19th century, in the South, it had become the fashion to raise only one staple crop, whereas in the North the crops were
_____.
   (A) diversified
   (B) unstable
   (C) fallow
   (D) uniform
   (E) wild

17. This author may be considered a cheerful and kindly sage: his writings are characterized by _____ but not by _____.
   (A) warmth—frustration
   (B) laconicism—zeal
   (C) levity—sincerity
   (D) moderation—consideration
   (E) insipidity—verbosity

18. The _____ demeanor of the crowd influenced the sheriff to
_____.
   (A) disciplined—arrest them
   (B) enthusiastic—commend them
   (C) wild—encourage
   (D) belligerent—pacify them
   (E) destructive—coddle them

19. If virtue were _____, the police would disappear and the courts would have nothing to do.
   (A) easy
   (B) admired
   (C) required
   (D) universal
   (E) attractive

20. William Seward was _____ as a _____ because he sought the purchase of Alaska, which had been labeled "Seward's Folly."
   (A) prescribed—nut
   (B) lampooned—warmonger
   (C) inscribed—traveler
   (D) condemned—fool
   (E) proscribed—gambler

21. A certain television actor amuses his audience because of the
    _____ of his _____. His audience laughs hysterically when he
    seems "to put his foot in his mouth."
    (A) impartiality—actions
    (B) malapropisms—speech
    (C) animation—face
    (D) clumsiness—movement
    (E) sting—satire

22. Such _____ habits of dress would not be imitated by a(n) _____
    person.
    (A) peculiar—erratic
    (B) intolerable—effusive
    (C) careless—fastidious
    (D) ornate—garish
    (E) meticulous—energetic

23. A wise person will not _____ sectional habits or customs; he will
    _____ those practices or actions that he enjoys.
    (A) deprecate—participate in
    (B) countenance—join in
    (C) disapprove—depreciate
    (D) question—denounce
    (E) enjoy—find pleasure in

24. Since there was inadequate grazing area for the herds, the land
    was _____ populated.
    (A) inadequately
    (B) sparsely
    (C) rustically
    (D) unconditionally
    (E) disproportionately

25. It is a custom in France on July 14th for the President of the
    Republic to offer _____ to certain prisoners in full _____.
    (A) acquittal—amnesty
    (B) amnesty—pardon
    (C) parole—acquittal
    (D) restitution—clemency
    (E) clemency—amnesty

Reading Comprehension

Directions: Read the following passages and answer each of the questions·
that come after them. Choose the *best* answer. Then mark the
appropriate space in the answer column.

Of all the areas of learning the most important is the development
of attitudes. Emotional reactions as well as logical thought processes
affect the behavior of most people. "The burnt child fears the fire" is
one instance; another is the rise of despots like Hitler. Both these examples also point up the fact that attitudes stem from experience. In the
one case the experience was direct and impressive; in the other it was indirect and cumulative. The Nazis were indoctrinated largely by the
speeches they heard and the books they read.

The classroom teacher in the elementary school is in a strategic
position to influence attitudes. This is true partly because children acquire attitudes from these adults whose word they respect. Another
reason it is true is that pupils often delve somewhat deeply into a subject in school that has only been touched upon at home or has possibly
never occurred to them before. To a child who had previously acquired
little knowledge of Mexico, his teacher's method of handling such a
unit would greatly affect his attitude toward Mexicans.

The media through which the teacher can develop wholesome attitudes are innumerable. Social studies (with special reference to races,
creeds and nationalities), science, matters of health and safety, the very
atmosphere of the classroom . . . these are a few of the fertile fields for
the inculcation of proper emotional reactions.

However, when children come to school with undesirable attitudes, it is unwise for the teacher to attempt to change their feelings by
cajoling or scolding them. She can achieve the proper effect by helping
them obtain constructive experiences. To illustrate, first-grade pupils
afraid of policemen will probably alter their attitudes after a classroom
chat with the neighborhood officer in which he explains how he pro-
tects them. In the same way, a class of older children can develop attitudes through discussion, research, outside reading and all-day trips.

Finally, a teacher must constantly evaluate her own attitude because her influence can be deleterious if she has personal prejudices.
This is especially true in respect to controversial issues and questions
on which children should be encouraged to reach their own decisions
as a result of objective analysis of all the facts.

26. The central idea conveyed in the above passage is that
    (A) attitudes affect our actions
    (B) teachers play a significant role in developing or changing pupils' attitudes
    (C) by their attitudes, teachers inadvertently affect pupils' attitudes
    (D) attitudes can be changed by some classroom experiences
    (E) attitudes are affected by experience

27. The author implies that
    (A) children's attitudes often come from those of other children
    (B) in some aspects of social studies a greater variety of methods can be used in the upper grades than in the lower grades
    (C) the teacher should guide all discussions by revealing her own attitude
    (D) people usually act on the basis of reasoning rather than on emotion
    (E) parents' and teachers' attitudes are more often in harmony than in conflict

28. A statement *not* made or implied in the passage is that
    (A) attitudes cannot easily be changed by rewards and lectures
    (B) a child can develop in the classroom an attitude about the importance of brushing his teeth
    (C) attitudes can be based on the learning of falsehoods
    (D) the attitudes of children are influenced by all the adults in their environment
    (E) the children should accept the teacher's judgment in controversial matters

29. The passage specifically states that
    (A) teachers should always conceal their own attitudes
    (B) whatever attitudes a child learns in school have already been introduced at home
    (C) direct experiences are more valuable than indirect ones
    (D) teachers can sometimes have an unwholesome influence on children
    (E) it is unwise for the teacher to attempt to change children's attitudes

30. The first and fourth paragraphs have all the following points in common *except*
    (A) how reading affects attitudes
    (B) the importance of experience in building attitudes
    (C) how attitudes can be changed in the classroom
    (D) how fear sometimes governs attitudes
    (E) how differences in approach change attitudes

Semanticists point out that words and phrases often acquire connotations tinged with emotions. Such significances are attached because of the context, the history of the usage of the expression, or the background of the person reading or listening. Thus, "the hills of home" may evoke a feeling of nostalgia or a pleasant sensation; but "Bolshevik" may arouse derision or disgust in the minds of many people.

The term "progressive education" has gone through several stages in the connotative process. At one time progressive education was hailed as the harbinger of all that was wise and wholesome in classroom practice, such as the recognition of individual differences and the revolution against formalized dictatorial procedures. However, partly because of abuses on the fanatical fringe of the movement, many people began to associate progressive schools with frills, fads, and follies. What had been discovered and developed by Froebel in Germany, by Pestalozzi in Switzerland, by Montessori in Italy, and by men like Parker and Dewey in the United States was muddled in a melange of mockery and misunderstanding and submerged in satirical quips. As a result, many educators have recently avoided the expression and have chosen to call present educational practices "new" or "modern" rather than "progressive."

Actually "progressive" ideas in any field are as ancient as the history of mankind. As long as individuals question the old ways of doing things and use their intelligence to experiment, advancement will take place. But since every new action produces a reaction, periods of confusion and criticism are to be expected. What we need is a method for distinguishing fact from fancy and arriving at judgments through a consideration of the average rather than of the extreme. If such a method were applied to "progressive education," the term would probably enjoy a better reputation than it has today.

31. The title which best fits the sense of the passage is
     (A) The Influence of Progressive Education
     (B) The Misinterpretation of Progressive Education
     (C) The Progress of Mankind in Education
     (D) The History of Progressive Education
     (E) Progressive vs. Traditional Education

32. A conspicuous feature of the style of this passage is
     (A) alliteration
     (B) metaphors
     (C) satire
     (D) oxymoron
     (E) similes

33. The author implies that
  (A) progressive education is full of silly activities
  (B) progressive ideas in any field are associated with the present era
  (C) periods of confusion and criticism are a natural result of the introduction of a new idea
  (D) inherent in progressive education is a method of distinguishing fact from fancy
  (E) progressive education has reached its greatest popularity in the schools today

34. All of the following are explanations of the acquisition by a word of additional connotations, according to the author, *except*
  (A) the context in which the word appears
  (B) the use to which the word has been put over a period of time
  (C) a desire on the part of the user to feel a pleasant sensation
  (D) the experience of the user
  (E) the events of the period

35. All of the following are offered by the author as reasons for the avoidance by many educators of the term "progressive education" *except* the fact that
  (A) progressive education is confused because its origin stemmed from many countries
  (B) extremists who called themselves "progressives" engaged in distorted practices
  (C) it was widely ridiculed
  (D) it was judged incorrectly
  (E) it was associated with extravagant and foolish notions

GO ON TO THE NEXT PAGE

Analogies

Directions: In each of the following questions choose the pair of words that *best* completes the analogy. Then mark the appropriate space in the answer column.

---

36. BURGLAR : ALARM ::
- (A) snake : hiss
- (B) air raid : siren
- (C) trespasser : bark
- (D) ship : buoy
- (E) crossing : bell

37. LOOM : DISASTER ::
- (A) impend : catastrophe
- (B) howl : storm
- (C) question : puzzle
- (D) hurt : penalty
- (E) imminent : eminent

38. REMORSELESS : COMPASSION ::
- (A) unscrupulous : qualms
- (B) opportunist : opportunity
- (C) impenitent : sin
- (D) intrepid : rashness
- (E) querulous : lamentation

39. CONVINCE : GULLIBLE ::
- (A) cheat : unassuming
- (B) suffer : fatigued
- (C) insult : sensitive
- (D) fear : frightened
- (E) steal : starved

40. CONDONE : ERROR ::
- (A) extenuate : crime
- (B) moderate : tone
- (C) placate : pardon
- (D) reprisal : retaliation
- (E) expiate : sin

41. PACT : FEUD ::
- (A) alliance : organization
- (B) conciliation : revolution
- (C) treaty : covenant
- (D) entreaty : parity
- (E) concord : discord

42. POSTERIOR : SIMULTANEOUS ::
- (A) posthumous : following
- (B) consecutive : ensuing
- (C) prolonged : before
- (D) now : there
- (E) subsequent : coincidental

43. EPILOGUE : PROLOGUE ::
- (A) glossary : index
- (B) progeny : proletariat
- (C) preface : table of contents
- (D) footnote : emendation
- (E) appendix : preface

44. ENTHUSIASTIC : FERVOR ::
- (A) affectionate : adumbration
- (B) eager : sentimentality
- (C) calm : listless
- (D) glib : fluency
- (E) fond : infatuation

45. GANG : HIJACK ::
- (A) rat : eat
- (B) trooper : lurk
- (C) monkey : mimic
- (D) wolf : prowl
- (E) reader : browse

IF YOU FINISH THIS SECTION OF THE SAT BEFORE YOUR TIME IS UP, YOU MAY LOOK BACK AT YOUR WORK IN THIS SECTION ONLY. YOU ARE NOT PERMITTED TO LOOK AT ANY OTHER SECTION OF THE TEST. WHEN THE TIME IS UP, TURN TO THE NEXT SECTION AND START WORK ON THAT SECTION.

Section 5: Mathematics Questions

Time: 30 minutes

Directions: Each question in this section is followed by five choices lettered (A) through (E). Choose the correct answer. Then mark the appropriate space in the answer column.

The following information may be useful to you in solving some of the mathematics problems in this part:

Circle, radius = r:
Area $= \pi r^2$.
Circumference $= 2\pi r$.
A circle has 360 degrees of arc.

Triangle:
The sum of the three angles in a triangle is 180 degrees.
Area $= \frac{1}{2}$(any side $\times$ altitude to that side).

Right Triangle:
The sum of the squares of the legs $=$ the square of the hypotenuse.

Definitions of certain mathematical symbols:

$>$ is greater than
$<$ is less than
$\geqq$ is greater than or equal to
$\leqq$ is less than or equal to
$\perp$ is perpendicular to
$\parallel$ is parallel to

Important Note: Figures in this section are not always drawn to scale. All numbers are real numbers and all figures lie in a plane unless otherwise stated.

1. A taxi ride costs $.30 for the first quarter mile and $.10 for each additional half mile or fraction thereof. How much does a 2-mile ride cost?
    (A) $1.50
    (B) $.85
    (C) $1.70
    (D) $.70
    (E) $1.80

2. A circle is inscribed in a square. The radius of the circle is 4. What is the area of the shaded portion?
    (A) $16 - 4\pi$
    (B) $4 - 2\pi$
    (C) 16π
    (D) 64
    (E) $16 - 64\pi$

3. John receives the following grades in English: 75, 95, 80, 75, and 65. What is his average?
    (A) 80
    (B) 74
    (C) 82
    (D) 84
    (E) 78

4. $\dfrac{5 - 3\sqrt{2}}{3 + \sqrt{2}} =$
    (A) $4 - 3\sqrt{2}$
    (B) $9 + 3\sqrt{2}$
    (C) $6 + 5\sqrt{2}$
    (D) $3 - 2\sqrt{2}$
    (E) none of these

5. If we let $a * * b$ represent a^b, then for which pair of a and b is $* *$ a commutative operation?
    (A) $a = 1$
         $b = 2$
    (B) $a = 2$
         $b = 4$
    (C) $a = 4$
         $b = 3$
    (D) $a = 0$
         $b = 1$
    (E) $a = 2$
         $b = 3$

6. What is the value of $\begin{vmatrix} 3 & 5 \\ -2 & -1 \end{vmatrix}$ if for any a,b,c,d, $\begin{vmatrix} a & b \\ c & d \end{vmatrix} = ad - bc$?

(A) −7

(B) 3

(C) 7

(D) 10

(E) −13

7. In a school, 10 students take Russian and 15 students take French. There are 20 students in the school. How many take both languages, assuming that everyone takes a language and that these are the only two given?

(A) 10

(B) 5

(C) 15

(D) 12

(E) 20

8. On the coordinate system shown, what is the slope of AC plus the slope of AB?

(A) −2

(B) 2

(C) 0

(D) $\dfrac{1}{2}$

(E) $-\dfrac{1}{2}$

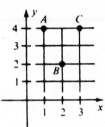

9. ABCD is a rectangle. Triangle BCE is a right triangle. AB = 4; EC = 12; and EB = 20. Find the length of the diagonal BD.

(A) $\sqrt{272}$

(B) $\sqrt{262}$

(C) $\sqrt{252}$

(D) $\sqrt{242}$

(E) $\sqrt{232}$

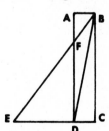

10. A can do a job in r days and B, who works faster, can do the same job in s days. Which of the following expressions represents the number of days it would take A and B to do the job if they worked together?

(A) $\dfrac{r+s}{2}$

(B) $r-s$

(C) $\dfrac{1}{r}+\dfrac{1}{s}$

(D) $\dfrac{r+s}{rs}$

(E) none of these

11. A circular lawn is surrounded by a walk in such a way that the lawn and the walk form 2 concentric circles. The difference in the circumferences of the 2 circles is 22 yd. What is the width of the walk? (Use $\pi = 22/7$.)

(A) 5 yd.
(B) 6 yd.
(C) 3.5 yds.
(D) 7 yd.
(E) 9 yd.

12. Find the value of x in the equation $\sqrt{2x-1} = 3\sqrt{6-x}$.

(A) 5

(B) $3\dfrac{4}{19}$

(C) $4\dfrac{1}{12}$

(D) 7

(E) $3\dfrac{3}{4}$

13. A large circular disc completes a rotation every 9 sec., and a smaller disc every 7 sec. How often do specific points on their respective circumferences begin rotating together?

(A) every 56 sec.

(B) every $1\dfrac{1}{20}$ min.

(C) every $1\dfrac{1}{4}$ min.

(D) every 48 sec.

(E) none of these

14. Two sides of a parallelogram are $12''$ and $\frac{2}{3}''$. These sides meet at an angle of $60°$. What is the area of the parallelogram?
    (A)   12 sq. in.
    (B) $4\sqrt{3}$ sq. in.
    (C)   8 sq. in.
    (D) $12\sqrt{3}$ sq. in.
    (E)   none of these

15. The numerator and the denominator of a certain fraction are in the ratio of 3:4. If the numerator is reduced by 1 and the denominator is increased by 2, the resulting fraction has the value of $\frac{2}{3}$. What is the denominator of the original fraction?

    (A)   21
    (B)   18
    (C)   35
    (D)   28
    (E)   32

GO ON TO THE NEXT PAGE

Directions: This section requires you to compare two quantities—the quantity in Column A and the quantity in Column B. After you have compared the two quantities, select

(A) if the quantity in Column A is greater than the quantity in Column B;

(B) if the quantity in Column B is greater than the quantity in Column A;

(C) if the quantities in the two columns are equal;

(D) if the information is not sufficient to make a valid comparison.

Any information that appears in a central position above the two quantities to be compared refers to both quantities.

(A) if the quantity in Column A is greater than the quantity in Column B

(B) if the quantity in Column B is greater than the quantity in Column A

(C) if the quantities in the two columns are equal

(D) if the information is not sufficient to make a valid comparison

	Column A	**Column B**
16.	$\dfrac{1}{2} + \dfrac{1}{3}$	$1\dfrac{1}{2} - \dfrac{5}{6}$
17.	$\dfrac{20}{36}$	$\dfrac{32}{48}$
18.	$(72 \div 2) + 4$	$72 \div (2 + 4)$

$$x = 3; \, y = 5; \, z = 7$$

19.	$7x + 3y + 2z$	$2z^2 - 3y - 10x$
20.	The price of an article in a store listing at \$16 and discounted 20%	The price of an article in a store listing at \$15 and discounted $33\dfrac{1}{3}\%$
21.	$\dfrac{2\sqrt{3}}{\sqrt{5}}$	$\dfrac{3\sqrt{2}}{\sqrt{5}}$

$$y = 2x; \, 1 < x < 9$$

22.	y	6
23.	The perimeter of a semicircle with radius of 5 in. $\left(\text{Use } \pi = \dfrac{22}{7}\right)$	The perimeter of a hexagon with each side 5 in. long

$$ab = 1$$

24.	$\dfrac{a}{b}$	a^2

(A) if the quantity in Column A is greater than the quantity in Column B
(B) if the quantity in Column B is greater than the quantity in Column A
(C) if the quantities in the two columns are equal
(D) if the information is not sufficient to make a valid comparison

Column A	Column B

n is an odd positive number

25. $(-2)^n$ $(1)^n$

26. $\dfrac{2}{\frac{1}{2}}$ $\dfrac{\frac{2}{1}}{2}$

Questions 27–30 are based on this bar graph.

COFFEE PRODUCTION OF FIVE LARGEST PRODUCERS

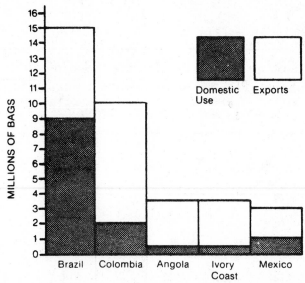

27. Amount exported by Brazil   Amount exported by Ivory Coast and Angola together

28. Percentage of total production exported by largest producer   Percentage of total production exported by smallest producer

29.   37,500,000   total world production

30. Percentage of total production used at home by Colombia   Percentage of total production used at home by Angola

(A) if the quantity in Column A is greater than the quantity in Column B
(B) if the quantity in Column B is greater than the quantity in Column A
(C) if the quantities in the two columns are equal
(D) if the information is not sufficient to make a valid comparison

Column A   **Column B**

Questions 31–32 refer to this diagram.

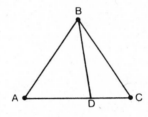

$$\angle A = \angle C$$

31.	AB	AC
32.	$\angle C$	$\angle ADB$

$$2x + 3y = 7$$
$$-4x - 6y = -14$$

33.	x	y
34.	$2 - (2 - 2) - 2 + 2$	$2 - (-2 + 2) + 2 - 2$
35.	$x^2 + y^2$	$x^2 + (-y)^2$

IF YOU FINISH THIS SECTION OF THE SAT BEFORE YOUR TIME IS UP, YOU MAY LOOK BACK AT YOUR WORK IN THIS SECTION ONLY. YOU ARE NOT PERMITTED TO LOOK AT ANY OTHER SECTION OF THE TEST. WHEN THE TIME IS UP, TURN TO THE NEXT SECTION AND START WORK ON THAT SECTION.

Section 6: Verbal Questions

Time: 30 minutes

Antonyms

Directions: Each question in this test consists of a word printed in capital letters followed by five words lettered (A) through (E). Choose the word that has most nearly the OPPOSITE meaning from the word in capital letters. Then mark the appropriate space in the answer column.

1. CALUMNY
   (A) calamity
   (B) aspersion
   (C) justification
   (D) foulness
   (E) rejection

2. MALEDICTION
   (A) wrath
   (B) significance
   (C) curse
   (D) blessing
   (E) slander

3. INEPT
   (A) unkempt
   (B) unskilled
   (C) insincere
   (D) calm
   (E) adroit

4. IMPIOUS
   (A) profane
   (B) secular
   (C) devout
   (D) lacking strength
   (E) not holy

5. PALLID
   (A) glowing
   (B) sleek
   (C) rejected
   (D) bedded
   (E) flung

6. CAPTIOUS
   (A) uncritical
   (B) carping
   (C) titular
   (D) lost
   (E) insinuating

7. ADAMANT
   (A) flexible
   (B) just
   (C) official
   (D) persistent
   (E) arrogant

8. FRUGALITY
   (A) economy
   (B) banality
   (C) age
   (D) generosity
   (E) strength

9. RECUMBENT
   (A) at ease
   (B) upright
   (C) reclined
   (D) horizontal
   (E) prostrate

10. QUAIL
    (A) discourage
    (B) cower
    (C) gain courage
    (D) shake
    (E) conquer

Sentence Completions

Directions: Each question in this test consists of a sentence or group of sentences in which one or two words are missing. Beneath the question are five pairs of words lettered (A) through (E). Choose the word or the pair of words that *best* completes the sentence or sentences. Then mark the appropriate space in the answer column.

11. The industrialists in the East feared that migration would make workers scarce and wages high, and regarded the abundance of land open to settlement as a(n) _____ to themselves.
    - (A) challenge
    - (B) advantage
    - (C) guide
    - (D) directive
    - (E) threat

12. The rights of citizens include the following: the right to life, liberty, the pursuit of happiness, and the free exercise of worship. _____ in these rights is the _____ to preserve and defend them to the best of their ability.
    - (A) Extraneous—duty
    - (B) Implicit—responsibility
    - (C) Obligatory—opportunity
    - (D) Precluded—principle
    - (E) Inherent—privilege

13. The queen was the _____ of all eyes as she entered the room.
    - (A) blight
    - (B) misery
    - (C) miracle
    - (D) cynosure
    - (E) tribulation

14. During the postwar period, _____ firms met with great difficulty in maintaining their business as soon as the standard brands of _____ companies became generally available.
    - (A) foreign—established
    - (B) newer—established
    - (C) specialized—rationalized
    - (D) manufacturing—agricultural
    - (E) ordinance—missile

15. One of the mistakes in our educational jargon is the common fault of stressing the interests of _____ and eliding over the interests of the _____.
(A)   the commonwealth—republic
(B)   the girls—boys
(C)   the aristocracy—oligarchy
(D)   society—individual
(E)   the community—state

Reading Comprehension

Directions: Read the following passages and answer each of the questions that come after them. Choose the *best* answer. Then mark the appropriate space in the answer column.

In the late 18th and early 19th centuries, the doctrine of individualism and competition was set forth in a really powerful way for the first time. The economists and the rising manufacturers rebelled against the limitations of mercantilism, and their views were expressed by Adam Smith in his *Wealth of Nations,* and by Ricardo and John Stuart Mill. Darwin in his *Origin of Species* and Herbert Spencer in his *Social Statics* both expounded the doctrine of natural selection and survival of the fittest. Thus, the groundwork was laid for Nietzsche's *Zarathustra* and the violence of the modern German approach based on the doctrine of the superiority of certain germ plasms.

The forces that Darwin, Adam Smith and John Stuart Mill let loose in the biological and economic worlds, combined with those originated by Hegel in the philosophic world, produced in the mind of Karl Marx one of the most powerful books of the 19th century, *Das Kapital.* Whether we like it or not, everyone in the world today is different because of *Das Kapital.* Without this book, there would have been neither the communist nor the fascist experiments. More than any other book of the 19th century, Karl Marx's great work continues to influence all of us.

16.   Which fields most influenced the late 18th and early 19th centuries?
   (A)   science and economics
   (B)   religion and art
   (C)   economics and constitutional law
   (D)   science and symbolic poetry
   (E)   religion and science

17.   Nietzsche's work was a precursor to
   (A)   Russian communism
   (B)   Italian fascism
   (C)   the theory of the German master race
   (D)   mercantilism
   (E)   democracy

18. According to the passage, life in the 20th century
   (A)   is not affected by past experience
   (B)   was profoundly affected by literary works
   (C)   is filled with violence
   (D)   is moving toward economic communism
   (E)   is simpler than life in the 19th century

19. Karl Marx was influenced by
   (A)   philosophy and hate
   (B)   philosophy and communism
   (C)   communism and fascism
   (D)   economics and philosophy
   (E)   none of these

20. Which of the following led to the development of 19th-century economic theory?
   (A)   hate
   (B)   competition
   (C)   communism
   (D)   violence
   (E)   none of these

It is a common belief that a thing is desirable because it is scarce and thereby has ostentation value. The notion that such a standard of value is an inescapable condition of settled social existence rests on one of two implicit assumptions. The first is that the attempt to educate the human race so that the desire to display one's possessions is not a significant feature of man's social behavior, is an infringement against personal freedom. The greatest obstacle to lucid discourse in these matters is the psychological anti-vaccinationist who uses the word freedom to signify the natural right of men and women to be unhappy and unhealthy through scientific ignorance instead of being healthy and happy through the knowledge which science confers. Haunted by a perpetual fear of the dark, the last lesson which man learns in the difficult process of growing up is "ye shall know the truth, and the truth shall make you free." The professional economist who is too sophisticated to retreat into the obscurities of this curious conception of liberty may prefer to adopt the second assumption, that the truth does not and cannot make us free because the need for ostentation is a universal species characteristic, and all attempts to eradicate the unconscionable nuisance and discord which arise from overdeveloped craving for personal distinction artificially fostered by advertisement, propaganda and so-called good breeding are therefore destined to failure. It may be earnestly hoped that those who entertain this view have divine guidance. No rational basis for it will be found in textbooks of economics. Whatever can be said with any plausibility in the existing state of knowledge rests on the laboratory materials supplied by anthropology and social history.

21. The author's purpose in writing this paragraph is most probably to
   (A)   denounce the psychological anti-vaccinationists
   (B)   demonstrate that the question under discussion is an economic rather than a psychological problem
   (C)   prove the maxim "ye shall know the truth, and the truth shall make you free"
   (D)   prove that ostentation is not an inescapable phenomenon of settled social existence
   (E)   prove the inability of economics to account for ostentation

22. The writer implies that
   (A)   neither the psychological anti-vaccinationist nor the professional economist recognizes the undesirability of ostentation
   (B)   our cultural standards are at fault in enhancing ostentation value
   (C)   scarcity as a criterion of value is an inexplicable concept
   (D)   his main objection is to the inescapable standard of values
   (E)   the results of studies of ostentation in anthropology and social history are irrational

23. In his reference to divine guidance, the writer is
   (A)   being ironic
   (B)   implying that only divine guidance can solve the problem
   (C)   showing how the professional economist is opposing divine laws
   (D)   referring to opposition which exists between religion and science
   (E)   indicating that the problem is not a matter for divine guidance

24. The writer believes that personal freedom
   (A)   is less important than is scientific knowledge
   (B)   is a requisite for the attainment of truth
   (C)   is attained by eradicating false beliefs
   (D)   is no concern of the professional economist
   (E)   is an unsophisticated concept

25. The writer would consider as most comparable to the effect of a vaccination on the body, the effect of
   (A)   fear upon personality
   (B)   science upon the supposed need for ostentation
   (C)   truth upon the mind
   (D)   knowledge upon ignorance
   (E)   knowledge upon happiness

Many experiences and data have been cited indicative of possible dolphin intelligence. For one, the mammal has lived at sea, completely removed from land forms, for 60,000,000 years. Thus, it is about as alien to mankind as any mammal on earth. Its forehead is oil-filled and contains complex sound-generating devices. Underwater sound is produced within the body with mouth and blowhole closed so that no air bubble appears. Tests indicate that the dolphin is sensitive to sound at frequencies up to 120 kilocycles. Whereas human vocal cords pulsate at 60 to 120 cycles per second with about 50 selective harmonics, the dolphin's pulsate at about 600 cycles per second with a choice of many more harmonics. Then, too, the dolphin has at least two separately controlled, independent sound mechanisms.

The dolphin's brain, located aft of the blowhole, generally exceeds the human brain in weight, and has a many-convoluted cortex that weighs about 1100 grams. Research indicates that, in humans, 600 to 700 grams of cortex is necessary for a vocabulary. Absolute weight of the cortex, rather than the ratio of brain weight to total body weight, is thought to be indicative of intelligence potential. (Large-headed humans usually have large sinus regions rather than proportionally larger brains.) In this regard, the sperm whale's 9000-gram brain could raise some interesting speculation. The dolphin apparently enjoys equal visual acuity in air and water, a remarkable feat when one considers the refractive index involved. Porpoises sleep with only one eye closed at a time for a maximum length of 30 seconds (between breaths). Their sleep totals about three hours out of each 24. (Space research has indicated that man's sleep requirement reduces to this figure when he is kept in water to eliminate energy expended in supporting himself against gravity.)

26. Assuming that the upper range for human hearing is about 20,000 cycles per second, the dolphin can
     (A) hear higher pitched sounds than can humans
     (B) hear no sounds
     (C) hear only human sounds
     (D) hear only in the lower frequency registers
     (E) hear only frequencies below the human audio spectrum

27. The dolphin produces sounds
     (A) by use of different sound-producing mechanisms
     (B) by one and only one sound-producing mechanism
     (C) the same way humans produce sounds
     (D) with less than 50 selective harmonics
     (E) so low that humans cannot hear them

28. If man's environment were the same as that of the dolphin's, man would require
    (A) the same amount of sleep as the dolphin
    (B) much less sleep than the dolphin
    (C) a much greater amount of sleep than the dolphin
    (D) an amount of sleep that cannot be estimated from the passage
    (E) an amount of sleep that would vary greatly

29. The ratio of brain weight to body weight determines
    (A) intelligence
    (B) cortex weight
    (C) sleep potential
    (D) all of the above
    (E) none of the above

30. Which of the following is true?
    (A) Not much is known about the intelligence of the sperm whale.
    (B) A human with 500 grams of cortex can speak only as well as an average eight-year-old child.
    (C) The dolphin can respond to airborne sound waves as well as to waterborne sound waves.
    (D) The human is less intelligent than the dolphin.
    (E) None of the above is true.

GO ON TO THE NEXT PAGE

Analogies

Directions: In each of the following questions choose the pair of words that *best* completes the analogy. Then mark the appropriate space in the answer column.

31. LINKS : CHAIN : :
(A) sugar : cane
(B) train : cars
(C) warp : woof
(D) rivers : ocean
(E) strands : rope

32. CORRAL : CATTLE : :
(A) dog : kennel
(B) apiary : bees
(C) fish : aquarium
(D) breviary : priest
(E) mortuary : people

33. MOVEMENT : SYMPHONY : :
(A) notes : staff
(B) melody : harmony
(C) harmony : counterpoint
(D) key : piano
(E) act : play

34. STAR : GALAXY : :
(A) electron : proton
(B) regiment : soldier
(C) shelf : book
(D) atom : molecule
(E) sea : fish

35. BITTER : SOUR : :
(A) disliking : liking
(B) enthusiastic : approving
(C) pink : red
(D) apathetic : disapproving
(E) frigid : cool

36. DRUNK : DRINK : :
(A) arisen : arise
(B) sang : sing
(C) rung : ring
(D) clang : cling
(E) stroke : strike

37. SUNSET : SUNRISE : :
(A) coming : going
(B) spring : autumn
(C) ten : five
(D) despair : hope
(E) evening : morning

38. BULLET : TRIGGER : :
(A) rope : pulley
(B) current : switch
(C) drawer : handle
(D) gun : holster
(E) light : bulb

39. DISASTER : PREMONITION : :
(A) event : prophecy
(B) life : dream
(C) fact : opinion
(D) expectation : hope
(E) religion : faith

40. SQUARE : CUBE : :
(A) oblong : square
(B) irregular : symmetrical
(C) trapezoid : parallel
(D) area : perimeter
(E) circle : sphere

IF YOU FINISH THIS SECTION OF THE SAT BEFORE YOUR TIME IS UP, YOU MAY LOOK BACK AT YOUR WORK IN THIS SECTION ONLY. YOU ARE NOT PERMITTED TO LOOK AT ANY OTHER SECTION OF THE TEST. WHEN TIME IS UP, THE SAT IS OVER.

AFTER YOU HAVE FINISHED PRACTICE TEST 1:

1. Look at the Answer Key on pages 60-61.
2. Determine your number of CORRECT answers for the MATH and VERBAL parts. DO NOT count Section 2.
3. Determine your number of INCORRECT answers for the MATH and VERBAL parts. DO NOT count Section 2.
4. To obtain the RAW SCORE for each part (VERBAL or MATH), deduct ¼ the number of INCORRECT answers from the number of CORRECT answers.
5. Find what your SCALED SCORES are by using your Raw Score and referring to the TABLES on pages 86 and 87.

Answer Key For Practice Test 1

Section 1

1. D	6. D	11. E	16. E	21. D
2. B	7. C	12. B	17. B	22. E
3. E	8. C	13. D	18. B	23. D
4. D	9. C	14. D	19. A	24. C
5. A	10. B	15. E	20. D	25. E

Section 2

1. D	9. A	17. D	25. B	33. C
2. B	10. A	18. A	26. B	34. B
3. E	11. D	19. C	27. C	35. E
4. E	12. E	20. E	28. C	36. B
5. A	13. A	21. D	29. C	37. E
6. A	14. E	22. A	30. D	38. B
7. C	15. D	23. B	31. C	39. B
8. B	16. E	24. A	32. A	40. D

Section 4

1. B	10. A	19. D	28. D	37. A
2. B	11. E	20. D	29. D	38. A
3. A	12. E	21. B	30. C	39. C
4. B	13. A	22. C	31. B	40. A
5. C	14. B	23. A	32. A	41. E
6. C	15. A	24. B	33. C	42. E
7. B	16. A	25. B	34. C	43. E
8. C	17. A	26. B	35. A	44. E
9. A	18. D	27. B	36. C	45. D

Section 5

1. D	8. A	15. D	22. D	29. D
2. A	9. A	16. A	23. B	30. A
3. E	10. E	17. B	24. C	31. D
4. D	11. C	18. A	25. B	32. B
5. B	12. A	19. B	26. A	33. D
6. C	13. B	20. A	27. C	34. C
7. B	14. B	21. B	28. B	35. C

Section 6

1. C	9. B	17. C	25. C	33. E
2. D	10. C	18. B	26. A	34. D
3. E	11. E	19. D	27. A	35. B
4. C	12. B	20. B	28. A	36. C
5. A	13. D	21. D	29. E	37. E
6. A	14. B	22. B	30. A	38. B
7. A	15. D	23. A	31. E	39. A
8. D	16. A	24. C	32. B	40. E

Explanatory Answers for Practice Test 1

Section 1: Mathematics Questions

1. **(D)**

    Formula: Rate $\times$ Time $=$ Distance

    He ran a total of 10 mi. $(4 \times 2\frac{1}{2})$.

    $$\frac{10}{6} = \frac{\text{distance}}{\text{time}} = \text{walking rate} = 1\frac{2}{3}$$

2. **(B)**

    Angles AOB $+$ BOC $+$ COD $=$ angle AOD $= 180°$.

    $$60 + 40 + \text{BOC} = 180$$
    $$\text{BOC} = 180 - 100$$
    $$\text{BOC} = 80$$

3. **(E)**

    The following coordinates of x and y may be obtained from the graph:

x	0	1	2	3
y	-4	-2	0	2

    (A) TRUE (by inspection). As x increases, y increases.

    (B) TRUE (by inspection). When $x = 0$, $y = 4$; when $y = 0$, $x = 2$.

    (C) TRUE. The angle marked θ is greater than $45°$. A right triangle is formed by the straight line $2x - y - 4 = 0$, the X axis, and the line $x = 3$. The leg opposite angle θ consists of 2 units and the adjacent leg of 1 unit. θ would be $45°$ if the legs were equal (the acute angles of an isosceles right triangle are each $45°$). The angle must be more than $45°$ since the leg opposite the angle θ is the greater.

    (D) TRUE. The graph, if continued, would pass through the point $x = 15$, $y = 26$.

    The coordinates of a point that lies on a graph will satisfy the equation of the graph,

    $2x - y - 4 = 0$ or $2(15) - (26) - 4 = 0$ or
    $30 - 30 = 0$
    $0 = 0$

4. **(D)**

    One orange costs $\frac{c}{n}$.

    Cost of x oranges $= x$ times the cost of 1 orange.

    $x \left(\frac{c}{n}\right)$ or $\frac{xc}{n}$ is the cost of x oranges.

5. (A)
Circumference $= \pi \times$ Diameter
$$72\pi = \pi \times \text{Diagonal}$$
$$72 = \text{Diagonal}$$

6. (D)
Area $=$ Length $\times$ Width   Perimeter $=$ 2(Length) $+$ 2(Width)

$$2(l) + 2(w) = 44$$
$$l + w = 22$$
$$w = 22 - l$$
$$(22 - l)l = 57 \quad \text{(substituting value of } w \text{ in area formula)}$$
$$22l - l^2 = 57$$
$$l^2 - 22l + 57 = 0$$
$$(l - 3)(l - 19) = 0 \therefore l = 3 \text{ (reject)}; l = 19$$

7. (C)

$$5a + 3p = 1.10 \quad \text{(multiply by 5)}$$
$$3a + 5p = 1.30 \quad \text{(multiply by 3)}$$

$$25a + 15p = 5.50$$
$$9a + 15p = 3.90$$
$$\overline{}$$
$$16a \quad\quad = 1.60 \quad \text{(subtracting)}$$
$$a = .10 \text{ or } \$.10$$

8. (C)
Substitute different numbers for x.

9. (C)
Since AB $=$ BC, $\angle$C $= \angle$BAC. The 50° angle is a remote exterior angle of $\angle$CAB and $\angle$C. Thus 50° $= \angle$CAB $+ \angle$C. Since $\angle$CAB $= \angle$C, $\angle$CAB $= \angle$C $= 25°$. Now surely, $y°$ $+ 25° = 180°$ (straight angle). Therefore $y° = 155°$.

10. (B)
Because EF is parallel to BC, triangle AEF is similar to triangle ABC. Therefore, triangle AEF is isosceles with AE $=$ AF. Because base angles of isosceles triangles are equal, angle x equals angle AFE. The sum of the 3 angles of a triangle is 180°, so:

$$42 + x + \text{angle AFE} = 180$$
$$42 + 2x = 180 \quad \text{(angle AFE} = x°\text{)}$$
$$2x = 138 \quad \text{(subtracting 42° from both sides)}$$
$$x = 69 \quad \text{(dividing both sides by 2)}$$

11. (E)

In square feet, the room measures 14 feet by 10 feet, or 140 square feet. Since the carpeting costs $.12 per square foot, the total cost would be $.12 times 140, or $16.80.

12. (B)

Call A' the new value of A:

$$A' = \frac{C}{3(2B)} \qquad \text{(substituting B doubled (2B) for B)}$$

$$A' = \frac{1}{2}\left(\frac{C}{3B}\right) \qquad \left(\text{taking out } \frac{1}{2}\right)$$

$$A' = \frac{1}{2}A \qquad \left(\text{substituting A for } \frac{C}{3B}\right)$$

Therefore, the new value of A is half the old.

13. (D)

Since there are 12 edges to a cube and each edge is increased by 2 in., the total increase is 24 in. (12×2).

14. (D)

$$\frac{a-b}{a^2-b^2} = \frac{a-b}{(a-b)(a+b)} = \frac{\cancel{(a-b)}}{\cancel{(a-b)}(a+b)} = \frac{1}{a+b}$$

15. (E)

$$8y = \frac{6y+2}{2x+1}$$

Multiply both sides by $(2x+1)$.

$$(8y)(2x+1) = 6y+2$$

Divide both sides by $8y$.

$$2x+1 = \frac{6y+2}{8y}$$

Subtract 1 from each side.

$$2x = \frac{6y+2}{8y} - 1$$

Find a common denominator.

$$2x = \frac{6y+2}{8y} - \frac{8y}{8y} = \frac{2-2y}{8y}$$

Divide both sides by 2.

$$x = \frac{1-y}{8y}$$

16.   (E)
Since the distance between two parallel lines is constant, the altitude of the triangle from C to AB is constant. The area of a triangle is one-half the base times the height. In this case, both base and height are constant, so $\frac{1}{2}bh$ is constant.

17.   (B)
Any product in which one of the factors is divisible by three, will be divisible by three. This reduces the problem to finding a number m such that at least one of m consecutive integers will be divisible by three. Clearly, it is possible to choose two consecutive integers such that neither will be divisible by three, but the third one chosen must then be divisible by three.

18.   (B)
Let the number of writing elements be 100. 1% are pencils— that is, there is one pencil in 100 writing tools. In 25% (or $\frac{1}{4}$) of the cases, that one pencil is yellow. Accordingly, $\frac{1}{4}$ of 1% of the writing elements are yellow pencils. This is 0.25%.

19.   (A)
$$-(1 - x^3) \geq 2$$
$$x^3 - 1 \geq 2$$
$$x^3 \geq 3$$
$$x \geq 3^{\frac{1}{3}}$$

20.   (D)
$$\frac{6m - 2}{4m^2} = \frac{3 - 2m}{2m} + \frac{2m^2 - 1}{2m^2}$$
$$= \frac{3m - 2m^2 + 2m^2 - 1}{2m^2}$$
$$= \frac{3m - 1}{2m^2}$$
$$= \frac{6m - 2}{4m^2}$$

This equality is an *identity*. It is true except when it is undefined, when $m = 0$.

21.   (D)
The coordinates of A, (5, 0), satisfy the equation. So do B, (0, −5), and D, (−4, 3). Equation: $x^2 + y^2 = 25$. This is the graph of a circle with radius 5 and center at the origin.

22. (E)

If c is positive, then c^5 is positive. Since b^4 is always positive, c^5b^4 is positive. For the entire expression to be negative, a^3 must be negative. This implies that a is negative.

23. (D)

The only time an implication, p implies q, is false is when p is true and q is false.

24. (C)

Multiply both sides of $\frac{4ab}{a+b} = a + b$ by $(a + b)$.

We get

$$4ab = (a + b)(a + b)$$

Now multiply out $(a + b)(a + b)$. We get

$$4ab = (a + b)(a + b) = a^2 + 2ab + b^2$$

Subtract $4ab$ from both sides of the above:

$$0 = a^2 + 2ab + b^2 - 4ab$$
$$= a^2 - 2ab + b^2$$
$$= (a - b)(a - b)$$

This last equation says that $a - b = 0$, or that $a = b$.

25. (E)

I is true. The square root of a fraction always equals the square root of the numerator over the square root of the denominator.

II is false. The square root of a sum is not equal to the sum of the square roots.

III is true.

$$(\sqrt{c})^2 = c$$

Since

$$(\sqrt{c})(\sqrt{c}) = \sqrt{c^2} = c$$

Section 2: Verbal Questions

1. **(D)**
   Decorous: proper; *antonym:* unsuitable

2. **(B)**
   Ribald: vulgar, coarse; *antonym:* polished

3. **(E)**
   Edify: to instruct and improve; *antonym:* confuse

4. **(E)**
   Seditious: pertaining to revolt against the government; *antonym:* loyal

5. **(A)**
   Munificent: generous, lavish; *antonym:* illiberal

6. **(A)**
   Laconic: brief; *antonym:* discursive

7. **(C)**
   Guile: deceit; *antonym:* honesty

8. **(B)**
   Adherent: one who maintains loyalty; *antonym:* opponent

9. **(A)**
   Recalcitrant: stubborn, hard to handle; *antonym:* amenable

10. **(A)**
    Lithe: flexible, limber; *antonym:* clumsy

11. **(D)**
    Cubism is a form of *art* as an *epic* is a type of a *poem.*

12. **(E)**
    A *train* stops at a *station* as a *ship* stops at a *dock.*

13. **(A)**
    A *mermaid* is part human, part *fish.* A *centaur* is part human, part *horse.*

14. **(E)**
    A *slave* is subservient to his *owner* as a *vassal* is subservient to his *master.*

15. (D)

A *priest* has an *ordination* as a *president* has an *inauguration*.

16. (E)

A *dirigible* moves through the *air* as a *boat* moves on the *water*.

17. (D)

Immortality refers to an *infinite* life whereas *mortality* refers to a *finite* life.

18. (A)

We have a *paperweight* and we have a *doorstopper*.

19. (C)

A *wail* (an audible and loud cry): *whimper* : : *guffaw* (a hearty burst of laughter) : *laugh*

20. (E)

Your *conscience* sets the course for your *conduct* as a *navigator* sets the course for the *ship*.

21. (D)

Choice (A) is incorrect because the author stops short of outright despair in the last sentence of the first paragraph by tempering the outbursts of the Renaissance scholar with the milder "our times are out of joint." Choices (B) and (E) are incorrect because there is no positive feeling expressed in the first paragraph. Choice (C) is incorrect because there is no feeling of attraction toward an earlier age. Choice (D) is correct because the negative feeling is not quite full-bodied.

22. (A)

There is no mention of energy sources at any point in the selection. Therefore, this answer is correct. Choices (B), (C), (D), and (E) are mentioned in paragraph 2.

23. (B)

The positive outlook of the words "Trend Is Not Destiny" is best exemplified by choice (B), which implies that man can improve his situation. The other statements are negative or pessimistic pronouncements.

24. (A)

The author cites choices (B), (C), (D), and (E) in paragraphs 5 and 8 as examples of renewed public awareness. The reference to the news media in the next to last paragraph is one in which the media are considered the vehicle of the public's knowledge of problems—not the result of that knowledge.

25. (B)
Choices (A) and (C) are incorrect because the author is consistently expressing optimism in man's ability to learn from past mistakes. Choice (B) is the correct answer. Choice (D) contradicts the realistic tone of the essay. Choice (E) is not at all characteristic of the writer's attitude.

26. (B)
See the fourth paragraph.

27. (C)
See the fourth paragraph.

28. (C)
See the last paragraph, where the author mentions that natural selection favored those infants who could produce tears.

29. (C)
Choice (C) is correct. See the fourth paragraph: "The nasal mucous membrane must withstand the impact of respired air . . ." Choice (A) is incorrect: see paragraph 1. Choice (B) is incorrect because, according to the passage, human infants do not usually cry with tears until they are about 6 weeks of age. Choice (D) is incorrect. See the fourth paragraph, last sentence.

30. (D)
The passage deals mainly with the need for weeping in humans from a survival point of view. The passage deals with crying but mainly *tearful* crying. Thus choice (C) is incorrect.

31. (C)
She ascribed its cause to fate because the tragedy was *unavoidable*.

32. (A)
The *residuum* is what is left.

33. (C)
Though he was romantic and sensual, his life was a life of strictness (*austerity*).

34. (B)
One would *reject* something that is repugnant when one is able to.

35. (E)
Scarcity is smallness in number or amount (*paucity*). Since economics deals with demands, scarcity is defined as *paucity* of amount or supply in *relation* to demands or wants.

36. (B)
Students who display a *stubborn* attitude cannot expect to receive praise (*plaudits*) for their efforts.

37. (E)
In accordance with the decree or edict (*ukase*), the restrictions against freedom of worship were repealed (*rescinded*).

38. (B)
The electrician worked like a *"natural."*

39. (B)
The closet poured forth (*exuded*) a reprehensible odor from *stifling* fumes.

40. (D)
Mandates and *accredit* are the only combination of words that make sense when inserted in the blanks of the sentence.

Section 4: Verbal Questions

1. **(B)**
    Quixotic: romantic and idealistic; *antonym:* realistic

2. **(B)**
    Extrovert: one whose interest is directed outside himself; *antonym:* withdrawn person

3. **(A)**
    Allay: to calm; *antonym:* provoke

4. **(B)**
    Snare: to entrap; *antonym:* to free

5. **(C)**
    Mundane: worldly; *antonym:* spiritual

6. **(C)**
    Parsimonious: stingy; *antonym:* extravagant

7. **(B)**
    Demur: to delay, to object; *antonym:* consent

8. **(C)**
    Acrimony: bitterness; *antonym:* sweetness

9. **(A)**
    Tenacious: holding fast; *antonym:* vacillating

10. **(A)**
    Secession: withdrawal; *antonym:* joining

11. **(E)**
    Repellent: tending to repel; *antonym:* inviting

12. **(E)**
    Impervious: impenetrable; *antonym:* vulnerable

13. **(A)**
    Generic: pertaining to a whole class; *antonym:* individual

14. **(B)**
    Innocuous: harmless, noncontroversial; *antonym:* harmful, deleterious

15. (A)

Wary: cautious; *antonym:* foolhardy

16. (A)

Here we are contrasting the raising of one staple crop (in the South) to diversification (in the North).

17. (A)

The best choice is (A): *warmth* but not by *frustration.*

18. (D)

The sheriff had to *pacify* the *belligerent* crowd.

19. (D)

If virtue were *universal,* we would not need police and there would be no need for a judicial court system.

20. (D)

Choice (D) is the most appropriate one consistent with the rest of the sentence.

21. (B)

A malapropism is a humorous misuse of a word. Thus, choice (B) is correct.

22. (C)

Such careless habits of dress would not be imitated by a meticulous (*fastidious*) person.

23. (A)

A wise person will not express disapproval or (*deprecate*) sectional habits or customs; he will *participate* in those practices or actions that he enjoys.

24. (B)

Since there was inadequate grazing area for the herds, the land was not dense or crowded (*sparsely* populated).

25. (B)

Choice (B) is most appropriate in light of the rest of the material presented.

26. (B)

The second paragraph sets the stage: "The classroom teacher in the elementary school is in a strategic position to influence attitudes."

27.   (B)
See paragraph 3: "Social studies (with special reference to races, creeds, and nationalities), . . ."

28.   (D)
Nowhere in the passage does the author imply that the attitudes of children are influenced by all the adults in their environment.

29.   (D)
See the last paragraph: "Finally, a teacher must constantly evaluate her own attitude because her influence can be deleterious if she has personal prejudices."

30.   (C)
The fourth paragraph does describe how attitudes can be changed in the classroom, but the first paragraph does not mention a classroom situation. Thus, choice (C) is correct. Each of the other choices relates to both the first and fourth paragraphs.

31.   (B)
The author is concerned mainly with the misinterpretation of progressive education.

32.   (A)
The author uses phrases such as "the hills of home," "fanatical fringe," "frills, fads, and follies." This is alliteration.

33.   (C)
The author states: "But since every new action produces a reaction, periods of confusion and criticism are to be expected."

34.   (C)
The author states that " 'Bolshevik' may arouse derision or disgust in the minds of many people." Thus choice (C) is correct.

35.   (A)
Nowhere in the passage does the author suggest that a reason for the avoidance of the term "progressive education" was that progressive education was confused because its roots were in many countries.

36.   (C)
A *burglar* can be stopped by an *alarm;* a *trespasser* can be stopped by the *bark* of a dog.

37. (A)

Loom (to seem imminent) : *disaster* : : *impend* (to hang or hover over menacingly) : *catastrophe*.

38. (A)

Here we are comparing opposites. *Remorseless* (no remorse) : *compassion* : : *unscrupulous* (without scruples) : *qualms* (pangs of conscience).

39. (C)

It is easy to *convince* a *gullible* person as it is easy to *insult* a *sensitive person*.

40. (A)

One *condones* an *error* as one *extenuates* (minimizes the seriousness of) a *crime*.

41. (E)

These are opposites : *pact* : *feud* : : *concord* : *discord*.

42. (E)

Posterior (later) : *simultaneous* (same time) : : *subsequent* (after) : *coincidental* (the same time or place).

43. (E)

Epilogue (the last part of a story) : *prologue* (the first part of a story) : : *appendix* (usually at the end of a book) : *preface* (usually at the beginning of a book).

44. (E)

enthusiastic : *fervor* (much enthusiasm) : : *fond* : *infatuation* (much fondness).

45. (D)

A *gang hijacks* as a *wolf prowls*.

Section 5: Mathematics Questions

1. **(D)**
    The fare is \$.30 for the first quarter mile.
    The fare is \$.10 for the next half mile.
    2 miles $= \frac{1}{4} + \frac{1}{2} + \frac{1}{2} + \frac{1}{2} + \frac{1}{4}$ miles.
    In terms of cents this is
    \$.30 + .10 + .10 + .10 + .10 = \$.70.
    Note that the remaining quarter mile costs \$.10 because it costs
    \$.10 for each half mile or *fraction thereof*.

2. **(A)**
    Area of the circle $= \pi r^2 = \pi(4)^2 = 16\pi$
    Area of the square $= \text{side}^2 = (2r)^2 = (8)^2 = 64$
    $$\text{Area of shaded portion} = \frac{\text{Area of square} - \text{Area of circle}}{4}$$
    $$\frac{64 - 16\pi}{4} = 16 - 4\pi$$

3. **(E)**
    The average is obtained by the sum of the scores divided by the
    number of terms.
    $$\frac{75 + 95 + 80 + 75 + 65}{5} = \frac{390}{5} = 78$$

4. **(D)**
    $$\frac{5 - 3\sqrt{2}}{3 + \sqrt{2}} \times \frac{3 - \sqrt{2}}{3 - \sqrt{2}} = \frac{15 - 14\sqrt{2} + 6}{9 - 2} = \frac{21 - 14\sqrt{2}}{7} =$$
    $3 - 2\sqrt{2}$

5. **(B)**
    $a = 2, b = 4$. For $* *$ to be commutative, a^b must be equal to b^a.
    $2^4 = 16 = 4^2$.

6. **(C)**
    $\begin{vmatrix} a & b \\ c & d \end{vmatrix}$ is $ad - bc$. Therefore, $3(-1) - 5(-2) = -3 + 10 = 7$.

7. **(B)**
    There are only 20 students in the school, but 25 were counted
    as taking a language. Thus, 5 were counted twice. These five
    are taking both languages.

8. (A)
Since it is a horizontal line, AC has a slope of 0. AB has a slope of $\frac{(4-2)}{(1-2)} = -2$.

9. (A)

$(BD)^2 = (CD)^2 + (BC)^2$
Since $AB = 4$, $CD = 4$.
Therefore, $(BD)^2 = 4^2 + (BC)^2$
Now $(BC)^2 = (BE)^2 - (CE)^2$
$(BC)^2 = (20)^2 - (12)^2$
So $(BD)^2 = 4^2 + (20)^2 - (12)^2$
$= 16^2 + 400 - 144$
$= 272$; $BD = \sqrt{272}$

10. (E)
Formula: $\frac{\text{Time worked}}{\text{Time required}} = \text{Part of job done}$
Let x = number of days needed when A and B work together.
$\frac{1}{r} + \frac{1}{s} = \frac{1}{x}$ This equals the amount of work done by A and B in one day.
lowest common denominator $= rsx$

$sx + rx = rs$

$x = \frac{rs}{s + r}$

11. (C)
Let d_1 = the diameter of the larger circle.
Let d_2 = the diameter of the smaller circle.
Let c_1 = the circumference of the larger circle.
Let c_2 = the circumference of the smaller circle.

$\pi d_1 = c_1$; $\pi d_2 = c_2$
$c_1 - c_2 = \pi d_1 - \pi d_2$
$c_1 - c_2 = 22$
$22 = \frac{22}{7}d_1 - \frac{22}{7}d_2 \quad (\pi = \frac{22}{7})$

$\frac{d_1}{7} - \frac{d_2}{7} = 1$; $d_1 - d_2 = 7$

Width of walk is $\frac{1}{2}$ the difference. $\therefore \frac{7}{2} = 3.5$ yd.

12. (A)

$2x - 1 = 9(6 - x)$ (squaring both sides)
$2x - 1 = 54 - 9x$
$11x = 55$
$x = 5$

13. **(B)**

The larger disc begins its rotation every 9, 18, 27, . . . seconds.
The smaller disc begins its rotation every 7, 14, 21, . . . seconds.
The answer can be obtained by multiplying the 2 numbers:
$9 \times 7 = 63$ sec.

$$\frac{63}{60} = 1\frac{1}{20} \text{ min.}$$

14. **(B)**

Area = Base $\times$ Altitude.
The altitude forms a 30-60-90 triangle.

The altitude is $\dfrac{\sqrt{3}}{3}$.

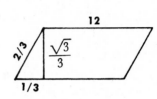

Area $= 12 \times \dfrac{\sqrt{3}}{3} = 4\sqrt{3}$ sq. in.

15. **(D)**

Let $3x =$ the numerator and $4x =$ the denominator.

$$\frac{3x - 1}{4x + 2} = \frac{2}{3}$$

$9x - 3 = 8x + 4$ (cross-multiplying)

$x = 7$

$4x = 28$

16. **(A)**

$$\frac{1}{2} + \frac{1}{3} = \frac{3 + 2}{6} = \frac{5}{6} \textbf{ (Column A)}$$

$$1\frac{1}{2} - \frac{5}{6} = \frac{3}{2} - \frac{5}{6} = \frac{9}{6} - \frac{5}{6} = \frac{4}{6} \textbf{ (Column B)}$$

17. **(B)**

$$\frac{20}{36} = \frac{5}{9} \textbf{ (Column A)}$$

$$\frac{32}{48} = \frac{2}{3} = \frac{6}{9} \textbf{ (Column B)}$$

18. **(A)**

$(72 \div 2) + 4 = 36 + 4 = 40$ **(Column A)**
$72 \div (2 + 4) = 72 \div 6 = 12$ **(Column B)**

19. **(B)**

Column A	Column B
$7x + 3y + 2z$	$2z^2 - 3y - 10x$
$= 7(3) + 3(5) + 2(7)$	$= 2(7^2) - 3(5) - 10(3)$
$= 21 + 15 + 14$	$= 2(49) - 15 - 30$
$= 50$	$= 53$

20. **(A)**

Column A	Column B
$\$16.00 \times .20 = \$3.20$	$\dfrac{2}{3} \times \$15 = \$10$
$\$16.00 - \$3.20 = \$12.80$	

21. **(B)**
For each quantity, square the expression and place it under a radical sign:

$$\sqrt{\left(\frac{2\sqrt{3}}{\sqrt{5}}\right)^2} = \sqrt{\frac{4(3)}{5}} = \sqrt{\frac{12}{5}} \text{ (Column A)}$$

$$\sqrt{\left(\frac{3\sqrt{2}}{\sqrt{5}}\right)^2} = \sqrt{\frac{9(2)}{5}} = \sqrt{\frac{18}{5}} \text{ (Column B)}$$

22. **(D)**
Since the value of x is not definite, there is no basis on which to compare the two expressions y and 6.

23. **(B)**
In Column A, the perimeter of a semicircle is equal to one-half the perimeter of a circle, or $\frac{1}{2}(2\pi r) = \pi r$.

$$\pi r = \pi(5) = \frac{22}{7} \times 5 = \frac{22 \times 5}{7} = \frac{110}{7} = 15\frac{5}{7} \text{ in.}$$

In Column B, the perimeter of a hexagon is 6 times the length of a side, or $6(5) = 30$ in.

24. **(C)**

$$b = \frac{1}{a}$$

Therefore

$$\frac{a}{b} = \frac{a}{\frac{1}{a}} = a^2$$

25. (B)

If n is an odd number, $(-2)^n$ is negative. 1 raised to any power equals 1, which is bigger than any negative number.

26. (A)

$$\frac{\frac{2}{1}}{\frac{1}{2}} = 2 \times \frac{2}{1} = 4$$

$$\frac{\frac{2}{1}}{\frac{1}{2}} = \frac{2}{2} = 1$$

27. (C)

Brazil exports 6 million bags. Angola and Ivory Coast each export 3 million bags. Accordingly, together they export 6 million bags.

28. (B)

Brazil, the largest producer, produces 15 million bags and exports 6 million bags, so the percentage is $\frac{6}{15} = 40\%$. Mexico, the smallest producer, produces 3 million bags and exports 2 million bags, so the percentage is $\frac{2}{3} = 66\frac{2}{3}\%$.

29. (D)

The answer cannot be determined because the graph shows only the world's five largest producers.

30. (A)

Colombia produces 10 million bags and keeps 2 million for home use for a percentage of $\frac{2}{10} = 20\%$. Angola produces 3.5 million bags and keeps .5 million for home use for a percentage of $.5/3.5 = 14.2857\frac{1}{7}\%$.

31. (D)

$\angle A = \angle C$ so we know $AB = BC$. It cannot be determined from the given information whether $AB = AC$.

32. (B)

$\angle ADB = 180° - \angle A - \angle ABD$.
$\angle C = 180° - \angle A - \angle B$.
$\angle ABD < \angle B$.
Therefore $\angle ADB > \angle C$.

33. (D)

Since the second equation is just -2 times the first equation, we really have only one equation in two unknowns. Therefore, the values of x and y cannot be determined.

34. (C)

Column A is
$$2 - 0 - 2 + 2 = 2 - 2 + 2 = 0 + 2 = 2$$
Column B is
$$2 - 0 + 2 - 2 = 2 + 2 - 2 = 2 + 0 = 2$$

35. (C)

Since $(-y)^2 = y^2$, these two expressions are equal.

Section 6: Verbal Questions

1. **(C)**
   Calumny: slander; *antonym:* justification

2. **(D)**
   Malediction: a curse; *antonym:* blessing

3. **(E)**
   Inept: unfit, clumsy; *antonym:* adroit

4. **(C)**
   Impious: lacking reverence; *antonym:* devout

5. **(A)**
   Pallid: pale; *antonym:* glowing

6. **(A)**
   Captious: quick to find fault; *antonym:* uncritical

7. **(A)**
   Adamant: unyielding; *antonym:* flexible

8. **(D)**
   Frugality: stinginess; *antonym:* generosity

9. **(B)**
   Recumbent: resting, lying down; *antonym:* upright

10. **(C)**
    Quail: to lose courage; *antonym:* gain courage

11. **(E)**
    The tone is that of fear. Thus the appropriate choice is *threat*.

12. **(B)**
    It would stand to reason that *implicit* in these rights is the *responsibility* to preserve and defend them to the best of their ability.

13. **(D)**
    The queen was the center of interest (*cynosure*) of all eyes as she entered the room.

14. **(B)**
    Choice (B) represents the most appropriate choice of words consistent with the idea of the sentence.

15. (D)

Here we are comparing the interests of the *individual* and of *society*.

16. (A)

It can be seen that science and economics most influenced the late 18th and 19th centuries. See the second paragraph.

17. (C)

See the last sentence of the first paragraph.

18. (B)

See the last paragraph, especially the last sentence.

19. (D)

Karl Marx was influenced by Hegel (a philosopher) and by Adam Smith (an economist).

20. (B)

It can be seen that the "survival of the fittest," or, in general, the competitive aspect of man, led to the development of 19th century economic theory.

21. (D)

The author discusses ostentation and implies that ostentation is not an inescapable phenomenon of settled social existence.

22. (B)

It can be seen that because of society's cultural standards, ostentation is enhanced.

23. (A)

The writer says, "It may be earnestly hoped that those who entertain this view have divine guidance. No rational basis for it will be found in textbooks of economics." Thus, in the context of the passage, when the author refers to "divine guidance," he is being ironic.

24. (C)

The writer stresses that the truth makes one free, and so personal freedom is attained by eradicating false beliefs.

25. (C)

The effect of a vaccination on the body, according to the passage, is comparable to the effect of truth upon the mind. ". . . ye shall know the truth, and the truth shall make you free."

26. **(A)**

The dolphin is sensitive to sound frequencies up to 120 kilocycles. This is 120,000 cycles per second. Since the upper range for humans is 20,000 cycles per second, Choice (A) is correct.

27. **(A)**

See the last sentence of the first paragraph: "Then, too, the dolphin has at least two separately controlled, independent sound mechanisms."

28. **(A)**

According to the passage, space research has indicated that man's sleep requirement reduces to the dolphin's sleep requirement when man is kept in water.

29. **(E)**

See the third sentence of the second paragraph.

30. **(A)**

See the sentence: "In this regard, the sperm whale's 9000-gram brain could raise some interesting speculation."

Choice (B) is incorrect. As stated in the passage, research indicates that in humans, 600 to 700 grams of cortex is necessary for a vocabulary. Thus, a human with 500 grams of cortex will not have a vocabulary and, in turn, will not speak like an average eight-year-old child.

Choice (C) is not necessarily true since this is nowhere implied or contradicted in the passage.

Choice (D) also is not necessarily true. The passage does not tell us the weight of the human cortex. Thus, we cannot judge whether the human may be more or less intelligent than the dolphin.

31. **(E)**

Links make up a *chain* as *strands* make up a *rope*.

32. **(B)**

Cattle are kept in a *corral* as *bees* are kept in an *apiary*.

33. **(E)**

A *symphony* is made up of *movements* as a *play* is made up of *acts*.

34. **(D)**

Stars make up a *galaxy* as *atoms* make up a *molecule*.

35. **(B)**
Bitter is slightly sharper than *sour*. *Enthusiastic* is slightly more intense than *approving*.

36. **(C)**
Drunk can have a different meaning than *drink* although it may also represent a different tense of drink. *Rung* can have a different meaning than *ring* although it may represent a different tense of ring. Also, there is an "ru" in *drunk* and an "ri" in *drink,* as there is an "ru" in *rung* and an "ri" in *ring*.

37. **(E)**
Sunset is the beginning of *evening*. *Sunrise* is the beginning of *morning*.

38. **(B)**
A *trigger* sets a *bullet* in motion. A *switch* sets a *current* in motion.

39. **(A)**
One may have a *premonition* of a *disaster* as one may have a *prophecy* of an *event*.

40. **(E)**
A *square* is two dimensional. A *cube* is three dimensional. When projected on a plane surface, a *cube* appears as a *square*. A *circle* is two dimensional. A *sphere* is three dimensional. When projected on a plane surface, a *sphere* appears as a *circle*.

How to Improve Your SAT Score

1. Find out what your scaled score is by looking at the RAW SCORE–SCALED SCORE CONVERSION TABLES on pages 86 and 87.
2. Refer to the SELF-APPRAISAL TABLE on page 94.
3. Read the section on VERBAL ABILITY beginning on page 319.
4. Take the 7 DIAGNOSTIC MATH TESTS beginning on page 359. These are coded to the Math Refresher (Part V) so you may assess and improve your math ability by taking the Diagnostic Tests and then referring to the Math Refresher.
5. Read the section on MATHEMATICAL ABILITY beginning on page 403.
6. Read the section: ABOUT THE SUBTESTS OF THE SAT beginning on page 299 for more specific help in dealing with each question type on the SAT.
7. Read the section on THE MINIMUM SETS OF MATH RULES AND CONCEPTS WITH WHICH YOU MUST BE FAMILIAR on page 516
8. Read WHAT THE SAT IS TESTING IN MATH AND HOW TO BE ONE STEP AHEAD, on page 522
9. Read MATHEMATICAL SHORTCUTS YOU SHOULD KNOW, on page 537
10. Read SHORTCUTS AND TECHNIQUES FOR ANSWERING THE QUANTITATIVE COMPARISON TYPE QUESTION, pages 540–548.
11. Work on the 80 ADDITIONAL QUANTITATIVE COMPARISON PRACTICE QUESTIONS, beginning on page 557.
12. Take PRACTICE TESTS 2, 3, and 4.

Raw Score-Scaled Score Conversion Table

When you receive your test results from the College Entrance Examination Board, you will see a VERBAL score (graded on a scale of 200 to 800) and a MATH score (also graded on a scale from 200 to 800). These are your SCALED SCORES. The Scaled Score is related to the Raw Score. The number of CORRECT answers minus one-fourth the number of INCORRECT answers is the RAW SCORE. If you get a Scaled Score of 500, you can expect to be in the 50th percentile—half the students taking the SAT scored above you, and the other half scored below you.

On the following pages are unofficial tables from which you may convert your RAW SCORE to your SCALED SCORE for the SAT practice tests that you take.

PRACTICE TEST 1   Verbal Part

Raw Score*	Scaled Score	Raw Score*	Scaled Score	Raw Score*	Scaled Score
85	800	63	580	42	380
84	790	62	570	41	380
83	780	61	560	40	370
82	770	60	550	39	370
81	760	59	540	38	360
80	750	58	530	37	360
79	740	57	520	36	355
78	730	56	510	35	350
77	720	55	500	34	340
76	710	54	490	33	340
75	700	53	480	32	335
74	690	52	470	31	330
73	680	51	460	30	320
72	670	50	450	29	320
71	660	49	440	28	310
70	650	48	430	27	310
69	640	47	420	26	300
68	630	46	410	25	300
67	620	45	400	20	270
66	610	44	390	10	230
65	600	43	390	0–10	200
64	590				

* Add the total number of CORRECT answers for Sections 4 and 6 and deduct from this one-fourth the total number of INCORRECT answers for Sections 4 and 6.

PRACTICE TEST 1   Math Part

Raw Score*	Scaled Score	Raw Score*	Scaled Score	Raw Score*	Scaled Score
60	800	45	650	31	400
59	790	44	640	30	390
58	780	43	620	29	380
57	770	42	610	28	370
56	760	41	600	27	360
55	750	40	580	26	350
54	740	39	560	25	340
53	730	38	540	24	330
52	720	37	520	23	320
51	710	36	500	22	320
50	700	35	480	21	310
49	690	34	460	20	300
48	680	33	440	10	250
47	670	32	420	0–10	200
46	660				

* Add the total number of CORRECT answers for Sections 1 and 5 and deduct from this one-fourth the total number of INCORRECT answers for Sections 1 and 5.

PRACTICE TEST 2   Verbal Part

Raw Score*	Scaled Score	Raw Score*	Scaled Score	Raw Score*	Scaled Score
85	800	63	580	42	380
84	790	62	570	41	380
83	780	61	560	40	370
82	770	60	550	39	370
81	760	59	540	38	360
80	750	58	530	37	360
79	740	57	520	36	350
78	730	56	510	35	350
77	720	55	500	34	340
76	710	54	490	33	340
75	700	53	480	32	330
74	690	52	470	31	330
73	680	51	460	30	320
72	670	50	450	29	320
71	660	49	440	28	310
70	650	48	430	27	310
69	640	47	420	26	300
68	630	46	410	25	300
67	620	45	400	20	270
66	610	44	390	10	230
65	600	43	390	0–10	200
64	590				

* Add the total number of CORRECT answers for Sections 1 and 5 and deduct from this one-fourth the total number of INCORRECT answers for Sections 1 and 5.

PRACTICE TEST 2   Math Part

*Raw Score**	*Scaled Score*	*Raw Score**	*Scaled Score*	*Raw Score**	*Scaled Score*
60	800	45	650	31	400
59	790	44	640	30	390
58	780	43	620	29	380
57	770	42	610	28	370
56	760	41	600	27	360
55	750	40	580	26	350
54	740	39	560	25	340
53	730	38	540	24	330
52	720	37	520	23	320
51	710	36	500	22	320
50	700	35	480	21	310
49	690	34	460	20	300
48	680	33	440	10	250
47	670	32	420	0–10	200
46	660				

* Add the total number of CORRECT answers for Sections 2 and 3 and deduct from this one-fourth the total number of INCORRECT answers for Sections 2 and 3.

PRACTICE TEST 3   Verbal Part

Raw Score*	Scaled Score	Raw Score*	Scaled Score	Raw Score*	Scaled Score
85	800	63	580	42	380
84	790	62	570	41	380
83	780	61	560	40	375
82	770	60	550	39	370
81	760	59	540	38	360
80	750	58	530	37	360
79	740	57	520	36	350
78	730	56	510	35	350
77	720	55	500	34	340
76	710	54	490	33	340
75	700	53	480	32	330
74	690	52	470	31	330
73	680	51	460	30	320
72	670	50	450	29	320
71	660	49	440	28	310
70	650	48	430	27	310
69	640	47	420	26	300
68	630	46	410	25	300
67	620	45	400	20	270
66	610	44	390	10	230
65	600	43	390	0–10	200
64	590				

* Add the total number of CORRECT answers for Sections 2 and 4 and deduct from this one-fourth the total number of INCORRECT answers for Sections 2 and 4.

PRACTICE TEST 3   Math Part

Raw Score*	Scaled Score	Raw Score*	Scaled Score	Raw Score*	Scaled Score
60	800	45	650	31	400
59	790	44	640	30	390
58	780	43	620	29	380
57	770	42	610	28	370
56	760	41	600	27	360
55	750	40	580	26	350
54	740	39	560	25	340
53	730	38	540	24	330
52	720	37	520	23	320
51	710	36	500	22	320
50	700	35	480	21	310
49	690	34	460	20	300
48	680	33	440	10	250
47	670	32	420	0–10	200
46	660				

* Add the total number of CORRECT answers for Sections 1 and 5 and deduct from this one-fourth the total number of INCORRECT answers for Sections 1 and 5.

PRACTICE TEST 4 Verbal Part

Raw Score*	Scaled Score	Raw Score*	Scaled Score	Raw Score*	Scaled Score
85	800	63	580	42	380
84	790	62	570	41	380
83	780	61	560	40	370
82	770	60	550	39	370
81	760	59	540	38	360
80	750	58	530	37	360
79	740	57	520	36	350
78	730	56	510	35	350
77	720	55	500	34	340
76	710	54	490	33	340
75	700	53	480	32	330
74	690	52	470	31	330
73	680	51	460	30	320
72	670	50	450	29	320
71	660	49	440	28	310
70	650	48	430	27	310
69	640	47	420	26	300
68	630	46	410	25	300
67	620	45	400	20	270
66	610	44	390	10	230
65	600	43	390	0–10	200
64	590				

* Add the total number of CORRECT answers for Sections 1 and 6 and deduct from this one-fourth the total number of INCORRECT answers for Sections 1 and 6.

PRACTICE TEST 4   Math Part

Raw Score*	Scaled Score	Raw Score*	Scaled Score	Raw Score*	Scaled Score
60	800	45	650	31	400
59	790	44	640	30	390
58	780	43	620	29	380
57	770	42	610	28	370
56	760	41	600	27	360
55	750	40	580	26	350
54	740	39	560	25	340
53	730	38	540	24	330
52	720	37	520	23	320
51	710	36	500	22	320
50	700	35	480	21	310
49	690	34	460	20	300
48	680	33	440	10	250
47	670	32	420	0–10	200
46	660				

* Add the total number of CORRECT answers for Sections 2 and 5 and deduct from this one-fourth the total number of INCORRECT answers for Sections 2 and 5.

Self-Appraisal Tables

Practice Test 1

Use the table below to find out how you performed on each of the question types of the SAT Practice Test. The numbers in the boxes refer to the *total* number of CORRECT answers for the respective question type.

	Antonyms	Sentence Completions	Reading Comprehension	Analogies	Regular Math	Quantitative Comparison
EXCELLENT	33–35	22–25	33–35	27–30	37–40	18–20
GOOD	27–32	18–21	27–32	22–26	30–36	14–17
FAIR	18–26	13–17	18–26	16–21	22–29	10–13
POOR	11–17	8–12	11–17	10–15	13–21	7–9
VERY POOR	0–10	0–7	0–10	0–9	0–12	0–6

Practice Test 2

Use the table below to find out how you performed on each of the question types of the SAT Practice Test. The numbers in the boxes refer to the *total* number of CORRECT answers for the respective question type.

	Antonyms	Sentence Completions	Reading Comprehension	Analogies	Regular Math	Quantitative Comparison
EXCELLENT	22–25	14–15	22–25	18–20	60–65	18–20
GOOD	18–21	11–13	18–21	14–17	50–59	14–17
FAIR	13–17	8–10	13–17	10–13	37–49	10–13
POOR	8–12	5–7	8–12	7–9	20–36	7–9
VERY POOR	0–7	0–4	0–7	0–6	0–19	0–6

Practice Test 3

Use the table below to find out how you performed on each of the question types of the SAT Practice Test. The numbers in the boxes refer to the *total* number of CORRECT answers for the respective question type.

	Antonyms	Sentence Completions	Reading Comprehension	Analogies	Regular Math	Quantitative Comparison
EXCELLENT	22–25	14–15	22–25	18–20	55–60	27–30
GOOD	18–21	11–13	18–21	14–17	50–59	22–26
FAIR	13–17	8–10	13–17	10–13	37–49	16–21
POOR	8–12	5–7	8–12	7–9	20–36	10–15
VERY POOR	0–7	0–4	0–7	0–6	0–19	0–9

Practice Test 4

Use the table below to find out how you performed on each of the question types of the SAT Practice Test. The numbers in the boxes refer to the *total* number of CORRECT answers for the respective question type.

	Antonyms	Sentence Completions	Reading Comprehension	Analogies	Regular Math	Quantitative Comparison
EXCELLENT	33–35	22–25	33–35	27–30	37–40	18–20
GOOD	27–32	18–21	27–32	22–26	30–36	14–17
FAIR	18–26	13–17	18–26	16–21	22–29	10–13
POOR	11–17	8–12	11–17	10–15	13–21	7–9
VERY POOR	0–10	0–7	0–10	0–9	0–12	0–6

SAT PRACTICE TEST 2 $\longrightarrow$

Tear out the answer sheet for this test at the end of the book.

Section 1: Verbal Questions

Antonyms

Directions: Each question in this test consists of a word printed in capital letters followed by five words lettered (A) through (E). Choose the word that has most nearly the OPPOSITE meaning from the word in capital letters. Then mark the appropriate space in the answer column.

1. PAUCITY
   - (A) scarcity
   - (B) obesity
   - (C) dearth
   - (D) abundance
   - (E) truth

2. MODISH
   - (A) unfashionable
   - (B) stylish
   - (C) momentous
   - (D) conventional
   - (E) artful

3. OPIATE
   - (A) deadener
   - (B) narcotic
   - (C) optician
   - (D) glass
   - (E) stimulant

4. MUTE
   - (A) silent
   - (B) dumb
   - (C) loud
   - (D) vocal
   - (E) taunting

5. FETID
   - (A) malodorous
   - (B) distasteful
   - (C) fragrant
   - (D) unappetizing
   - (E) enigmatic

6. STAID
   - (A) exuberant
   - (B) serene
   - (C) sedate
   - (D) solid
   - (E) drunk

7. INDOLENT
   - (A) active
   - (B) insolent
   - (C) opposite
   - (D) feverish
   - (E) greed

8. QUAINT
   - (A) unusual
   - (B) different
   - (C) ordinary
   - (D) stale
   - (E) coarse

9. ALTERCATION
   - (A) argument
   - (B) mixture
   - (C) agreement
   - (D) accumulation
   - (E) carom

10. NOCTURNAL
    - (A) at night
    - (B) diurnal
    - (C) sleepless
    - (D) tired
    - (E) alert

Sentence Completions

Directions: Each question in this test consists of a sentence or group of sentences in which one or two words are missing. Beneath the question are five pairs of words lettered (A) through (E). Choose the word or the pair of words that *best* completes the sentence or sentences. Then mark the appropriate space in the answer column.

---

11. Although our country is a land of plenty, we still have much to do to assure to all of our people _____ to develop their _____ for personal, group, and community usefulness.
    (A) obligations—interests
    (B) caprices—interests
    (C) resources—impartiality
    (D) opportunities—ambitions
    (E) opportunities—capacities

12. There is much justification for the _____ forecast made by the officers of the corporation: compared with the earnings of the past three years, the income of the corporation was _____ than ever before.
    (A) casual—less
    (B) pessimistic—larger
    (C) studied—more
    (D) sanguine—greater
    (E) long-term—far more

13. His success in converting the people to his way of thinking was largely a result of his _____ criticisms of the existing order.
    (A) substantial
    (B) emotional
    (C) indiscreet
    (D) persuasive
    (E) unbridled

14. This teacher has little regard for factual learning on the part of his students; his goal is to build men, not to make _____.
    (A) television contestants
    (B) thinkers
    (C) encyclopedias
    (D) theorists
    (E) martinets

15. While it may appear at the present time that the Soviets exceed us in missile production, I am certain that this _____ will _____ in due course.
    (A) superiority—increase
    (B) advantage—decline
    (C) inferiority—diminish
    (D) situation—defeat itself
    (E) propaganda—develop

16. The crowded cities and the concentration of industry in our country make us a _____ target of any _____ who can take us by surprise.
    (A) difficult—enemy
    (B) hostile—dictator
    (C) easy—friend
    (D) vulnerable—adversary
    (E) bristling—planes

17. Only the rich can save money without _____.
    (A) distinction
    (B) shame
    (C) compulsion
    (D) privation
    (E) argument

18. Man has added much to the science of horticulture. In particular, he has accomplished a great deal in the selection and breeding of flowers through _____ and _____.
    (A) protection—incision
    (B) modification—adaptation
    (C) sheltering—pruning
    (D) grafting—restriction
    (E) colonizing—selection

19. A strike is usually resorted to only when less _____ measures fail.
    (A) mercenary
    (B) drastic
    (C) urgent
    (D) meaningful
    (E) preferable

20. A _____ point is one that is _____.
    (A) subjective—objective
    (B) disputed—untenable
    (C) rejected—argumentative
    (D) valid—reliable
    (E) moot—disputable

Reading Comprehension

Directions: Read the following passages and answer each of the questions that come after them. Choose the *best* answer. Then mark the appropriate space in the answer column.

In the terminology of the Domesday Inquest we find the villeins as the most numerous element of the English population. Out of about 240,000 households enumerated in Domesday, 100,000 are marked as belonging to villeins. They are rustics performing, as a rule, work services for their lords. But not all the inhabitants of the villages were designated by that name. Villeins are opposed to socmen and freemen on one hand, to *bordarii,* cottagers, and slaves on the other. The distinction in regard to the first two of these groups was evidently derived from their greater freedom, although the difference is only one in degree and not in kind. In fact, the villein is assumed to be a person free by birth, but holding land of which he can not dispose freely. The distinction as against *bordarii* and cottagers is based on the size of the holding: the villeins are holders of regular shares in the village—that is, of the virgates, bovates, or half-hides which constitute the principal subdivisions in the fields and contribute to form the plough-teams—whereas the *bordarii* hold smaller plots of some five acres, more or less, and *cottarii* are connected with mere cottages and crofts. Thus the terminology of Domesday takes note of two kinds of differences in the status given to rustics: a legal one in connection with the right to dispose of property in land, and an economic one reflecting the opposition between the holders of shares in the fields and the holders of auxiliary tenements. The feature of personal serfdom is also noticeable, but it provides a basis only for the comparatively small group of *servi,* of whom only about 25,000 are enumerated in Domesday Book. The contrast between this exceptionally situated class and the rest of the population shows that personal slavery was rapidly disappearing in England about the time of the Conquest. It is also to be noticed that the Domesday Survey constantly mentions the *terra villanorum* as opposed to the demesne of the estates or manors of the time, and that the land of the rustics is taxed separately for the gold, so that distinction between the property of the lord and that of the peasant dependent on him is clearly marked and is by no means devoid of practical importance.

21.   What would you choose as the best title for this paragraph?
- (A)   Serfdom in England
- (B)   The Domesday Inquest
- (C)   The Status of the Villein at the Time of the Norman Conquest
- (D)   Socman, Freeman, and Villein
- (E)   The Rights of the People of England

22. What sort of services did the villeins perform for their lords?
(A) agricultural labor
(B) household work
(C) land-rental services
(D) military services
(E) special obligations

23. What is the name of the class who held shares in the fields?
(A) villeins
(B) socmen
(C) freemen
(D) *servi*
(E) cottagers

24. What is the name of a class who held auxiliary tenements?
(A) lords
(B) socmen
(C) freemen
(D) *bordarii*
(E) *servi*

25. Which of these do you think would be nearest to the number of personal serfs in England 50 years before the Domesday Survey?
(A) 5,000
(B) 15,000
(C) 25,000
(D) 35,000
(E) 20,000

Even in early times there was a certain variety in biography, but it was mostly written for political or moral purposes in Greek and Roman times and much later. In the 4th century B.C., Xenophon wrote a defense of his master Socrates that is called *Memorabilia*—a title something like the word "memoirs" as it is used today. In the 1st century A.D., Plutarch wrote his *Parallel Lives,* comparing the careers of a score of Romans with the same number of Greeks, pair by pair, and countless later writers (Shakespeare among them) drew on this work for facts and characterization. In Latin, Cornelius Nepos (1st century B.C.) wrote brief lives of illustrious men in a simple clear style; Tacitus, the great historian, wrote a life of his father-in-law Agricola that is a classic; and Suetonius's *Twelve Caesars* (written about 120 A.D.) is gossipy and full of scandal. These are samples of what is called "antique biography," written to emphasize certain moral qualities or to teach a political lesson.

Biography in English begins in the 16th century with William Roper's *Life of Sir Thomas More* and George Cavendish's *Life of Cardinal Wolsey*. In the 17th century, Izaak Walton wrote the *Lives* of Donne, Hooker, Herbert and others that are the forerunners of modern personal biography. James Boswell's *Life of Samuel Johnson* (1791) is interesting, personal, detailed, and minute. Johnson's own *Life of Cowley* was written, he said, because in a former biography "all was confused and enlarged through a mist of panegyric."

26. Shakespeare utilized the works of
    I.   Xenophon
    II. Tacitus
    III. Suetonius
    IV. William Roper
    (A) I and II only
    (B) III and IV only
    (C) I, II, and III only
    (D) I, II, III, and IV
    (E) none of those mentioned

27. Antique biography
    (A) utilizes factual material
    (B) teaches a lesson
    (C) tells about the lives of famous people
    (D) contains the author's own life story
    (E) is relevant to none of these

28. The writing of biography is
    (A) relatively modern
    (B) not popular
    (C) very common
    (D) found early in history
    (E) associated primarily with England

29. A book which contains several biographies was written by
    (A) Xenophon
    (B) Plutarch
    (C) Roper
    (D) Boswell
    (E) Sir Thomas More

30. Shakespeare was influenced by the Greek and Roman authors, especially by
    (A) Plutarch
    (B) Suetonius
    (C) Tacitus
    (D) Xenophon
    (E) none of these

Analogies

Directions: In each of the following questions choose the pair of words that *best* completes the analogy. Then mark the appropriate space in the answer column.

---

31. SPARSE : DENSE ::
(A) clever : shrewd
(B) California : New York
(C) bald : stupid
(D) Nevada : Java
(E) obtuse : acute

32. FREQUENTLY : SELDOM ::
(A) happy : sad
(B) intermittently : occasionally
(C) always : never
(D) constantly : ubiquitously
(E) never : always

33. DISEASE : IMMUNITY ::
(A) obligation : debt
(B) change : adaptation
(C) custom : conformity
(D) transgression : pardon
(E) tax : exemption

34. GLANCE : SCRUTINIZE ::
(A) watch : search
(B) eye : sight
(C) look : see
(D) touch : grasp
(E) ponder : examine

35. MUSCLE : CRAMP ::
(A) stone : crack
(B) machine : jam
(C) pain : throb
(D) lightning : flash
(E) order : cancel

36. PLATEAU : PLAIN ::
(A) lake : river
(B) water : lake
(C) country : state
(D) mountain : valley
(E) order : cancel

37. POODLE : KENNEL ::
(A) pugilist : ring
(B) bird : nest
(C) canary : cage
(D) fish : tackle
(E) tiger : zoo

38. WALL : MASON ::
(A) cement : bricklayer
(B) magic : magician
(C) friendship : stranger
(D) picture : painter
(E) cure : doctor

39. AUTOMOBILE : BRAKE ::
(A) doer : thinker
(B) man : conscience
(C) horse : ride
(D) carburetor : choke
(E) society : detergent

40. BIGOTRY : TOLERANCE ::
(A) urgency : exigency
(B) profession : avocation
(C) ribaldry : prodigality
(D) unselfish : selfish
(E) parsimony : magnanimity

Reading Comprehension

Directions: Read the following passage and answer each of the questions that comes after it. Choose the *best* answer. Then mark the appropriate space in the answer column.

Gentlemen, should not any anthropologist be attracted by an institution such as yours, which combines within itself the characteristics peculiar to those historical concretions without which no society could survive nor even come into existence, devoid as it would be of any internal framework?

Institutions give the body politic its solidity and durability; but they can only fulfill this role if their legitimacy is unquestionable. This legitimacy rests at once upon a principle of continuity and a requirement of filiation.

A principle of continuity, since the value of institutions does not correspond, at any particular moment, to the value of the individuals of whom they are composed.

On the contrary, as soon as these individuals seek to become members and are accepted by the institutions, they fuse their personal value with that of the organism it is their mission to maintain, until such time as others replace them and accept in their turn the responsibility of perpetuating it.

Filiation, since you bestow on each of your members the advantage of a line of descent composed of all those who, over almost three and a half centuries, have sat in the seat he has the honor of occupying; this line of descent is partly fictitious, but the anthropologist knows that the same is true of those genealogies he has traveled to the ends of the world to record, at least in all cases where they claim to go back any distance in time.

And although the immortality which, according to another legend, you bestow upon your elect may be more rightly termed *ante* than *post mortem* (the Academic function, being synonymous with life, at least allows those who exercise it to escape the social death of retirement), this privilege, which is attributed to you somewhat ironically, bears witness even in our society to the strength of the link binding so many institutions to the domain of magic and the supernatural.

Yet, whatever illusory objective institutions may proclaim or be credited with, they have another very real aim. They organize individuals into a system and give contours and perspective to social life.

They mold its amorphous matter and allow society to acquire dimensions in which it would have been lacking had it remained unstructured. Institutions construct the social order. As a sheet of paper can be folded, opened up and turned inside out to create a certain shape or form, an institution such as yours, gentlemen, gathers up a surface into a volume. It shortens distances and brings together types of minds and individuals in an unexpected manner.

By creating and re-creating orders different from the empirical order, it bestows form on the seething chaos of events; it filters the flow of time, modulates the uniform course of the generations, breaks down these groups and then rebuilds their elements into more firmly organized entities, thus bringing into being new social and moral configurations which differ from the primitive dispensation, while preserving, interpreting and enriching its potentialities.

41. According to this passage, an institution derives its *raison d'etre* from
(A) the value of its current membership
(B) the value and continuity of its historical mission
(C) the body politic
(D) a purely fictitious genealogy
(E) the expertise of past members

42. The writer affirms that once an individual becomes part of an institution, he
(A) seeks to become a more creative human being
(B) searches for ways to become immortal
(C) submits his personality to the will of the group at large
(D) makes his goals synonymous with those of the institution into which he has been accepted
(E) postpones his retirement from social life indefinitely

43. The writer maintains that one goal of institutions is to
(A) help interpret the magic and the supernatural
(B) mold society into predestined dimensions
(C) provide society with substantial form extracted from the undetermined matter of which it is constituted
(D) insure a scientific approach to the interpretation of a chaotic world
(E) create a stopgap action so that generations are ultimately destroyed and must be rebuilt

44. Judging from the comments of the author, he is directing his remarks to
(A) the inmates of a prison
(B) the members of a lawmaking body
(C) the members of a college fraternity
(D) the members of a medical association
(E) the members of a select academic society

45. One may safely conclude from the writer's remarks that he regards membership in the organization with
(A) awe
(B) envy
(C) respect
(D) regret
(E) confusion

IF YOU FINISH THIS SECTION OF THE SAT BEFORE YOUR TIME IS UP, YOU MAY LOOK BACK AT YOUR WORK IN THIS SECTION ONLY. YOU ARE NOT PERMITTED TO LOOK AT ANY OTHER SECTION OF THE TEST. WHEN THE TIME IS UP, TURN TO THE NEXT SECTION AND START WORK ON THAT SECTION.

Section 2: Mathematics Questions

Time: 30 minutes

Directions: Each question in this section is followed by five choices lettered (A) through (E). Choose the correct answer. Then mark the appropriate space in the answer column.

The following information may be useful to you in solving some of the mathematics problems in this part:

Circle, radius = r:
   Area $= \pi r^2$.
   Circumference $= 2\pi r$.
   A circle has 360 degrees of arc.

Triangle:
   The sum of the three angles in a triangle is 180 degrees.
   Area $= \frac{1}{2}$(any side $\times$ altitude to that side).

Right Triangle:
   The sum of the squares of the legs $=$ the square of the hypotenuse.

Definitions of certain mathematical symbols:

   $>$ is greater than
   $<$ is less than
   $\geq$ is greater than or equal to
   $\leq$ is less than or equal to
   $\perp$ is perpendicular to
   $\parallel$ is parallel to

Important Note: Figures in this section are not always drawn to scale. All numbers are real numbers and all figures lie in a plane unless otherwise stated.

1. The average of a number together with two-fifths of that number and 30, is 31. Find the number.
   (A)   70
   (B)   61
   (C)   31
   (D)   25
   (E)   45

2. The graph of $y = x^2 + 4x + 1$ intersects the line $y = 1$ at which of the following points?
   (A)   (0, 1) and (−4, 1)
   (B)   (0, 0) and (−4, 0)
   (C)   (1, 1)
   (D)   (4, 1)
   (E)   (1, 0)

3. A man wishes to dig a rectangular hole whose dimensions will be 3 ft. wide, 5 ft. long, and 6 ft. deep. If the chest to be buried there measures 2 ft. wide, 5 ft. long, and 2 ft. high, how much earth will remain after burying the chest?
   (A)   70 cu. ft.
   (B)   110 cu. ft.
   (C)   50 cu. ft.
   (D)   60 cu. ft.
   (E)   20 cu. ft.

4. Find the value of $(4^{\frac{1}{2}})\,(2^3)^2(2^{-2})$.
   (A) $16\sqrt{2}$
   (B)   64
   (C)   4
   (D)   16
   (E)   32

5. Solve the set of equations $x + 2y = 7$ and $2x + 4y = 8$.
   (A) $x = 1$ and $y = 3$
   (B) $x = 0$ and $y = 2$
   (C) $x = 0$ and $y = 0$
   (D) $x = 1$ and $y = 1$
   (E)   no solution

6. If $a * b = a^2 + ab + b$, then $1 * x =$
   (A) x
   (B)   1
   (C) $1 + 2x$
   (D) x^2
   (E) $x^2 + x + 1$

7. In the diagram below, rectangle ABCD and square DEFG both have areas of p^2. If the length of AD is m units, what is the length of EC?

(A) mp

(B) $m - p$

(C) $p - m$

(D) $\dfrac{p^2}{m}$

(E) $\dfrac{p^2}{m} - p$

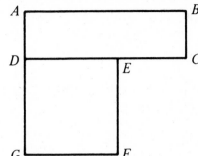

8. The area of the triangle formed by the line $x + 3y = 6$, and the X and Y axes is

(A) 2

(B) 12

(C) 6

(D) 3

(E) 10

9. Which of the following is a subset of the integers?

  I. null set

 II. positive integers

III. reals

(A) I only

(B) III only

(C) I and II only

(D) II and III only

(E) I, II, and III

10. Mr. Smith bought a tape recorder for $700. He had it insured for 80% of the full value at a rate of $.80 per $100. What was his annual premium?

(A) $3.96

(B) $5.34

(C) $2.64

(D) $4.48

(E) $5.64

11. What is the area of a triangle whose vertices are $(-1, 1)$, $(2, 1)$ and $(0, -3)$?

(A) 2

(B) 6

(C) 1

(D) 12

(E) 8.5

12. If $|x + 2| < 2$ then
(A) $x < 0$
(B) $-4 < x < 0$
(C) $x > 4$
(D) $x = -1$
(E) $x = 2$

13. Which of the lines on the graph represents the equation
$y = 2x - 4$?
(A) a
(B) b
(C) c
(D) d
(E) e

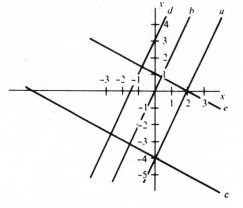

14. Which of the choices below is greater than $\frac{1}{4}$?

(A) $-\frac{1}{2}$

(B) $.04$

(C) $\sqrt{\frac{1}{4}}$

(D) $(\frac{1}{4})^2$

(E) $\frac{0.4}{4}$

15. If $a \neq 0$, $b \neq 0$, and $ab \neq 1$, then $\dfrac{ab - 1}{a - \dfrac{1}{b}} =$

(A) a
(B) $a - b$
(C) ab
(D) $1 - ob$
(E) b

16. If 2 feet of wood cost $.80, how much do 4 yards of wood cost?
(A) $9.60
(B) $.40
(C) $4.80
(D) $6.40
(E) $3.20

17. In the triangle below, line DE is parallel to line BC. If angle
    B = 60° and angle A = 50°, what is angle x?
    (A) 60°
    (B) 110°
    (C) 10°
    (D) 70°
    (E) 90°

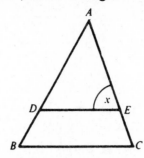

18. To paint 2 square yards of wall with a special fluid costs $1.00.
    How much would it cost to cover a wall 9 feet by 15 feet?
    (A) $7.50
    (B) $15.00
    (C) $67.50
    (D) $22.50
    (E) $100.00

19. If $x = \dfrac{1}{y}$ and y is tripled, then the value of x
    (A) is tripled
    (B) is reduced by two-thirds of its original value
    (C) is multiplied by 9
    (D) is decreased by 3
    (E) remains the same

20. In triangle ABC, angle A is twice angle C and angle B is three
    times angle C. What is the size of angle A?
    (A) 30°
    (B) 45°
    (C) 60°
    (D) 120°
    (E) 90°

21. Which of the following is greater than x for all $x > 1$.
    (A) $-x$
    (B) $\dfrac{1}{x}$
    (C) $\sqrt{x}$
    (D) x^2
    (E) $\frac{1}{2}x$

22.   What percent of 300 is 450?
   (A) $66\frac{2}{3}\%$
   (B) 150%
   (C) $133\frac{1}{3}\%$
   (D) 50%
   (E) 75%

23.   In the diagram shown, each unit on the X-axis represents 2 feet. Each unit on the Y-axis represents $\frac{1}{2}$ foot. What is the distance between a point 6 units along the X-axis and a point 10 units along the Y-axis?
   (A)   13 feet
   (B)   17 feet
   (C)   26 feet
   (D)   18 feet
   (E)   4 feet

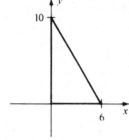

24.   According to the graph, what percent of the people in the group had brown eyes?
   (A) 40%
   (B) 10%
   (C) 50%
   (D) $33\frac{1}{3}\%$
   (E) 5%

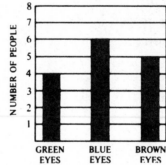

25. A car rides d miles for h hours. It then continues for x miles for y hours. What is the average rate of speed for the entire trip?

(A) $\dfrac{dx + hy}{h - y}$

(B) $\dfrac{d + x}{h + y}$

(C) $\dfrac{dh + xy}{hy}$

(D) $\dfrac{dy + xh}{2}$

(E) $(d + h)(x + y)$

IF YOU FINISH THIS SECTION OF THE SAT BEFORE YOUR TIME IS UP, YOU MAY LOOK BACK AT YOUR WORK IN THIS SECTION ONLY. YOU ARE NOT PERMITTED TO LOOK AT ANY OTHER SECTION OF THE TEST. WHEN THE TIME IS UP, TURN TO THE NEXT SECTION AND START WORK ON THAT SECTION.

Section 3: Mathematics Questions

Directions: Each question in this section is followed by five choices lettered (A) through (E). Choose the correct answer. Then mark the appropriate space in the answer column.

The following information may be useful to you in solving some of the mathematics problems in this part:

Circle, radius = r:
Area $= \pi r^2$.
Circumference $= 2\pi r$.
A circle has 360 degrees of arc.

Triangle:
The sum of the three angles in a triangle is 180 degrees.
Area $= \frac{1}{2}$(any side $\times$ altitude to that side).

Right Triangle:
The sum of the squares of the legs $=$ the square of the hypotenuse.

Definitions of certain mathematical symbols:

$>$ is greater than
$<$ is less than
$\geq$ is greater than or equal to
$\leq$ is less than or equal to
$\perp$ is perpendicular to
$\parallel$ is parallel to

Important Note: Figures in this section are not always drawn to scale. All numbers are real numbers and all figures lie in a plane unless otherwise stated.

1. Find the length of a rectangle whose perimeter is 42 and whose diagonal is 15.
    (A) 21
    (B) 18
    (C) 16
    (D) 14
    (E) 12

2. A circle is inscribed in a square whose side is 6. Find the area of the shaded portion.
    (A) $36 - 18\pi$
    (B) $36 - 9\pi$
    (C) $36 - \pi$
    (D) 36
    (E) none of these

    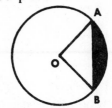

3. The radius (OA and OB) of the circle below is 20. Angle AOB = 90 degrees. Find the area of the shaded portion.
    (A) 100π
    (B) $100\pi - 200$
    (C) $100(\pi - 1)$
    (D) 200π
    (E) $100 - \pi(20)$

4. If 45 is added to a 2-digit number, the digits are reversed. If the original number is divided by the difference of the digits, the quotient is 7 and the remainder is 3. What is the original number? (The ten's digit is smaller than the unit's digit.)
    (A) 44
    (B) 36
    (C) 71
    (D) 26
    (E) 38

5. If the number of square inches in the area of a circle is equal to the number of inches in its circumference, the diameter of the circle is
    (A) 4 in.
    (B) 6 in.
    (C) 3 in.
    (D) 8 in.
    (E) 2 in.

6. Two congruent right triangles have their right angles meeting at the center of a circle. The circumference of the circle intersects the legs of the triangles at their midpoints as shown in the diagram. What is the area of the shaded portions?

(A) 8π

(B) $\dfrac{\pi r^2}{4} - 2r$

(C) $4\pi - r^2$

(D) $4r^2 - \dfrac{\pi r^2}{2}$

(E) $2r^2 - \dfrac{\pi r^2}{2}$

radius of circle $= r$

7. If the shipping charges to a certain point are $.62 for the first 5 oz. and $.08 for each additional ounce, the weight of a package for which the charges are $1.66 is
(A) 13 oz.
(B) $1\frac{1}{8}$ lb.
(C) $1\frac{1}{4}$ lb.
(D) 1 lb. 8 oz.
(E) none of these

8. A man is planning to build a rectangular enclosure at the rear of a building and to fence it in on 3 sides as shown in the figure. There is available 60 ft. of fencing. The width of the enclosure is represented by x and the length by y.

All of the following statements are true EXCEPT
(A) $2x + y = 60$
(B) The area of the enclosure is xy
(C) The area of the enclosure is $60x - 2x^2$
(D) When $x = 15$, the enclosed area is 450 sq. ft.
(E) The enclosed area is greatest when $x = y$

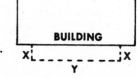

9. Find the value of x in the equation $\sqrt{7} + \sqrt{5} = x$.
(A) $\sqrt{12}$
(B) $\sqrt{60}$
(C) $\sqrt{2}$
(D) $\sqrt{10}$
(E) none of these

10. Simplify $\sqrt{0^2 + (\sqrt{10})^2 + 3^2 + (\sqrt{6})^2}$.

    (A) $\sqrt{19}$

    (B) 5

    (C) 0

    (D) $\sqrt{89}$

    (E) 6

11. If $\dfrac{a - b}{a} = b + 2$, express b in terms of a.

    (A) $2a + 1$

    (B) $\dfrac{a}{2} - 1$

    (C) $\dfrac{-a}{a + 1}$

    (D) $\dfrac{a - 1}{a}$

    (E) $2a$

12. For what values of x is x^3 negative?

    (A) $x = 0$

    (B) $x < 0$

    (C) $x > 0$

    (D) x is a fraction

    (E) x is a prime

13. Which of the following fractions is closest to 1?

    (A) $\dfrac{8}{9}$

    (B) $\dfrac{5}{7}$

    (C) $\dfrac{3}{4}$

    (D) $\dfrac{7}{8}$

    (E) $\dfrac{11}{10}$

14. $4 - (7 - d) = 3 - d(4 - d)$. Solve for d.
   (A)   3 and 2
   (B)   2 and -3
   (C)   4 and 3
   (D)   4 and 2
   (E)   4 and -2

15. If an event can succeed in p ways (all equally probable) and fail in q ways, the probability that the event will succeed is $\dfrac{p}{p + q}$.
   Which, if any, of the following statements is true?
   (A)   The probability of drawing a glass marble in a single draw from a bag containing 8 glass marbles and 12 clay marbles is $\frac{2}{3}$.
   (B)   The letters x, y, and z can be arranged in 6 different orders: xyz, zyx, yxz, etc. If one of these arrangements is chosen at random, the probability that z will be the middle letter is $\frac{1}{6}$.
   (C)   If one of the integers from 8 to 15 inclusive is chosen at random, the probability that the integer is even is equal to the probability that it is odd.
   (D)   The probability that a man, aged 40, will live to reach the age of 70 is $\frac{4}{7}$.
   (E)   none of these

Directions: This section requires you to compare two quantities—the quantity in Column A and the quantity in Column B. After you have compared the two quantities, select

(A) if the quantity in Column A is greater than the quantity in Column B;

(B) if the quantity in Column B is greater than the quantity in Column A;

(C) if the quantities in the two columns are equal;

(D) if the information is not sufficient to make a valid comparison.

Any information that appears in a central position above the two quantities to be compared refers to both quantities.

(A) if the quantity in Column A is greater than the quantity in Column B
(B) if the quantity in Column B is greater than the quantity in Column A
(C) if the quantities in the two columns are equal
(D) if the information is not sufficient to make a valid comparison

	Column A	**Column B**
16.	5%	$\dfrac{25}{500}$
17.	The average of the heights $5'2''$, $5'6''$, $5'8''$, $5'10''$, and $6'2''$	$5'6''$
18.	5^2	2^5
19.	$\sqrt{196}$	13
20.	$(+15)(-5)$	$(+18)(+4)$

$$y = x + 2$$

	Column A	**Column B**
21.	$x + 4$	$y - 1$

$$s < 0;\ r = 2s$$

	Column A	**Column B**
22.	$2r^2 s$	$3rs^2$

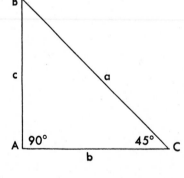

	Column A	**Column B**
23.	$\dfrac{b}{a}$	$\dfrac{c}{a}$

(A) if the quantity in Column A is greater than the quantity in Column B

(B) if the quantity in Column B is greater than the quantity in Column A

(C) if the quantities in the two columns are equal

(D) if the information is not sufficient to make a valid comparison

	Column A	**Column B**
24.	$\dfrac{4}{\sqrt{2}}$	$2\sqrt{2}$
25.	$\dfrac{5}{6}$ of $\dfrac{5}{6}$	$\left(\dfrac{1}{36}\right) \times (24)$
26.	$x^2 + 1$	$x^3 + 1$

Laura bought a dozen
batteries for $3.00

27.	Cost of one battery	$.24

$$3x - y = 3$$
$$x + 2y = 8$$

28.	x	y

Questions 29–30 refer to this diagram.

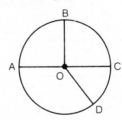

O is center of circle
AC is a straight line
BO and OD are straight lines

29.	AC	BO + DO

$$AO = 2$$

30.	π^2	circumference of the circle

(A) if the quantity in Column A is greater than the
quantity in Column B
(B) if the quantity in Column B is greater than the
quantity in Column A
(C) if the quantities in the two columns are equal
(D) if the information is not sufficient to make a
valid comparison

Column A   **Column B**

Questions 31–33 refer to the following circle graph.

FAMILY INCOME DISTRIBUTION FOR ONE YEAR

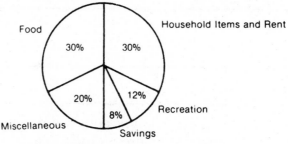

Total Family Income = $12,000

31. Amount spent on Food,   Amount spent on everything
Household Items, and   else
Rent together

32. Amount spent on bowling $1,000.00

33. $2,500   Amount spent on
miscellaneous items

34. $(x + 3)^2$ $(x - 3)^2$

35. $7 \times (12 + 14)$ $14 \times (6 + 7)$

IF YOU FINISH THIS SECTION OF THE SAT BEFORE YOUR
TIME IS UP, YOU MAY LOOK BACK AT YOUR WORK IN THIS
SECTION ONLY. YOU ARE NOT PERMITTED TO LOOK AT
ANY OTHER SECTION OF THE TEST. WHEN THE TIME IS UP,
TURN TO THE NEXT SECTION AND START WORK ON THAT
SECTION.

Section 4: Standard Written English Test

Time: 30 minutes

Because the SWET (Standard Written English Test) does not count toward your score but is only used for Freshman English placement when you get into college, questions of this type are not included.

TURN TO THE NEXT SECTION AND START WORK ON THAT SECTION.

Section 5: Verbal Questions

Antonyms

Time: 30 minutes

Directions: Each question in this test consists of a word printed in capital letters followed by five words lettered (A) through (E). Choose the word that has most nearly the OPPOSITE meaning from the word in capital letters. Then mark the appropriate space in the answer column.

1. AUSTERE
   (A) dull
   (B) gray
   (C) difficult
   (D) indulgent
   (E) severe

2. RANCID
   (A) sour
   (B) rapid
   (C) fetid
   (D) tasty
   (E) fresh

3. BLANDISHMENT
   (A) charity
   (B) flattery
   (C) insult
   (D) wit
   (E) hope

4. TRUCULENT
   (A) sadistic
   (B) fierce
   (C) harmless
   (D) uncouth
   (E) putrid

5. PEERLESS
   (A) unexcelled
   (B) visionary
   (C) myopic
   (D) rich
   (E) equal

6. NOXIOUS
   (A) odious
   (B) harmless
   (C) quaint
   (D) affluent
   (E) mercerized

7. CANDOR
   (A) impartiality
   (B) truth
   (C) law
   (D) bird
   (E) fraudulence

8. ENCROACH
   (A) impose
   (B) avoid
   (C) exterminate
   (D) annoy
   (E) select

9. IMPECCABLE
   (A) neat
   (B) flawless
   (C) attractive
   (D) blemished
   (E) smart

10. PROMULGATE
    (A) veil
    (B) announce
    (C) increase
    (D) create
    (E) arrest

11. COMMODIOUS
    (A) cramped
    (B) luxurious
    (C) expedient
    (D) hesitant
    (E) roomy

12. ENCOMIUM
    (A) economy
    (B) hoard
    (C) reproach
    (D) praise
    (E) paradox

13. ABASE
    (A) structure
    (B) operate
    (C) lose
    (D) extol
    (E) top

14. LAMPOON
    (A) satire
    (B) plaudit
    (C) weapon
    (D) symbol
    (E) paper

15. FERVENT
    (A) godless
    (B) evil
    (C) pathetic
    (D) benign
    (E) phlegmatic

Sentence Completions

Directions: Each question in this test consists of a sentence or group of sentences in which one or two words are missing. Beneath the question are five pairs of words lettered (A) through (E). Choose the word or the pair of words that *best* completes the sentence or sentences. Then mark the appropriate space in the answer column.

16. Many citizens objected vigorously to the _____ of the county offices, which, for the most part, could not be reached without traveling considerable distances.
    (A) inaccessibility
    (B) lack
    (C) inefficiency
    (D) corruption
    (E) layout

17. It is the _____ man who is usually dependent upon popular favor.
    (A) aspiring
    (B) sensitive
    (C) elected
    (D) career
    (E) prosperous

18. One of the deleterious effects of failing to permit children to exercise _____ is the danger that they may remain so immature that they fail to successfully _____ school, home, and community.
    (A) belligerence—overcome
    (B) self-judgment—adjust to
    (C) discipline—adjust to
    (D) initiative—depreciate
    (E) freedom of action—re-make

19. The student of human nature knows that its components are, for the most part, _____; but he is also aware that events—pleasant or unpleasant—do play a part in bringing to the fore at one time or another certain _____.
    (A) fixed—reactions
    (B) unstable—traits
    (C) immutable—characteristics
    (D) ephemeral—people
    (E) general—instincts

20. When the democratic principle shall have become firmly established in all nations, then we shall witness the _____ of prejudice, intolerance, and _____.

(A)   culmination—bigotry

(B)   nationalization—animosity

(C)   denunciation—crime

(D)   cessation—bigotry

(E)   condemnation—license

Analogies

Directions: In each of the following questions choose the pair of words that *best* completes the analogy. Then mark the appropriate space in the answer column.

21. REWARD : CAPTURE : :
    (A) deed : crime
    (B) dance : movement
    (C) play : plot
    (D) criminal : reward
    (E) prize : victory

22. OVAL : CIRCLE : :
    (A) line : perimeter
    (B) circle : square
    (C) triangle : square
    (D) rectangle : square
    (E) square : diamond

23. SEA : OCEAN : :
    (A) land : water
    (B) stream : river
    (C) village : suburb
    (D) city : country
    (E) cape : continent

24. GRADE : MOUNTAIN : :
    (A) altitude : hill
    (B) depth : valley
    (C) pitch : roof
    (D) height : hill
    (E) shingles : roof

25. VEGETABLES : PORTION : :
    (A) medicine : dose
    (B) water : glass
    (C) oatmeal : spoon
    (D) fish : vitamins
    (E) bread : loaf

26. FAILURES : EXAMINATION : :
    (A) water : faucet
    (B) quality : denier
    (C) impurities : filter
    (D) wheat : chaff
    (E) remedies : petition

27. EARTH : AXIS : :
    (A) wheel : hub
    (B) earth : sun
    (C) state : nation
    (D) orbit : firmament
    (E) mountain : sea

28. TERSE : TURGID : :
    (A) cow : pig
    (B) tremendous : prodigious
    (C) state : nation
    (D) slim : obese
    (E) mountain : sea

29. SKY : CLOUD : :
    (A) crime : sex
    (B) ugly : thought
    (C) sun : shade
    (D) knowledge : obtuse
    (E) mind : prejudice

30. INCONSTANT : VACILLATION : :
    (A) unstable : stability
    (B) variable : wind
    (C) vacillating : steadfastness
    (D) aberrant : constancy
    (E) capricious : vagary

Reading Comprehension

Directions: Read the following passages and answer each of the questions that come after them. Choose the *best* answer. Then mark the appropriate space in the answer column.

The principles of operationism provide a procedure by which the concepts of science can be cast in rigorous form. This procedure consists of defining each concept in terms of the concrete operations by which the concept is arrived at, and in rejecting all notions founded upon impossible operations. Operational doctrine makes explicit recognition of the fact that a concept or proposition has empirical meaning only if it stands for definite, concrete operations capable of re-execution by normal human beings. The principles which must guide operational science are, briefly: 1. Science is knowledge agreed upon by members of society. Only those constructs based upon operations which are public and repeatable are admitted to the body of science. 2. Science regards all observations, including those which a scientist makes upon himself, as made upon "the other one," and thereby makes explicit the distinction between the experimenter and the thing observed. 3. A term or proposition has meaning (denotes something) if, and only if, criteria of its applicability or truth consist of concrete operations, which can be performed. 4. Discrimination or differential response is the fundamental operation. It is prerequisite even to the operation of denoting or "pointing to." 5. By discrimination we mean the concrete differential reactions of the living organism to environmental states, either internal or external. Discrimination is, therefore, a "physical" process or series of natural events, and all knowledge is obtained, conveyed, and verified by means of this process.

31. Science is meaningful if its subject matter is capable of
    (A)   repetition
    (B)   an artistic representation
    (C)   a philosophical orientation
    (D)   being understood by everyone
    (E)   being understood by the majority of scientists

32. A scientific concept lacks validity unless it is made part of
    (A)   the common store of knowledge
    (B)   studies in all major countries
    (C)   a relation between art and science
    (D)   everyday work
    (E)   the philosophy of man

33. The statement "Truth is dependent upon performable acts"
   (A) can be derived from the first principle (principle 1)
   (B) can be derived from the second principle (principle 2)
   (C) can be derived from the third principle (principle 3)
   (D) can be derived from the fourth and fifth principles (principles 4 and 5)
   (E) cannot be derived from any of the principles 1, 2, 3, 4, or 5

34. The statement "The primary tool of science is concept formation"
   (A) can be derived from the first principle (principle 1)
   (B) can be derived from the second principle (principle 2)
   (C) can be derived from the third principle (principle 3)
   (D) can be derived from the fourth and fifth principles (principles 4 and 5)
   (E) cannot be derived from any of the principles 1, 2, 3, 4, or 5

35. The statement "Science is based on a physical process"
   (A) can be derived from the first principle (principle 1)
   (B) can be derived from the second principle (principle 2)
   (C) can be derived from the third principle (principle 3)
   (D) can be derived from the fourth and fifth principles (principles 4 and 5)
   (E) cannot be derived from any of the principles 1, 2, 3, 4 or 5

The discouragement and disillusionment that followed the Franco-Prussian War of 1870–71 and a decline in material prosperity brought a new type of literature and an almost complete abandonment of the old realism based upon the worship of science. Foreign influences were strong—Freud, Wagner, Nietzsche, Tolstoy, and Dostoevsky all left their imprints upon French literature. There was a revival of music and of conversation in salons reminiscent of the seventeenth century. The influence of Pascal, emphasizing human life and faith, finally replaced that of Descartes. Henri Bergson (1859–1941), who received the Nobel Prize in 1927, denied that science was all-powerful. He emphasized intuition and belief and gave art a new purpose, the expression of intuition and instinct. Bergson's influence was great and particularly noticeable in the revival of Catholicism, featured by many dramatic conversions. Literary and dramatic criticism flourished in the hands of Francisque Sarcey (1828–1899), Ferdinand Brunetiere (1849–1906), Jules Lemaître (1853–1914), Gustave Lanson (1857–1934), and Julien Benda (1867–1956).

In poetry, the symbolists—Stéphane Mallarmé (1842–1898), Paul Verlaine (1844–1896), Jean Arthur Rimbaud (1854–1891)—abandoned conventional syntax and meters for more personal expression. Their poetry is essentially vague, fluid, musical, often abstract, and filled with veiled symbols. Their sucessors are Emile Verhaeren (1855–1916), Henri de Régnier (1854–1936), the Comtesse de Noailles (1876–1933), Paul Claudel (1868–1955), and Paul Valéry (1871–1945). Claudel, an ardent Catholic and essentially mystic, sought a hidden reality. Valéry's poetry is purely intellectual; he seems to sit apart from a physical world and set himself word problems in space. In 1920 the dadaist movement denied everything because it felt incapable of solving anything. It was essentially an outgrowth of World War I and could not last long. Poets turned again to symbolism and Catholicism, and, as with Jean Cocteau (1891–1963), to a new classicism.

36. Henri Bergson, a Nobel Prize winner of 1927, believed in
    (A) the continued worshiping of science
    (B) the expression of intuition and instinct
    (C) Descartes' principles
    (D) the all-powerful work of scientists
    (E) the relationship of science and art

37. Which of these did NOT happen during the time of Freud, Tolstoy, and the modernists?
    (A) the revival of Catholicism
    (B) vague, musical and abstract poetry
    (C) a renewed interest in the arts
    (D) a decline in prosperity
    (E) none of these

38. Which of these men did NOT influence the modern movements?
    (A) Freud
    (B) Wagner
    (C) Nietzsche
    (D) Tolstoy
    (E) none of these

39. The literary and dramatic critics included all of the following EXCEPT
    (A) Sarcey
    (B) Lemaître
    (C) Lanson
    (D) Rimbaud
    (E) Benda

40.   The poetry of Valéry is characterized by
     I.   a discovery of space
    II.   purely intellectual writing
   III.   an apartness of the physical world
   IV.   influences from the symbolists
  (A)   I only
  (B)   II only
  (C)   III only
  (D)   IV only
  (E)   all of the above

IF YOU FINISH THIS SECTION OF THE SAT BEFORE YOUR TIME IS UP, YOU MAY LOOK BACK AT YOUR WORK IN THIS SECTION ONLY. YOU ARE NOT PERMITTED TO LOOK AT ANY OTHER SECTION OF THE TEST. WHEN THE TIME IS UP, TURN TO THE NEXT SECTION AND START WORK ON THAT SECTION.

Section 6: Mathematics Questions

Time: 30 minutes

Directions: Each question in this section is followed by five choices lettered (A) through (E). Choose the correct answer. Then mark the appropriate space in the answer column.

The following information may be useful to you in solving some of the mathematics problems in this part:

Circle, radius = r:
Area $= \pi r^2$.
Circumference $= 2\pi r$.
A circle has 360 degrees of arc.

Triangle:
The sum of the three angles in a triangle is 180 degrees.
Area $= \frac{1}{2}$(any side $\times$ altitude to that side).

Right Triangle:
The sum of the squares of the legs $=$ the square of the hypotenuse.

Definitions of certain mathematical symbols:

$>$ is greater than
$<$ is less than
$\geqq$ is greater than or equal to
$\leqq$ is less than or equal to
$\perp$ is perpendicular to
$\parallel$ is parallel to

Important Note: Figures in this section are not always drawn to scale. All numbers are real numbers and all figures lie in a plane unless otherwise stated.

132

1. A storekeeper purchased an article for \$36. In order to include 10% of cost for overhead and to provide \$9 for net profit, the markup should be
    (A) 25%
    (B) 35%
    (C) $37\frac{1}{2}$%
    (D) 40%
    (E) 48%

2. If $ax + b = cx + d$, which of the following is the correct expression for x in terms of a, b, c, and d?

    (A) $\dfrac{b - d}{a - e}$

    (B) $\dfrac{d - b}{a - c}$

    (C) $\dfrac{b + d + c}{a}$

    (D) $a + b + c$

    (E) $\dfrac{c}{a}$

3. If a is 20% of b and $2c$ is 80% of b, what percent of c is a?
    (A) 20%
    (B) 100%
    (C) 200%
    (D) 25%
    (E) 50%

4. The rate at which Philip is traveling is 20 miles per *hour*. How many miles per *minute* must Philip increase his speed in order to cover a 200-mile distance in 8 hours?

    (A) $\dfrac{1}{10}$

    (B) $\dfrac{1}{12}$

    (C) $\dfrac{1}{5}$

    (D) $\dfrac{1}{3}$

    (E) $\dfrac{1}{2}$

5. Which of the choices below is less than $\frac{1}{3}$?

    (A) $\dfrac{0.3}{0.1}$

    (B) 0.3

    (C) $\dfrac{1}{0.3}$

    (D) 3^3

    (E) $\dfrac{1}{2}$

6. Which of the following is equal to $\dfrac{x - \dfrac{1}{y}}{y - \dfrac{1}{x}}$?
    $(x \neq 0 \text{ and } y \neq 0;\ xy \neq 1)$

    (A) 1

    (B) $\dfrac{x}{y}$

    (C) $\dfrac{y}{x}$

    (D) $y - x$

    (E) $x - y$

7. At which point does the graph of $y = 4 - x^2$ intersect the Y axis?

    (A)   D and E
    (B)   B and C
    (C)   A
    (D)   D
    (E)   E

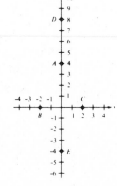

8. If a pint of ice cream costs $.50, how much will 3 quarts cost?
    (A) $3.00
    (B) $1.50
    (C) $6.00
    (D)   more than $6.00
    (E)   less than $1.50

9. In the diagram below, angle $a = 50°$ and angle $b = 70°$. If the lines at points X, Y, and Z intersect at right angles, find the value of angle d.

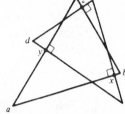

   (A)   50°
   (B)   70°
   (C)   120°
   (D)   90°
   (E)   60°

10. One-inch square tiles sell for $.05 a piece. How much would it cost to cover an area 2 feet by 10 feet?

   (A) $12.00
   (B) $1.00
   (C) $144.00
   (D) $100.00
   (E) $5.00

11. The sum of the digits of a 3-digit number is 16. The unit's digit is 3 times the hundred's digit. If the digits are reversed, the resulting number exceeds the original number by 594. What is the original number?

   (A)   682
   (B)   349
   (C)   163
   (D)   286
   (E)   943

12. In the triangle below, angle ACB contains x degrees, angle CAD contains $3x$ degrees, and angle CBA contains 20 degrees. Find the value of x.

   (A)   5
   (B)   30
   (C)   20
   (D)   10
   (E)   cannot be determined
          with information given

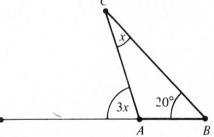

13. $\left(\dfrac{\sqrt{3^2 + 4^2}}{\sqrt{13^2 - 12^2}} \right)^2$

   (A)   1
   (B)   49
   (C) $\sqrt{3}$
   (D) $\sqrt{17}$
   (E)   11

14. One side of a rectangle has a length of p. The other side has a length of $3p$. If you double p, what happens to the area?
(A) It doubles.
(B) It triples.
(C) It remains the same.
(D) It quadruples.
(E) It is cut in half.

15. A boy has 9 pennies and 1 nickel in his drawer. He cannot see the coins. What is the least number of coins he must remove to be certain he will have at least $.05?
(A) 2
(B) 6
(C) 10
(D) 1
(E) 5

16. If John buys a 2-lb. apple pie with ingredients distributed as shown, how much of his pie is water?

(A) $\frac{1}{4}$ lb.

(B) $\frac{1}{2}$ lb.

(C) $\frac{3}{4}$ lb.

(D) 1 lb.

(E) $1\frac{1}{4}$ lb.

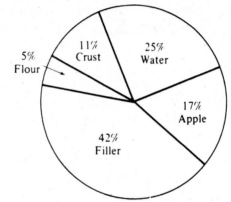

Apple Pie Ingredients

17. Which of the following is closed under addition?
  I. even numbers
 II. odd numbers
III. integers
(A) I and III only
(B) II only
(C) I and II only
(D) III only
(E) I, II, and III

18. A dealer wishes to mix candy worth $.85 per pound with candy worth $.35 per pound to yield a mixture of 60 pounds worth $.75 per pound. How many pounds of the $.85 candy must he use in the mixture?

(A) 40
(B) 35
(C) 30
(D) 25
(E) 48

19. The average of 4 numbers is 10. If two of the numbers are 8 and 11, find the sum of the other 2 numbers.

(A) 8
(B) 21
(C) 10
(D) $10\frac{1}{2}$
(E) 40

20. In the triangle below, BD is an altitude to AC. AC is 10 units long and BD is 10 units long. ·If the area of triangle BDA is three times the area of triangle BDC, find the length of AD.

(A) $7\frac{1}{2}$

(B) 5

(C) $6\frac{2}{3}$

(D) $3\frac{1}{3}$

(E) $2\frac{1}{2}$

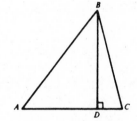

21. Three-quarters of the perimeter of an isosceles right triangle is 18. The perimeter of the triangle is

(A) 24
(B) 25
(C) 26
(D) 27
(E) 28

22. If 32 is a factor of y, which of the following is necessarily a factor of y?

(A) 17
(B) 20
(C) 100
(D) 18
(E) 8

23. A map is scaled so that 1 inch represents 2 miles. A square area of land consists of 16 square miles. Give the length in inches of one side of that area of the map.

(A) 8
(B) 16
(C) 1
(D) 4
(E) 2

24. If *ab* is negative, then you can say about *a* and/or *b*

(A) *a* is positive
(B) *a* is negative
(C) if *a* is positive, *b* is negative
(D) *b* = 0 or *a* = 0
(E) *a* is negative and *b* is negative

25. If $(x - 2) \leq 0$, then which of the following represents *x* on a number line?

(A)
(B)
(C)
(D)
(E)

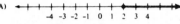
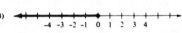
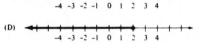

IF YOU FINISH THIS SECTION OF THE SAT BEFORE YOUR TIME IS UP, YOU MAY LOOK BACK AT YOUR WORK IN THIS SECTION ONLY. YOU ARE NOT PERMITTED TO LOOK AT ANY OTHER SECTION OF THE TEST. WHEN TIME IS UP. THE SAT IS OVER.

AFTER YOU HAVE FINISHED PRACTICE TEST 2:

1. Look at the Answer Key on pages 139-140.
2. Determine your number of CORRECT answers for the MATH and VERBAL parts. DO NOT count Section 6.
3. Determine your number of INCORRECT answers for the MATH and VERBAL parts. DO NOT count Section 6.
4. To obtain the RAW SCORE for each part (VERBAL or MATH) deduct ¼ the number of INCORRECT answers from the number of CORRECT answers.
5. Find what your SCALED SCORES are by using your Raw Score and referring to the TABLES on pages 88 and 89.

Answer Key for Practice Test 2

Section 1

1. D	10. B	19. B	28. D	37. C
2. A	11. E	20. E	29. B	38. D
3. E	12. D	21. C	30. A	39. B
4. D	13. D	22. A	31. D	40. E
5. C	14. C	23. A	32. C	41. B
6. A	15. B	24. D	33. E	42. D
7. A	16. D	25. D	34. D	43. C
8. C	17. D	26. E	35. B	44. E
9. C	18. B	27. B	36. D	45. A

Section 2

1. E	6. C	11. B	16. C	21. D
2. A	7. E	12. B	17. D	22. B
3. E	8. C	13. A	18. A	23. A
4. E	9. C	14. C	19. B	24. D
5. E	10. D	15. E	20. C	25. B

Section 3

1. E	8. E	15. C	22. B	29. C
2. B	9. E	16. C	23. C	30. B
3. B	10. B	17. A	24. C	31. A
4. E	11. C	18. B	25. A	32. D
5. A	12. B	19. A	26. D	33. A
6. D	13. E	20. B	27. A	34. D
7. B	14. A	21. A	28. B	35. C

Section 5

1. D	9. D	17. C	25. A	33. C
2. E	10. A	18. B	26. C	34. E
3. C	11. A	19. C	27. A	35. D
4. C	12. C	20. D	28. D	36. B
5. E	13. D	21. E	29. E	37. E
6. B	14. B	22. D	30. E	38. E
7. E	15. E	23. B	31. A	39. D
8. B	16. A	24. C	32. A	40. E

Section 6

1. B	6. B	11. B	16. B	21. A
2. B	7. C	12. D	17. A	22. E
3. E	8. A	13. A	18. E	23. E
4. B	9. E	14. D	19. B	24. C
5. B	10. C	15. E	20. A	25. D

Explanatory Answers for Practice Test 2

Section 1: Verbal Questions

1. **(D)**
   Paucity: scarcity; *antonym:* abundance

2. **(A)**
   Modish: in style; *antonym:* unfashionable

3. **(E)**
   Opiate: something that quiets or deadens; *antonym:* stimulant

4. **(D)**
   Mute: silent; *antonym:* vocal

5. **(C)**
   Fetid: stinking; *antonym:* fragrant

6. **(A)**
   Staid: grave, sober; *antonym:* exuberant

7. **(A)**
   Indolent: lazy, idle; *antonym:* active

8. **(C)**
   Quaint: unfamiliar or unusual; *antonym:* ordinary

9. **(C)**
   Altercation: an angry argument; *antonym:* agreement

10. **(B)**
    Nocturnal: pertaining to night; *antonym:* daily or diurnal

11. **(E)**
    Choice (E) contains the most appropriate combination of words that completes the sentence.

12. (D)

There is much justification for the eagerly optimistic (*sanguine*) forecast . . . the income of the corporation was *greater* than ever before.

13. (D)

The success was attributed to his *persuasive* criticisms of the existing order.

14. (C)

Note that the teacher has little regard for factual learning. Thus he doesn't care to make *encyclopedias* of the students.

15. (B)

From the context, the words *advantage* and *decline* are most appropriate.

16. (D)

The crowded cities . . . make us a *vulnerable* target of any *adversary* who can take us by surprise.

17. (D)

Only the rich can save money without the lack of the basic necessities of life (*privation*).

18. (B)

Modification and *adaptation* when inserted in the blanks produce the most consistent and logical sentence.

19. (B)

We rely on an almost last resort when less *drastic* measures fail.

20. (E)

An arguable (*moot*) point is one that is *disputable*.

21. (C)

The passage essentially deals with the status of the villein during the Norman Conquest.

22. (A)

See the seventh and eighth sentences.

23. (A)

See the eighth sentence: "The villeins are holders of regular shares in the village. . . ."

24. (D)

See the eighth sentence.

25. (D)

It is stated that there is a small group of *servi,* of whom only 25,00 are enumerated in the Domesday Book. It is also stated that personal slavery was rapidly disappearing in England about the time of the Conquest. Thus, we can estimate the number of personal serfs in England 50 years before the Domesday survey to be *greater* than 25,000, perhaps 35,000, the only appropriate choice.

26. (E)

From the passage, it can be seen that Shakespeare did not utilize the works (I), (II), (III), or (IV).

27. (B)

See the last sentence of the first paragraph.

28. (D)

It is mentioned in the first paragraph that biography was written as early as the 4th century B.C.

29. (B)

See the sentence, "In the first century A.D., Plutarch wrote his *Parallel Lives,* comparing the careers of a score of Romans. . . ."

30. (A)

See the third sentence of the first paragraph.

31. (D)

Nevada is *sparse* in population compared to the *density* of people in *Java.*

32. (C)

Here we are comparing antonyms with respect to time. *Frequently* is to *seldom* as *always* is to *never.*

33. (E)

We would like an *immunity* against *disease* as we would like an *exemption* against *taxes.*

34. (D)

Scrutinize is much more intense than *glance* as a *grasp* is much more intense than a *touch.*

35. (B)

A *cramp* thwarts a normal *muscle* movement, as a *jam* thwarts a normal *machine* process.

36. (D)

Plateau is a peak; *plain* is below. *Mountain* is high as *valley* is below.

37.   (C)
A *poodle,* which is a pet, is boarded in a *kennel.* A *canary,* which is a pet, is boarded in a *cage.*

38.   (D)
A *mason* works with stone or brick and is likely to work on a *wall.* A *painter* is likely to work on a *picture.* Choice (A) is incorrect because a bricklayer works *with* cement; he doesn't make the cement or work on the synthesis of the cement.

39.   (B)
A *brake* is used to stop an *automobile* from moving. A *conscience* is used to stop a *man* from wrongdoing.

40.   (E)
Here we are comparing levels of intensity. *Bigotry* is intense prejudice. *Tolerance* is the generous respect for the behavior or opinions of others. *Parsimony* is extreme economy. *Magnanimity* is generosity and nobleness in forgiving.

41.   (B)
(A) is incorrect becase it is directly contradicted by paragraph 3. Choice (B) is correct, and the concept of continuity is reinforced in paragraphs 3 and 4. Choice (C) is incorrect because it reverses the cause and effect procedure stated in paragraph 2. Choice (D) is incorrect because it is irrelevant to the statement under consideration. Choice (E) is incorrect because the topic was not discussed in the reading selection.

42.   (D)
Choices (A) and (B) are incorrect because they are not discussed in the reading selection. Choice (C) is incorrect because it is a misinterpretation of the content of paragraph 4. Choice (D) is correct according to paragraph 4. Choice (E) is incorrect because it distorts the intent of the last several paragraphs.

43.   (C)
Choice (A) is incorrect because it is an inaccurate version of the material in the selection. Choice (B) is incorrect because there is no mention in the selection of a preordained direction for society. Choice (C) is a correct statement of the material in the last paragraph. Choice (D) is an incorrect conclusion, contradicted by the phrase "different from the empirical order" in the last paragraph. Choice (E) is also directly contradicted by the material in the last paragraph.

44.   (E)
Choice (A) is incorrect because the author refers to the "honor" (paragraph 5), "immortality" (paragraph 6), and "privilege" (paragraph 6) attendant upon belonging to the institution. Choices (B) and (D) are incorrect because the author mentions the "Academic function," the role of "magic" (paragraph 6), and an order which differs from the empirical (last paragraph). Choice (C) is incorrect because of the reference to retirement, hardly relevant to those of college age. Choice (E) is correct.

45.   (A)
Choice (A) is correct because the author is ecstatic throughout the article about the role of the institution. Choice (B) is incorrect because in the opening sentence the anthropologist admits his own membership and thus would have no reason to envy others. Choice (C) is incorrect because the rather mild connotation of respect does not suit the laudatory tone of the selection. Choice (D) is incorrect because there is nothing in the selection to indicate a feeling of dissatisfaction. Choice (E) is incorrect because the author is consistent throughout the article in his praise of the institution.

Section 2: Mathematics Questions

1.   (E)
Call the number n. Then

$$\frac{n + \frac{2}{5}n + 30}{3} = 31$$

because the average is the sum of the elements divided by the number of elements. Cross-multiplying and adding:

$$\frac{7}{5}n + 30 = 93$$
$$\frac{7}{5}n = 63$$
$$n = 45.$$

2.   (A)
If $y = x^2 + 4x + 1$ and $y = 1$, then they intersect at the points where $1 = x^2 + 4x + 1$, or $x^2 + 4x = 0$. This can be factored into $x(x + 4) = 0$, which is satisfied by $x = 0$ and $x = -4$. At these points $y = 1$, so the points are $(0, 1)$ and $(-4, 1)$.

3.   (E)
Only the volume of earth equal to the volume of the chest will be left after burying the chest.
$2 \times 5 \times 2 = 20$ cu. ft.

4. **(E)**

$$4^{\frac{1}{2}} = 2$$

$$2^3 = 8$$

$$2^{-2} = \frac{1}{4}$$

Thus:

$$(4^{\frac{1}{2}})(2^3)^2(2^{-2}) =$$

$$(2)(8)^2 \frac{1}{4} =$$

$$(2)(64)\frac{1}{4} = 32$$

Alternatively, we could solve the problem like this:

$$4^{\frac{1}{2}} = (2^2)^{\frac{1}{2}} = 2^1$$

$$(2^3)^2 = 2^6$$

Thus:

$$(4^{\frac{1}{2}})(2^3)^2(2^{-2}) = (2^1)(2^6)(2^{-2})$$

Adding exponents, keeping the base, we get:

$$(2^1)(2^6)(2^{-2}) = 2^5 = 32$$

5. **(E)**

$x + 2y = 7$ and $2x + 4y = 8$. Dividing the second equation by 2 gives $x + 2y = 4$. From the first equation, $x + 2y = 7$, so $4 = 7$, which is false. Therefore, there is no solution to this set of equations.

6. **(C)**

$$a * b = a^2 + ab + b$$
$$1 * x = 1^2 + 1(x) + x = 1 + 2x$$

7. **(E)**

Let $EC = x$. Since the area of the square is p^2, side DE of the square is p. Now $p + x$ is the length of the rectangle (side DC). Since $AD = m$, the area of the rectangle is

$$(m)(p + x)$$

But the area of the rectangle is given as p^2. Thus:

$$(m)(p + x) = p^2$$
$$mp + mx = p^2$$
$$mx = p^2 - mp$$
$$x = \frac{p^2 - mp}{m}$$
$$x = \frac{p^2}{m} - p$$

8. (C)

If the line is sketched, it can be seen that the x intercept is 6 and the y intercept is 2. The area is $\frac{1}{2}$(base) (height) $= \frac{1}{2}$(6) (2) $= 6$.

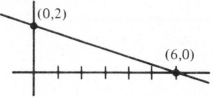

9. (C)

The null or empty set is a subset of all sets. The positive integers constitute a subset of the integers. The reals include such numbers as the fractions, which are not part of the integers.

10. (D)

80% of 700 $= .80 \times 700 =$ \$560 (the amount insured)

$\dfrac{560}{100} \times 80\cancel{c} = 5.6 \times .80 =$ \$4.48

11. (B)

If we sketch the points, we see that the length of the base is 3 and the height is 4. The area is $\frac{1}{2}$(base) (height) $= \frac{1}{2}$(3) (4) $= 6$.

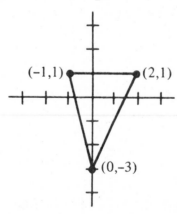

12. (B)

$|\,a\,|$ means a if a is positive and $-a$ if a is negative. (The absolute value sign always makes the number positive.) There are two cases for $|\,x + 2\,|$: either $x + 2 \geq 0$ or $x + 2 < 0$.

If $x + 2 > 0$, then $|\,x + 2\,| = x + 2$ and $|\,x + 2\,| < 2$ is $x + 2 < 2$, which is the same as $x < 0$.

If $x + 2 < 0$, then $|\,x + 2\,| = -(x + 2)$ and $-(x + 2) < 2$, which is the same as $x + 2 > -2$, or $x > -4$. The entire solution is $-4 < x < 0$.

13. (A)
From the equation $y = 2x - 4$, when $x = 0$, $y = -4$, and when $y = 0$, $x = 2$. The only line through these points is a.

14. (C)
Convert $\frac{1}{4}$ and all the choices to decimals and compare them. $\frac{1}{4} = 0.25$. $-\frac{1}{2}$ is less than $\frac{1}{4}$ because negative numbers are always less than positive numbers. 0.04 is less than 0.25. $(\frac{1}{4})^2$ is 0.0625. $\frac{0.4}{4}$ is 0.10. $\sqrt{\frac{1}{4}} = \frac{1}{2} = 0.5$, which is larger than 0.25.

15. (E)
$\dfrac{ab - 1}{a - \dfrac{1}{b}}$. Multiply the numerator and denominator by b to get

$\dfrac{b(ab - 1)}{ab - 1}$. Cancelling the $ab - 1$ gives b.

16. (C)
If 2 feet of wood cost $.80, then 1 foot costs $.40. There are 3 feet in one yard, so 4 yards have 12 feet. The cost of 12 feet of wood is (12) ($.40) = $4.80.

17. (D)
Angle ADE = angle B because line AB cuts two parallel lines, and a line that cuts two parallel lines makes equal angles with the parallel lines. Therefore, angle ADE = 60°. Angle A + angle ADE + angle x = 180° since there are 180° in a triangle. Therefore, 50° + 60° + x = 180° or x = 70°.

18. (A)
There are 3 feet in one yard, so in an area one yard square there are 9 square feet (3 × 3 = 9). To paint 2 square yards, or 18 square feet, costs $1.00. In an area 9 feet by 15 feet there are 135 square feet, so to paint this area costs (135 square feet) × $\dfrac{\$1.00}{18 \text{ square feet}} = \$7.50$.

19. (B)
$x = \dfrac{1}{y}$. Call the new value of x, x'. Then $x' = \dfrac{1}{3y}$. Substitute x for $\dfrac{1}{y}$ to get $x' = \frac{1}{3}x$, so the new value of x is $\frac{1}{3}$ of the old. $x - \frac{2}{3}x = \frac{1}{3}x$.

20. (C)
Call angle C, x. Then angle A $= 2x$ and angle B $= 3x$. Angle A + angle B + angle C $= 180°$ since there are $180°$ in a triangle. Therefore, $2x + 3x + x = 180$, $6x = 180$, $x = 30$. Angle A $= 2x = 60°$.

21. (D)
If we choose $x = 4$, we get

$$-x = -4$$

$$\frac{1}{x} = \frac{1}{4}$$

$$\sqrt{x} = 2$$

$$x^2 = 16$$

$$\frac{1}{2}x = 2$$

The only one greater than 4 is 16, or x^2. Similarly, this is true of all x greater than 1.

22. (B)
The percentage, x, is that number that forms the same ratio with 100 as the two original numbers form with each other.

Therefore, $\dfrac{x}{100} = \dfrac{450}{300}$, and $x = 150$, or 150%.

23. (A)
If each unit along the X-axis represents 2 feet and there are 6 units, there is a total distance of 12 feet. Along the Y-axis the distance is 5 feet. The distance between the points is the hypotenuse of a right triangle. Using the relationship for a right triangle $c^2 = a^2 + b^2$, you get $c^2 = 5^2 + 12^2 = 169$, or $c = 13$.

24. (D)
According to the graph, 4 people had green eyes, 6 people had blue eyes, and 5 had brown eyes, so there were 15 people in the group. The percentage, x, can be found by setting up the ratio $\dfrac{x}{100} = \dfrac{5}{15} = \dfrac{1}{3}$, or $x = 33\frac{1}{3}$. $33\frac{1}{3}$% had brown eyes.

25. (B)
The total distance is $d + x$. The total time is $h + y$. Thus, the average rate is given by

$$\frac{d + x}{h + y}$$

Section 3: Mathematics Questions

1. **(E)**

   Let L = the length and W = the width.

   $$2L + 2W = 42$$
   $$L + W = 21$$
   $$W = 21 - L$$

   According to the Pythagorean theorem:

   $$L^2 + W^2 = 15^2$$
   $$L^2 + W^2 = 225$$
   $$L^2 + (21 - L)^2 = 225 \quad \text{(substituting the value of W}$$
   $$L^2 + 441 - 42L + L^2 = 225 \quad \text{in terms of L)}$$
   $$2L^2 - 42L + 216 = 0$$
   $$L^2 - 21L + 108 = 0 \quad \text{(dividing by 2)}$$
   $$(L - 9)(L - 12) = 0$$
   $$L = 9 \quad \text{(reject)}$$
   $$L = 12$$

2. **(B)**

   Side = 6

   Area of square = side^2 or 36

   Area of circle = πr^2 or 9π

   Area of shaded portion = $36 - 9\pi$

3. **(B)**

   Area of sector AOB = $\dfrac{n}{360} \times \pi r^2 = \dfrac{90}{360} \times \pi(20)^2 =$

   $$\dfrac{400\pi}{4} = 100\pi$$

   Area of triangle AOB = $\dfrac{1}{2}bh = \dfrac{400}{2} = 200$

   Area of segment = area of sector − area of triangle
   $100\pi - 200$

4. **(E)**

Let $t =$ the ten's digit and $u =$ the unit's digit.

$$10t + u + 45 = 10u + t$$
$$9t + 45 = 9u$$

$$\frac{10t + u}{u - t} = 7 + \frac{3}{u - t}$$

$$\frac{10t + (t + 5)}{(t + 5) - t} = 7 + \frac{3}{(t + 5) - t}$$

$$\frac{11t + 5}{5} = 7 + \frac{3}{5}$$

$$11t + 5 = 35 + 3$$
$$11t = 33$$
$$t = 3$$
$$t + 5 = u \therefore u = 8$$
$$10t + u = 38$$

5. **(A)**

$$\pi r^2 = 2r\pi$$
$$r = 2$$
$$d = 4 \text{ in.}$$

6. **(D)**

Shaded portion $=$ Area of the 2 triangles $- \frac{1}{2}$ Area of circle

Area of 2 triangles $= 2\left(\frac{2r \times 2r}{2}\right) = 4r^2$

Area of $\frac{1}{2}$ circle $= \frac{\pi r^2}{2}$; Shaded portion $= 4r^2 - \frac{\pi r^2}{2}$

7. **(B)**

Total charges $=$ \$1.66
Charge for 1st ounce $= \underline{\quad .62}$
$\quad$ \$1.04 remaining charges at the rate
$\quad$ of \$.08 an ounce

$$\frac{1.04}{.08} = 13 \text{ oz.}$$

5 oz. $+$ 13 oz. $=$ 18 oz. (total number of ounces in weight of package)

$$\frac{18}{16} = 1\frac{1}{8} \text{ lb.}$$

8. **(E)**
Each statement must be tested individually. We will find that statement (E) is false.

The perimeter is given by $2x + y = 60$. Thus, statement (A) is true. The area of enclosure is xy. Thus, statement (B) is true. Since the area is xy and $2x + y = 60$, the area can be represented by $x(60 - 2x) = 60x - 2x^2$. Thus, statement (C) is true. When $x = 15$, $60x - 2x^2 = (60)(15) - 2(15)(15) = 900 - 450 = 450$. Thus, statement (D) is true. If $x = y$, the perimeter $= 3x$. Since the perimeter is given as 60 ft., $3x = 60$ and $x = 20$. Therefore, $y = 20$. The area would be computed by multiplying 20×20, or 400 sq. ft. But in statement (D) we found that when $x = 15$, the enclosed area is 450 sq. ft. Therefore, statement (E) is false.

9. **(E)**
Square both sides:

$$x^2 = (\sqrt{7} + \sqrt{5})^2$$
$$x^2 = 12 + 2\sqrt{35}$$
$$x = \sqrt{12 + 2\sqrt{35}}$$

10. **(B)**
Any number raised to the second power means that number multiplied by itself, so $0^2 = 0 \times 0 = 0$, $3^2 = 3 \times 3 = 9$. $(\sqrt{10})^2 = 10$ and $(\sqrt{6})^2 = 6$ because the square root of x is the number that, when multiplied by itself, gives x. Therefore:

$$\sqrt{0^2 + (\sqrt{10})^2 + 3^2 + (\sqrt{6})^2} =$$
$$\sqrt{0 + 10 + 9 + 6} = \sqrt{25} = 5.$$

11. **(C)**
$\dfrac{a - b}{a} = b + 2$. Multiply both sides by a. Then $a - b = ab + 2a$. Adding b and $-2a$ to both sides gives $a - 2a = ab + b$. $a - 2a = -a$, so $-a = ab + b$. Factoring the b on the left gives $-a = b(a + 1)$. Dividing by $a + 1$ gives $b = \dfrac{-a}{a + 1}$.

12. **(B)**
x^3 means $(x)(x)(x)$. This is negative when x is negative because you have a negative times a negative times a negative. The product of two negatives is a positive. The product of a positive times a negative is a negative.

13. **(E)**

$$\frac{8}{9} = .888$$

$$\frac{5}{7} = .714$$

$$\frac{3}{4} = .75$$

$$\frac{7}{8} = .875$$

$$\frac{11}{10} = 1.10$$

14. **(A)**

$$4 - (7 - d) = 3 - d(4 - d)$$
$$4 - 7 + d = 3 - 4d + d^2 \quad \text{(eliminating parentheses)}$$
$$d^2 - 5d + 6 = 0 \quad \text{(performing operations and}$$
$$(d - 3)(d - 2) = 0 \qquad \text{transposing)}$$
$$d - 3 = 0; d - 2 = 0$$
$$d = 3 \qquad d = 2$$

15. **(C)**

If one of the integers from 8 to 15 inclusive is chosen at random, the probability that the integer is even, is equal to the probability that it is odd.

$$p_{even} = 4 \ (8, 10, 12, 14)$$
$$q_{even} = 4 \ (9, 11, 13, 15)$$

$$\frac{p}{p + q} = \frac{4}{4 + 4} = \frac{1}{2}$$

$$p_{odd} = 4 \ (9, 11, 13, 15)$$
$$q_{odd} = 4 \ (8, 10, 12, 14)$$

$$\frac{p}{p + q} = \frac{4}{4 + 4} = \frac{1}{2}$$

(C) is true inasmuch as $\frac{1}{2} = \frac{1}{2}$

16. **(C)**

$$5\% = \frac{5}{100} = \frac{25}{500}$$

17. **(A)**
Find the average of the 5 heights in Column A:

$$5'\ 2''$$
$$5'\ 6''$$
$$5'\ 8''$$
$$5'10''$$
$$\underline{6'\ 2''}$$
$$26'28'' = 340''$$
$$340'' \div 5 = 68'' = 5'8''$$

18. **(B)**

$5^2 = 5 \times 5 = 25$ (Column A)
$2^5 = 2 \times 2 \times 2 \times 2 \times 2 = 32$ (Column B)

19. **(A)**

$13^2 = 169$
$\sqrt{196} > \sqrt{169}$

20. **(B)**

$(+15)(-5) = -75$ (Column A)
$(+18)(+4) = +72$ (Column B)
A positive whole number is larger than a negative whole number.

21. **(A)**
In column B:

$y - 1 = x + 2 - 1 = x + 1$. $x + 4 > x + 1$, so $x + 4 > y - 1$.

22. **(B)**

$2r^2s = 2(2s)^2s = 2(4s^2)s = 8s^3$ (Column A)
$3rs^2 = 3(2s)s^2 = 6s^3$ (Column B)
But s is negative, so $6s^3 > 8s^3$.

23. **(C)**
In a right triangle in which the other two angles are each $45°$, the two sides other than the hypotenuse are equal. Since $b = c$,
$\dfrac{b}{a} = \dfrac{c}{a}$.

24. **(C)**
Multiplying the numerator and denominator of the fraction $\dfrac{4}{\sqrt{2}}$ by $\sqrt{2}$, we get $\dfrac{4\sqrt{2}}{2}$, which equals $2\sqrt{2}$.

25. **(A)**

$$\frac{5}{6} \text{ of } \frac{5}{6} = \frac{5}{6} \times \frac{5}{6} = \frac{25}{36}$$

$$\frac{1}{36} \times 24 = \frac{24}{36}$$

26. **(D)**
If $x = 0$, the quantities are equal.
If $0 < x < 1$, then $x^2 + 1 > x^3 + 1$.
If $x > 1$, then $x^3 + 1 > x^2 + 1$.

27. **(A)**
Dividing $3.00 by 12, we get the cost of one battery, $.25, which is greater than $.24.

28. **(B)**
Multiplying the second equation by 3 and subtracting the result from the first equation, we get $-7y = -21$. Therefore, $y = 3$. Substituting in the second equation, we get $x + 6 = 8$. There-fore, $x = 2$.

29. **(C)**
AC is a diameter of the circle. BO and DO are radii. The length of a diameter is twice the length of a radius.

30. **(B)**
The circumference of a circle is $2\pi r$. The circumference of this circle, then, is $2\pi(2) = 4\pi$. π is less than 4. Therefore, the circumference is greater than π^2.

31. **(A)**
30% of income is spent on Food. 30% is spent on Household Items and Rent. Together, these entries account for 60% of income. Everything else, therefore, accounts for 40%.

32. **(D)**
Since the graph specifies only recreation, we cannot determine how much is spent on bowling.

33. **(A)**
The amount spent on miscellaneous items is 20% of $12,000.00. That amounts to $2,400.00.

34. **(D)**
If $x < 0$, then $(x + 3)^2 < (x - 3)^2$. If $x > 0$, then $(x + 3)^2 > (x - 3)^2$. Therefore, the answer cannot be determined.

35. **(C)**

$(12 + 14) = 2 \times (6 + 7)$

Therefore, Column A equals

$7 \times 2 \times (6 + 7) = 14 \times (6 + 7)$

Further computation is unnecessary.

Section 5: Verbal Questions

1. **(D)**
Austere: severe; *antonym:* indulgent

2. **(E)**
Rancid: sour; *antonym:* fresh

3. **(C)**
Blandishment: flattery; *antonym:* insult

4. **(C)**
Truculent: cruel, rude; *antonym:* harmless

5. **(E)**
Peerless: unmatched; *antonym:* equal

6. **(B)**
Noxious: harmful; *antonym:* harmless

7. **(E)**
Candor: frankness; *antonym:* fraudulence

8. **(B)**
Encroach: trespass; *antonym:* avoid

9. **(D)**
Impeccable: flawless; *antonym:* blemished

10. **(A)**
Promulgate: to make known; *antonym:* conceal, veil

11. **(A)**
Commodious: spacious; *antonym:* cramped

12. **(C)**
Encomium: high praise; *antonym:* reproach

13. **(D)**

Abase: to degrade; *antonym:* to praise, to extol

14. **(B)**

Lampoon: to attack or ridicule; *antonym:* plaudit

15. **(E)**

Fervent: hot, ardent; *antonym:* sluggish, calm, phlegmatic

16. **(A)**

Choice (A) is consistent with the rest of the sentence.

17. **(C)**

A man is *elected* by popular vote.

18. **(B)**

Choice (B) is consistent with the rest of the sentence.

19. **(C)**

The student . . . knows that its components are, for the most part, not susceptible to change (*immutable*); but he is also aware that events . . . do play a part in bringing to the fore at one time or another certain *characteristics.*

20. **(D)**

Cessation of prejudice, intolerance, and *bigotry* is what will be witnessed.

21. **(E)**

There is a *reward* for a *capture* as there is a *prize* for a *victory.*

22. **(D)**

An *oval* is a stretched *circle* as a *rectangle* is a stretched *square.*

23. **(B)**

A *sea* is a body of water smaller than an *ocean*. A *stream* is a body of water smaller than a *river.*

24. **(C)**

We speak of the *grade* of a *mountain* as we speak of the *pitch* of a *roof.*

25. **(A)**

We speak of a *portion* of *vegetables* as we speak of a *dose* of *medicine.*

26. (C)
An *examination* filters out *failures* as a *filter* filters out *impurities*.

27. (A)
The *earth* revolves about its *axis* as a *wheel* revolves about its *hub*.

28. (D)
Terse (concise) : *turgid* (over-ornate in style or language) : :
slim (thin) : *obese* (fat).

29. (E)
A *cloud* blocks the *sky* as *prejudice* blocks the *mind*.

30. (E)
Here we are dealing with words that have similar meanings.

31. (A)
See principle 1: "Only those constructs based upon operations
which are public and repeatable are admitted to the body of
science."

32. (A)
See principle 1: "Science is knowledge agreed up by members
of society . . ." and "Only those constructs based upon operations
which are public. . . ."

33. (C)
See principle 3: ". . . if, and only if, the criteria of its applicability
or truth consist of concrete operations, which can be performed."

34. (E)
This statement cannot be derived from any of the principles in the
passage.

35. (D)
See the discussion on discrimination: ". . . discrimination is, therefore, a 'physical' process. . . ."

36. (B)
See the fifth and sixth sentences.

37. (E)
The revival of Catholicism, vague, musical, and abstract poetry, a
renewed interest in the arts, and a decline in prosperity happened
during the time of Freud, Tolstoy, and the modernists.

38. (E)
Freud, Wagner, Nietzsche, and Tolstoy all influenced the modern movements.

39. (D)
Rimbaud is not mentioned as one of the literary and dramatic critics.

40. (E)
I, II, III, and IV all characterize Valéry's poetry. See the second paragraph.

Section 6: Mathematics Questions

1. (B)
Cost = $36
Overhead = 10% of Cost = $3.60
Profit = $9.00
Selling price = $48.60 (36 + 3.60 + 9)
Markup = 12.60 (48.60 − 36)
$$\frac{\text{Markup}}{\text{Cost}} = \% \text{ of Markup} = \frac{12.60}{36.00} = 35\%$$

2. (B)
$ax + b = cx + d$ and adding $-b$ and $-cx$ to both sides gives $ax - cx = d - b$. Factoring out the x yields $x(a - c) = d - b$. Dividing both sides by $a - c$ gives $x = \dfrac{d - b}{a - c}$.

3. (E)
$a = 0.20b$, which can be written as $4a = 0.80b$. $2c = 0.80b$, so $2c = 4a$, or $\frac{1}{2}c = a$. $\frac{1}{2}$ is 50%, so a is 50% of c.

4. (B)
20 miles per hour is $\frac{20}{60}$ miles per minute. 200 miles in 8 hours is a rate of 25 miles per hour, or $\frac{25}{60}$ miles per minute. $\frac{25}{60} - \frac{20}{60} = \frac{5}{60}$, or $\frac{1}{12}$ of a mile per minute.

5. **(B)**
By examining each choice, it can be seen that

(A) $\dfrac{0.3}{0.1} = \dfrac{3}{1} = 3$

(B) $0.3 = \dfrac{3}{10} = \dfrac{9}{30}$ $\left(\dfrac{1}{3} = \dfrac{10}{30}\right)$

(C) $\dfrac{1}{0.3} = \dfrac{10}{3}$

(D) $3^3 = 27$

(E) $\dfrac{1}{2} = \dfrac{3}{6}$ $\left(\dfrac{1}{3} = \dfrac{2}{6}\right)$

Choice (B) is the only answer less than $\dfrac{1}{3}$.

6. **(B)**
$\dfrac{x - \dfrac{1}{y}}{y - \dfrac{1}{x}}$. Multiplying the numerator and denominator by xy gives

$\dfrac{x^2 y - x}{xy^2 - y}$. Factoring the numerator and denominator gives

$\dfrac{x(xy - 1)}{y(xy - 1)}$. Cancelling the $(xy - 1)$ from the numerator and

denominator gives $\dfrac{x}{y}$.

7. **(C)**
At the point where a graph intersects the Y axis, $x = 0$. If $x = 0$ in the equation, $y = 4 - x^2$, then $y = 4$, which is point A.

8. **(A)**
There are two pints in a quart. Therefore, there are 6 pints in 3 quarts. The price of 6 pints is $6 \times \$.50 = \$3.00$.

9. (E)

There are 180° in a triangle, so angle *c* must equal 60°. Angle 1 must be 30° since it is part of a right triangle and the other angle is 60°. Angle 1 = angle 2 = 30°. Angle *d* equals 60° since it is part of a right triangle with angle 2.

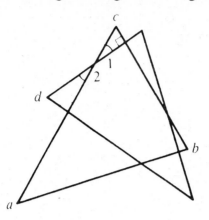

10. (C)

There are 12 inches in one foot, and 12 × 12 = 144 square inches in one square foot. In a 2-foot by 10-foot area there are 20 square feet, or 2880 square inches. At $.05 a square inch, it would cost $144.00 to cover the given area.

11. (B)

Let h = the hundred's digit, t = the ten's digit, and u = the unit's digit.

$$h + t + u = 16 \quad \text{(first equation)}$$
$$u = 3h \quad \text{(second equation)}$$
$$100u + 10t + h = 100h + 10t + u + 594 \quad \text{(third equation)}$$
$$99u - 99h = 594 \quad \text{(transposing and combining terms)}$$
$$99(3h) - 99h = 594 \quad \text{(substitution)}$$
$$198h = 594$$
$$h = 3$$
$$u = 3h = 9$$
$$3 + t + 9 = 16 \quad \text{(substitution)}$$
$$t = 4$$

The original number is 349.

12. (D)

$x + 20 + $ angle CAB $= 180°$ since there are 180° in a triangle. $3x + $ angle CAB $= 180°$ since $3x$ and angle CAB form a straight angle. Therefore, $x + 20 = 3x$ and $x = 10$.

13. (A)

$$\frac{\sqrt{3^2 + 4^2}}{\sqrt{13^2 - 12^2}} = \frac{\sqrt{9 + 16}}{\sqrt{169 - 144}} = \frac{\sqrt{25}}{\sqrt{25}} = \frac{5}{5} = 1$$

14. **(D)**

The original area is $p \times 3p = 3p^2$. If you double p, the new area is $2p \times 3(2p) = 12p^2$. This is four times the original.

15. **(E)**

If he pulls out five coins, he will be certain to have at least 5 pennies. If he pulled out fewer than 5 coins, he would not be sure of having $.05.

16. **(B)**

From the diagram, 25% is water, so 0.25×2 lb. $= \frac{1}{2}$ lb. is water.

17. **(A)**

An even number is one that can be expressed as 2N where N is an integer. Accordingly, if you add two even numbers such as 2M and 2P, you get $2(M + P)$, which must be even since $M + P$ is an integer. (If you add any two integers, you get an integer.) The odd numbers are not closed since $3 + 5 = 8$, which is not odd.

18. **(E)**

Let x be the number of pounds of the $.85 candy. Then:

$$85x + 35(60 - x) = 75(60)$$
$$85x + 2100 - 35x = 4500$$
$$50x = 2400$$
$$x = 48$$

19. **(B)**

Let the sum of the two numbers be x. Then $\dfrac{8 + 11 + x}{4} = 10$

because an average is the sum of the elements divided by the number of elements. Solving for x gives us $19 + x = 40$, or $x = 21$.

20. **(A)**

Let length $AD = x$. Then $DC = 10 - x$. The area of a triangle $= \frac{1}{2}$ (base) (height), so the area of triangle BDA $= \frac{1}{2}(x)(10) = 5x$. The area of the triangle BDC $= \frac{1}{2}(10 - x)(10) = 50 - 5x$. The area of triangle BDA is three times the area of triangle BDC, or $5x = 3(50 - 5x)$.

$$5x = 150 - 15x$$
$$20x = 150$$
$$x = 7\frac{1}{2}$$

21. (A)

Let the perimeter of the triangle be denoted by P. Then we get

$$\frac{3}{4}P = 18$$
$$3P = 4 \times 18$$
$$P = \frac{4 \times 18}{3}$$
$$P = 4 \times 6 = 24$$

Note that we really *didn't need the fact* that the triangle was an *isosceles right triangle*. Sometimes on the SAT, information that makes the problem appear more difficult, or actually appear impossible to solve, or extraneous information is presented with the problem.

22. (E)

If 32 divides y, then 8×4 must also divide y because $8 \times 4 = 32$. Therefore 8 must also be a factor because if 32 divides y a total of p times, with p a whole number, then 8, which is one-fourth of 32, divides y a total of $4p$ times.

23. (E)

The area of a square of side s is s^2.
On the land $s^2 = 16$ square miles.

$$s = 4 \text{ miles}$$

Each inch represents 2 miles, so 2 inches represents 4 miles.

24. (C)

For the product of two numbers to be negative, one must be positive and one must be negative.

25. (D)

If $(x - 2) \leq 0$, then $x \leq 2$. x is the part of the line that is equal to 2 or less, or that portion of the line which is at 2 or to the left of 2.

SAT PRACTICE TEST 3 ⟶

Tear out the answer sheet for this test at the end of the book.

Section 1: Mathematics Questions

Time: 30 minutes

Directions: Each question in this section is followed by five choices lettered (A) through (E). Choose the correct answer. Then mark the appropriate space in the answer column.

The following information may be useful to you in solving some of the mathematics problems in this part:

Circle, radius $= r$:

Area $= \pi r^2$.

Circumference $= 2\pi r$.

A circle has 360 degrees of arc.

Triangle:

The sum of the three angles in a triangle is 180 degrees.

Area $= \frac{1}{2}$(any side $\times$ altitude to that side).

Right Triangle:

The sum of the squares of the legs $=$ the square of the hypotenuse.

Definitions of certain mathematical symbols:

$>$ is greater than

$<$ is less than

$\geq$ is greater than or equal to

$\leq$ is less than or equal to

$\perp$ is perpendicular to

$\parallel$ is parallel to

Important Note: Figures in this section are not always drawn to scale. All numbers are real numbers and all figures lie in a plane unless otherwise stated.

1. John received the following marks on math tests: 70, 60, 95, 95.
    What mark must he get on a fifth test in order to have an 80
    average?
    (A) 75
    (B) 80
    (C) $83\frac{1}{2}$
    (D) 85
    (E) 90

2. If $a + by = cb$, express y in terms of a, b, and c.
    (A) $ab - a - b$

    (B) $\dfrac{c - b}{a}$

    (C) $\dfrac{cb + a}{a}$

    (D) $\dfrac{cb}{a} - b$

    (E) $\dfrac{cb - a}{b}$

3. If 10% of s is $\frac{1}{2}r$ and 5% of s is $2q$, then $r - q$ is what percent
    of s?
    (A) 15%
    (B) 10%
    (C) $17\frac{1}{2}\%$

    (D) $22\frac{1}{2}\%$

    (E) 20%

4. A train travels from City A to City B in 4 hours. It travels at
    50 miles per hour. Another train goes from City B to City A
    in 5 hours. How fast does it go?
    (A) 20 mph
    (B) 25 mph
    (C) 35 mph
    (D) 40 mph
    (E) 60 mph

5. Which is less than 3?

(A) $\dfrac{22}{7}$

(B) $\sqrt{8}$

(C) $\dfrac{10}{3}$

(D) $(1.8)^2$

(E) $\dfrac{0.3}{0.01}$

6. $\dfrac{\dfrac{1}{x} + \dfrac{1}{y}}{xy} =$

(A) $\dfrac{xy}{x + y}$

(B) $\dfrac{y + x}{(xy)^2}$

(C) $\dfrac{(x + y)xy}{x - y}$

(D) $x + y$

(E) $xy(x + y)$

7. In the diagram below, AB is parallel to DE. What is the measure of angle D if angle A is 50° and angle ACD is 70°?

(A) 15°
(B) 20°
(C) 30°
(D) 50°
(E) 60°

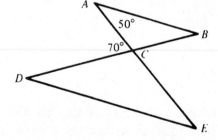

8. If $A = \dfrac{10}{B}$ and B is tripled, then the initial value of A is

(A) tripled

(B) multiplied by $\dfrac{10}{3}$

(C) divided by $\dfrac{10}{3}$

(D) divided by 30

(E) divided by 3

9. In the diagram below, GCA is a straight line and EC bisects angle GCB. What is $d° + \frac{1}{2}c°$?

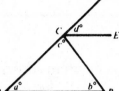

   (A) $a° + b° - c°$
   (B) $180° - a° - b°$
   (C) $90°$
   (D) $90° + a° + b°$
   (E) $180° + \frac{1}{2}(a° + b°)$

10. $\frac{1}{2} + 4x = 10$. Solve for x.

   (A) $-\dfrac{9}{8}$

   (B) $\dfrac{5}{2}$

   (C) $\dfrac{11}{2}$

   (D) $-\dfrac{19}{4}$

   (E) $\dfrac{19}{8}$

11. According to the table below, of Harry's collection, U.S. air mail stamps make up

   (A) 4.00%
   (B) 8.05%
   (C) 15.50%
   (D) 16.00%
   (E) 21.35%

   Distribution of Stamps in Harry's Collection

English	22%
French	18%
South American	25%
U.S.	35%

   Distribution of U.S. Stamps in Harry's Collection

Commemoratives	52%
Special Delivery	10%
Postage Due	15%
Air Mail	23%

12. Evaluate $\dfrac{(4x^2 - 2x)(y + 2x)(3y)}{(x + y)(x - y)}$. Let $x = 2y$ and $y = 1$.

   (A) -10
   (B) 1
   (C) 25
   (D) 30
   (E) 60

13. If $1 + \dfrac{5}{p} + \dfrac{3}{p-1} = \dfrac{p^2 + 2}{p^2 - p}$, then what value(s) can p take on?

    (A) -2 only
    (B) 1 only
    (C) 1 and -1 only
    (D) no values
    (E) cannot be determined from the given information

14. $\dfrac{\sqrt{2} + \sqrt{3}}{\sqrt{2} - \sqrt{3}} =$

    (A) $\sqrt{2} - \sqrt{3}$
    (B) $-(\sqrt{2} - \sqrt{3})$
    (C) $\sqrt{3} + \sqrt{2}$
    (D) 1
    (E) $-5 - 2\sqrt{6}$

15. Which of the following statements is (are) *false*?
    I.   An odd number raised to an even power is odd.
    II. The sum of any even number of odd terms is even.
    III. The square of an even number is always divisible by 4.
    (A) I and II only
    (B) II only
    (C) III only
    (D) II and III only
    (E) none

16. If $\dfrac{r}{3}$ is an even integer and $\dfrac{r}{6}$ is an odd integer, which of the following values could r be?
    (A) 60
    (B) 18
    (C) 12
    (D) 24
    (E) 36

17. Provided $a \neq b$, $-\left[\dfrac{(a+b)(a-b)}{b^2 - a^2}\right] =$

    (A) $-(a+b)$
    (B) $+1$
    (C) $a - b$
    (D) -1
    (E) $\dfrac{a+b}{a-b}$

18. Find r in terms of p if $p + r = \dfrac{5p - r}{0.5}$.

(A) $\frac{3}{2}p$

(B) $\dfrac{p}{p + 5}$

(C) $10p$

(D) $\dfrac{2p + 5}{2}$

(E) $3p$

19. If $a^2 > b^2$ then
(A) a is always greater than b
(B) a is sometimes greater than b
(C) a is never greater than b
(D) a can be zero
(E) a and b must both be greater than zero

20. The average of a set of 30 numbers is 100. What is their average if each term is halved?
(A) 50
(B) 60
(C) 100
(D) 25
(E) 15

21. 9 is 150% of
(A) 3
(B) 6
(C) 12
(D) 15
(E) $7\frac{1}{2}$

22. In the figure below, angle A is a right angle, AC = 4, AB = 3. If the length of CD is 80% of the length of DE and CDEB is a rectangle, find the area of the shaded region.
(A) 25
(B) 15
(C) 8
(D) 14
(E) 12

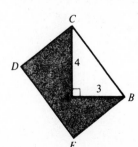

23. What is the minimum value of $\frac{a}{b}$ if $0.05 \geqq a \geqq 0.005$ and $0.005 \leqq b \leqq 0.05$?
(A)   1.0
(B)   0.01
(C)   0.1
(D)   0.001
(E)   0.0001

24. If Q is divisible by both 30 and 35, then we know it is also divisible by
(A)   65
(B)   21
(C)   8
(D)   90
(E)   11

25. On the coordinate system below, the units on the *y*-axis are yards and the units on the *x*-axis are feet. What is the area of the triangle shown in square inches?
(A)   27
(B)   186
(C)   722
(D)   1944
(E)   3888

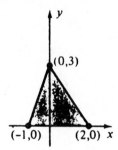

IF YOU FINISH THIS SECTION OF THE SAT BEFORE YOUR TIME IS UP, YOU MAY LOOK BACK AT YOUR WORK IN THIS SECTION ONLY. YOU ARE NOT PERMITTED TO LOOK AT ANY OTHER SECTION OF THE TEST. WHEN THE TIME IS UP, TURN TO THE NEXT SECTION AND START WORK ON THAT SECTION.

Section 2: Verbal Questions

Time: 30 minutes

Antonyms

Directions: Each question in this test consists of a word printed in capital letters followed by five words lettered (A) through (E). Choose the word that has most nearly the OPPOSITE meaning from the word in capital letters. Then mark the appropriate space in the answer column.

1. TYRO
   - (A) novice
   - (B) expert
   - (C) amateur
   - (D) militant
   - (E) anchor

2. LACKADAISICAL
   - (A) listless
   - (B) bored
   - (C) enthusiastic
   - (D) uninterested
   - (E) lazy

3. GENIAL
   - (A) cheerful
   - (B) unable
   - (C) sardonic
   - (D) sarcastic
   - (E) unfriendly

4. INTREPID
   - (A) inclusive
   - (B) fearless
   - (C) fearful
   - (D) explained
   - (E) solved

5. FURTIVE
   - (A) secret
   - (B) brief
   - (C) apparent
   - (D) awake
   - (E) beneficial

6. ANTIPATHY
   - (A) dislike
   - (B) fondness
   - (C) apathy
   - (D) objection
   - (E) idolatry

7. DEBILITATE
   - (A) weaken
   - (B) strengthen
   - (C) in debt
   - (D) owe
   - (E) pay

8. HACKNEYED
   - (A) trite
   - (B) inane
   - (C) novel
   - (D) flat
   - (E) shapeless

9. GARRULOUS
   - (A) wordy
   - (B) loquacious
   - (C) verbose
   - (D) laconic
   - (E) prolix

10. SATIATE
    - (A) starve
    - (B) endow
    - (C) satisfy
    - (D) torture
    - (E) harm

11. MENDICANT
(A) doctor
(B) pauper
(C) philanthropist
(D) beggar
(E) miser

12. CHOLERIC
(A) spotted
(B) healthy
(C) serene
(D) splenetic
(E) pretty

Sentence Completions

Directions: Each question in this test consists of a sentence or group of sentences in which one or two words are missing. Beneath the question are five pairs of words lettered (A) through (E). Choose the word or the pair of words that *best* completes the sentence or sentences. Then mark the appropriate space in the answer column.

13. Since the judge feels that the defendant's offense is ———, he will, probably, give him a light sentence.
(A) vindictive
(B) venal
(C) militant
(D) venial
(E) heinous

14. Most estimates of the incidence of chicken pox in communities are ———, not because of poor statistical techniques but because the disease is not well reported.
(A) unnecessary
(B) heartening
(C) unreliable
(D) variable
(E) made

15. As often happens with those who rule by emotion rather than by reason, their discussion soon retrogressed from ——— to ———.
(A) argument—controversy
(B) consideration—rationalization
(C) disagreement—altercation
(D) dispute—disagreement
(E) squabbling—wrangling

16. A good axiom to remember, to serve as a source of consolation, is that a single _____ does not constitute _____.
(A) apple—a meal
(B) winter—old age
(C) misfortune—victory
(D) loss—defeat
(E) flower—spring

17. Some beliefs are patently and clearly false even though there is little evidence to _____ them.
(A) verify
(B) clarify
(C) disprove
(D) substantiate
(E) impute

18. The _____ base of the giant tree is _____ evidence of its antiquity.
(A) red—vivid
(B) round—tacit
(C) concrete—definite
(D) complete—striking
(E) gnarled—mute

19. A fortunate but small number of people work at jobs which are in themselves _____ and are not performed chiefly for the return they bring
(A) painful
(B) useful
(C) wearisome
(D) necessary
(E) pleasurable

20. The lawyer attempted to _____ the gravity of his client's offense by ascribing it to a condition of _____.
(A) condone—premeditation
(B) mitigate—temporary insanity
(C) minimize—malevolence
(D) aggravate—unawareness
(E) soften—intolerance

Reading Comprehension

Directions: Read the following passage and answer each of the questions that come after it. Choose the *best* answer. Then mark the appropriate space in the answer column.

When an animal is presented with food, he will salivate. If a bell is repeatedly rung shortly before the food is presented, the animal will begin to salivate soon after the sound of the bell, even if the food is not offered. With repeated trials of the bell followed by the food (conditioning trials), the latency of the response (that is, the time interval between the advent of the bell and the beginning of salivation) decreases. This process is called conditioning, and salivation to the sound of the bell is termed the conditioned response. The conditioned response may be unlearned or extinguished if the bell is presented a number of times without being followed by food (extinction trials). Under such conditions, the latency of the conditioned response gradually increases until it does not take place at all. Trials which are separated by an interval of time are called distributed trials, while those which follow immediately one upon the other are called massed trials. One theory holds that after each conditioning trial a finite amount of excitation is left which facilitates the occurrence of the conditioned response, and also that a finite amount of inhibition is left which inhibits the occurrence of the conditioned response. During the conditioning trials, the excitation is built up faster than the inhibition, whereas during the extinction trials, the reverse is held to be true. The strength of the conditioned response, as measured, for example, in terms of how quickly it begins after the bell is sounded, is said to be a function of the magnitude of the difference between the quantity of excitation and the quantity of inhibition. The inhibitory component disappears more quickly with the passage of time than does the excitatory component. It has been assumed that 50 percent of the inhibition is spontaneously dissipated after a few hours, while the excitation remains practically intact. The inhibitory component is also more readily destroyed upon the occurrence of some novel stimulus than is the excitation component.

21.   In Experiment A the conditioning trials are massed, and in Experiment B they are distributed. On the basis of the theory, after the same number of trials, the latency of the conditioned response in Experiment A as compared with Experiment B should be

(A)   longer

(B)   shorter

(C)   the same

(D)   unpredictable

(E)   irrelevant

22. If the conditioned response, salivation, is extinguished
    (A) its latency decreases
    (B) the food was presented without the bell
    (C) the amount of inhibition is greater than the amount of excitation
    (D) the animal is no longer hungry
    (E) the amount of inhibition is less than the amount of excitation

23. In Experiment E an unusual tone was sounded immediately after the bell. On that trial the conditioned response failed to occur. This means that the tone was sufficiently loud to
    (A) dissipate all the excitation, but none of the inhibition
    (B) dissipate all the excitation, and leave some of the inhibition
    (C) dissipate all the excitation and all of the inhibition
    (D) increase the excitation, but increase the inhibition more
    (E) dissipate some of the excitation but none of the inhibition

24. On the basis of the theory, the rapidity with which a hungry animal should adopt a conditioned response as compared with a satiated animal should be
    (A) less
    (B) greater
    (C) the same
    (D) unpredictable
    (E) irrelevant

25. After the bell sounds, the conditioned response of trial 7 of the conditioning series as compared with trial 30 should take place
    (A) quicker
    (B) slower
    (C) after the same interval
    (D) sometimes more quickly and sometimes more slowly
    (E) instantaneously

GO ON TO THE NEXT PAGE

Analogies

Directions: In each of the following questions choose the pair of words
that *best* completes the analogy. Then mark the appropriate space
in the answer column.

26. FABULOUS : REAL ::
 (A) descendant : ancestor
 (B) creditable : veritable
 (C) medieval : prehistoric
 (D) amphibian : reptile
 (E) dragon : dinosaur

27. FRIGHTFUL : HORRID ::
 (A) death : demise
 (B) life : breath
 (C) resistance : invasion
 (D) might : right
 (E) asylum : insane

28. LITERAL : FREE ::
 (A) intrinsic : extrinsic
 (B) translate : paraphrase
 (C) communicate : express
 (D) simile : metaphor
 (E) news : hearsay

29. CITADEL : VAULT ::
 (A) virtue : disgrace
 (B) prop : cornice
 (C) building : foundation
 (D) head : foot
 (E) tower : dungeon

30. EXPOSITION : PRECIS ::
 (A) genuine : synthetic
 (B) volume : booklet
 (C) tome : epitaph
 (D) obese : slender
 (E) synopsis : compendium

31. IMPLICIT : EXPLICIT ::
 (A) suggestion : recommendation
 (B) state : hint
 (C) innuendo : assertion
 (D) allusion : insinuation
 (E) indirect : devious

32. HOG : PORK ::
 (A) lion : jackal
 (B) mutton : sheep
 (C) beef : stew
 (D) lamb : chops
 (E) deer : venison

33. PHILOLOGIST : LANGUAGE ::
 (A) ornithologist : birds
 (B) botanist : animals
 (C) biologist : cells
 (D) etymologist : insects
 (E) pediatrician : feet

34. DIME : DOLLAR ::
 (A) decade : century
 (B) penny : dime
 (C) time : number
 (D) decalogue : triology
 (E) little : much

35. PROSPEROUS : PRODIGAL ::
 (A) rich : gorgeous
 (B) poor : frugal
 (C) wealth : prosperous
 (D) lachrymose : indolent
 (E) well-to-do : heedless

Reading Comprehension

Directions: Read the following passages and answer each of the questions that come after them. Choose the *best* answer. Then mark the appropriate space in the answer column.

Origins of the seventeenth-century scientific revolution have been disputed by historians for the past two centuries. Some have seen it as the result of the liberation of the European mind by the Protestant Reformation; others have attributed it to the rise of the middle class, with its characteristic curiosity and quantitative penchant. Still a third school prefers to view modern science as a philosophical revolution in which the elements of science were entirely redefined. Finally, there is the view that modern science arose from a technological revolution which, by focusing attention upon the exploitation of nature, stimulated the search for natural laws. There are elements of truth in all these interpretations. While the Protestants were no more friendly or hostile to science than the Catholics, the very proliferation of Protestant sects made it possible for the holders of heterodox views to gain a hearing. The middle class, too, made its contribution. From its ranks came much of the driving force behind the attack on nature, which was provided by the vision of economic reward attendant upon eventual victory.

More important than these factors, however, was the reorientation in philosophy. The Copernican system owed far more to philosophical presuppositions than it did to anything else, and classical dynamics was founded by challenging a fundamental tenet of Aristotelian philosophy. The technological innovations of the Renaissance were also to make an important contribution to seventeenth-century science. By the seventeenth century, fairly complicated machinery was in use in a number of industries. Machines provided the analogy upon which science was to call for two centuries. The universe and its component processes could be likened to a machine and, like a machine, the universe could be understood in terms of the separate operations of its parts.

36.   The cause of scientific discovery during the seventeenth century
   (A)   is agreed to by most historians
   (B)   is agreed to by some historians
   (C)   has been argued among historians
   (D)   has something to do with religious developments
   (E)   is none of these

37. The factor that did NOT affect the scientific revolution was
  (A)   philosophy
  (B)   the middle class
  (C)   economic motives
  (D)   industrial development
  (E)   none of these

38. The Protestant Reformation gave rise to
  (A)   different opinions
  (B)   victory of science over nature
  (C)   a challenge to Copernican doctrine
  (D)   economic wealth
  (E)   none of these

39. One theory maintains that the advance in scientific thought was brought about by
  (A)   inventions
  (B)   religious toleration
  (C)   economic theories
  (D)   Aristotle
  (E)   none of these

40. One contribution of the scientific revolution was
  (A)   political freedom
  (B)   a rise in the middle class
  (C)   a rejection of Aristotle's ideas
  (D)   a rejection of philosophy in scientific matters
  (E)   none of these

The solar system is the total system of the sun. Our solar system is made up of nine principal planets, thirty-one known natural satellites or moons that circle some of the planets, thousands of tiny planetoids or asteroids, millions of comets, innumerable meteoroids, and vast quantities of interplanetary dust and gas. The magnetic and radiation fields around the sun and the planets are also important parts of the system.

The volume of space our solar system occupies can be visualized as a sphere more than ten billion miles across, with the sun at its center. Only minor parts of the system extend to the extreme borders of this sphere. The planets are located relatively close to the sun; they lie in a plane, and all revolve around the sun in the same direction.

All material particles in the solar system, from the giant planet Jupiter to those no bigger than a grain of sand, pursue individual orbits or paths around the sun. Our moon revolves around the earth, but it also revolves with earth around the sun. Viewed from the earth, the moon's orbit appears as a near circle. Viewed from the sun, the path of the moon would appear much like earth's but with "wiggles" in it.

Material particles orbit the sun because of the gravitational pull that the sun's large mass exerts over them. This force is continuous and would, theoretically, pull all members of the solar system into the sun if they themselves were not moving. A planet can be visualized as a stone tied to a string; the sun, as a boy swinging the stone in a circle over his head. The pull of the string on the stone keeps the stone from flying off its orbit. If the stone were not moving, however, the same amount of pull would quickly bring the stone to the boy in the same way that a planet, if not moving, would be pulled into the sun.

41. Which of the following statements is FALSE?
  (A)   The moon revolves around the sun.
  (B)   The earth tends to fall into the sun.
  (C)   The components of the solar system follow definite paths.
  (D)   The force of gravity has little effect in the solar system.
  (E)   none of these

42. The diameter of the solar system is about
  (A)   10,000,000 miles across
  (B)   10,000,000,000 miles across
  (C)   10,000,000,000,000 miles across
  (D)   100,000,000,000 miles across
  (E)   none of these

43. From the above passage, it would appear that
  (A)   the sun is the largest body in the solar system
  (B)   the sun is not in the center of the solar system
  (C)   the earth is in the center of the solar system
  (D)   the moon is in the center of the solar system
  (E)   none of these is true

44. The main reason for the attraction of bodies to the sun is
  (A)   that the sun is hot
  (B)   the sun's rotation
  (C)   the sun's size
  (D)   the sun's distance from the body
  (E)   none of these

45. The main reason that bodies do not fall into the sun is that
  (A)   they are small
  (B)   they are too big
  (C)   they are in motion
  (D)   they follow orbits around the sun
  (E)   none of these

IF YOU FINISH THIS SECTION OF THE SAT BEFORE YOUR TIME IS UP, YOU MAY LOOK BACK AT YOUR WORK IN THIS SECTION ONLY. YOU ARE NOT PERMITTED TO LOOK AT ANY OTHER SECTION OF THE TEST. WHEN THE TIME IS UP, TURN TO THE NEXT SECTION AND START WORK ON THAT SECTION.

Section 3: Mathematics Questions

Time: 30 minutes

Directions: Each question in this section is followed by five choices lettered (A) through (E). Choose the correct answer. Then mark the appropriate space in the answer column.

The following information may be useful to you in solving some of the mathematics problems in this part:

Circle, radius $= r$:
 Area $= \pi r^2$.
 Circumference $= 2\pi r$.
 A circle has 360 degrees of arc.

Triangle:
 The sum of the three angles in a triangle is 180 degrees.
 Area $= \frac{1}{2}$(any side $\times$ altitude to that side).

Right Triangle:
 The sum of the squares of the legs $=$ the square of the hypotenuse.

Definitions of certain mathematical symbols:

 $>$ is greater than
 $<$ is less than
 $\geq$ is greater than or equal to
 $\leq$ is less than or equal to
 $\perp$ is perpendicular to
 $\parallel$ is parallel to

Important Note: Figures in this section are not always drawn to scale. All numbers are real numbers and all figures lie in a plane unless otherwise stated.

1. Which of the following proves that x^5y is positive?
(A) y is positive
(B) x^3y is positive
(C) x^2 is positive
(D) x^4y is positive
(E) x is positive

2. In the figure shown, at which point does the graph of the equation $y^2 + y - 6 = x$ cross or touch the y axis?
(A) D only
(B) E and D
(C) B and E
(D) A and D
(E) A and B

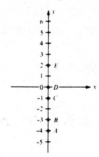

3. If $2\pi rh + \pi r^2 = 30$ and $V = \pi r^2h$, what is V?

(A) $\pi r^2\left(\dfrac{15}{\pi r} - \dfrac{r}{2}\right)$

(B) $\pi r\left(\dfrac{\pi}{15r} - r\right)$

(C) $\pi r^3\left(15\pi - \dfrac{r}{2}\right)$

(D) $\pi r^3\left(\dfrac{15}{\pi} - \dfrac{r^2}{2}\right)$

(E) $\pi r\left(\dfrac{15\pi}{r} - 2\right)$

4. In the diagram, the isosceles triangle has an angle of 60° between the two equal sides; and one of the legs equals 4. The area of this triangle is equal to the area of the shaded region in the diagram. What is the area of the triangle labeled ABC?

(A) $\dfrac{8}{3}\sqrt{3}$

(B) $\dfrac{8}{5}\sqrt{3}$

(C) $\dfrac{1}{3}\sqrt{3}$

(D) $\dfrac{4\sqrt{3}}{3}$

(E) 1.732

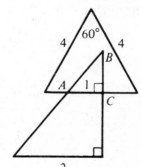

5. A relation R is said to be symmetric if when *a* R *b* is true, *b* R *a* is also true. In which of the following relations is R symmetric?

   I.   less than
  II.   is a multiple of
 III.   is relatively prime to

(A) I only
(B) III only
(C) II and III only
(D) I and III only
(E) none

6. A line parallel to $y = \dfrac{x}{3} + 7$ and passing through the origin is

(A) $y = -3x + 1$
(B) $y = 3x$
(C) $y = \dfrac{x}{3} + \dfrac{7}{3}$
(D) $x = \dfrac{y}{3} + 7$
(E) $x = 3y$

7. If the remainder is 3 when *n* is divided by 7, then what is the remainder when $5n$ is divided by 7?

(A) 0
(B) 1
(C) 3
(D) 4
(E) $\dfrac{3}{5}$

8. In the diagram below, AB is tangent to circle O. The distance from A to B is 15 and the radius of circle O is 8. Find the cosine of angle AOB.

(A) $\dfrac{15}{17}$

(B) $\dfrac{15}{8}$

(C) $\dfrac{8}{12}$

(D) $\dfrac{8}{17}$

(E) $\dfrac{17}{8}$

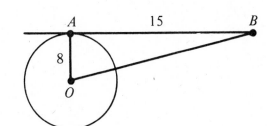

9. What is the probability that a pair of fair dice tossed will show a 12?

    (A) $\dfrac{1}{6}$

    (B) $\dfrac{1}{4}$

    (C) $\dfrac{1}{36}$

    (D) $\dfrac{1}{8}$

    (E) 1

10. Which of the following systems of equations has no solution?
    (A) $4x + 7y = 2$
         $3x + 5y = 7$
    (B) $x = 3$
         $y = 7x + 2$
    (C) $14x + 6y = 22$
         $7x + 3y = 9$
    (D) $x + y = 0$
         $x - y = 0$
    (E) $9x + 12y = 21$
         $3x + 4y = 7$

11. For real numbers x and y, let $x * y = \dfrac{x + y}{xy}$. Then, when $x = 2$ and $y = 7$, $x * y =$

    (A) $\dfrac{9}{14}$

    (B) $\dfrac{5}{9}$

    (C) $\dfrac{5}{14}$

    (D) 0

    (E) $\dfrac{14}{9}$

12. What is the total number of positive and negative integer divisors of 12?
    (A) 2
    (B) 3
    (C) 4
    (D) 6
    (E) 12

13. Through which of the lettered points would the graph of $y = \frac{1}{2}x + 2$ go?

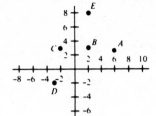

   (A) A
   (B) B
   (C) C
   (D) D
   (E) E

14. How many pairs of positive integers (x, y) will satisfy $x^2 - 4 = -3y$?

   (A) 0
   (B) 1
   (C) 2
   (D) 3
   (E) The number of pairs is infinite.

15. The intersection point of the two lines, $y = 3x + 2$ and $y = -x + 10$, is

   (A) (3, 7)
   (B) (2, 8)
   (C) (−4, 5)
   (D) (6, 9)
   (E) (1, 7)

16. The average of six sales that a door-to-door salesman made was $8.00. If five of the sales were respectively $7.40, $9.50, $6.80, $7.10, and $7.60, what was the sixth sale?

   (A) $6.50
   (B) $8.00
   (C) $9.80
   (D) $9.60
   (E) $10.40

17. If $qx + rx - t = s$, what is x in terms of q, r, t and s?

   (A) $s + t - q - r$

   (B) $\dfrac{s + t}{q + r}$

   (C) $\dfrac{s - t}{q - r}$

   (D) $\dfrac{s}{t} + q$

   (E) $\dfrac{s + q}{r + t}$

18. If $m = 2x + y$ and x is 38% of m, what percent of m is y?
(A) 76%
(B) 62%
(C) 24%
(D) 52%
(E) 28%

19. If, in a factory, 20 machines can do 40 jobs in one day, how many additional machines should the owner buy to get 64 jobs done in a day?
(A) 2
(B) 24
(C) 12
(D) 32
(E) 16

20. If AB is greater than 0, then $\dfrac{AB}{\sqrt{AB}} =$

(A) $(AB)\frac{3}{2}$

(B) $\sqrt{AB}$

(C) $\dfrac{A}{\sqrt{B}}$

(D) $\dfrac{1}{AB}$

(E) $\dfrac{1}{\sqrt{AB}}$

Directions: This section requires you to compare two quantities—the quantity in Column A and the quantity in Column B. After you have compared the two quantities, select

(A) if the quantity in Column A is greater than the quantity in Column B;

(B) if the quantity in Column B is greater than the quantity in Column A;

(C) if the quantities in the two columns are equal;

(D) if the information is not sufficient to make a valid comparison.

Any information that appears in a central position above the two quantities to be compared refers to both quantities.

(A) if the quantity in Column A is greater than the quantity in Column B
(B) if the quantity in Column B is greater than the quantity in Column A
(C) if the quantities in the two columns are equal
(D) if the information is not sufficient to make a valid comparison

Column A	Column B

21. $\dfrac{3\sqrt{98}}{7\sqrt{3}}$ $\qquad\qquad$ $\sqrt{6}$

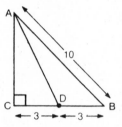

22. Area of triangle ABD $\qquad\qquad$ 13

$$3a + 2b = 11$$
$$6a - b = 7$$

23. $b - a$ $\qquad\qquad$ 1

24. .0002 $\qquad\qquad$ $\dfrac{50\% \text{ of } 0.4\%}{10\%}$

25. $5648 \times 25 \times 10$ $\qquad\qquad$ $15 \times 20 \times 5648$

$$x \neq 4;\ x \neq -2$$

26. $\dfrac{4}{x-4} \div \dfrac{2}{x^2 - 2x - 8}$ $\qquad\qquad$ $x + 2$

(A) if the quantity in Column A is greater than the quantity in Column B
(B) if the quantity in Column B is greater than the quantity in Column A
(C) if the quantities in the two columns are equal
(D) if the information is not sufficient to make a valid comparison

Column A   **Column B**

Questions 27–28 are based on the following chart.

Population of City A and City B from 1970 to 1976

Year	Population of City A (*in thousands of persons*)	Population of City B (*in thousands of persons*)
1970	106	128
1971	110	124
1972	113	118
1973	115	109
1974	122	108
1975	119	112
1976	127	105

27. Greatest one year change in the population of City A | Greatest one year change in the population of City B

28. The difference between the population of City A in 1975 and the population of City B in 1971 | 5,000

29. 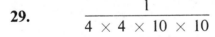 |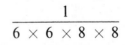

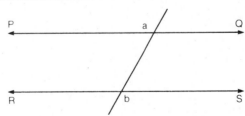

Line PQ parallel to line RS

30. $a + b$ 240°

IF YOU FINISH THIS SECTION OF THE SAT BEFORE YOUR TIME IS UP, YOU MAY LOOK BACK AT YOUR WORK IN THIS SECTION ONLY. YOU ARE NOT PERMITTED TO LOOK AT ANY OTHER SECTION OF THE TEST. WHEN THE TIME IS UP, TURN TO THE NEXT SECTION AND START WORK ON THAT SECTION.

Section 4: Verbal Questions

Time: 30 minutes

Antonyms

Directions: Each question in this test consists of a word printed in capital letters followed by five words lettered (A) through (E). Choose the word that has most nearly the OPPOSITE meaning from the word in capital letters. Then mark the appropriate space in the answer column.

1. SAVORY
   - (A) tasty
   - (B) iiked
   - (C) baked
   - (D) smelly
   - (E) unpalatable

2. CAPACIOUS
   - (A) wide
   - (B) spacious
   - (C) captious
   - (D) not limited
   - (E) crowded

3. GRATIS
   - (A) free
   - (B) enslaved
   - (C) great
   - (D) costly
   - (E) positive

4. NOMINAL
   - (A) inexpensive
   - (B) named
   - (C) insignificant
   - (D) temperamental
   - (E) exorbitant

5. ADVOCATE
   - (A) affirm
   - (B) urge
   - (C) judge
   - (D) opponent
   - (E) relaxation

6. HUSBANDRY
   - (A) mismanagement
   - (B) planning
   - (C) domesticity
   - (D) frugality
   - (E) agronomy

7. RABID
   - (A) animal
   - (B) composed
   - (C) mad
   - (D) eager
   - (E) lazy

8. BANAL
   - (A) original
   - (B) bitter
   - (C) vapid
   - (D) faded
   - (E) hurt

9. HILARITY
   (A) mirth
   (B) solemnity
   (C) poverty
   (D) anger
   (E) cruelty

10. MENDACITY
    (A) truthfulness
    (B) vengeance
    (C) medicine
    (D) prevarication
    (E) sickness

11. DOGMATIC
    (A) imperious
    (B) fluctuating
    (C) religious
    (D) persistent
    (E) atheist

12. IMMINENT
    (A) distant
    (B) important
    (C) unimportant
    (D) threatening
    (E) distressful

13. ARTISAN
    (A) tyro
    (B) painter
    (C) performer
    (D) novice
    (E) unskilled worker

Sentence Completions

Directions: Each question in this test consists of a sentence or group of sentences in which one or two words are missing. Beneath the question are five pairs of words lettered (A) through (E). Choose the word or the pair of words that *best* completes the sentence or sentences. Then mark the appropriate space in the answer column.

14. Despite the many bribes they offered the player, the "fixers" did not succeed in _____ his integrity.
    (A) undermining
    (B) discouraging
    (C) discovering
    (D) reducing
    (E) enhancing

15. Beauty is only skin-deep, but _____ goes all the way to the bone.
    (A) disease
    (B) blood
    (C) ugliness
    (D) fright
    (E) liniment

16. One who _____ to excess may correctly be called _____.
    (A) curses—immoral
    (B) grumbles—querulous
    (C) drinks—teetotaller
    (D) gambles—lecher
    (E) speaks—laconic

17. It is not easy to _____ a story. One must exercise real judgment and knowledge in determining where to _____ it.
    (A) augment—digest
    (B) shorten—aggravate
    (C) analyze—expose
    (D) abridge—modify
    (E) expurgate—enhance

18. The _____ of a person is officially called his _____.
    (A) face—countenance
    (B) speed—celerity
    (C) demeanor—regard
    (D) decease—termination
    (E) residence—domicile

19. At the trial, the defendant maintained a manner that could be best described as _____; but the revelations concerning his actions in the commission of the crime portrayed a personality that could only be described as _____.
    (A) sanctimonious—imperious
    (B) continent—self-possessed
    (C) suffering—emotional
    (D) impassive—impassioned
    (E) belligerent—jocose

20. Newton's picture of the universe was not one in which there was _____, and, in accordance with his teaching, the universe might very likely have been created out of one piece.
    (A) examination
    (B) verification
    (C) inevitability
    (D) development
    (E) uniformity

Analogies

Directions: In each of the following questions choose the pair of words that *best* completes the analogy. Then mark the appropriate space in the answer column.

21. POPE : PAPACY ::
     (A) leader : executive
     (B) president : democracy
     (C) clansman : tribe
     (D) queen : aristocracy
     (E) king : monarchy

22. MYRIAD : SPARSE ::
     (A) many : few
     (B) plethora : innumerable
     (C) major : minor
     (D) predominant : sporadic
     (E) minority : plurality

23. RELIGION : RITES ::
     (A) government : army
     (B) legislature : judiciary
     (C) men : men
     (D) table : legs
     (E) manuscript : thesis

24. FALL : RISE ::
     (A) callow : mature
     (B) moon : sun
     (C) light : murky
     (D) dusk : dawn
     (E) diurnal : nocturnal

25. SYMPATHY : SORROW ::
     (A) pain : agony
     (B) water : fire
     (C) ointment : burn
     (D) medicine : doctor
     (E) powder : face

26. TRIUMPH : EXULTATION ::
     (A) war : victory
     (B) emergency : desolation
     (C) calamity : distress
     (D) news : gratification
     (E) tidings : jubilation

27. DISSIPATION : DEPRAVITY ::
     (A) callowness : inexperience
     (B) repetition : monotony
     (C) attempt : achievement
     (D) familiarity : recognition
     (E) interest : boredom

28. SPECTACLES : VISION ::
     (A) statement : contention
     (B) airplane : locomotion
     (C) canoe : paddle
     (D) hay : horse
     (E) hero : worship

29. RAZOR : BLADE ::
     (A) lighter : fluid
     (B) book : page
     (C) keys : typewriter
     (D) pencil : lead
     (E) cup : coffee

30. BOOK : COVER ::
     (A) window : door
     (B) write : compose
     (C) ink : crayon
     (D) spelling : grammar
     (E) body : skin

Reading Comprehension

Directions: Read the following passages and answer each of the questions that come after them. Choose the *best* answer. Then mark the appropriate space in the answer column.

"A standard comprises characteristics attached to an aspect of a process or product by which it can be evaluated. Standardization is the development and adoption of standards. When they are formulated, standards are not usually the product of a single person, but represent the thoughts and ideas of a group, leavened with the knowledge and information which are currently available. Standards which do not meet certain basic requirements become a hindrance rather than an aid to progress. Standards must not only be correct, accurate, and precise in requiring no more and no less than what is needed for satisfactory results, but they must also be workable in the sense that their usefulness is not nullified by external conditions. Standards should also be acceptable to the people who use them. If they are not acceptable, they cannot be considered to be satisfactory, although they may possess all the other essential characteristics."

31. According to the above paragraph, a processing standard that requires the use of materials that cannot be procured, is most likely to be
(A)   incomplete
(B)   inaccurate
(C)   unworkable
(D)   unacceptable
(E)   unnatural

32. According to the above paragraph, the construction of standards to which the performance of job duties should conform is most often
(A)   the work of the people responsible for seeing that the duties are properly performed
(B)   accomplished by the person who is best informed about the functions involved
(C)   the responsibility of the people who are to apply them
(D)   attributable to the efforts of various informed persons
(E)   the result of someone's haphazard direction

33. According to the above paragraph, when standards call for finer tolerances than those essential to the conduct of successful production operations, the effect of the standards on the improvement of production operations is
(A) negative
(B) nullified
(C) negligible
(D) beneficial
(E) lessened

34. The one of the following which is the most suitable title for the above paragraph is
(A) The Evaluation of Formulated Standards
(B) The Attributes of Satisfactory Standards
(C) The Adoption of Acceptable Standards
(D) The Use of Process or Product Standards
(E) The Origins of Standards

"For the ease and pleasure of treading the old road, accepting the fashions, the education, the religion of society, he takes the cross of making his own, and, of course, the self-accusation, the faint heart, the frequent uncertainty and loss of time, which are the nettles and tangling vines in the way of the self-relying and self-directed, and the state of virtual hostility in which he seems to stand to society, and especially to educated society. For all this loss and scorn, what offset? He is to find consolation in exercising the highest functions of human nature. He is one who raises himself from private consideration and breathes and lives on public and illustrious thoughts. He is the world's eye. He is the world's heart. He is to resist the vulgar prosperity that retrogrades ever to barbarism, by preserving and communicating heroic sentiments, noble biographies, melodious verse, and the conclusions of history. Whatsoever oracles the human heart, in all emergencies, in all solemn hours, has uttered as its commentary on the world of actions—these he shall receive and impart. And whatsoever new verdict Reason from her inviolable seat pronounces on the passing men and events of today —this he shall hear and promulgate.

"These being his functions, it becomes him to feel all confidence in himself, and to defer never to the popular cry. He and he only knows the world. The world of any moment is the merest appearance. Some great decorum, some fetish of a government, some ephemeral trade, or war, or man, is cried up by half mankind and cried down by the other half, as if all depended on this particular up or down. The odds are that the whole question is not worth the poorest thought which the scholar has lost in listening to the controversy. Let him not quit his belief that a popgun is a popgun, though the ancient and honorable of the earth affirm it to be the crack of doom. In silence, in steadiness, in severe abstraction, let him hold by himself; add observation to observation, patient of neglect, patient of reproach, and bide his own time— happy enough if he can satisfy himself alone that this day he has seen something truly. Success treads on every right step. For the instinct is sure, that prompts him to tell his brother what he thinks. He then learns that in going down into the secrets of his own mind he has descended into the secrets of all minds. He learns that he who has mastered any law in his private thoughts, is master to that extent of all translated. The poet, in utter solitude remembering his spontaneous thoughts and recording them, is found to have recorded that which men in crowded cities find true for them also. The orator distrusts at first the fitness of his frank confessions, his want of knowledge of the persons he addresses, until he finds that he is the complement of his hearers—that they drink his words because he fulfills for them their own nature; the deeper he dives into his privatest, secretest presentiment, to his wonder he finds this is the most acceptable, most public, and universally true. The people delight in it; the better part of every man feels. This is my music; this is myself."

35. It is a frequent criticism of the scholar that he lives by himself, in an "ivory tower," remote from the problems and business of the world. Which of these below constitutes the best refutation by the writer of the passage to the criticism here noted?
    (A) The world's concerns being ephemeral, the scholar does well to renounce them and the world.
    (B) The scholar lives in the past to interpret the present.
    (C) The scholar at his truest is the spokesman of the people.
    (D) The scholar is not concerned with the world's doings because he is not selfish and therefore not engrossed in matters of importance to himself and neighbors.
    (E) The scholar's academic researches of today are the businessman's practical products of tomorrow.

36. The scholar's road is rough, according to the passage read. Which of these is his greatest difficulty?
    (A) He must renounce religion.
    (B) He must pioneer new approaches.
    (C) He must express scorn for, and hostility to, society.
    (D) He is uncertain of his course.
    (E) There is a pleasure in the main-traveled roads in education, religion, and all social fashions.

37. When the writer speaks of the "world's eye" and the "world's heart" he means
   (A)   the same thing
   (B)   culture and conscience
   (C)   culture and wisdom
   (D)   a scanning of all the world's geography and a deep sympathy for every living thing
   (E)   mind and love

38. By the phrase "nettles and tangling vines" the author probably refers to
   (A)   "self-accusation" and "loss of time"
   (B)   "faint heart" and "self-accusation"
   (C)   "the slings and arrows of outrageous fortune"
   (D)   a general term for the difficulties of a scholar's life
   (E)   "self-accusation" and "uncertainty"

39. The various ideas in the passage are best summarized in which of these groups?
   I.   truth versus society
          the scholar and books
          the world and the scholar
   II.   the ease of living traditionally
          the glory of a scholar's life
          true knowledge versus trivia
   III.   the hardships of the scholar
          the scholar's functions
          the scholar's justifications for
              disregarding the world's business
   (A)   I and III together
   (B)   I only
   (C)   III only
   (D)   I, II, and III together
   (E)   I and II together

40. "seems to stand" (line 6) means
   (A)   is
   (B)   ends probably in becoming
   (C)   gives the false impression of being
   (D)   is seen to be
   (E)   the quicksands of time

IF YOU FINISH THIS SECTION OF THE SAT BEFORE YOUR TIME IS UP, YOU MAY LOOK BACK AT YOUR WORK IN THIS SECTION ONLY. YOU ARE NOT PERMITTED TO LOOK AT ANY OTHER SECTION OF THE TEST. WHEN THE TIME IS UP, TURN TO THE NEXT SECTION AND START WORK ON THAT SECTION.

Section 5: Mathematics Questions

Time: 30 minutes

Directions: Each question in this section is followed by five choices lettered (A) through (E). Choose the correct answer. Then mark the appropriate space in the answer column.

The following information may be useful to you in solving some of the mathematics problems in this part:

Circle, radius = r:
Area $= \pi r^2$.
Circumference $= 2\pi r$.
A circle has 360 degrees of arc.

Triangle:
The sum of the three angles in a triangle is 180 degrees.
Area $= \frac{1}{2}$(any side $\times$ altitude to that side).

Right Triangle:
The sum of the squares of the legs $=$ the square of the hypotenuse.

Definitions of certain mathematical symbols:

$>$ is greater than
$<$ is less than
$\geq$ is greater than or equal to
$\leq$ is less than or equal to
$\perp$ is perpendicular to
$\parallel$ is parallel to

Important Note: Figures in this section are not always drawn to scale. All numbers are real numbers and all figures lie in a plane unless otherwise stated.

1. Four years from now a mother will be 3 times as old as her son. Six years ago she was 24 years older than her son was then. How old is her son now?
    (A)   16
    (B)   12
    (C)   8
    (D)   10
    (E)   14

2.
x	2	3	4	5
y	4	7	10	13

    If $x = 9$, what is the value of y?
    (A)   16
    (B)   17
    (C)   19
    (D)   25
    (E)   31

3. If $ab + 15 = 20 + 15$, the pair (a, b) *could not* be
    (A)   (10, 2)
    (B) $(-10, -2)$
    (C)   (5, 4)
    (D)   (4, 5)
    (E)   (10, 10)

4. Successive discounts of 40% and 20% are equal to a single discount of
    (A)   24%
    (B)   30%
    (C)   52%
    (D)   64%
    (E)   86%

5. A line is tangent to 2 contiguous equal circles. If the radius of each circle is 7 in., what is the area of the shaded portion? (Use $\pi = 22/7$.)
    (A)   44 sq. in.
    (B)   33 sq. in.
    (C)   35 sq. in.
    (D)   21 sq. in.
    (E)   14 sq. in.

6. A circle with a radius of 1 is inscribed in an equilateral triangle. The area of the shaded portion is

(A) $\sqrt{3 - \pi}$

(B) $\dfrac{\pi}{3}$

(C) $3\pi\sqrt{3}$

(D) $\dfrac{3\pi}{\sqrt{3}}$

(E) $\dfrac{3\sqrt{3} - \pi}{3}$

7. John can do a job in s hours, and David can do the same job in t hours. How long will it take them to do the job if they work together?

(A) $\dfrac{s + t}{st}$

(B) $s + t$

(C) $st(s + t)$

(D) $\dfrac{st}{s + t}$

(E) $s - t$

8. A bird flew 5 kilometers west and 6 kilometers north from its starting point. If the bird wanted to return to its starting point, what direction must it fly?
(A) Southwest
(B) Northwest
(C) Southeast
(D) Northeast
(E) South

9. $\sqrt{\dfrac{1}{36} - \dfrac{1}{100}} =$

(A) $\dfrac{2}{15}$

(B) $\dfrac{1}{4}$

(C) $\dfrac{3}{10}$

(D) $\dfrac{5}{6}$

(E) none of these

10. A motorist travels 120 mi. to his destination at the average speed of 60 mph and returns to his starting point at the average speed of 40 mph. His average speed for the entire trip is
    (A) 40 mph
    (B) 48 mph
    (C) 50 mph
    (D) 54 mph
    (E) 60 mph

11. In the figure below, what is $180° - (x + y)$?
    (A) z
    (B) x
    (C) w
    (D) $90 - z$
    (E) $90 - x$

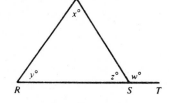

12. In the diagram below, if OA = AB and the area of the shaded portion of circle O is 3π, then what is the area of the square?
    (A) $\frac{4}{3}\pi$
    (B) 4
    (C) $16\pi^2$
    (D) 16
    (E) 32π

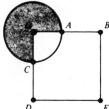

13. All of the boxes have equal volume *except* the rectangular box that measures
    (A) 6 x 2 x 12
    (B) 3 x 4 x 12
    (C) 18 x 1 x 8
    (D) 16 x 3 x 8
    (E) 9 x 4 x 4

14. If 48 is a multiple of N, which of the following is necessarily a multiple of N?
    (A) 144
    (B) 12
    (C) 72
    (D) 68
    (E) 80

15. A picture, 5 inches by 3 inches, is going to be enlarged so that the new area of the picture will be 135 square inches. What will the longest side of the enlarged picture be?
    (A) 45 inches
    (B) 15 inches
    (C) 27 inches
    (D) 39 inches
    (E) 65 inches

Directions: This section requires you to compare two quantities—the quantity in Column A and the quantity in Column B. After you have compared the two quantities, select

(A) if the quantity in Column A is greater than the quantity in Column B;

(B) if the quantity in Column B is greater than the quantity in Column A;

(C) if the quantities in the two columns are equal;

(D) if the information is not sufficient to make a valid comparison.

Any information that appears in a central position above the two quantities to be compared refers to both quantities.

(A) if the quantity in Column A is greater than the quantity in Column B
(B) if the quantity in Column B is greater than the quantity in Column A
(C) if the quantities in the two columns are equal
(D) if the information is not sufficient to make a valid comparison

Column A	**Column B**
16. 2^3	6
17. $5\frac{1}{2}\%$ interest on \$3,000 for one year	4% interest on \$5,000 for one year
18. $7 - \dfrac{8 + \dfrac{1}{2}}{3}$	$\dfrac{21 - 8}{3} - \dfrac{1}{6}$
19. The price per ounce of a 1-lb. loaf of bread costing \$.32	The price per ounce of a $1\frac{1}{2}$-lb. loaf of bread costing \$.46
20. The perimeter of a square 4 inches on a side	The perimeter of a pentagon 3 inches on a side

$$\angle A = \angle B; \; DE \parallel AB; \; AC = BC$$

21. $\angle C - \angle EDC$	$\angle C - \angle B$

$$x > 2$$

22. $\dfrac{1}{x}$	$\dfrac{1}{x-1}$

(A) if the quantity in Column A is greater than the quantity in Column B
(B) if the quantity in Column B is greater than the quantity in Column A
(C) if the quantities in the two columns are equal
(D) if the information is not sufficient to make a valid comparison

Column A   **Column B**

$$a = .35$$
$$b = .65$$
$$c = .85$$

23. $(-a)(b)(2c)$ $(a)(b)(c)$

$$2r + 6 < 18$$
24. $6 - r$ 0

There are 40 quarters in a roll.
There are 50 dimes in a roll.
25.   Value of 2 rolls of quarters   Value of 3 rolls of dimes

$$xy = 2$$
26. x^2y^2 4

Larry bought a TV set for
$80.00 at a discount store.
The store charges 20% under
the list price.
27.   List price of the TV set $96.00

A car gets 17 miles per gallon.
28.   Number of gallons used to   20 gallons
drive 350 miles

GO ON TO THE NEXT PAGE

(A) if the quantity in Column A is greater than the quantity in Column B
(B) if the quantity in Column B is greater than the quantity in Column A
(C) if the quantities in the two columns are equal
(D) if the information is not sufficient to make a valid comparison

Column A	Column B

Questions 29–30 refer to this diagram.

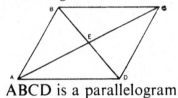

ABCD is a parallelogram

29. $\angle AEB + \angle BEC$ $160°$

30. $\angle CAD$ $\angle BCA$

31. The average of $(x - 2)$, $(x - 1)$, x, $(x + 1)$, $(x + 2)$ The average of $(x - 17)$, $(x - 13)$, $(x + 12)$, $(x + 18)$

$$p < q$$

32. $-2p$ $-2q$

33. $[(3 \times 2) + (4 \times 3)] + (5 \times 4)$ $(3 \times 2) + [(4 \times 3) + (5 \times 4)]$

34. $3x^2 + 9x + 6$ $3(x + 1)(x + 2)$

35. $\dfrac{\frac{1}{5}}{\frac{1}{5} + \frac{1}{\frac{1}{5}}}$ $\dfrac{1}{26}$

IF YOU FINISH THIS SECTION OF THE SAT BEFORE YOUR TIME IS UP, YOU MAY LOOK BACK AT YOUR WORK IN THIS SECTION ONLY. YOU ARE NOT PERMITTED TO LOOK AT ANY OTHER SECTION OF THE TEST. WHEN THE TIME IS UP, TURN TO THE NEXT SECTION AND START WORK ON THAT SECTION.

Section 6: Standard Written English Test

Time: 30 minutes

Because the SWET (Standard Written English Test) does not count toward your score but is only used for Freshman English placement when you get into college, questions of this type are not included.

THE SAT IS NOW OVER.

AFTER YOU HAVE FINISHED PRACTICE TEST 3:

1. Look at the Answer Key on pages 208 and 209.

2. Determine your number of CORRECT answers for the MATH and VERBAL parts. DO NOT count Section 3.

3. Determine your number of INCORRECT answers for the MATH and VERBAL parts. DO NOT count Section 3.

4. To obtain the RAW SCORE for each part (VERBAL or MATH) deduct ¼ the number of INCORRECT answers from the number of CORRECT answers.

5. Find what your SCALED SCORES are by using your Raw Score and referring to the TABLES on pages 90 and 91.

Answer Key for Practice Test 3

Section 1

1.	B	6.	B	11.	B	16.	B	21.	B
2.	E	7.	B	12.	E	17.	B	22.	D
3.	C	8.	E	13.	D	18.	E	23.	C
4.	D	9.	C	14.	E	19.	B	24.	B
5.	B	10.	E	15.	E	20.	A	25.	D

Section 2

1.	B	10.	A	19.	E	28.	B	37.	E
2.	C	11.	C	20.	B	29.	E	38.	A
3.	E	12.	C	21.	A	30.	B	39.	A
4.	C	13.	D	22.	C	31.	C	40.	C
5.	C	14.	C	23.	C	32.	E	41.	D
6.	B	15.	C	24.	D	33.	A	42.	B
7.	B	16.	D	25.	B	34.	A	43.	A
8.	C	17.	C	26.	E	35.	B	44.	C
9.	D	18.	E	27.	A	36.	C	45.	C

Section 3

1.	B	7.	B	13.	B	19.	C	25.	B
2.	C	8.	D	14.	B	20.	B	26.	D
3.	A	9.	C	15.	B	21.	C	27.	B
4.	D	10.	C	16.	D	22.	B	28.	C
5.	B	11.	A	17.	B	23.	A	29.	A
6.	E	12.	E	18.	C	24.	B	30.	D

Section 4

1.	E	9.	B	17.	D	25.	C	33.	A
2.	E	10.	A	18.	E	26.	C	34.	B
3.	D	11.	B	19.	D	27.	B	35.	C
4.	E	12.	A	20.	D	28.	B	36.	B
5.	D	13.	E	21.	E	29.	D	37.	C
6.	A	14.	A	22.	A	30.	E	38.	E
7.	B	15.	C	23.	D	31.	C	39.	C
8.	A	16.	B	24.	D	32.	D	40.	C

Section 5

1. C	8. C	15. B	22. B	29. A
2. D	9. A	16. A	23. B	30. C
3. E	10. B	17. B	24. A	31. C
4. C	11. A	18. C	25. A	32. A
5. D	12. D	19. A	26. C	33. C
6. E	13. D	20. A	27. A	34. C
7. D	14. A	21. C	28. A	35. C

Explanatory Answers for Practice Test 3

Section 1: Mathematics Questions

1. **(B)**
   He must receive an 80 on his fifth test. If his average is to be 80, then the sum of his five marks must be $5 \times 80 = 400$. The sum of 70, 60, 95, and 95 is 320. Thus, his fifth mark must be $400 - 320 = 80$.

2. **(E)**
   $a + by = cb$ is given. Subtract a from both sides: $by = cb - a$. Divide both sides by b:
   $$y = \frac{cb - a}{b}.$$

3. **(C)**
   $$\frac{1}{2}r = 10\% \; s; \text{ therefore, } r = 20\% \; s.$$
   $$2q = 5\% \; s; \text{ therefore, } q = 2\frac{1}{2}\% \; s.$$
   $$r - q = (20\% \; s - 2\frac{1}{2}\% \; s) = 17\frac{1}{2}\% \; s.$$

4. **(D)**
   Both trains cover the same distance. Since distance = rate $\times$ time, the distance from A to B is $50 \times 4 = 200$. Let x equal the speed of the second train. Then $5x = 200$, or $x = 40$.

5. **(B)**
   Since $\sqrt{9} = 3$, $\sqrt{8}$ is less than three.

6. (B)

To simplify, multiply both numerator and denominator by xy:

$$\frac{\left(\frac{1}{x} + \frac{1}{y}\right)xy}{(xy)xy} = \frac{y + x}{(xy)^2}.$$

7. (B)

Since AB is parallel to DE, angle A equals angle E (they are alternate interior angles). Thus, angle E equals 50°. The sum of angle ACD and angle DCE equals 180° since they form a straight line. Therefore, angle DCE equals $180 - 70 = 110°$. Then, since the sum of the angles in a triangle always equals 180°, angle D equals $180 - 110 - 50 = 20°$.

8. (E)

Let the new value of A be A′. If B is tripled, the result is $\frac{10}{3B}$, which equals $\frac{1}{3} \times \frac{10}{B}$. As $\frac{10}{B}$ was the initial value of A, the value of A is $\frac{A}{3}$.

9. (C)

It is known that angle GCB equals $a + b$ (ext. angle is equal to the sum of the two remote interior angles). This means that $2d = a + b$ or $d = \frac{1}{2}(a + b)$.

$$d + \frac{1}{2}c = \frac{1}{2}(a + b) + \frac{1}{2}c = \frac{1}{2}(a + b + c) = \frac{1}{2}(180) = 90°.$$

You may have noticed another way to do this problem:
$\angle$ GCA $= 180°$ since GCA is a straight line.
Thus $c + d + d = 180°$ or $c + 2d = 180°$.
Dividing by 2, we get $\frac{1}{2}c + d = 90°$.

10. (E)

Subtract $\frac{1}{2}$ from both sides and then divide by 4.

$$\frac{1}{2} + 4x = 10$$
$$4x = 9\frac{1}{2} = \frac{19}{2}$$
$$x = \frac{19}{8}$$

11. (B)

35% of all of Harry's stamps are American, and 23% of these are air mail. 23% of 35% equals

$$\frac{23}{100} \times \frac{35}{100} = \frac{805}{10,000} = \frac{8.05}{100}$$

which equals 8.05%.

12. (E)

Since $y = 1$, $x = 2$.

$$\frac{[4(4) - 2(2)] \, [1 + 2(2)] \, [3(1)]}{(2 + 1) \, (2 - 1)} = \frac{(12) \, (5) \, (3)}{(3) \, (1)} = 60$$

13. (D)

Solve for p by multiplying both sides by $p(p - 1)$:

$$p(p - 1) \left[1 + \frac{5}{p} + \frac{3}{p - 1} \right] = p(p - 1) \frac{p^2 + 2}{p^2 - p}$$
$$p^2 - p + 5p - 5 + 3p = p^2 + 2$$
$$7p = 7$$
$$p = 1$$

But p cannot equal 1 because it would mean dividing by zero. Thus, there are no solutions.

14. (E)

Rationalizing by multiplying the numerator and the denominator by the conjugate yields

$$\frac{\sqrt{2} + \sqrt{3}}{\sqrt{2} - \sqrt{3}} \times \frac{\sqrt{2} + \sqrt{3}}{\sqrt{2} + \sqrt{3}} = \frac{(2 + 3 + 2\sqrt{6})}{-1} =$$
$$-(2 + 3 + 2\sqrt{6}) = -5 - 2\sqrt{6}$$

15. (E)

All three statements are true.

   I.   Since an odd times an odd is odd, an odd raised to any power is odd.

   II. Since an odd plus an odd is even, group the terms in pairs and we have the sum of a set of even terms, which is even.

  III. An even has a factor of 2. Therefore, the square of an even has the factor $2 \times 2 = 4$.

16. (B)

If $\frac{r}{3}$ is an even integer, it must be exactly divisible by 2. Note that all the choices make $\frac{r}{3}$ an even integer:

$$\frac{60}{3} = 20; \frac{18}{3} = 6; \frac{12}{3} = 4; \frac{24}{3} = 8; \frac{36}{3} = 12$$

However, only one choice (B) makes $\frac{r}{6}$ an odd integer:

$$\frac{18}{6} = 3$$

17. (B)

$$-\left[\frac{(a+b)(a-b)}{b^2-a^2}\right] = -\left[\frac{(a+b)(a-b)}{(b+a)(b-a)}\right]$$

$$= -\left[\frac{a-b}{b-a}\right] = -(-1) = +1$$

18. (E)

Since dividing by 0.5 is the same as multiplying by 2, the answer is

$$p + r = 2(5p - r)$$
$$p + r = 10p - 2r$$
$$3r = 9p$$
$$r = 3p$$

19. (B)

It is true that $5^2 > 3^2$ and $5 > 3$. But it is also true that $(-5)^2 > (-3)^2$ and $-5 < -3$.

20. (A)

The sum of the numbers is 30 times 100, or 3000. If each term is halved, the sum is 1500. Thus, the average is $\frac{1500}{30}$, or 50.

21. (B)

$$9 = 150\%x$$
$$9 = 1\frac{1}{2}x$$
$$\frac{2}{3} \times 9 = x = 6$$

22. (D)

By the Pythagorean theorem

$$CB^2 = AB^2 + AC^2$$
$$= 3^2 + 4^2 = 9 + 16 = 25$$

Thus, CB equals 5.
This means that DE also equals 5 and that CD equals 80% of 5, or 4. The area of CDEB is $5 \times 4 = 20$. The area of the triangle is $\frac{1}{2} \times 3 \times 4 = 6$. The area of the shaded portion is $20 - 6 = 14$.

23. (C)

The minimum value of $\frac{a}{b}$ occurs when a is smallest and b is largest. a is smallest at the lower range of the scale, that is when $a = 0.005$. b is largest when b is at the higher end of the scale, that is, when $b = 0.05$. Thus, the minimum value of $\frac{a}{b}$ is $\frac{.005}{.05} = .1$

24. **(B)**

Since Q is divisible by 30, it is divisible by the prime factors of 30—that is, 2, 3, and 5. Since it is divisible by 35, it is also divisible by 5 and 7. Thus, Q is divisible by 2, 3, 5, and 7. This means

$$\frac{Q}{2 \times 3 \times 5 \times 7} = \text{integer}$$

In the denominator there is a 21, that is, (3×7). Thus, Q is divisible by 21.

25. **(D)**

The base of the triangle is 3 feet and the height is 3 yards, or 9 feet. Thus, the area is $\frac{1}{2} \times 3 \times 9$ square feet. Since each square foot has 144 square inches, the number of square inches is $\frac{1}{2} \times 3 \times 9 \times 144 = 1944$.

Section 2: Verbal Questions

1. **(B)**
   Tyro: a beginner; *antonym:* expert

2. **(C)**
   Lackadaisical: spiritless; *antonym:* enthusiastic

3. **(E)**
   Genial: kindly; *antonym:* unfriendly

4. **(C)**
   Intrepid: fearless; *antonym:* fearful

5. **(C)**
   Furtive: stealthy; *antonym:* apparent

6. **(B)**
   Antipathy: a strong dislike; *antonym:* fondness

7. **(B)**
   Debilitate: to weaken; *antonym:* strengthen

8. **(C)**
   Hackneyed: trite; *antonym:* novel

9. **(D)**
   Garrulous: talkative; *antonym:* laconic

10.   (A)
Satiate: glut; *antonym:* starve

11.   (C)
Mendicant: receiver of alms; *antonym:* philanthropist

12.   (C)
Choleric: quick-tempered; *antonym:* serene

13.   (D)
The judge feels that the defendant's offense is small (*venial*), so he will probably give him a light sentence.

14.   (C)
Unreliable is the best choice for a word that is consistent with the complete sentence.

15.   (C)
. . . the discussion soon retrogressed from *disagreement* to a heated argument (*altercation*).

16.   (D)
Choice (D) contains the most appropriate words.

17.   (C)
Some beliefs clearly may be false even though one cannot produce much evidence to *disprove* them.

18.   (E)
The knotted (*gnarled*) base of the giant tree is silent (*mute*) evidence of its antiquity.

19.   (E)
A job not performed chiefly for the return is probably enjoyable (*pleasureable*).

20.   (B)
The lawyer attempted to lessen (*mitigate*) the gravity of his client's offense by ascribing it to a condition that showed that the client was not aware of what he had been doing (e.g., *temporary insanity*).

21. (A)

It is stated that the inhibitory component disappears more quickly with the passage of time than does the excitatory component. It is also stated that after each conditioning trial, a finite amount of excitation is left, which facilitates the occurrence of the conditioned response. It is also stated that a finite amount of inhibition is left, which inhibits the occurrence of a conditioned response. Since the distributed trials are performed over a period of time, the inhibitory component disappears more quickly than the excitatory component, so the latency of conditioned response in Experiment A, as compared with Experiment B, should be longer.

22. (C)

It is stated that during the extinction trials, the inhibition is built up faster than the excitation.

23. (C)

It is stated that the inhibitory component is more readily destroyed upon the occurrence of some novel stimulus than is the excitatory component. Since the conditioned response failed to occur, all the excitation and all the inhibition must have been dissipated.

24. (D)

There is nothing in the passage that compares the response of a hungry animal to a satiated animal.

25. (B)

It is stated that with repeated trials the latency of response decreases. Thus, trial 7 should have a greater latency of response than trial 30.

26. (E)

Fabulous is legendary (fable), and a *dragon* is legendary (a fable); whereas, a *dinosaur* is *real*.

27. (A)

Frightful and *horrid* are synonyms. *Death* and *demise* are synonyms.

28. (B)

We *translate* word for word (*literally*). We *paraphrase* more *freely*.

29. (E)

A *citadel* (fortress) is to a dark place below (a *vault*) as a *tower* is to a *dungeon* (below).

30.   (B)

An *exposition* is to a concise summary (a *precis*) as a *volume* is to a *booklet*.

31.   (C)

Implicit is contrasted with *explicit* as *innuendo* (an indirect implication) is to an *assertion* (a direct statement).

32.   (E)

Pork comes from a *hog* as *venison* comes from a *deer*.

33.   (A)

Philology is the study of historical linguistics. Thus, a *philologist* would study *language*. An *ornithologist* would study *birds*. Note that choice (C) is incorrect since a biologist studies biology, of which *cells* are but one subject.

34.   (A)

Dime is to *dollar* as 10 is to 100 (or *decade* is to *century*).

35.   (B)

The opposite of *prosperous* is *poor*. The opposite of *prodigal* (extravagant) is *frugal* (thrifty).

36.   (C)

See the first sentence of the first paragraph.

37.   (E)

Philosophy, the middle class, economic motives, and industrial developments affected the scientific revolution.

38.   (A)

It is seen that the Protestant Reformation gave rise to different opinions.

39.   (A)

See the second paragraph.

40.   (C)

See the second paragraph.

41.   (D)

See the fourth paragraph: "Material particles orbit the sun because of the gravitational pull that the sun's large mass exerts over them." The statements in choices (A), (B), and (C) are all correct according to the passage.

42. **(B)**

See the second paragraph: "The volume of space our solar system occupies can be visualized as a sphere more than ten billion miles across, with the sun at its center."

43. **(A)**

From the statements 1) "Material particles orbit the sun because of the gravitational pull that the sun's large mass exerts over them," and 2) "All material particles in the solar system, from the giant planet Jupiter . . . , pursue individual orbits or paths around the sun," it can be implied that the sun is the largest body in the solar system.

44. **(C)**

"Material particles orbit the sun because of the gravitational pull that the sun's large mass exerts over them." Thus, the main reason for the attraction is the sun's large mass. In this case, we can say that the sun's possessing a large mass implies that it has a large size and vice versa.

45. **(C)**

See the statement, "This force is continuous and would, theoretically, pull all members of the solar system into the sun if they themselves were not moving."

Section 3: Mathematics Questions

1. **(B)**

A positive number times a positive number is always positive. Any number squared is also positive. x^5y can be expressed as the product of x^2 and x^3y. Since we know that x^2 is positive, if we are given x^3y positive, x^5y must always be positive.

2. **(C)**

In order to find where the graph touches the x axis, it is necessary to set x equal to zero and solve for y:

$$y^2 + y - 6 = 0 \quad \text{(setting } x = \text{to zero)}$$
$$(y + 3)(y - 2) = 0 \quad \text{(factoring)}$$
$$y = -3 \text{ or } y = 2$$

3. **(A)**

Solve first for h, and then plug into the given equation for V:

$$2\pi rh + \pi r^2 = 30$$
$$2\pi rh = 30 - \pi r^2 \qquad \text{(subtracting } \pi r^2 \text{ from each side)}$$
$$h = \frac{30 - \pi r^2}{2\pi r} \qquad \text{(dividing both sides by } 2\pi r)$$
$$h = \frac{15}{\pi r} - \frac{r}{2}$$
$$V = \pi r^2 \left(\frac{15}{\pi r} - \frac{r}{2} \right)$$

4. **(D)**

Since the included angle is 60°, the triangle is equilateral, and the area is the side squared times the square root of three divided by four. This means the area of the shaded region is $4\sqrt{3}$. The shaded region is a trapezoid, and its area is one-half the height times the sum of the bases: $4\sqrt{3} = \frac{1}{2}h(1 + 2)$. Therefore, $h = \left(\frac{8}{3} \right) \left(\sqrt{3} \right)$. Since ABC is similar to the large triangle (right triangle),

$$\frac{BC}{1} = \frac{h + BC}{2}$$

Thus:

$$2BC = h + BC$$
$$BC = h$$

The area of triangle ABC is given as

$$\frac{(BC)(1)}{2} = \frac{h}{2} = \frac{4\sqrt{3}}{3}$$

5. **(B)**

Simple examples will show that neither I nor II is a symmetric relation:

I. If 4 is less than 5, it does not follow that 5 is less than 4.
II. If 27 is a multiple of 3, it does not follow that 3 is a multiple of 27.

However, III is a symmetric relation. If a is relatively prime to b, then a has no factors in common with b. It follows immediately that b has no factors in common with a.

6. **(E)**
    In the y-intercept form of the equation for a line, $y = mx + b$, m is the slope of the line, and b is the y-intercept. A line parallel to a given line has the same slope; a line passing through the origin has y-intercept zero. The line needed then has the equation

    $$y = \frac{x}{3} + 0, \text{ or } x = 3y.$$

7. **(B)**
    Since n has a remainder of 3 when divided by 7, n can be expressed as $7k + 3$, where k is an integer. Then $5n$ will be $35k + 15$, or $7(5k + 2) + 1$. The remainder, when this is divided by 7, is clearly 1.

8. **(D)**
    The figure forms an 8, 15, 17 right triangle. The cosine of AOB is adjacent over hypotenuse, or $\frac{8}{17}$.

9. **(C)**
    There is only one way for a pair of dice to show a 12—each die must show a six. The probability that one die will show a six is one-sixth. The probability that two dice will show sixes is $\frac{1}{6}$ times $\frac{1}{6}$, or $\frac{1}{36}$.

10. **(C)**
    The two lines in choice (C) have the same slope and different y-intercepts. The lines are therefore parallel. This means that they do not touch and that, solved simultaneously, they have no solution.

11. **(A)**
    To find $x * y$ when $x = 2$ and $y = 7$, substitute 2 and 7 for x and y in the given definition:

    $$\frac{2 + 7}{2 \times 7} = \frac{9}{14}$$

12. **(E)**
    The integer divisors of 12 are: $-12, -6, -4, -3, -2, -1, 1, 2, 3, 4, 6, 12$. There are 12.

13. (B)
By substituting into the equation for each of the lettered points, it can be found that point B is the only lettered point that satisfies the equation:

(A) $1 \neq \frac{1}{2}(6) + 2 = 5$

(B) $3 = \frac{1}{2}(2) + 2 = 3$

(C) $3 \neq \frac{1}{2}(-2) + 2 = 1$

(D) $-2 \neq \frac{1}{2}(-3) + 2 = \frac{1}{2}$

(E) $8 \neq \frac{1}{2}(1) + 2 = 2\frac{1}{2}$

14. (B)
Only one pair of positive integers, namely (1, 1), will satisfy $x^2 - 4 = -3y$. This is because $1^2 - 4 = -3(1)$, and when $x = 2, y = 0$; when $x = 3, 4, 5$, etc., $x^2 - 4 > 0$, but $-3y < 0$.

15. (B)
To find the intersection point, it is necessary to solve the equations simultaneously:

$$y = 3x + 2$$
$$y = -x + 10$$
$$3x + 2 = -x + 10$$
$$4x = 8$$
$$x = 2$$

Since $x = 2, y = 8$. The intersection point is (2, 8).

16. (D)
Since the average of the six sales was $8.00, the *total* amount of the sales must have been 6 times $8.00, or $48.00. When the amounts of the five given sales are added together, the result is $38.40. In order for the total sales to be $48.00, the last sale must be $48.00 minus $38.40, or $9.60.

17. (B)
To express x in terms of $q, r, s,$ and t, it is necessary to isolate x on one side of the equation:

$$qx + rx - t = s$$
$$qx + rx = s + t$$
$$(q + r)x = s + t$$
$$x = \frac{s + t}{q + r}$$

18.   (C)
Since x is 38% of m, $2x$ is 2 times 38% of m, or 76% of m.
Since m is

$$2x + y, \frac{100}{100}m = \frac{76}{100}m + y$$

Subtracting $\frac{76}{100}m$ from both sides yields

$$\frac{24}{100}m = y \text{ or } y = 24\% \text{ of } m$$

19.   (C)
If 20 machines can do 40 jobs in one day, then each machine must do 40 divided by 20, or two jobs in one day. At this rate, it would take 32 machines to do 64 jobs in one day. The factory already has 20 machines; therefore, it needs 32 minus 20, or 12 more machines.

20.   (B)
Multiply numerator and denominator by $\sqrt{AB}$:

$$\frac{AB}{\sqrt{AB}} \times \frac{\sqrt{AB}}{\sqrt{AB}} = \frac{AB\sqrt{AB}}{AB}$$

Divide numerator and denominator by AB:

$$\frac{AB\sqrt{AB}}{AB} = \sqrt{AB}$$

21.   (C)

$$3\sqrt{98} = 3\sqrt{49 \times 2} =$$
$$3 \times 7\sqrt{2} = 21\sqrt{2}$$
$$\frac{3\sqrt{98}}{7\sqrt{3}} = \frac{21\sqrt{2}}{7\sqrt{3}} = \frac{3\sqrt{2}}{\sqrt{3}}$$

Multiplying $\frac{3\sqrt{2}}{\sqrt{3}}$ by $\frac{\sqrt{3}}{\sqrt{3}}$, we get

$$\frac{3\sqrt{2} \times \sqrt{3}}{3} = \sqrt{2} \times \sqrt{3} = \sqrt{6}$$

22.   (B)
By the Pythagorean theorem, we can figure out that side $AC = 8$. Therefore, the area of triangle $ABC = \frac{1}{2} \times 8 \times 6 = 24$. Since triangle ACD and triangle ABD have the same altitude and equal bases, the area of triangle ACD equals the area of triangle $ABD = \frac{1}{2} \times 24 = 12$.

23. (A)
Solving the equations simultaneously, we get the following:

$$2 \times (3a + 2b) = 2 \times 11 =$$

$$\begin{array}{r} 6a + 4b = 22 \\ -(6a - b = 7) \\ \hline 5b = 15 \end{array}$$

$$b = 3, a = 1\frac{2}{3}$$

$$b - a = 1\frac{1}{3}$$

24. (B)

$$\frac{50\% \text{ of } 0.4\%}{10\%} = \frac{(.5)(.004)}{.1} = \frac{.002}{.1} = .02$$

$$.02 > .0002$$

Thus, $\dfrac{50\% \text{ of } 0.4\%}{10\%} > .0002$

25. (B)
Since 5648 is common to both quantities, we only have to solve the relationship between 25×10 and 15×20:

$25 \times 10 = 250$
$15 \times 20 = 300$
$300 > 250$
Thus, $5648 \times 300 > 5648 \times 250$.

26. (D)

$$\frac{4}{x-4} \div \frac{2}{x^2 - 2x - 8} =$$

$$\frac{4}{x-4} \times \frac{(x-4)(x+2)}{2} = 2(x+2)$$

If $x + 2$ is less than 0,
then $2(x + 2) < x + 2$.
If $x + 2$ is greater than 0,
then $2(x + 2) > x + 2$.
Thus, the relationship cannot be determined.

27. (B)
The greatest one year change in City A's population is 8,000. This occurred in 1975–76 when the population went from 119,000 to 127,000. The greatest one year change in City B's population came in 1972–73 when the population went from 118,000 to 109,000. This was a change of 9,000.

28.   (C)
The population of City A in 1975 was 119,000. The population of City B in 1971 was 124,000. Thus, the difference is 5,000.

29.   (A)

$$\frac{1}{4 \times 4 \times 10 \times 10} = \frac{1}{4 \times 10 \times 4 \times 10} = \frac{1}{(4 \times 10)^2} = \frac{1}{40^2}$$

$$\frac{1}{6 \times 6 \times 8 \times 8} = \frac{1}{6 \times 8 \times 6 \times 8} = \frac{1}{(6 \times 8)^2} = \frac{1}{48^2}$$

$$40^2 < 48^2$$

Thus, $\frac{1}{40^2} > \frac{1}{48^2}$

30.   (D)
Since line PQ is parallel to line RS, we can determine that $a = b$. However, that is all we know about these angles. Given no further information, we cannot determine what $a + b$ equals.

Section 4: Verbal Questions

1.   (E)
Savory: tasty; *antonym:* unpalatable

2.   (E)
Capacious: roomy; *antonym:* crowded

3.   (D)
Gratis: free; *antonym:* costly

4.   (E)
Nominal: slight; *antonym:* exorbitant

5.   (D)
Advocate: supporter; *antonym:* opponent

6.   (A)
Husbandry: careful management; *antonym:* mismanagement

7.   (B)
Rabid: violent, fanatical; *antonym:* composed

8.   (A)
Banal: trite, commonplace; *antonym:* original

9. (B)

Hilarity: mirth; *antonym:* solemnity

10. (A)

Mendacity: falseness; *antonym:* truthfulness

11. (B)

Dogmatic: positive in manner; *antonym:* fluctuating

12. (A)

Imminent: about to happen; *antonym:* distant

13. (E)

Artisan: a skilled craftsman; *antonym:* unskilled worker

14. (A)

. . . the "fixers" did not succeed in weakening (*undermining*) his integrity.

15. (C)

Here we are contrasting beauty to *ugliness.*

16. (B)

Choice (B) describes the only appropriate group of words.

17. (D)

If we *abridge* a story, we must be careful where we want to *modify* the story.

18. (E)

The *residence* is called the person's *domicile.*

19. (D)

Here we are contrasting *impassive* (emotionless) to *impassioned* (filled with emotion).

20. (D)

In accordance with Newton's teaching, the universe might very likely have been created out of one piece. Thus, Newton's picture of the universe was probably not one in which there was *development.*

21. (E)

The jurisdiction and office of the *pope* is the *papacy.* The jurisdiction of a *king* is a *monarchy.*

22. **(A)**
Myriad (large number) : *sparse* (small number) : : *many* : *few*.

23. **(D)**
A *religion* has *rites* as a *table* has *legs*.

24. **(D)**
The sun *falls* at *dusk*, and the sun *rises* at *dawn*.

25. **(C)**
We give *sympathy* for *sorrow* and give an *ointment* for a *burn*.

26. **(C)**
A *triumph* brings *exultation* as a *calamity* brings *distress*.

27. **(B)**
Dissipation (waste) leads to *corruption* as *repetition* leads to *monotony*.

28. **(B)**
Spectacles are used for *vision* as an *airplane* is used for *locomotion*.

29. **(D)**
A *razor* works only with a *blade* as a *pencil* works only with *lead*.

30. **(E)**
A *book* has a *cover*. The body's *cover* is the *skin*.

31. **(C)**
See "Standards must not only be correct. . . ."

32. **(D)**
See "When they are formulated, standards are not usually the product of a single person. . . ."

33. **(A)**
See the last three sentences of the passage.

34. **(B)**
It can be seen that choice (B) is most appropriate.

35. **(C)**
See the sentence in the second paragraph: "He and only he knows the world."

36. (B)

See the first paragraph.

37. (C)

From the context, we see that "world's eye" and "world's heart" refer to culture and wisdom, respectively.

38. (E)

See the first sentence: ". . . the self-accusation, the faint heart, the frequent uncertainty and loss of time, which are the nettles and tangling vines. . . ." Here "nettles and tangling vines" refer to "self-accusation" and "uncertainty."

39. (C)

The most appropriate groups are: the hardships of the scholar, the scholar's functions, and the scholar's justifications for disregarding the world's business, as can be seen from the structure and content of the passage.

40. (C)

From the context of the rest of the sentence, the author uses the phrase "seems to stand" as "giving the false impression of being."

Section 5: Mathematics Questions

1. (C)

Let m = the mother's age and s = the son's age.
The mother is 24 years older, and this is a constant difference.

$$m = s + 24$$
$$m + 4 = 3(s + 4)$$
$$(s + 24) + 4 = 3s + 12$$
$$2s = 16$$
$$s = 8$$

2. (D)

This type of problem is solved by determining the relationship between the numbers:

$y = 3x - 2$
$y = 3(9) - 2$
$y = 25$

3. **(E)**

In the equation $ab + 15 = 20 + 15$, get rid of the 15 from both sides of the equation. We are then left with

$$ab = 20$$

This means that for the pair, (a, b), $a \times b = 20$. This is true for Choice A: $10 \times 2 = 20$, for Choice B: $- 10 \times - 2 = 20$, for Choice C: $5 \times 4 = 20$, for Choice D: $4 \times 5 = 20$. However $a \times b \neq 20$ for Choice E since $10 \times 10 = 100$. Therefore Choice E is correct.

4. **(C)**

$$
\begin{array}{rl}
\$100 & \text{(list price)} \\
\times\ .40 & \\
\hline
\$\ 40 & \text{(1st discount)} \\
\\
.\$\ 60 & \text{(1st selling price [100} - 40]) \\
\\
\$\ 60 & \\
\times\ .20 & \\
\hline
\$\ 12 & \text{(2nd discount)} \\
\\
\$\ 48 & \text{(2nd selling price [60} - 12]) \\
\\
\$100 & \text{(list price)} \\
-\ \ 48 & \text{(selling price)} \\
\hline
\$\ 52 & \text{(total discount)}
\end{array}
$$

$$\frac{52}{100} = 52\%$$

5. **(D)**

The area of the rectangle − the area of the sectors = the area of the shaded portion.

Area of the rectangle $= 2r^2 (2r = \text{length}, r = \text{width})$

Area of sector $= \dfrac{\pi r^2}{2}$ (area of sector = semicircle)

$2r^2 - \dfrac{\pi r^2}{2} =$ area of shaded portion

$2(7)^2 - \dfrac{\pi(7)^2}{2} = 2(49) - \dfrac{49\pi}{2}$

Now $\pi = \dfrac{22}{7}$

$$98 - \frac{\overset{7}{\cancel{49}}}{\underset{1}{\cancel{2}}} \times \frac{\overset{11}{\cancel{22}}}{\underset{1}{\cancel{7}}} = 98 - 77 = 21 \text{ sq. in.}$$

6. **(E)**

Angle EOF = angle EOD = angle FOD = 120°

∴ Angle AOD = 60°

Triangle AOD is a 30-60-90 triangle.

If OD = 1, AD = $\sqrt{3}$ and AC = $2\sqrt{3}$.

Altitude BD = 3:

AO = BO = 2OD = 2OE = 2OF.

∴ BO = 2 since OD = 1. Thus, BO + OD = 3 = BD.

The area of the shaded portion = $\dfrac{\text{the area of triangle}}{3}$ −

the area of the circle.

$$\frac{\frac{1}{2}bh - \pi r^2}{3} = \frac{\frac{1}{2}2\sqrt{3}(3) - \pi}{3} = \frac{3\sqrt{3} - \pi}{3}$$

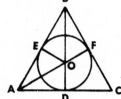

7. **(D)**

Working together for 1 hr., the boys can do $\dfrac{s + t}{st}$ of a job. To

complete the job, they need $\dfrac{st}{s + t}$ hours since $\dfrac{st}{s + t} \times \dfrac{s + t}{st} = 1$.

8. **(C)**

We draw a diagram. The bird flew 5 kilometers west and 6 kilometers north so that the diagram looks like the following:

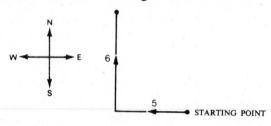

If the bird wanted to return to its starting point, according to the diagram below, it would have to go *southeast*.

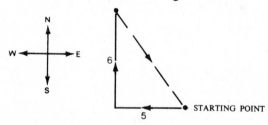

9. **(A)**

Combine the fractions. The lowest common denominator is 36 × 100, or 3,600

$$\sqrt{\frac{100 - 36}{3,600}} = \sqrt{\frac{64}{3,600}} =$$

$\dfrac{8}{60}$ (extracting the square root) = $\dfrac{2}{15}$ (reducing)

10. **(B)**
Formula: Rate × Time = Distance

The first part of his trip takes 2 hr. $\left(\dfrac{120}{60}\right)$.

The second part of his trip takes 3 hr. $\left(\dfrac{120}{40}\right)$.

The entire trip (240 mi.) takes 5 hr.

$\dfrac{240}{5} = 48$ mph

11. **(A)**
The sum of the angles of a triangle is 180°. Therefore, 180° minus two of the three angles is the third angle, which is z.

12. **(D)**
The area of the shaded portion is $\dfrac{3}{4}$ of the area of the entire circle. Since the formula for the area of a circle is πr^2, the formula for the area of the shaded region is $\dfrac{3}{4}\pi r^2$.

$3\pi = \dfrac{3}{4}\pi r^2$

$4 = r^2$ $\quad\left(\text{multiplying each side by } \dfrac{4}{3\pi}\right)$

$2 = r$ $\quad$ (taking square root of each side)

Since OA = AB, the length of each side of the square is 2 + 2, or 4. The area of the square is, therefore, 4 times 4, or 16.

13. **(D)**
To find the volume of a box, you must multiply the three numbers (given in each choice). All the choices except Choice D give the same result (144).

14. **(A)**
The easiest way to do this problem would be to consider the least favorable special case. Since N must be a factor of 48, any conditions which held for the special case N = 48 would also hold for all other values of N. 144 is divisible by 48 (144 ÷ 48 = 3); all other answers are not.

15. (B)

The proportions of the new picture must be the same as those of the old picture. If we call x the constant of proportionality, the sides of the enlarged picture can then be expressed as $5x$ inches by $3x$ inches. We know that the area of the enlarged picture is 135 square inches. Since the formula for the area of a rectangle is length times width, an equation can be set up:

$$
\begin{aligned}
5x \times 3x &= 135 \\
15x^2 &= 135 \quad \text{(multiplying)} \\
x^2 &= 9 \quad \text{(dividing both sides by 15)} \\
x &= 3 \quad \text{(taking the square root of each side)}
\end{aligned}
$$

Since the constant of proportionality is 3, the longest side is 5 times 3, or 15.

16. (A)

$$2^3 = 2 \times 2 \times 2 = 8$$

17. (B)

$\$3,000 \times .055 = \$165$ (Column A)
$\$5,000 \times .04 \;\; = \$200$ (Column B)

18. (C)

$$7 - \frac{8\frac{1}{2}}{3} = 7 - \left(\frac{17}{2} \times \frac{1}{3}\right) = 7 - \frac{17}{6} = \frac{42 - 17}{6} = \frac{25}{6}$$
(Column A)

$$\frac{21 - 8}{3} - \frac{1}{6} = \frac{13}{3} - \frac{1}{6} = \frac{26}{6} - \frac{1}{6} = \frac{25}{6} \quad \text{(Column B)}$$

19. (A)

$$\frac{\$.32}{16 \text{ oz.}} = \$.02 \text{ per oz. (Column A)}$$

$$\frac{\$.46}{24 \text{ oz.}} = \$.0192 \text{ per oz. (Column B)}$$

20. (A)

$4 \times 4 = 16$ (Column A)
$5 \times 3 = 15$ (Column B)

21. (C)

$$
\begin{aligned}
\angle A &= \angle B \\
\angle A &= \angle EDC \quad \text{(call } \angle EDC, \angle D) \\
\angle D &= \angle B \\
\angle C - \angle D &= \angle C - \angle B
\end{aligned}
$$

22. **(B)**
The denominator in Column B $(x - 1)$ < the denominator in Column A (x). When the denominator decreases and the numerator stays constant, the fraction increases.

23. **(B)**
The value in Column A is negative. The value in Column B is positive. Therefore, the value in Column B is greater than the value in Column A. It is not necessary to multiply out.

24. **(A)**
Subtracting 6 from each side of the inequality, we get $2r < 12$. Dividing each side by 2, we get $r < 6$. Subtracting r from each side, we get $0 < 6 - r$.

25. **(A)**
40 quarters equal $10.00. Therefore, 2 rolls of quarters equal $20.00. 50 dimes equal $5.00. Therefore, 3 rolls of dimes equal $15.00.

26. **(C)**
$x^2 y^2 = (xy)^2 = 2^2 = 4$

27. **(A)**
If Larry got a 20% discount, the price he paid was 80% of the list price. That is, $.8x = \$80.00$. Dividing each side of the equation by .8, we get the list price, $x = \$100.00$.

28. **(A)**
To drive 350 miles, you need $\frac{350}{17} = 20\frac{10}{17}$ gallons.

29. **(A)**
$\angle AEB + \angle BEC$ form a straight angle, which has $180°$.

30. **(C)**
These angles are alternate interior angles formed by a line cutting two parallel lines. Hence, they are equal.

31. **(C)**
The sum of the terms in Column A is $5x$. There are 5 terms, so the average is x. The sum of the terms in Column B is $4x$. There are 4 terms, so the average is x.

32. **(A)**
Multiplying both sides of the inequality by -2, we get $-2p > -2q$. Remember, when an equality is multiplied by a negative number, the direction of the inequality changes.

33. (C)

Since addition is associative, the positioning of the parentheses does not affect the sum. The sums, therefore, are equal. It is not necessary to multiply out and add.

34. (C)

$$3x^2 + 9x + 6 =$$
$$3(x^2 + 3x + 2) =$$
$$3(x + 1)(x + 2)$$

35. (C)

$$\frac{1}{\frac{1}{5}} = 5$$

$$\frac{1}{5} + 5 = \frac{26}{5}$$

Therefore:

$$\frac{\frac{1}{5}}{\frac{1}{5} + \frac{1}{\frac{1}{5}}} = \frac{\frac{1}{5}}{\frac{26}{5}} = \frac{1}{5} \times \frac{5}{26} = \frac{1}{26}$$

SAT PRACTICE TEST 4 ➡️

Tear out the answer sheet for this test at the end of the book.

Section 1: Verbal Questions

Time: 30 minutes

Antonyms

Directions: Each question in this test consists of a word printed in capital letters followed by five words lettered (A) through (E). Choose the word that has most nearly the OPPOSITE meaning from the word in capital letters. Then mark the appropriate space in the answer column.

1. DEMURE
   (A) brazen
   (B) decorous
   (C) shy
   (D) wavery
   (E) friendly

2. ONEROUS
   (A) single
   (B) facile
   (C) weighty
   (D) burdensome
   (E) slow

3. AGILE
   (A) light
   (B) clumsy
   (C) fast
   (D) graceful
   (E) charming

4. LEVITY
   (A) solemnity
   (B) lightness
   (C) brevity
   (D) gaiety
   (E) balm

5. NEPOTISM
   (A) favoritism
   (B) family
   (C) fairness
   (D) contrast
   (E) retreat

6. VENIAL
   (A) unforgivable
   (B) unkind
   (C) hard
   (D) bloody
   (E) hateful

7. CAPRICIOUS
   (A) fretful
   (B) rocky
   (C) limited
   (D) bouncing
   (E) dependable

8. ALACRITY
   (A) activity
   (B) sharpness
   (C) protection
   (D) slowness
   (E) suppleness

9. ZEPHYR
   (A) sail
   (B) typhoon
   (C) boat part
   (D) musical instrument
   (E) harmony

10. WHET
    (A) dry
    (B) stimulate
    (C) sharpen
    (D) thicken
    (E) dull

Sentence Completions

Directions: Each question in this test consists of a sentence or group of sentences in which one or two words are missing. Beneath the question are five pairs of words lettered (A) through (E). Choose the word or the pair of words that *best* completes the sentence or sentences. Then mark the appropriate space in the answer column.

---

11. If a young man says that he is a _____, he most likely means that he is _____.
    (A) doctor—reliable
    (B) philanthropist—parsimonious
    (C) teacher—scholarly
    (D) celibate—a hermit
    (E) celibate—a bachelor

12. A(n) _____ may be defined as the perpetration of (a) _____.
    (A) maxim—saw
    (B) witticism—banality
    (C) murder—assault
    (D) cliche—conspiracy
    (E) offense—calumny

13. When he saw his brother approach, he _____; he was sorry to have made such a show of his true feelings. He would have given much to have been able to suppress the _____ at the same moment.
    (A) shouted—reaction
    (B) sighed—fervor
    (C) grimaced—action
    (D) laughed—jeer
    (E) exulted—distortion

14. The syndicalists who would introduce anarchy are unconcerned about the _____ such a form of government will bring with it.
    (A) plutocracy
    (B) republicanism
    (C) chaos
    (D) dictatorship
    (E) democracy

15. If oxygen were lacking, plants would die because oxygen _____ plant life.
    (A) is dependent upon
    (B) derives from
    (C) is a by-product of
    (D) is concerned with
    (E) is basic to

16. Labor unions hold that capital is only the _____ of labor, and that its origin is subsequent to that of _____.
- (A) fruit—freedom
- (B) product—labor
- (C) machinery—labor
- (D) tool—wealth
- (E) slave—labor

17. Today, although we are witnessing a period of _____ employment, we still find that many people are unemployed, particularly since labor is relatively _____.
- (A) high scale—high priced
- (B) high level—scarce
- (C) optimum—immobile
- (D) industrial—rural
- (E) continuing—unskilled

18. _____ all the hardships the people had gone through, they would not give up.
- (A) In addition to
- (B) Inasmuch as
- (C) In spite of
- (D) For
- (E) Pursuant to

19. He may be deemed _____ who _____ considers the consequences before he acts.
- (A) impetuous—always
- (B) wary—generally
- (C) intrepid—casually
- (D) circumspect—occasionally
- (E) diffident—usually

20. We are not wont to regard with favor those _____ who perform their duties principally for _____ reasons.
- (A) altruists—business
- (B) mercenaries—financial
- (C) managers—social
- (D) leaders—creditable
- (E) business men—impractical

Reading Comprehension

Directions: Read the following passages and answer each of the questions that come after them. Choose the *best* answer. Then mark the appropriate space in the answer column.

In the Federal Convention of 1787, the members were fairly well agreed as to the desirability of some check on state laws; but there was sharp difference of opinion whether this check should be political in character as in the form of a congressional veto, or whether the principle of judicial review should be adopted.

Madison was one of the most persistent advocates of the congressional veto and in his discussion of the subject he referred several times to the former imperial prerogative of disallowing provincial statutes. In March, 1787, he wrote to Jefferson, urging the necessity of a federal negative upon state laws. He referred to previous colonial experience in the suggestion that there should be "some emanation" of the federal prerogative "within the several states, so far as to enable them to give a temporary sanction to laws of immediate necessity." This had been provided for in the imperial system through the action of the royal governor in giving immediate effect to statutes, which nevertheless remained subject to royal disallowance. In a letter to Randolph a few weeks later, Madison referred more explicitly to the British practice, urging that the national government be given "a negative, in all cases whatsoever, on the Legislative acts of the States, as the King of Great Britain heretofore had." Jefferson did not agree with Madison; on practical grounds rather than as a matter of principle, he expressed his preference for some form of judicial control.

On July 17, Madison came forward with a speech in support of the congressional veto, again supporting his contention by reference to the royal disallowance of colonial laws: "Its utility is sufficiently displayed in the British System. Nothing could maintain the harmony and subordination of the various parts of the empire, but the prerogative by which the Crown stifles in the birth every Act of every part tending to discord or encroachment. It is true the prerogative is sometimes misapplied thro' ignorance or a partiality to one particular part of the empire: but we have not the same reason to fear such misapplications in our System." This is almost precisely Jefferson's theory of the legitimate function of an imperial veto.

This whole issue shows that the leaders who wrestled with confederation problems during and after the war understood, in some measure at least, the attitude of British administrators when confronted with the stubborn localism of a provincial assembly.

21. Madison was advocating
   (A)   royal disallowance of state legislation
   (B)   a political check on state laws
   (C)   the supremacy of the states over the federal government
   (D)   the maintenance of a royal governor to give immediate effect to statutes
   (E)   discord and encroachment among the states

22. From this passage there is no indication
   (A)   of what the British System entailed
   (B)   of Jefferson's stand on the question of a check on state laws
   (C)   that the royal negative had been misapplied in the past
   (D)   that Jefferson understood the attitude of British administrators
   (E)   of what judicial review would entail

23. According to this passage, Madison believed that the federal government
   (A)   ought to legislate for the states
   (B)   should recognize the sovereignty of the several states
   (C)   ought to exercise judicial control over state legislation
   (D)   should assume the king's former veto power
   (E)   was equivalent to a provincial assembly

24. Madison's main principle was that
   (A)   the national interest is more important than the interests of any one state
   (B)   the national government should have compulsive power over the states
   (C)   the king can do no wrong
   (D)   the United States should follow the English pattern of government
   (E)   the veto power of the royal governor should be included in the federal prerogative

25. Which of the following is the best argument that could be made against Madison's proposition?
   (A)   The United States has no king.
   (B)   The federal government is an entity outside the jurisdiction of the states.
   (C)   Each state has local problems concerning which representatives from other states are not equipped to pass judgment.
   (D)   The federal prerogative has been misused in the past.
   (E)   It provides no means of dealing with stubborn localism.

The wings of insects, unlike their analogs in other aerial animals, appear to have arisen solely in connection with flight and not from pre-existing locomotor appendages. During flight, the shape of the thorax is altered by the contraction of two massive sets of muscles within, the movement being transmitted to the wings by a hinge mechanism. Flight may be studied in suspended insects, which can be made to beat their wings by removing a platform from beneath their feet. Wing-beat frequencies of several hundred per second are commonplace among flies, *Drosophila* being capable of continuous flight for 1½ hours, during which the wings may beat 1½ million times.

In the course of such a flight, *Drosophila* may deplete glycogen reserves to the extent of 3.5 percent of its body weight. The extraordinary speed at which metabolic reserves are mobilized during this drastic expenditure of energy is shown by the observation that an exhausted *Drosophila* is able to resume flight 45 seconds after drinking a glucose solution, 1 μg of glucose maintaining flight for 6.3 minutes. The extent of the energy expenditure during flight may be judged from the oxygen consumption, which may be as much as 50 times that of the resting insect. Little is yet known of the mechanisms of oxygen transfer and heat dissipation or of the systems of metabolic enzymes associated with such prodigious activity, although large numbers of sarcosomes containing enzymes in concentrated form are present in the flight muscles of those insects with the highest wing-beat frequencies. It is also significant that the oxidation and reduction of cytochrome were first observed in the flight muscles of a moth. Analyses of the aerodynamic efficiency and power output of flying insects should be of immense value when they can be fully correlated with metabolic studies.

26. What is the efficiency of transformation of glycogen into energy expended in flight in *Drosophila?*
    (A) 3.5%
    (B) 45 seconds
    (C) 6.3:1
    (D) 20%
    (E) There is not enough information in the passage to answer this question.

27. Which of the following statements best summarizes the information in the section regarding the origin of insect wings?
    (A) Insect wings were developed from the need for locomotion.
    (B) Insect wings were developed through specialization of the legs.
    (C) No evolutionary changes appear in the development of insect wings.
    (D) Structures that preceded wings in the evolution of insects were related to flight.
    (E) None of the above is appropriate.

28. The muscles which move the wings in flight are in the
- (A) hinge mechanisms
- (B) thorax
- (C) wing hinges
- (D) wings
- (E) legs

29. *Drosophila* has a wing-beat frequency of
- (A) 20 beats per second
- (B) 40 beats per second
- (C) 60 beats per second
- (D) 100 beats per second
- (E) over 100 beats per second

30. According to the author, the efficiency of flight of insects should be related to
- (A) metabolism
- (B) temperature
- (C) power output
- (D) wing-beat frequency
- (E) color

Analogies

Directions: In each of the following questions choose the pair of words that *best* completes the analogy. Then mark the appropriate space in the answer column.

---

31. SAILOR : PIRATE : :
    - (A) transient : permanent
    - (B) plant : fungus
    - (C) mate : captain
    - (D) police : thief
    - (E) wolf : prey

32. SPRINTER : GUN : :
    - (A) butterfly hunter : net
    - (B) dog : whistle
    - (C) fencer : sword
    - (D) fighter : bell
    - (E) writer : pen

33. WRINKLE : FOLD : :
    - (A) tear : cut
    - (B) steal : lose
    - (C) paper : refuse
    - (D) sprinkle : rub
    - (E) wrinkle : smooth

34. WIND : GALE : :
    - (A) storm : sea
    - (B) atmospheric pressure : clear day
    - (C) affection : passion
    - (D) contraction : dilation
    - (E) breeze : gale

35. FRAME : PICTURE : :
    - (A) sash : window
    - (B) painting : canvas
    - (C) setting : diamond
    - (D) border : exile
    - (E) shell : egg

36. TRAIN : WHISTLE : :
    - (A) air raid : siren
    - (B) car : horn
    - (C) swimmer : bell buoy
    - (D) ship : anchor
    - (E) singer : tune

37. REFUGEE : HAVEN : :
    - (A) child : bed
    - (B) fish : bowl
    - (C) exile : sanctuary
    - (D) prisoner : dungeon
    - (E) berth : stowaway

38. WAIT : LOITER : :
    - (A) bum : thief
    - (B) diligent : tardy
    - (C) late : laggard
    - (D) work : putter
    - (E) regress : ingress

39. SHRUB : PRUNE : :
    - (A) beard : shave
    - (B) hair : trim
    - (C) lawnmower : mow
    - (D) scissors : cut
    - (E) wool : shear

40. FACADE : BUILDING : :
    - (A) personality : qualities
    - (B) vestibule : apartment
    - (C) aspect : appearance
    - (D) demeanor : character
    - (E) front : affront

IF YOU FINISH THIS SECTION OF THE SAT BEFORE YOUR TIME IS UP, YOU MAY LOOK BACK AT YOUR WORK IN THIS SECTION ONLY. YOU ARE NOT PERMITTED TO LOOK AT ANY OTHER SECTION OF THE TEST. WHEN THE TIME IS UP, TURN TO THE NEXT SECTION AND START WORK ON THAT SECTION.

Section 2: Mathematics Questions

Time: 30 minutes

The following information may be useful to you in solving some of the mathematics problems in this part:

Circle, radius $= r$:
Area $= \pi r^2$.
Circumference $= 2\pi r$.
A circle has 360 degrees of arc.

Triangle:
The sum of the three angles in a triangle is 180 degrees.
Area $= \frac{1}{2}$(any side $\times$ altitude to that side).

Right Triangle:
The sum of the squares of the legs $=$ the square of the hypotenuse.

Definitions of certain mathematical symbols:

$>$ is greater than
$<$ is less than
$\geq$ is greater than or equal to
$\leq$ is less than or equal to
$\perp$ is perpendicular to
$\parallel$ is parallel to

Important Note: Figures in this section are not always drawn to scale. All numbers are real numbers and all figures lie in a plane unless otherwise stated.

1. Calculate $(2^3)^2 + 3^3 + 4^2$.
    (A) 14
    (B) 555
    (C) 31
    (D) 81
    (E) 107

2. The graph of $y = (x - 2)(x - 1)(x)$ intersects the x-axis in how many points?
    (A) 1
    (B) 2
    (C) 3
    (D) 4
    (E) 0

3. What is the negation of the statement "if $a = 0$, then $b = 0$"?
    (A) if $b \neq 0$, then $a \neq 0$
    (B) if $a \neq 0$, then $b \neq 0$
    (C) $a \neq 0$ or $b \neq 0$
    (D) $a = 0$ and $b \neq 0$
    (E) if $b = 0$, then $a = 0$

4. Which of the following sets of equations has no solution?
      I. $2x + y = 7$ and $x = 1$
     II. $x - y = 3$ and $2x = 2y + 6$
    III. $x + 3y = 2$ and $2x + 6y = 2$
    (A) I only
    (B) II only
    (C) I and III only
    (D) III only
    (E) I, II, and III

5. Let the operation $*$ be defined as $a * b = a - b^2$. Find the numerical value of $2 * [3 * (5 * 1)]$.
    (A) 0
    (B) 167
    (C) 30
    (D) -167
    (E) -18

6. Vertex Q of a triangle is at coordinate (2, 0) and vertex P is at $(-2, 0)$. Which of the following is a possible coordinate for the third vertex, Z, if the area of the triangle is 8?
    (A) (2, 2)
    (B) (0, 4)
    (C) (0, 8)
    (D) (4, 2)
    (E) (8, 8)

7. If $a + b = 21$ and b is an integral multiple of a, how many such positive integer pairs of a and b satisfy the equation?
   (A) 1
   (B) 0
   (C) 21
   (D) 9
   (E) 3

8. $|x| = x$ if and only if
   (A) $x < 0$
   (B) $x \geqq 0$
   (C) $x = 0$
   (D) $-1 \leqq x \leqq 1$
   (E) x is an integer

9. In the accompanying diagram, a semicircle is placed alongside a square in such a way that the side of the square is equal to the diameter of the semicircle. What is the area of the semicircle if the diagonal of the square is 4 in.?

   (A) $\dfrac{\pi}{2}$ sq. in.

   (B) $\dfrac{\pi}{3}$ sq. in.

   (C) π sq. in.
   (D) 2π sq. in.
   (E) 3π sq. in.

10. The average of three numbers is 14. If 2 is added to the first number, 5 is added to the second number, and 8 is added to the third number, by how much is the average increased?
    (A) 5
    (B) 0
    (C) 15
    (D) 19
    (E) cannot be determined from the information given

11. If $\dfrac{x}{a} + b = c$, express x in terms of a, b, and c.
    (A) $ca - ba$
    (B) $ca - b$

    (C) $\dfrac{c - b}{a}$

    (D) $\dfrac{c}{b} - a$

    (E) $\dfrac{bc}{a}$

12. If 20% of p is $2m$ and 45% of p is $\frac{1}{2}n$, what percent of p is $m + n$?

(A) 80%
(B) 100%
(C) 65%
(D) 50%
(E) 25%

13. The area of the square is 64, and the area of the triangle is $3\frac{1}{2}$.

If FB = AE = x, find x.

(A) 3
(B) 6 or 2
(C) 5
(D) 7 or 1
(E) 8

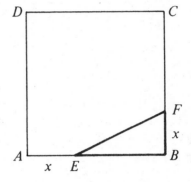

14. If $abc = 1$, where a, b, c, d, and e are all real numbers, which of the following must be *false?*

(A) $a^2c = 0$
(B) $a^2e = 0$
(C) $adc = 0$
(D) $aed = 0$
(E) $acb = 1$

15. Which of the following is the least common multiple of 24 and 20?

(A) 80
(B) 120
(C) 20
(D) 480
(E) 1

16. The blackened arrow on the number line shown represents which of the following?.

(A) $\frac{x}{2} \geqq 0$
(B) $x + 2 = 0$
(C) $5x \leqq 0$
(D) $x - 3 \geqq 0$
(E) $x \leqq 4$

17. On the graph shown, which point(s) does the graph of $x^2 + y^2 = 4$ go through?

(A)   A only
(B)   E only
(C)   D only
(D)   B and D only
(E)   B, C, D and E

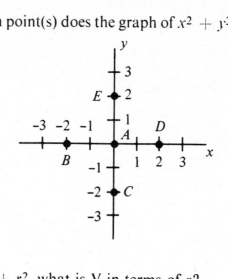

18. If $V = \pi r^2 h$ and $rh = 5r + r^2$, what is V in terms of r?

(A) $\dfrac{\pi r^3}{5}$

(B) $(5 + r)^2$
(C) $5\pi r^3$
(D) $5r^3 + \pi r$
(E) $5\pi r^2 + \pi r^3$

19. Compute the value of $(p - q)^2 + (p - 2)q + (q - 1)p^8$ if $p = 2$ and $q = 1$.

(A)   20
(B)   9
(C)   1
(D)   258
(E)   0

20. $1 + \dfrac{1}{x - 1} = \dfrac{x}{x - 1}$. Solve for x.

(A) $x = 1$ only
(B) $x = 2$ only
(C) $x = 0$ only
(D) $x = \sqrt{2}$ only
(E)   All values of x except $x = 1$

21. If a number n can be expressed as 4 times some whole number, then what can you say about n?

(A) n is a prime
(B) n is even
(C) n is odd
(D) n is a perfect square
(E) n is divisible by 8

22. ABCD, DEHC and EFGH in the diagram below are rectangles. DC = y and AF = ED = x. If the area of rectangle ABCD is y square units, what is the length of EF?
    (A) xy
    (B) $y + 2x$
    (C) $2x$
    (D) $1 - 2x$
    (E) $y - 2x$

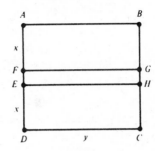

23. The identity element e for an operation * is defined as $e * a = a$ for all a. (An example is 0 for addition because $0 + a = a$ for all a.) If $x * y$ is defined as $x + y - 3$, then what is the identity element?
    (A) 0
    (B) 1
    (C) −3
    (D) 6
    (E) 3

24. A line parallel to $2y = x + 8$ going through the origin is
    (A) $y = -2x + 8$
    (B) $y = x$
    (C) $y + 2 = x$
    (D) $y = \frac{1}{2}x$
    (E) $y = -2$

25. When p is divided by 5, the remainder is 4. What is the remainder when $2p$ is divided by 5?
    (A) 0
    (B) 3
    (C) 4
    (D) 2
    (E) 1

IF YOU FINISH THIS SECTION OF THE SAT BEFORE YOUR TIME IS UP, YOU MAY LOOK BACK AT YOUR WORK IN THIS SECTION ONLY. YOU ARE NOT PERMITTED TO LOOK AT ANY OTHER SECTION OF THE TEST. WHEN THE TIME IS UP, TURN TO THE NEXT SECTION AND START WORK ON THAT SECTION.

Section 3: Verbal Questions

Time: 30 minutes

Antonyms

Directions: Each question in this test consists of a word printed in capital letters followed by five words lettered (A) through (E). Choose the word that has most nearly the OPPOSITE meaning from the word in capital letters. Then mark the appropriate space in the answer column.

1. CLANDESTINE
   (A) covert
   (B) spying
   (C) open
   (D) dark
   (E) analyzed

2. NEOPHYTE
   (A) virtuoso
   (B) tyro
   (C) novice
   (D) novel
   (E) scholar

3. ABSOLVE
   (A) pardon
   (B) recreate
   (C) convict
   (D) pollute
   (E) spoil

4. DESULTORY
   (A) permanent
   (B) discursive
   (C) irregular
   (D) erratic
   (E) ruinous

5. CONTUMACY
   (A) dominancy
   (B) obstinacy
   (C) interdependence
   (D) willingness
   (E) translation

6. ZEST
   (A) yen
   (B) creation
   (C) sleep
   (D) plaudit
   (E) distaste

7. PARSIMONIOUS
   (A) greedy
   (B) stingy
   (C) extravagant
   (D) vacant
   (E) spicy

8. ITINERANT
   (A) steadfast
   (B) wandering
   (C) guiding
   (D) tolerant
   (E) judicial

9. DECRY
   (A) discredit
   (B) censure
   (C) weep
   (D) trot
   (E) exalt

10. LANGUOR
    (A) indolence
    (B) pallor
    (C) petulance
    (D) intimacy
    (E) vivacity

Analogies

Directions: In each of the following questions choose the pair of words that *best* completes the analogy. Then mark the appropriate space in the answer column.

11. PARCHED : DESERT : :
    (A) captive : jail
    (B) inundated : flood
    (C) penurious : slum
    (D) glum : outlook
    (E) withered : plant

12. PARAGRAPH : GIST : :
    (A) play : outcome
    (B) matter : essence
    (C) matter : particle
    (D) epitome : paraphrase
    (E) molecule : atom

13. BUOY : DETOUR : :
    (A) ship : hurricane
    (B) ocean : road
    (C) canal : road
    (D) warning : signal
    (E) storm : accident

14. MOTORIST : ROAD SIGN : :
    (A) telegraph operator : Morse code
    (B) English : pronunciation
    (C) vocabulary : alphabet
    (D) bicyclist : roadblock
    (E) reader : punctuation

15. SYNONYM : SAME : :
    (A) antonym : unlike
    (B) antonym : opposite
    (C) metaphor : poetry
    (D) metonymy : versification
    (E) triangle : pyramid

16. LEG : KNEE : :
    (A) angle : elbow
    (B) hand : wrist
    (C) compound sentence : conjunction
    (D) ribs : breastbone
    (E) simile : metaphor

17. SUPPLENESS : ACROBAT : :
    (A) paint : artist
    (B) fleetness : runner
    (C) imagination : artist
    (D) strength : detective
    (E) grace : chess-player

18. LAUGH : SMILE : :
    (A) grumble : scowl
    (B) lament : condole
    (C) express : restrain
    (D) entice : endow
    (E) cry : sigh

19. ANARCHY : CHAOS : :
    (A) hierarchy : peace
    (B) oppression : confusion
    (C) disturbance : problem
    (D) dictator : democrat
    (E) government : order

20. CEILING : PILLAR : :
    (A) steel : girder
    (B) society : law
    (C) apex : climax
    (D) prices : subsidy
    (E) tree : trunk

Reading Comprehension

In any country the wages commanded by laborers who have comparable skills but who work in various industries are determined by the productivity of the least productive unit of labor, i.e., that unit of labor which works in the industry which has the greatest economic disadvantage. We will represent the various opportunities of employment in a country like the United States by symbols: A, standing for a group of industries in which we have exceptional economic advantages over foreign countries; B, for a group in which our advantages are less; C, one in which they are still less; D, the group of industries in which they are least of all.

When our population is so small that all our labor can be engaged in the group represented by A, productivity of labor (and therefore wages) will be at their maximum. When our population increases so that some of the labor will have to be set to work in group B, the wages of all labor must decline to the level of the productivity in that group. But no employer, without government aid, will yet be able to afford to hire labor to exploit the opportunities represented by C and D, unless there is a further increase in population.

But suppose that the political party in power holds the belief that we should produce everything that we consume, that the opportunities represented by C and D should be exploited. The commodities that the industries composing C and D will produce have been hitherto obtained from abroad in exchange for commodities produced by A and B. The government now renders this difficult by placing high duties upon the former class of commodities. This means that workers in A and B must pay higher prices for what they buy, but do not receive higher prices for what they sell.

After the duty has gone into effect and the prices of commodities that can be produced by C and D have risen sufficiently, enterprisers will be able to hire labor at the wages prevailing in A and B, and establish industries in C and D. So far as the remaining laborers in A and B buy the products of C and D, the difference between the price which they pay for those products and the price that they would pay if they were permitted to import those products duty-free is a tax paid not to the government, but to the producers in C and D, to enable the latter to remain in business. It is an uncompensated deduction from the natural earnings of the laborers in A and B. Nor are the workers in C and D paid as much, estimated in purchasing power, as they would have received if they had been allowed to remain in A and B under the earlier conditions.

21. When C and D are established, workers in these industries
     (A) receive higher wages than do the workers in A and B
     (B) receive lower wages than do the workers in A and B
     (C) must be paid by government funds collected from the duties
          on imports
     (D) are not affected so adversely by the levying of duties as are
          workers in A and B
     (E) receive wages equal to those workers in A and B

22. "No employer, without government aid, will yet be able to afford
     to hire labor to exploit the opportunities represented by C and D"
     because
     (A) productivity of labor is not at the maximum
     (B) we cannot produce everything we consume
     (C) the population has increased
     (D) enterprisers would have to pay wages equivalent to those
          obtained by workers in A and B, while producing under
          greater economic disadvantages
     (E) productivity would drop correspondingly with the wages of
          labor

23. When it places high duties on imported commodities of classes C
     and D, the government
     (A) raises the price of commodities produced by A and B
     (B) is, in effect, taxing the workers in A and B
     (C) raises the wages of workers in C and D at the expense of the
          workers in A and B
     (D) does not affect the productivity of the workers in A and B,
          although the wages of these workers are reduced
     (E) is adopting a policy made necessary by the stability of the
          population

24. The author's main point is that
     (A) it is impossible to attain national self-sufficiency
     (B) the varying productivity of the various industries leads to
          the inequalities in wages of workers in these industries
     (C) a policy that draws labor from the fields of greater natural
          productiveness to fields of lower natural productiveness
          tends to reduce purchasing power
     (D) wages ought to be independent of international trade
     (E) the government ought to subsidize C and D

25. The author's arguments in this passage could best be used to
(A) refute the belief that it is theoretically possible for us to produce everything that we consume
(B) disprove the theory that national self-sufficiency can be obtained by means of protective tariffs
(C) advocate the levying of duties on imported goods
(D) advocate equal wages for workers who have comparable skills but who work in various industries
(E) advocate free trade

Sentence Completions

Directions: Each question in this test consists of a sentence or group of sentences in which one or two words are missing. Beneath the question are five pairs of words lettered (A) through (E). Choose the word or the pair of words that *best* completes the sentence or sentences. Then mark the appropriate space in the answer column.

26. Liberty and slavery differ only in the nature of the controlling authority. As a result, freedom can be easily perverted into _____.
(A) servitude
(B) humility
(C) arrogance
(D) defeat
(E) liberty

27. The tornado left all the buildings a(n) _____ mass of destruction.
(A) massive
(B) motley
(C) destitute
(D) unrecognizable
(E) incomparable

28. Although a tenet may be _____ in nature, it cannot be considered a _____.
(A) colored—miniature
(B) ceremonial—relic
(C) incorrect—lie
(D) simple—rite
(E) ridiculous—doctrine

29. I have never heard _____ so _____.
    (A) strikes—complete
    (B) an explosion—ear-shattering
    (C) revolutions—successful
    (D) detonations—atomized
    (E) redundancy—sanctified

30. The administration of President Grant is _____ as marking a
    _____ in American government.
    (A) admitted—zenith
    (B) revealed—departure
    (C) refuted—chasm
    (D) acknowledged—nadir
    (E) accepted—panacea

31. Measures that are taken _____ to anticipate trouble or to assure
    success come under the heading of _____.
    (A) beforehand—ingenuity
    (B) in advance—precaution
    (C) afterwards—ingenuousness
    (D) previously—sagacity
    (E) prematurely—anticipation

32. Certain community groups on the East Side have opposed plans
    to _____ its slums and replace them with modern "projects."
    (A) reconstruct
    (B) resurrect
    (C) raze
    (D) alleviate
    (E) alter

33. There are stories and highly _____ suppositions that the Hyksos
    built a considerable empire in Egypt, although there are few writ-
    ten records or definite evidences of their conquests.
    (A) plausible
    (B) peculiar
    (C) challenging
    (D) improbable
    (E) historical

34. An impediment which makes _____ more difficult is _____.
    (A) achievement—a strike
    (B) efficiency—over-production
    (C) peace—the UN
    (D) accomplishment—a handicap
    (E) success—gambling

35. Among the baseball players of his time, Joe DiMaggio was _____ to be without a(n) _____.
- (A) declared—inferior
- (B) recognized—peer
- (C) acclaimed—flaw
- (D) described—emotion
- (E) assailed—equal

Reading Comprehension

Directions: Read the following passage and answer each of the questions that come after it. Choose the *best* answer. Then mark the appropriate space in the answer column.

Physico-chemical investigations lead to the idea that life has been entirely adapted to terrestrial conditions from its very beginning, and probably has arisen from the earth. This conception is somewhat contradictory to a theory widely accepted formerly, the so-called theory of panspermia according to which life was propagated from spores scattered through the universe. The beginnings of life and evolution were supposed to depend on the condition that such germ cells were dropped on a planet like the earth where conditions were favorable for germination. Since such germ cells were supposed to be carried by radiation pressure from planet to planet and from solar system to solar system, life was considered to be eternal like time and matter; it should never have been generated anew (radiation pressure has been demonstrated experimentally by a movement of dust particles in a vacuum following radiation from one side). This theory, popularized by extensive physical discussions by such an authority as S. Arrhenius, has been invented on account of the widely accepted doctrine that life can never arise from inanimate matter. As is well known this doctrine dates back to the famous experiments by which Pasteur exposed the delusion of the old time "life creators," viz., those careless experimenters who drew conclusions from observations on nutritive media, handled without adequate control of asepsis. The reason given for the impossibility of spontaneous generation was simply that so far nobody had ever observed it. But such a negative inductive proof cannot be convincing!

36. The theory of panspermia holds that
    (A) life is independent of terrestrial conditions
    (B) germ cells are immortal
    (C) spontaneous generation on earth is impossible
    (D) radiation pressure from some source disperses the germ cells
    (E) radiation pressure has no effect on germ cells

37. The most effective proof for a theory of terrestrial generation would be
    (A) demonstration that spontaneous life creation was inconceivable
    (B) production of animate matter from inanimate matter
    (C) disproof of radiation pressure
    (D) unanimous testimony of competent authorities
    (E) a chemical reaction

38. Pasteur's investigations proved
    (A) that spontaneous generation was impossible
    (B) that no one had yet observed spontaneous generation
    (C) that microorganisms are practically omnipresent
    (D) that the creation of life was supra-human
    (E) none of the above

39. If life were adapted to terrestrial conditions from the outset,
    (A) panspermia is still a possibility
    (B) the theories of Arrhenius are disproved
    (C) Pasteur's experiments are irrelevant
    (D) a change in these conditions, even though gradual, would inhibit it
    (E) two of the above are correct

40. The theory of terrestrial generation holds that
    (A) life is a purely terrestrial phenomenon
    (B) life on earth is eternal like time and matter
    (C) a negative inductive proof is insufficient
    (D) genetic competence for survival can be assumed
    (E) genetic competence for survival cannot be assumed

TURN TO THE NEXT SECTION AND START WORK ON THAT SECTION.

Section 4: Standard Written English Test

Time: 30 minutes

> Because the SWET (Standard Written English Test) does not count toward your score but is only used for Freshman English placement when you get into college, questions of this type are not included.

TURN TO THE NEXT SECTION AND START WORK ON THAT SECTION.

Section 5: Mathematics Questions

Directions: Each question in this section is followed by five choices lettered (A) through (E). Choose the correct answer. Then mark the appropriate space in the answer column.

The following information may be useful to you in solving some of the mathematics problems in this part:

Circle, radius $= r$:
  Area $= \pi r^2$.
  Circumference $= 2\pi r$.
  A circle has 360 degrees of arc.

Triangle:
  The sum of the three angles in a triangle is 180 degrees.
  Area $= \frac{1}{2}$(any side $\times$ altitude to that side).

Right Triangle:
  The sum of the squares of the legs $=$ the square of the hypotenuse.

Definitions of certain mathematical symbols:

  $>$ is greater than
  $<$ is less than
  $\geq$ is greater than or equal to
  $\leq$ is less than or equal to
  $\perp$ is perpendicular to
  $\parallel$ is parallel to

Important Note: Figures in this section are not always drawn to scale. All numbers are real numbers and all figures lie in a plane unless otherwise stated.

1. If $\dfrac{1}{n} = \dfrac{p}{q} + \dfrac{1}{p}$, then $n =$

(A) $\dfrac{p^2 + q}{pq}$

(B) $\dfrac{p^2 + pq}{1 - p}$

(C) $\dfrac{pq}{p^2 + q}$

(D) $\dfrac{1 - p^2}{pq}$

(E)   none of these

2. $\dfrac{5\sqrt{2}}{\sqrt{5}} =$

(A) $\sqrt{10}$

(B) $\sqrt{\dfrac{10}{5}}$

(C) $\dfrac{\sqrt{2}}{5}$

(D) $\sqrt{\dfrac{2}{10}}$

(E) $\sqrt{2}$

3. In rectangle ABCD, E is the midpoint of AD; DC is 4 in.; angle ABE is 45°. Find the area of the shaded portion.

(A)   36 sq. in.
(B)   32 sq. in.
(C)   18 sq. in.
(D)   20 sq. in.
(E)   24 sq. in.

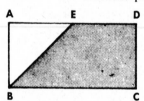

4. In a graduating class of 620 students, 35% plan to seek employment and the rest plan to attend college. How many plan to go to college?

(A)   217
(B)   334
(C)   365
(D)   403
(E)   521

5. Triangle ABC is inscribed in a circle. DE is a tangent to the circle at point A. If angle CAE = 36°, how many degrees are there in angle B?

(A) 18°
(B) 24°
(C) 36°
(D) 72°
(E) 90°

6. Find the area of an equilateral triangle whose side is 10.
(A) $5\sqrt{3}$
(B) $10\sqrt{3}$
(C) $15\sqrt{3}$
(D) $25\sqrt{3}$
(E) $50\sqrt{3}$

7.

Y	4	3	6	?
X	12	16	8	24

Find the value of the missing number.

(A) 18
(B) 24
(C) 16
(D) 8
(E) 2

8. Angles a, b, and c are in the ratio of 4:5:6. Angle c is
(A) 72°
(B) 60°
(C) 48°
(D) 24°
(E) 36°

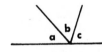

9. In right triangle ABC, angle C is 90°. If the altitude CD divides the hypotenuse into lengths of 3 and 12 respectively, what is the altitude?
(A) 8
(B) 7
(C) 6
(D) 5
(E) 4

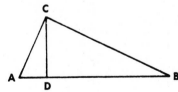

10. A purse contains $2.55 in nickels and dimes. If the number of dimes exceeds twice the number of nickels by 8, how many nickels are there?

(A) 6
(B) 7
(C) 8
(D) 12
(E) 14

11. Two stations, A and B, are located 6 mi. apart on a railroad. The rates of cartage of coal are $.50 per ton per mile from A and $.75 per ton per mile from B. At a certain consumer's home, located on the railroad between A and B, the cost for cartage is the same whether the coal is delivered from A or from B. What is the distance from this home to A?

(A) 3 mi.

(B) $3\frac{1}{2}$ mi.

(C) $3\frac{3}{5}$ mi.

(D) 4 mi.
(E) 5 mi.

12. Boys and girls attend a school dance. Each boy is charged $.25 and each girl $.10 for admission. The boys and girls pay a total of $12.60 for admission. If the total number of boys had been 8 less and each had payed $.05 less, and if the total number of girls had been 8 more and each had payed $.05 more, the money collected from the boys would have been twice that collected from the girls. How many girls attend the dance?

(A) 38
(B) 30
(C) 24
(D) 20
(E) 16

13. Find the average of $\frac{3}{5}, \frac{2}{3}, \frac{5}{6}$, and $\frac{1}{2}$.

(A) $\dfrac{9}{10}$

(B) $10\frac{2}{5}$

(C) $\dfrac{13}{20}$

(D) $12\frac{4}{7}$

(E) $\dfrac{17}{20}$

14. The figure below consists of 5 equal squares. If the area of the figure is 180 sq. in., what is the length of the perimeter?

(A)   36 in.
(B)   45 in.
(C)   72 in.
(D)   90 in.
(E)   108 in.

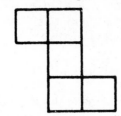

15. What is the sum of 7 hr. 42 min. and 3 hr. 34 min.?

(A)   10 hr. 16 min.
(B)   11 hr. 8 min.
(C)   10 hr. 8 min.
(D)   11 hr. 16 min.
(E)   11 hr. 20 min.

GO ON TO THE NEXT PAGE

Directions: This section requires you to compare two quantities—the quantity in Column A and the quantity in Column B. After you have compared the two quantities, select

- (A) if the quantity in Column A is greater than the quantity in Column B;
- (B) if the quantity in Column B is greater than the quantity in Column A;
- (C) if the quantities in the two columns are equal;
- (D) if the information is not sufficient to make a valid comparison.

Any information that appears in a central position above the two quantities to be compared refers to both quantities.

(A) if the quantity in Column A is greater than the quantity in Column B
(B) if the quantity in Column B is greater than the quantity in Column A
(C) if the quantities in the two columns are equal
(D) if the information is not sufficient to make a valid comparison

Column A   **Column B**

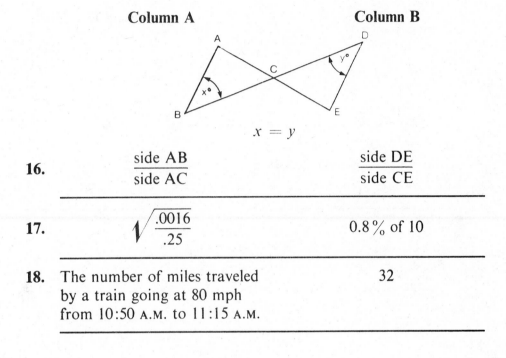

$$x = y$$

16. $\dfrac{\text{side AB}}{\text{side AC}}$ $\dfrac{\text{side DE}}{\text{side CE}}$

17. $\sqrt{\dfrac{.0016}{.25}}$ 0.8 % of 10

18. The number of miles traveled by a train going at 80 mph from 10:50 A.M. to 11:15 A.M.   32

$$-1 < n < 0$$

19. n^4 $\left(\dfrac{1}{n}\right)^4$

20. The average speed of a car that travels at 30 mph for the first hour, 50 mph for the next 3 hours, and 60 mph for the last 2 hours   50 mph

(A) if the quantity in Column A is greater than the
   quantity in Column B
(B) if the quantity in Column B is greater than the
   quantity in Column A
(C) if the quantities in the two columns are equal
(D) if the information is not sufficient to make a
   valid comparison

Column A 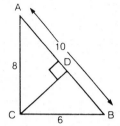 **Column B**

Angle ACB is a right angle.

21.   CD   5

$$x^2 - 4x = -4$$
$$3y^2 + 12 = 12y$$

22. x y

$$\sqrt{x} = 1.6$$

23. x $\dfrac{2^3}{3}$

Questions 24 and 25 refer to the following diagram.

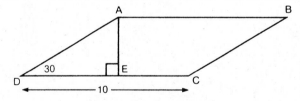

Area of parallelogram ABCD = 30.

24.   AD   5

25. $\angle DAB + \angle DCB$ 320°

26. $1\dfrac{7}{24} + \dfrac{7}{12} + 2\dfrac{3}{8}$ 4

(A) if the quantity in Column A is greater than the quantity in Column B

(B) if the quantity in Column B is greater than the quantity in Column A

(C) if the quantities in the two columns are equal

(D) if the information is not sufficient to make a valid comparison

Questions 27–30 are based on the following graph.

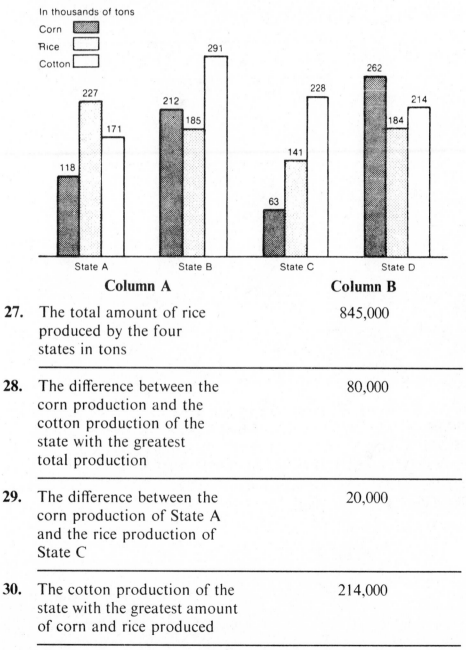

1975 PRODUCTION OF CORN, RICE, AND COTTON IN STATES A, B, C, AND D

	Column A	**Column B**
27.	The total amount of rice produced by the four states in tons	845,000
28.	The difference between the corn production and the cotton production of the state with the greatest total production	80,000
29.	The difference between the corn production of State A and the rice production of State C	20,000
30.	The cotton production of the state with the greatest amount of corn and rice produced	214,000

(A) if the quantity in Column A is greater than the quantity in Column B
(B) if the quantity in Column B is greater than the quantity in Column A
(C) if the quantities in the two columns are equal
(D) if the information is not sufficient to make a valid comparison

Column A	Column B

$$p^2 + q^2 = 100$$
$$-6 \leqq q \leqq 0$$

31. The lowest possible value of p 0

32. $[(\sqrt{2} + 6) \div (3 - 1)] + 4$ $\sqrt{2} + [(6 \div 3) - 1 + 4]$

$$0 < x < y < z$$

33. $\dfrac{y}{xz}$ $\dfrac{z}{xy}$

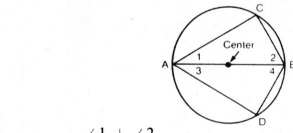

34. $\angle 1 + \angle 2$ $\angle 3 + \angle 4$

$$y \neq 0$$

35. $x^2 + y^2$ $x^2 - y^2$

IF YOU FINISH THIS SECTION OF THE SAT BEFORE YOUR TIME IS UP, YOU MAY LOOK BACK AT YOUR WORK IN THIS SECTION ONLY. YOU ARE NOT PERMITTED TO LOOK AT ANY OTHER SECTION OF THE TEST. WHEN THE TIME IS UP, TURN TO THE NEXT SECTION AND START WORK ON THAT SECTION.

Section 6: Verbal Questions

Time: 30 minutes

Antonyms

Directions: Each question in this test consists of a word printed in capital letters followed by five words lettered (A) through (E). Choose the word that has most nearly the OPPOSITE meaning from the word in capital letters. Then mark the appropriate space in the answer column.

1. ABEYANCE
   (A) revival
   (B) dormancy
   (C) carriage
   (D) conveyance
   (E) choice

2. JOCOSE
   (A) happy
   (B) jesting
   (C) jocund
   (D) small
   (E) serious

3. ERUDITE
   (A) unlearned
   (B) scholarly
   (C) erupted
   (D) insightful
   (E) vacuous

4. AVERSION
   (A) sign
   (B) attraction
   (C) avarice
   (D) appellate
   (E) dolt

5. CHASTE
   (A) pure
   (B) devoted
   (C) licentious
   (D) common
   (E) inviolable

6. FULSOME
   (A) abhorrent
   (B) plentiful
   (C) pleasing
   (D) empty
   (E) wasted

7. ACERBITY
   (A) acidity
   (B) servility
   (C) possessor
   (D) sharpener
   (E) mildness

8. IGNEOUS
   (A) volcanic
   (B) aflame
   (C) sedimentary
   (D) firm
   (E) solid

9. SPORADIC
   (A) pausing
   (B) latent
   (C) natal
   (D) seedlike
   (E) frequent

10. NIGGARDLY
    (A) miserly
    (B) stingy
    (C) lazy
    (D) dark
    (E) giving

11. CACOPHONY
    (A) harmony
    (B) discord
    (C) dissonance
    (D) noise
    (E) beauty

12. INSIPID
    (A) dull
    (B) flat
    (C) boring
    (D) witty
    (E) foolish

13. BELLICOSE
    (A) warlike
    (B) peaceful
    (C) overweight
    (D) underweight
    (E) loud

14. CHAGRIN
    (A) annoyance
    (B) pleasure
    (C) acclaim
    (D) support
    (E) irascibility

15. BRAGGADOCIO
    (A) boast
    (B) conceit
    (C) modesty
    (D) pride
    (E) hate

Sentence Completions

Directions: Each question in this test consists of a sentence or group of sentences in which one or two words are missing. Beneath the question are five pairs of words lettered (A) through (E). Choose the word or the pair of words that *best* completes the sentence or sentences. Then mark the appropriate space in the answer column.

---

16. A _____ is a minute particle of a(n) _____.
    (A) second—matter
    (B) protozoa—fish
    (C) molecule—substance
    (D) millimeter—ammeter
    (E) dyne—energy

17. History tells us that Demosthenes made several long speeches warning the Greeks against Philip of Macedon. Since these _____ were strongly worded, personal in nature, and full of abuse, a new word, _____, has passed over into our language.
    (A) speeches—demonstration
    (B) invectives—geriatrics
    (C) outbursts—genocide
    (D) paeans—acrimonious
    (E) declamations—philippics

18. The old actor lived in a world of his own, characterized by senility and garrulity. In particular, his speech pattern was affected. Whatever he said was marked by _____. One could not say that he was _____ in nature.
    (A) laconicism—rambling
    (B) inconsistency—incompetent
    (C) wisdom—foolish
    (D) circumlocution—disciplined
    (E) arrogance—concise

19. Many of our pioneer American writers were confronted with the choice of striving for originality or emulating the masters of the old world with _____ skill and technique.
    (A) consummate
    (B) individual
    (C) pecuniary
    (D) sustained
    (E) foolish

20. The greatest of men have honestly admitted in their autobiographies that they were not _____ of virtue; that, merely, some of their abilities had received a striking _____.

 (A) exemplars—emphasis
 (B) paragons—aggravation
 (C) destructive—reaction
 (D) contemptuous—rejection
 (E) unmindful—upturn

Reading Comprehension

Directions: Read the following passages and answer each of the questions that come after them. Choose the *best* answer. Then mark the appropriate space in the answer column.

The nucleus of its population is the local businessmen, whose interests constitute the municipal policy and control its municipal administration. These local businessmen are such as the local bankers, merchants of many kinds and degrees, real estate promoters, local lawyers, local clergymen. . . . The businessmen, who take up the local traffic in merchandising, litigation, church enterprise and the like, commonly begin with some share in real estate speculation. This affords a common bond and a common ground of pecuniary interest, which commonly masquerades under the name of local patriotism, public spirit, civic pride, and the like. This pretense of public spirit is so consistently maintained that most of these men come presently to believe in their own professions on that head. Pecuniary interest in local land values involves an interest in the continued growth of the town. Hence any creditable misrepresentation of the town's volume of business traffic, population, tributary farming community, or natural resources, is rated as serviceable to the common good. And any member of this businesslike community will be rated as a meritorious citizen in proportion as he is serviceable to this joint pecuniary interest of these "influential citizens."

21. The tone of the paragraph is
    (A) bitter
    (B) didactic
    (C) complaining
    (D) satirical
    (E) informative

22. The foundation for the "influential citizens' " interest in their community is
    (A) their control of the municipal administration
    (B) their interests in trade and merchandising
    (C) their natural feeling of civic pride
    (D) a pretense of public spirit
    (E) ownership of land for speculation

23. The "influential citizens' " type of civic pride may be compared with the patriotism of believers in
    (A) a balance of power in international diplomacy
    (B) racial superiority
    (C) a high tariff
    (D) laissez faire
    (E) dollar diplomacy

24. The important men in the town
    (A) are consciously insincere in their local patriotism
    (B) are drawn together for political reasons
    (C) do not scruple to give their community a false boost
    (D) regard strict economy as a necessary virtue
    (E) are extremely jealous of their prestige

25. The writer considers that the influential men of the town
    (A) are entirely hypocritical in their conception of their motives
    (B) are blinded to facts by their patriotic spirit
    (C) have deceived themselves into thinking they are altruistic
    (D) look upon the welfare of their community as of paramount importance
    (E) form a closed corporation devoted to the interests of the town

26. Probably the author's own view of patriotism is that it
    (A) should be a disinterested passion untinged by commercial motives
    (B) is found only among the poorer classes
    (C) is usually found in urban society
    (D) grows out of a combination of the motives of self-interest and altruism
    (E) consists in the main of a feeling of local pride

The objection likely to be made to this argument would probably take some such form as the following: There is no greater assumption of infallibility in forbidding the propagation of error, than in any other thing which is done by public authority on its own judgment and responsibility. Judgment is given to men that they may use it. Because it may·be used erroneously, are men to be told that they ought not to use it at all? To prohibit what they think pernicious, is not claiming exemption from error, but fulfilling the duty incumbent on them, although fallible, of acting on their conscientious conviction. If we were never to act on our opinions, because those opinions may be wrong, we should leave all our interests uncared for, and all our duties unperformed. An objection which applies to all conduct, can be no valid objection to any conduct in particular. It is the duty of governments, and of individuals, to form the truest opinions they can; to form them carefully, and never impose them upon others unless they are quite sure of being right. But when they are sure (such reasoners may say), it is not conscientiousness but cowardice to shrink from acting on their opinions, and allow doctrines which they honestly think dangerous to the welfare of mankind, either in this life or in another, to be scattered abroad without restraint, because other people, in less enlightened times, have persecuted opinions now believed to be true. Let us take care, it may be said, not to make the same mistake: but governments and nations have made mistakes in other things, which are not denied to be fit subjects for the exercise of authority: they have laid on bad taxes, made unjust wars. Ought we therefore to lay on no taxes, and, under whatever provocation, make no wars? Men, and governments, must act to the best of their ability. There is no such thing as absolute certainty, but there is assurance sufficient for the purposes of human life. We may, and must, assume our opinion to be true for the guidance of our own conduct: and it is assuming no more when we forbid bad men to pervert society by the propagation of opinions which we regard as false and pernicious.

I answer, that it is assuming very much more. There is the greatest difference between presuming an opinion to be true, because, with every opportunity for contesting it, it has not been refuted, and assuming its truth for the purpose of not permitting its refutation. Complete liberty of contradicting and disproving our opinion, is the very condition which justifies us in assuming its truth for purposes of action; and on no other terms can a being with human faculties have assurance of being right.

27. We may assume that it is the writer's contention that
- (A) one must not publish doctrines inimical to the welfare of mankind
- (B) one must permit every doctrine, false or true, to be published
- (C) it is the duty of governments and of individuals to form the truest opinion possible, then to act upon it
- (D) because government may, on occasion, exercise its powers injudiciously, it should not therefore be forbidden of such powers
- (E) we assume infallibility in forbidding the propagation of error

28. The meaning of the first sentence is
- (A) nothing is more erroneous than the thought that anything done by public authority is infallible
- (B) believing that things may be done by public authority on its own authority, without recourse to any other sanction, is a prime error
- (C) government has no more opportunity for error in censorship than in its other exercises of power
- (D) there is no such thing as absolute certainty
- (E) the government is infallible and may forbid the propagation of error

29. The case for censorship is in part justified by
- (A) syllogism: deduction from a major hypothesis and a minor hypothesis
- (B) inductive reasoning: reasoning to a conclusion from relevant instances
- (C) analogy: reasoning by comparison with similar situations
- (D) experience: citing of instances of successful censorship
- (E) rhetoric: persuasive skill in the use of language

30. The argument given against censorship runs as follows:
- (A) censorship is a form of cowardice—a refusal to obey the promptings of one's conscience
- (B) censorship is, in effect, a begging of the question. It assumes what it should prove—namely, that an opinion is wrong.
- (C) on no other terms than complete liberty of contradicting and disproving an opinion can a being with human faculties have the sense of being a rational, complete individual
- (D) we may not prohibit the free play of mind on the pretext that it may be used erroneously; that is the risk a free society takes
- (E) truth is good; censorship is bad

Analogies

Directions: In each of the following questions choose the pair of words that *best* completes the analogy. Then mark the appropriate space in the answer column.

31. CLIMAX : BATTLE : :
    (A) prelude : interlude
    (B) coup d'etat : revolution
    (C) emergency : decision
    (D) apex : flight
    (E) crisis : disease

32. FAILURE : TIMOROUSNESS : :
    (A) sagacity : experience
    (B) smarting : ointment
    (C) study : book
    (D) experiment : hypothesis
    (E) heredity : wisdom

33. AFFIRMATION : REPORT : :
    (A) acknowledgment : rumor
    (B) reputation : gossip
    (C) testify : certify
    (D) servility : dependability
    (E) probably : possible

34. TEPID : TORRID : :
    (A) turgid : horrid
    (B) pool : placid
    (C) cool : frigid
    (D) tumid : turbid
    (E) livid : lurid

35. MILLENNIUM : CENTURY : :
    (A) year : month
    (B) hour : minute
    (C) month : day
    (D) decade : year
    (E) minute : second

36. GILLS : LUNGS : :
    (A) water : air
    (B) tail : feathers
    (C) tongue : teeth
    (D) wings : arms
    (E) mouth : ears

37. FATHER : DAUGHTER : :
    (A) aunt : nephew
    (B) mother : daughter-in-law
    (C) uncle : niece
    (D) minor : adult
    (E) nephew : niece

38. RIBS : UMBRELLA : :
    (A) rafters : roof
    (B) spokes : hub
    (C) roof : rafters
    (D) skeleton : frame
    (E) garret : house

39. MERIDIAN : SETTING : :
    (A) start : finish
    (B) baptism : birth
    (C) pinnacle : climax
    (D) culminate : terminate
    (E) maturity : homestretch

40. HARBINGER : SPRING : :
    (A) fight : might
    (B) tail : comet
    (C) telegram : event
    (D) spring : winter
    (E) dawn : day

Reading Comprehension

Directions: Read the following passage and answer each of the questions that come after it. Choose the *best* answer. Then mark the appropriate space in the answer column.

Ants have not been incriminated as vectors of pathogenic bacteria affecting man, though medical entomology abounds with citations of flies as carriers of many species of bacteria. Even cockroaches have been suspected, but ants have not been mentioned. No reference is found in the available literature as to their role in this respect. Theoretically, if flies can convey pathogens mechanically from infected to non-infected material, other insects should be able to do likewise. Recently, in the course of experiments on native food as a culture medium for Shigella, accidentally ants were found to carry these organisms. Portions of the native food, rice and beans cooked together with onions and tomato sauce, were inoculated with various strains of Shigella to determine whether this food was a favorable medium for the growth of the pathogens and thus a source of the dysentery so common in Puerto Rico. Following a 24-hour incubation of the plates streaked from this food, which had been inoculated with Flexner strains of Shigella, they were read, covered and left inverted on the laboratory table until the next morning. At that time unusual growths of non-lactose fermenting colonies, later identified as Shigella, were observed in a pattern similar to miniature rabbit tracks. Examination revealed a few ants on the table, leaving the plates. These were caught and allowed to walk on sterile agar plates which, upon incubation, produced a growth pattern similar to the original. Some ants, demonstrated to be sterile, were obtained. Food inoculated with Shigella was placed in one container. These ants fed readily during a period of four hours, then the food was removed and sterile plates introduced long enough to allow ants to walk over the surfaces. These plates produced Shigella. Twenty-four hours after feeding on the infected material, sterile plates were again introduced. These, too, produced the typical growth of Shigella marking the footprints of the ants. The process was repeated after forty-eight hours, but on these last plates no colonies appeared. About twenty ants of this group were then macerated and inoculated on plates; others were placed in nutrient broth, which again failed to produce Shigella.

41. Shigella is a
    (A) protozoan
    (B) bacterium
    (C) food
    (D) disease
    (E) person

42. From the above paragraph one may conclude that
    (A) ants, as well as houseflies, should be eradicated
    (B) ants transmit dysentery in Puerto Rico
    (C) ants may carry bacteria on their feet for at least 24 hours
         after feeding on or traversing infected material
    (D) ants may carry bacteria in their digestive tracts after feeding
         on or traversing infected material
    (E) none of the above is true

43. The experiment reported above was designed to investigate
    (A) native food as a source of dysentery
    (B) native food as a culture medium
    (C) the possibility that ants could carry pathogenic bacteria
    (D) the possibility that Shigella could be a cause of dysentery
    (E) none of the above

44. The experiment showed that
    (A) ant tracks are similar in pattern to rabbit tracks
    (B) ants do not normally carry infections
    (C) ants may carry infectious materials more than 24 hours
    (D) ants carry only non-lactose fermenting bacteria
    (E) we cannot make any of the above inferences about ants

45. The best reason that no Shigella colonies appeared after 48 hours
    is that
    (A) the ants were no longer hungry
    (B) other bacteria destroyed the Shigella
    (C) the life cycle of the Shigella is less than 48 hours
    (D) the sterile plates were contaminated by flies
    (E) the experiment was not controlled

IF YOU FINISH THIS SECTION OF THE SAT BEFORE YOUR TIME IS UP, YOU MAY LOOK BACK AT YOUR WORK IN THIS SECTION ONLY. YOU ARE NOT PERMITTED TO LOOK AT ANY OTHER SECTION OF THE TEST. WHEN TIME IS UP, THE SAT IS OVER.

AFTER YOU HAVE FINISHED PRACTICE TEST 4:

1. Look at the Answer Key on pages 277 and 278.

2. Determine your number of CORRECT answers for the MATH and VERBAL parts. DO NOT count Section 3.

3. Determine your number of INCORRECT answers for the MATH and VERBAL parts. DO NOT count Section 3.

4. To obtain the RAW SCORE for each part (VERBAL or MATH) deduct ¼ the number of INCORRECT answers from the number of CORRECT answers.

5. Find what your SCALED SCORES are by using your Raw Score and referring to the TABLES on pages 92 and 93.

Answer Key for Practice Test 4

Section 1

1. A	9. B	17. C	25. C	33. A
2. B	10. E	18. C	26. E	34. C
3. B	11. E	19. B	27. D	35. C
4. A	12. B	20. B	28. B	36. B
5. C	13. C	21. B	29. E	37. C
6. A	14. C	22. E	30. A	38. D
7. E	15. E	23. D	31. B	39. B
8. D	16. B	24. B	32. D	40. D

Section 2

1. E	6. B	11. A	16. C	21. B
2. C	7. E	12. B	17. E	22. D
3. D	8. B	13. D	18. E	23. E
4. D	9. C	14. A	19. C	24. D
5. D	10. A	15. B	20. E	25. B

Section 3

1. C	9. E	17. B	25. E	33. A
2. A	10. E	18. A	26. A	34. D
3. C	11. C	19. E	27. D	35. B
4. A	12. B	20. D	28. C	36. D
5. D	13. B	21. E	29. B	37. B
6. E	14. E	22. D	30. D	38. C
7. C	15. B	23. B	31. B	39. A
8. A	16. B	24. C	32. C	40. D

Section 5

1. C	8. A	15. D	22. C	29. A
2. A	9. C	16. C	23. B	30. C
3. E	10. B	17. C	24. A	31. B
4. D	11. C	18. A	25. B	32. A
5. C	12. E	19. B	26. A	33. B
6. D	13. C	20. C	27. B	34. C
7. E	14. C	21. B	28. B	35. A

Section 6

1. A	10. E	19. A	28. C	37. C
2. E	11. A	20. A	29. C	38. A
3. A	12. D	21. B	30. B	39. D
4. B	13. B	22. E	31. E	40. E
5. C	14. B	23. E	32. A	41. B
6. C	15. C	24. C	33. A	42. C
7. E	16. C	25. C	34. C	43. C
8. C	17. E	26. A	35. D	44. C
9. E	18. D	27. B	36. A	45. C

Explanatory Answers for Practice Test 4

Section 1: Verbal Questions

1. **(A)**
Demure: serious, prim; *antonym:* shameless, brazen

2. **(B)**
Onerous: burdensome; *antonym:* facile

3. **(B)**
Agile: nimble; *antonym:* clumsy

4. **(A)**
Levity: gaiety; *antonym:* solemnity

5. **(C)**
Nepotism: favoritism; *antonym:* fairness

6. **(A)**
Venial: forgivable; *antonym:* unforgivable

7. **(E)**
Capricious: erratic, changeable; *antonym:* dependable

8. **(D)**
Alacrity: eagerness; *antonym:* slowness

9. **(B)**
Zephyr: a breeze; *antonym:* typhoon

10. **(E)**
Whet: to sharpen; *antonym:* dull

11. **(E)**
If a young man says that he will be always unmarried (a *celibate*), he most likely means that he is a bachelor.

12. **(B)**
A *witticism* (a witty remark or saying) may be defined as the perpetration of a *banality* (trite remark).

13. **(C)**
In light of the rest of the sentence, *grimaced* and *action* are the best choices of words to insert in the blanks.

14. (C)

. . . are unconcerned about the total disorder or confusion (*chaos*) such a form of government will bring with it.

15. (E)

Since the plants would die, oxygen must be *basic to* plant life.

16. (B)

The combination of the words *product* and *labor,* in that order, makes for the most logical and consistent sentence.

17. (C)

Choice (C) gives us the best combination of words to make the sentence sensible.

18. (C)

They would not give up *in spite of* all the hardships.

19. (B)

A *wary* person would *generally* consider the consequences before he acts.

20. (B)

Mercenaries are motivated by money for material gain. Thus, they perform their duties principally for *financial* reasons.

21. (B)

The congressional veto was a political check on state laws. Madison was advocating the congressional veto.

22. (E)

The passage does not describe what judicial review entails.

23. (D)

See the next to last sentence of the second paragraph.

24. (B)

It can be seen that Madison was concerned with the fact that the national government should have compulsive power over the states. See the next to last sentence of the second paragraph.

25. (C)

Choice (C) is the most appropriate. It is true that the individual state may have problems peculiar to itself. Thus, a member of another state may not be able to pass judgment on the problems of a particular state.

26. (E)
There is not enough data in the passage to enable one to calculate this efficiency.

27. (D)
See the first sentence of the first paragraph.

28. (B)
See the second sentence of the first paragraph.

29. (E)
It is stated in the fourth sentence that "Wing-beat frequencies of several hundred per second are commonplace among flies. *Drosophila* being capable of continuous flight. . . ." Thus it is apparent that, in context, *Drosophila* must have a wing-beat frequency of at least more than 100 beats per second.

30. (A)
See the last sentence of the passage in which the author states that analyses of aerodynamic efficiency should be of immense value when they can be fully correlated with metabolic studies.

31. (B)
A *sailor* is threatened by a *pirate* as a *plant* is threatened by a *fungus*.

32. (D)
A *sprinter* starts running at the sound of a *gun*. A *fighter* starts fighting at the sound of a *bell*.

33. (A)
A *wrinkle* is a weak *fold*. A *tear* is a weak *cut*.

34. (C)
A *gale* is a strong *wind*. A *passion* is a strong *affection*.

35. (C)
You put a *picture* in a *frame*. You put a *diamond* in a *setting*.

36. (B)
A *train* uses a *whistle* as a *car* uses a *horn*.

37. (C)
A *refugee* looks for a *haven* as an *exile* looks for a *sanctuary*.

38. (D)

When one *loiters,* one stands idly about, unlike *waiting* for somebody. When one *putters,* one moves about aimlessly, unlike when one *works.*

39. (B)

One *prunes* a *shrub* as one *trims hair.*

40. (D)

A *building* has a *façade* as a *character* has a *demeanor.*

Section 2: Mathematics Questions

1. (E)

A number to the n power means that number times itself n times. Thus, $2^3 = 2 \times 2 \times 2 = 8$, and $(2^3)^2 = 8^2 = 64$
Similarly, $3^3 = 27$, and $4^2 = 16$
The sum is $64 + 27 + 16 = 107$

2. (C)

A graph of an equation intersects the x-axis whenever a value of x makes $y = 0$. This occurs when $x = 1$, $x = 2$, and $x = 0$, or 3 points.

3. (D)

The statement "If $a = 0$, then $b = 0$," means that $b = 0$ will occur whenever $a = 0$. The negation of this is to say that $b \neq 0$ while $a = 0$. This is $a = 0$ and $b \neq 0$.

4. (D)

The equations in I have a definite solution, $x = 1$, and substituting $x = 1$ into $2x + y = 7$, gives $y = 5$. Both the equations in II are the same. The solution consists of all the points that satisfy these equations, and there is an infinite set of such points. If the first equation of III is multiplied by 2, the result is $2x + 6y = 4$. The second equation of III is $2x + 6y = 2$. If these equations are equated, the result is $2 = 4$, which is a contradiction, so there is no solution to this set of equations.

5. (D)

$a * b = a - b^2$
Therefore, $5 * 1 = 5 - 1^2 = 4$
$3 * (5 * 1) = 3 * 4 = 3 - 4^2 = -13$
$2 * [3 * (5 * 1)] = 2 * (-13) =$
$2 - (-13)^2 = -167$

6. **(B)**
    If we sketch the triangle, it will help us in doing the problem. We see that the base is 4 units long. The area of a triangle is $\frac{1}{2}$ (base) (height), so $\frac{1}{2}$ (4) (height) = 8, or the height must be 4. This must be 4 units perpendicular to the X-axis, so a possible solution is (0, 4).

7. **(E)**
    The positive integral solutions of $a + b = 21$, with b being an integral multiple of a, are $a = 1$, $b = 20$; $a = 3$, $b = 18$; $a = 7$, $b = 14$.

8. **(B)**
    The absolute value of x, $|x|$, is defined as x if x is positive or equal to 0 and $-x$ if x is negative. Thus, $|x| = x$ if and only if $x \geq 0$.

9. **(C)**
    Let d = diameter of semicircle. Then, since the two equal adjacent sides of the square form a right angle, we have

    $$d^2 + d^2 = 4^2$$
    $$\text{or} \qquad 2d^2 = 16$$
    $$d^2 = 8$$

    The area of the semicircle is $\frac{\pi}{2}\left(\frac{d}{2}\right)^2 = \frac{\pi d^2}{8}$.

    Since $d^2 = 8$, $\frac{\pi d^2}{8} = \pi$.

10. **(A)**
    If the average of three numbers is 14, then the sum of the three numbers is 42. Each number is increased by 2, 5, and 8 respectively, so the new sum is 57. The average of three numbers whose sum is 57 is 19. Therefore, the average is increased by 5. Or, alternatively, the average increase is $\frac{2 + 5 + 8}{3} = \frac{15}{3} = 5$.

11. **(A)**
    $\frac{x}{a} + b = c$. Multiply both sides of the equation by a. Then $x + ba = ca$. Subtract ba from both sides, and the result is $x = ca - ba$.

12. (B)

$2m$ is 20% of p, or $2m = (0.20)p$, so $m = (0.10)p$. $\frac{1}{2}n$ is 45% of p, or $\frac{1}{2}n = (0.45)p$, so $n = (0.90)p$. Therefore, $m + n = (0.10)p + (0.90)p = (1.00)p$ or $m + n = p$. That means that $m + n$ is 100% of p.

13. (D)

The area of the square is Side $\times$ Side, so each side of the square is 8. The area of the triangle is $\frac{1}{2}$ (base) (height) or $\frac{1}{2}$ (EB) (x). From the diagram, EB $= 8 - x$ since AB $= 8$. Therefore, $\frac{1}{2}(8 - x)(x) = 3\frac{1}{2}$ or $8x - x^2 = 7$. Rearranging gives $x^2 - 8x + 7 = 0$ or $(x - 7)(x - 1) = 0$. The solutions to this equation are $x = 7$ or $x = 1$.

14. (A)

If $abc = 1$, this implies that $a \neq 0$, $b \neq 0$ and $c \neq 0$. If $a \neq 0$ then $a^2 \neq 0$ and since $c \neq 0$, a^2c could not be 0. Thus Choice A is correct. Note that since e or d could be 0, the equations in Choices B, C, and D may be true. Since $abc = 1 = acb$, the equation in Choice E is clearly true.

15. (B)

The least common denominator of 2 numbers is the lowest product of all the factors into which the two numbers can be divided.

$24 = 3 \cdot 2 \cdot 2 \cdot 2$
$20 = 2 \cdot 2 \cdot 5$

Thus, $3 \cdot 2 \cdot 2 \cdot 2 \cdot 5 = 120$, into which both 24 and 20 may be divided.

16. (C)

The graph represents all the numbers that are less than or equal to 0. This is written as $x \leq 0$. This is the same as $5x \leq 0$ because it is possible to multiply an inequality on both sides by a positive number without changing the value of the inequality.

17. (E)

The coordinates of point A are $(0, 0)$ or $x = 0$ and $y = 0$. This point does not satisfy the equation $x^2 + y^2 = 4$. The coordinates of B, C, D, and E are $(-2, 0)$, $(0, -2)$, $(2, 0)$, and $(0, 2)$ respectively. All these pairs satisfy the equation.

18. (E)

If $rh = 5r + r^2$, then dividing by r gives $h = 5 + r$. Substituting this value of h into $V = \pi r^2 h$, yields $V = \pi r^2(5 + r)$, or $V = 5\pi r^2 + \pi r^3$.

19. **(C)**
Substituting $p = 2$ and $q = 1$ into
$(p - q)^2 + (p - 2) q + (q - 1) p^8$, gives
$(2 - 1)^2 + (2 - 2) (1) + (1 - 1) 2^8 =$
$1^2 + (0) (1) + (0) 2^8 = 1^2 = 1$.

20. **(E)**
$1 + \dfrac{1}{x - 1} = \dfrac{x}{x - 1}$. 1 cannot be a solution because a 0 in the denominator is not defined. Assume $x \neq 1$ and multiply both sides by $x - 1$ to get $(x - 1) + 1 = x$ or $x = x$. This is an identity in x, so all values (except the 1 that was eliminated) will satisfy this.

21. **(B)**
If n is 4 times a whole number, then $n = 4a$ where a is a whole number. $n = 4a$ is the same as $n = 2b$ where $b = 2a$. Now n is being expressed as a multiple of 2. Any number that is a multiple of 2 is an even number.

22. **(D)**
Call EF, a. Then the length of AD $=$ AF $+$ FE $+$ ED, or AD $= x + a + x$, or AD $= 2x + a$. The area of rectangle ABCD is (AD) (DC) $= (2x + a) (y)$. This area is equal to y, or $(2x + a) (y) = y$. Dividing by y gives us $2x + a = 1$, or $a = 1 - 2x$.

23. **(E)**
Call the identity element e. Then $e * a = a$, or $e + a - 3 = a$, or $e = 3$.

24. **(D)**
If the original equation is put into the form $y = mx + b$, the result is $y = \frac{1}{2}x + 4$, and the slope (m) is $\frac{1}{2}$. A line parallel to this must have the same slope, $\frac{1}{2}$. The family of lines parallel to $y = \frac{1}{2}x + 4$ is $y = \frac{1}{2}x + b$ where b is any constant. For the line to go through the origin $(0, 0)$; then $0 = \frac{1}{2}(0) + b$, or $b = 0$. The equation is $y = \frac{1}{2}x$.

25. **(B)**
If p is divisible by 5 with a remainder of 4, then $p = 5a + 4$ where a is an integer. $2p$ is then $10a + 8$. When $10a + 8$ is divided by 5, you get $2a + 1$ with a remainder of 3.

Section 3: Verbal Questions

1. **(C)**
   Clandestine: secret; *antonym:* open

2. **(A)**
   Neophyte: a beginner; *antonym:* virtuoso

3. **(C)**
   Absolve: to free of guilt; *antonym:* convict

4. **(A)**
   Desultory: aimless, random; *antonym:* permanent

5. **(D)**
   Contumacy: disobedience; *antonym:* willingness

6. **(E)**
   Zest: spirited enjoyment, gusto; *antonym:* distaste

7. **(C)**
   Parsimonious: stingy; *antonym:* extravagant

8. **(A)**
   Itinerant: traveling; *antonym:* steadfast

9. **(E)**
   Decry: to speak against publicly; *antonym:* exalt

10. **(E)**
    Languor: languidness; *antonym:* vivacity

11. **(C)**
    A *desert* will make one *parched*. A *slum* will make one *penurious* (stingy, miserly).

12. **(B)**
    The *gist* (central idea) of a *paragraph* is analagous to the *essence* of the *matter*.

13. **(B)**
    A buoy is a marker placed in a body of water (or ocean) as a warning. A detour is another road used as a main route. Thus, we have the analogy: *buoy : detour :: ocean : road.*

14. (E)
A *motorist* uses the language of *road signs* as communication. A *reader* uses the language of *punctuation* as communication.

15. (B)
A *synonym* is a word that has the *same* meaning as another word. An *antonym* is a word *opposite* in meaning to another word.

16. (B)
The *knee* is a joint in the *leg*. The *wrist* is a joint in the *hand*.

17. (B)
An *acrobat* must be *supple* as a *runner* must have *fleetness*.

18. (A)
A *laugh* is much more intense than a *smile* as a *grumble* is much more intense than an angry frown (*scowl*).

19. (E)
An *anarchy* creates *chaos* as a *government* creates *order*.

20. (D)
A *ceiling* can be held up by a *pillar* as *prices* can be held up by *subsidies*.

21. (E)
See the fourth paragraph: "After the duty has gone into effect and the prices of commodities that can be produced by C and D have risen sufficiently, enterprisers will be able to hire labor at the wages prevailing in A and B and establish industries in C and D."

22. (D)
The enterpriser would have to pay what A and B make, and production would be under more economic disadvantage.

23. (B)
See the last paragraph. The high duties on imported commodities of classes C and D result, in effect, in taxing the workers in A and B.

24. (C)
It can be seen that choice (C) is the most appropriate.

25. **(E)**

The passage describes arguments that show that free trade may be the best solution.

26. **(A)**

It is seen that, as a result, freedom easily can be perverted into *servitude*.

27. **(D)**

The tornado destroyed the buildings so that they were *unrecognizable*.

28. **(C)**

Although a tenet may be *incorrect*, it cannot be considered a *lie*.

29. **(B)**

We *hear* an *earth-shattering explosion*.

30. **(D)**

We *acknowledge* that the administration of President Grant marked a low point (*nadir*) in American government.

31. **(B)**

We take *precautions* by taking measures *in advance*.

32. **(C)**

Community groups have opposed plans to tear down (*raze*) their slums and replace them with modern projects.

33. **(A)**

The suppositions were highly *plausible* (likely, or apparently valid).

34. **(D)**

Accomplishment is thwarted by a *handicap*.

35. **(B)**

Since we are talking about baseball and a baseball player, choice (B) describes the only correct combination of words that fits the sentence.

36. **(D)**

See the first four sentences of the passage.

37. (B)

According to the passage, there are two types of generation: Panspermia and Terrestrial Generation. Panspermia has been invented on account of the widely used doctrine that life can never arise from inanimate matter. A theory that there could be production of animate matter from inanimate matter would be the most effective proof for a theory of terrestrial generation.

38. (C)

Asepsis refers to the control of infection caused by microorganisms. Choice (C) is, therefore, correct.

39. (A)

If life were adapted to terrestrial conditions from the outset, extraterrestrial origins of life would still be possible. Thus, choice (A) is correct. Note that this does not disprove the theories of Arrhenius.

40. (D)

Choices (A), (B), and (C) are clearly incorrect. Genetic competence for survival certainly can be assumed.

Section 5: Mathematics Questions

1. (C)

$$\frac{1}{n} = \frac{p^2 + q}{pq}$$

$$n = \frac{pq}{p^2 + q}$$

2. (A)

Rationalize the denominator $\dfrac{5\sqrt{2}}{\sqrt{5}} \times \dfrac{\sqrt{5}}{\sqrt{5}} = \dfrac{5\sqrt{10}}{5} = \sqrt{10}$

3. (E)

Triangle ABE is a 45-45-90 triangle. AB and AE $= 4$
Since E is a midpoint, AD $= 8$
Area of ABCD $= 32$ sq. in. (8×4)
Area of triangle ABE $= \frac{1}{2}bh = \frac{1}{2}\, 4 \times 4 = 8$
$32 - 8 = 24$ sq. in.

4. **(D)**
   35% plan to work; 100% − 35% = the number who plan to go to college = 65%. 65% of 620 = 620 × .65 = 403

5. **(C)**
   Angle CAE is measured by $\frac{1}{2}$ its intercepted arc ($\overset{\frown}{AC}$)

   Angle B is measured by $\frac{1}{2}$ its intercepted arc ($\overset{\frown}{AC}$)
   Angle B = Angle CAE   Angle B = 36°

6. **(D)**
   $\frac{1}{2}bh = \dfrac{10 \times 5\sqrt{3}}{2} = 25\sqrt{3}$

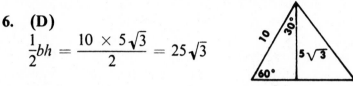

7. **(E)**
   The formula for each set of values is $xy = 48$.
   $24y = 48$
   $y = 2$

8. **(A)**
   Let angle $a = 4x$, angle $b = 5x$, and angle $c = 6x$.

   $4x + 5x + 6x = 180°$
   $15x = 180°$
   $x = 12°$
   $6x = 72°$

9. **(C)**
   In a right triangle, the altitude of the hypotenuse is the mean proportional between the segments of the hypotenuse.

   $\dfrac{AD}{CD} = \dfrac{CD}{DB}$ or $\dfrac{3}{x} = \dfrac{x}{12}$ $x^2 = 36$ and $x = 6$

10. **(B)**
    Let d = the number of dimes and n = the number of nickels.

    $d = 2n + 8$
    $.10d + .05n = 2.55$
    $10d + 5n = 255$ (multiplying by 100)
    $2d + n = 51$ (dividing by 5)
    $2(2n + 8) + n = 51$ (substituting the value of d in terms
    $4n + 16 + n = 51$ of n)
    $5n = 35$
    $n = 7$

11. (C)

Given: distance between A and B = 6 mi.

Then x = number of miles from A, and $6 - x$ = number of miles from B

Cost of cartage from A = .50(x); cost of cartage from B = .75($6 - x$)

$$\ldots .50(x) = .75(6 - x), \text{ or } .50x = 4.5 - .75x$$
$$1.25x = 4.5$$
$$x = 3\tfrac{3}{5} \text{ mi.}$$

12. (E)

Let b = the number of boys and g = the number of girls.

$$.25b + .10g = 12.60$$
$$25b + 10g = 1260 \quad \text{(multiplying by 100 to eliminate decimal points)}$$

① $\qquad 5b + 2g = 252 \quad$ (dividing by 5)

$$20(b - 8) = 2[15\,(g + 8)]$$
$$20b - 160 = 30g + 240$$
$$20b = 30g + 400$$
$$2b = 3g + 40$$
$$b = \frac{3g + 40}{2}$$

$$5\left(\frac{3g + 40}{2}\right) + 2g = 252 \quad \text{(substituting value of } b \text{ in ①)}$$
$$15g + 200 + 4g = 504$$
$$19g = 304$$
$$g = 16$$

13. (C)

$$\text{Average} = \frac{\text{Sum of numbers}}{\text{Number of terms}}$$

$$\frac{3}{5} + \frac{2}{3} + \frac{5}{6} + \frac{1}{2} = \frac{36 + 40 + 50 + 30}{60} = \frac{156}{60}$$

$$\frac{156}{60} \div 4 = \frac{156}{60} \times \frac{1}{4} = \frac{156}{240} = \frac{13}{20}$$

14. (C)

The area of each square is 36 sq. in. $\left(\dfrac{180}{5}\right)$

Each side is, therefore, 6 in. ($\sqrt{36}$)

Since there are 12 sides in the perimeter, $(12 \times 6) = 72$ in.

15. **(D)**

$$
\begin{aligned}
&\quad 7 \text{ hr. } 42 \text{ min.}\\
+&\quad 3 \text{ hr. } 34 \text{ min.}\\
\hline
&10 \text{ hr. } 76 \text{ min.}
\end{aligned}
$$

Since 60 min. = 1 hr., 76 min. = 1 hr. 16 min.
Therefore, the sum is 11 hours 16 minutes

16. **(C)**
Angle ACB and angle DCE are equal because they are vertical angles. Since we now have two pairs of congruent angles, we know that triangle ABC is similar to triangle CDE. Therefore, their corresponding sides form equal ratios.

17. **(C)**

$$\sqrt{\frac{.0016}{.25}} = \frac{\sqrt{.0016}}{\sqrt{.25}} = \frac{.04}{.5} = .08$$

0.8 % of 10 = .008 × 10 = .08

18. **(A)**
The time between 10:50 A.M. and 11:15 A.M. is 25 minutes, or $\frac{5}{12}$ of an hour. The number of miles traveled in this time equals the rate × time = $80 \times \frac{5}{12} = \frac{100}{3} = 33\frac{1}{3}$ miles.

19. **(B)**
Since n is between -1 and 0, $\frac{1}{n}$ will always be less than -1. However, when both of these negative numbers are raised to a positive even power, such as 4, their sign also changes to positive. Thus $\left(\frac{1}{n}\right)^4$ will always be greater than 1, while n^4 will always be between 0 and $+1$.

20. **(C)**

$$
\begin{aligned}
30 \times 1 &= 30\\
50 \times 3 &= 150\\
60 \times 2 &= \underline{120}\\
&\ 300\\
300 \div 6 &= 50
\end{aligned}
$$

21. **(B)**
The area of triangle ABC equals $\frac{1}{2} \times$ base $\times$ height $= \frac{1}{2} \times 6 \times 8 = 24$. Line segments AB and CD can be considered as another base and altitude, respectively, of the same triangle. Thus, the area $= 24 = \frac{1}{2} \times 10 \times$ CD. Solving for CD, we get CD $= \frac{24}{5} = 4\frac{4}{5}$.

22.   (C)

$x^2 - 4x = -4$
$x^2 - 4x + 4 = 0$
$(x - 2)(x - 2) = 0$
$x = 2$

The equation for y is exactly the same as that for x except that every term is multiplied by 3. Thus, y is also equal to 2.

23.   (B)

$\sqrt{x} = 1.6$
Thus, $x = (1.6)^2 = 2.56$
$\dfrac{2^3}{3} = \dfrac{8}{3} = 2\dfrac{2}{3}$

$2\dfrac{2}{3}$ is approximately equal to 2.67

24.   (A)

The area of a parallelogram equals its base × height. Since the area is given as 30 and the base as 10, the height, or AE, equals 3. AE is also the side opposite the 30° angle of right triangle ADE. Thus the hypotenuse AD equals 2 × 3 = 6.

25.   (B)

Since consecutive angles in a parallelogram are supplementary (add up to 180°), <DCB = 150°. Also, <DCB = <DAB since any two opposite angles of a parallelogram are congruent. Thus, <DAB + <DCB = 150° × 2 = 300°.

26.   (A)

First, change all three fractions into improper fractions:

$1\dfrac{7}{24} + \dfrac{7}{12} + 2\dfrac{3}{8} = \dfrac{31}{24} + \dfrac{7}{12} + \dfrac{19}{8}$

Since the lowest common denominator of all three is 24, multiply $\dfrac{7}{12}$ by $\dfrac{2}{2}$ and $\dfrac{19}{8}$ by $\dfrac{3}{3}$:

$= \dfrac{31}{24} + \dfrac{14}{24} + \dfrac{57}{24}$

Finally, add up all the numbers:

$= \dfrac{102}{24} = \dfrac{17}{4} = 4\dfrac{1}{4}$

27.   (B)

The total amount of rice produced equals:

$(227 + 185 + 141 + 184) \times 1000 = 737 \times 1000 = 737{,}000$

28.   (B)

The state with the greatest total production is State B, which produced 688,000 tons of produce. The difference between the corn and cotton production = 291,000 − 212,000 = 79,000.

29. (A)
The corn production of State A is 118,000 tons. The rice production of State C is 141,000 tons. Thus, their difference is $141,000 - 118,000 = 23,000$.

30. (C)
The state with the greatest corn and rice production is State D, with a combined production total of $262,000 + 184,000 = 446,000$ tons. State D's cotton production is 214,000 tons.

31. (B)
The lowest possible value of p, which will be negative, will exist when q^2 is at a minimum. In this case, the minimum value of q^2 is 0. Thus, $p^2 = 100$ and $p = -10$. (Lowest value of p.)

32. (A)
$$[(\sqrt{2} + 6) \div (3 - 1)] + 4 =$$
$$[(\sqrt{2} + 6) \div 2] + 4 =$$
$$\frac{\sqrt{2}}{2} + 3 + 4 = \frac{\sqrt{2}}{2} + 7$$
$$\sqrt{2} + [(6 \div 3) - 1 + 4] =$$
$$\sqrt{2} + [2 + 3] = \sqrt{2} + 5$$

33. (B)
Since both quantities have a common factor of x, x can be eliminated from both sides. This leaves us with $\frac{y}{z}$ on one side and $\frac{z}{y}$ on the other. Since $z > y$, $\frac{y}{z}$ will always be less than 1, while $\frac{z}{y}$ will always be greater than 1. Thus, $\frac{z}{y} > \frac{y}{z}$.

34. (C)
Angles ACB and ADB are right angles since they are both inscribed in semicircles. Therefore, angles 1 and 2 are complementary, as are angles 3 and 4. Their sums are equal to 90° each, despite the difference in the lengths of the sides of the two triangles.

35. (A)
Subtract x^2 from both columns. We are left with y^2 for Column A and $-y^2$ for Column B. Since $y \neq 0$, and $y^2 > 0$, $y^2 > -y^2$.

Section 6: Verbal Questions

1. **(A)**
   Abeyance: temporary suspension; *antonym:* revival

2. **(E)**
   Jocose: humorous; *antonym:* serious

3. **(A)**
   Erudite: scholarly; *antonym:* unlearned

4. **(B)**
   Aversion: opposition; *antonym:* attraction

5. **(C)**
   Chaste: pure; *antonym:* licentious, morally unrestrained

6. **(C)**
   Fulsome: offensive; *antonym:* pleasing

7. **(E)**
   Acerbity: sharpness; *antonym:* mildness

8. **(C)**
   Igneous: pertaining to or produced by fire; *antonym:* sedimentary

9. **(E)**
   Sporadic: infrequent; *antonym:* frequent

10. **(E)**
    Niggardly: stingy; *antonym:* giving

11. **(A)**
    Cacophony: harsh sound; *antonym:* harmony

12. **(D)**
    Insipid: tasteless, dull; *antonym:* witty

13. **(B)**
    Bellicose: warlike; *antonym:* peaceful

14. **(B)**
    Chagrin: embarrassment; *antonym:* pleasure

15. **(C)**
    Braggadocio: a braggart; *antonym:* modesty

16. (C)

A *molecule* is a part of the whole *substance*.

17. (E)

Only choice (E) gives us the correct choice of words consistent with the first and second sentences.

18. (D)

The combination of words *circumlocution* and *disciplined,* when inserted in the blanks, creates meaningful sentences consistent with the rest of the passage.

19. (A)

Consummate is a possible choice. None of the other choices are appropriate.

20. (A)

Choice (A) gives the only combination of appropriate words.

21. (B)

It can be seen that the author is trying to teach or instruct, especially concerning moral issues. Thus, the tone of the paragraph is *didactic*.

22. (E)

See the sentence "The businessmen, who take up the local traffic in merchandising, litigation, church enterprise, and the like, commonly begin with some share in real estate speculation."

23. (E)

The comparison is with the patriotism of believers in dollar diplomacy.

24. (C)

See the sentences "Pecuniary interest in local land values involves an interest in the continued growth of the town. Hence any creditable misrepresentation. . . ."

25. (C)

See the sentence "This pretense of public spirit is so consistently maintained that most of these men come presently to believe in their own professions on that head."

26. (A)

The author is against the commercial motives of influential society, and it is implied that the author's view of patriotism is that it should be unbiased.

27. **(B)**

Choice (B) is most appropriate. See, for example, the sentences "It is the duty of governments, and of individuals, to form the truest opinions they can. . . ." and "If we were never to act on our opinions, because those opinions may be wrong, we should leave all our interests uncared for, and all our duties unperformed."

28. **(C)**

It can be seen that choice (C) describes the essence of the first sentence.

29. **(C)**

The author makes an analogy to other situations.

30. **(B)**

See the sentence "If we were never to act on our opinions, because those opinions may be wrong, we should leave all our interests uncared for, and all our duties unperformed."

31. **(E)**

The point of greatest intensity and turning point in a *battle* is the *climax*. The point of greatest intensity and turning point in a *disease* is a *crisis*.

32. **(A)**

Failure is due to apprehensiveness (*timorousness*) as wiseness (*sagacity*) is due to *experience*.

33. **(A)**

One *affirms* a *report* as one *acknowledges* a *rumor*.

34. **(C)**

Lukewarm (*tepid*) : scorching (*torrid*) : : *cool* : *frigid*.

35. **(D)**

Millenium (1000) : *century* (100) : : *decade* (10) : year (1).

36. **(A)**

Gills are associated with *water* as *lungs* are associated with *air*.

37. **(C)**

Father : *daughter* : : *uncle* : *niece* (daughter of uncle).

38. **(A)**

A *rib* supports the *umbrella* as a *rafter* supports a *roof*.

39. (D)

Meridian (observer's zenith) : *setting* (lowest point at the descent of the sun) : : *culminate* (to reach the highest point) : *terminate* (end, lowest point).

40. (E)

A *harbinger* is a plant that blooms in early spring and is a signal of the beginning of *spring*. *Dawn* is a signal of the beginning of *day*.

41. (B)

It is evident from the context that Shigella is a bacterium.

42. (C)

The passage does not give any supporting evidence for choices (A), (B), or (D). There is mention that 24 hours after feeding, the typical growth of Shigella marking the footprints of the ants was observed.

43. (C)

Choice (C) is the only correct possibility since all the experimentation directly addresses itself to this question.

44. (C)

There is no supporting evidence for choices (A), (B), or (D). The passage does discuss the length of time that ants could carry Shigella.

45. (C)

Choice (C) would be the most probable reason. The other choices are possible but not probable.

part II

ABOUT THE SUBTESTS
OF THE SAT

Read this part to get an idea of the various question types and how best to answer them.

ABOUT ANTONYM TESTS

Antonym questions often appear on scholastic aptitude examinations because they are an excellent means of testing vocabulary skills. In antonym questions, you must choose a word that has the opposite or nearly the opposite meaning of a given word.

Study the Following Sample

Directions: The following question consists of a word printed in capital letters followed by five words lettered (A) through (E). Choose the word that has most nearly the OPPOSITE meaning from the word in capital letters. Then mark the appropriate space in the answer column.

MUNDANE
    (A) real
    (B) proprietary
    (C) languorous
    (D) spiritual
    (E) torpid

                                           A B C D E

Answer: (D) spiritual is the correct answer, so you would mark space D in the answer column.

                                         A B C D E

Explanation: *mundane* is a favorite word on scholastic aptitude and vocabulary tests. It comes from the Latin *mundus*, meaning *the world*. *Mundane* means *worldly* or *earthly*. At a glance, you can see that *spiritual* is the only antonym. Choice (A), *real* (actual, true), has little relationship to the general, broad meaning contained in *mundane* and does not even qualify as a suitable synonym. Choice (B), *proprietary*, means *of or pertaining to a proprietor, property, or ownership*. Choice (C), *languorous* (sluggish, dull), has no connection with *mundane* or *worldly*. Choice (E), *torpid* (inert, dull, apathetic, numb), must also be discarded.

Most of the words you will encounter on the SAT can be found in the VOCABULARY REVIEW LIST beginning on page 331. It may be a good idea to learn 50 of these words a day. It is also useful to learn the COMMON PREFIXES, SUFFIXES, AND ROOTS beginning on Page 320.

ABOUT ANALOGY TESTS

The main purpose of verbal analogy tests is to judge your ability to *reason*. As a result, they do not necessarily include difficult or tricky vocabulary words. They concentrate, instead, on *relationships*—the relationship of one word to another or of one idea to another.

On exams, analogy questions are designed so that either one or two words are missing, and you are given choices from which you must complete the analogy. Solving an analogy problem involves three skills. First, you have to understand the meaning of the question words. Second, you have to figure out the relationship between the question words. Third, and most difficult, you have to be able to complete the analogy by choosing two words that have the same relationship to one another as the question words have to each other.

Analogies are often written in an abbreviated form, using symbols such as those in a mathematical ratio. In an analogy, a colon (:) stands for the words "is to." Two colons (::) stand for the words "in the same way as." Look at this analogy.

THIEF : PRISON :: juvenile delinquent : reformatory

With the symbols written out, the analogy reads, *A thief is to a prison in the same way as a juvenile delinquent is to a reformatory.* And the meaning is that a thief is punished by being sent to prison in the same way as a juvenile delinquent is punished by being sent to a reformatory. The key strategy is to put the analogy in the form of a sentence relating to the words: a *thief* is sent to *prison* as a *juvenile delinquent* is sent to a *reformatory*.

For the most part, the analogies that appear on exams can be classified into specific categories. For example, some analogies compare parts of speech. Others compare family relationships. Still others compare time elements. Some common types of analogies are listed below with specific examples that fall within each type. You will find it helpful to study this list and the relationships shown in the examples. But don't try to memorize these categories or to classify the analogies you are given on the exam. Instead, reason out the relationships shown in the first pair of analogies in each exam question, and then carefully choose a second pair that has a corresponding relationship.

Typical Kinds of Analogies on the SAT

A part is compared to a whole
Example—LEG : BODY :: wheel : car
        (part) (whole)   (part) (whole)

A cause is compared to its effect
Example—CLOUD : RAIN :: sun : heat
        (cause)   (effect)   (cause) (effect)

The general is compared to the specific
Example—PERSON : BOY :: vehicle : bus
(general)   (specific)   (general) (specific)

A word is compared to a synonym of itself
Example—VACUOUS : EMPTY :: seemly : fit
(word)   (synonym)   (word) (synonym)

A word is compared to an antonym of itself
Example—SLAVE : FREEMAN :: desolate : joyous
(word)   (antonym)   (word) (antonym)

A word is compared to a definition of itself
Example—ASSEVERATE : AFFIRM :: segregate : separate
(word)   (definition)   (word) (definition)

A male is compared to a female
Example—COLT : FILLY :: buck : doe
(male)   (female)   (male) (female)

An object is compared to the material of which it is made
Example—COAT : WOOL :: dress : cotton
(object)   (material)   (object) (material)

One element of time is compared to another element of time
Example—DAY : NIGHT :: sunrise : sunset
(time   (time   (time   (time
element)   element)   element)   element)

A lesser degree is compared to a greater degree
Example—HAPPY : ECSTATIC :: warm : hot
(lesser   (greater   (lesser   (greater
degree)   degree)   degree)   degree)

A user is compared to his tool
Example—FARMER : HOE :: dentist : drill
(user)   (tool)   (user)   (tool)

A creator is compared to a creation
Example—ARTIST : PICTURE :: poet : poem
(creator)   (creation)   (creator) (creation)

A broad category is compared to a narrower category
Example—RODENT : SQUIRREL :: fish : flounder
(broad   (narrower   (broad   (narrower
category)   category)   category)   category)

A person is compared to a characteristic
Example—GIANT : BIGNESS : : baby : helplessness
      (person) (characteristic) (person) (characteristic)

A person is compared to his profession
Example—TEACHER : EDUCATION : : doctor : medicine
      (person)   (profession)   (person) (profession)

An instrument is compared to a function it performs
Example—CAMERA : PHOTOGRAPHY : :
      (instrument)   (function)
      yardstick : measurement
      (instrument)   (function)

The plural is compared to the singular
Example— WE : I : : they : he
      (plural) (singular) (plural) (singular)

A symbol is compared to an institution
Example—FLAG : GOVERNMENT : : cross ·: Christianity
      (symbol)   (institution)   (symbol) (institution)

A reward is compared to an action
Example—MEDAL : BRAVERY : : trophy : championship
      (reward)   (action)   (reward)   (action)

An object is compared to an obstacle that hinders it
Example—AIRPLANE : FOG : : car : rut
      (object)   (obstacle) (object) (obstacle)

Something is compared to a need that it satisfies
Example—WATER : THIRST : : food : hunger
      (thing)   (need)   (thing)   (need)

A family relationship is compared to a similar family relationship
Example—FATHER : SON : : uncle : nephew
      (family relationship)   (family relationship)

Something is compared to its natural medium
Example—SHIP : WATER : : airplane : air
      (thing) (natural   (thing) (natural
            medium)   medium)

Something is compared to something else that can operate it
Example—DOOR : KEY : : safe : combination

A virtue is compared to a failing
Example—FORTITUDE : COWARDICE : :
            (virtue)   (failing)
        honesty : dishonesty
        (virtue)   (failing)

An element is compared to an extreme of itself
Example—WIND : TORNADO : : water : flood
        (element)   (extreme¹   (element) (extreme)

Do's and Don'ts for Answering Analogy Tests

DO be sure you understand what an analogy is before you enter the exam. Every analogy expresses a relationship between two things. It is this relationship that you must figure out as you look for the correct fill-in to complete the analogy.

DO follow these principles in answering verbal analogy questions: First, try to understand the relationship expressed in the pair of question words. Next, look for a pair of answer words that *best* expresses a similar relationship in terms of meaning, order, or function.

DO be familiar with the symbols and forms of analogy questions. Sometimes analogies are completely written out in this way—*BLUE is to SKY in the same way as green is to grass.* More often, colons (:) are used as symbols to replace words in analogy questions in this way—*BLUE : SKY : : green : grass.*

DO remember that the order of the answer words must be the same as the order of the question words. For example, the analogy *INAUGURATION : PRESIDENT : : ordination : priest* is ·correct. But *INAUGURATION : PRESIDENT : : priest : ordination* is incorrect because the order in the second pair of words is the reverse of the order in the first pair of words.

DO check to see that the parts of speech used in the two sections of an analogy are consistent and follow in the same sequence. For example, if the first pair of words contains a noun and an adjective in that order, the second pair of words should contain a noun and an adjective in that order. Thus, *GOD : GOOD : : devil : bad* is correct. But *GOD : GOOD : : devil : badly* is incorrect.

DON'T expect the second pair of words in an analogy always to be of the same class, type, or species as the first pair of words. For example, in the analogy *PUPPY : DOG :: sapling : tree,* the first pair of words refers to an animal and the second pair refers to a plant. But the *relationship* between the words in both pairs is the same—a puppy is a young dog in the same way as a sapling is a young tree.

DON'T be fooled by a common tester's trick of reversing word sequence in answer choices. The answer words *must* follow the same order as the question words. Thus *TRAIN : TRACK :: automobile : highway* is a correct analogy. But *TRAIN : TRACK :: highway : automobile* is incorrect.

DON'T waste time pondering each of the answer choices in any analogy. Scan the pair of words given as answer choices, and then choose the pair that seems *best* to you. If you cannot answer a question, leave it and go on to the next question. Come back to the more difficult questions after you have finished the easier ones.

Study the Following Sample

Directions: In the following question, choose the pair of words that best completes the analogy. Then mark the appropriate space in the answer column.

TRAIN : WHISTLE : :
    (A)   air raid : siren
    (B)   swimmer : raft
    (C)   car : horn
    (D)   singer : song
    (E)   airplane : propeller

A B C D E

Answer: (C) car : horn. The correct answer is car : horn, so you would mark space C in the answer column.

A B C D E

Explanation: A train uses its whistle for warning purposes just as a car uses its horn as a warning. None of the other choices suits the analogy in the same way. Choices (B) *swimmer : raft,* (D) *singer : song,* and (E) *airplane : propeller* can quickly be ruled out. Choice (A) *air raid : siren* might seem like a possibility at first glance. But it is incorrect because an air raid is an event, not an object or concrete thing the way a train or car is. The only possible answer, then, is choice (C).

ABOUT READING COMPREHENSION TESTS

Reading comprehension tests are becoming ever more important in all kinds of examinations. Their purpose is to test your ability to read and understand passages that are typical of the kinds of material you would read at your level of education. The questions on these exams test seven major skills. These are the ability to (1) find errors in logic, (2) draw conclusions from information given, (3) develop generalizations, (4) search out hidden meanings, (5) form value judgments, (6) detect bias in writing, and (7) think critically.

The reading materials given and the types of questions asked throughout the examination vary in difficulty. The easiest kind of question simply tests your understanding of what you have read by asking you to list facts or explain the meaning of words.

At the next stage of difficulty, the questions call for you to interpret materials by giving the central thought of the passage or noting contradictions.

The third stage of difficulty consists of questions in which you must apply principles or opinions expressed in the reading passage to other situations.

The final and most difficult kind of question asks you to evaluate what you have read and to agree or differ with the point of view of the author.

Because all these levels of questions appear on the reading sections of the examination, your study tests include many questions of each type.

Understanding Passages

In your high school studies, you have learned many things about reading for comprehension. To help you review what you know, here is a summary of the important features of written passages and some suggestions for approaching passages critically.

Any written passage contains two main elements: main ideas and supporting details. A main idea is the subject of a passage—what the passage is about. Details support, expand, or limit the main idea.

The placement of main ideas and details in a passage is important. In fact, the placement of these elements often makes the difference between an interesting, effective passage and a dull, unimaginative one.

Sometimes the writer states his main idea first and then goes on to support it with details; sometimes he presents a series of details and concludes with a main summarizing statement. In still other cases, the main idea is stated somewhere in the middle of the passage. In others, the main idea may not be stated at all, and the reader will have to infer it.

The design the writer uses depends on his purpose and on the effect he wants his words to have. As a reader, it is important for you to understand the main idea, whether stated or implied.

It is also important for you to understand the writer's vocabulary. In your reading, you may encounter words with which you are not familiar. For example, you may read a sentence such as this: "At first, Muller refused to accept the new interpretation of events, but later he succumbed to the scholars' opposing arguments and wrote in support of them." The word *succumbed* means "gave in" or "yielded." You can readily determine its meaning by looking for clues or hints in the context—that is, in the words and phrases surrounding the unfamiliar word. One context clue in the example above is the word *but*, which signals a contrast between the unfamiliar word *succumbed* and a phrase you do know—*refused to accept*. Another context clue is the supporting detail—"and wrote in support of them"—which follows the word *succumbed*. These modifying words, together with the signal *but*, help you figure out the meaning of *succumbed*.

Writers often provide other kinds of context clues. One kind involves the use of examples. Notice how examples are used to help you understand the meaning of *artifact* in the following sentence: "Next to the bones of animals were artifacts such as arrowheads, spears, pottery, and tools." Artifacts are man-made objects, as you can infer from the sentence.

Another important context clue is restatement—repetition of the meaning of the unfamiliar words in other words. This technique is used to help you understand the meaning of *hyperbole* in the following passage:

> The story was filled with many metaphors and similes. It also contained several hyperboles, or exaggerations, such as "He was centuries old" and "He ran with the speed of lightning."

As you understand the writer's meaning, it will often become clear to you that he is expressing a particular opinion or arguing for a certain point of view. Note the writer's argument. Is it sound? Do his statements support his opinion or point of view?

Sometimes you will have to go one step further and tell, on the basis of the author's stated opinions, how he would probably feel about a situation other than the one he writes about. Imagine, for example, that a writer argues that the United States should increasingly withdraw from international affairs, devoting its time and resources to solving domestic problems. How would this writer probably feel if the United States began arming a South American country and supplying it with troops to protect itself against a neighboring country? He would probably oppose this action.

As you read, try to keep in mind more than just the words on the page. Look for the writer's point of view, his arguments, and the implications in the passage. Before you begin taking the Reading Comprehension Tests, you can get additional hints in the Do's and Don'ts for Answering Reading Comprehension Tests.

Developing Reading Speed

In addition to understanding passages thoroughly, it is important for you to be able to read with reasonable speed and efficiency. The SAT, as you know, is a timed test, so it is to your advantage to be able to do the work well in as short a time as possible.

Many people are poor readers. They look at each word on each line and say it to themselves as they cover the reading material. Good readers do not look at each word. They take in phrases and ideas as their eyes skim the lines. They do not spend time vocalizing, or saying words to themselves, as they go.

You can improve your reading speed by being aware of your reading habits and consciously improving them. You can practice every day as you read magazines, newspapers, or fiction.

For practice, find a newspaper story with narrow columns. Your first goal will be to read each line in two "fixations" of your eyes. That is, you will try to stop your eyes just *twice* on each line and make your eyes pick up the rest of the line without looking directly at all the words. To do this, use your hand or a pencil as a marker underneath the words you are reading. First move it to a spot about one-fourth of the way along the first line. That will be the point of your first fixation. Then move it to a spot about three-fourths of the way along. That will be the point of your second fixation. Continue in the same way with each line, pushing yourself to keep up a steady speed. Do not allow yourself to "back up" to pick up words you think you missed. Concentrate on moving forward, taking in ideas rather than words.

At first, you may feel that you are missing a lot of material. With practice, however, you will probably find not only your speed improving but your comprehension, too.

Next try to take in each line of a newspaper column with just *one* fixation. Again, use your hand or a pencil underneath each line and concentrate on moving forward steadily. Continue practicing whenever you read.

Your reading speed depends, of course, on the kind of material you are reading. You can probably cover newspaper stories and light fiction very quickly. Science or history textbooks, on the other hand, require slower speed and more careful attention, since they are often packed with names, terms, dates, and other details that you must learn.

You will find reading materials of many kinds on the different parts of the SAT. Read everything as quickly as you can with understanding. Answer the questions carefully, referring back to the passages when necessary.

Do's and Don'ts for Answering Reading Comprehension Tests

DO follow these three steps in beginning a reading comprehension test: *First*, scan the passage quickly to get the general idea. *Second*, read the passage carefully and critically, *underlining leading phrases and ideas*. *Third*, read each question carefully, then look for the answer in the text, if you cannot answer the question directly.

DO be sure to answer the questions only on the basis of the information given to you in the passage and not from outside information you may happen to know.

DO notice whether a question refers to a specific line, sentence, or quotation from the reading passage. The answer to such a question is almost certain to be found in or near this reference in the passage.

DO be suspicious of words such as *never, always, wholly, forever* in the answer choices. Usually, answers that use such categorical terms are incorrect.

DO watch out for the too-easy answer. Be especially on your guard when the question seems to follow word for word the reference in the text.

DO leave the more difficult questions for last. Try to answer the easier ones first so that you have time to spend thinking about the harder ones.

DON'T expect the answers to follow the order of the text. In most cases, you have to skip from one part of the passage to another to find an answer.

DON'T look in just one sentence or paragraph for an answer. Often the thread of an answer flows through the whole passage.

DON'T give your opinion in an answer unless specifically asked to do so. If a question asks you to choose the writer's opinion from a list of choices, make sure it is his opinion.

DON'T be disturbed if none of the passages deals with your subject field or areas of interest. Even if you have no familiarity with the subject matter in a passage, you should be able to read through it and work out the answers.

DON'T waste time by worrying about sections or questions you do not understand. Just work as quickly and methodically as you can.

Study the Following Sample

Directions: Read the following passage and answer the question that comes after it. Choose the *best* answer. Then mark the appropriate space in the answer column.

It is pitifully easy to prove our rules of grammar arbitrary, unintelligent, and inconsistent. One mistake or change gets by, another gets stopped. The adjective *like* may freely become a preposition; the adjective *near* is admitted with some reluctance to the same class; but the adjective *worth* must remain an adjective though its use is plainly prepositional. The phrase *already* may be written as one word, but not the phrase *all right*. Scores of verbs, such as *write, incline, begin, end*—the list is endless—may be either transitive or intransitive, but not *lay* or *set*. We may *lay a floor* but not *lay down, set the table* but not *just set*. We may use what was originally a past tense as a past participle when we say "I have fought," but we must not say "I have fell." Why not?

The best title for this selection is:
(A)   Poor Grammar
(B)   The Meaning of Words
(C)   Idioms
(D)   Prepositions
(E)   Adjectives

A B C D E

Answer: (C) Idioms. The correct answer is (C), so you would mark space (C) in the answer column.

A B C D E

Explanation: In general, title selection is based upon the broadest interpretation of the passage as a whole. Do not be misled by a title that characterizes *part* of the passage but does not encompass the whole.

ABOUT SENTENCE COMPLETION TESTS

Sentence completion questions are probably the best test of your ability to understand and use words. In them, you are tested on your understanding of words in sentences and paragraphs. Because you are expected to be able to reason out the meaning of words in context, many of the words used in sentence completion tests are more difficult than the test words used in antonym tests.

Sentence completion questions consist of a sentence in which one word or two words are missing. It is your job to fill in the missing words from among a number of choices given. To do so, you have to read and understand the section of the sentence given and then choose the word or words that best complete the thought expressed in the sentence. The answer you choose must be idiomatically suited to the rest of the sentence. It also must be grammatically correct and in keeping with the mood of the sentence.

Sentences in which two words are missing are more difficult to answer than those in which only one word is missing. Because most verbal ability exams include both types of questions, the practice tests in this book also include both types. They are designed to familiarize you with how to answer sentence completion tests and to train you to meet successfully even the most challenging questions.

Key Words in Sentence Completion Questions

It is very important to watch for *key words* in the sentence completion questions. Here are some examples of typical SAT sentence completion questions which you can answer rapidly, once you are aware of these key words.

1. It is important that you envision the correct approach to the problem, as that will _____ you to solve the problem correctly.
    (A) entice
    (B) enable
    (C) convince
    (D) believe
    (E) make

The *key word* is "as" because this word links the two ideas—"that you envision the correct approach to the problem" and "that will _____ you to solve the problem correctly." The first idea *implies* the second idea (because of the word "as.") It is then obvious that *enable* is the missing word. Therefore Choice B is correct.

2. Let us not _____ the students as being childish, even though they are very _____ in their behavior.
    (A) classify—compulsive
    (B) assess—calm
    (C) dedicate—presumptuous
    (D) categorize—systematic
    (E) discuss—simple

The *key words* are "even though" and "as being." The words "as being" refer to some type of *classification*. The words "even though" represent a contrast to the first idea, "Let us not (classify) the students as being childish." Therefore, let's look for something that contrasts with or contradicts the students *not* being childish. This would be the student's *compulsive* behavior. Thus, the correct choices are *classify* and *compulsive*. Therefore, Choice A is correct.

3. The government is trying to _____ with the energy crisis, but it is going to be quite some time before real _____ is made.
    (A)   deal—effort
    (B)   cease—energy
    (C)   coordinate—efforts
    (D)   cope—progress
    (E)   contend—acknowledgement

Here the *key words* are "trying" and "but." The word "but" shows that something will happen which is contrary to the first idea. The words "cope" and "progress" are the best choices. Thus Choice D is correct.

4. Even a _____ pianist has many hours of practicing to do in order to perform well.
    (A)   clever
    (B)   poor
    (C)   knowledgeable
    (D)   tired
    (E)   talented

The *key word* is "Even." The word "Even" is introducing something that you may not usually think is correct. Normally, one might think that a "talented" pianist is so good that he or she doesn't have to practice much to perform well. So the word "Even" is essentially telling you that that is not altogether true. "Even a talented pianist has many hours of practicing to do to perform well." is like saying "You might not think that a talented pianist must practice many hours but he or she really does have to." Thus Choice E is correct.

Notice that it is not always necessary to completely analyze every choice. If you get the jist of the sentence completion and see the *key words*, you may immediately spot the correct word or word set, without looking closely at every other choice.

Do's and Don'ts for Answering Sentence Completion Tests

DO consider three things when choosing a fill-in for a sentence completion question: *First*, the answer you choose must make sense in the sentence. *Second*, the answer must help carry out the meaning of the sentence. *Third*, the answer must be idiomatic and grammatically correct.

DO be especially careful of sentences that call for conjunctions in the answer. The conjunction must be just the right one to connect the various elements of the sentence.

DO follow this rule when answering two-blank questions: Try inserting both words of your answer choice into the sentence at the same time. Usually, one word in each pair of possible answers fits the sentence, so you gain nothing from trying one word at a time. It is up to you to find the *pair* of words best suited to the sentence.

DO be alert for paired words that cancel each other in meaning or content. Such words can be discarded at once from among the choices given.

DO make sure that the words you choose to fill a two-blank sentence appear in the same order that the blank spaces occur in the sentence. If the order of the words is wrong, that choice is incorrect in the sentence.

DO choose words that fit the tone or style of the sentence.

DON'T skip parts of the sentence or group of sentences that make up a sentence completion question. Sometimes there are three or four sentences, or even a paragraph, included in a single sentence completion question. Some of these sentences may have no blanks. But they have an important purpose and must be read carefully to get the exact meaning and purpose of the question. You will have difficulty choosing the correct answer unless you read all the sentences involved in the question.

DON'T—in answering two-blank questions—choose answers in which only one of the words really fits the sentence. Both words in an answer pair should be meaningful within the sentence.

DON'T use up all your time on two-blank questions. The one-blank questions are usually easier to answer. When possible, answer these questions first and then go on to the two-blank questions.

DON'T ponder each answer choice. Read the sentence carefully, then scan through the possible answers. Choose the answer that *best* completes the sentence. If you cannot decide on an answer, go on to the next question and come back to the harder questions later.

Study the Following Samples

Directions: The following question consists of a sentence in which one word is missing. Beneath the sentence are five words lettered (A) through (E). Choose the word that *best* completes the sentence. Then mark the appropriate space in the answer column.

A strike, like a war, should be resorted to only when less _____ measures have failed.

(A) drastic
(B) important
(C) derogatory
(D) objective
(E) eventful

A B C D E

Answer: (A) drastic. Drastic is the correct answer, so you would mark space A in the answer column.

A B C D E

Explanation: This question tests your ability to distinguish between words in order to choose the very best word for the sentence. Choice (B), *important*, and choice (E), *eventful*, might have been used. But on careful examination you can see that *drastic* (extreme in effect) is most suitable. Choice (C), *derogatory*, and choice (D), *objective*, have little meaning within the sentence.

Directions: The following question consists of a sentence in which two words are missing. Beneath the sentence are five pairs of words lettered (A) through (E). Choose the pair of words that *best* completes the sentence. Then mark the appropriate space in the answer column.

Hannibal's efforts came to _____ when he was defeated by Scipio, principally because he was too hot-headed to agree with those who counseled _____ while he hastened to engage in battle.

(A) wisdom-defeat
(B) victory-speed
(C) discretion-nothing
(D) naught-circumspection
(E) fiasco-prudence

A B C D E

Answer: (D) naught-circumspection. Naught-circumspection is the correct answer, so you would mark space D in the answer column.

A B C D E

Explanation: *Naught* means *nothing* or *failure. Circumspection* means *caution, prudence,* or *wariness.* This combination of words best suits the meaning of the sentence. Choice (A), *wisdom—defeat,* and choice

(C), *discretion—nothing,* invert the order of words and, therefore, must be discarded immediately. Choice (B), *victory—speed,* is incorrect because the word *victory* makes no sense in the sentence. Choice (E), *fiasco—prudence,* suits the theme of the sentence, but must be discarded because the word *fiasco* is grammatically incorrect following the words "came to." Had the sentence read "Hannibal's efforts resulted in a _____," this choice would have been an acceptable one.

ABOUT THE REGULAR MATHEMATICS TESTS

Math questions appear on almost all aptitude and general and mental abilities tests. They are designed to test not only your mathematical skills but also your ability to think quickly and to grasp the meaning of a problem. Some of the problems on math tests involve only arithmetic. Some seem deceptively easy at first glance. Don't be fooled. Many of the "easy" problems turn out to be far more complex than they appear.

On the examination, you will probably find it helpful to work out your own solutions to each math problem *first,* before you look at the answer choices given. The answer choices may confuse you unless you've arrived at a solution on your own.

To solve problems at the Scholastic Aptitude Test level, you should know the following numerical information. Be sure to memorize this information if you have not already done so.

Square root of 2 = 1.414
Square root of 3 = 1.732
π (Pi)   = 3.14
In a 30–60–90 triangle, the ratio of sides is $1 : \sqrt{3} : 2$
In a 45–45–90 triangle, the ratio of sides is $1 : 1 : \sqrt{2}$

Study the Following Sample

Directions: The following question is followed by five possible answers lettered (A) through (E). Choose the correct answer. Then mark the appropriate space in the answer column.

What is the cost of 4 pounds of meat at $.75 a pound?

    (A) $1.95
    (B) $3.00
    (C) $3.25
    (D) $3.50
    (E)   none of these

A B C D E

Answer: (B) $3.00. The correct answer is $3.00, so you would mark space B in the answer column.

A B C D E

Solution: $.75
            $\times$ 4
            ———
            $3.00

Do's and Don'ts for Answering Mathematics Tests

DO take an entire practice exam before turning to the correct answers at the end of the exam. You will learn more by actually working through each problem yourself.

DO study the explanations given with each answer in the practice tests. These explanations are carefully designed so that you can follow the solutions step-by-step and repeat them on your own in reviewing.

DO review, as often as possible, problems that you missed or that you found especially difficult. In math, perhaps more than any other subject, practice is essential to improving your skill.

DON'T just guess at answers. Here, as in other subjects, you are penalized for wrong answers. Work out your answers before choosing the one you consider best.

DON'T forget details. Sometimes a key piece of information is just mentioned briefly in a math problem. Read the questions carefully, and try to figure out why each piece of information is given.

DON'T panic if you cannot answer a question. Go on to the next question, and come back to the more difficult one later if you have time.

FOR MATH DIAGNOSIS, MATH REVIEW, AND SPECIAL MATH STRATEGIES AND SHORTCUTS, REFER TO PARTS IV, V, AND VI OF THIS BOOK.

ABOUT QUANTITATIVE COMPARISON TESTS

Quantitative comparison tests are designed to measure the candidate's ability to understand mathematical principles. In a quantitative comparison question, the candidate is asked to study two quantities and tell whether one is larger than the other, whether they are equal, or whether it is impossible to tell how they relate from the information given.

To give you additional practice, this book contains eighty extra quantitative comparison questions. Solutions as well as answers are given at the end of the eighty questions.

Study the Following Sample

Directions: This section requires you to compare two quantities—the quantity in Column A and the quantity in Column B. After you have compared the two quantities, select
   (A) if the quantity in Column A is greater than the quantity in Column B;
   (B) if the quantity in Column B is greater than the quantity in Column A;
   (C) if the quantities in the two columns are equal;
   (D) if the information is not sufficient to make a valid comparison.
Any information that appears in a central position above the two quantities to be compared refers to both quantities.

Column A	Column B	A B C D
$2 + (7 \times 8)$	$2(7 \times 8)$	

Answer: (B) the quantity in Column B is greater than that in Column A. The correct answer is (B), so you would mark space (B) in the answer column.

A B C D

Explanation: This is a relatively easy question. In Column A, the numbers in parentheses are multiplied together and 2 is added to them: $7 \times 8 = 56$; $56 + 2 = 58$. In the second quantity, all three numbers are multiplied together: $2 \times 7 \times 8 = 112$.

Do's and Don'ts for Answering Quantitative Comparison Tests

DO be sure you fully understand the directions before beginning the quantitative comparison tests. The directions for these tests are somewhat different from those for most other kinds of tests you have been taking. If you are uncertain how to answer the questions, study the sample question and solution again.

DO aim for both speed and accuracy. Remember that your examination time will be limited.

DON'T work out the actual solutions to the questions *unless it is necessary to do so in order to answer the question.* Some answers require computation; others require only an understanding of mathematical principles.

DON'T waste time on questions you cannot answer. When you run into difficulties, go on to the next question. Go back to the difficult questions after completing and scoring the practice tests.

DON'T make haphazard guesses. As on the other parts of the actual exam, a percentage of your wrong answers will be subtracted from the number of right answers as a correction for guessing. However, it will be to your advantage to answer questions of which you have *some* knowledge since your chances of choosing the correct answer will be greater.

For additional practice in quantitative comparison type questions, refer to page 557, where you will find 80 ADDITIONAL QUANTITATIVE COMPARISON PRACTICE QUESTIONS.

For SPECIAL SHORTCUTS AND STRATEGIES FOR THE QUANTITATIVE COMPARISON TYPE QUESTION, refer to pages 537–539 and pages 540–555.

part III

VERBAL ABILITY

Further develop your verbal skills by reading this part.

Tests in verbal ability make up one part of the Scholastic Aptitude Test.

A variety of tests may be included in the testing of verbal ability. They are designed to discover your knowledge of word meanings, your vocabulary level, your ability to reason, and your skill at understanding what you read.

Although the exact forms of the questions may vary from exam to exam, tests on certain basic skills appear time and again in verbal ability examinations. These include vocabulary tests on synonyms (words that have the same meaning) and antonyms (words that have opposite meanings), sentence completion tests, analogy tests (word relationships), and reading comprehension tests.

DEVELOPING YOUR VOCABULARY

Because verbal ability tests require that you understand the meanings of words, it is important for you to have a strong vocabulary. In high school you have doubtless learned the meanings of many words, and you have probably learned to figure out the meanings of words you do not know.

The following pages provide aids to vocabulary building. First you will find lists of prefixes, suffixes, and common roots and their meanings. Knowing these word elements will help you work out the meanings of unfamiliar words. Next is a list of over 2,300 words to help you review many words that generally appear in high school course work. You probably know the meanings of many of the words, so use the list to help yourself recall the ones you know and learn the ones you do not know.

COMMON PREFIXES

Prefix	Meaning	Examples
ab-, a-, abs-	away from	abhor—to withdraw from in fear or disgust
		abscond—to run away
ad- (also a-, ac-, af-, ag-, an-, ap-, ar-, as-, at-)	to; toward	adapt—to fit to
		accede—to attain to
ambi-	both	ambivalent—having two feelings
amphi-	on both sides; around	amphibian—an animal that lives first in the water and then adapts to land life
		amphitheater—a theater with seats on all sides
ante-	before	antebellum—before the war
anti-	against	antifreeze—a substance added to a liquid to prevent freezing
auto-	self	automobile—a self-propelled vehicle

bi-	two	*bifocals*—glasses with lenses for two focuses
circum-	around	*circumscribe*—to draw around
com-, con-, co-, col-	with; together	*combine*—to bring together
		conjoin—to join together
		co-worker—one who works with
contra-, contro-, counter-	against	*contradict*—to say the opposite
		counteract—to act against
de-	away from; down; the opposite of	*depart*—to go away from
		decline—to turn down
		deactivate—to make inactive
di-	twice	*dioxide*—an oxide with two atoms of oxygen in a molecule
dia-	across; through	*diagonal*—across or through a figure
		diagnose—to determine what is wrong through knowledge
dis-	apart; not	*disperse*—to scatter widely
		dishonest—not honest
dys-	bad; ill	*dysfunction*—a poor functioning
epi-	upon	*epitaph*—an inscription on a tombstone (upon burial)
equi-	equal; equally	*equitable*—fair
ex-, e-, ef-	out; from	*excavate*—to hollow out
		eject—to throw out
		effuse—to pour out
extra-	outside; beyond	*extraordinary*—outside the usual
fore-	before; in front of	*foresee*—to anticipate
geo-	earth	*geology*—the study of the earth
homo-	same; equal; like	*homonym*—a word with the same pronunciation as another word
hyper-	over; too much	*hypertension*—unusually high tension
hypo-	under; too little	*hypodermic*—under the skin
in-, il-, ig-, ir-, im-	not	*inactive*—not active
		illegal—not legal
		ignoble—not noble
		irreverent—not reverent
		improbable—not probable
in-, il-, ir-, im-	in; into	*inject*—to put in
		illuminate—to light up
		irradiate—to shine light on
		implant—to fix firmly (in)
inter-	between; among	*interurban*—between cities
intra-, intro-	within; inside of	*intravenous*—directly into a vein
		introvert—one who looks inside himself
mal-, male-	bad; wrong; ill	*malfunction*—to fail to function correctly
		malevolent—wishing harm to others

Prefix	*Meaning*	*Examples*
mis-	wrong; badly	*mistreat*—to treat badly
mis-, miso-	hatred	*misanthrope*—one who hates men
mono-	one; alone	*monologue*—a speech by one person
neo-	new	*neologism*—a new word or a new meaning for an old word
non-	not; the reverse of	*nonsense*—something that makes no sense
omni-	all; everywhere	*omnipresent*—present everywhere
pan-	all	*pandemic*—existing over a whole area
per-	by; through; throughout	*pervade*—to be present throughout
poly-	many	*polyglot*—speaking or writing several languages
post-	after	*postwar*—after the war
pre-	before; earlier than	*preview*—a preliminary viewing *prehistorical*—before written history
pro-	forward; going ahead of; supporting	*proceed*—to go forward *proboscis*—a snout *prowar*—supporting the war
re-	again; back	*retell*—to tell again *recall*—to call back
retro-	backward	*retroactive*—applying to things that have already taken place
se-	apart	*secede*—to withdraw
semi-	half; partly	*semicircle*—half a circle *semiliterate*—able to read and write a little
sub-	under; less than	*submarine*—underwater *subconscious*—beneath the consciousness
super-	over; above; greater	*superimpose*—to put something over something else *superstar*—a star greater than the others
syn-, sym-, syl-, sys-	with; at the same time	*synchronize*—to make things agree *symmetry*—balance on two sides of a dividing line
tele-	far	*telepathy*—communication by thoughts alone
trans-	across	*transcontinental*—across the continent
un-	not	*unhelpful*—not helpful

COMMON SUFFIXES

Suffix	Meaning	Examples
-able, -ible, -ble	able to; capable of being	*viable*—able to live *edible*—capable of being eaten
-acious, -cious	having the quality of	*tenacious*—holding firmly
-al	of; like	*nocturnal*—of the night
-ance, -ancy	the act of; a state of being	*performance*—the act of performing *truancy*—the act of being truant
-ant, -ent	one who	*occupant*—one who occupies *respondent*—one who responds
-ar, -ary	connected with; concerning	*ocular*—pertaining to the eye *beneficiary*—one who receives benefits
-ence	the act, fact, or quality of	*existence*—the quality of being
-er, -or	one who does	*teacher*—one who teaches *visitor*—one who visits
-ful	full of; having qualities of	*fearful*—full of fear *masterful*—having the qualities of a master
-fy	to make	*deify*—to make into a god
-ic, -ac	of; like; pertaining to	*cryptic*—hidden *cardiac*—pertaining to the heart
-il, -ile	pertaining to	*civil*—pertaining to citizens *infantile*—pertaining to infants or infancy
-ion	the act or condition of	*correction*—the act of correcting
-ism	the philosophy, act, or practice of	*patriotism*—support of one's country
-ist	one who does, makes, or is occupied with	*artist*—one who is occupied with art
-ity, -ty, -y	the state or character	*unity*—the state of being one *novelty*—the quality of being novel or new
-ive	containing the nature of; giving or leaning toward	*pensive*—thoughtful
-less	without; lacking	*heartless*—cruel; without a heart
-logue	a particular kind of speaking or writing	*dialogue*—a conversation or interchange
-logy	a kind of speaking; a study or science	*eulogy*—a speech or writing in praise of someone *theology*—the study of God and related matters
-ment	the act of; the state of	*alignment*—the act of aligning *retirement*—the state of being retired

Suffix	Meaning	Examples
-ness	the quality of	*eagerness*—the quality of being eager
-ory	having the nature of; a place or thing for	*laudatory*—showing praise *laboratory*—a place where work is done
-ous, -ose	full of; having	*dangerous*—full of danger *verbose*—wordy
-ship	the art or skill of; the state or quality of being	*leadership*—the ability to lead
-some	full of; like	*troublesome*—full of trouble
-tude	the state or quality of	*servitude*—slavery or bondage
-y	full of; somewhat; somewhat like	*musty*—having a stale odor *chilly*—somewhat cold *willowy*—like a willow

COMMON ROOTS

Root	Meaning	Examples
acr	sharp; bitter	*acrid*—sharp; bitter
act, ag	to do; to act	*activity*—action *agent*—one who does
acu	sharp; keen	*acuity*—keenness
alt	high	*exalt*—to raise or lift up
anim	life; mind	*animate*—to make alive
ann	year	*annual*—yearly
anthrop	man	*misanthrope*—one who hates men
apt	fit	*adapt*—to fit to
arch	to rule	*patriarch*—a father and ruler
aud	to hear	*audience*—those who hear
bas	low	*debase*—to make lower
belli	war	*bellicose*—hostile; warlike
ben, bene	well; good	*benevolent*—doing or wishing good
bio	life	*biology*—the study of living things
brev	short	*abbreviate*—to shorten
cad, cas	to fall	*cadence*—the fall of the voice in speaking; movement in sound *cascade*—a small waterfall
cap, capt, cip, cept, ceive, ceit	to take or hold	*captive*—one who is caught and held *receive*—to take
cav	hollow	*excavate*—to hollow out
cede, ceed, cess	to go; to give in	*precede*—to go before *access*—a means of going to
chrom	color	*chromatic*—having color
chron, chrono	time	*synchronize*—to make agree in time *chronology*—the order of events
cid, cis	to cut; to kill	*homicide*—the killing of a man by another *incisive*—cutting into; sharp

Root	Meaning	Examples
clin	to lean; to bend	*decline*—to bend or turn downward
clud, clus, clos, claud, claus	to close; to shut	*exclude*—to shut out *claustrophobia*—fear of closed places
cogn, cognit	to know; to learn	*cognizant*—aware *recognition*—knowing on sight
cor, cord	heart	*accord*—agreement
corp, corpor	body	*corporal*—bodily
cred, credit	to believe	*credible*—believable
crypt	hidden	*cryptic*—with hidden meaning
cum	to heap up	*cumulative*—increasing by additions
cur	to care	*accurate*—careful and precise
curr, curs, cours	to run	*current*—the flow of running water *cursory*—hastily done
da, date	to give	*date*—a given time
dem, demo	people	*demography*—a statistical study of population
di	day	*diary*—a daily record
dic, dict	to say	*diction*—wording; verbal expression *indict*—to make a formal accusation
doc, doct	to teach	*doctrine*—something taught
dol	grief; pain	*doleful*—sorrowful
domin	to rule; to master	*dominion*—rule; a ruled territory
dorm	to sleep	*dormant*—sleeping; inactive
duc, duct	to lead	*induce*—to lead to action *aqueduct*—a pipe or waterway
dynam	power	*dynamite*—a powerful explosive
ego	I	*egocentric*—seeing everything in relation to oneself
eu	good; beautiful	*euphonious*—having pleasant sound
fac, fact, fic, fec, fect	to make; to do	*facile*—easy to do *artifact*—an object made by man *fiction*—something that has been made up
fer, ferr, lat	to carry, bring, or bear	*refer*—to carry to something or somebody else *translate*—to bring from one language to another
fid	faith; trust	*confide*—to tell a trusted person
fin	end; limit	*final*—coming at the end
fort, force	strong	*fortitude*—strength *enforce*—to give strength to
frag, fract	to break	*fragment*—a part broken from the whole *fracture*—a break
gen	birth	*gender*—classification of words by sex

Root	Meaning	Examples
gen, gener	kind; race	*general*—applying to a whole class or kind
		generate—to give birth to
gnos	to know	*agnostic*—one who believes people cannot know whether God exists
grad, gress	to step; to go	*graduate*—to go from one state to another
		progress—to move forward
graph, gram	writing	*graphic*—relating to writing
		telegram—a written message sent over a distance
helio	sun	*heliolatry*—sun worship
hydro	water	*hydrant*—a pipe from which one draws water
jac, jact, jec, ject	to throw	*trajectory*—the path of an object that has been thrown or shot
		project—to propose; to put forward
junct	to join	*junction*—a joining
jur	to swear	*perjure*—to lie under oath
labor	to work	*elaborate*—worked out carefully
leg, lect	to gather; to choose	*legion*—a large number gathered together
		elect—to choose
leg	law	*legislate*—to make laws
liber	book	*library*—a book collection
liber	free	*liberation*—freedom
loc	place	*dislocate*—to displace
loqu, locut	to talk	*loquacious*—talkative
		elocution—style of speaking
luc	light	*elucidate*—to clarify ("throw light on")
magn	great	*magnanimous*—of noble mind; generous
		magnate—an important person
man, mani, manu	hand	*manipulate*—to work with the hands
		manuscript—a document written by hand
mar	the sea	*maritime*—having to do with the sea
medi	middle	*intermediate*—in the middle
meter, metr, mens	to measure	*thermometer*—an instrument to measure temperature
		symmetry—similarity of measurement on both sides
		immense—very large (unmeasurable)
micro	small	*microbe*—an organism too small to be seen with the naked eye

Root	Meaning	Examples
min, mini	small	*minute*—very tiny
		miniature—a small copy of something
mit, mitt, miss	to send	*admit*—to allow in
		missile—a projectile
mon, monit	to advise, warn, remind	*monument*—a plaque, statue, building, etc., set up to remind of someone or something
		premonition—an advance warning
mort, mori	to die	*mortal*—destined to die
		moribund—dying
mov, mot, mob	to move	*remove*—to move away
		emotion—strong (moving) feelings
		immobile—not movable
mut	to change	*immutable*—never changing
nat, nasc	born	*prenatal*—before birth
		nascent—coming into being; being born
nav	ship	*circumnavigate*—to sail around
nocturn	night	*nocturnal*—taking place at night
nomy	law; arranged order	*astronomy*—the science of the stars
nov, novus	new	*innovation*—something new
onym	name	*anonymous*—without a name
oper	to work	*operative*—capable of working
pac	peace	*pacify*—to calm
par	equal	*disparate*—not alike; distinct
pars, part	part	*parse*—to separate into parts
		depart—to go away from
pater, patr	father	*paternal*—fatherly
		patriarch—a father and ruler
path, pat, pas	feeling, suffering	*empathy*—"feeling with" another person
		patient—suffering without complaint
		passion—strong emotion
ped, pede, pod	foot	*pedestal*—the bottom of a statue, column, etc.
		impede—to hinder
		podium—a platform on which to stand
pel, puls	to drive	*expel*—to drive out
		repulse—to drive back
pend, pens	to hang; to weigh; to pay	*pendulous*—hanging loosely
		pensive—thoughtful
		pension—a payment to a person after a certain age
pet, petit	to seek	*impetus*—a motive
		petition—to request

Root	Meaning	Examples
phil, philo	loving	*philanthropy*—a desire to help mankind
		philosophy—love of knowledge
phobia	fear	*hydrophobia*—fear of water
phon, phone	sound	*symphony*—harmony of sounds
		telephone—an instrument for sending sound over a distance
plac	to please	*placate*—to stop from being angry
polis	city	*metropolis*—a major city
pon, pos, posit, pose	to place	*proponent*—a person who makes a suggestion or supports a cause
		deposit—to place
port, portat	to carry	*porter*—one who carries
		transportation—a means of carrying
psych, psycho	mind	*psychology*—the science of the mind
quer, quisit	to ask	*query*—a question
		inquisition—a questioning
quies	quiet	*acquiesce*—to agree without protest
radi	ray	*irradiate*—to shine light on
rap, rapt	to seize	*rapine*—the act of seizing others' property by force
		rapture—being seized or carried away by emotion
rid, ris	to laugh	*ridiculous*—laughable
		risible—causing laughter
rog, rogate	to ask	*prerogative*—a prior right
		interrogate—to question
rupt	break	*disrupt*—to break up
sat, satis	enough	*satiate*—to provide with enough or more than enough
		satisfy—to meet the needs of
schis, schiz	to cut	*schism*—a split or division
		schizophrenia—a mental disorder characterized by a separation of the thoughts and emotions
sci	to know	*science*—knowledge
scop	to watch; to view	*telescope*—an instrument for seeing things from a distance
scrib, script	to write	*describe*—to tell or write about
		transcript—a written copy
sec, sect	to cut	*sectile*—cutable with a knife
		bisect—to cut in two
sed, sess, sid	to sit	*sediment*—material that settles to the bottom (in liquid)
		session—a meeting
		preside—to have authority

Root	Meaning	Examples
sent, sens	to feel; to think	*sentiment*—feeling *sensitive*—responding to stimuli
sequ, secu, secut	to follow	*sequence*—order *consecutive*—one following another
solv, solut	to loosen	*absolve*—to free from guilt *solution*—the method of working out an answer
soph	wise; wisdom	*sophisticate*—a worldly wise person
spec, spect, spic	to look; to appear	*specimen*—an example *inspect*—to look over *perspicacious*—having sharp judgment
spir, spirit	to breathe	*expire*—to exhale; to die *spirit*—life
sta, stat	to stand	*stable*—steady *stationary*—fixed; unmoving
stru, struct	to build	*construe*—to explain or deduce the meaning *structure*—a building
suas, suad	to urge	*persuasive*—having the power to cause something to change *dissuade*—to change someone's course
sum, sumpt	to take	*assume*—to take on *resumption*—taking up again
tact, tang	to touch	*tactile*—able to be touched or felt *intangible*—unable to be touched
tempor	time	*temporal*—lasting only for a time; temporary
ten, tent, tain	to hold	*untenable*—unable to be held *retentive*—holding *maintain*—to keep or keep up
tend, tens	to stretch	*extend*—to stretch out or draw out *tension*—tautness
terr	land	*territory*—a portion of land
the, theo	god	*atheist*—one who believes there is no God *theocracy*—rule by God or by persons claiming to represent Him
thermo	heat	*thermal*—having to do with heat
tract	to draw	*attract*—to draw
trud, trus	to thrust	*protrude*—to stick out *intrusive*—pushing into or upon something
un, uni	one	*unanimous*—of one opinion *uniform*—of one form

Root	Meaning	Examples
urb	city	*suburb*—a district near a city
ut, util	to use; useful	*utile*—useful
		utility—the quality of being useful
vac	empty	*vacuum*—empty space
ven, vent	to come	*convene*—to meet together
		advent—an arrival
ver	true	*verify*—to prove to be true
verd	green	*verdant*—green
vert, vers	to turn	*avert*—to turn away
vi, via	way	*deviate*—to turn off the prescribed way
		via—by way of
vid, vis	to see	*evident*—apparent; obvious
		invisible—unable to be seen
vinc, vict	to conquer	*convince*—to overcome the doubts of
		victory—an overcoming
vit, viv	to live	*vital*—alive
		vivacious—lively
voc, voke, vocat	to call	*vocal*—spoken or uttered aloud
		invoke—to call on
		vocation—a calling
void	empty	*devoid*—without
vol	to fly	*volatile*—vaporizing quickly
volv, volut	to roll or turn around	*evolve*—to develop by stages; to unfold
		convoluted—coiled

VOCABULARY REVIEW LIST

A

abase—to degrade

abash—to embarrass

abate—to decrease

abattoir—a slaughter-house

abdicate—to give up

aberration—a deviation

abet—to aid

abeyance—temporary suspension

abhor—to detest

abject—miserable

abjure—to give up on oath

ablution—washing the body

abnegate—to renounce

abominate—to loathe

aboriginal—first; existing someplace since the beginning

abort—to cut short

abrade—to rub off

abridge—to shorten

abrogate—to cancel by authority

abscond—to run away

absolve—to free of guilt

abstemious—moderate in eating and drinking

abstract—a summary

abstruse—hard to understand

abut—to border on

abysmal—bottomless; wretched

accede—to take on the duties (of); to attain (to)

acclivity—an upward slope

accolade—a demonstration of honor

accouterments—one's clothes

accretion—accumulation

accrue—to accumulate

acerbity—sharpness

acme—a peak

acquiesce—to yield

acquit—to clear of a charge

acrid—sharp

acrimony—bitterness

actuate—to put into motion

acumen—keenness

adage—an old saying

adamant—unyielding

adduce—to give as proof

adept—skilled; expert

adhere—to stay fast

adipose—fatty

adjudicate—to judge

adjunct—something added

adjure—to charge under oath

admonish—to warn

adroit—skillful

adulation—flattery

adulterate—to make impure

adumbration—a foreshadowing; an outlining

advent—an arrival

adventitious—accidental

adversity—misfortune

advocate—to support

aesthetic—pertaining to beauty

affable—friendly

affected—artificial

affidavit—a sworn statement in writing

affinity—a close relationship

affirmation—assertion

affluent—wealthy

affray—a noisy quarrel

affront—an insult

agenda—a program

agglomerate—to gather into a mass

aggrandize—to make greater

aggravate—to make worse

aggregate—a group of things together

aggrieved—wronged

aghast—horrified

agile—nimble

agnostic—one who doesn't know

agrarian—agricultural

akimbo—with hands on hips

alacrity—eagerness

albeit—although

alchemy—early chemistry

alienate—to make unfriendly

allay—to calm

allege—to declare

allegory—a symbolic story

alleviate—to relieve

allocate—to distribute

allude—to refer indirectly

alluvial—pertaining to soil deposits left by water

altercation—an angry argument

altruism—unselfish concern for others

amass—to accumulate

amatory—showing love

331

ambidextrous—skillful; able to use both hands equally well

ambrosia—the food of the gods

ambulant—moving about

ameliorate—to improve

amenable—easily led

amenity—a pleasant quality

amiable—friendly

amity—friendship

amnesty—pardon

amorphous—shapeless

amplify—to increase

amulet—a charm

anachronism—something misplaced in time

analgesic—a pain-reliever

analogous—comparable

anarchy—absence of government

anathema—a curse

anchorite—a recluse

ancillary—serving as an aid

animadversion—a critical comment

animate—to bring to life

animosity—hatred

annals—yearly records

anneal—to heat and then cool; to strengthen

annuity—a yearly payment

annul—to invalidate

anomaly—an abnormality

antediluvian—before the Biblical Flood; very old

anterior—toward the front

anthropoid—resembling man

antipathy—a strong dislike

antipodes—exact opposites

antithesis—opposite

apathetic—indifferent

aperture—an opening

apex—a peak

aphorism—an adage

aplomb—self-possession; poise

apocryphal—of doubtful authenticity

apogee—the highest point

apoplexy—sudden paralysis

apostate—one who abandons his faith or cause

apothecary—druggist

apothegm—a saying

apotheosis—deification

appall—to shock or dismay

apparition—a ghost

appease—to pacify

appellation—a name or title

append—to attach

apposite—apt

apprise—to notify

appurtenance—an accessory or possession

aquiline—curved or hooked

arabesque—an elaborate architectural design

arable—plowable (land)

arbiter—a judge or umpire

arbitrary—left to one's judgment; despotic

arboreal—pertaining to trees

archaic—ancient or old-fashioned

archetype—an original model or perfect example

archipelago—a group of islands

archives—a place where records are kept; records

ardor—passion

arduous—laborious

argot—jargon

armada—a fleet of warships

arraign—to bring to court to answer charges

arrant—complete; out-and-out

arrears—unpaid debts

arrogate—to appropriate

articulate—to join; to speak clearly

artifact—a manmade object, particularly a primitive one

artifice—ingenuity; trickery

artisan—a skilled craftsman

ascendant—rising

ascetic—self-denying

ascribe—to assign or attribute

aseptic—free of bacteria

askance—with a sideways look; suspiciously

askew—crookedly

asperity—harshness

aspersion—a slanderous remark

assail—to assault

assay—to test or analyze; to try

asseverate—to assert

assiduous—diligent

assimilate—to incorporate

assuage—to lessen

astral—pertaining to the stars

astute—clever; shrewd

atavism—a throwback to an earlier state; a reappearance of a characteristic from an earlier generation

atheist—one who believes there is no God

athwart—across

atrophy—to waste away

attenuate—to weaken

attest—to confirm

attribute—a characteristic
attrition—wearing away
atypical—abnormal
audacious—bold
audible—loud enough to be heard
augment—to enlarge
augur—to foretell
august—inspiring reverence and respect
aural—pertaining to the ear or hearing
auspices—sponsorship
auspicious—favorable
austerity—severity; the condition of denying oneself
autocrat—a dictator
autonomy—self-government; independence
auxiliary—a thing or person that gives aid
avarice—greed
aver—to affirm
averse—opposed
avid—greedy
avocation—a hobby
avoirdupois—weight
avow—to acknowledge
avuncular—pertaining to an uncle; like an uncle
awry—not straight

B

bacchanal—a drunken party
badger—to tease or annoy
badinage—playful talk; banter
baffle—to perplex
baleful—harmful
balk—to obstruct; to refuse to move
balm—something that soothes or heals
banal—trite; commonplace
bandy—to toss back and forth; exchange
baneful—deadly

barbaric—uncivilized
baroque—very ornate
barrage—a prolonged attack of artillery fire or words
barrister—a man of the legal profession
bastion—a fortification or defense
bate—to lessen

bathos—sentimentality
batten—to thrive
bayou—a marshy body of water
beatific—blissful
beatitude—perfect happiness
bedizen—to dress in a showy way
bedlam—a madhouse; a place of chaos
beguile—to charm or deceive
behemoth—a large and powerful animal or thing
behoof—behalf; interest
belabor—to beat; to scold or criticize
beleaguer—to besiege
belie—to contradict
bellicose—warlike
belligerent—warlike
benediction—a blessing
benefactor—one who provides benefits
benevolent—kindly
benighted—surrounded by darkness; unenlightened
benign—kindly; harmless
benison—a blessing
berate—to scold
berserk—frenzied
beset—to attack
bestial—like a beast; brutish
bestow—to present (as a gift); to confer
bestride—to mount with one leg on each side

bête noire—something or someone hated or feared
bibliophile—one who loves books
bibulous—inclined to drink alcoholic beverages
biennial—every two years
bigot—an intolerant person
bilious—bad-tempered
billingsgate—vulgar, abusive talk
binate—paired
bivouac—a temporary encampment
bizarre—odd; eccentric
blanch—to make white; to bleach; (a person) to turn white
bland—mild
blandishment—flattery
blasphemy—profanity
blatant—unpleasantly loud
blazon—to make known; to adorn or decorate
bleak—unsheltered; bare
blight—anything that kills, withers, or stunts
blithe—gay
bloated—swollen
bludgeon—a club
bluster—to act in a noisy manner
bode—to foreshadow
boisterous—rowdy
bolster—to support
bombastic—using unnecessarily pompous language
bondage—slavery
boor—a rude person
bootless—useless
bounty—generosity
bourgeois—pertaining to the middle class
bovine—cowlike
bowdlerize—to remove offensive passages (from a book)

braggadocio—a braggart
brandish—to shake or wave (something) in a menacing way
brash—impudent
bravado—a show of bravery
brazen—shameless
breach—a violation
brevity—briefness
brigand—a bandit
broach—to open or introduce
bromidic—dull
bruit—to rumor
brusque—abrupt in manner
bucolic—rural; pastoral
buffoonery—clowning
bullion—gold or silver in bars
bulwark—a defense
bumptious—conceited or forward
burgeon—to grow
burlesque—to imitate in order to ridicule
burnish—to polish
buttress—a support
buxom—healthy; plump

C

cabal—a small group of conspirators
cache—a hiding place; hidden things
cacophony—harsh sound
cadaver—a corpse
cadence—rhythm
cadre—a basic structure; a nucleus or framework
caitiff—a mean person
cajole—to coax or wheedle
caliber—quality or value
calk, caulk—to fill cracks or seams
calligraphy—penmanship
callous—unfeeling
callow—immature

calumny—slander
camaraderie—fellowship
canaille—rabble; mob
canard—a false, often malicious report
candor—frankness
canny—shrewd
cant—slang or argot
canvass—to go through for opinions, votes, etc.
capacious—roomy
capitulate—to surrender
capricious—erratic, changeable
captious—quick to find fault
captivate—to fascinate
careen—to lean to the side or from side to side
caricature—an imitation or drawing that exaggerates certain features of the subject
carmine—red
carnage—slaughter
carnal—bodily
carousal—a rowdy drinking party
carp—to make petty complaints
carrion—decaying flesh
carte blanche—a free hand; unlimited authority
castigate—to punish
casualty—a mishap
casuistry—false reasoning
cataclysm—an upheaval
catalyst—an agent of change
catapult—to shoot or launch; to leap
catastrophe—a calamity
categorical—absolute
catholic—universal
causerie—a chat
caustic—corrosive
cauterize—to burn
cavalcade—a procession
caveat—a warning

cavil—to quibble
cede—to give up one's rights to (something); to transfer ownership of
celerity—speed
celestial—heavenly

celibate—unmarried
censure—to blame or criticize
cerebration—thought; thinking
cessation—stopping
cession—the giving up (of something) to another
chafe—to rub for warmth; to irritate
chaff—husks of grain; anything worthless
chagrin—embarrassment
chaotic—totally disorderly
charlatan—imposter; quack
charnel—a place where corpses or bones are put
chary—watchful
chaste—pure
chastise—to punish
chattel—personal property
chauvinism—fanatical patriotism or partisanship
checkered—characterized by diverse experiences
chicanery—trickery or deception
chide—to rebuke
chimerical—imaginary
choleric—quick-tempered
chronic—long-lasting or perpetual
chronicle—a historical record arranged in order of time
churlish—rude
circuitous—roundabout

circumlocution—an indirect or lengthy way of saying something
circumscribe—to encircle
circumspect—cautious
circumvent—to surround; to prevent (something) by cleverness
citadel—a fortress
cite—to quote
civility—politeness
clandestine—secret
clarion—clear (sound) like a trumpet
cleave—to split
cleft—a split
clemency—leniency
cliché—an overworked expression
climacteric—a crucial period or event
climactic—pertaining to the climax, or high point
clique—an exclusive group of people
cloister—a monastery or convent
cloy—to satiate
coadjutor—an assistant
coalesce—to unite or merge
codicil—an addition or supplement
coerce—to force
coffer—a strongbox
cogent—forceful
cogitate—to think over
cognate—related
cognizant—aware
cognomen—a name
cohesion—tendency to stick together
cohort—a group or band; an associate
coincident—happening at the same time
collaborate—to work together
collateral—side by side; parallel

collocation—an arrangement
colloquial—conversational; informal (speech)
colloquy—a formal discussion or conference
collusion—conspiracy
colossal—huge
comatose—pertaining to a coma
comely—attractive
comestible—edible
comity—politeness
commensurate—equal in size or measure
comminuted—powdered
commiseration—sympathy or sorrow
commodious—spacious
commutation—an exchange or substitution
compassion—deep sympathy
compatible—able to get along well together
compendious—brief but comprehensive
compile—to gather in an orderly form
complacent—self-satisfied
complaisant—obliging; agreeable
complement—that which completes something
compliant—submissive
component—a part of the whole
comport—to behave or conduct (oneself)
compunction—guilt; remorse
concatenate—linked together; connected
concede—to acknowledge or admit as true
conciliate—to make up with
concise—brief and clear
conclave—a private or secret meeting

conclusive—decisive
concoct—to devise
concomitant—accompanying
concordat—an agreement
concourse—a crowd; a space for crowds to gather
concupiscent—having strong sexual desire or lust
concurrent—running together or at the same time
condescend—to deal with someone beneath oneself on his own level, sometimes patronizingly
condign—deserved or suitable
condolence—expression of sympathy
condone—to pardon or overlook
conducive—tending or leading
conduit—a pipe or channel for liquids
configuration—an arrangement
confiscate—to seize by authority
conflagration—a large fire
confute—to prove wrong
congeal—to solidify
congenital—existing from birth
conglomerate—a mass or cluster
congruent—corresponding
congruous—suitable, fitting
conjecture—a guess
conjoin—to unite
conjugal—pertaining to marriage
conjure—to produce by magic

connive—to pretend not to see another's wrong-doing; to cooperate or conspire in wrong-doing

connoisseur—one with expert knowledge and taste in an area

connotation—an idea suggested by a word or phrase that is different from the literal meaning of the word or phrase

consanguinity—blood relationship; close relationship

conscript—to draft (as for military service)

consecrate—to dedicate

consensus—general agreement

consign—to hand over; to put in the care of another

consonance—agreement

consort—a spouse, particularly of a king or queen; a traveling companion

consternation—great emotion that leaves one helpless and confused

constituency—the people served by an elected official

constrain—to confine or hold back

constrict—to make smaller by applying pressure; to restrict

construe—to interpret

consummate—to bring to completion; to finish

contaminate—to pollute

contemn—to scorn

contentious—quarrelsome; controversial

context—the words around a particular portion of a speech or passage; surroundings and background

contiguous—touching along one side; adjacent

continence—self-restraint; moderation

contingent—possible; accidental; depending on something else

contortion—a twisting

contraband—smuggled merchandise

contravene—to oppose; to dispute

contrition—remorse or repentance

contrivance—something that is thought up or devised; an invention

controvert—to contradict; to debate

contumacious—insubordinate; disobedient

contumely—humiliating rudeness

contusion—bruise

conundrum—a puzzling question or problem

convene—to assemble

conversant—familiar (with)

conveyance—a vehicle or other means of carrying

convivial—pertaining to festivity; sociable

convoke—to call together

convolution—a twisting together; a twist or coil

copious—plentiful

corollary—a proposition that follows from another that has been proved

corporeal—bodily

corpulent—very fat

correlation—a mutual relationship; a correspondence

corroborate—to confirm

corrosive—capable of eating or wearing away; sarcastic; biting

corsair—a pirate or pirate ship

cortege—a procession

coterie—a clique

countermand—to revoke (an order)

coup d'état—an overthrow of a government

covenant—an agreement

covert—hidden

covetous—envious

cower—to shrink in fear

coy—bashful; reserved; coquettish

cozen—to cheat or deceive

crabbed—ill-tempered

crass—grossly stupid or dull

craven—cowardly

credence—belief

credulous—easily or too easily convinced

creed—a statement of belief, religious or otherwise

crepitate—to crackle

criterion—a standard for judging

crone—a hag

crony—a close companion

crux—a problem; the deciding point

cryptic—hidden

cudgel—a stick or club

culinary—pertaining to the kitchen or cooking

cull—to pick out or select

culmination—the highest point

culpable—blameworthy

cumbersome—burdensome; clumsy

cuneate—wedge-shaped

cupidity—greed

curmudgeon—a bad-tempered person

curry—to try to obtain favor by flattery

cursory—superficial

curtail—to cut short

cynic—a person who believes all actions are motivated by selfishness

D

dais—a platform in a hall or room

dally—to play or trifle; to waste time

dank—damp

dastard—a mean coward

daunt—to intimidate

dauntless—bold

dearth—scarcity

debacle—an overwhelming defeat or failure

debase—to lower in dignity, quality, or value

debauch—to corrupt

debilitate—to weaken

debonair—courteous; gay

decadence—decay

decamp—to break camp; to run away

deciduous—falling off at a certain time or yearly (as leaves from trees)

decimate—to kill a large part of

declivity—a downgrade; a slope

decorous—proper

decoy—a lure or bait

decrepit—weak from age

decry—to speak against publicly

deduce—to reason out logically; to conclude from known facts

de facto—actual

defalcate—to misuse money left in one's care; to embezzle

defamation—slander

default—neglect; failure to do what is required

defection—desertion

deference—regard for another's wishes

defile—to make dirty or pollute; to dishonor

definitive—conclusive; distinguishing

deflect—to turn aside; to deviate

defunct—dead; no longer operating

deign—to condescend

delete—to strike out or erase

deleterious—harmful

delineate—to sketch or or design; to portray

delude—to mislead

delusion—a false belief

demagogue—one who stirs people up by emotional appeal in order to gain power

demarcate—to mark the limits of

demean—to degrade

demeanor—bearing or behavior

demise—death

demolition—destruction

demonic—pertaining to a demon or demons

demur—to delay; to object

demure—serious; prim

denizen—an inhabitant

denouement—the outcome or solution of a plot

depict—to portray

depilate—to rid of hair

deplete—to reduce or exhaust

deplore—to lament or feel sorry about

deploy—to station forces or troops in a planned way

depravity—corruption

deprecate—to express disapproval of

depreciate—to lessen in value

depredate—to plunder or despoil

deranged—insane

derelict—abandoned

deride—to mock; to laugh at

derogatory—expressing a low opinion

descant—to discuss at length

descry—to detect (something distant or obscure)

desecrate—to make profane

desiccate—to dry up

desist—to stop

despicable—contemptible

despoil—to strip; to pillage

despotism—tyranny

destitute—lacking; in extreme need of things

desuetude—state of disuse

desultory—aimless; random

deterrent—something that discourages (someone) from an action

detonate—to explode

detraction—belittling the worth of something or someone

detriment—injury; hurt

deviate—to turn aside

devious—winding; going astray

devoid—lacking

devolve—to transfer to another person

devout—pious

dexterous—skillful

diabolical—devilish

diadem—a crown

diapason—the entire range of musical sounds

diaphanous—transparent or translucent

diatribe—a bitter denunciation

dichotomy—a division into two parts

dictum—an authoritative statement

didactic—instructive

diffident—unconfident; timid

diffusion—the act of spreading (something) out in all directions

digress—to turn aside or deviate, especially in writing or speaking

dilapidation—a state of disrepair

dilate—to expand

dilatory—tending to delay; tardy

dilemma—a choice of two unsatisfactory alternatives

dilettante—one who involves himself in the arts as a pastime

diligent—hard-working

diminution—a lessening

dint—means

dire—terrible; fatal; extreme

dirge—funereal music

disavowal—a denial

discernible—able to be seen or distinguished

discerning—having good judgment; astute

disclaim—to disown

discomfit—to frustrate the plans of

disconcert—to upset or confuse

disconsolate—sad; dejected

discordant—not harmonious

discountenance—to make ashamed; to discourage

discreet—showing good judgment in conduct; prudent

discrete—separate; not connected

discretion—individual judgment; quality of being discreet

discursive—passing from one subject to another

disdain—to think (someone or something) unworthy

disheveled—messy

disingenuous—insincere

disinterested—not influenced by personal advantage

disjointed—disconnected

disparage—to belittle

disparity—inequality

disperse—to scatter or distribute

disport—to amuse or divert

disputatious—inclined to dispute

disquisition—a formal inquiry; an elaborate essay

dissemble—to disguise or pretend

disseminate—to scatter

dissident—not agreeing

dissimulate—to dissemble; to pretend

dissipate—to scatter or disperse

dissolute—loose in morals

dissonance—discord

dissuade—to advise against; to divert by persuasion

distend—to expand

distrait—absent-minded; preoccupied

distraught—troubled; confused; harassed

diurnal—daily

diverge—to extend from one point in separate directions

diverse—differing; various

divest—to strip or deprive

divination—the act of foreseeing or foretelling

divulge—to reveal

docile—easy to teach or discipline

doff—to take off

doggerel—poorly written verse

dogma—a belief or doctrine; a positive statement of opinion

dogmatic—positive in manner or in what one says

doldrums—low spirits

dolorous—sorrowful

dolt—a stupid fellow

domicile—a home

dormant—sleeping; inactive

dorsal—pertaining to the back

dossier—collected documents on a person

dotage—senility

doughty—valiant

dour—stern; sullen

dregs—sediment; the most worthless part of something

drivel—silly talk

droll—amusing and strange

dross—waste or refuse

drudgery—tiresome work

dubious—doubtful

ductile—able to be drawn or hammered thin without breaking

dulcet—sweet-sounding

duplicity—deception; double-dealing

durance—imprisonment

duress—imprisonment; compulsion

E

ebullient—enthusiastic

eccentricity—oddity

éclat—brilliant success; acclaim

eclectic—made up of material collected from many sources

ecumenical—universal; intended to bring together the Christian churches

edict—a decree

edifice—a (usually large) building
edify—to instruct and improve
educe—to elicit or draw forth
efface—to rub out
effectual—efficient
effervesce—to bubble; to be lively or boisterous
effete—exhausted; worn out
efficacy—power to have effect
effigy—an image or figure that represents a disliked person
effluence—a flowing forth
effrontery—shameless boldness
effulgent—radiant
effusive—pouring out; gushing
egotism—constant reference to oneself
egregious—flagrant
egress—emergence; exit
elation—high spirits
eleemosynary—pertaining to charity
elegy—a poem, particularly a lament for the dead
elicit—to draw out
elucidate—to explain; to throw light on
elusive—hard to grasp
emaciated—very thin
emanate—to flow forth
embellish—to ornament or beautify
embody—to give bodily form to; to make concrete
embroil—to confuse by discord; to involve in confusion
embryonic—undeveloped
emend—to correct
eminent—lofty; distinguished

emollient—something that soothes or softens (the body)
emolument—one's fees or salary
empirical—based on observation or experience
empyreal—heavenly
emulate—to imitate with the hope of equaling or surpassing
enclave—an area enclosed inside a foreign territory
encomium—high praise
encompass—to encircle; to contain
encroach—to trespass
encumber—to impede or burden
endemic—native to a particular area
endue—to invest or endow
enervate—to weaken
engender—to cause or produce
engrossed—absorbed; fully occupied
engulf—to swallow up or overwhelm
enhance—to make greater; to heighten
enigma—a puzzle
enjoin—to order; to prohibit
ennui—boredom
enormity—great wickedness
ensconce—to shelter; to settle comfortably
ensue—to follow right after
enthrall—to captivate
entity—a being or thing
entourage—a group of associates or attendants
entreaty—a serious request
entrepreneur—a man of business

envenom—to make poisonous; to embitter
environs—surroundings; vicinity
ephemeral—short-lived
epicure—a connoisseur of food and drink
epigram—a short, pointed poem or saying
epistle—a long, formal letter
epithet—a descriptive phrase; an uncomplimentary name
epitome—an abstract; a part that represents the whole
epoch—a period of time
equable—uniform; tranquil
equanimity—even temper
equestrian—pertaining to horses
equilibrium—a state of balance between various forces or factors
equity—fairness
equivocal—ambiguous; doubtful
equivocate—to deceive; to lie
erode—to eat away
errant—wandering

erudite—scholarly
escarpment—a steep slope
eschew—to avoid
esculent—edible
esoteric—for a limited, specially initiated group
espouse—to marry; to advocate (a cause)
esprit de corps—group spirit
estimable—worthy of respect or esteem
estival—pertaining to summer

estranged—separated

ethereal—celestial; spiritual

ethnic—pertaining to races or cultures

eugenic—pertaining to the bearing of genetically healthy offspring

eulogy—high praise

euphemism—an inoffensive expression substituted for an unpleasant one

euphoria—a feeling of well-being

euthanasia—painless death

evanescent—fleeting

evasive—not frank or straightforward

evince—to make evident; to display

eviscerate—to disembowel

evoke—to call forth

evolve—to develop gradually; to unfold

exacerbate—to make more intense; to aggravate

exact—to call for; to require

exasperate—to vex

excise—to cut away

excoriate—to strip of skin; to denounce harshly

exculpate—to free from blame

execrable—detestable

exemplary—serving as a good example

exhort—to urge

exigency—an emergency

exiguous—meager

exonerate—to acquit

exorbitant—excessive; extravagant

exorcise—to drive out (an evil spirit)

expatiate—to talk freely and at length

expedient—advantageous

expedite—to speed up or make easy

expeditious—efficient and quick

expiate—to atone for

expound—to set forth

expunge—to blot out; to erase

expurgate—to rid (a book) of offensive material

extant—in existence

extemporaneous—not planned

extenuate—to make thin; to diminish

extirpate—to pluck out

extol—to praise

extort—to take from a person by force

extradition—the surrender by one state to another of an alleged criminal

extraneous—not essential

extricate—to free

extrinsic—unessential; extraneous

extrovert—one whose interest is directed outside himself

extrude—to force or push out

exuberant—profuse; effusive

exude—to discharge or ooze; to radiate; to diffuse

F

fabricate—to build; to lie

façade—the front of a building

facet—a small plane of a gem; an aspect

facetious—humorous; joking

facile—easy; expert

facilitate—to make easier

faction—a clique or party

factious—producing or tending to dissension

factitious—artificial

factotum—an employee with many duties

faculty—an ability; a sense

fain—gladly

fallacious—misleading; containing a fallacy

fallible—capable of error

fallow—(land) left unplanted during a growing season

falter—to move unsteadily; to stumble or stammer

fanaticism—excessive enthusiasm

fastidious—hard to please; easy to offend

fatalism—the belief that all events are ruled by fate

fatuous—foolish

fauna—animal life

faux pas—an error in social behavior

fawn—to seek favor by demeaning oneself

fealty—loyalty

feasible—practical

feckless—weak; careless

feculent—filthy; foul

fecundity—fertility; productiveness

feign—to pretend

feint—a move intended to throw one's opponent off guard

felicitous—apt; happy in expression

fell—cruel; fierce

felonious—wicked

ferment—a state of unrest

ferret—to search out

fervent, fervid—hot; ardent

fete—a lavish entertainment, often in someone's honor

fetid—stinking

fetish—an object supposed to have magical power; any object of special devotion
fetter—to shackle or restrain
fettle—state of the body and mind
fiasco—a complete failure
fiat—a command
fickle—changeable
fidelity—faithfulness
fiduciary—pertaining to one who holds something in trust for another
figment—an invention; a fiction
filch—to steal
filial—pertaining to a son or daughter
finale—a conclusion
finesse—skill; cunning
finite—limited
fissure—a narrow opening or cleft
flaccid—flabby
flag—to droop or lose vigor
flagellate—to whip or flog
flagitious—wicked and vile
flagrant—glaring (as an error)
flail—to beat
flamboyant—ornate; showy
flatulent—gas-producing; windy in speech
flaunt—to show off; to display
flay—to skin; to pillage; to censure harshly
fledgling—a young bird that has his feathers; an immature person
flippant—pert
florid—flowery; ornate
flotsam—ship wreckage floating on the sea; drifting persons or things

flout—to reject
fluctuate—to waver
fluent—fluid; easy with words
flux—a moving; a flowing
foible—a failing or weakness
foist—to pass off fraudulently
foment—to stir up
foppish—like a dandy
foray—a raid
forbearance—patience
foreboding—a feeling of coming evil
formidable—threatening
forswear—to renounce
forte—strong point
fortitude—strength; courage
fortuitous—accidental
foster—to rear; to promote
fractious—unruly
fraught—filled
fray—a commotion or fight
freebooter—a plunderer; a pirate
frenetic—frantic; frenzied
frenzy—violent emotional excitement
fresco—a painting done on fresh plaster
freshet—a stream or rush of water
frigid—very cold
fritter—to waste
frivolous—of little importance or value; trivial
froward—obstinate
fructify—to bear fruit
frugal—thrifty
fruition—use or realization; enjoyment
frustrate—to counteract; to prevent from achieving something
fulminate—to explode suddenly; to thunder forth verbally

fulsome—offensive, particularly because of insincerity
funereal—appropriate to funerals
furor—a fury or frenzy
furtive—stealthy
fusion—union
futile—useless

G

gadfly—a fly that attacks livestock; a person who annoys people or moves them to action
gainsay—to deny
gambol—to skip and frolic
gamut—the whole range
gape—to open wide
Gargantuan—gigantic
garish—gaudy
garner—to gather or store
garnish—to decorate
garrulous—talkative
gasconade—boastful talk
gelid—icy; frozen
generality—a broad, vague statement
generic—pertaining to a whole class, kind, or group
genial—favorable to growth; kindly
genre—a kind or category
gentility—of the upper classes; having taste and refinement
gentry—people of education and good birth
germane—relevant and pertinent to the case at hand
germinal—in the first stage of growth
gesticulation—gesture
ghastly—horrible
gibbet—gallows

gibe—to scoff at; to deride

gist—the main point in a debate or question

glaucous—bluish- or yellowish-green

glean—to gather what has been left in a field after reaping; to pick up, little by little

glib—fluent

gloaming—dusk

gloat—to look at with evil satisfaction or greed

glut—to overfill

glutinous—gluey

gluttony—excess in eating

gnarled—twisted

gnomic—wise and pithy

goad—to urge; to drive

gorge—to stuff

gouge—to scoop out; to tear out

gradation—arrangement by grades or steps

gradient—a slope; the degree of a slope

graphic—vivid; pertaining to writing

granary—a storehouse for grain

grandiloquent—using pompous language

grandiose—imposing; splendid

gratis—free

gratuitous—given freely; unwarranted

gregarious—tending to flock together

grimace—an expression that twists the face

grotesque—distorted; bizarre; absurd

grotto—a cave

grovel—to lie prone; to act humble or abject

grueling—punishing

gudgeon—a person who is easy to trick

guerdon—a reward

guile—deceit

guileless—innocent

gullible—easily tricked

gustatory—pertaining to tasting

gusto—liking; great appreciation or relish

guttural—pertaining to the throat

H

habiliments—clothing; equipment

habitable—able or fit to be lived in

hackneyed—trite

haggard—unruly; looking worn and wasted from exertion or emotion

haggle—to bargain

halcyon—peaceful

hale—healthy and sound

hallucination—a perception of something imaginary

hamper—to obstruct or hinder

haphazard—random

hapless—unlucky

harangue—a long speech; a tirade

harass—to worry or torment

harbinger—a forerunner

harp—to persist in talking or writing (about something)

harridan—a shrewish old woman

harrow—to rob or plunder

harry—to raid; to torment or worry

haughty—showing scorn for others; proud

hauteur—haughtiness

hawser—a large rope or cable for mooring or anchoring a ship

hector—to bully

hedonism—the pursuit of pleasure as the primary goal of life

heedless—careless; unmindful

hegemony—leadership; dominance

heinous—abominable

herbaceous—pertaining to herbs or leaves

herculean—of great size, strength, or courage

heresy—a religious belief opposed by the church

heterodox—unorthodox; inclining toward heresy

heterogeneous—dissimilar; varied

hiatus—a gap or break

hibernal—pertaining to winter

hierarchy—an arrangement in order of rank

hieratic—priestly

hieroglyphic—written in symbols; hard to read or understand

hilarity—mirth

hinder—to restrain or hold back

hirsute—hairy

histrionic—theatrical

hoary—white; white-haired

holocaust—destruction by fire

homage—allegiance or honor

homicide—the killing of one person by another

homily—a long, dull sermon

homogeneous—similar; uniform

hone—to sharpen

hortatory—encouraging; giving advice

horticulture—the growing of plants

hybrid—of mixed or unlike parts

hydrous—containing water

hyperbole—exaggeration

hypercritical—too critical

hypochondriac—one who constantly believes he is ill

hypocritical—pretending to be what one is not

hypothetical—assumed; supposed

I

iconoclast—one who attacks traditional ideas

ideology—a body of ideas

idiom—a language or dialect; a particular phrasing that is accepted in use, although its meaning may be different from the literal meaning of the words

idiosyncrasy—a personal peculiarity

idolatry—worship

idyll—a poem based on a simple scene

igneous—pertaining to or produced by fire

ignoble—dishonorable; base

ignominious—shameful; degrading

illicit—unlawful; prohibited

illusory—unreal; deceptive

imbibe—to drink, drink in, or absorb

imbroglio—a confusion; a misunderstanding

imbue—to color; to inspire (with ideas)

immaculate—spotless; clean

immanent—existing within

imminent—about to happen

immolate—to sacrifice

immutable—unchangeable

impair—to make worse or weaker; to reduce

impale—to fix on a pointed object

impalpable—not capable of being felt; not capable of being grasped by the mind

impasse—a situation with no escape or solution

impassive—not feeling pain; calm

impeccable—faultless

impecunious—poor; penniless

impede—to obstruct or delay

impending—about to happen

impenitent—without regret

imperious—domineering

impermeable—unable to be penetrated

impertinent—irrelevant; impudent

imperturbable—unable to be disturbed; impassive

impervious—impenetrable; not affected (by something)

impetuous—rushing; rash or impulsive

impetus—a force; a driving force

impiety—lack of reverence (for God or parents)

implacable—incapable of being pacified

implicate—to involve; to imply

implicit—implied; absolute

impolitic—unwise

import—meaning; significance

importune—to urge persistently

impotent—weak; powerless

imprecate—to pray for (evil)

impregnable—unable to be conquered or entered

impresario—a manager in the performing arts

impromptu—offhand

impropriety—being improper

improvident—not providing for the future

impugn—to oppose or challenge

impunity—freedom from punishment or harm

impute—to charge another (with a negative trait)

inadvertent—heedless; unintentional

inane—empty; foolish

inarticulate—unable to speak understandably or at all

incantation—a chant supposed to work magic

incapacitate—to disable

incarcerate—to imprison

incendiary—pertaining to destruction by fire

inception—beginning

incessant—never-ending

inchoate—just begun; incipient

incipient—in the first stage of existence

incisive—keen, sharp

inclement—stormy; harsh

incognito—disguised

incongruous—incompatible; inappropriate

inconsequential—unimportant

incontrovertible—undeniable

incorrigible—unreformable

increment—increase; the amount of increase

incriminate—to accuse of a crime; to involve in a crime

incubus—a nightmare; an oppressive burden

inculcate—to instill

inculpate—to incriminate

incursion—an inroad; a brief raid

indefatigable—untiring

indemnify—to insure; to reimburse

indict—to charge formally with

indigenous—growing or living in a particular area

indite—to compose and write

indolent—lazy; idle

indomitable—hard to discourage or defeat

indubitable—unquestionable

indulgent—giving in to one's own desires; kind or lenient

indurate—hardened

ineffable—inexpressible

ineluctable—unavoidable

inept—unfit; clumsy

inert—powerless to move; slow

inexorable—unrelenting; unalterable

infallible—incapable of error

infamous—notorious

inference—something that is drawn as a conclusion

infernal—pertaining to hell; diabolical

infidel—one who doesn't believe in a particular doctrine or religion

infinite—limitless; vast

infirmity—weakness

influx—a flowing in

infringe—to violate

ingenious—having genius; clever; original

ingenuous—candid; frank

ingrate—an ungrateful person

ingratiate—to win another's favor by efforts

inherent—innate; characteristic

inhibit—to hold back or repress

inimical—hostile; in opposition

iniquitous—wicked

injunction—a command; an order enjoining, or prohibiting, (someone) from doing something

innate—existing in someone from birth or in something by its nature

innocuous—harmless; noncontroversial

innuendo—an indirect remark or reference

inordinate—unregulated; immoderate

inscrutable—obscure; not easily understood

insensate—not feeling; inanimate; insensitive

insidious—crafty

insinuate—to work gradually into a state; to hint

insipid—tasteless; dull

insolent—impudent; disrespectful

insolvent—bankrupt; unable to pay debts

insouciant—carefree; indifferent

instigate—to urge on to some action; to incite

insular—like an island; isolated; narrow-minded

insuperable—unable to be overcome

insurgent—a person who rises up against (political) authority

intangible—unable to be touched; impalpable

integrity—wholeness; soundness; honesty

intelligentsia—intellectuals as a group

inter—to bury

interdict—to prohibit; to restrain or impede

interim—meantime

interjection—something thrown in or interrupted with; an exclamation

intermittent—periodic; starting and stopping

internecine—mutually harmful or destructive

interpolate—to insert

interregnum—a break, as between governments or regimes

intestate—without a (legal) will to distribute one's property after death

intimate—to hint

intractable—unruly or stubborn

intransigent—refusing to agree or compromise

intrepid—fearless

intrinsic—inherent; of the nature of a thing

introvert—a person who looks inside himself more than outside

intuition—immediate understanding

inundate—to flood

inured—habituated (to something unpleasant)

invective—a violent verbal attack

inveigh—to talk or write strongly (against)

inveigle—to trick or entice

inverse—opposite

investiture—the giving of office to someone
inveterate—of long standing
invidious—offensive
inviolable—not to be violated; unable to be violated
invulnerable—unable to be injured or wounded
iota—a tiny amount
irascible—quick-tempered
irksome—tiresome; annoying
irony—humor in which one says the opposite of what he means; an occurrence that is the opposite of what is expected
irremediable—incurable or irreparable
irrevocable—unable to be called back or undone
iterate—to repeat
itinerant—traveling

J

jaded—tired; satiated
jargon—incoherent speech; a mixed language; the particular vocabulary of one group
jaundiced—yellow; prejudiced
jeopardy—peril
jettison—to throw overboard
jetty—a wall built out into the water
jocose—humorous
jocular—joking
jocund—cheerful
journeyman—a worker who has learned a trade
judicious—wise

juggernaut—any extremely strong and irresistible force
juncture—a point of joining; a critical point in the development of events
junket—a feast or picnic; a pleasure excursion
junta—men engaged in political intrigue
juxtapose—to place side by side

K

ken—understanding
kinetic—pertaining to motion
kith—friends
knavery—dishonesty; deceit
knell—to ring solemnly
knoll—a small hill

L

labyrinth—a maze
lacerate—to tear or mangle
lachrymose—tearful
lackadaisical—spiritless; listless
laconic—brief; using few words
lacuna—a gap where something is missing
laggard—one who is slow
laity—all the people who are not clergy
lambent—flickering; glowing
lampoon—to attack or ridicule
languid—weak; listless
languish—to lose vigor; to droop
larceny—theft
largess—generosity
lascivious—lewd; lustful
lassitude—weariness
latent—hidden or undeveloped

lateral—pertaining to the side or sides
latitude—freedom to act
laudatory—praising
leaven—to spend something throughout something else to bring about a gradual change
lecherous—lustful
legerdemain—trickery
lesion—an injury
lethal—deadly
lethargic—dull, sluggish

levity—gaiety
liaison—a linking up
libel—false printed material intended to harm a person's reputation
libertine—one who lives a morally unrestrained life
libidinous—lustful; lewd
licentious—morally unrestrained
liege—a name for a feudal lord or his subject
lieu—place (in lieu of)
limn—to paint or draw; to describe in words
limpid—clear
literal—word-for-word; actual
lithe—flexible; limber
litigation—carrying out a lawsuit
littoral—pertaining to the shore or coast
livid—black-and-blue; lead-colored
loath—reluctant
loathe—to detest
locution—a word or phrase; a style of speech
logistics—the part of military science having to do with obtaining and moving men and materiel
longevity—long life
loquacious—talkative

lout—a stupid person

lubricity—smoothness; trickiness

lucent—shining; giving off light

lucid—transparent; clear

lucrative—profitable

lucre—money

ludicrous—absurd

lugubrious—mournful

luminary—a body that sheds light; a person who enlightens; any famous person

lurid—sensational

lustrous—shining

luxuriant—lush; rich

M

macabre—gruesome; horrible

macerate—to soften by soaking; to break or tear into small pieces

Machiavellian—crafty and deceitful

machination—a secret plot or scheme

magnanimous—generous; not petty

magnate—an important person, often in a business

magniloquent—lofty or pompous

maim—to disable or mutilate (a person)

maladroit—clumsy

malaise—a vague feeling of illness

malcontent—discontented

malediction—a curse

malefactor—one who does evil

malevolent—wishing ill to others

malfeasance—a wrongdoing

malicious—spiteful

malign—to slander

malignant—evil; harmful

malinger—to pretend to be ill to avoid doing something

malleable—able to be hammered; pliable

mammoth—enormous

mandate—an official order or command

mandatory—required

maniacal—insane; raving

manifest—apparent or evident

manipulate—to work with the hands; to control by unfair means

manumission—liberation from slavery

marauder—a raider

maritime—pertaining to the sea

martial—pertaining to war or the military; warlike

martinet—a strict disciplinarian

masochist—one who enjoys suffering

masticate—to chew up

maternal—pertaining to a mother or motherhood

matrix—a die or mold

maudlin—foolishly sentimental

maunder—to act dreamily or vaguely

mauve—purple

maverick—one who refuses to go along with his group

mawkish—sickeningly sweet

maxim—a principle or truth precisely stated; a saying

mayhem—maiming another person; violence or destruction

meander—to wind or wander

mecca—a place where many people visit

mediate—to help two opposing sides come to agreement

mediocre—ordinary; average

mélange—a mixture

melee—a noisy fight among a lot of people

meliorate—to improve

mellifluous—sweet and smooth

mendacious—lying

mendicant—a beggar

menial—pertaining to servants; servile

mentor—a wise advisor or teacher

mercantile—pertaining to merchants or trade

mercenary—motivated by money; greedy

mercurial—like mercury; quick; changeable

meretricious—superficially alluring

mesa—a high, flat land with steep sides

metamorphosis—a change or transformation

metaphysical—pertaining to the nature of being or reality

mete—to distribute

meticulous—very careful about details

mettle—quality of character, especially good character

miasma—a vapor rising from a swamp; an unwholesome atmosphere

mien—manner or bearing

migrant—a person or an animal that moves from place to place

militate—to work (against)

mimetic—imitative

mimic—to imitate

minatory—threatening

mincing—acting overly dainty or elegant

minion—a favorite (follower); a subordinate

ministration—the carrying out of a minister's duties; service

minutiae—minor details

misadventure—a bit of bad luck

misanthrope—one who dislikes other people

misapprehension—misunderstanding

miscegenation—marriage between a man and a woman of different races

miscellany—a collection of varied things

misconstrue—to misinterpret

miscreant—an evil person

misdemeanor—a minor offense

misgiving—a doubt or fear

mishap—an unfortunate accident

misnomer—the wrong name applied to something

misogynist—one who hates women

mitigate—to make less painful

mnemonic—helping the memory

mobile—capable of moving or being moved

mode—a manner or style

modicum—a bit

modish—in style

modulate—to adjust or regulate

moiety—a share

mollify—to pacify

molt—to shed skin or other outer parts

molten—melted

momentous—very important

monetary—pertaining to money

monolith—a large piece of stone

moot—debatable

morbid—pertaining to disease; gruesome

mordant—biting; sarcastic

mores—ways or customs that are quite important to a culture

moribund—dying

morose—gloomy

mortify—to punish (oneself) by self-denial; to make (someone) feel ashamed

mote—a speck

motif—a main feature or theme

motility—ability to move by itself

motley—of many colors; made up of many unlike parts

mountebank—a quack

mufti—civilian clothes

mulct—to fine; to get money from someone by deceit

multiplicity—a great number (of various things)

mundane—worldly; commonplace

munificent—generous; lavish

muse—to ponder

mutable—changeable

mute—silent

mutilate—to damage by cutting off or injuring vital parts

mutinous—inclined to rebel or revolt

myopia—nearsightedness

myriad—a great number

N

nadir—the lowest point

naiad—a water nymph; a female swimmer

naiveté—simplicity; lack of sophistication

narcissism—love for and interest in the self

nascent—being born; starting to develop

natal—pertaining to one's birth

nauseous—sickening

nebulous—vague; indefinite

necromancy—black magic

nefarious—wicked

negation—denial; the absence of a positive quality

negligible—so unimportant that it can be neglected

nemesis—fair punishment; something that seems to defeat a person constantly

neolithic—pertaining to the Stone Age

neophyte—a beginner

nepotism—special consideration to relatives, particularly in assignment to offices or positions

nettle—to sting; to irritate or annoy

neurosis—a mental disorder

nexus—a connection

nicety—exactness and delicacy

niggardly—stingy

nihilist—one who believes there is no basis for knowledge; one who rejects common religious beliefs

nocturnal—pertaining to night

noisome—harmful; offensive

nomadic—moving from place to place

nomenclature—a system for naming

nominal—pertaining to names; slight

nonchalant—cool; indifferent

noncommittal—not aligning oneself with any side or point of view

nondescript—having few distinguishing qualities; hard to classify

nonentity—something that exists only in the mind; something or someone of little importance

nonpareil—without equal

nonplus—to perplex

non sequitur—something that does not follow logically from what went before

nostalgia—homesickness

notorious—well-known (often unfavorably)

novice—a beginner

noxious—harmful; unwholesome

nuance—a slight variation of color, tone, etc.

nugatory—worthless

nullify—to make invalid or useless

nurture—to feed and/or raise (a child)

nutrient—a food

O

oaf—a clumsy, stupid person

obdurate—hardhearted; hardened; inflexible

obeisance—a motion of reverence

obese—very fat

obfuscate—to make unclear; to confuse

objurgate—to rebuke

oblation—an offering

oblique—slanting; indirect

obliquity—the state of being oblique

obliterate—to wipe out

oblivion—forgetfulness

obloquy—verbal abuse or the disgrace that results from it

obnoxious—offensive

obscure—dim; unclear

obsequious—too servile or submissive

obsession—an idea that persists in the mind

obsolete—out-of-date; no longer used

obstreperous—unruly

obtrude—to push out

obtrusive—pushy in calling attention to oneself

obtuse—blunt; dull

obviate—to make unnecessary

occlude—to close; to shut in or out

occult—hidden; secret; mysterious

odious—offensive

odoriferous—having a (pleasant) odor

odyssey—a long journey

officious—providing help that is not wanted

ogle—to look at openly and with desire

oleaginous—oily

olfactory—pertaining to the sense of smell

oligarchy—a state ruled by a few persons

ominous—threatening

omnipotent—all-powerful

omniscient—all-knowing

omnivorous—eating both animals and vegetables

onerous—burdensome

onslaught—an attack

opaque—letting no light through

opiate—a medicine or anything else that quiets and deadens

opportune—at the right time

opprobrium—disgrace

optimum—best

opulence—wealth; abundance

oracular—wise; prophetic

ordure—filth

orifice—a mouth or opening

ornate—heavily decorated; showy

ornithologist—one who studies birds

orthodox—holding the accepted beliefs of a particular group

oscillate—to move back and forth

osculate—to kiss

ossify—to harden into bone; to settle into a habit

ostensible—apparent

ostentatious—showy; pretentious

ostracize—to banish or exclude

overt—open; observable

overweening—extremely proud

P

pacifist—one who opposes war

paean—a song of joy or praise

palatable—suitable for eating

palatial—like a palace

palaver—idle talk

pall—to become boring or otherwise bothersome

palliate—to lessen or ease (pain); to excuse

pallid—pale

palpable—able to be felt or to be grasped by the senses

paltry—insignificant

panacea—a cure-all

pander—to cater to another's unworthy desires, especially sexual

panegyric—a formal tribute

panoply—a suit of armor; a protective or showy covering

paradigm—an example or model

paradox—a statement that appears false but may be true; a statement that contradicts itself and is false

paragon—a model of perfection

paramount—chief; dominant

paranoia—a state in which one believes that others are against him or that he is a great or famous person

paraphernalia—personal possessions; equipment or gear

parasite—one who lives off another without giving anything in return

paregoric—a medicine

pariah—an outcast

parity—equality

parlance—a manner of speaking or writing

paroxysm—an attack or convulsion

parricide—the killing of a parent

parry—to ward off (a blow); to evade

parsimony—stinginess

partiality—bias; prejudice

parvenu—one who has risen in wealth or power quickly

passive—yielding; non-resisting

pastoral—pertaining to shepherds or rural life in general

patent—obvious

pathetic—pitiful

pathos—a feeling of pity or sorrow

patriarch—a father and ruler

patricide—the killing of one's father

patrimony—an inheritance

paucity—scarcity

pecadillo—a minor fault

peculate—to embezzle

pecuniary—pertaining to money

pedagogue—a teacher, often a narrow-minded one

pedantic—narrow-minded in teaching

pedestrian—ordinary and uninteresting

pejorative—derogatory

pellucid—clear; easy to understand

penance—voluntary self-punishment

penchant—a taste or liking

pendant—something that hangs

pendent—hanging

penitent—sorry or ashamed

pensive—thoughtful

penurious—stingy; poverty-stricken

penury—poverty

percussion—the impact of one thing against another

perdition—damnation; hell

peregrinations—travels

peremptory—final; undeniable or unopposable; dictatorial

perennial—lasting all through the year; lasting a long time

perfidious—treacherous

perforce—necessarily

perfunctory—without care; superficial

perigee—the point nearest the earth in an orbit

peripatetic—moving or walking about

periphery—the boundary of something; the perimeter

perjury—telling a lie under oath

permeable—able to be passed through

permeate—to pass through; to spread through

permutation—a complete change

pernicious—deadly

perpetrate—to do (something bad)

perpetual—eternal

perquisite—a benefit in addition to one's regular pay; prerogative

persiflage—a light style of talking; banter

perspective—the appearance of things caused by their positions and distances; a way of seeing things in their true relation to each other

perspicacious—keen; acute in judgment

pertinacious—persistent

pertinent—relevant

perturb—to upset or alarm

peruse—to study; to read casually

pervade—to spread throughout

perverse—wrong or corrupt; perverted; stubborn

perversion—an abnormal form; a twisting or distortion

pervious—able to be passed through or penetrated; open-minded

pessimist—one who looks on the dark side and expects the worst

pestilence—an epidemic; anything harmful

petrify—to turn to stone; to harden; to stun with fear

petulant—pert; irritable

phalanx—military ranks in close formation; a group of individuals

philander—to carry on light love affairs

philanthropist—one who gives money to help others

philistine—a narrow and conventional person who ignores the arts and culture

phlegmatic—sluggish; calm

phobia—an irrational, unwarranted fear (of something)

physiognomy—one's face and facial expressions

pied—spotted

piety—faithfulness to religious duties; devotion to family

pillage—to loot or plunder

pinion—to cut or tie a bird's wings to keep it from flying; to bind a man's arms; to shackle

pious—devout

piquant—sharp or biting to the taste; stimulating

pique—to offend or provoke

pithy—meaningful; concise

pittance—a meager amount

placate—to pacify

placid—calm; quiet

plaintive—mournful

plait—to pleat or braid

platitude—a dull or commonplace remark

platonic—intellectual or spiritual but not sexual (relationship)

plaudit—applause; an expression of approval

plausible—apparently true

plebeian—a common man

plebiscite—a vote by the people on a political issue

plenary—full; complete

plenipotentiary—a man who has full power as a governmental representative

plethora—excess

plutocracy—government by the wealthy

poach—to trespass; to steal

pogrom—a systematic persecution or killing of a group

poignant—sharply affecting the senses or feelings

politic—prudent; crafty

poltroon—a coward

polygamy—having more than one husband or wife

polyglot—speaking or writing several languages

pommel—the knob on the end of a sword or on a saddle

pompous—stately; self-important

ponder—to consider carefully

portend—to foreshadow

portent—an omen

portly—stout

posit—to place in position; to set forth as fact

posterity—all future generations

posthumous—born after one's father is dead; published after the writer's death; happening after death

postprandial—after-dinner

potable—drinkable

potentate—a ruler

potential—possible; latent

potpourri—a collection of varied things

poultice—a hot, soft mass, sometimes put on sore parts of the body

practicable—feasible; usable

pragmatic—practical; dealing with daily matters

prate—to chatter

precarious—uncertain; risky

precedent—a legal occurrence that is an example for future ones

precept—a rule of conduct

precipitate—to throw downward, to bring on

precipitous—like a precipice; abrupt

preclude—to make impossible; to prevent

precocious—developing earlier than usual

precursor—a forerunner

predatory—living by robbing or exploiting others; feeding on other animals

predicate—to state as a quality of someone or something; to affirm

predilection—a preference

predispose—to make receptive

preeminent—better than others in a particular quality

prefatory—introductory

prelude—opening

premeditate—to think out ahead of time

premise—a statement on which an argument is based

premonition—a forewarning; a foreboding

preponderate—to sink downward; to predominate

preposterous—absurd

prerogative—a right or privilege

presage—to warn; to predict

prescience—foreknowledge

presentiment—a premonition or foreboding

presumption—taking something upon oneself without permission; forwardness

pretentious—claiming greatness; showing off

preternatural—abnormal; supernatural

prevaricate—to avoid the truth; to lie

primordial—existing from the beginning; original

pristine—in original condition; pure and unspoiled

privy (to)—told about (something) in secret

probity—honesty

proboscis—a long snout; a nose

proclivity—a slope; a tendency

procrastinate—to delay or postpone

prodigal—wasteful; generous

prodigious—wonderful; huge

profane—nonreligious; irreverent

proffer—to offer

proficient—skilled

profligate—immoral; wasteful

profound—very deep

profusion—a great abundance

progenitor—a forefather

progeny—children or descendants

prognosis—a forecast

proletarian—a worker

prolific—producing a lot (of children, fruit, or ideas)

prolix—wordy; long-winded

promiscuous—containing many various elements; engaging in indiscriminate sexual affairs

promontory—a headland

promulgate—to make known

prone—lying face downward; disposed (to do something)

propagate—to breed or reproduce

propensity—a natural tendency

propinquity—nearness; kinship

propitiate—to appease

propitious—gracious; boding well; advantageous

proponent—one who puts forth an idea

propound—to propose

propriety—suitability

prosaic—commonplace

proscribe—to outlaw or forbid

prosody—the study or the art of verse or versification

prostrate—lying face downward; overcome

protégé—one who is helped in his career by another

protocol—a document outlining points of agreement; a system of proper conduct in diplomatic encounters

prototype—a model

protract—to prolong

protrude—to stick out

protuberant—sticking out

provident—providing for future needs

proviso—a condition (that one must meet)

provoke—to excite; to anger

prowess—boldness; skill

proximity—nearness

proxy—a person who acts for another

prudent—careful; wise

puerile—childish

pugnacious—quarrelsome

puissant—powerful

pulchritude—beauty

pulmonary—pertaining to the lungs

punctilious—careful about detail; exact

pungent—sharp; biting

punitive—pertaining to punishment

purloin—to steal
purport—to claim
purveyor—one who supplies
purview—scope; range
pusillanimous—timid; uncourageous
putative—reputed
putrid—rotten; stinking

Q

quack—one who practices medicine without training; a charlatan
quaff—to drink
quagmire—a bog; a difficult situation
quail—to lose courage
qualm—a sudden ill feeling; a sudden misgiving
quandary—a dilemma
queasy—nauseous; uneasy
quell—to subdue; to quiet
querulous—complaining
query—a question
quibble—to object to something for petty reasons
quiescent—inactive
quietude—quiet; rest
quintessence—the most perfect example
quip—a witty remark
quirk—a twist (as of luck); an evasion; a peculiarity
quixotic—like Don Quixote; romantic and idealistic
quizzical—comical; teasing; questioning

R

rabble—a mob; the masses
rabid—violent; fanatical
raillery—satire; teasing

raiment—clothing
ramification—a branching; a consequence or result of something
rampant—growing or spreading richly; wild and uncontrollable in behavior
rancid—spoiled, as stale fat
rancor—hate
rankle—to provoke anger or rancor
rant—to rave
rapacious—greedy; predatory
rapine—taking away people's property by force; plunder
rapprochement—a bringing together
rarefied—thin; refined
ratiocination—reasoning
rationalize—to explain rationally; to find motives for one's behavior that are not the true ones
raucous—loud and rowdy
ravage—to ruin
ravening—look greedily for prey
ravenous—extremely hungry
rebate— to return (part of money paid); to deduct (from a bill)
rebuke—to scold sharply
recalcitrant—stubborn; hard to handle
recant—to take back (a belief or statement)
recapitulate—to summarize
recidivist—one who falls back into crime or other bad behavior
reciprocal—done in return; occurring on both sides
recision—the act of rescinding

recluse—one who lives apart from others
reconcile—to bring together again; to make consistent
recondite—not understandable by most people; obscure
reconnaissance—looking over a situation to get information
recourse—turning to (someone or something) for help
recreant—cowardly; disloyal
recrimination—answering an attack by attacking in return
rectify—to make right
rectitude—moral uprightness
recumbent—lying down; resting
recurrent—happening again one or more times
redeem—to get back; to save from sin; to make (oneself) worthy again by making amends
redolent—sweet-smelling
redoubtable—fearful
redress—to rectify
redundant—more than enough; wordy
refection—refreshment
refraction—the bending of a light ray or sound wave
refractory—stubborn
refulgent—shining
refutation—disproof
regale—to entertain with a feast
regeneration—renewal; rebirth
regime—a system or period of government
regimen—a system of diet and other physical care designed to aid the health

regressive—going backward
reimburse—to pay back
reiterate—to repeat over and over
rejuvenate—to make seem young again
relegate—to send away (to someplace)
relevant—pertaining to the matter in question
relinquish—to give (something) up
relish—to enjoy
remediable—curable; correctable
reminisce—to remember
remiss—careless in one's duty
remission—forgiveness; a letting up
remnant—remainder
remonstrate—to protest
remunerative—profitable
render—to give over; to give up; to cause to become
renegade—one who gives up his religion or cause and joins the opposition
renounce—to give up (a right, for example)
renovate—to renew
reparable—able to be repaired
reparation—a repairing; making up for a wrong
repartee—a clever reply; clever conversation back and forth
repast—a meal
repercussion—an effect of an event
repertoire—the selection of works a performer or group is prepared to perform
replenish—to refill
replete—full; stuffed
repository—a place where things are kept
reprehensible—deserving criticism

reprieve—a postponement of punishment
reprimand—a formal rebuke
reprisal—force used in retaliation for an act by another country
reproach—to make (someone) feel ashamed
reprobate—a person of no principles
reprove—to rebuke or disapprove
repudiate—to disown; to deny
repugnant—contradictory; offensive
requiem—a Mass or music for the dead
requisite—required
requite—to return or repay
rescind—to repeal (an order)
resilient—elastic; buoyant
respite—a delay; a letup
resplendent—splendid
restitution—restoration; reimbursement
restive—balky; unruly; restless
resurgent—rising again
resuscitate—to revive
retaliate—to return injury or evil in kind
retentive—holding; able to remember
reticent—speaking very little
retinue—a group of followers or attendants
retort—to answer in kind; to reply sharply or cleverly
retract—to take back
retribution—just punishment or reward
retrieve—to recover (something); to save
retroactive—applying to the past

retrograde—going backward
retrospective—looking backward
revelry—merrymaking
reverberate—to echo
reverie—a daydream
revert—to go back to a former state
revile—to abuse; to scold
revoke—to withdraw; to rescind
revulsion—a sudden change in feeling; disgust
rheumy—watery
ribald—vulgar; coarse
rife—occurring everywhere; plentiful
rigor—strictness; exactness
risible—laughable
risqué—daring
robust—healthy and strong
rococo—an elaborate architectural style
roseate—rosy; cheerful
rote—routine
rotund—rounded; stout
rubicund—reddish
rudiment—a basic principle; a first stage
rueful—pitiable; mournful
ruminate—to ponder
rummage—to search through
ruse—a trick
ruthless—cruel

S

sable—black
saccharine—pertaining to sugar; too sweet
sacerdotal—priestly
sacrilegious—in violation of something sacred
sacrosanct—holy; not to be violated
sadist—one who gets pleasure from hurting others

sagacious—perceptive; shrewd

sage—wise

salacious—lecherous; pornographic

salient—leaping; standing out; prominent

saline—salty

sallow—having a sickly, yellowish coloring

salubrious—healthful

salutary—conducive to good health

sanctity—holiness

sang-froid—coolness; calmness

sanguine—blood-colored; cheerful and optimistic

sapient—wise

sardonic—sarcastic

sartorial—pertaining to tailors or clothing

sate—to satisfy completely

satiate—to glut

saturate—to soak

saturnine—gloomy

savant—a scholar

savoir-faire—tact

savor—to season; to taste or smell appreciatively

scabrous—scaly; improper

scapegoat—one who is blamed for the wrongs of another

scathing—harsh; biting

schism—a split

scintilla—a tiny bit

scintillate—to sparkle; to show verbal brilliance

scion—an offspring

scoff—to jeer (at)

scourge—a whip; a punishment

scruple—a qualm or doubt

scrupulous—very careful in doing what is correct

scrutiny—close inspection

scurrilous—coarse; vulgar

scuttle—to scurry; to sink (a ship); to abandon (a plan)

sebaceous—pertaining to fat

secede—to withdraw

secular—worldly

sedate—calm; serious

sedentary—sitting much of the time

seditious—pertaining to revolt against the government

sedulous—diligent

seethe—to boil; to foam

seine—a fishing net

seismic—pertaining to earthquakes

semantic—pertaining to meaning

semblance—appearance

senile—showing mental deterioration due to old age

sensual—pertaining to the body or the senses

sententious—pointed; full of trite wordings

sentient—feeling; conscious

sepulcher—a tomb

sequester—to set apart; to withdraw

serene—calm

serrated—having notches along the edge

servile—slavelike

sever—to separate; to cut in two

shackle—to hold back; to restrain

shambles—a slaughterhouse; a place of disorder

shard—a broken piece (of pottery)

sheathe—to put (a knife or sword) into its covering

shibboleth—a phrase or a practice that is observed by a particular group

shoddy—cheap; poorly made

shunt—to turn aside

sidereal—pertaining to the stars or constellations

simian—pertaining to monkeys

simile—a figure of speech that compares things by using *like* or *as*

simper—to smile in a silly way

simulate—to pretend or fake

sinecure—a job that requires little work

sinister—threatening; evil

sinuous—winding; devious

skeptical—doubting

skittish—playful; jumpy

skulk—to slink

slake—to satisfy

slatternly—dirty; untidy

sleazy—flimsy (as a fabric); cheap or shoddy

slothful—lazy

slough—to shed; a swamp

slovenly—careless or untidy

sluggard—a lazy person

sobriety—soberness

sojourn—a temporary stay

solecism—a misuse of grammar; a breach of manners

solicitous—expressing care; eager

soliloquy—a talking to oneself

solstice—the point at which the sun is farthest north or south of the equator

solvent—able to pay one's debts
somatic—pertaining to the body
somnambulism—sleepwalking
somnolent—sleepy; making one sleepy
sonorous—rich and full (sound)
soothsayer—one who predicts the future
sophisticated—urbane; not naive
sordid—dirty; ignoble
soupçon—a trace or hint
spasmodic—intermittent
specious—appearing correct but not really so
specter—a ghost
spectral—ghostly
splenetic—bad-tempered
spontaneous—arising naturally or by its own force
sporadic—occasional
sportive—playful
spurious—false; not real
squalid—filthy; sordid
squander—to waste
staid—sober
stalwart—sturdy; brave; firm
stamina—endurance
stark—prominent; barren; blunt
status—position or state
staunch, stanch—to stop (blood) flowing from a wound; to stop or check
stellar—pertaining to the stars
stentorian—very loud
stigma—a sign of disgrace
stilted—elevated; pompous
stint—to hold back in distributing or using
stipend—a salary or allowance

stoical—showing no reaction to various emotions or events
stolid—unexcitable
strait—a narrow waterway; a difficult situation
strategem—a scheme or trick
striated—striped or furrowed
stricture—censure; a limitation
strident—having a harsh or shrill sound
stringent—strict
stultify—to make stupid, dull, or worthless
suave—urbane; polished
subaltern—a subordinate
subjugate—to conquer
sublimate—to purify
sublime—exalted; grand
suborn—to get someone to do something illegal
sub rosa—in private
subsequent—coming later
subservient—servile
subsidiary—supplementary; secondary
subsidy—a grant of money
subsistence—a means of providing one's basic needs
substantiate—to confirm
subterfuge—any means by which one conceals his intentions
subtle—thin; characterized by slight differences and qualities; not obvious
subversive—inclined to overthrow or harm the government
succinct—clear and brief
succor—to aid
succulent—juicy
suffuse—to spread throughout

sully—to soil
sultry—hot and close
summation—adding up
sumptuous—lavish
sunder—to split apart
sundry—miscellaneous
superannuated—too old to be of use; outdated
supercilious—haughty
superficial—pertaining to the surface aspects of something
superfluous—more than the amount needed
superlative—of the best kind; supreme
supersede—to take the place of
supine—lying on the back
supple—flexible
supplicant—one who prays for or asks for (something)
surcease—an end
surfeit—to provide too much of something; to satiate
surly—rude and ill-tempered
surmise—a guess made on the basis of little evidence
surreptitious—secret
surrogate—a substitute
surveillance—a watch over someone
sustenance—maintenance
sybaritic—loving luxury
sycophant—one who flatters to gain favor of important people
sylvan—pertaining to the woods
symmetry—balance
symposium—a meeting for the exchange of ideas
synchronize—to regulate several things so they will correspond in time

synopsis—a summary

synthesis—a putting together

synthetic—not natural; artificial

T

tacit—unspoken; understood rather than declared

taciturn—reluctant to speak

tactful—saying and doing the appropriate thing when people's feelings are involved

tactile—pertaining to the sense of touch

taint—to infect or spoil

talisman—a charm supposed to have magic power

tangible—touchable; objective

tantamount—equal (to)

tantalize—to tempt (someone) with something he cannot have

tautological—employing needless repetition of an idea

tawdry—cheap and gaudy

tawny—tan in color

tedious—tiresome

temerity—foolish boldness

temperate—moderate

template—a pattern

temporal—temporary; worldly

tenacious—holding fast

tenet—a principle

tentative—proposed but not final; hesitant

tenuous—thin; slight

tenure—the period of time for which something is held; a permanent status in a job based on length of service

tepid—lukewarm

termagant—a shrewish old woman

terminal—pertaining to the end

terrestrial—earthly; pertaining to land

terse—concise

tertiary—third

testy—irritable

theocracy—rule of a state by God or by God's authority

therapeutic—curing

thermal—pertaining to heat

thespian—pertaining to drama; an actor

thralldom—slavery

throes—pangs

thwart—to obstruct or prevent

tirade—a lengthy, violent speech

titanic—huge

tithe—a tenth of something

titular—pertaining to a title; in name only

toady—one who tries to gain another's favor; sycophant

tome—a book, especially a large one

torpid—dormant; slow-moving

tortuous—twisting; devious

toxic—poisonous

tract—a stretch of land

tractable—easy to manage or control

traduce—to slander

trammel—to confine or entangle

tranquil—calm; peaceful

transcend—to go beyond

transcribe—to write out in one form from another

transgression—a breaking of a rule; a violation of a limit

transient—not permanent

transition—a change from one thing to another

transitory—fleeting

translucent—allowing light through

transmute—to change from one form to another

transpire—to become known

transverse—lying across

trappings—one's clothes and equipment

trauma—a severe injury or shock

travail—hard work; pain

traverse—to go across

travesty—a burlesque; a distortion (of something)

treatise—a formal, written presentation of a subject

trek—to travel slowly

tremor—a trembling; a vibration

tremulous—trembling; afraid

trenchant—keen; forceful

trepidation—uncertainty and anxiety

tribulation—great unhappiness; a trying circumstance

tribunal—a law court

trite—overworked; no longer novel

troth—truth; one's word, as a promise

truckle—to submit and be servile

truculent—cruel; rude

truism—a statement that is known to be true

trumpery—something pretentious but not worth anything

truncate—to cut off part of

truncheon—a club
tryst—a meeting
tumid—swollen; inflated
turbid—muddy; dense
turbulence—a state of commotion or agitation
turgid—swollen; pompous
turncoat—a renegade; a traitor
turnkey—a jailer
turpitude—vileness
tutelage—care; guardianship
tyro—a beginner

U

ubiquitous—omnipresent
ulterior—on the far side; later; beyond what is said
ultimate—the farthest, final, or highest
ultimatum—a nonnegotiable demand
umbrage—offense
unadulterated—pure
unanimity—agreement
unassuming—modest
unbridled—uncontrolled; free
uncanny—strange; weird
unconscionable—done without applying one's conscience
uncouth—clumsy; not having culture or polish
unction—ointment; an intense manner of behavior; unctuousness
unctuous—oily; displaying fake religious feeling
undulate—to move in waves
unearth—to dig up
unequivocal—clear
unfaltering—unhesitating

unfathomable—not understandable
ungainly—awkward
unguent—an ointment
unimpeachable—undoubtable; above reproach
unique—unlike any other
unkempt—untidy
unmitigated—unrelieved
unprecedented—never having occurred before
unremitting—not letting up
unruly—unmanageable
unseemly—not proper
untenable—unable to be held
unwitting—unconscious; unaware
unwonted—rare
upbraid—to rebuke
urbane—polished and refined
usurp—to take by force
usury—lending money at outrageously high interest rates
utilitarian—useful
utopian—idealistic; perfect
uxorious—overly fond of one's wife

V

vacillate—to move one way and then the other; to waver
vacuous—empty; stupid
vagary—a peculiarity
vainglorious—vain and boastful
valiant—brave
validate—to confirm legally
vanguard—the group in front
vapid—dull
variegated—having a variety of colors in splotches; diverse
vaunt—a boast

veer—to change direction
vegetate—to have a dull, inactive existence
vehement—having great force or passion
venal—bribable
vendetta—a feud
vendor—a seller
vengeance—punishment; revenge
veneer—a thin covering of fine wood over cheaper wood; a thin and superficial display of a noble quality
venerable—old and honorable
venerate—to respect deeply
venial—forgivable
vent—to allow (steam or feelings) to escape
veracious—truthful
verbatim—word-for-word
verbiage—wordiness
verbose—wordy
verdant—green
verily—truly
verisimilar—appearing to be true
verity—truth
vernacular—the common speech of an area or its people
versatile—changeable; adaptable
vertigo—dizziness
vestige—a trace
viable—able or likely to live
viand—something to eat
vicarious—substitute; done or experienced by one person through another
vicissitudes—changes
victuals—food
vie—to compete
vigilant—watchful
vilify—to slander
vindicate—to free of blame

vindictive—seeking revenge

virile—manly; masculine

virtuoso—a skilled performer

virulent—deadly

visage—one's face

viscid—sticky; viscous

viscous—sticky; viscid

visionary—like a vision; unrealistic

vitiate—to spoil or debase

vitriolic—bitter

vituperation—harsh language

vivacious—lively

vivid—lively; intense

vociferous—loud

volatile—turning to vapor quickly; changeable

volition—employing one's will

voluble—talkative

voluptuous—sensual; inclined toward luxury

voracious—greedy

votary—one who has taken a vow; a follower or supporter of a cause

vouchsafe—to grant

vulnerable—in a position to be attacked or injured

W

waggish—playful

waive—to give up (a right, etc.)

wan—pale

wane—to decrease

wanton—morally loose; unwarranted

warranty—a guarantee

wary—cautious

wastrel—one who wastes (money)

weal—welfare

wheedle—to coax

whet—to sharpen

whimsical—fanciful

whit—(the) least bit

wily—sly

windfall—a surprising bit of good luck

winnow—to pick out the good elements or parts of something

winsome—charming

witless—foolish

witticism—a clever remark

wizened—withered; dried up

wont—accustomed

wraith—a ghost

wreak—to allow to be expressed; to inflict

wrest—to take away by force

wry—twisted; stubborn

Y

yeoman—a man who has a small amount of land

Z

zany—clownish; crazy

zealot—one who is extremely devoted to his cause

zenith—the highest point

zephyr—a breeze

zest—spirited enjoyment

part IV

7 DIAGNOSTIC MATH TESTS

Use these tests to diagnose your weaknesses in math. Then use the code numbers following each explanatory answer to guide you to the section in Part V that offers instruction in your weak areas.

The purpose of these Diagnostic Math Tests is to pinpoint your weaknesses in math. Once you know in just which areas you are shaky, you may use to good advantage the Math Refresher Section in Part V of this book. After practicing in your weak areas, you should score much higher on the practice SAT tests.

Take these Diagnostic Math Tests under strict examination conditions, with no interruptions. Allow yourself exactly the number of minutes allotted, and answer every one of the ten questions in each test.

All explanatory answers include a number, e.g., (4.21) in parenthesis after *each* answer. The number refers to a specific section in Part V, the Math Refresher Section, where the rules and principles involved in the question are explained simply and clearly. These explanations are invaluable for strengthening your weaknesses in specific math topics.

DIAGNOSTIC TEST 1

Fraction, Decimal, Percentage, Deviation, Ratio, and Proportion Problems

Time: 30 minutes
Correct answers and solutions follow each test.

1. What is the product of the fractions $\frac{21}{16}$, $\frac{15}{8}$, and $\frac{32}{27}$?

1. A B C D E

(A) $\frac{15}{2}$

(B) $\frac{15}{4}$

(C) $\frac{35}{2}$

(D) $\frac{35}{4}$

(E) $\frac{35}{12}$

2. A ball club has played 12 games and won 4. How many additional games must it win *in a row* to achieve a 50% winning record?

(A) 3
(B) 4
(C) 5
(D) 6
(E) 7

3. A stationer buys 1500 pens at $1.00 a dozen, and 1500 pencils at $.90 a dozen. He then packages them into 1500 pen-and-pencil sets, which he sells for $.50 a set. What is his fractional profit on the whole transaction?

(A) $\dfrac{\$512.50}{\$237.50}$

(B) $\dfrac{\$512.50}{\$750.00}$

(C) $\dfrac{\$237.50}{\$750.00}$

(D) $\dfrac{\$750.00}{\$512.50}$

(E) $\dfrac{\$750.00}{\$237.50}$

4. If, on a map, one inch represents 1000 feet, how many yards are represented by a line $\frac{3}{4}$ of a foot long?

(A) 9000
(B) 3000
(C) 750
(D) $\dfrac{125}{6}$
(E) none of these

5. If, in the formula $P = \frac{1}{2}Ac^2$, the value of c is increased by 20%, by what percent does P increase, assuming that A remains constant?

(A) 22%
(B) 66%
(C) $33\frac{1}{3}\%$
(D) 88%
(E) 44%

6. Which of the following fractions is the largest?

6. A B C D E

(A) $\dfrac{11}{19}$

(B) $\dfrac{13}{21}$

(C) $\dfrac{7}{11}$

(D) $\dfrac{15}{23}$

(E) $\dfrac{9}{13}$

7. An object in a store is marked up to 125% of the original cost. During a sale, the item is discounted to 80% of its marked-up price. What is the ratio of the original cost to the final price?

7. A B C D E

(A) 1 : 1.25
(B) 1.25 : 0.8
(C) 0.8 : 1
(D) 0.8 : 1.25
(E) 1 : 1

8. Find 2.5% of 0.04.

8. A B C D E

(A) 0.01
(B) 0.001
(C) 0.0001
(D) 0.0016
(E) 0.16

9. In certain states, there is a 5% sales tax on all purchases. If an entire bill added up to $44.52, what was the cost of the purchase *without* tax?

9. A B C D E

(A) $44.60
(B) $41.80
(C) $42.00
(D) $42.20
(E) $42.40

10. On a certain army base, 30% of the men were from New York State, and 40% of those were from New York City. What percent of all the men on the base were from New York City?

10. A B C D E

(A) 10%
(B) 12%
(C) 15%
(D) 18%
(E) 24%

Answer Key for Diagnostic Test 1

1. E

2. B

3. A

4. B

5. E

6. E

7. E

8. B

9. E

10. B

All explanatory answers below include a number (or numbers) in parentheses after *each* answer. The number refers to a specific section in Part V, Math Refresher, where the rules and principles involved in the question are explained simply and clearly. These explanations are invaluable for strengthening your weaknesses in specific math topics.

Explanatory Answers for Diagnostic Test 1

1. **(E)**
$\frac{21}{16} \times \frac{15}{8} \times \frac{32}{27} = \frac{21 \times 15 \times 32}{16 \times 8 \times 27}$. We can divide both the numerator and denominator of a fraction by the same number without changing the value of the fraction. First, dividing by 16 gives us $\frac{21 \times 15 \times 2}{1 \times 8 \times 27}$. Dividing this by 3 gives us $\frac{7 \times 15 \times 2}{1 \times 8 \times 9}$, and dividing by 3 again gives us $\frac{7 \times 5 \times 2}{1 \times 8 \times 3}$. Then, dividing by 2 gives us $\frac{7 \times 5}{1 \times 4 \times 3} = \frac{35}{12}$. **(1.14)**

2. (B)

To achieve a 50% winning record, a team must win half the games it plays. Thus, letting g represent the number of additional games to be played, $4 + g$ = total games won, and $12 + g$ = total games played. Games won divided by games played must equal 50%. Thus, $\dfrac{4 + g}{12 + g} = 50\% = \dfrac{1}{2}$. Cross-multiplying: $2(4 + g) = 1(12 + g)$. $8 + 2g = 12 + g$. Subtracting $8 + g$ from both sides, $g = 4$. The club must win four more games in a row to achieve a 50% winning record.   **(2.4, 1.1)**

3. (A)

1500 equals 12×125, or 125 dozen. Original cost equals 125 dozen pens at \$1.00 per dozen plus 125 dozen pencils at \$.90 per dozen, for a total of \$125.00 + \$112.50, or \$237.50. Total gross receipts = 1500 sets at \$.50 a set, or \$750.00. Thus, net profit = \$750.00 − \$237.50 = \$512.50. Fractional profit = $\dfrac{\text{net profit}}{\text{cost}} = \dfrac{\$512.50}{\$237.50}$.   **(2.4)**

4. (B)

$\dfrac{3}{4}$ foot = $\dfrac{3}{4}$ of 12 inches = 9 inches. Given 1 inch on map = 1000 feet; therefore, 9 inches = 9000 feet. Since 3 feet = 1 yard, $\dfrac{9000 \text{ feet}}{\dfrac{3 \text{ feet}}{\text{yard}}} = 3000$ yards.   **(1.14)**

5. (E)

$P = \dfrac{1}{2}Ac^2$. If we replace c by c', which is the new c, and P by P', the new P, we have $P' = \dfrac{1}{2}A(c')^2$. But $c' = 120\% \times c = \dfrac{6c}{5}$.

Thus, $P' = \dfrac{1}{2}A\left(\dfrac{6c}{5}\right)^2 = \dfrac{1}{2}A\left(\dfrac{36}{25}\right)(c^2) = \left(\dfrac{36}{25}\right)(P) = 144\% \times P$. Therefore, P increases by 44%.   **(1.14)**

6. **(E)**
The easiest way to compare fractions is to convert them to decimals, which can be readily compared at sight. To do this, divide the numerator of each fraction by its denominator. Thus:

$$\frac{11}{19} = 19 \overline{)11.00} .57$$

$$\frac{13}{21} = 21 \overline{)13.00} .62$$

$$\frac{7}{11} = 11 \overline{)7.00} .637 \approx .64$$

$$\frac{15}{23} = 23 \overline{)15.00} .65$$

$$\frac{9}{13} = 13 \overline{)9.00} .69$$

Since 0.69 is the largest decimal, $\frac{9}{13}$ is the largest fraction.   **(1.2)**

7. **(E)**
Call the original cost C and the final price FP. The object is then marked up to 125% of C, or 1.25 × C. This new price is then marked down to 80%, or 0.8 of the new price: (0.8) × (1.25) × C = 1.00 × C = FP, or C = FP. Therefore, the ratio of the original cost to the final price is 1 : 1.   **(1.24)**

8. **(B)**
Since 2.5% = 0.025, then 2.5% of 0.04 = 0.025 × 0.04 = 0.001.   **(1.35)**

9. **(E)**
Call the cost, excluding tax, C. Then we have the equation 105% × C = $44.52. Since 105% = 1.05, this equation can be rewritten as 1.05 × C = $44.52. Dividing by 1.05 gives us C = $42.40.   **(1.35)**

10. **(B)**
The number of men from New York City was 40% of 30% of the number of men on the base. "Of" means "times," so we multiply 40% × 30%. Since 40% = $\frac{40}{100}$ and 30% = $\frac{30}{100}$, 40% × 30% = $\frac{40}{100} \times \frac{30}{100} = \frac{1200}{10,000} = \frac{12}{100}$, or 12%.

An alternate solution uses decimals. Since 40% = 0.40 and 30% = 0.30, we multiply 0.40 × 0.30 and get 0.12. Then we convert 0.12 back to a percent by multiplying it by 100: 100 × 0.12 = 12, or 12%.   **(1.3)**

DIAGNOSTIC TEST 2

Rate Problems: Distance and Time, Work, Mixture, and Cost

Time: 30 minutes
Correct answers and solutions follow each test.

1. If a man can run m miles in n minutes, what is his speed in miles per hour?
   - (A) mn
   - (B) $60mn$
   - (C) $\dfrac{m}{n}$
   - (D) $\dfrac{m}{60n}$
   - (E) $\dfrac{60m}{n}$

   1. A B C D E

2. A man spent $2.00 on $.08 stamps and $.10 stamps. If he bought 23 stamps in all, how many $.08 stamps did he buy?
   - (A) 5
   - (B) 8
   - (C) 10
   - (D) 13
   - (E) 15

   2. A B C D E

3. If 6 identical faucets turned on simultaneously can fill a tub in 8 minutes, how long will it take 9 such faucets to do the same job?
   - (A) 5 minutes
   - (B) $5\frac{1}{3}$ minutes
   - (C) 6 minutes
   - (D) 9 minutes
   - (E) 12 minutes

   3. A B C D E

4. A plane takes 5 hours to complete a 1200-mile trip if it travels in the same direction as the wind. If it travels against the wind, the trip takes 6 hours. What is the speed of the wind?
   - (A) 25 mph
   - (B) 100 mph
   - (C) 30 mph
   - (D) 200 mph
   - (E) 20 mph

   4. A B C D E

5. If you mix a certain amount of a 40% solution of sulfuric acid with an equal amount of pure sulfuric acid, what will be the concentration (percentage) of the resulting solution?
   (A) 40%
   (B) 50%
   (C) 60%
   (D) 70%
   (E) 80%

6. Machine A can do a job in 10 minutes, and Machine B can do the same job in 5 minutes. How many minutes does it take the two machines working together to complete the job?
   (A) 3
   (B) 15
   (C) $2\frac{1}{2}$
   (D) $3\frac{1}{3}$
   (E) $7\frac{1}{2}$

7. Jim can run 100 yards in 18 seconds, while Billy takes 20 seconds to run the same distance. If Jim gives Billy a 4-second head start, which of them will win a 220-yard race, and by how many seconds?
   (A) Jim will win by a second or more.
   (B) Jim will win by less than a second.
   (C) The race will end a tie.
   (D) Billy will win the race by less than a second.
   (E) Billy will win the race by a second or more.

8. In how many different ways can you add up ten coins to get $1.50? (The coins include pennies, nickels, dimes, and quarters *only*.)
   (A) none
   (B) one
   (C) two
   (D) three
   (E) four

9. Which method of financing a car will be more expensive, and by how much:

1) a down payment of $500, with twelve monthly installments of $180.00 or

2) a down payment of $100.00, with eighty weekly installments of $32.00?

(A)   The first method will cost more by over $50.00.

(B)   The first method will cost more by $50.00 or less.

(C)   The two methods will cost exactly the same.

(D)   The second method will cost more by $50.00 or less.

(E)   The second method will cost more by over $50.00.

10. John can paint a fence in 30 minutes. Steve can paint the same fence in 40 minutes. Approximately how many minutes will it take them, working together, to paint the fence?

(A)   12

(B)   17

(C)   35

(D)   50

(E)   70

Answer Key for Diagnostic Test 2

1. E		**6.** D	
2. E		**7.** B	
3. B		**8.** C	
4. E		**9.** C	
5. D		**10.** B	

All explanatory answers below include a number (or numbers) in parentheses after *each* answer. The number refers to a specific section in Part V, Math Refresher, where the rules and principles involved in the question are explained simply and clearly. These explanations are invaluable for strengthening your weaknesses in specific math topics.

Explanatory Answers for Diagnostic Test 2

1. (E)

Converting minutes to hours, n minutes $= \dfrac{n}{60}$ hours.

rate	$\times$ time	$=$ distance
mi. /hr.	hr.	miles
r	$\dfrac{n}{60}$	m

From the table, $r \times \dfrac{n}{60} = m$; $r = m \times \dfrac{60}{n}$; and $r = \dfrac{60m}{n}$. Since speed is the same as rate, the man's speed is $\dfrac{60m}{n}$ mph.   **(2.45)**

2. (E)

	rate $\times$ number $=$ value		
	¢ /stamp	stamps	cents
$.08 stamp	8	x	$8x$
$.10 stamp	10	y	$10y$

Let $x =$ number of $.08 stamps.
Let $y =$ number of $.10 stamps.
Total number of stamps: $x + y = 23$
Total value of stamps: $8x + 10y = 200$
Solve these simultaneous equations by multiplying $x + y = 23$ by 10 to get $10x + 10y = 230$ and subtracting:

$$\begin{array}{r} 10x + 10y = 230 \\ -(8x + 10y = 200) \\ \hline 2x = 30 \\ x = 15 \end{array}$$

Therefore, the man bought fifteen $.08 stamps.   **(2.42)**

3.   (B)

	rate	×	time	=	work
	tub /min.		min.		tubs
6 faucets	$6r$		8		1
9 faucets	$9r$		t		1

Let r = rate of one faucet.

Let t = time for 9 faucets to fill one tub.

$6r \times 8 = 1$; $48r = 1$; $r = \dfrac{1}{48}$

Then, for 9 faucets: $9r \times t = 1$: $9 \times \dfrac{1}{48} \times t = 1$: $\dfrac{9}{48}t = 1$;

$t = \dfrac{48}{9} = 5\dfrac{1}{3}$ minutes   **(2.410)**

4.   (E)

Speed × time = distance. Let p = speed of the plane in still air and w = speed of the wind. Then:

	speed	×	time	=	distance
	mi. /hr.		hours		miles
with wind	$p + w$		5		1200
against wind	$p - w$		6		1200

Thus, $(p + w) \times 5 = 1200$; $(p + w) \dfrac{1200}{5} = 240$

$(p - w) \times 6 = 1200$; $(p - w) \dfrac{1200}{6} = 200$

Then, $p + w = 240$

$\underline{p - w = 200}$

subtracting, $2w = 40$

$w = 20$ mi. /hr. (speed of the wind)   **(2.45)**

5.   (D)

In this problem, the units we use for the amounts of acid and solution are arbitrary and do not affect the answer. We have chosen the gallon to be the unit.

Let p = the percent of acid in the mixture, and let a = the amount of the 40% solution and also of the pure sulfuric acid (100% solution). The concentration (percent) of acid in any solution multiplied by the amount of solution equals the total amount of acid in that solution, thus:

	concentration ×	amount of solution =	amount of acid
	%	gal.	gal.
in 40% solution	40	a	.40a
in pure acid	100	a	1.00a
in mixture	p	2a	1.40a

Then, $p \times 2a = 1.40a$; $p = \dfrac{1.40a}{2a} = .70$. Thus, 70% is the concentration of the mixture.   **(2.49)**

6. **(D)**

	rate ×	time =	work
	job/min.	min.	jobs
Machine A	a	10	1
Machine B	b	5	1
together	$a + b$	t	1

Let a = rate at which Machine A does the job.

Let b = rate at which Machine B does the job.

Let t = time it takes the two machines working together to do the job.

To find the rate at which Machine A works, we substitute its data in the equation as follows: $10 \times a = 1$; $a = \frac{1}{10}$, or Machine A does $\frac{1}{10}$ of its job per minute.

We do the same to find the rate at which Machine B works: $5 \times b = 1$; $b = \frac{1}{5}$, or Machine B does $\frac{1}{5}$ of its job per minute. Using the same equation and substituting the values we have found, we can find t: $(a + b) \times t = 1$; $\left(\frac{1}{10} + \frac{1}{5}\right)t = 1$; $\left(\frac{1}{10} + \frac{2}{10}\right)t = 1$; $\frac{3}{10}t = 1$. Multiplying both sides of the equation by 10, we get $10 \times \frac{3}{10}t = 10 \times 1$; $3t = 10$; $t = \frac{10}{3}$ or $3\frac{1}{3}$ minutes.   **(2.410)**

7. **(B)**

We are told that Jim's time for 100 yards is 18 seconds, and Billy's time for the same distance is 20 seconds.

Let j = Jim's speed, and z = Jim's time for 220 yds.

Let b = Billy's speed, and y = Billy's time for 220 yds.

We have the following equation and data:

speed $\times$ time = distance

	yds. /sec.	sec.	yds.
Jim	j	18	100
Billy	b	20	100
Jim	j	z	220
Billy	b	y	220

Find Jim's and Billy's speeds on the 100-yd. run:

$j \times 18 = 100; j = \dfrac{100}{18}; j = \dfrac{50}{9}$ yds. /sec., Jim's speed

$b \times 20 = 100; b = \dfrac{100}{20}; b = 5$ yds. /sec., Billy's speed

Knowing the values for j and b, we again use the equation to find the values for the two runners' times for 220 yds.

For Jim:

$j \times z = 220; \dfrac{50}{9} \times z = 220; z = \dfrac{220}{\frac{50}{9}}; z = \overset{22}{\cancel{220}} \times \dfrac{9}{\underset{5}{\cancel{50}}} = 39.6$

sec., Jim's running time for 220 yds. Since Jim gave Billy a 4-second handicap, Jim's total time for the race was 39.6 + 4 = 43.6 seconds.

For Billy:

$b \times y = 220; 5 \times y = 220; y = \dfrac{220}{5}; y = 44$ sec., Billy's time for 220 yds. Billy's time − Jim's time = 44 − 43.6 = 0.4 sec. Thus, Jim's total time is less than a second better than Billy's time.

(2.45)

8.   (C)

value of coin × number = total value

	¢/coin	coins	cents
pennies	1	p	$1p$
nickels	5	n	$5n$
dimes	10	d	$10d$
quarters	25	q	$25q$

Let p = number of pennies.
Let n = number of nickels.
Let d = number of dimes.
Let q = number of quarters.
Total number of coins = $p + n + d + q = 10$
Total value = $p + 5n + 10d + 25q = 150$

We could have 0, 1, 2, 3, 4, 5, or 6 quarters. We will examine each of these possibilities. First if $q = 0$, then $p + n + d + 0 = 10$, and $p + 5n + 10d = 150$. This is impossible because even if the 10 coins were all dimes, giving the highest total value, they would add up to only 100¢—not 150¢. If $q = 1$, $p + n + d + 1 = 10$, or $p + n + d = 9$, and $p + 5n + 10d + 25 = 150$, or $p + 5n + 10d = 125$. This is also impossible because even if the remaining 9 coins were all dimes, giving the highest possible total value, the 10 coins would add up to only 115¢. If $q = 2$, $p + n + d = 8$ and $p + 5n + 10d = 100$. This is still not enough because, using a maximum number of dimes, 8, we have 80¢ + 50¢ (2 quarters), which equals 130¢. If $q = 3$, $p + n + d = 7$ and $p + 5n + 10d = 75$. This still does not provide the needed value. If $q = 4$, $p + n + d = 6$ and $p + 5n + 10d = 50$. So, 4 dimes and 2 nickels will work. This is one correct solution. If $q = 5$, $p + n + d = 5$ and $p + 5n + 10d = 25$, so we need 5 nickels only. This is another correct solution. If $q = 6$, $p + n + d = 4$, $p + 5n + 10d = 0$, which is impossible. Thus, there are only two correct combinations: 4 quarters, 4 dimes, and 2 nickels or 5 quarters and 5 nickels.

(2.42)

9. (C)

rate $\times$ installments $=$ payment

	$ /inst.	number	dollars	
first way	500	1	500	(down payment)
	180	12	2160	
second way	100	1	100	(down payment)
	32	80	2560	

Total payment, first method $= 500 + 2160 = 2660$
Total payment, second method $= 100 + 2560 = 2660$
The two methods cost the same.   **(2.4)**

10. (B)

rate $\times$ time $=$ work

	fnc. /min.	min.	fences
John	r	30	1
Steve	s	40	1
together	$r + s$	t	1

Let $r =$ John's rate of painting.
Let $s =$ Steve's rate of painting.
Let $t =$ time it takes them to paint the fence together.

John's rate: $r \times 30 = 1$; $r = \frac{1}{30}$, or $\frac{1}{30}$ of a fence per minute.

Steve's rate: $s \times 40 = 1$; $s = \frac{1}{40}$, or $\frac{1}{40}$ of a fence per minute.

When John and Steve work together, their rate is the sum of their individual rates: $(r + s)$. Using this joint rate and substituting the results of our calculations in the equation we used above, we get:

$(r + s) \times t = 1$; $\left(\frac{1}{30} + \frac{1}{40}\right)t = 1$; $\left(\frac{4}{120} + \frac{3}{120}\right)t = 1$; $\frac{7}{120}t = 1$;

$7t = 120$; $t = \frac{120}{7} = 17$ minutes, approximately.   **(2.410)**

DIAGNOSTIC TEST 3

Area, Perimeter, and Volume Problems

Time: 35 minutes
Correct answers and solutions follow each test.

1. The area of a certain equilateral triangle is equal to that of a square. What is the ratio of one side of the triangle to one side of the square?
(A) $4 : \sqrt{3}$
(B) $16 : 3$
(C) $\sqrt{3} : 4$
(D) $2 : \sqrt{3}$
(E) $2 : \sqrt[4]{3}$

2. Which of the following figures has the greatest area?

(A) A
(B) B
(C) C
(D) D
(E) E

3. On a bull's-eye target the largest ring has an inner radius of 10 inches and an outer radius of 12 inches. What is the area of the largest ring in square inches?
(A) 40π
(B) 42π
(C) 44π
(D) 46π
(E) 48π

4. What is the area of the largest circle that can be cut out of a rectangular piece of paper measuring 30 inches by 32 inches?
    (A) 225π square inches
    (B) 256π square inches
    (C) 450π square inches
    (D) 512π square inches
    (E) 900π square inches

    4. A B C D E

5. How many 1-inch by 2-inch tiles will it take to cover a rectangular floor measuring 13 feet by 17 feet?
    (A) 7956
    (B) 13,151
    (C) 15,912
    (D) 26,302
    (E) 31,824

    5. A B C D E

6. What is the ratio of the shaded area in Figure A to the shaded area in Figure B, assuming that the radius of the circle in each figure is one inch?
    (A) $\pi : 2$
    (B) $(4 - \pi) : (\pi - 2)$
    (C) $1 : 1$
    (D) $(\pi - 2) : (4 - \pi)$
    (E) $2 : \pi$

    6. A B C D E

7. It takes a wheel 14 revolutions to roll 35 feet. What is the diameter of the wheel?

    (A) $\dfrac{5}{2\pi}$ feet

    (B) $\dfrac{5}{4\pi}$ feet

    (C) $\dfrac{2\pi}{5}$ feet

    (D) $\dfrac{4\pi}{5}$ feet

    (E) none of the above

    7. A B C D E

8. How many gallons can be put into a rectangular tank measuring 42 inches $\times$ 17 inches $\times$ 22 inches if one gallon equals 231 cubic inches?
    (A) 17 gallons
    (B) 34 gallons
    (C) 49 gallons
    (D) 68 gallons
    (E) 84 gallons

    8. A B C D E

9. Originally, the volume of a certain cube was exactly equal to that of a cylinder. If the radius of the cylinder is doubled and the height of the cylinder is reduced by half, what has to be done to the length of one side of the cube if the new cube's volume is to equal the new cylinder's volume?

9. A B C D E

(A) It has to be multiplied by 2.
(B) It has to be multiplied by π.
(C) It has to be multiplied by $\sqrt{2}$.
(D) It has to be multiplied by 4.
(E) none of the above

10. What is the ratio of the shaded area in Figure A to the shaded area in Figure B, assuming that the two squares are congruent?

10. A B C D E

(A) 2 : 1
(B) $\sqrt{2}$: 1
(C) 1 : 1
(D) 1 : $\sqrt{2}$
(E) 1 : 2

Figure A

Figure B

Answer Key for Diagnostic Test 3

1. E   6. B

2. C   7. A

3. C   8. D

4. A   9. E

5. C   10. C

All explanatory answers below include a number (or numbers) in parentheses after *each* answer. The number refers to a specific section in Part V, Math Refresher, where the rules and principles involved in the question are explained simply and clearly. These explanations are invaluable for strengthening your weaknesses in specific math topics.

Explanatory Answers for Diagnostic Test 3

1. **(E)**
Let S be the side of the square and T be the side of the triangle. The square's area is S^2. By using the Pythagorean Theorem we find that the triangle's area is $\dfrac{T^2\sqrt{3}}{4}$. $\left(A = \tfrac{1}{2}bh. \quad b = \tfrac{1}{2}T. \right.$ $\left. h = \dfrac{T\sqrt{3}}{2}.\right)$ Thus, $\dfrac{T^2\sqrt{3}}{4} = S^2$ and $T^2\sqrt{3} = 4S^2$. Therefore, $T^2 : S^2 = 4 : \sqrt{3}$. Taking square roots, we find that $T : S = 2 : \sqrt[4]{3}$. **(3.22, 3.31)**

2. **(C)**
The area of these figures can be found by breaking them up into rectangles and right triangles. All the figures have areas of 4 square units, except for Figure C, which covers 5 square units. **(3.31)**

3. **(C)**
The area of a circular ring (for example, one ring of a bull's-eye target) is equal to the difference between the areas of the circles that form its boundaries. Thus, the area of the ring here is $\pi(12)^2 - \pi(10)^2 = 144\pi - 100\pi = 44\pi$. **(3.31)**

4. **(A)**
The area of a circle is πr^2. The largest circle that could be cut from a 30- by 32-inch rectangular piece of paper would have a diameter of 30 inches and, thus, a radius of 15 inches. Substituting 15 for r in the formula, we get $\pi(15)^2 = 225\pi$ square inches. **(3.31)**

5. **(C)**
The area of the floor is 13 feet $\times$ 17 feet, which equals 221 square feet. Since 1 square foot $= 12^2$ inches, or 144 square inches, 221 square feet $= 221 \times 144 = 31,824$ square inches. The area of each tile is 1 inch $\times$ 2 inches, or 2 square inches. Then, the number of tiles needed to cover a floor of 31,824 square inches is $31,824 \div 2$, which equals 15,912 tiles. **(3.31)**

6. (B)
Since the radius of each circle is 1 inch, the length of one side of the square in Figure A is 2 inches, and its area is 4 square inches; the area of the circle in Figure A is $\pi 1^2$, or π square inches. Therefore, the area of the shaded region is $4 - \pi$ square inches. The diagonal of the square in Figure B is 2 inches because it is equal to the diameter of the circle. Since the area of a square is one-half the square of the diagonal, the area of the square in Figure B is $\frac{1}{2}(2)^2$, or 2 square inches. Since the area of the circle in Figure B is π square inches, the area of the shaded area in B is $\pi - 2$ square inches. Thus, the ratio of the shaded portion of Figure A to that of the shaded portion of Figure B is $(4 - \pi) : (\pi - 2)$.   **(3.31)**

7. (A)
Each revolution moves the wheel through a distance equal to its circumference. Thus, the wheel's circumference is 35 feet $\div$ 14, or $\frac{5}{2}$ feet. Diameter equals circumference divided by π, so the diameter of the wheel is $\frac{5}{2\pi}$ feet.   **(3.31)**

8. (D)
The volume of a rectangular tank is the product of the length, width, and depth. Therefore, the volume of the rectangular tank is $42 \times 17 \times 22$ cubic inches. The number of gallons the tank can hold equals the volume of the tank (in cubic inches) divided by the number of cubic inches in one gallon. Thus, $\frac{42 \times 17 \times 22}{231}$.

Factoring the 231, we obtain 21×11. Then, $\frac{\overset{2}{\cancel{42}} \times 17 \times \overset{2}{\cancel{22}}}{\cancel{21} \times \cancel{11}} = 2 \times 17 \times 2 = 68$ gallons.   **(3.32)**

9. (E)
Call one side of the cube s; call the radius of the cylinder r and the height of the cylinder h. The problem states that the volume of the cube equals the volume of the cylinder, or $s^3 = \pi r^2 h$. Then, replacing r by $2r$ (because the radius of the cylinder is doubled), and h by $\frac{1}{2}h$ (because the height of the cylinder is halved), we solve for the new value of s, which we can call S.

Substituting, $S^3 = \pi(2r)^2\left(\frac{1}{2}h\right)$, and $S^3 = \pi(\overset{2}{\cancel{4}}r^2)\left(\frac{1}{\cancel{2}}h\right) : S^3 = 2\pi r^2 h$. Since $s^3 = \pi r^2 h$, $2\pi r^2 h = 2s^3$. But S^3 also equals $2\pi r^2 h$, so $S^3 = 2s^3$. Thus, $S = \sqrt[3]{2s^3} = s\sqrt[3]{2}$. In other words, s must be multiplied by $\sqrt[3]{2}$, which is not one of the given choices.   **(3.32)**

10. **(C)**
Let the length of one side of the square in each diagram be s. The radius of the circle in Figure A is $\frac{s}{2}$, and the radius of each of the four circles in Figure B is $\frac{s}{4}$. Thus, the area of the large circle is $\frac{\pi s^2}{4}$, and the area of each of the small circles is $\frac{\pi s^2}{16}$. But there are four small circles, so their total area is four times $\frac{\pi s^2}{16}$, or $\cancel{4}\frac{\pi s^2}{\cancel{16}}_{4} = \frac{\pi s^2}{4}$. Thus, the shaded areas of Figure A and Figure B are equal and their ratio is 1 : 1.   (3.31)

DIAGNOSTIC TEST 4

Algebra Problems

Time: 35 minutes
Correct answers and solutions follow each test.

1. Find the value of $a^2 - 2ab + b^2$ if $a = 1$ and $b = -1$.
   (A) 6
   (B) 0
   (C) 4
   (D) 2
   (E) −2

   1. A B C D E

2. If $xy = 4y^2$ when $y = 9$, what is the value of x?
   (A) 4
   (B) 9
   (C) 24
   (D) 36
   (E) 64

   2. A B C D E

3. Which of the following expressions is equivalent to $(2a - 3b)^2$?
   (A) $2a^2 - 3b^2$
   (B) $4a^2 - 9b^2$
   (C) $4a^2 + 9b^2$
   (D) $4a^2 - 6ab + 9b^2$
   (E) $4a^2 - 12ab + 9b^2$

4. If we let n represent a man's height in inches, then which of the following will represent his height in feet?
   (A) $3n$
   (B) $12n$
   (C) $\dfrac{n}{3}$
   (D) $\dfrac{n}{12}$
   (E) none of these

5. Which of the following is not a factor of $x^4 - 5x^2 + 4$?
   (A) $x - 1$
   (B) $x^2 - 1$
   (C) $x - 2$
   (D) $x + 2$
   (E) $x^2 + 2$

6. If $ax + b = by - a$, what is the ratio of x to y (in terms of a and b)?
   (A) $\dfrac{a}{b}$
   (B) $-\left(\dfrac{a}{b}\right)$
   (C) $\dfrac{b}{a}$
   (D) $-\left(\dfrac{b}{a}\right)$
   (E) cannot be determined from the given information

7. If $m + 2n = 8$ and $2m - n = 6$, what is the value of n?
   (A) 2
   (B) 4
   (C) $\dfrac{2}{3}$
   (D) $\dfrac{14}{5}$
   (E) cannot be determined from the given information

8. Which of the following equations has no real solution?

    (A) $x^2 - 9 = 0$
    (B) $x^3 - 9 = 0$
    (C) $x^2 + 9 = 0$
    (D) $x^3 + 9 = 0$
    (E) none

    8. A B C D E

9. If a car travels p feet in q seconds, what is its speed in miles per hour?

    (A) $(5280)(3600)pq$

    (B) $\dfrac{(5280)(3600)p}{q}$

    (C) $\dfrac{(5280)p}{(3600)q}$

    (D) $\dfrac{(3600)p}{(5280)q}$

    (E) $\dfrac{p}{(5280)(3600)q}$

    9. A B C D E

10. Which of the following is the graph of the equation $4x + 3y = 0$?

    (A) a single point
    (B) a straight vertical line
    (C) a straight horizontal line
    (D) a straight line with a positive slope
    (E) a straight line with a negative slope

    10. A B C D E

Answer Key for Diagnostic Test 4

1. C		6. E	
2. D		7. A	
3. E		8. C	
4. D		9. D	
5. E		10. E	

All explanatory answers below include a number (or numbers) in parentheses after *each* answer. The number refers to a specific section in Part V, Math Refresher, where the rules and principles involved in the question are explained simply and clearly. These explanations are invaluable for strengthening your weaknesses in specific math topics.

Explanatory Answers for Diagnostic Test 4

1. **(C)**

   If we substitute $a = 1$ and $b = -1$ in the expression $a^2 - 2ab + b^2$, we get $(1)^2 - 2(1)(-1) + (-1)^2$, or $1 + 2 + 1 = 4$. Another way to solve this problem is to observe that the original expression is equal to $(a - b)^2$. If we substitute the values for a and b, we get $[1 - (-1)]^2$, or 2^2, which equals 4.

   (2.2)

2. **(D)**

   First divide the original equation by y, which gives $x = 4y$. Substituting 9 for y gives $x = 4(9)$; therefore, $x = 36$.   **(2.2)**

3. **(E)**

   $(2a - 3b)^2 = (2a)(2a) + (2a)(-3b) + (-3b)(2a) + (-3b)(-3b) = 4a^2 - 6ab - 6ab + 9b^2 = 4a^2 - 12ab + 9b^2$.

   (2.52)

4. **(D)**

   12 inches $= 1$ foot; therefore, 1 inch $= \frac{1}{12}$ foot. Multiplying both sides of the equation by n, we obtain: n inches $= \frac{n}{12}$ feet.

   (4.5)

5. **(E)**

   $x^4 - 5x^2 + 4 = (x^2 - 4)(x^2 - 1)$. Thus, choice (B) is a factor of the given expression. Factoring each of these two terms, we get $(x^2 - 4)(x^2 - 1) = (x - 2)(x + 2)(x - 1)(x + 1)$. Thus, (A), (C), and (D) are also factors of the given expression. Choice (E), however, is not a factor of the original expression.

   (2.6)

6. **(E)**

   Subtracting b from both sides of the equation gives us $ax = by - a - b$. Dividing first by a gives us $x = \frac{by}{a} - 1 - \frac{b}{a}$. Then dividing by y gives us $\frac{x}{y} = \frac{b}{a} - \frac{1}{y} - \frac{b}{ay}$. Now we see that the ratio of x to y $\left(\frac{x}{y}\right)$ is dependent on finding a value of y in terms of a and b only. Since we do not know the value of y in terms of a and b, the ratio of x to y cannot be determined from the given information.

   (2.11)

7. **(A)**
    The two equations are $m + 2n = 8$ and $2m - n = 6$. We subtract $2n$ from both sides of the first equation: $m + 2n - 2n = 8 - 2n$, giving $m = 8 - 2n$; and we add n to both sides of the second equation: $2m - n + n = 6 + n$, giving $2m = 6 + n$. Now we multiply the first equation by 2, which is the coefficient of m in the second equation. Our equations now are: $2m = 16 - 4n$ and $2m = 6 + n$. Equating $16 - 4n$ and $6 + n$, because they are both equal to $2m$, gives $16 - 4n = 6 + n$. Solving this equation for n gives us $10 = 5n$, or $n = 2$.   **(2.3)**

8. **(C)**
    The equation $x^2 + 9 = 0$ cannot have any real solutions because x^2 must be greater than or equal to zero. (If x were less than zero, that is, negative, its square would be positive and therefore more than zero.) But 9 is greater than zero, so the sum of x^2 and 9 must be greater than zero and therefore cannot equal zero. Thus, no real value of x satisfies the condition $x^2 + 9 = 0$.   **(2.11)**

9. **(D)**
    1 mile = 5280 feet, so 1 foot = $\dfrac{1}{5280}$ mile, and p feet = $\dfrac{p}{5280}$ miles. Similarly, 1 hour = 3600 seconds, so 1 second = $\dfrac{1}{3600}$ hour, and q seconds equals $\dfrac{q}{3600}$ hours. Thus, the speed, which equals the distance divided by the time, equals $\dfrac{p \text{ feet}}{q \text{ seconds}} =$

    $$\dfrac{\dfrac{p}{5280} \text{ mi.}}{\dfrac{q}{3600} \text{ hr.}} = \dfrac{3600p}{5280q} \text{ miles /hour.} \qquad \textbf{(2.51)}$$

10. **(E)**
    Transforming this equation to standard form, we obtain the equation $y = \left(-\dfrac{4}{3} \right)x + 0$, which is the equation of the straight line. Since the coefficient of x in the standard equation is equal to the slope of the line represented by this equation, our slope is equal to $-\dfrac{4}{3}$, a negative number.   **(4.1)**

DIAGNOSTIC TEST 5

Geometry Problems

Time: 35 minutes
Correct answers and solutions follow each test.

1. In Mr. Jones' garden, there is a circular flower bed with a diameter of 20 feet. If a boy walks across the middle of the flower bed instead of walking around the circumference, how much walking will he save in going from one point on the edge of the flower bed to a point that is exactly opposite?
   (A) $10\pi - 10$ feet
   (B) $10\pi - 20$ feet
   (C) $20\pi - 10$ feet
   (D) $20\pi - 20$ feet
   (E) none of these

1. A B C D E

2. In triangle PQR, angle P is acute and angle R equals 30°. Which of the following *best* describes the range of possible values for angle Q?
   (A) $\angle Q$ must be less than 60°.
   (B) $\angle Q$ must be greater than 60°.
   (C) $\angle Q$ must be less than 150°.
   (D) $\angle Q$ must be greater than 150°.
   (E) $\angle Q$ must be greater than 60° but less than 150°.

2. A B C D E

3. If the midpoints of a parallelogram are joined, what type of figure will be formed?
   (A) a square
   (B) a rectangle, but not necessarily a square
   (C) a rhombus (all sides equal), but not necessarily a square
   (D) a parallelogram, but not necessarily a rectangle or a rhombus
   (E) none of the above

3. A B C D E

385

4. A regular hexagon is inscribed inside a circle. What fraction of the circle's area is included in the hexagon?

4. A B C D E

(A) $\dfrac{3\sqrt{3}}{2\pi}$

(B) $\dfrac{6\sqrt{3}}{\pi}$

(C) $\dfrac{\sqrt{3}}{4\pi}$

(D) $\dfrac{\sqrt{3}}{\pi}$

(E) cannot be determined from the given information

5. How many degrees are there between the hands of a clock at 9:30?

5. A B C D E

(A) 90°
(B) 95°
(C) 100°
(D) 105°
(E) 110°

6. In a pentagon, the angles are in the ratio 3 : 4 : 5 : 6 ; 7. What is the number of degrees in the smallest angle?

6. A B C D E

(A) 21.6°
(B) 43.2°
(C) 57.6°
(D) 64.8°
(E) 82.2°

7. If a central angle of 60° cuts off an arc of 3 inches on the circumference of a circle, what is the circle's diameter?

7. A B C D E

(A) 9 inches
(B) $\dfrac{9}{\pi}$ inches
(C) 18 inches
(D) 18π inches
(E) $\dfrac{18}{\pi}$ inches

8. Through how many degrees does the minute hand of a clock move in 25 minutes?

8. A B C D E

(A) 25°
(B) 50°
(C) 75°
(D) 125°
(E) 150°

9. In the following diagram, AB, FC, and ED are all perpendicular to BD. If AB = 6 and FC = 2, what is the length of ED?

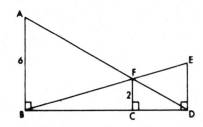

(A) 2
(B) 3
(C) 4
(D) 6
(E) cannot be determined from the given information

10. How many degrees are there in each angle of a regular polygon with twelve sides?

(A) 120°
(B) 132°
(C) 144°
(D) 150°
(E) 172°

Answer Key for Diagnostic Test 5

1. B   6. D

2. E   7. E

3. D   8. E

4. A   9. B

5. D   10. D

All explanatory answers below include a number (or numbers) in parentheses after *each* answer. The number refers to a specific section in Part V, Math Refresher, where the rules and principles involved in the question are explained simply and clearly. These explanations are invaluable for strengthening your weaknesses in specific math topics.

Explanatory Answers for Diagnostic Test 5

1. (B)

If the boy walks around the flower bed, he will have to travel half of the circle's circumference, or $\frac{1}{2}(\pi)$ (20 feet) $= 10\pi$ feet. Walking through the center in a straight line, he reaches the point opposite by walking only 20 feet. Thus, he has saved the difference: 10π feet $-$ 20 feet.   **(3.31)**

2. (E)

The sum of angles P and R must be greater than 30° but less than 120° since P is acute. Since the three angles of a triangle always add up to 180°, the third angle, Q, must be less than 150° but still greater than 60°. If angle Q were more than 150°, the sum of angles R and Q alone would be more than 180°, which is impossible; and if angle Q were less than 60°, angle P could not be acute (150° $-$ 60° $=$ 90°).   **(3.3)**

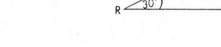

3. (D)

As this diagram illustrates, the figure need not be a rectangle (including a square) or a rhombus. To prove that it must be a parallelogram, draw in one diagonal of the original parallelogram. This divides the original parallelogram into two triangles. Two opposite sides of the *new* figure are both parallel to this diagonal. They are both lines joining the midpoints of two sides of a triangle, and a line joining the midpoints of two sides of a triangle is parallel to the third side. Since they are both parallel to the diagonal, they are also parallel to each other. Repeat this for the other diagonal, and you will see that opposite sides of the new figure are parallel. Therefore, this new figure, being four-sided and having opposite sides parallel, must be a parallelogram.   **(3.3)**

4. (A)

Let the radius of the circle be r. Then the circle's area is πr^2. The area of the hexagon is equal to the sum of the areas of six equilateral triangles with sides equal to r. The area of each triangle is $\dfrac{r^2\sqrt{3}}{4}$, so the six triangles will have a total area of $\overset{3}{\cancel{6}} \times \dfrac{r^2\sqrt{3}}{\underset{2}{\cancel{4}}}$, or $\dfrac{3r^2\sqrt{3}}{2}$, which is the area of the hexagon. To find the fraction of the circle's area that is included in the hexagon, divide the area of the hexagon by that of the circle: $\dfrac{3r^2\sqrt{3}}{2\pi r^2}$, or $\dfrac{3\sqrt{3}}{2\pi}$.

(3.31)

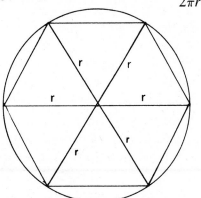

5. (D)

At 9:30, the hour hand is halfway between the 9 and the 10, while the minute hand is on the 6. Since the space between 2 numerals represents a 30-degree interval (360 degrees ÷ 12), and the two hands are three-and-a-half numerals apart, there will be $3\frac{1}{2} \times 30$ degrees, or 105 degrees between the two hands.

(3.3)

6. (D)

The sum of the angles of an n-sided polygon is $(n - 2) \times 180°$. Therefore, the sum of the angles in a pentagon = $(5 - 2) \times 180° = 3 \times 180° = 540°$.

Let the angles of the pentagon be $3x$, $4x$, $5x$, $6x$, and $7x$. Then their sum, $25x$, equals the sum of the angles of the pentagon, or $25x = 540°$, and $x = 540° \div 25 = 21.6°$. The smallest angle, $3x$, equals $3 \times 21.6° = 64.8°$.   **(3.3)**

7. (E)

If a 60° angle cuts off an arc of 3 inches, then a 360° angle will cut off the entire circumference of 18 inches (360° ÷ 60° = 6; 6 × 3 inches = 18 inches). Since the diameter of a circle is equal to the circumference divided by π, the diameter of the given circle will be $\dfrac{18}{\pi}$ inches.   **(3.14, 3.3)**

8. **(E)**

   During 25 minutes, the minute hand moves through five numeral-intervals on the face of the clock. Since the interval between two numerals equals $30°$, the hand moves through $150°$. **(3.3)**

9. **(B)**

   Triangle ADB and triangle FDC are similar because they have equal angles. This may be shown as follows: (1) $\angle ADB = \angle FDC$ because these angles are identical; (2) $\angle ABC = 90°$ because AB is given as being perpendicular to BD, and $\angle FCD = 90°$ because FC is given as being perpendicular to BD. Therefore, the two angles are equal; (3) $\angle DAB = \angle DFC$ because if two angles of one triangle are equal to two angles of another triangle, the third angle of the first triangle is equal to the third angle of the second triangle. Then, $CD : BD = 2 : 6$ because if the angles of two triangles are equal, their sides are proportional. If we let $x = CD$, then we have $x : BD = 2 : 6$; $x : BD = 1 : 3$; $BD = 3x$. Now, $BD = BC + CD$; $3x = BC + x$; $BC = 2x$. But triangles EDB and FCB are similar, as can be proved by using the same reasoning as in the first paragraph of this answer. Then, $ED : FC = BD : BC$; $FC = 2$ (given) and $BC = 2x$ (as shown above). Thus, $ED : 2 = 3x : 2x$;

   $ED (2x) = 6x$; $ED = \dfrac{6x}{2x}$; $ED = 3$. **(3.31)**

10. **(D)**

    A regular polygon with twelve sides has angles that total $(12 - 2)(180°)$, or $1800°$. The angles of a regular polygon are equal. Therefore, each angle in the 12-sided polygon $= 1800 \div 12 = 150°$. **(3.3)**

DIAGNOSTIC TEST 6

Miscellaneous Problems, Including Averages, Properties of Integers, Series, and Approximation Problems

Time: 30 minutes
Correct answers and solutions follow each test.

1. A man drives 180 miles to his destination at an average speed of 60 mph and returns to the starting point at an average speed of 30 mph. His average speed for the entire trip is
   (A) 42 mph
   (B) 45 mph
   (C) 40 mph
   (D) 48 mph
   (E) none of these

   1. A B C D E

2. A certain class has 5 girls and 10 boys. The girls average 85% on a certain test. What must be the boys' average if the entire class averages 89%?
   (A) 90%
   (B) 91%
   (C) 92%
   (D) 93%
   (E) 97%

   2. A B C D E

3. The average of four consecutive integers is *always*
   (A) divisible by four
   (B) divisible by two, but not necessarily by four
   (C) an odd integer
   (D) an integer
   (E) none of the above

   3. A B C D E

4. What is the sum of 8.97, 67.542, and 9.85 to the nearest whole number?
   (A) 86.4
   (B) 86.7
   (C) 85
   (D) 86
   (E) 87

   4. A B C D E

392   DIAGNOSTIC TEST 6

5. What is the next term in the sequence: −1, 3, −9, 27, . . .?

5. A B C D E

(A) 36
(B) −36
(C) −81
(D) 81
(E) 49

6. What is the next number in the sequence: 1, 2, 4, 3, 7, 4, 10, . . .?

6. A B C D E

(A) 5
(B) 7
(C) 8
(D) 10
(E) 16

7. If the average of 12 numbers is 25 and none of the numbers is smaller than 15, what is the largest possible value any one of the numbers can have?

7. A B C D E

(A) 35
(B) 50
(C) 85
(D) 135
(E) there is no limit to the size of the largest number

8. Find the next term in the series: 3, 7, 0, 5, 3, 3, 0, ...

8. A B C D E

(A) 0
(B) 1
(C) 3
(D) 5
(E) 9

9. Find the average of 2, 20, 200, 2000, 20,000, and 200,000.

9. A B C D E

(A) 20,000
(B) 2000
(C) 10,000
(D) 43,907
(E) 37,037

10. If the average of two numbers is 60 and the average of these two numbers along with a third number is 54, find the third number.

10. A B C D E

(A) 42
(B) 114
(C) 8
(D) 38
(E) 44

Answer Key for Diagnostic Test 6

1.	C	**6.**	A
2.	B	**7.**	D
3.	E	**8.**	B
4.	D	**9.**	E
5.	C	**10.**	A

All explanatory answers below include a number (or numbers) in parentheses after *each* answer. The number refers to a specific section in Part V, Math Refresher, where the rules and principles involved in the question are explained simply and clearly. These explanations are invaluable for strengthening your weaknesses in specific math topics.

Explanatory Answers for Diagnostic Test 6

1. **(C)**
180 miles at 60 mph = 3 hours driving time.
180 miles at 30 mph = 6 hours driving time.
360 miles in 9 hours = 40 mph average speed.   **(1.51, 2.45)**

2. **(B)**
Since the five girls average 85%, the sum of their marks was $5 \times 85\% = 425\%$. To have an average of 89%, the sum of the marks of the entire class must be $15 \times 89\% = 1335\%$. Since the sum of the marks of the whole class was 1335% and the sum of the marks of the girls was 425%, then the sum of the marks of the boys must be 910%. ($1335\% - 425\% = 910\%$.) Since the sum of the marks of the boys must be 910% and there are 10 boys, the average for the boys was $910\% \div 10$, or 91%.
    (1.51)

3. **(E)**
Let us call the first consecutive integer n. Then the next integers are $n + 1$, $n + 2$, and $n + 3$. The sum of the four integers is therefore $4n + 6$. The average is then $(4n + 6) \div 4$, or $n + 1\frac{1}{2}$.

Since n is an integer, $n + 1\frac{1}{2}$ cannot be an integer, so the answer is (E).   **(1.51, 1.53)**

4. **(D)**
First we round off the numbers 8.97, 67.542 and 9.85 to 9.0, 67.5, and 9.9 respectively. The sum of the rounded off numbers is 86.4, which we round off to the nearest whole number, 86.
(1.21)

5. **(C)**
This series is a geometric progression in which each term is -3 times the term before it: -1 times $-3 = 3$, 3 times $-3 = -9$, -9 times $-3 = 27$. Thus the next term is -81 (27 times -3).
(1.53)

6. **(A)**
This sequence can be broken down into two sub-sequences: the odd-numbered terms form the arithmetic series: 1, 4, 7, 10, . . . ; the even-numbered terms form the arithmetic series: 2, 3, 4, ... Thus, the next term, an even-numbered term, would be 5.   **(1.53)**

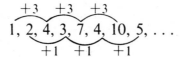

7. **(D)**
If the average of 12 numbers is 25, their sum must be 12×25, or 300. If one number has the largest possible value, then it is obvious that the rest should all have the smallest possible value, which in this case is 15. Since eleven numbers each equal 15 for a total of 11×15, or 165, the twelfth number must be $300 - 165$, or 135.
(1.51)

8. **(B)**
The odd-numbered terms form the beginning of the alternating series: 3, 0, 3, 0, . . . while the even-numbered terms form the beginning of the arithmetic series: 7, 5, 3, ... Thus, the next term, an even-numbered one, should be 1.
(1.53)

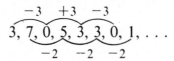

9. **(E)**
Imagining the 6 numbers listed in a column, one can see at once that their sum is 222,222. Dividing this quantity by 6, we find that the average is 37,037.
(1.51)

10. (A)

The average of the first 2 numbers is 60, so their sum must be 2 × 60, or 120. The average of the 3 numbers is 54, so their sum is 3 × 54, or 162. Thus, the third number must be 162 — 120, or 42.   **(1.51)**

DIAGNOSTIC TEST 7

Graph (or Chart) and Table Problems

Time: 30 minutes
Correct answers and solutions follow each test.

HOW YOUR SAVINGS WORK FOR YOU

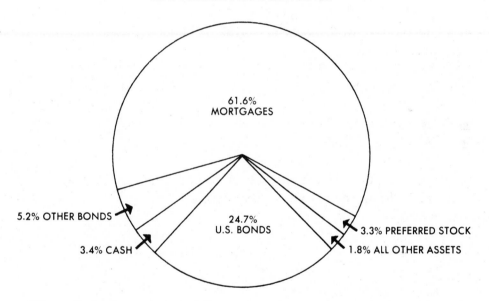

The graph above was published by a bank in a large city to show its depositors how it invests their savings.

1. What percent of the bank's assets are invested in preferred stock?
(A) 33%
(B) 3.4%
(C) 3.3%
(D) 1.8%
(E) none of these

1. A B C D E

2. In what single way is approximately one-fourth of the bank's assets invested?

   (A)   other bonds
   (B)   preferred stock
   (C)   cash
   (D)   United States bonds
   (E)   none of these

3. Which fraction is nearest to the bank's total investment in mortgages?

   (A) $\frac{1}{2}$

   (B) $\frac{3}{4}$

   (C) $\frac{5}{8}$

   (D) $\frac{3}{5}$

   (E)   none of these

4. The bank's total assets are $162,575,800. Of this total, what amount is kept in cash?

   (A) $5,526,577.20
   (B) $5,536,577.20
   (C) $5,526,567.20
   (D) $5,537,576.20
   (E)   none of these

5. Approximately how many times as much money is invested in United States bonds as in other bonds?

   (A)   5
   (B)   25
   (C)   7
   (D)   6
   (E)   none of these

GROWTH IN MOTOR VEHICLE REGISTRATION

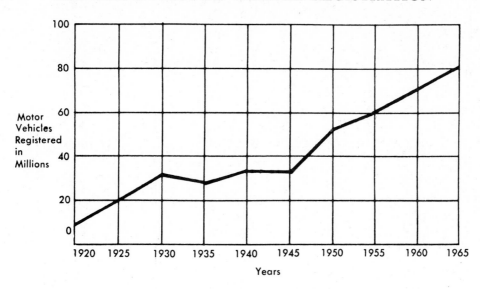

The graph above shows the growth in motor vehicle registration from 1920 through 1965.

6. Approximately how many motor vehicles were registered in 1930?
(A) 10 million
(B) 20 million
(C) 40 million
(D) 25 million
(E) none of these

6. A B C D E

7. How many motor vehicles were registered in 1955?
(A) 80 million
(B) 70 million
(C) 20 million
(D) 60 million
(E) none of these

7. A B C D E

8. Approximately how many times as many motor vehicles were registered in 1955 as in 1925?
   - (A) 40
   - (B) 3
   - (C) 2
   - (D) 4
   - (E) none of these

8. A B C D E

9. How many more motor vehicles were registered in 1965 than in 1955?
   - (A) 10 million
   - (B) 15 million
   - (C) 20 million
   - (D) 25 million
   - (E) none of these

9. A B C D E

10. What percent of increase in registration occurred between 1955 and 1965?
   - (A) 10%
   - (B) $\frac{1}{3}$%
   - (C) 20%
   - (D) $33\frac{1}{3}$%
   - (E) none of these

10. A B C D E

Answer Key for Diagnostic Test 7

1.	C	6.	E
2.	D	7.	D
3.	C	8.	B
4.	E	9.	C
5.	A	10.	D

All explanatory answers below include a number (or numbers) in parentheses after *each* answer. The number refers to a specific section in Part V, Math Refresher, where the rules and principles involved in the questions are explained simply and clearly. These explanations are invaluable for strengthening your weaknesses in specific math topics.

Explanatory Answers for Diagnostic Test 7

1. **(C)**
   See graph.   **(1.42)**

2. **(D)**
   24.7% (United States bonds) is approximately one-fourth of
   100%   **(1.42)**

3. **(C)**
   61.6% (mortgages) is closest to 62.5%, or $\frac{5}{8}$.   **(1.42)**

4. **(E)**
   None of these. The correct answer is $5,527,577.20.
   $162,575,800 $\times$ 0.034 = $5,527,577.20.   **(1.42)**

5. **(A)**
   24.7% was invested in United States bonds; 5.2% was invested
   in other bonds.

$$\frac{24.7\%}{5.2\%} = 52 \overline{)247.00} \quad \begin{array}{c} 4.75 \end{array}$$

   About 5 times as much was invested in United States bonds.
                                                                 (1.42)

6. **(E)**
   None of these. The correct answer is 30 million.   **(1.43)**

7. **(D)**
   See graph.   **(1.43)**

8. **(B)**
   60 million motor vehicles were registered in 1955; 20 million
   motor vehicles were registered in 1925; $\frac{60}{20}$ = 3 times as many
   motor vehicles registered in 1955 as in 1925.   **(1.43)**

9. **(C)**
   80 million motor vehicles were registered in 1965; 60 million
   motor vehicles were registered in 1955. 80 million − 60 million = 20 million.   **(1.43)**

10. **(D)**
    $\frac{20 \text{ million}}{60 \text{ million}} = \frac{1}{3} = 33\frac{1}{3}\%$.   **(1.43)**

STEPS TO TAKE AFTER YOU HAVE COMPLETED THE DIAGNOSTIC MATH TESTS

Step One

After you have taken a diagnostic test, compare each of your answers with the answer given in the explanatory answers section that follows each test. Tally the number you answered correctly. Then go over the solutions to the questions—especially the solutions to the problems you answered incorrectly. Note the number in parentheses that appears after each solution. This number refers you to a specific section in Part V, Math Refresher, of this book. These sections explain simply and clearly the rules and principles involved in solving each problem. You will find these rules and principles invaluable for strengthening the areas of math in which you are weak.

Step Two

Pinpoint the areas in which you are weakest. The following checklist will help you spotlight the areas where you need the most study and practice.

CHECKLIST

Math Area	Strong (8–10 Correct)	Average (5–7 Correct)	Weak (0–4 Correct)
	Write Your Score Below		
Fractions, Decimals, Percentages, Deviations, Ratios and Proportions			
Rate (including Time, Distance, Work, Cost, Mixture)			
Area, Perimeter, and Volume			
Algebra			
Geometry			
Miscellaneous (Including Averages, Properties of Integers, Series, Approximations)			
Tables and Graphs (or charts)			

Use the checklist in this way:

1. Write your score (number correct) for each of the diagnostic tests you have just taken in the appropriate box.

2. If you have a score in the 0 to 4 (*weak*) column, place one check ($\sqrt{}$) after a score of 3 or 4 to indicate that you are *moderately weak* in that area. Place two checks ($\sqrt{}$ $\sqrt{}$) after a score of 0, 1, or 2; this means that you are *seriously weak* in that area. *Do not be discouraged in any case.* You will definitely eliminate your math "soft spots"—perhaps sooner than you think—if you follow the procedures suggested here.

Step Three

Turn to Part V, Math Refresher, to find instructional material in the math area in which you showed your greatest weakness. Go over the solutions to the questions you missed. Then (just as you did in STEP 1), note the *number* in parentheses following each incorrect answer. This will lead you to those sections that will explain the rules and principles for the problems that gave you trouble.

Step Four

When you finish the section that covers your weakest area, turn to the section that covers your next weakest area and proceed as above. Continue until you have studied every section that is noted as "weak" in your checklist. Then you may want to work on some of your "average" areas.

part V

MATHEMATICAL ABILITY
(Math Refresher)

Further develop your math skills by reading this part.

Another part of the Scholastic Aptitude Test consists of a series of problems that measures mathematical ability. The subject matter of these problems is based on standard high school mathematics courses, including elementary algebra and elementary geometry. The questions are designed to measure (1) your knowledge of elementary mathematics, (2) your ability to apply your mathematical knowledge to new situations, and (3) the extent of your mathematical insight when presented with nonroutine concepts and problems.

The following review section is designed to sharpen your skills and refresh your memory for handling a great variety of mathematical problems.

On the examination, you are instructed to do your scratch work in the margins of your question booklet. For your practice exams, use the margins of this book as you would the exam booklet. Use additional scratch paper only if you run out of margin space.

1. ARITHMETIC

1.1 Fractions

A fraction is a piece of something. In arithmetic, a fraction is made up of two parts—one part above a line and the other part under the line. The number below the line in a fraction is called the *denominator*, and the number above the line is called the *numerator*. The *denominator* tells the number of equal pieces into which something has been divided. For example, if the denominator is 4, it tells you that something has been divided into 4 equal pieces. The *numerator* tells how many of the pieces are in the fraction.

$$\frac{3}{4} \quad \begin{array}{l} \text{numerator} \\ \text{denominator} \end{array}$$

You read this fraction as three-fourths. The 4 in the denominator tells you that something has been divided into 4 equal parts. The 3 in the numerator means the fraction represents 3 of these parts. For example, if you have $\frac{3}{4}$ of a pie, it means the pie has been cut into four equal pieces and you have three of these pieces. This type of fraction is called a *common fraction*.

If a number includes both a whole number and a fraction, it is called a *mixed number*. Thus, $3\frac{1}{2}$ is a mixed number. If a fraction's numerator is larger than its denominator, it is called an *improper fraction*: $\frac{8}{3}$, $\frac{17}{4}$, and $\frac{89}{67}$ are all improper fractions.

1.11 Reducing Fractions

All solutions to fraction problems must be reduced to *lowest terms*. This may be done by dividing the numerator and the denominator by the *highest* number that will go into both evenly.

Examples:

(1) $\frac{8}{32}$ may be reduced by dividing the numerator and denominator both by 8. Thus, $\frac{8}{32} = \frac{1}{4}$, since $8 \div 8 = 1$ and $32 \div 8 = 4$.

(2) $\frac{12}{28}$ may be reduced by dividing both the numerator and denominator by 4. Thus, $\frac{12}{28} = \frac{3}{7}$, since $12 \div 4 = 3$ and $28 \div 4 = 7$. Notice that if we divided both the numerator and denominator in this problem by 2, we would get $\frac{6}{14}$, which could again be reduced, by dividing by 2, to $\frac{3}{7}$. For this reason it is important when reducing fractions to try to find the *highest* number that will divide into the numerator and denominator to avoid having to reduce more than one time.

Practice Exercises 1:

Reduce the following fractions to lowest terms.

ANSWERS TO PRACTICE EXERCISES APPEAR AT END OF SECTION.

(1) $\frac{4}{36}$

(2) $\frac{7}{42}$

(3) $\frac{12}{90}$

(4) $\frac{51}{85}$

1.12 Addition of Fractions

To add fractions it is necessary to find the *lowest common denominator*, or L.C.D. This is the *smallest* number that can be divided evenly by all the denominators in the problem. Sometimes the L.C.D. will be one of the denominators in the problem and sometimes it will be an entirely new number. All problems in addition of fractions fall into one of the following three categories.

Type I: All the Denominators Are the Same

To get the answer, simply add the numerators and place the sum over the common denominator.

Examples:

(1)
$$\frac{2}{13}$$
$$\frac{7}{+13}$$
$$\frac{9}{13}$$

(2)
$$\frac{3}{20}$$
$$\frac{7}{20}$$
$$+\frac{5}{20}$$
$$\frac{15}{20} = \frac{3}{4}$$

Type II: One of the Denominators Is the L.C.D.

To get the answer, use the denominator of the fraction that all the other denominators will divide into evenly as the L.C.D. Then change all the other fractions to fractions with this denominator. This can be done by dividing the L.C.D. by each denominator of each fraction and multiplying this answer by the respective numerators of the fractions. Although this may sound complicated, the following example shows that it is easier than it sounds.

Example: Add

(1) $4\frac{3}{8}$

$1\frac{1}{4}$

$5\frac{5}{24}$

The smallest number that can be divided evenly by all the denominators is 24, which is the L.C.D. Dividing 24 by each denominator and multiplying the answer by the numerator, we have:

$$\frac{3}{8} = \frac{9}{24} \qquad 4\frac{9}{24}$$
$$\frac{1}{4} = \frac{6}{24} \qquad 1\frac{6}{24}$$
$$\frac{5}{24} = \frac{5}{24}; \text{ then adding: } \quad 5\frac{5}{24}$$
$$\overline{10\frac{20}{24}},$$

and reducing the fraction: $10\frac{5}{6}$ is the answer.

Type III: None of the Denominators Is the L.C.D.

To get the answer, it is usually sufficient to find the L.C.D. by multiplying all the denominators together and then proceeding as in Type II problems.

Examples:
(1) *Add*

$$2\frac{3}{4}$$

$$+5\frac{1}{9}$$

We use 36 as the L.C.D., since it is the product of the denominators, 4 and 9. Then,

$$2\frac{27}{36}$$

$$+5\frac{4}{36}$$

$$7\frac{31}{36} \text{ Ans.}$$

(2)

$$\frac{1}{3}$$

$$\frac{1}{4}$$

$$+\frac{1}{5}$$

We use 60 as the L.C.D., since it is the product of the denominators, 3, 4, and 5 ($3 \times 4 \times 5 = 60$). Then,

$$\frac{20}{60}$$

$$\frac{15}{60}$$

$$+\frac{12}{60}$$

$$\frac{47}{60} \text{ Ans.}$$

Multiplying all the denominators together, however, sometimes gives a common denominator larger than the *lowest* common denominator.

Example:

$$\frac{3}{12} + \frac{4}{18}$$

Multiplying the denominators, $12 \times 18 = 216$, but the L.C.D. is 36, not 216. In such a case the L.C.D. can be found by inspection or by trial and error. When you look at the problem, think of multiples of 12 that might be divisible by 18. $2 \times 12 = 24$ is not divisible but $3 \times 12 = 36$ is.

Note: If fractions add up to more than 1 (i.e., the answer is an improper fraction), change the answer to a mixed number by (1) dividing the numerator by the denominator, and (2) writing the remainder as a fraction:

Example:

$$\frac{1}{3} = \frac{2}{6}$$

$$+\frac{5}{6} = \frac{5}{6}$$

$$\frac{7}{6} = 6\overline{)7} = 1\frac{1}{6}$$
$$\frac{6}{1}$$

Practice Exercises 2:

ANSWERS TO PRACTICE EXERCISES APPEAR AT END OF SECTION.

(1)   If Marie adds $3\frac{3}{5}$ cups of sugar to $2\frac{7}{15}$ cups of sugar, how many cups of sugar will she have altogether?

(2)   Emmanuel has cut three pieces of wood of lengths $\frac{1}{3}$ ft., $\frac{2}{6}$ ft., $\frac{5}{18}$ ft., which he intends to use to make a coffee table. What is the total length of the three pieces?

(3)   What is the sum of $\frac{5}{6}$ and $\frac{6}{7}$?

(4)   The number of inches of rainfall on three successive days was $4\frac{1}{5}''$, $3\frac{2}{7}''$, and $1\frac{1}{2}''$. What was the total number of inches of rainfall for the three days?

1.13 Subtraction of Fractions

To subtract one fraction from another, you use the same general procedure as in addition of fractions.

Examples:

(1)
$$\begin{array}{r} \frac{11}{12} \\ -\frac{7}{12} \\ \hline \frac{4}{12} = \frac{1}{3} \end{array}$$

(2)
$$\begin{array}{r} 5\frac{5}{18} = 5\frac{5}{18} \\ -2\frac{1}{6} = -2\frac{3}{18} \\ \hline 3\frac{2}{18} = 3\frac{1}{9} \end{array}$$

In the subtraction of mixed numbers, if the number you are subtracting (lower) has a fraction in it larger than the fraction that is in the number you are subtracting from (upper), you must: (1) find the L.C.D., (2) borrow 1 from the upper whole number, (3) change 1 to a fraction with the L.C.D., (4) add it to the upper fraction. Then, proceed as in previous examples. Thus,

$$\begin{array}{r} 7\frac{1}{3} \\ -3\frac{5}{6} \\ \hline \end{array}$$

The L.C.D. is 6. Borrow 1 $\left(=\frac{6}{6}\right)$ from 7, and to $\frac{1}{3}\left(=\frac{2}{6}\right)$ add $\frac{6}{6}$, thus: $\frac{2}{6} + \frac{6}{6} = \frac{8}{6}$. Now, the upper mixed number is $6\frac{8}{6}\left(\text{that is, } 7\frac{1}{3} = 6\frac{8}{6}\right)$. Then,

$$\begin{array}{r} 6\frac{8}{6} \\ -3\frac{5}{6} \\ \hline 3\frac{3}{6} = 3\frac{1}{2}. \end{array}$$

Practice Exercises 3:

ANSWERS TO PRACTICE EXERCISES APPEAR AT END OF SECTION.

(1) Find the difference between $\frac{7}{8}$ and $\frac{3}{16}$.

(2) What is the remainder, if from a piece of cloth $3\frac{3}{4}$ feet long, a piece $1\frac{1}{3}$ feet long has been cut away?

(3) Subtract: $6\frac{3}{8}$

$$-2\frac{3}{4}$$

(4) If a job takes $4\frac{2}{9}$ days to do and the men on the job have already worked $2\frac{3}{5}$ days, how many days of work remain to complete the job?

(5) Subtract $3\frac{3}{4}$ from 8.

1.14 Multiplication of Fractions

To multiply fractions, simply find the products of their numerators and denominators.

Examples:

(1) $\frac{4}{7} \times \frac{3}{5} = \frac{12}{35}$

(2) $\frac{3}{8} \times \frac{5}{6} = \frac{15}{48} = \frac{5}{16}$

(3) $3 \times \frac{5}{8} = \frac{3}{1} \times \frac{5}{8} = \frac{15}{8} = 1\frac{7}{8}$

To change a mixed number to an improper fraction, (1) multiply the whole number part of the mixed number by the denominator of the fraction, (2) add the product of the fraction's numerator, and (3) place the sum over the denominator.

Example:

Change $7\frac{5}{6}$ to an improper fraction.

(1) $6 \times 7 = 42$

(2) $42 + 5 = 47$

(3) $\frac{47}{6}$

Thus, $7\frac{5}{6} = \frac{47}{6}$.

To multiply mixed numbers, change each mixed number to an improper fraction and proceed as indicated above.

Examples:

(1) $4\frac{2}{3} \times \frac{2}{7} = \frac{14}{3} \times \frac{2}{7} = \frac{28}{21} = 1\frac{7}{21} = 1\frac{1}{3}$

(2) $3\frac{1}{2} \times 2\frac{2}{3} = \frac{7}{2} \times \frac{8}{3} = \frac{56}{6} = 9\frac{2}{6} = 9\frac{1}{3}$

Practice Exercises 4:

ANSWERS TO PRACTICE EXERCISES APPEAR AT END OF SECTION.

(1) Find the product of $\frac{4}{9}$ and $\frac{5}{8}$.

(2) If Carlos cuts off $\frac{1}{3}$ of a metal pipe $12\frac{3}{4}''$ long, how much has he cut off?

(3) Multiply $6\frac{3}{5}$ by $2\frac{3}{11}$.

(4) Raymond was absent from school $\frac{1}{6}$ of the total number of school days in November. If there were 21 school days that month, how many days was he absent?

1.15 Division of Fractions

To divide fractions, simply *invert* (turn upside down) the *divisor* (the fraction to be divided into the given fraction) and then proceed as in multiplication. Convert mixed numbers to fractions and proceed in the same way.

Examples:

(1) $\frac{2}{3} \div \frac{1}{4} = \frac{2}{3} \times \frac{4}{1} = \frac{8}{3} = 2\frac{2}{3}$

(2) $\frac{2}{9} \div 8 = \frac{2}{9} \div \frac{8}{1} = \frac{2}{9} \times \frac{1}{8} = \frac{2}{72} = \frac{1}{36}$

(3) $7 \div 5\frac{5}{6} = \frac{7}{1} \div \frac{35}{6} = \frac{7}{1} \times \frac{6}{35} = \frac{42}{35} = 1\frac{7}{35} = 1\frac{1}{5}$

(4) $3\frac{7}{8} \div 1\frac{11}{20} = \frac{31}{8} \div \frac{31}{20} = \frac{31}{8} \times \frac{20}{31} = \frac{20}{8} = 2\frac{4}{8} = 2\frac{1}{2}$

Practice Exercises 5:

ANSWERS TO PRACTICE EXERCISES APPEAR AT END OF SECTION.

(1)   Divide $\frac{9}{10}$ by $\frac{1}{5}$.

(2)   If 9 is divided by $\frac{3}{4}$, what is the result?

(3)   What is the quotient of $2\frac{1}{6} \div 26$?

(4)   How many times can $6\frac{2}{3}$ fit into 60?

Simplifying Complex Fractions

When the numerator or denominator of a fraction consists of the sum or difference of two numbers, the two numbers should be combined into one number in the interest of simplification.

Examples:

(1) $\dfrac{25 + 3}{4 + 3} = \dfrac{28}{7} = 4$

(2) $\dfrac{\frac{1}{3} + \frac{1}{2}}{8 + 4} = \dfrac{\frac{2+3}{6}}{12} = \dfrac{\frac{5}{6}}{12} = \dfrac{5}{6} \times \dfrac{1}{12} = \dfrac{5}{72}$

Practice Exercises 6:

ANSWERS TO PRACTICE EXERCISES APPEAR AT END OF SECTION.

(1)   Reduce to lowest terms: $\dfrac{2 + 24}{100}$

(2)   Reduce to lowest terms: $\dfrac{\frac{1}{2} - \frac{1}{4}}{\frac{5}{8}}$

(3)   Simplify: $\dfrac{3 + \frac{1}{2} + 2}{3 + \frac{1}{3}}$

(4)   Simplify: $\dfrac{\frac{1}{2} + \frac{1}{8}}{5}$

Answers and Solutions

Practice Exercises 1:

(1) $\dfrac{1}{9}$

(2) $\dfrac{1}{6}$

(3) $\dfrac{2}{15}$

(4) $\dfrac{3}{5}$

Practice Exercises 2:

(1) $6\dfrac{1}{15}$

$$3\tfrac{3}{5} = 3\tfrac{9}{15}$$
$$+2\tfrac{7}{15} = 2\tfrac{7}{15}$$
$$5\tfrac{16}{15} = 5 + 1\tfrac{1}{15} = 6\tfrac{1}{15}$$

(2) $\dfrac{17}{18}$

$$\tfrac{1}{3} = \tfrac{6}{18}$$
$$\tfrac{2}{6} = \tfrac{6}{18}$$
$$+\tfrac{5}{18} = \tfrac{5}{18}$$
$$\tfrac{17}{18}$$

(3) $1\dfrac{29}{42}$

$$\tfrac{5}{6} = \tfrac{35}{42}$$
$$+\tfrac{6}{7} = \tfrac{36}{42}$$
$$\tfrac{71}{42} = 1\tfrac{29}{42}$$

(4) $8\dfrac{69}{70}$

$$4\tfrac{1}{5} = 4\tfrac{14}{70}$$
$$3\tfrac{2}{7} = 3\tfrac{20}{70}$$
$$1\tfrac{1}{2} = 1\tfrac{35}{70}$$
$$8\tfrac{69}{70}$$

Practice Exercises 3:

(1) $\dfrac{11}{16}$

$$\tfrac{7}{8} = \tfrac{14}{16}$$
$$-\tfrac{3}{16} = -\tfrac{3}{16}$$
$$\tfrac{11}{16}$$

(2) $2\dfrac{5}{12}$

$$3\tfrac{3}{4} = 3\tfrac{9}{12}$$
$$-1\tfrac{1}{3} = -1\tfrac{4}{12}$$
$$2\tfrac{5}{12}$$

(3) $3\dfrac{5}{8}$

$$6\tfrac{3}{8} = 5\tfrac{3}{8} + \tfrac{8}{8} = 5\tfrac{11}{8}$$
$$-2\tfrac{3}{4} \qquad = -2\tfrac{6}{8}$$
$$3\tfrac{5}{8}$$

(4) $1\dfrac{28}{45}$

$$4\tfrac{2}{9} = 4\tfrac{10}{45} = 3\tfrac{10}{45} + \tfrac{45}{45} = 3\tfrac{55}{45}$$
$$-2\tfrac{3}{5} = -2\tfrac{27}{45} \qquad\qquad = -2\tfrac{27}{45}$$
$$1\tfrac{28}{45}$$

(5) $4\dfrac{1}{4}$

$$8 = \tfrac{8}{1} = \tfrac{32}{4}$$
$$-3\tfrac{3}{4} \quad = -\tfrac{15}{4}$$
$$\tfrac{17}{4} = 4\tfrac{1}{4}$$

Practice Exercises 4:

(1) $\dfrac{5}{18}$

$$\frac{4}{9} \times \frac{5}{8} = \frac{20}{72} = \frac{5}{18}$$

(2) $4\dfrac{1}{4}$

$$\frac{1}{3} \times 12\frac{3}{4} = \frac{1}{3} \times \frac{51}{4} = \frac{51}{12} = 4\frac{1}{4}$$

(3) **15**

$$6\frac{3}{5} \times 2\frac{3}{11} = \frac{\overset{3}{\cancel{33}}}{\underset{1}{\cancel{5}}} \times \frac{\overset{5}{\cancel{25}}}{\underset{1}{\cancel{11}}} = 15$$

(4) $3\dfrac{1}{2}$

$$\frac{1}{6} \times \frac{21}{1} = \frac{21}{6} = 3\frac{1}{2}$$

Practice Exercises 5:

(1) $4\dfrac{1}{2}$

$$\frac{9}{10} \div \frac{1}{5} = \frac{9}{10} \times \frac{5}{1} = \frac{45}{10} = 4\frac{1}{2}$$

(2) **12**

$$9 \div \frac{3}{4} = \frac{9}{1} \div \frac{3}{4} = \frac{\overset{3}{\cancel{9}}}{1} \times \frac{4}{\underset{1}{\cancel{3}}} = 12$$

(3) $\dfrac{1}{12}$

$$2\frac{1}{6} \div 26 = \frac{\overset{1}{\cancel{13}}}{6} \times \frac{1}{\underset{2}{\cancel{26}}} = \frac{1}{12}$$

(4) **9**

$$60 \div 6\frac{2}{3} = \frac{60}{1} \div \frac{20}{3} = \frac{\overset{3}{\cancel{60}}}{1} \times \frac{3}{\underset{1}{\cancel{20}}} = 9$$

Practice Exercises 6:

(1) $\dfrac{13}{50}$

$$\frac{2 + 24}{100} = \frac{26}{100} = \frac{13}{50}$$

(2) $\dfrac{2}{5}$

$$\frac{\dfrac{1}{2} - \dfrac{1}{4}}{\dfrac{5}{8}} = \frac{\dfrac{2-1}{4}}{\dfrac{5}{8}} = \frac{\dfrac{1}{4}}{\dfrac{5}{8}} = \frac{1}{\underset{1}{\cancel{4}}} \times \frac{\overset{2}{\cancel{8}}}{5} = \frac{2}{5}$$

(3) $1\dfrac{13}{20}$

$$\frac{3 + \dfrac{1}{2} + 2}{3 + \dfrac{1}{3}} = \frac{5\dfrac{1}{2}}{3\dfrac{1}{3}} = \frac{11}{2} \times \frac{3}{10} = \frac{33}{20} = 1\frac{13}{20}$$

(4) $\dfrac{1}{8}$

$$\frac{\dfrac{1}{2} + \dfrac{1}{8}}{5} = \frac{\dfrac{4+1}{8}}{5} = \frac{\dfrac{5}{8}}{5} = \frac{\overset{1}{\cancel{5}}}{8} \times \frac{1}{\underset{1}{\cancel{5}}} = \frac{1}{8}$$

1.2 Decimal Fractions

Another way of writing fractions is to use *decimal fractions*. Using a symbol called a *decimal point* before a number makes that number a fraction. The number of places to the right of the decimal point tells the size of the fraction. Whole numbers appear to the left of the decimal point. Below are the place units for decimal fractions up to a millionth.

.3	*tenths*
.03	*hundredths*
.003	*thousandths*
.0003	*ten thousandths*
.00003	*hundred thousandths*
.000003	*millionths*

Decimal fractions are based on the *decimal system*, a place-value system based on tens. In this system, each place is worth one-tenth of the value of the place to its left. For example, in the number 8.93, the 3 stands for $\frac{3}{100}$, the 9 stands for $\frac{9}{10}$, and the 8 stands for 8 ones.

Decimal fractions are related to common fractions in this way:

$$.3 = \frac{3}{10}$$

$$.03 = \frac{3}{100}$$

$$.003 = \frac{3}{1000}$$

$$.0003 = \frac{3}{10,000}$$

Remember that .01 is smaller than .1 and that .001 is smaller still. (One-hundredth of an inch is smaller than one-tenth of an inch, and one-thousandth of an inch is even smaller.)

By the decimal's position, or place, you know what size unit it stands for. Use the unit's name in reading or writing the numbers. For example:

.137 is one hundred thirty-seven *thousandths*, or $\frac{137}{1000}$

.43 is forty-three *hundredths*, or $\frac{43}{100}$

.9034 is nine thousand thirty-four *ten thousandths*, or $\frac{9034}{10,000}$

A *decimal mixed number* (both a whole number and a decimal fraction) is read or written by substituting the word "and" for the decimal point, and adding the proper decimal term at the end. For example:

5.07 is five *and* seven hundredths, or $5\frac{7}{100}$

14.107 is fourteen *and* one hundred seven thousandths, or $14\frac{107}{1000}$

325.0065 is three hundred twenty-five *and* sixty-five ten thousandths, or $325\frac{65}{10,000}$

1.21 Rounding Off Decimals

To round off a decimal to a given place, look at the number in the place immediately to the right of the given place. If this number is less than 5, leave the numbers before it as they are. If this number is 5 or more, increase the number just before it by one.

 4.438   rounds off to the nearest hundredth as 4.44
11.104   rounds off to the nearest hundredth as 11.10
 .2178   rounds off to the nearest thousandth as .218
 .4399   rounds off to the nearest tenth as .4
7.04   rounds off to the nearest tenth as 7.0

Practice Exercises 1:

ANSWERS TO PRACTICE EXERCISES APPEAR AT END OF SECTION.

(1)   Round off 4.76 to the nearest tenth.

(2)   Round off 3.893 to the nearest hundredth.

(3)   Round off 5.1198 to the nearest thousandth.

1.22 Addition of Decimals

Arrange the numbers of a problem so that decimals that stand for the same unit size are in the same column. Carelessness in writing the problem can lead to incorrect answers.

Example 1:   4.5 + .58 + 72.134 =

Written correctly:	Incorrectly:
4.5·	4.5
.58	.58
+72.134	+72.134
77.214	

Line up the decimal points in all the numbers. Remember to put the decimal point in the proper place in the sum.

If the sum of any column is more than ten, remember to put the carry number above the next column to the left before adding that column.

Example 2:   15.68 + 8.4 =

```
  1 1
 15.68
+ 8.4
───────
 24.08
```

Practice Exercises 2: Add

ANSWERS TO PRACTICE EXERCISES APPEAR AT END OF SECTION.

(1)   9.4 + .09 + 14.2 =
(2)   514.6 + 36.43 + .074 =
(3)   2.4 + 11.03 + 7.56 =

1.23 Subtraction of Decimals

Here again, decimals of the same unit size must be put in the same column and the decimal points lined up. In order to solve some problems, you may have to add zeros to a decimal. Any number of zeros may be added to the right of a decimal fraction. They do not change the value of the fraction. For example:

.5 = .50 = .500 = .5000
.02 = .020 = .0200

Example 1:
Two zeros are added to the minuend 5.7.

```
             69
5.7 − 3.241 =   5.700
             −3.241
             ───────
              2.459
```

Example 2:
Zeros need not be added to the bottom number.

```
5.234 − 3.1 =   5.234
              −3.1
              ───────
               2.134
```

The method of borrowing or regrouping decimals is the same as in subtraction of whole numbers.

Example 3:

$$9.2 - .7 = \begin{array}{r} \overset{8}{\cancel{9}.2} \\ - .7 \\ \hline 8.5 \end{array}$$

Example 4:

$$7.14 - 2.36 = \begin{array}{r} \overset{6\ 10}{7.\cancel{1}4} \\ -2.36 \\ \hline 4.78 \end{array}$$

Practice Exercises 3: Subtract

ANSWERS TO PRACTICE EXERCISES APPEAR AT END OF SECTION.

(1)   9.008
      −3.334

(2)   121.7
      −106.2

(3)   18.73
      − 9.006

1.24 Multiplication of Decimals

You work out problems in decimal multiplication the same way as you do in whole-number multiplication. The only difference is placing the decimal point in the final product. The number of decimal places in the answer must be equal to the sum of the decimal places in both numbers, the one you multiply and the one you multiply by.

Example 1:

      1.3   one decimal place in the multiplicand
  ×   .4   one decimal place in the multiplier
    ─────
      .52   there must be two decimal places in the product.

Example 2:

      .003   three decimal places in the multiplicand
  ×   .02   two decimal places in the multiplier
    ───────
    .00006   five decimal places are needed in the product.

Practice Exercises 4: Multiply

ANSWERS TO PRACTICE EXERCISES APPEAR AT END OF SECTION.

(1)   12.4
      $\times$ 3.6

(2)   .0003
      $\times$ .005

(3)   14.81
      $\times$ .906

1.25 Division of Decimals

You solve decimal division problems in the same way as whole-number division problems. The only difference is remembering to put the decimal point in the proper place in the quotient. This is done by moving the decimal point of the divisor (the number you are dividing by) to the right as many places as are necessary to make it a whole number. Then move the decimal point of the dividend (the number being divided) the same number of places and put the decimal point of the quotient directly above this new place. If necessary, add zeros to the dividend.

Examples:

(1) $2.4\overline{)72.48}$ Moving the decimal point one place to the right in both divisor and dividend gives $24\overline{)724.8}$, and dividing gives

$24\overline{)724.8}$ = 30.2 .

(2) $.314\overline{)1.570}$ = $314\overline{)1570.}$ = 5.

(3) $.006\overline{)72.600}$ = $6\overline{)72,600.}$ = 12,100.

Practice Exercises 5: Divide

ANSWERS TO PRACTICE EXERCISES APPEAR AT END OF SECTION.

(1) $3.6\overline{)1.0836}$

(2) $.07\overline{)2.849}$

(3) $.08\overline{)265.6}$

Answers and Solutions

Practice Exercises 1:

(1) **4.8**
(2) **3.89**
(3) **5.120**

Practice Exercises 2:

(1) **23.69**

$$\begin{array}{r} 9.4 \\ .09 \\ \underline{14.2} \\ \mathbf{23.69} \end{array}$$

(2) **551.104**

$$\begin{array}{r} 514.6 \\ 36.43 \\ \underline{.074} \\ \mathbf{551.104} \end{array}$$

(3) **20.99**

$$\begin{array}{r} 2.4 \\ 11.03 \\ \underline{7.56} \\ \mathbf{20.99} \end{array}$$

Practice Exercises 3:

(1) **5.674**

$$\begin{array}{r} 9.008 \\ \underline{-3.334} \\ \mathbf{5.674} \end{array}$$

(2) **15.5**

$$\begin{array}{r} 121.7 \\ \underline{-106.2} \\ \mathbf{15.5} \end{array}$$

(3) **9.724**

$$\begin{array}{r} 18.730 \\ \underline{-\ 9.006} \\ \mathbf{9.724} \end{array}$$

Practice Exercises 4:

(1) **44.64**

$$\begin{array}{r} 12.4 \\ \underline{3.6} \\ 744 \\ \underline{372} \\ \mathbf{44.64} \end{array}$$

(2) **.0000015**

$$\begin{array}{r} .0003 \\ \underline{.005} \\ \mathbf{.0000015} \end{array}$$

(3) **13.41786**

$$\begin{array}{r} 14.81 \\ \underline{.906} \\ 8886 \\ \underline{13329} \\ \mathbf{13.41786} \end{array}$$

Practice Exercises 5:

(1) **.301**

$$\begin{array}{r} \mathbf{.301} \\ 3.6\overline{)\,1.0836} \\ \underline{1\ 08} \\ 3 \\ \underline{0} \\ 36 \\ \underline{36} \end{array}$$

(2) **40.7**

$$\begin{array}{r} \mathbf{40.7} \\ .07\,\overline{)\,2.849} \end{array}$$

(3) **3320**

$$\begin{array}{r} \mathbf{3320.} \\ .08\,\overline{)\,265.60} \\ \underline{24} \\ 25 \\ \underline{24} \\ 16 \\ \underline{16} \\ 00 \end{array}$$

1.3 Percentage

1.31 Changing Decimals to Percents

To change a *decimal to a percent*, move the decimal point two places to the *right* of its original location, and add the percent sign.

Examples:
(1) $.03 = 3\%$
(2) $.094 = 9.4\%$
(3) $4.37 = 437\%$

1.32 Changing Fractions to Percents

To change a *fraction to a percent*, multiply the fraction by 100, and add the percent sign.

Examples:

(1) $\dfrac{2}{5} = \dfrac{2}{\cancel{5}} \times \cancel{100}\,^{20} = 40\%$

(2) $\dfrac{3}{8} = \dfrac{3}{\cancel{8}_2} \times \cancel{100}\,^{25} = \dfrac{3}{2} \times 25 = \dfrac{75}{2} = 37\tfrac{1}{2}\%$

Practice Exercises 1:

ANSWERS TO PRACTICE EXERCISES APPEAR AT END OF SECTION.

Change the following decimals or fractions to percents.
(1) .64
(2) 1.96
(3) .003

(4) $\dfrac{7}{20}$

(5) $\dfrac{17}{25}$

(6) $\dfrac{5}{6}$

1.33 Changing Percents to Decimals

To change *a percent to a decimal*, move the decimal point two places to the *left* of its original location.

Examples:
(1) $53\% = .53$
(2) $9\% = .09$
(3) $42.6\% = .426$

1.34 Changing Percents to Fractions

To change a percent to a fraction, place the percent over 100 and reduce to lowest terms.

Examples:

(1) $75\% = \dfrac{75}{100} = \dfrac{3}{4}$

(2) $33\frac{1}{3}\% = \dfrac{33\frac{1}{3}}{100} = \dfrac{\dfrac{100}{3}}{\dfrac{100}{1}} = \dfrac{100}{3} \times \dfrac{1}{100} = \dfrac{1}{3}$

Practice Exercises 2:

ANSWERS TO PRACTICE EXERCISES APPEAR AT END OF SECTION.

Change the following percents to decimals.
(1) 48%
(2) 1%
(3) 263%

Change the following percents to fractions.
(4) 65%
(5) $16\frac{2}{3}\%$
(6) 120%

1.35 Finding the Percent of a Quantity

1. Change the percent to a decimal (or fraction, if necessary).
2. Multiply the decimal (fraction) by the number in the problem.

Example 1:
What is 35% of 108?

$$\begin{array}{r} 108 \\ \times\ .35 \\ \hline 540 \\ 324 \\ \hline 37.80 \end{array}$$ Thus, 37.8 is 35% of 108.

Example 2:
29% of 340 is how much?

$$\begin{array}{r} 340 \\ \times\ .29 \\ \hline 3060 \\ 680 \\ \hline 98.60 \end{array}$$ Thus, 29% of 340 is 98.60.

Practice Exercises 3:

ANSWERS TO PRACTICE EXERCISES APPEAR AT END OF SECTION.

(1)   What is 30% of 160?
(2)   4% of 903 is?
(3)   512% of 300 is how much?

1.36 Finding What Percent One Quantity Is of Another

1. Decide which of the numbers is the *base* quantity in the problem, that is, the quantity *of* which you are to find the percent.
2. Decide which number is *part* of the base quantity, that is, which number is the percent *to be found*.
3. Make a fraction of the two numbers with the *part* as the numerator and the *base* as the denominator.
4. Multiply this fraction by 100 to get the final answer.

Examples:
(1)   8 is what percent of 20?

The base quantity is 20, and the part is 8; thus, we make the fraction $\frac{8}{20}$.

$$\frac{8}{20} \times \frac{100}{1} = 8 \times 5 = 40\%$$

(2)   What percent of 720 is 180?

$$\frac{\overset{18}{\cancel{180}}}{\underset{72}{\cancel{720}}} \times \frac{100}{1} = \frac{18}{72} \times \frac{100}{1} = \frac{1800}{72} =$$

$$\begin{array}{r} 25\% \\ 72\overline{\smash{)}1800} \\ \underline{144} \\ 360 \end{array}$$

Practice Exercises 4:

ANSWERS TO PRACTICE EXERCISES APPEAR AT END OF SECTION.

(1)   25 is what percent of 200?
(2)   What percent of 900 is 150?
(3) $60 is what percent of $180?
(4)   What % of 510 is 370?

1.37 Percent of Gain or Loss

These problems may be solved by using the following general formula:

$$\% \text{ Gain or Loss} = \frac{\text{difference between the two amounts}}{\text{original amount}} \times 100.$$

This is a common type of percentage problem.

Examples:

(1)   If a union contract increased John's weekly wage from $80 to $112 a week, what was the percent of increase in his wages?

$$\% \text{ Gain} = \frac{112 - 80}{80} \times \frac{100}{1} = \frac{32}{\underset{4}{\cancel{80}}} \times \frac{\overset{5}{\cancel{100}}}{1} = \frac{160}{4} = 40\%$$

(2)   Mr. Garcia bought some stocks for $3000. A year later they were worth $1200. What was his percent of loss?

$$\% \text{ Loss} = \frac{3000 - 1200}{3000} \times \frac{100}{1} =$$

$$\frac{\overset{3}{\cancel{1800}}}{\underset{5}{\cancel{3000}}} \times \frac{100}{1} = \frac{3}{\underset{1}{\cancel{5}}} \times \frac{\overset{20}{\cancel{100}}}{1} = 60\%$$

Miscellaneous Problems

(1)   The alcoholic content of a particular bottle of wine is 12%. If the bottle contains 32 ounces, how many ounces are alcohol?

$$
\begin{array}{r}
32 \\
\underline{.12} \\
64 \\
\underline{32} \\
3.84 \text{ ounces}
\end{array}
$$

(2)   What percent of the boxes below is shaded?

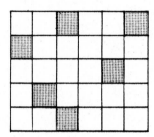

$$
\frac{6 \text{ (Shaded)}}{30 \text{ (Total)}} = \frac{1}{\cancel{5}_1} \times \frac{\overset{20}{\cancel{100}}}{1} = 20\%
$$

(3)   If on a test containing 45 questions Clara got 30 correct, what percent did she answer correctly?

$$
\frac{30 \text{ (Correct)}}{45 \text{ (Total)}} = \frac{2}{3} \times \frac{100}{1} = \frac{200}{3} = 66\frac{2}{3}\%
$$

Practice Exercises 5:

ANSWERS TO PRACTICE EXERCISES APPEAR AT END OF SECTION.

(1)   There are 300 enrollees in a job training program. If 85% of them are women, how many men are in the program?

(2)   What percent of the boxes below is *unshaded*?

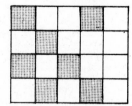

(3)   If Gloria got 3 problems wrong out of 24 on a mathematics test, what percent of the problems did she answer incorrectly?

(4)   If a color TV set cost $600 when it was first available on the market, and it can now be bought for $480, what is the percent of decrease (loss) in price?

Answers and Solutions

Practice Exercises 1:

(1) **64**%

(2) **196**%

(3) **.3**%

(4) **35**%

$$\frac{7}{\overset{}{\cancel{20}}} \times \frac{\overset{5}{\cancel{100}}}{1} = \mathbf{35}\%$$

(5) **68**%

$$\frac{17}{\overset{}{\cancel{25}}} \times \frac{\overset{4}{\cancel{100}}}{1} = \mathbf{68}\%$$

(6) **83$\frac{1}{3}$**%

$$\frac{5}{6} \times \frac{100}{1} = \frac{500}{6} = \mathbf{83\frac{1}{3}}\%$$

Practice Exercises 2:

(1) **.48**

(2) **.01**

(3) **2.63**

(4) **$\frac{13}{20}$**

(5) **$\frac{1}{6}$**

(6) **1$\frac{1}{5}$**

Practice Exercises 3:

(1) **48**

$$\begin{array}{r} 160 \\ .30 \\ \hline \mathbf{48.\cancel{00}} \end{array}$$

(2) **36.12**

$$\begin{array}{r} 903 \\ .04 \\ \hline \mathbf{36.12} \end{array}$$

(3) **1536**

$$\begin{array}{r} 5.12 \\ 300 \\ \hline \mathbf{1536.\cancel{00}} \end{array}$$

Practice Exercises 4:

(1) $\dfrac{25}{200} = 12\dfrac{1}{2}\%$

(2) $\dfrac{150}{900} = 16\dfrac{2}{3}\%$

(3) $\dfrac{60}{180} = 33\dfrac{1}{3}\%$

(4) $\dfrac{370}{510} = 72\dfrac{28}{51}\%$

Practice Exercises 5:

(1) **45**

$$\begin{array}{r} 300 \\ .85 \\ \hline 1500 \\ 2400 \\ \hline 255.00 \end{array} \text{ are women}$$

$300 - 255 = $ **45**

(2) **65%**

$$\dfrac{7}{\cancel{20}} \times \dfrac{\overset{5}{\cancel{100}}}{1} = 35\% \text{ shaded}$$

So $100\% - 35\% = $ **65% unshaded**

(3) $12\dfrac{1}{2}\%$

$$\dfrac{3}{24} = \dfrac{1}{8} \times \dfrac{100}{1} = \dfrac{100}{8} = 12\dfrac{1}{2}\%$$

(4) **20%**

$$\% \text{ loss} = \dfrac{600 - 480}{600} \times \dfrac{100}{1} = \dfrac{\overset{1}{\cancel{120}}}{\underset{5}{\cancel{600}}} \times \dfrac{100}{1} = \dfrac{1}{5} \times \dfrac{100}{1} = \mathbf{20\%}$$

1.4 Graphs

Graphs and charts show the relationship of numbers or quantities in visual form. By looking at a graph, you can see the relationship between two or more sets of information at a glance. If such information were presented in written form, it would be hard to read and understand.

To read a graph, you must know what *scale* the graph has been drawn to. Somewhere on the face of the graph there will be an explanation of what each division of the graph means. Sometimes the divisions will be labeled. At other times, this information will be given in a small box called a *scale* or *legend*. For instance, a map, which is a specialized kind of graph, will always carry a scale or legend on its face telling you such information as $1'' = 100$ miles or $\frac{1}{4}'' = 2$ miles.

1.41 Bar Graphs

The bar graph shows how the information is compared by using broad lines, called bars, of varying lengths. Sometimes single lines are used as well. Bar graphs are good for showing a quick comparison of the information involved; however, the bars are difficult to read accurately unless the end of the bar falls exactly on one of the divisions of the scale. If the end of the bar falls between divisions of the scale, it is not easy to arrive at the precise figure represented by the bar. In bar graphs, the bars can run either vertically or horizontally. The sample bar graph below is a horizontal graph.

EXPENDITURES PER PUPIL—1980

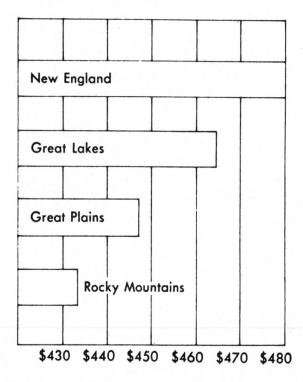

$430 $440 $450 $460 $470 $480

The individual bars in this kind of graph may carry a label within the bar, as in this example. The label may also appear alongside each bar. The scale used on the bars may appear along one axis, as in the example, or it may be noted somewhere on the face of the graph. Each numbered space on the *x*- (or horizontal) axis represents an expenditure of $10 per pupil. A wide variety of questions may be answered by a bar graph, such as:

(1)   Which area of the country spends least per pupil?   Rocky Mountains.

(2)   How much does the New England area spend per pupil? $480.

(3)   How much less does the Great Plains spend per pupil than the Great Lakes? $464 - 447 = 17$ $17/pupil.

(4)   How much more does New England spend on a pupil than the Rocky Mountain area? $480 - 433 = \$47$/pupil.

1.42 Circle Graphs

A circle graph shows how an entire quantity has been divided or apportioned. The circle represents 100% of the quantity; the different parts into which the whole has been divided are shown by sections, or wedges, of the circle. Circle graphs are good for showing how money is distributed or collected, and for this reason they are widely used in financial graphing. The information is usually presented on the face of each section, telling you exactly what the section stands for and the value of that section in comparison to the other parts of the graph.

SOURCES OF INCOME—PUBLIC COLLEGES OF U.S.

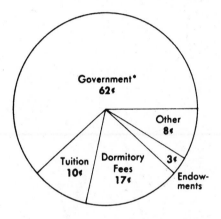

* Government refers to all levels of government—not exclusively the federal government.

The circle graph above indicates where the money originates that is used to maintain public colleges in the U.S. The size of the sections tells you at a glance which source is most important (government) and which is least important (endowments). The sections total 100¢ or $1.00. This graph may be used to answer the following questions:

(1) What is the most important source of income to the public colleges? Government
(2) What part of the revenue dollar comes from tuition? 10¢
(3) Dormitory fees bring in how many times the money that endowments bring in? $5\frac{2}{3}$ times $\left(\frac{17}{3} = 5\frac{2}{3}\right)$
(4) What is the least important source of revenue to public colleges? Endowments

1.43 Line Graphs

Graphs that have information running both across (horizontally) and up and down (vertically) can be considered to be laid out on a grid having a *y*-axis and an *x*-axis. One of the two quantities being compared will be placed along the *y*-axis, and the other quantity will be placed along the *x*-axis. When we are asked to compare two values, we subtract the smaller from the larger.

SHARES OF STOCK SOLD
NEW YORK STOCK EXCHANGE

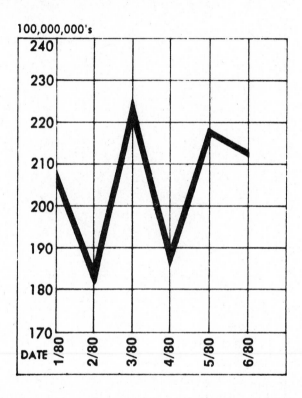

Our sample line graph represents the total shares of stock sold on the New York Stock Exchange between January and June. The months are placed along the *x*-axis, while the sales, in units of 100,000,000 shares, are placed along the *y*-axis.

(1) How many shares were sold in March?   225,000,000.
(2) What is the trend of stock sales between April and May?   The volume of sales rose.
(3) Compare the share sales in January and February.   25,000,000 fewer shares were sold in February.
(4) During which months of the period was the increase in sales largest?   February to March.

Practice Exercises

ANSWERS TO PRACTICE EXERCISES APPEAR AT END OF SECTION.

MORTALITY RATE OF AMERICANS BY RACE

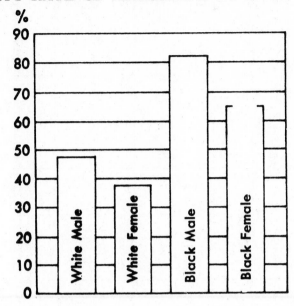

(1)   What is the mortality rate of white American males?
(2)   What is the mortality rate of black American females?
(3)   Approximately how many times greater is the black male mortality rate than the white male mortality rate?
(4)   Which group has the lowest mortality rate?

TEACHER SALARY—MASTER'S DEGREE SCALE

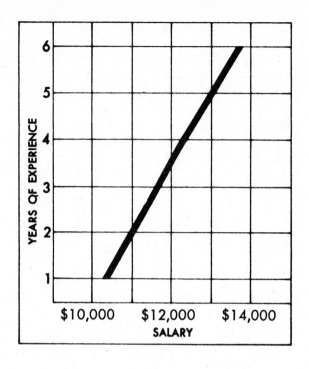

(1) A person with one year's teaching experience and a Master's degree will be earning how much?

(2) Compare the salaries of a person with one year's experience and six years' experience on this salary guide. What is the difference?

(3) If the same pattern holds, what should a person with seven years' experience be earning?

(4) If a teacher with a Master's degree is earning $12,200, how many years of experience does he or she have?

BELAFONTE ASSOCIATES BUSINESS COSTS

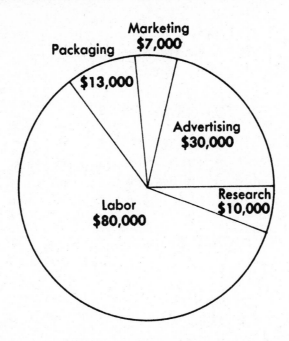

(1) What fraction of the advertising budget is the research budget?
(2) What is their largest single cost of doing business?
(3) What was their total cost of doing business?
(4) What fraction of their total cost was the cost of marketing?

Answers and Solutions

(1) Bar Graph

(1) **48%**
(2) **65%**
(3) **About two times as great**
(4) **White females**

(2) Line Graph

(1) **About $10,250**
(2) **About $3350 more by six years**
(3) **About $14,500**
(4) **4 years**

(3) Circle Graph

(1) $\frac{1}{3}$
(2) **labor**
(3) **$140,000**
(4) $\frac{1}{20}$

1.5 Properties of Numbers

Prime Numbers

Prime numbers are numbers that can be divided evenly only by themselves and the number 1. Thus, 13 is a prime because there is no number (factor) except 1 that will go into it without a remainder. The number 21 is *not* a prime since it is divisible by 3 and by 7. Below is a list of all the prime numbers from 1 to 50:

Table of Prime Numbers

3, 5, 7, 11, 13, 17, 19, 23, 29, 31, 37, 41, 43, 47.

Examples:
Which of the following numbers are prime?
(1) 91
(2) 59
(3) 87
(4) 71
59 and 71 are prime
91 is divisible by 7 and 13
87 is divisible by 3 and 29

434

Practice Exercises 1:

ANSWERS TO PRACTICE EXERCISES APPEAR AT END OF SECTION.

Which is the prime number in each of the following groups of numbers?
(1) 49, 51, 61, 93
(2) 63, 78, 117, 79
(3) 101, 105, 123, 119

1.51 Average of Numbers

There are two common types of average, the *mean* and the *median*. The mean of a number of figures is obtained by adding up all the figures and dividing the sum by the number of figures. When we speak of an *average*, we generally are speaking of a *mean*.

Examples:
(1) Mr. Calderon is a commercial artist who works on a free-lance basis. If his income for five successive weeks was $150, $175, $220, $160, and $185, find his mean earnings per week for that period.

$$\text{Mean:} \quad \frac{150 + 175 + 220 + 160 + 185}{5} = \frac{890}{5} = \$178.$$

(2) On three consecutive days in January it snowed $3\frac{1}{2}''$, $12\frac{1}{4}''$, and $4\frac{1}{2}''$.

What was the mean number of inches of snowfall per day?

$$\frac{3\frac{1}{2} + 12\frac{1}{4} + 4\frac{1}{2}}{3} = \frac{20\frac{1}{4}}{3} = \frac{81}{4} \div \frac{3}{1} = \frac{81}{4} \times \frac{1}{3} = \frac{81}{12} = 6\frac{3}{4}''$$

The *median* is an average obtained by counting. First you rearrange the numbers in rank order. It is most convenient to list them in a column with the largest number at the top. The median is defined as the number that divides the half of the numbers with the larger values from the half with the smaller values.

Examples:

(1)   Values
    39
    35
    33
    30   ← Median is 30 (7 is an *odd* number of values)
    26
    24
    22

(2)   Values
    21
    19
    16
    15
       ← Median is 14.5 (8 is an *even* number of values)
    14
    11
     9
     8

Practice Exercises 2:

ANSWERS TO PRACTICE EXERCISES APPEAR AT END OF SECTION.

(1)   What is the mean of 14.3, 6.5, 7.8, and 3.4?

(2)   On five examinations, Lisa scored 60, 80, 95, 75, and 90. What was her median score?

(3)   Stacy's weight has varied from September through February as follows: 105 lbs., 118 lbs., 110 lbs., 115 lbs., 112 lbs., and 106 lbs. What was her mean weight for this period of time?

1.52 Squares and Square Roots of Numbers

The *square* of a number is the result of multiplying a number by itself. For instance, the square of 7 is $7 \times 7 = 49$. It is useful to memorize the squares of the numbers from 1 to 20.

TABLE OF SQUARES

Number	Square	Number	Square
1	1	11	121
2	4	12	144
3	9	13	169
4	16	14	196
5	25	15	225
6	36	16	256
7	49	17	289
8	64	18	324
9	81	19	361
10	100	20	400

The symbol for the squaring operation is a small 2 written above and just to the right of the number to be squared. Thus for "eight squared equals 64" we write $8^2 = 64$.

The square root of a number is the number which, when multiplied by itself, will give the number under the square sign. Thus $\sqrt{16} = 4$ since $4 \times 4 = 16$. It is useful to memorize the exact square roots for the numbers from 1 to 20.

TABLE OF SQUARE ROOTS

$$\sqrt{1} = 1 \qquad \sqrt{121} = 11$$
$$\sqrt{4} = 2 \qquad \sqrt{144} = 12$$
$$\sqrt{9} = 3 \qquad \sqrt{169} = 13$$
$$\sqrt{16} = 4 \qquad \sqrt{196} = 14$$
$$\sqrt{25} = 5 \qquad \sqrt{225} = 15$$
$$\sqrt{36} = 6 \qquad \sqrt{256} = 16$$
$$\sqrt{49} = 7 \qquad \sqrt{289} = 17$$
$$\sqrt{64} = 8 \qquad \sqrt{324} = 18$$
$$\sqrt{81} = 9 \qquad \sqrt{361} = 19$$
$$\sqrt{100} = 10 \qquad \sqrt{400} = 20$$

...nes you will be asked to find the square root of a number ... exact square. In such a case it will be necessary to find ...nate answer by using the procedure explained below.

...ple:

...ind $\sqrt{671}$ to the nearest hundredth.

STEP 1.   Add four zeros to the right of the decimal point.
$\sqrt{671.0000}$

STEP 2.   Mark off the numbers in groups of two from the left and from the right of the decimal point.
$\sqrt{6'71.00'00'}$

STEP 3.   Determine what is the nearest square less than 6. Answer: 2 ($2 \times 2 = 4$). Place the 2 above the line, over the 6. This is a partial answer (square root) to the problem.

```
        2  5. 9  0
      √6 71.00 00
        4
  45  |2 71
        2 25
 509  | 46 00
        45 81
5180  |    19 00
```

STEP 4.   Square the 2 ($2 \times 2 = 4$) and place the square, 4, under the 6. Subtract, getting a remainder of 2.

STEP 5.   Bring down the next group of numbers (71) and place them to the right of the remainder obtained in Step 4, getting 271.

STEP 6.   Double the partial answer and place the result (4) to the left of the remainder.

STEP 7.   Put a trial zero to the right of the 4 obtained in Step 3 (getting 40), and determine how many times 40 goes into 271. Answer: 5. Place the 5 alongside the 2 in the partial answer. Now, substitute the 5 for the trial zero, getting 45.

STEP 8.   Multiply 45 by 5 ($5 \times 45 = 225$) and place the product below the 271.

STEP 9.   Subtract the 225 from 271, getting a remainder of 46.

STEP 10.   Bring down the next group of numbers (00) and place them to the right of the remainder obtained in Step 9, getting 4600.

STEP 11.   Double the partial answer you have found so far (25) and place the product (50) in the left-hand column.

STEP 12. Again add a trial zero to the right of the doubled partial answer (getting 500), and determine how many times 500 goes into 4600. Answer: 9. Place the 9 alongside the 5 in the partial answer. Now substitute the 9 for the trial zero, getting 509.

STEP 13. Multiply 509 by 9, and place the product (4581) below the 4600.

STEP 14. Subtract 4581 from 4600, getting a remainder of 19.

STEP 15. Bring down the next group of numbers (00) and place them to the right of the remainder obtained in Step 14, getting 1900.

STEP 16. Double the partial answer (259) you have found so far, and place the product (518) in the left-hand column.

STEP 17. Add a trial zero to the doubled partial answer (getting 5180), and determine how many times 5180 goes into 1900. Answer: 0. Place the zero alongside the 9 in the answer.

STEP 18. The square root of 671 is 25.90, correct to hundredths.

(*Note:* The decimal point in the answer is placed above the decimal point in the number whose square root is being found, as you do in division.)

Practice Exercises 3:

ANSWERS TO PRACTICE EXERCISES APPEAR AT END OF SECTION.

(1) What is the square of 317?

(2) Find $\sqrt{625}$.

(3) Find $\sqrt{40.1956}$.

1.53 Number Series

Number series (sometimes called *progressions*) are sequences of numbers having some regular pattern.

Arithmetic series are number series having a *common difference*. An example of such a series would be 3,6,9,12,15, . . . since each successive number may be obtained by adding 3 to the one before it. Hence, 3 is the common difference. The common difference may be found by subtracting any number in the series from the one immediately after it.

Geometric series are number series having a *common ratio*. An example of such a series would be 2,8,32,128, . . . since each successive number may be obtained by multiplying the one before it by 4. Hence, 4 is the common ratio. The common ratio may be found by dividing any number in the series by the one immediately preceding it.

Examples:

(1)   Find the eighth term in the series 27, 31, 35, 39, ...
The common difference is 4, so we add 4 to 39 in order to get the next term and continue to add 4 to each number until we get to the eighth term: 27, 31, 35, 39, 43, 47, 51, 55. So **55** is the eighth term.

(2)   Find the sixth term in the series 1, 3, 9, 27, ...
The common ratio is 3. If we continue the series, we have 1, 3, 9, 27, 81, 243. So **243** is the sixth term.

Practice Exercises 4:

ANSWERS TO PRACTICE EXERCISES APPEAR AT END OF SECTION.

(1)   Find the seventh term in the series 9, 14, 19, 24, ...
(2)   Find the ninth term in the series 2, 11, 20, 29, ...
(3)   Find the eighth term in the series 13, 26, 52, 104, ...
(4)   Find the sixth term in the series 1, 6, 36, 216, ...

Answers and Solutions

Practice Exercises 1:

(1)   **61**
(2)   **79**
(3)   **101**

Practice Exercises 2:

(1)   **8**

$$\frac{14.3 + 6.5 + 7.8 + 3.4}{4} = \frac{32}{4} = \mathbf{8}$$

(2)   **80**

60 75 **80** 90 95

(3)   **111 lbs.**

$$\frac{105 + 118 + 110 + 115 + 112 + 106}{6} = \frac{666}{6} = \mathbf{111 \text{ lbs.}}$$

Practice Exercises 3:

(1) **100,489**

```
   317
   317
  2219
   317
   951
100,489
```

(2) **25**

```
      2 5
   √6 25
    4
45 │2 25
    2 25
```

(3) **6.34**

```
          6.3  4
     √40.19 56
      36
123 │ 4 19
      3 69
1264│ 50 56
      50 56
```

Practice Exercises 4:

(1) **39**
9, 14, 19, 24, 29, 34, **39**

(2) **74**
2, 11, 20, 29, 38, 47, 56, 65, **74**

(3) **1664**
13, 26, 52, 104, 208, 416, 832, **1664**

(4) **7776**
1, 6, 36, 216, 1296, **7776**

1.6 Signed Numbers

For all of the arithmetic problems in the preceding chapters it was sufficient for us to use *positive* numbers such as 8, 15, $12\frac{1}{2}$, 9.4, etc. However, when we consider the difference between, say, having $50 and owing $50 or a temperature of 31 degrees above zero and 31 degrees below zero or throwing a ball 25 feet up from the roof of a house and having it fall 25 feet below the roof, we begin to see the need for having to enlarge our concepts of numbers to include numbers less than zero—*negative numbers*. If we do this with the situations just mentioned, then they may be represented numerically as follows.

1. Having $50: $+50$
   Owing $50: -50
2. 31° above zero: $+31°$
   31° below zero: $-31°$
3. Throwing a ball 25 feet above the roof: $+25$
   A ball falling 25 feet below the roof: -25

In order to deal with problems involving considerations such as those illustrated above, it will be necessary to know how to perform operations including both positive and negative numbers. All of the positive and negative numbers together are referred to as *signed numbers*.

A positive number has a *plus* sign before it, while a negative number has a *minus* sign before it. Any number without a sign is assumed to be *positive*. *Zero* is represented at all times as 0 without any sign.

1.61 Addition of Signed Numbers

When adding two signed numbers whose signs are the same (i.e., both are positive or both are negative), simply *add* the numbers and place the common sign in front of the answer.

When adding two signed numbers whose signs are different (i.e., one sign is positive and one sign is negative), find the *difference* between the two numbers and place the *sign of the larger number* in front of the answer.

Examples:

(1) $\begin{array}{r} +\ 9 \\ +\ 5 \\ \hline +14 \end{array}$

(2) $\begin{array}{r} -12 \\ -27 \\ \hline -39 \end{array}$

(3) $\begin{array}{r} +16 \\ -\ 7 \\ \hline +\ 9 \end{array}$

(4) $\begin{array}{r} +15 \\ -40 \\ \hline -25 \end{array}$

You may be asked to add more than two signed numbers together. In these cases first add the positive numbers and the negative numbers separately; then add the respective sums.

Examples:

(1) *Add*
$\begin{array}{r} +24 \\ -12 \\ +13 \\ -10 \end{array}$

(a) $\begin{array}{r} +24 \\ +13 \\ \hline +37 \end{array}$ $\begin{array}{r} -12 \\ -10 \\ \hline -22 \end{array}$

(b) $\begin{array}{r} +37 \\ -22 \\ \hline +15 \end{array}$

(2) *Add*
$\begin{array}{r} -45 \\ +13 \\ -41 \\ +18 \\ -63 \end{array}$

(a) $\begin{array}{r} +13 \\ +18 \\ \hline +31 \end{array}$ $\begin{array}{r} -45 \\ -41 \\ -63 \\ \hline -149 \end{array}$

(b) $\begin{array}{r} -149 \\ +\ 31 \\ \hline -118 \end{array}$

Practice Exercises 1: Add

ANSWERS TO PRACTICE EXERCISES APPEAR AT END OF SECTION.

(1) $+8$
       $+4$

(2) $-\ 9$
       -14

(3) $+48$
       -63

(4) $+12$
       -10

(5) $+49$
        13

(6) -12
       -12

(7) -70
       $+85$

(8) -63
       $+49$

(9) $+1$
       $+2$
       -3
       -4

(10) $+12$
       -13
       $+14$
       -15
       -16

1.62 Subtraction of Signed Numbers

To subtract signed numbers change the sign of the *subtrahend* (bottom number) after circling the original sign, and follow the rules of addition.

Examples:

Subtract

(1) $+\ 12$
    $-\ \oplus\ 17$
       $-\ \ 5$

(2) $-\ 50$
    $+\ \ominus\ 27$
       $-\ 23$

(3) $+\ \ 40$
    $+\ \ominus\ \ 65$
       $+\ 105$

(4) $-\ \ 20$
    $-\ \oplus\ 13$
       $-\ \ 33$

Practice Exercises 2: Subtract

ANSWERS TO PRACTICE EXERCISES APPEAR AT END OF SECTION.

(1) $+30$
     -14

(6) $+17$
     0

(2) -16
     $+\ 9$

(7) -63
     $+19$

(3) -28
     -28

(8) $+72$
     -69

(4) $+34$
     $+44$

(9) -16
     -15

(5) 0
     -14

(10) $+58$
      $+31$

1.63 Multiplication and Division of Signed Numbers

If the two signed numbers to be multiplied or divided have the *same sign*, perform the indicated operation and place a *plus sign* in front of the answer.

If the two signed numbers to be multiplied or divided have *different signs*, perform the indicated operation and place a *minus sign* in front of the answer.

Examples:

Multiply

(1) $(+14)(+3) = +42$
(2) $(-15)(-5) = +75$
(3) $(+10)(-3) = -30$
(4) $(-18)(+4) = -72$

Examples:

Divide

(1) $+14 \div +2 = +7$
(2) $\dfrac{-20}{-\ 5} = +4$
(3) $+100 \div -4 = -25$
(4) $\dfrac{-50}{+\ 5} = -10$

Practice Exercises 3:

Perform the indicated operation on the signed numbers below.

(1) $(+3)(+7)$

(2) $(-8)(-5)$

(3) $(+5)(-6)$

(4) $(-10)(+7)$

(5) $(-9)(0)$

(6) $\dfrac{+35}{+\ 5}$

(7) $-9 \div -9$

(8) $\dfrac{40}{-\ 8}$

(9) $\dfrac{-65}{+13}$

(10) $\dfrac{0}{-6}$

1.64 Parentheses

Parentheses are used to group terms (numbers or symbols) into a larger unit. If you wish to show addition of the group of terms, you precede the parentheses with a plus sign.

Example:

$4 + 5 + 7 = 4 + (5 + 7)$

Preceding parentheses by a minus sign changes the sign of every term inside the parentheses when you remove the parentheses. You can think of the minus sign as being a minus 1 multiplied by the numbers in parentheses.

Example:

$4 - (-5 - 7) = 4 + 5 + 7$

Practice Exercises 4:

Remove the parentheses from each expression below.

(1) $3 + (1 - 4)$

(2) $5 - (3 + 7)$

(3) $3 - (-4 + 6)$

(4) $9 + (10 + 1)$

(5) $10 - (-3 - 6)$

(6) $2 - (1 - 16)$

Answers and Solutions

Practice Exercises 1:

(1) $+12$
(2) -23
(3) -15
(4) $+ 2$
(5) $+62$
(6) -24
(7) $+15$
(8) -14
(9) $- 4$
(10) -18

Practice Exercises 2:

(1) $+ 44$
(2) $- 25$
(3) 0
(4) $- 10$
(5) $+ 14$
(6) $+ 17$
(7) $- 82$
(8) $+141$
(9) $- 1$
(10) $+ 27$

Practice Exercises 3:

(1) $+21$
(2) $+40$
(3) -30
(4) -70
(5) 0
(6) $+ 7$
(7) $+ 1$
(8) $- 5$
(9) $- 5$
(10) 0

Practice Exercises 4:

(1) $3 + 1 - 4$
(2) $5 - 3 - 7$
(3) $3 + 4 - 6$
(4) $9 + 10 + 1$
(5) $10 + 3 + 6$
(6) $2 - 1 + 16$

2. ALGEBRA

Algebra is that branch of mathematics that deals with the relationship of known and unknown quantities. Letters are used in algebra problems to stand for unknown quantities or numbers.

2.1 Algebraic Equations

The relationship of numbers or symbols in an algebra problem is expressed in a statement called an *equation*.

An example of an equation would be $y - 5 = 11$. This equation says that when you subtract 5 from the unknown number y, you will have 11 left. Therefore, you know that $y = 16$ because $16 - 5 = 11$.

You should remember that an equation in algebra is like a balance scale.

When a number and a letter are written together without any operation sign between them $(+, -, \times, \div)$ multiplication is understood. For example, 5X means 5 times X.

If you add, subtract, multiply, or divide on one side of an equation, then you must do the same thing on the other side of the equation.

2.11 Solution of Equations

You solve an equation by finding a value for the unknown quantity or quantities represented by letters or symbols. To solve an equation, you change it around (restructure it) so that all the known parts are on one side and the unknown is on the opposite side. By applying opposite operations, we can isolate the unknown and obtain the answer.

Example 1: What can you do to eliminate the -6 from the left? Use signed numbers.

$$
\begin{array}{rl}
t - 6 = & 8 \\
+ 6 = & +6 \\
\hline
t \quad = & 14
\end{array}
$$

STEP 1: Add $+6$ to -6.

STEP 2: However, you cannot change one side without doing the same to the other side, so add $+6$ to the other side.

STEP 3: Solution is complete. The value of the equation is not changed because the same amount (6) was added to both sides of the $=$ sign.

Example 2: What can you do to eliminate the $+7$ from the left side of the equation?

$$r + 7 = 9$$
$$\underline{ - 7 = -7}$$
$$r = 2$$

STEP 1: Add -7 to $+7$ to eliminate that term on the left.

STEP 2: You must add the same quantity (-7) to the opposite side.

STEP 3: Solution is complete. Remember, you added -7 to both sides.

Notice, in the next two examples, that when the unknown is multiplied by a number, we divide to get the solution, and when the unknown is divided by a number, we multiply to get the answer.

Note: In algebra a raised dot is used to indicate multiplication.

Example 3:

STEP 1: $7t = 84$

STEP 2: $\dfrac{7t}{7} = \dfrac{84}{7}$

STEP 3: $t = 12$

Example 4:

STEP 1: $\dfrac{g}{-4} = 13$

STEP 2: $-4 \cdot \dfrac{g}{-4} = 13 \cdot (-4)$

STEP 3: $g = -52$

Sometimes it is necessary to use two steps of opposite operations in order to solve for the unknown in an equation. This may be done as follows:

Example 5:

STEP 1: Subtract 9 from each side of the equation.

$$2a + 9 = 15$$
$$\underline{ - 9 = -9}$$
$$2a = 6$$

STEP 2: Divide each side by 2.

$$\dfrac{\cancel{2}a}{\cancel{2}} = \dfrac{\overset{3}{\cancel{6}}}{\cancel{2}}$$

$$a = 3$$

Example 6:

STEP 1: Add +2 to each side.

$$14t - 2 = 5$$
$$\underline{+2 = +2}$$
$$14t = 7$$

STEP 2: Divide each side by 14.

$$\frac{14t}{14} = \frac{7}{14}$$

$$t = \frac{1}{2}$$

Practice Exercises 1:

ANSWERS TO PRACTICE EXERCISES APPEAR AT END OF SECTION.

Solve for the unknown in each of the following equations.

(1) $x + 7 = 15$

(2) $6y = 78$

(3) $2m - 5 = 37$

(4) $\frac{x}{3} + 7 = 10$

2.12 Literal Equations

Sometimes equations have only letters, and you will be asked to solve for a particular letter. The procedure is exactly the same as that outlined above.

Examples:

(1) Solve for x if $rx - c = t$.

Add c to both sides:

$$rx - c = t$$
$$\underline{+c = +c}$$
$$rx = t + c$$

Divide each side by r, solving for x:

$$\frac{rx}{r} = \frac{t + c}{r}$$

$$x = \frac{t + c}{r}$$

(2)   Solve for y if $\dfrac{a}{y} = \dfrac{b}{c}$

Note: To solve this problem you must first *cross-multiply* the numerators and denominators of the fractions. This means that you (1) multiply the denominator of the fraction on the left side of the equation by the numerator of the fraction on the right side of the equation, and (2) multiply the numerator of the fraction on the left by the denominator of the fraction on the right. Thus,

if $\dfrac{a}{y} = \dfrac{b}{c}$, then

$$yb = ac$$

Then, dividing both sides by b,

$$\frac{yb}{b} = \frac{ac}{b}$$

$$y = \frac{ac}{b}$$

Practice Exercises 2:

ANSWERS TO PRACTICE EXERCISES APPEAR AT END OF SECTION.

(1)   Solve for t if $st + m = q - r$.

(2)   Solve for z if $\dfrac{b}{z} = \dfrac{d}{e}$.

Answers and Solutions

Practice Exercises 1:

(1) $x = \mathbf{8}$

$$
\begin{array}{r}
x + 7 = 15 \\
-7 = -7 \\
\hline
x = \mathbf{8}
\end{array}
$$

(2) $y = \mathbf{13}$

$$\frac{6y}{6} = \frac{78}{6}$$

$$y = \mathbf{13}$$

(3) $m = \mathbf{21}$

$$
\begin{array}{r}
2m - 5 = 37 \\
+5 = +5 \\
\hline
\dfrac{2m}{2} = \dfrac{42}{2} \\
m = \mathbf{21}
\end{array}
$$

(4) $x = \mathbf{9}$

$$\frac{x}{3} + 7 = 10$$

$$
\begin{array}{r}
-7 = -7 \\
\hline
3 \cdot \dfrac{x}{3} = 3\,(3) \\
x = \mathbf{9}
\end{array}
$$

Practice Exercises 2:

(1) $\dfrac{q - r - m}{s}$

$$st + m = q - r$$
$$\underline{ - m = - m}$$
$$\dfrac{st}{s} = \dfrac{q - r - m}{s}$$

$$t = \dfrac{q - r - m}{s}$$

(2) $z = \dfrac{be}{d}$

$$\dfrac{b}{z} = \dfrac{d}{e}$$

$$\dfrac{zd}{d} = \dfrac{be}{d}$$

$$z = \dfrac{be}{d}$$

2.2 Evaluation of Algebraic Expressions and Formulas

Evaluation means "finding the value of." Problems in evaluation may concern obtaining the value of (1) algebraic expressions, or (2) expressions that set forth a general fact, rule, or principle that deals with such things as finding roots of equations, converting temperatures, finding areas and volumes, and calculating interest. The latter type of expressions are called *formulas*. In both of these types, in order to carry out the evaluation, simply substitute the numerical values given for the letters in the problem and then perform the indicated operations.

Examples:
(1) If $t = 7$ and $b = 4$, simplify $3t + 5bt$.

Note: "Simplify" will sometimes be used instead of "evaluate."

$$3t + 5bt = 3\,(7) + 5\,(4)\,(7)$$
$$= 21 + 140 = 161$$

(2) If $a = 5$ and $b = 3$, evaluate

$$\dfrac{1}{b} + \dfrac{3}{a - b} - \dfrac{2}{a + b}$$

$$= \dfrac{1}{3} + \dfrac{3}{2} - \dfrac{2}{8}$$

$$= 1\dfrac{5}{6} - \dfrac{1}{4} = 1\dfrac{7}{12}$$

Practice Exercises 1:

(1)   If $a = 4$ and $b = 2$, find the value of $6ab + 5b - a$.

(2)   If $x = 5$ and $c = 3$, simplify $\dfrac{6}{x + c} - \dfrac{2}{x - c} + \dfrac{8}{c}$.

Example:

If $F = \dfrac{9}{5}(C + 32)$, find F when $C = 45°$.

$F = \dfrac{9}{5}C + 32$

$F = \dfrac{9}{5}(45) + 32$

$F = 81 + 32$

$F = 113°$

Example:

If $S = \dfrac{1}{2}gt^2$, find S when $g = 32$ and $t = 4$.

$S = \dfrac{1}{2}gt^2$

$S = \dfrac{1}{2}(32)(4)^2$

$S = 16 \cdot 16$

$S = 256$

Practice Exercises 2:

(1)   If $C = \dfrac{5}{9}(F - 32)$, find C when $F = 77°$.

(2)   If $I = prt$, find I when $p = \$400$, $r = 5\%$, and $t = 3$ yrs.

Answers and Solutions

Practice Exercises 1:

(1)   **54**

$6ab + 5b - a$, when $a = 4$, $b = 2$
$= 6 \cdot 8 + (5 \cdot 2) - 4$
$= 48 + 10 - 4$
$= \mathbf{54}$

(2) $2\frac{5}{12}$

$$\frac{6}{x+c} - \frac{2}{x-c} + \frac{8}{c}, \text{ when } x = 5, c = 3$$

$$= \frac{6}{8} - \frac{2}{2} + \frac{8}{3} = \frac{18}{24} - \frac{24}{24} + \frac{64}{24} = \frac{58}{24} = 2\frac{10}{24} = \mathbf{2\frac{5}{12}}$$

Practice Exercises 2:

(1) **25°**

$$C = \frac{5}{9}(F - 32)$$

$$C = \frac{5}{9}(77 - 32)$$

$$C = \frac{5}{\cancel{9}}(\cancel{45}^{5})$$

$$C = \mathbf{25°}$$

(2) **$60**

$$I = prt$$

$$I = \$\cancel{400}^{4} \times \frac{5}{\cancel{100}_{1}} \times \frac{3}{1}$$

$$I = 4 \times 5 \times 3$$

$$I = \mathbf{\$60}$$

2.3 Solving for Two Unknowns

When you are given *two* equations with the same two unknowns, you can solve for both unknowns.

Example 1:

$3a + 4b = 24$
$2a + b = 11$
Solve for a and b.

STEP 1. To solve the equations, you must change one or both of the equations in such a way that you can eliminate one of the unknowns by adding or subtracting the equations. In this problem, you can multiply the bottom equation through by -4.

$3a + 4b = 24$
$-8a - 4b = -44$

STEP 2. Add the equations.

$3a + 4b = 24$
$-8a - 4b = -44$
$-5a = -20$

STEP 3. Solve for a.

$-5a = -20$
$5a = 20$
$a = 4$

STEP 4. Substitute the value of a in one of the equations to solve for b.

$3a + 4b = 24$
$3(4) + 4b = 24$
$12 + 4b = 24$
$4b = 12$
$b = 3$

You can eliminate *either* unknown in order to solve a problem of this kind. Here is the same problem, worked by eliminating a.

Example 2:

$3a + 4b = 24$
$2a + b = 11$

STEP 1. Eliminate a by multiplying the first equation by 2 and the second by -3.

$6a + 8b = 48$
$-6a - 3b = -33$

STEP 2.   Add the equations.

$$6a + 8b = 48$$
$$\underline{-6a - 3b = -33}$$
$$ 5b = 15$$

STEP 3.   Solve for b.

$$5b = 15$$
$$b = 3$$

STEP 4.   Substitute to find the value of a.

$$2a + b = 11$$
$$2a + 3 = 11$$
$$ 2a = 8$$
$$ a = 4$$

Practice Exercises

ANSWERS TO PRACTICE EXERCISES APPEAR AT END OF SECTION.

Solve for a and b or x and y in each problem.

(1) $6a - 2b = 32$
 $3a + 2b = 22$

(2) $3a + 3b = 24$
 $2a + b = 13$

(3) $4x + 2y = 16$
 $2x + 3y = 14$

(4) $6x + 2y = 24$
 $x + y = 5$

Answers and Solutions

Practice Exercises

(1) $a = $ **6**, $b = $ **2**

$$6a - 2b = 32$$
$$\underline{3a + 2b = 22}$$
$$9a = 54$$
$$a = \mathbf{6}$$

Substitute to find b:

$$6a - 2b = 32$$
$$6(6) - 2b = 32$$
$$36 - 2b = 32$$
$$ -2b = -4$$
$$ b = \mathbf{2}$$

(2) $a = 5, b = 3$

$$
\begin{array}{rcr}
3a + 3b & = & 24 \\
2a + b & = & 13 \\
3a + 3b & = & 24 \\
-6a - 3b & = & -39 \\
\hline
-3a & = & -15 \\
a & = & 5
\end{array}
$$

Substitute to find b:

$$
\begin{array}{rcl}
2a + b & = & 13 \\
2(5) + b & = & 13 \\
10 + b & = & 13 \\
+ b & = & 3
\end{array}
$$

(3) $x = 2\tfrac{1}{2}, y = 3$

$$
\begin{array}{rcr}
4x + 2y & = & 16 \\
2x + 3y & = & 14 \\
4x + 2y & = & 16 \\
-4x - 6y & = & -28 \\
\hline
-4y & = & -12 \\
y & = & 3
\end{array}
$$

Substitute to find x:

$$
\begin{array}{rcl}
4x + 2y & = & 16 \\
4x + 2(3) & = & 16 \\
4x + 6 & = & 16 \\
4x & = & 10 \\
x & = & 2\tfrac{1}{2}
\end{array}
$$

(4) $x = 3.5, y = 1.5$

$$
\begin{array}{rcr}
6x + 2y & = & 24 \\
x + y & = & 5 \\
6x + 2y & = & 24 \\
-2x - 2y & = & -10 \\
\hline
4x & = & 14 \\
x & = & 3.5
\end{array}
$$

Substitute to find y:

$$
\begin{array}{rcl}
x + y & = & 5 \\
3.5 + y & = & 5 \\
y & = & 1.5
\end{array}
$$

2.4 Verbal Problems

Verbal problems are word problems. To solve word problems using basic arithmetic, you must remember to read and interpret carefully all the information that is given in the problem. Here is a basic step-by-step guide that you can follow in preparing to solve all word problems.

STEP 1.   *What are you told?* List on the paper on which you are doing your work all numbers discussed in the problem and what they stand for. This allows you to refer to them at any time while solving the problem.

STEP 2.   *What are you asked?* Read the problem carefully to find out what you are being asked to do. Otherwise, you may do a lot of work correctly and still come up with the wrong answer.

STEP 3.   *Which information do you need?* All the information given may not be needed to solve the problem. Choose the necessary information and ignore the rest.

STEP 4.   *Are there any key words in the problem?* They tell you what method of solution is needed. Learn the key words that usually mean add, subtract, multiply, or divide.

STEP 5.   *How can you organize the information for solution?* For example, do you have to change all measurements in the problem to the same unit? (All in feet, hours, miles, etc.)

2.41 Key Words and Phrases

Many word problems use words or phrases that give clues as to how the problem should be solved. The most common words or phrases are:

Add

sum—as in, the sum of 3, 6, and 10
total—as in, the total of three payments
addition—as in, if a recipe calls for the addition of 3 lbs.
plus—as in, 3 lbs. plus 6 lbs.
increase—as in, his rent was increased by $10
more than—as in, this week the attendance was 5 more than last week
added to—as in, if you added $16 to the cost
successive—as in, the total of five successive payments

Subtract

difference—as in, what is the difference between, or the difference of
fewer—as in, there were 16 fewer apples left
remainder—as in, what quantity remains, or is left
less—as in, if there are now 3 apples less than there were an hour ago
reduced—as in, the rent was reduced by
decreased—as in, if he decreased his car's speed by

Multiply

total—as in, if you spend $8 a week on cigarettes, what is the total for a four-week period
of—as in, $\frac{1}{8}$ of the class
times—as in, 3 times as many boys came to football practice today
at—as in, the cost of 12 yds. of cloth at $.85 a yd. is

Divide

ratio—as in, what is the ratio of
divide—as in, if the class were divided into 4 sections

All of the word problems below will require you to make use of your knowledge of algebra. The steps above indicate how you can mentally *prepare* to solve the problem. The following simple set of instructions will enable you to actually *solve* word problems.

2.42 Guidelines for Solving Verbal Problems

1. Represent all unknown quantities algebraically (with letters) based on the information provided about them in the problem.

2. Write down an equation expressing the relationship between the unknowns in the problem. This step is equivalent to changing some statement(s) in the problem into mathematical language.

3. Solve the equation to determine the value of the unknowns.

2.43 Number Problems

Example 1: If one number is three times as large as another and the smaller number is increased by 19, the result is 6 less than twice the larger. Find the two numbers.

Let t = the smaller number
Let $3t$ = the larger number

$$
\begin{aligned}
\text{Then } t + 19 &= 2(3t) - 6 \\
t + 19 &= 6t - 6 \\
-t &= -t \\
\hline
19 &= 5t - 6 \\
+6 &= +6 \\
\hline
25 &= 5t \\
\frac{25}{5} &= \frac{5t}{5} \\
5 &= t
\end{aligned}
$$

Since $t = 5$, $3t = 15$, so the two numbers are 5 and 15.

Example 2: One number exceeds another number by 5. If the sum of the two numbers is 39, find the numbers.

Let m = the smaller number
Let $m + 5$ = the larger number

$$
\begin{aligned}
\text{Then } m + m + 5 &= 39 \\
2m + 5 &= 39 \\
-5 &= -5 \\
\hline
2m &= 34 \\
\frac{2m}{2} &= \frac{34}{2} \\
m &= 17
\end{aligned}
$$

So, $m + 5 = 22$, and the two numbers are 17 and 22.

2.44 Age Problems

Example 1:   Lisa is 16 years younger than Kathy. If the sum of their ages is 30 years, how old is Lisa?

Let X = Kathy's age
Let X − 16 = Lisa's age

$$
\begin{aligned}
\text{Then } X + X - 16 &= 30 \\
2X - 16 &= 30 \\
+ 16 &= +16 \\
\hline
2X &= 46 \\
\frac{2X}{2} &= \frac{46}{2} \\
X &= 23
\end{aligned}
$$

But Lisa is X − 16, so Lisa is 23 − 16 = 7 yrs. old.

Example 2:   Clyde is four times as old as Douglas. If the difference between their ages is 39 years, find out how old Clyde is.

Let b = Douglas' age
Let $4b$ = Clyde's age

$$
\begin{aligned}
\text{Then } 4b - b &= 39 \\
3b &= 39 \\
\frac{3b}{3} &= \frac{39}{3} \\
b &= 13
\end{aligned}
$$

But Clyde is $4b$, so Clyde's age = 4 (13) = 52 yrs. old.

2.45 Motion Problems

These problems on the examination usually require you to represent some quantity such as rate, distance, or time algebraically rather than actually solving an entire problem.

Example 1:   Madelaine left her home and walked a distance of d miles at the rate of 5 mph. She then turned around and walked back home at the rate of 3 mph. Represent in terms of d the total time Madelaine spent walking.

Since Rate × Time = Distance, or $r \times t = d$, if we divide both sides of the equation by Rate we get

$$\text{Time} = \frac{\text{Distance}}{\text{Rate}}, \text{ or } t = \frac{d}{r}.$$

Therefore, the time Madelaine spent walking away from her house is $\frac{d}{5}$, while the time she spent walking back is $\frac{d}{3}$.

Hence, the total time is $\frac{d}{5} + \frac{d}{3}$, or $\frac{8d}{15}$.

Example 2: If Carl rows a boat upstream at the rate of 6 mph and the stream flows at the rate of b mph, represent the net rate at which Carl moves upstream.

Carl moves upstream at 6 mph, but the stream pushes back against his efforts at b mph. Therefore, his net speed upstream must be $(6 - b)$ mph.

2.46 Perimeter Problems

Example 1: The length of a rectangle is 6 less than four times the width. If the perimeter of the rectangle is 28 inches, find its length and width.

Let w = the width
Let $4w - 6$ = the length

Then $w + w + 4w - 6 + 4w - 6 = 28$

$$10w - 12 = 28$$
$$\underline{+ 12 = +12}$$
$$10w = 40$$
$$\frac{10w}{10} = \frac{40}{10}$$
$$w = 4''$$

$4w - 6 = 4 (4) - 6 = 16 - 6 = 10''$

Example 2: Each of the equal sides of an isosceles triangle (a triangle with two equal sides) is 5 more than twice the third side. If the perimeter of the triangle is 45 inches, find the sides of the triangle.

Let m = the base of the triangle
Let $2m + 5$ = each of the two equal sides

Then $m + 2m + 5 + 2m + 5 = 45$

$$5m + 10 = 45$$
$$\underline{- 10 = -10}$$
$$5m = 35$$
$$\frac{5m}{5} = \frac{35}{5}$$
$$m = 7$$

$2m + 5 = 2 (7) + 5 = 19$

So the base is 7 and each equal side is 19.

2.47 Ratio and Proportion Problems

A *ratio* is one kind of comparison between two numbers. It may be written as a fraction, as in $\frac{4}{7}$, or with a colon, as in 4 : 7. A *proportion* is a statement that two ratios are equal. For instance, $\frac{5}{10} = \frac{1}{2}$, or 5 : 10 = 1 : 2, and 3 : 4 = 6 : 8, or $\frac{3}{4} = \frac{6}{8}$.

Example 1:   A blueprint for a new high school is drawn to a scale of $\frac{1}{27}'' = 1''$. If the height of one of the windows is to be 6 ft., by what length will the window be represented on the blueprint?

Note: Bear in mind that all numbers should be represented in the same units, that is, in either inches or feet but not both in the same problem.

Blueprint	*Actual Size*
$\frac{1}{27}''$	$1''$
x''	6 ft. $= 72''$

We must change the following English sentence into an equation expressing a proportion: If $\frac{1}{27}''$ represents $1''$ of actual size, then x'' represents $72''$ of actual size. This may be done as follows:

$$\frac{\frac{1}{27}}{1} = \frac{x}{72}$$

Then cross-multiply to get:

$$x = \frac{1}{27} \cdot \frac{72}{1}$$
$$x = \frac{72}{27} = 2\frac{18}{27} = 2\frac{2}{3}''$$

Example 2: The following proportion, $\dfrac{a}{b} = \dfrac{c}{d}$ is equivalent to which equation below?

(a) $\dfrac{d}{c} = \dfrac{a}{b}$

(b) $c = \dfrac{ba}{d}$

(c) $\dfrac{c}{d} = \dfrac{a}{b}$

(d) $cb = \dfrac{a}{d}$

If we cross-multiply the given proportion, we get $ad = bc$. We then look at the choices given to see which one will give the same products when cross-multiplied. Inspecting the four possibilities, we see that the only one that will do this is choice (c), which is the answer.

Practice Exercises 1:

ANSWERS TO PRACTICE EXERCISES APPEAR AT END OF SECTION.

(1) Michael is three years older than twice Carol's age. If their ages added together total 42 years, how old is Michael?

(2) The difference between two numbers is 16 less than twice their sum. If the larger number is one more than twice the smaller, find the numbers.

(3) If on a map $\dfrac{1}{5}'' = 1''$, then a distance of 6 ft. would be represented by what distance on the map?

(4) If an airplane travels for 17 hours and goes a distance of $(e + 8)$ miles, represent its rate in terms of e.

(5) The perimeter of a rectangle is 54 inches. If the width is 3 inches less than half the length, find the dimensions of the rectangle.

(6) If Sharlene is three times as old as Maurice and their ages total 50 years, find out how old Sharlene is.

(7) Which of the following is an alternative way of writing the proportion $\dfrac{m}{t} = \dfrac{f}{s}$?

    (a) $mf = ts$

    (b) $\dfrac{s}{t} = \dfrac{f}{m}$

    (c) $\dfrac{st}{m}$

    (d) $\dfrac{m}{t} = \dfrac{s}{f}$

(8)   A boat in still water travels at K mph, but a 9 mph wind pushes it in the opposite direction. With what net rate does it move forward?

2.48 Interest Problems

Example 1:   What yearly interest would be earned on $500 at a rate of 5% interest?

Change 5% to a fraction by placing the 5 over 100, and multiply by the amount invested.

$$\frac{5}{\cancel{100}_{1}} \times \frac{\cancel{500}^{5}}{1} = \$25$$

Example 2:   How much money would be needed in a savings account to earn $100 per month at 6% interest per year?

$100 per month would be $1200 per year. Let M be the amount of money needed.

$$.06M = \$1200$$
$$M = \frac{\$1200}{.06} = \$20,000$$

2.49 Mixture Problems

A mixture problem gives a percentage or fractional composition of a substance in terms of its ingredients and asks questions about the composition of the substance. There are two basic relationships to remember about mixtures:

1. The percentage of a certain ingredient in a mixture times the amount of the mixture equals the amount of the ingredient.

2. When two mixtures are added together, the amount of one ingredient in the final mixture equals the sum of the amounts of that ingredient in the parts.

Example: A chemist has 2 quarts of 25% acid solution and 1 quart of 40% acid solution. If he mixes these, what will be the concentration of acid in the final mixture?

To understand this kind of problem, it is helpful to organize the information on a table. Enter the information you know, and systematically fill in the missing information.

	rate $\times$ $\dfrac{\text{qt. (acid)}}{\text{qt. (sol.)}}$	amount of solution qts. (sol.)	= amount of acid qts. (acid)
25% solution	0.25	2	0.50
40% solution	0.40	1	0.40
mixture	x	3	$3x$

Applying basic relationship number 2 above,

$3x = 0.50 + 0.40$
$3x = 0.90$
$x = 0.30$, a 30% concentration of acid in the final mixture

2.410 Work Problems

Work problems are based on the following relationship:

$$\text{rate} \times \text{time} = \text{work}$$

Example: Jack can chop down 20 trees in 1 hour. Ted can chop down 18 trees in $1\frac{1}{2}$ hours. If the two men work together, how long will it take them to chop down 48 trees?

As in the mixture problem, it is helpful to organize your work in a table. Let x be the length of time required for the two men together to chop down 48 trees. The x is entered under *time* for both Jack and Ted on lines 3 and 4 since each man works the same amount of time.

		rate	$\times$ time	$=$ work
		trees/hr.	hours	trees
1.	Jack	20	1	20
2.	Ted	12	$1\frac{1}{2}$	18
3.	Jack	20	x	$20x$
4.	Ted	12	x	$12x$

$$20x + 12x = 48$$
$$32x = 48$$
$$x = 1\frac{1}{2} \text{ hours}$$

Practice Exercises 2:

ANSWERS TO PRACTICE EXERCISES APPEAR AT END OF SECTION.

(1) Jack invested $1500 at $4\frac{1}{2}\%$ a year. How much interest will he earn in two years?

(2) If a chemist mixes 2 pints of 40% acid solution with 1 pint of pure acid, what will be the acid concentration of the final solution?

(3) Mary can complete 50 order forms in an hour. Jean can complete 60 in $1\frac{1}{2}$ hours. How long will it take them together to complete 180 forms?

Answers and Solutions

Practice Exercises 1:

(1) **29 yrs. old**

Let x = Carol's age
Let $2x + 3$ = Michael's age

$$x + 2x + 3 = 42$$
$$3x + 3 = 42$$
$$\underline{- 3 = -3}$$
$$3x = 39$$
$$\frac{3x}{3} = \frac{39}{3}$$
$$x = 13$$

So $2x + 3 = 2(13) + 3 = 26 + 3 =$ **29**

(2) **7 and 3**

Let q = the smaller number
Let $2q + 1$ = the larger number

$$(2q + 1) - q = 2(q + 2q + 1) - 16$$
$$q + 1 = 2(3q + 1) - 16$$
$$q + 1 = 6q + 2 - 16$$
$$q + 1 = 6q - 14$$
$$\underline{-q = -q}$$
$$1 = 5q - 14$$
$$\underline{+ 14 = + 14}$$
$$15 = 5q$$

$$\frac{\overset{3}{\cancel{15}}}{\cancel{5}} = \frac{\cancel{5}q}{\cancel{5}}$$
$$q = \mathbf{3}$$
$$2q + 1 = \mathbf{7}$$

(3) $\mathbf{14\frac{2}{5}''}$

6 ft. = 72 in.

$$\frac{\frac{1}{5}}{\frac{1}{1}} = \frac{x}{72}$$

$$x = \frac{1}{5} \cdot \frac{72}{1}$$
$$x = \frac{72}{5} = \mathbf{14\frac{2}{5}''}$$

(4) $\dfrac{e + 8}{17}$

$$\text{Rate} = \frac{\text{Distance}}{\text{Time}} = \frac{e + 8}{17}$$

(5) **Length = 20″, width = 7″**

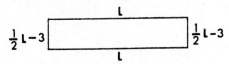

$$L + L + \tfrac{1}{2}L - 3 + \tfrac{1}{2}L - 3 = 54$$

$$3L - 6 = 54$$
$$\underline{+ 6 = + 6}$$
$$3L = 60$$

$$\frac{\cancel{3}L}{\cancel{3}} = \frac{\overset{20}{\cancel{60}}}{\cancel{3}}$$

$$L = 20″$$

$$\tfrac{1}{2}L - 3 = \tfrac{1}{2}(20) - 3 = 10 - 3 =$$

$$7″ = \textbf{width}$$

(6) $37\tfrac{1}{2}$ **yrs. old**

Let m = Maurice's age
Let $3m$ = Sharlene's age

$$3m + m = 50$$
$$4m = 50$$
$$\frac{\cancel{4}m}{\cancel{4}} = \frac{50}{4}$$
$$m = 12\tfrac{1}{2}$$

$$\text{So } 3m = 3\left(12\tfrac{1}{2}\right) = 37\tfrac{1}{2}$$

(7) **(b)**

If we cross-multiply in (b) $\dfrac{s}{t} \diagdown\!\!\!\!\diagup \dfrac{f}{m}$, we get $sm = tf$, which is the same set of products that results from cross-multiplying the given proportion $\dfrac{m}{t} = \dfrac{f}{s}$.

(8) **(K − 9) mph**

Practice Exercises 2:

(1) **$135**

Let I equal the interest.

$I = 4\frac{1}{2}\% \times \$1500 \times 2$ years

$I = .045 \times \$1500 \times 2$

$I = .045 \times \$3000$

$I = \$135$

(2) **60%**

Set up a table:

	rate $\times$	amount of solution $=$	amount of acid
	$\dfrac{\text{pt. (acid)}}{\text{pt. (sol.)}}$	pts. (sol.)	pts. (acid)
40% solution	0.40	2	0.80
100% solution	1.00	1	1.00
mixture	x	3	$3x$

$3x = 1.80$

$x = .60$, a **60%** concentration

(3) **2 hours**

Let x = the time it will take the two women together, and set up a table:

	rate $\times$	time $=$	work
	forms /hr.	hours	forms
1. Mary	50	1	50
2. Jean	40	$1\frac{1}{2}$	60
3. Mary	50	x	$50x$
4. Jean	40	x	$40x$

$50x + 40x = 180$

$90x = 180$

$x = $ **2 hours**

2.5 Monomials and Polynomials

2.51 Monomials

Monomials are algebraic expressions consisting of only one term. Examples of monomials are $8t$, $-3b$, $4xy^2$, and $.7r^3$.

Adding and Subtracting Monomials

To add or subtract monomials, simply follow the rules of signed numbers in order to determine which number to place in front of the particular monomial in the problem.

Examples:

Add

(1)
$$\begin{array}{r} -9m^2t \\ +5m^2t \\ \hline -4m^2t \end{array}$$

(2)
$$\begin{array}{r} +\ 5rmx \\ -\ 9rmx \\ +14rmx \\ \hline 10rmx \end{array}$$

Examples:

Subtract

(1)
$$\begin{array}{r} -\ 7x^2y \\ +\ominus 5x^2y \\ \hline -\ 2x^2y \end{array}$$

(2)
$$\begin{array}{r} +\ 18ab^3c^2 \\ +\ominus 12ab^3c^2 \\ \hline 30ab^3c^2 \end{array}$$

Multiplying Monomials

To multiply monomials of the same base (letter or letters), find the exponent of the product by *adding* the exponents of the monomials involved. An exponent tells how many times a number is multiplied by itself. Thus, $2^3 = 2 \times 2 \times 2$. The ^{3} is the exponent. If the monomials are preceded by factors, multiply the factors as in arithmetic.

Examples:

(1) $e^4 \cdot e^5 = e^{4+5} = e^9$

(2) $5^2 \cdot 5^3 = 5^5 = 5 \times 5 \times 5 \times 5 \times 5 = 3,125$

(3) $m^6 \cdot m^8 \cdot m^{12} = m^{26}$

(4) $(-7a^3b)(+5a^2b^2) = -35a^5b^3$

Note that in example (4) the product of -7 and $+5$ is -35, the product of a^3 and a^2 is a^5, and the product of b and b^2 is b^3 since any monomial having no exponent indicated is assumed to have an exponent of one.

When monomials are being *raised to a power*, the answer is obtained by multiplying the exponents of each part of the monomial by the power to which it is being raised.

Examples:

(1) $(A^7)^3 = A^{21}$

(2) $(X^3Y^2)^4 = X^{12}Y^8$

Dividing Monomials

To divide monomials of the same base, divide any factor as in arithmetic, and then find the exponent of the quotient by taking the difference of the exponents of the monomials involved.

Examples:

(1) $\dfrac{m^{10}}{m^3} = m^7$

(2) $\dfrac{7^4}{7^3} = 7^1 = 7$

(3) $\dfrac{-20t^9b^8}{+4t^7b^5} = -5t^2b^3$

Note that in (3) the quotient of -20 and $+4$ is -5, the quotient of t^9 and t^7 is t^2, and the quotient of b^8 and b^5 is b^3.

Practice Exercises: Monomials

ANSWERS TO PRACTICE EXERCISES APPEAR AT END OF SECTION.

(1) *Add* $-8m^2bt$
                  $-4m^2bt$
                  $+5m^2bt$

(2) *Subtract* $-17abcd$
                  $-17abcd$

(3) *Multiply* $(b^2cd^4)^5$

(4) *Multiply* $(-8b^2c^4)(+2b^2c)$

(5) *Divide* $\dfrac{-30ab^3d^4}{-15b^2d}$

2.52 Polynomials

A *polynomial* is an algebraic expression consisting of two or more terms, that is, two or more monomials. Examples of polynomials are $7b + 8$, $X^2 + Y^2 + Z^2$, and $9c^2 + 4c - 3$.

Adding and Subtracting Polynomials

To add or subtract polynomials, arrange as monomials in columns. Then simply add or subtract the columns of monomials.

Examples:

Add

(1) $5X - 7Y$
     $9X + 4Y$
     ─────────
     $14X - 3Y$

(2) $a^2 + 5b + 7$
     $2a^2 - 6b - 3$
     $-5a^2 + 4b + 6$
     ──────────────
     $-2a^2 + 3b + 10$

Subtract

(1) $3cd \quad\quad\; - 6mt$
     $+\ominus 2cd -\; \oplus 9mt$
     ──────────────────
     $5cd \quad\quad - 15mt$

(2) $8s^2 \quad\quad - 5st \quad\quad + 4t^3$
     $+\ominus 5s^2 + \ominus 3st - \oplus 2t^3$
     ──────────────────────────
     $13s^2 \quad\quad - 2st \quad\quad + 2t^3$

Multiplying Polynomials

To multiply polynomials, place the smaller polynomial beneath the larger polynomial. Then multiply each term in the larger polynomial by each term in the smaller polynomial. Arrange the results of these successive multiplications in columns containing the same type of monomials. Add up each column for the final answer.

Examples:

Multiply

(1) $(3m + 6)$ by $(2m - 4)$

$$
\begin{array}{l}
3m\ + 6 \\
\underline{2m\ - 4} \qquad\qquad \text{(multiplying)} \\
6m^2 + 12m \\
\qquad\ \ \underline{-\ 12m - 24} \qquad \text{(adding)} \\
6m^2 \qquad\quad - 24
\end{array}
$$

(2) $(a^2 + 2ab - 3)\,(a + 4b)$

$$
\begin{array}{l}
a^2 + 2ab - 3 \\
\underline{a\ + 4b} \\
a^3 + 2a^2b - 3a \\
\underline{\quad + 4a^2b \qquad\quad + 8ab^2 - 12b} \\
a^3 + 6a^2b - 3a + 8ab^2 - 12b
\end{array}
$$

Dividing Polynomials

To divide a *polynomial by a monomial*, simply divide each term in the polynomial by the monomial.

To divide a *polynomial by a polynomial*, the procedure to be used is comparable to long division of whole numbers.

Example 1:

Divide

$(16a^7 - 12a^5) \div 4a^2$

$$
\frac{\overset{4}{\cancel{16a^7}} - \overset{3}{\cancel{12a^5}}}{\cancel{4a^2}} = 4a^5 - 3a^3
$$

Example 2:

Divide

$(X^2 + 18X + 45)$ by $(X + 3)$

(Note similarity to long division.)

$$24\,\overline{)\,1512} \qquad\qquad X + 3\,\overline{)\,X^2 + 18X + 45}$$

$$\begin{array}{r} 6 \\ 24\,\overline{)\,1512} \end{array} \qquad\qquad \begin{array}{r} X \\ X + 3\,\overline{)\,X^2 + 18X + 45} \end{array}$$

$$\begin{array}{r} 6 \\ 24\,\overline{)\,1512} \\ 144 \\ \hline 72 \end{array} \qquad\qquad \begin{array}{r} X \\ X + 3\,\overline{)\,X^2 + 18X + 45} \\ \underline{X^2 + 3X} \\ + 15X + 45 \end{array}$$

$$\begin{array}{r} 63 \\ 24\,\overline{)\,1512} \\ 144 \\ \hline 72 \end{array} \qquad\qquad \begin{array}{r} X\ + 15 \\ X + 3\,\overline{)\,X^2 + 18X + 45} \\ \underline{X^2 + 3X} \\ 15X + 45 \end{array}$$

$$\begin{array}{r} 63 \\ 24\,\overline{)\,1512} \\ 144 \\ \hline 72 \\ 72 \end{array} \qquad\qquad \begin{array}{r} X\ + 15 \\ X + 3\,\overline{)\,X^2 + 18X + 45} \\ \underline{X^2 + 3X} \\ 15X + 45 \\ 15X + 45 \end{array}$$

Practice Exercises: Polynomials

ANSWERS TO PRACTICE EXERCISES APPEAR AT END OF SECTION.

(1) *Add*
$$\begin{array}{r} 5x^2y^2 - 4ab \\ -6x^2y^2 + 3ab \\ \underline{+2x^2y^2 -\ ab} \end{array}$$

(2) *Subtract*
$$\begin{array}{r} 5X^2 - 3XY - 2Y^2 \\ \underline{-3X^2 - 3XY + 2Y^2} \end{array}$$

(3) *Multiply* $(a^2 + m)\,(a - 2)$

(4) Find the product of $(X^2 + 3X - 9)$ and $(X - 2)$.

(5) Find the quotient of $(20X^3b^2 - 10X^2b^3) \div 10X^2b^2$.

(6) *Divide* $(X^2 + 22X + 85)$ by $(X + 17)$

Answers and Solutions

Practice Exercises: Monomials

(1) $-7m^2bt$

(2)   **0**

(3) $b^{10}c^5d^{20}$

(4) $-16b^4c^5$

(5) $2abd^3$

Practice Exercises: Polynomials

(1) $x^2y^2 - 2ab$

(2) $8X^2 - 4Y^2$

$$
\begin{array}{ccc}
5X^2 & -\ 3XY & -\ 2Y^2 \\
+\ominus 3X^2\ + & \ominus 3XY\ - & \oplus 2Y^2 \\
\hline
8X^2 & & -\ 4Y^2
\end{array}
$$

(3) $a^3 + am - 2a^2 - 2m$

$a^2 + m$
$\underline{a\ -\ 2}$
$a^3 + am$
$\underline{\qquad\qquad -\ 2a^2 - 2m}$
$a^3 + am - 2a^2 - 2m$

(4) $X^3 +\ X^2 - 15X + 18$

$X^2 + 3X\ -\ 9$
$\underline{X\ -\ 2}$
$X^3 + 3X^2 -\ 9X$
$\underline{\qquad -\ 2X^2 -\ 6X + 18}$
$X^3 +\ X^2 - 15X + 18$

(5) $-2X + b$

(6) $X + 5$

$$
\begin{array}{r}
X\ +\ 5 \\
X + 17\ )\ \overline{X^2 +\quad 22X + 85} \\
\underline{X^2 -\ \oplus 17X\quad} \\
5X + 85 \\
\underline{5X + 85}
\end{array}
$$

2.6 Factoring

To *factor* an algebraic expression means to find the two or more quantities whose product will give the original quantity. There are three basic types of expressions you ought to be able to factor. These, and the methods for factoring each, are outlined below.

Type I: The Difference Between Two Squares

1. Determine the square roots of the letter term and the perfect numerical square.
2. Place these square roots within the brackets of the factors, one with a *plus* sign and one with a *minus* sign.

Examples:

Factor

(1) $m^2 - 64$
$= (m + 8)(m - 8)$

(2) $A^4 - 144$
$= (A^2 + 12)(A^2 - 12)$

Type II: Expressions Containing Common Unknown Factor

1. The unknown in the expression is one factor.
2. Find the remaining factor by dividing the expression by the first factor.

Examples:

Factor

(1) $b^2 - 13b$
$= b(b - 13)$

(2) $X^4 - 25X^2$
$= X^2(X^2 - 25)$
$= X^2(X + 5)(X - 5)$

Note: Since $(X^2 - 25)$ can be factored further, the result is *three* rather than the usual *two* factors.

3. In expressions of more than two terms, any coefficient held in common by all terms can be factored.

Example:

Factor

$4b^3 + 2b^2 - 3b$
$= b(4b^2 + 2b - 3)$

Type III: Quadratic Expressions Containing Three Terms

Quadratic expressions are expressions containing an unknown whose highest degree is 2. Such expressions as $4X^2 + 3$, $X^2 - 7$, and $2X^2 + 3X - 5$ are all examples of quadratic expressions. It is particularly important to be able to factor these expressions since this is a necessary step in solving quadratic equations.

Procedure

1. If the sign of the last number of the expression is *positive:*

    (a) Find two numbers whose *product* is the last number of the expression and whose *sum* is the coefficient (number) in the middle term.

    (b) Give *both* factors the sign of the *middle* term of the expression.

2. If the sign of the last number of the expression is *negative:*

    (a) Find two numbers whose *product* is the last number of the expression and whose *difference* is the coefficient (number) in the middle term.

    (b) Give the larger of these two numerical factors the sign of the middle term. Give the remaining numerical factor the opposite sign.

Examples:

Factor

(1) $X^2 + 8X + 15$
     $(X + 3)(X + 5)$

Notice that $3 \times 5 = 15$ and $3 + 5 = 8$, the coefficient of the middle term. Also note that the signs of both factors are $+$, the sign of the middle term.

(2) $X^2 - 5X - 14$
     $(X - 7)(X + 2)$

Notice that $7 \times 2 = 14$, and $7 - 2 = 5$, the coefficient of the middle term. Also note that the sign of the larger factor, 7, is $-$, while the other factor, 2, has a $+$ sign.

(3) $X^2 + 2X - 24$
     $(X - 4)(X + 6)$

(4) $X^2 - 17X + 72$
     $(X - 8)(X - 9)$

Practice Exercises:

Factor the following quadratic expressions:
(1) $a^2 + 26a$
(2) $X^2 - 121$
(3) $C^4 - 49$
(4) $t^2 - 35t$
(5) $X^2 - X - 30$
(6) $r^2 + 14r + 45$
(7) $t^2 + 5t - 24$
(8) $m^2 - 16m + 48$

Answers and Solutions

Practice Exercises:

(1) **a(a + 26)**
(2) **(X + 11) (X − 11)**
(3) **(C² + 7) (C² − 7)**
(4) **t(t − 35)**
(5) **(X + 5) (X − 6)**
(6) **(r + 9) (r + 5)**
(7) **(t + 8) (t − 3)**
(8) **(m − 4) (m − 12)**

2.7 Solving Quadratic Equations

Quadratic equations are equations in which the highest degree of the unknown is 2. Examples of such equations are:

(a) $x^2 + 4x - 5 = 0$
(b) $m^2 - 3m = 0$
(c) $t^2 - 81 = 0$
(d) $Y^2 - 3Y = 28$

In all the examples above, with the exception of (d), the equation is set equal to zero. When this is the case, the equation is considered to be in *standard form*. If the equation is not set equal to zero, we rearrange the terms by the method of opposite operations so that the equation will equal zero.

Below you will see how this can be done for example (d) by subtracting 28 from both sides of the equation.

$$Y^2 - 3Y = 28$$
$$\underline{ -28 = -28}$$
$$Y^2 - 3Y - 28 = 0$$

Now equation (d) is in standard form. Notice that when an equation is in standard form, the square term is written first (Y^2), the first degree term is written second ($-3Y$), and the number is written last (-28).

The equations you solved in the chapter on algebraic equations were first degree, or *linear*, equations and had one, and only one, solution. Quadratic equations are second degree equations, and therefore they each have *two* solutions.

Procedure for Solving Quadratic Equations

1. Factor the equation.

2. Set each factor equal to zero.

3. Solve each of the resulting first degree equations by the method outlined in "Solving Equations."

4. Check your solution by substituting your answers in the original equation.

Examples:
Solve the following quadratic equations:

(1) $M^2 - 256 = 0$

(Factor into two linear equations. The only way for the whole expression to equal zero is for *at least* one of the factors to be zero. So set *both* equal to zero to obtain both possible answers [roots].)

$$(M + 16) = 0 \qquad\qquad (M - 16) = 0$$
$$M + 16 = 0 \qquad\qquad M - 16 = 0$$
$$\underline{ -16 = -16} \qquad\qquad \underline{ +16 = +16}$$
$$M = -16 \qquad\qquad M = +16$$
$$M = +16, -16$$

Check:

$$M^2 - 256 = 0 \qquad\qquad M^2 - 256 = 0$$
$$(-16)^2 - 256 = 0 \qquad\qquad (+16)^2 - 256 = 0$$
$$256 - 256 = 0 \qquad\qquad 256 - 256 = 0$$
$$0 = 0 \qquad\qquad\qquad\qquad 0 = 0$$

(2) $q^2 - 8q = 0$
$\quad q(q - 8) = 0$
$\qquad\qquad q = 0,$ and
$\quad (q - 8) = 0$
$\qquad\quad +8 = +8$
$\overline{\qquad q \qquad\quad = \quad 8}$
$\quad q = 0, 8$

Check:

$$q^2 - 8q = 0 \qquad\qquad q^2 - 8q = 0$$
$$(0)^2 - 8(0) = 0 \qquad\qquad (8)^2 - 8(8) = 0$$
$$\text{and}$$
$$0 - 0 = 0 \qquad\qquad 64 - 64 = 0$$
$$0 = 0 \qquad\qquad\qquad 0 = 0$$

(3) $d^2 - 13d + 36 = 0$
$\quad (d - 9)(d - 4) = 0$
$\quad d - 9 = 0 \qquad\qquad d - 4 = 0$
$\quad\underline{+9 = +9} \quad \text{and} \quad \underline{+4 = +4}$
$\quad d \qquad = +9 \qquad\qquad d \qquad = +4$
$\quad d = 9, 4$

Check:

$$d^2 - 13d + 36 = 0$$
$$(9)^2 - 13(9) + 36 = 0$$
$$81 - 117 + 36 = 0$$
$$117 - 117 = 0$$
$$0 = 0$$
$$d^2 - 13d + 36 = 0$$
$$(4)^2 - 13(4) + 36 = 0$$
$$16 - 52 + 36 = 0$$
$$52 - 52 = 0$$
$$0 = 0$$

(4) $X^2 + 5X = 84$

First put the equation in standard form:

$X^2 + 5X - 84 = 0$

$(X + 12)(X - 7) = 0$

$X + 12 =$	0		$X - 7 =$	0
$- 12 =$	-12		$+ 7 =$	$+7$
X $=$	-12		X $=$	7

$X = -12, 7$

Check:

$$X^2 + 5X = 84$$
$$(7)^2 + 5(7) = 84$$
$$49 + 35 = 84$$
$$84 = 84$$
$$X^2 + 5X = 84$$
$$(-12)^2 + 5(-12) = 84$$
$$144 - 60 = 84$$
$$84 = 84$$

Practice Exercises:

ANSWERS TO PRACTICE EXERCISES APPEAR AT END OF SECTION.

(1) $t^2 - 289 = 0$

(2) $M^2 + 47M = 0$

(3) $Y^2 - 18Y + 45 = 0$

(4) $X^2 + 13X = -40$

Answers and Solutions

Practice Exercises:

(1)   **t = +17, −17**

$t^2 - 289 = 0$

$(t + 17) = \quad 0$	$(t - 17) = \quad 0$
$t + 17 = \quad 0$	$t - 17 = \quad 0$
$\underline{\quad - 17 = -17}$	$\underline{\quad + 17 = +17}$
$t \qquad = -17$	$\mathbf{t} \qquad = \quad \mathbf{17}$

(2)   **M = 0, −47**

$M^2 + 47M \ = 0$	$M + 47 = \quad 0$
$\underline{M(M + 47) = 0}$	$\underline{\quad - 47 = -47}$
$\mathbf{M} \qquad\quad = \mathbf{0}$	$\mathbf{M} \qquad = -\mathbf{47}$

(3)   **Y = 3, 15**

$Y^2 - 18Y + 45 = 0$

$Y - 15 = \quad 0$	$Y - 3 = \quad 0$
$\underline{\quad + 15 = +15}$	$\underline{\quad + 3 = +3}$
$\mathbf{Y} \qquad = \quad \mathbf{15}$	$\mathbf{Y} \qquad = \quad \mathbf{3}$

(4)   **X = −5, −8**

$X^2 + 13X = -40$

$X^2 + 13X + 40 = 0$

$(X + 8)(X + 5) = 0$

$X + 8 = \quad 0$	$X + 5 = \quad 0$
$\underline{\quad - 8 = -8}$	$\underline{\quad - 5 = -5}$
$\mathbf{X} \qquad = -\mathbf{8}$	$\mathbf{X} \qquad = -\mathbf{5}$

2.8 Inequalities

Just as we can perform the following operations with *equalities*:

$a + b = c$	$3 + 4 = 7$
$\underline{+ \qquad d = d}$	$\underline{+ \qquad 2 = 2}$
$a + b + d = c + d$	$3 + 4 + 2 = 9$

we can do the same with *inequalities*:

("$>$" means greater than, "$<$" means less than)

$b > c$	$4 > 3$	$4 > \quad 3$
$\underline{+ \quad d > e}$	$\underline{7 > 6}$	$\underline{-6 > -7}$
$b + d > c + e$	$11 > 9$	$-2 > -4$

Also just as "equals multiplied by equals are equal":

$$a = b \qquad\qquad 5 = 5$$
Thus $ca = cb \qquad\quad 6(5) = 6(5);$

the following is true:

$$5 > 4 \qquad\qquad a > b$$

Therefore $6(5) > 6(4) \qquad ca > cb$ (if $c > 0$)
$\qquad$ or $30 > 24$

Note if $5 > 4$, $(-6)(5) < (-6)(4)$ or $-30 < -24$. Thus when we multiply by a negative number, we *reverse* the inequality sign.

$$-5 < -4$$
Thus $-(-5) > -(-4)$
$\qquad$ or $5 > 4$
$\qquad\qquad$ So if $-2 < x < +2$
$\qquad\qquad\qquad$ Then $+2 > -x > -2$

Practice Exercises:

ANSWERS TO PRACTICE EXERCISES APPEAR AT END OF SECTION.

(1)   If $1 > y > 0$, prove that $y > y^2$

(2)   If $-3 < y < +3$, prove that $-y > -3$

(3)   If $4m + 3 > 4n + y$, prove that $m - n > \dfrac{y - 3}{4}$

(4)   If $a + b > 0$, prove that
$$\frac{2ab}{a + b} \leqq \frac{a + b}{2}$$
where "$\leqq$" means "less than or equal to."

Answers and Solutions
Practice Exercises:

(1) $1 > y$
$\quad$ $y = y$
$\quad$ Now multiply both sides:
$\quad$ $1 \times y \geqq y \times y = y^2$ (Noting y is *not* negative)
$\quad$ Thus: $y > y^2$

(2)   Multiply the inequality $-3 < y < +3$ by (-1). Thus we get:
$(-1)(-3) > (-1)(y) > (-1)(+3)$
or $+3 > -y > -3$
Thus: $-y > -3$

(3)   Given: $4m + 3 > 4n + y$:
Subtract $4n$ from both sides:
We get: $4m - 4n + 3 > y$
Subtract 3 from both sides:
$4m - 4n > y - 3$
Divide by 4:
$$m - n > \frac{y - 3}{4}$$

(4)   We want to show
$$\frac{2ab}{a + b} \leqq \frac{a + b}{2}$$
Multiply the above by $a + b$ (Noting $a + b > 0$).
We get: $2ab \leqq \dfrac{(a + b)(a + b)}{2}$
Multiply by 2 and we get:
$4ab \leqq (a + b)(a + b)$
Now $(a + b)(a + b) = a^2 + 2ab + b^2$
So we have: $4ab \leqq a^2 + 2ab + b^2$
Subtract $4ab$ from both sides and we get:
$0 \leqq a^2 + 2ab - 4ab + b^2$
Or: $0 \leqq a^2 - 2ab + b^2$
Now $a^2 - 2ab + b^2 = (a - b)^2$
So we have: $0 \leqq (a - b)^2$
This is because $(a - b)^2$ is always greater than 0 (positive) or
equal to 0 (if $a = b$).
Thus our original inequality
$$\frac{2ab}{a + b} \leqq \frac{a + b}{2}$$
must be true, since we can always work backwards (given $(a - b)^2$
$\geqq 0$ and proving $\dfrac{2ab}{a + b} \leqq \dfrac{a + b}{2}$).

3. GEOMETRY

Geometry is the study of solid and plane shapes and figures. *Solid figures* have length, width, and thickness. They occupy space in three dimensions. *Plane figures* have only length and width. For example, a square is a plane figure and a cereal box is a solid figure.

This section on geometry will be divided into three sub-sections:

(1) Angles
(2) Triangles
(3) Plane and solid figures

3.1 Angles

An *angle* is formed by two straight lines that have the same end-point, called the *vertex*. The side that is horizontal is called the *initial side*. The side that rotates to form the size of the angle is called the *terminal side*. Thus, an angle may be represented as follows:

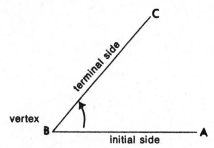

When the terminal side rotates once completely about the vertex, it has passed through 360 degrees. Thus, the sizes of all angles range from 0° to 360°.

3.11 Types of Angles

1. *Acute angle*—any angle measuring more than 0° and less than 90°

2. *Obtuse angle*—any angle measuring more than 90° and less than 180°.

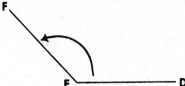

3. *Straight angle*—any angle measuring exactly 180°.

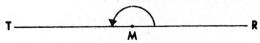

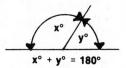

$x° + y° = 180°$

4. *Right angle*—any angle measuring exactly 90°.

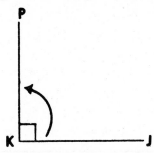

Practice Exercises 1: Types of Angles

ANSWERS TO PRACTICE EXERCISES APPEAR AT END OF SECTION.

(1) What kind of angle is formed between the hands of a clock when it is
 (a) 6 o'clock?
 (b) 2 o'clock?
 (c) 3 o'clock?
 (d) 8 o'clock?

3.12 Pairs of Angles

1. *Vertical Angles*—The opposite pair of angles formed by two intersecting lines are called *vertical angles*. Vertical angles are equal.

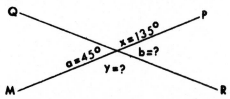

In the diagram above, lines QR and MP intersect, forming two pairs of angles, x and y, and a and b. If $a = 45°$, then $b = 45°$, and if $x = 135°$, then $y = 135°$ since vertical angles are equal to each other.

2. *Complementary angles*—Two angles that add up to 90° are *complementary* angles. If angle $x = 60°$ and angle $y = 30°$, then x and y are complementary angles since $60° + 30° = 90°$.

3. *Supplementary angles*—Two angles that add up to 180° are *supplementary* angles. If angle $s = 73°$ and angle $t = 107°$, then s and t are supplementary angles since $73° + 107° = 180°$.

Examples:

(1)   If lines AB and CD intersect at E and if angle AEC measures 53°, then how many degrees are there in angle BED?

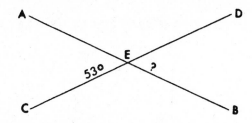

      Angle BED contains 53° since AEC and BED are vertical angles.

(2)   Find the complement of the following angles:
    (a) 17°   (b) $t°$

    (a) $90 - 17 = \mathbf{73}°$
    (b) $\mathbf{(90 - t)}°$

(3)   Find the supplement of the following angles:
    (a) 124°   (b) $(x + 9)°$

    (a) $180 - 124 = \mathbf{56}°$
    (b) $180 - (x + 9)$
           $= 180 - x - 9$
           $= \mathbf{(171 - x)}°$

Practice Exercises 2: Pairs of Angles

ANSWERS TO PRACTICE EXERCISES APPEAR AT END OF SECTION.

(1)   In the diagram below, angle XTM and angle _____ are *vertical* with respect to each other.

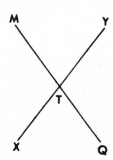

(2) Find the complement of
  (a) $74\frac{1}{2}°$
  (b) $(q - 5)°$

(3) Find the supplement of
  (a) $180°$
  (b) $(m - 30)°$

3.13 Parallel Lines and Their Angles

Two or more lines are said to be *parallel* if they never meet no matter how far they are extended. A line drawn cutting across parallel lines is called a *transversal*. In the diagram below, lines AB and CD are parallel and are cut by transversal T.

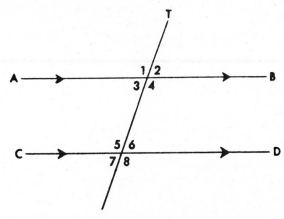

You can see that a transversal cutting through two parallel lines causes eight angles to be formed. These angles are related to each other in several ways, as follows:

1. *Corresponding Angles* (matching angles)
  $\angle 2 = \angle 6$
  $\angle 4 = \angle 8$
  $\angle 1 = \angle 5$
  $\angle 3 = \angle 7$

2. *Alternate Interior Angles*
  $\angle 3 = \angle 6$
  $\angle 4 = \angle 5$

3. *Consecutive Interior Angles*
  $\angle 4 + \angle 6 = 180°$
  $\angle 3 + \angle 5 = 180°$

You will notice that corresponding and alternate interior angles are *equal*, while consecutive interior angles are *supplementary*.

A *radian* is an angle formed when its vertex is at the center of a circle and the length of the arc of the intercepted angle is equal to the radius of the circle.

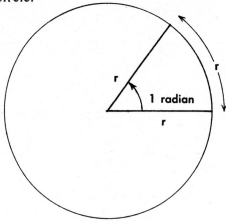

Practice Exercises 3:

(1)   In the figure, name all the pairs of the following types of angles.

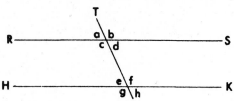

(a)   Vertical angles
(b)   Consecutive interior angles
(c)   Corresponding angles
(d)   Alternate interior angles

3.14 Angles in Circles

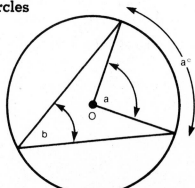

If O is the center of the circle above, then the *central* angle a is measured by its arc. That is, if $a° = 50°$, its arc is $50°$. The *inscribed* angle b is measured by $\frac{1}{2}$ its arc. Thus $b° = \frac{1}{2}a°$. If $b° = 25°$, then its arc will be $50°$. Note that if the inscribed angle is $90°$, the arc is $180°$.

Answers and Solutions

Practice Exercises 1: Types of Angles

(1) (a) **Straight angle**
     (b) **Acute angle**
     (c) **Right angle**
     (d) **Obtuse angle**

Practice Exercises 2: Pairs of Angles

(1) **Angle QTY**

(2) (a) $\mathbf{15\frac{1}{2}}^{\circ}$

     $90 - 74\frac{1}{2} = \mathbf{15\frac{1}{2}}^{\circ}$

     (b) $\mathbf{(95 - q)}^{\circ}$

     $90^{\circ} - (q - 5)^{\circ}$
     $= 90^{\circ} - q + 5$
     $= \mathbf{(95 - q)}^{\circ}$

(3) (a) $\mathbf{0}^{\circ}$

     $180 - 180 = \mathbf{0}^{\circ}$

     (b) $\mathbf{(210 - M)}^{\circ}$

     $180 - (M - 30)$
     $= 180 - M + 30$
     $= \mathbf{(210 - M)}^{\circ}$

Practice Exercises 3:

(1) (a) **Vertical Angles**
          $\angle a = \angle d$
          $\angle b = \angle c$
          $\angle e = \angle h$
          $\angle f = \angle g$
     (b) **Consecutive Interior Angles**
          $\angle d + \angle f = 180^{\circ}$
          $\angle c + \angle e = 180^{\circ}$
     (c) **Corresponding Angles**
          $\angle b = \angle f$
          $\angle d = \angle h$
          $\angle a = \angle e$
          $\angle c = \angle g$
     (d) **Alternate Interior Angles**
          $\angle d = \angle e$
          $\angle c = \angle f$

3.2 Triangles

A triangle is a flat, closed, three-sided figure. The sum of the angles of any triangle is 180°.

3.21 Types of Triangles

1. A *scalene* triangle is a triangle whose *three* sides are of different lengths.

2. An *isosceles* triangle is a triangle that has *two* equal sides, and thus two equal base angles.

3. An *equilateral* triangle is a triangle that has *three* equal sides, and thus three equal angles.

4. A *right* triangle is a triangle that has a right angle (90°).

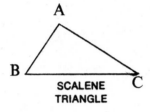

If AC > AB,
Then ∠B > ∠C

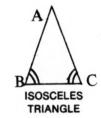

If AB = AC
∠B = ∠C
or if ∠B = ∠C
AB = AC

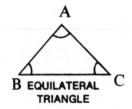

If AB = BC = AC
Then ∠A = ∠B = ∠C = 60°
If ∠A = ∠B = ∠C
Then AB = BC = AC

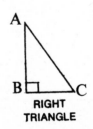

If ∠B = 90°,
$(AB)^2 + (BC)^2 = (AC)^2$
and ∠A + ∠C = 90°

Example 1:

Two angles of a triangle measure 45° and 85°. How many degrees are there in the third angle?

The angles of a triangle add up to 180°. The sum of 45° and 85° is 130°. Therefore, the remaining angle must be 180° — 130° = 50°.

Example 2:

Find what z is in terms of x and y in the following diagram:

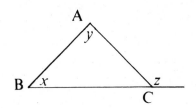

Call $\angle BCA = p$

Then $p + z = 180°$

But $x + y + p = 180°$

Subtract equations:

$p + z - x - y - p = 180° - 180° = 0$

$z - x - y = 0; z = x + y$

What we have just proven is a good thing to memorize, that for the triangle above, $z = x + y$.

Example 3:

In triangle ABC below, angle C is three times angle A, and angle B is five times angle A. Find the number of degrees in each angle of the triangle.

Let y = the number of degrees in angle A. Then $3y$ = the number of degrees in angle C.

Then $5y$ = the number of degrees in angle B.

Since the sum of the angles of the triangle is $180°$, we can say:

$$y + 3y + 5y = 180$$
$$\frac{9y}{9} = \frac{180}{9}$$
$$y = 20° \ (\angle A)$$
$$3y = 60° \ (\angle C)$$
$$5y = 100° \ (\angle B)$$

Notice that $20 + 60 + 100 = 180°$.

Practice Exercises 1: Angles of a Triangle

ANSWERS TO PRACTICE EXERCISES APPEAR AT END OF SECTION.

(1) If two angles of a triangle are $23\frac{1}{2}°$ and $143\frac{1}{2}°$, find the third angle.

(2) One angle of a triangle is $44°$. The second angle is $4°$ larger than the third angle. Determine the number of degrees in the second and third angles.

3.22 The Pythagorean Theorem

In any right angle triangle (triangle containing a $90°$ angle) the side opposite the $90°$ angle is called the *hypotenuse*. The other two sides are called the *legs* of the triangle.

The Greek mathematician Pythagoras discovered that a particular relation exists among the three sides of *all* right triangles. This relation is known as the Pythagorean theorem.

Statement of the Pythagorean Theorem:

In any right triangle the square of the hypotenuse is equal to the sum of the squares of the legs.

Formula of the Pythagorean Theorem

$$a^2 + b^2 = c^2$$

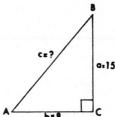

Thus, if we are told the lengths of the two legs of a right triangle, it is possible to find the length of the hypotenuse.

Also, if the lengths of the hypotenuse and one leg are given, it is possible to find the length of the second leg.

Example 1:

Find the hypotenuse of a right triangle whose legs are 8″ and 15″ respectively.

$a^2 + b^2 = c^2$
$15^2 + 8^2 = c^2$
$225 + 64 = c^2$
$289 = c^2$
$\sqrt{289} = c$
Therefore, $c = 17''$

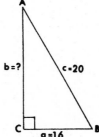

Example 2:

Find the third side of a right triangle that has a hypotenuse of 20″ and one leg 16″ long.

$a^2 + b^2 = c^2$
$16^2 + b^2 = 20^2$
$256 + b^2 = 400$
$-256 \qquad = -256$
_____
$b^2 = 144$
$b = \sqrt{144}$
$b = 12''$

Practice Exercises 2: Pythagorean Theorem

ANSWERS TO PRACTICE EXERCISES APPEAR AT END OF SECTION.

(1) Find the diagonal of a rectangle whose width is 5″ and whose length is 12″.

(2) A ladder 25 feet long rests against the wall of a building at a point 24 feet above the ground. How far from the wall is the bottom of the ladder?

Answers and Solutions

Practice Exercises 1: Angles of a Triangle

(1) **13°**

$$180 - \left(143\tfrac{1}{2} + 23\tfrac{1}{2}\right)$$
$$= 180 - 167$$
$$= \mathbf{13°}$$

(2) **66°, 70°**

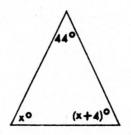

Let x = the third angle
Let $x + 4$ = the second angle
Then $x + x + 4 + 44 = 180$

$$2x + 48 = 180$$
$$\underline{-48 = -48}$$
$$\frac{\cancel{2}x}{\cancel{2}} = \frac{132}{2}$$
$$x = \mathbf{66°}$$
and $x + 4 = \mathbf{70°}$

Practice Exercises 2: Pythagorean Theorem

(1) **13″**

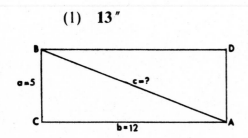

$$a^2 + b^2 = c^2$$
$$25 + 144 = c^2$$
$$169 = c^2$$
$$\sqrt{169} = c$$
$$\mathbf{13''} = c$$

(2) **7 feet**

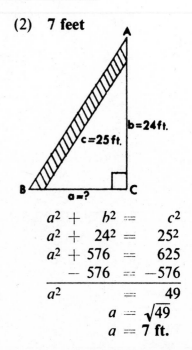

$$a^2 + b^2 = c^2$$
$$a^2 + 24^2 = 25^2$$
$$a^2 + 576 = 625$$
$$\underline{-576 = -576}$$
$$a^2 = 49$$
$$a = \sqrt{49}$$
$$a = \mathbf{7\ ft.}$$

3.3 Plane and Solid Figures

Plane figures have only two dimensions: length and width. They have no thickness. They are not three-dimensional. The most common plane figures and their characteristics are:

Triangle—a three-sided figure. The sum of the interior angles (angles inside the triangle) = 180°.

Right Triangle—a triangle that has one interior right angle and two acute angles.

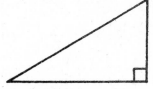

Quadrilateral—any four-sided figure.

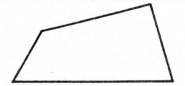

Rectangle—a four-sided figure. The opposite sides are parallel and equal in length. Each interior angle = 90°. The sum of the interior angles = 360°.

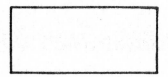

Square—a four-sided figure. The opposite sides are parallel and all sides are equal in length. Each interior angle = 90°. The sum of the interior angles = 360°.

Parallelogram—a four-sided figure. The opposite sides are parallel and equal in length. There are no interior right angles. Opposite angles are equal in size. The sum of the interior angles = 360°.

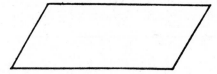

Trapezoid—a four-sided figure. The bases only are parallel. No sides necessarily are equal in length. The sum of the interior angles = 360°.

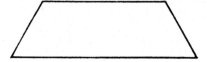

Circle—a figure formed by a single curved line. Every point is of equal distance from the center point of the figure. The total number of degrees of arc is 360°.

3.31 Perimeter and Area

You now have some idea of what the most elementary plane figures look like. Most often you will be asked to find either the *perimeter* or the *area* of one of these figures. The *perimeter* means the sum of the distances around the outside (edge) of any plane figure. The *area* is the number of square units of space contained within a plane figure.

Below is a table of formulas for the perimeters and areas of the most common plane figures. The letters used in these formulas and what they represent are: l = length, w = width, s = side, b = base, h = height, r = radius, and d = diameter. The symbol π (pi) is a Greek letter and is a *mathematical constant*, that is, its value never changes. It is always equal to the fraction $\frac{22}{7}$ $\left(\text{or } 3\frac{1}{7}\right)$ or, in decimal form, 3.14 +. Its value is obtained from the ratio of the circumference (perimeter) of a circle to its diameter. This means that the circumference of *any* circle is about $3\frac{1}{7}$ times its diameter.

AREAS OF PLANE FIGURES

Figure	Perimeter	Area
Square	$P = 4s$	$A = s^2$
Rectangle	$P = 2l + 2w$	$A = lw$
Triangle	$P = s_1 + s_2 + s_3$	$A = \frac{1}{2} bh$
Parallelogram	$P = 2l + 2w$	$A = bh$
Circle	$C = 2\pi r$	$A = \pi r^2$
Trapezoid	$P = b_1 + b_2 + s_1 + s_2$	$A = \frac{1}{2} h(b_1 + b_2)$

Examples:

Find the *perimeters* of the figures below:

(*Note:* Parentheses and the multiplication sign are used interchangeably, as they are on the examination.)

(1) **Square**

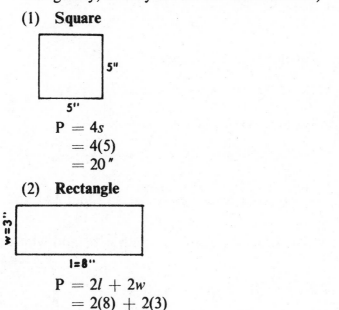

$$P = 4s$$
$$= 4(5)$$
$$= 20''$$

(2) **Rectangle**

$$P = 2l + 2w$$
$$= 2(8) + 2(3)$$
$$= 16 + 6$$
$$= 22''$$

(3) **Circle**

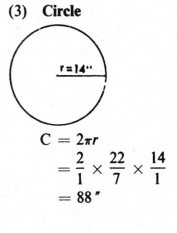

$$C = 2\pi r$$
$$= \frac{2}{1} \times \frac{22}{7} \times \frac{14}{1}$$
$$= 88''$$

Find the *areas* of the figures below:

(4) **Triangle**

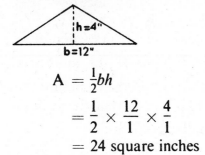

$$A = \tfrac{1}{2}bh$$
$$= \frac{1}{2} \times \frac{12}{1} \times \frac{4}{1}$$
$$= 24 \text{ square inches}$$

(6) **Parallelogram**

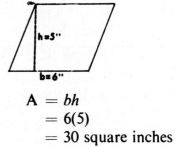

$$A = bh$$
$$= 6(5)$$
$$= 30 \text{ square inches}$$

(5) **Trapezoid**

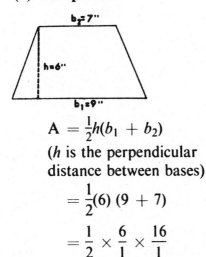

$$A = \tfrac{1}{2}h(b_1 + b_2)$$
(*h* is the perpendicular
distance between bases)
$$= \frac{1}{2}(6)\,(9 + 7)$$
$$= \frac{1}{2} \times \frac{6}{1} \times \frac{16}{1}$$
$$= 48 \text{ square inches}$$

Practice Exercises 1: Perimeters and Areas

ANSWERS TO PRACTICE EXERCISES APPEAR AT END OF SECTION.

(1) Find the area of a square whose side is $6\tfrac{1}{2}''$.

(2) Find the perimeter of a triangle whose sides are $2\tfrac{1}{2}''$, $3\tfrac{3}{4}''$, and $5\tfrac{1}{6}''$ long.

(3) Find the area of a trapezoid whose bases are $11''$ and $14''$ and whose height is $5''$.

(4) Find the perimeter of a rectangle whose length is $8''$ and whose width is $2\tfrac{1}{2}''$.

(5) Find the area of a circle whose radius is $10''$.

Congruence and Similarity

Two plane geometric figures are said to be *congruent* if they are identical in size and shape. They are said to be *similar* if they have the same shape but are not identical in size.

Examples:

All squares are similar.

These triangles are congruent.

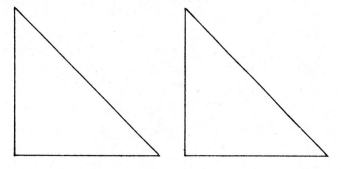

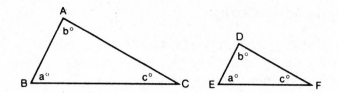

The two triangles above are *similar*. This is because the two triangles have at least *two* angles in common. Because they are similar

$$\frac{AB}{DE} = \frac{AC}{DF} = \frac{BC}{EF}$$

That is, their sides are proportional.

Example:

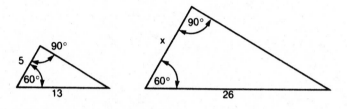

Find *x*, above.

Solution: The triangles are similar.

Thus: $\dfrac{5}{x} = \dfrac{13}{26}$

$13x = (26)(5)$

$x = \dfrac{(26)\ (5)}{13}$

$x = (2)(5)$

$x = 10$

3.32 Volumes of Solid Figures

Three of the most common solid geometric figures are the cube, the rectangular solid, and the cylinder. Each of these figures may be thought of as the three-dimensional extensions of flat two-dimensional figures, namely, the square, rectangle, and circle.

The table below indicates the formulas to be used to find the volumes of these figures. The volume of a solid is the amount of cubic units of space the figure contains.

Formulas for Volumes of Solid Figures

Figure	*Volume*
Cube	$V = s^3 = s \times s \times s$
Rectangular Solid	$V = lwh$
Cylinder	$V = \pi r^2 h$

Examples:

Find the volumes of the solid figures below whose dimensions are indicated.

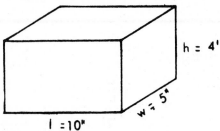

(1) **Rectangular Solid**

$V = lwh = 10(5)\,(4) = 200$ cubic inches

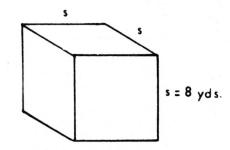

(2) **Cube**

$V = s^3 = 8 \times 8 \times 8 = 512$ cubic yards

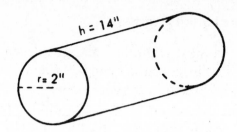

(3)   Cylinder

$$V = \pi r^2 h = \frac{22}{\cancel{7}} \times \frac{2}{1} \times \frac{2}{1} \times \frac{\cancel{14}^2}{1} = 22(8) = 176 \text{ cubic inches}$$

Practice Exercises 2: Volumes of Solid Figures

ANSWERS TO PRACTICE EXERCISES APPEAR AT END OF SECTION.

(1)   What is the volume of a cube whose side is $5\frac{1}{2}$"?

(2)   If a rectangular solid has a length of 4 inches, a width of 3 inches, and a height of 2 feet, find its volume.

(3)   Given that a cylinder's height is 42" and its radius is 3". Determine its volume.

Answers and Solutions

Practice Exercises 1: Perimeters and Areas

(1)   **$42\frac{1}{4}$ square inches**

$$A = s^2$$
$$= \left(6\frac{1}{2}\right)\left(6\frac{1}{2}\right)$$
$$= \frac{13}{2} \times \frac{13}{2} = \frac{169}{4}$$
$$= 42\frac{1}{4} \text{ sq. in.}$$

(2)   **$11\frac{5}{12}$"**

$$P = s_1 + s_2 + s_3$$
$$= 2\frac{1}{2} + 3\frac{3}{4} + 5\frac{1}{6}$$
$$= 11\frac{5}{12}\text{"}$$

(3) **$62\frac{1}{2}$ square inches**

$$A = \frac{1}{2}h(b_1 + b_2)$$

$$= \frac{1}{2}(5)\,(14 + 11)$$

$$= \frac{1}{2} \times \frac{5}{1} \times \frac{25}{1}$$

$$= \frac{125}{2} = 62\frac{1}{2} \text{ sq. in.}$$

(4) **21″**

$$P = 2l + 2w$$

$$= 2(8) + 2\left(2\frac{1}{2}\right)$$

$$= 16 + 5$$

$$= \mathbf{21″}$$

(5) **314 square inches**

$$A = \pi r^2$$

$$= 3.14 \times 10 \times 10$$

$$= 3.14 \times 100$$

$$= \mathbf{314 \text{ sq. in.}}$$

Note: Here 3.14 is more convenient than $\frac{22}{7}$ as a value of pi.

Practice Exercises 2: Volumes of Solid Figures

(1) **$166\frac{3}{8}$ cubic inches**

$$V = s^3$$

$$= 5\frac{1}{2} \times 5\frac{1}{2} \times 5\frac{1}{2}$$

$$= \frac{11}{2} \times \frac{11}{2} \times \frac{11}{2}$$

$$= \frac{1331}{8}$$

$$= 166\frac{3}{8} \text{ cubic inches}$$

(2) **288 cubic inches**

$$V = l \times w \times h$$
$$= 4 \times 3 \times 24$$
$$= \textbf{288 cu. in.}$$

Notice that 2 feet had to be converted to 24 inches so that all dimensions would be expressed in the same units.

(3) **1188 cubic inches**

$$V = \pi r^2 h$$

$$= \frac{22}{\cancel{7}} \times \frac{3}{1} \times \frac{3}{1} \times \frac{\cancel{42}^{\,6}}{1}$$
$$= \textbf{1188 cu. in.}$$

4. ADDITIONAL TOPICS AND REVIEW AIDS

4.1 Coordinate Geometry

Coordinate geometry allows us to see relationships between algebra and geometry and to solve some types of problems by graphs.

A graph (see the figure below) is a two-way (horizontal and vertical) chart. Usually the horizontal dimension is called the x-axis, and the vertical dimension is called the y-axis. The location of any point on the graph can be given by its x and y values. For example, point 0 at the center is at location (0, 0). In the parentheses the x coordinate comes first and the y coordinate second.

Three other points, P_1, P_2, and P_3, are plotted on the graph. Their coordinates are shown in parentheses. P_1P_2 represents a straight line segment. If you draw in the dotted lines, P_1P_3 and P_2P_3, you have a right triangle. You can solve for the length of P_1P_2 by using the Pythagorean Theorem.

FIGURES FOR COORDINATE GEOMETRY

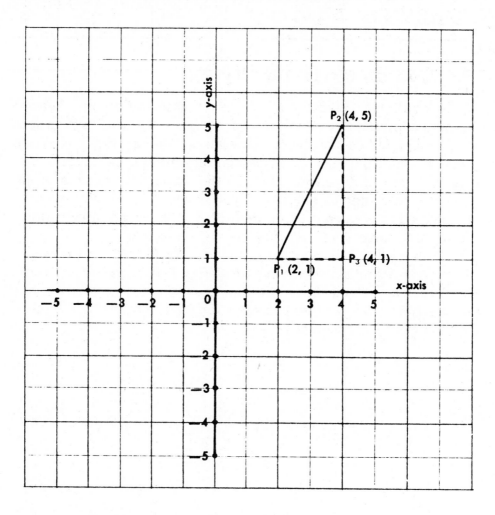

$$P_1P_2 = \sqrt{(P_1P_3)^2 + (P_2P_3)^2}$$
$$= \sqrt{2^2 + 4^2} = \sqrt{20}$$

Lengths P_1P_3 and P_2P_3 are found by taking the differences in their x coordinates and y coordinates, respectively.

In addition to straight lines whose equations are *first degree* (*x* and *y* having exponents of 1 understood), there are *second degree* equations. In a second degree equation at least one term in *x* or *y* has an exponent of 2. The simplest equations for several types of second degree equations and their corresponding shapes on a graph are shown here.

Second Degree Equations and Figures

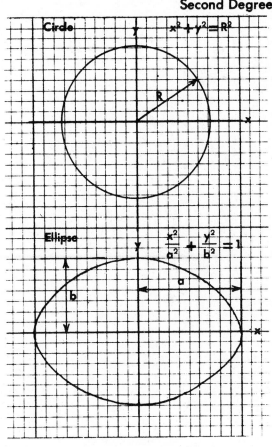

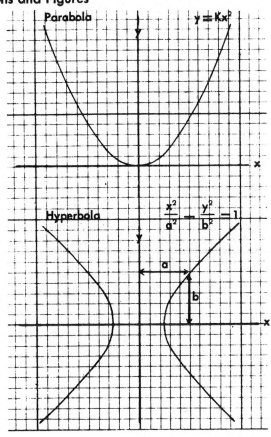

4.2 Trigonometry

There are six trigonometric functions that are ratios of pairs of sides in a right triangle.

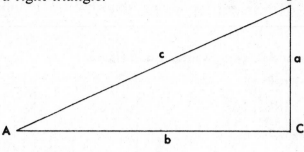

sine of A (abbreviated sin A) $= \dfrac{a}{c}$

cosine of A (abbreviated cos A) $= \dfrac{b}{c}$

tangent of A (abbreviated tan A) $= \dfrac{a}{b}$

cotangent of A (abbreviated cot A) $= \dfrac{b}{a}$

secant of A (abbreviated sec A) $= \dfrac{c}{b}$

cosecant of A (abbreviated csc A) $= \dfrac{c}{a}$

In general, for any angle the following relationships hold:

Function	Relation (ratio)
sin	opposite side over hypotenuse
cos	adjacent side over hypotenuse
tan	opposite side over adjacent side
cot	adjacent side over opposite side
sec	hypotenuse over adjacent side
csc	hypotenuse over opposite side

When an angle exceeds 90°, you can still find the values of trigonometric functions, but you must consider which of four quadrants the hypotenuse is in. The quadrants are numbered consecutively by Roman numerals in a counterclockwise direction in the figure below.

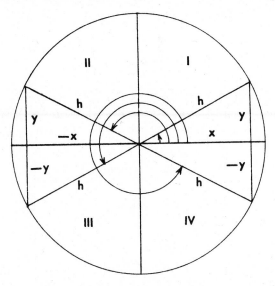

Four congruent triangles are shown, one in each quadrant. The numerical value for each trigonometric function is the same in all four quadrants. However, the algebraic signs are negative in some instances. The following table summarizes the signs for all functions in all quadrants.

ALGEBRAIC SIGNS OF FUNCTIONS

Quadrant	Sin	Cos	Tan
I	+	+	+
II	+	−	−
III	−	−	+
IV	−	+	−

There are several relationships among functions of the same angle.

$$\sin x = \frac{1}{\csc x}$$

$$\cos x = \frac{1}{\sec x}$$

$$\sec x = \frac{1}{\cos x}$$

$$\csc x = \frac{1}{\sin x}$$

$$\tan x = \frac{\sin x}{\cos x} = \frac{1}{\cot x}$$

$$\cot x = \frac{\cos x}{\sin x} = \frac{1}{\tan x}$$

$$\sin^2 x + \cos^2 x = 1$$

$$1 + \tan^2 x = \frac{1}{\cos^2 x}$$

$$1 + \cot^2 x = \frac{1}{\sin^2 x}$$

$$\sin(-x) = -\sin x$$

$$\cos(-x) = \cos x$$

$$\tan(-x) = -\tan x$$

$$\sin(90 - x) = \cos x$$

$$\cos(90 - x) = \sin x$$

$$\tan(90 - x) = \cot x$$

There are three common cases of right triangles for which the sine, cosine, and tangent functions should be memorized. In a right triangle with two angles each equal to 45° the functions are:

$$\sin 45° = \frac{1}{\sqrt{2}}$$

$$\cos 45° = \frac{1}{\sqrt{2}}$$

$$\tan 45° = 1$$

where AC = BC = 1

$$AB = \sqrt{1^2 + 1^2} = \sqrt{2}$$

In a right triangle with two angles equal to 30° and 60° the short side is half as long as the hypotenuse.

$$(AC)^2 + (BC)^2 = (AB)^2$$

$$(AC)^2 = (AB)^2 - (BC)^2$$

$$AC = \sqrt{(AB)^2 - (BC)^2}$$

$$AC = \sqrt{2^2 - 1^2}$$

$$AC = \sqrt{3}$$

The functions to remember are:

$$\sin 30° = \frac{1}{2}$$

$$\cos 60° = \frac{1}{2}$$

4.3 Binary System

The *binary system* is a place-value system. Unlike the decimal system, which is based on *ten*, the binary system is based on *two*. Only two symbols are used, *zero* and *one*. In this system each place is worth one-half of the value of the place to its left. Following are some examples of numbers in the binary system and their equivalents in the decimal system.

Eights	Fours	Twos	Units	Decimal Equivalent
1	1	0	0	12
	1	1	0	6
		1	1	3

4.4 Logarithms

The *logarithm* of a given number is a power or exponent to which a *base* must be raised to yield the given number. The most common base is 10. The word logarithm is abbreviated *log*.

$$\log 10 = \log 10^1 = 1$$
$$\log 100 = \log 10^2 = 2$$
$$\log 1000 = \log 10^3 = 3$$
$$\log 0.1 = \log 10^{-1} = -1$$
$$\log 0.01 = \log 10^{-2} = -2$$
$$\log 0.001 = \log 10^{-3} = -3$$

4.5 Weights and Measures

Dry Measure

2 cups = 1 pint (pt.)
2 pints = 1 quart (qt.)
8 quarts = 1 peck (pk.)
4 pecks = 1 bushel (bu.)

Liquid Measure

2 cups = 1 pint
16 fluid ounces (oz.) = 1 pint
2 pints = 1 quart
4 quarts = 1 gallon

Weight

16 ounces = 1 pound (lb.)
2000 pounds = 1 ton (T.)

Distance

12 inches (in.) = 1 foot (ft.)
3 feet = 1 yard (yd.)
1,760 yards = 1 mile (mi.)
5,280 feet = 1 mile

Area

144 square inches = 1 square foot (sq. ft.)
9 square feet = 1 square yard (sq. yd.)
43,560 square feet = 1 acre
640 acres = 1 square mile (sq. mi.)

Volume

1,728 cubic inches = 1 cubic foot (cu. ft.)
27 cubic feet = 1 cubic yard (cu. yd.)

Counting Units

12 units = 1 dozen (doz.)
12 dozens = 1 gross
144 units = 1 gross

4.6 Table of Equivalents

Fraction	Decimal	Percentage
$\frac{1}{2}$	.50	50%
$\frac{1}{3}$	.333	$33\frac{1}{3}\%$
$\frac{1}{4}$	.25	25%
$\frac{1}{5}$	.20	20%
$\frac{1}{6}$	.167	$16\frac{2}{3}\%$
$\frac{1}{8}$	.125	$12\frac{1}{2}\%$
$\frac{3}{4}$	.75	75%
$\frac{2}{3}$	.667	$66\frac{2}{3}\%$
$\frac{3}{8}$	.375	$37\frac{1}{2}\%$

4.7 The Metric System

Linear Measure

10 millimeters	= 1 centimeter	=	0.3937	inch
10 centimeters	= 1 decimeter	=	3.937	inches
10 decimeters	= 1 meter	=	39.37	inches or 3.28 feet
10 meters	= 1 decameter	=	393.7	inches
10 decameters	= 1 hectometer	=	328 feet 1 inch	
10 hectometers	= 1 kilometer	=	0.621	mile
10 kilometers	= 1 myriameter	=	6.21	miles

Volume Measure

1,000 cubic millimeters	= 1 cubic centimeter	=	.06102	cubic inch
1,000 cubic centimeters	= 1 cubic decimeter	=	61.02	cubic inches
1,000 cubic decimeters	= 1 cubic meter	=	35.314	cubic feet

Capacity Measure

10 milliliters	= 1 centiliter	=	.0338	fluid ounce
10 centiliters	= 1 deciliter	=	.338	fluid ounce
10 deciliters	= 1 liter	=	1.0567	liquid quarts or
			0.9081	dry quart
10 liters	= 1 decaliter	=	2.64	gallons or 0.284 bushel
10 decaliters	= 1 hectoliter	=	26.418	gallons or 2.838 bushels
10 hectoliters	= 1 kiloliter	=	264.18	gallons or 35.315 cubic feet

Weights

10 milligrams	= 1 centigram	=	0.1543	grain
10 centigrams	= 1 decigram	=	1.5432	grains
10 decigrams	= 1 gram	=	15.432	grains
10 grams	= 1 decagram	=	0.3527	ounce
10 decagrams	= 1 hectogram	=	3.5274	ounces
10 hectograms	= 1 kilogram	=	2.2046	pounds
10 kilograms	= 1 myriagram	=	22.046	pounds
10 myriagrams	= 1 quintal	=	220.46	pounds
10 quintals	= 1 metric ton	=	2,204.6	pounds

part VI

SPECIAL MATH TECHNIQUES AND SHORTCUTS

THE MINIMUM SETS OF MATH RULES AND CONCEPTS WITH WHICH YOU MUST BE FAMILIAR

Make sure that you understand each of the following math rules and concepts. It is a good idea to memorize them all. Refer to the section of the Math Refresher (Part V, page 403) shown in parentheses, *e.g.*, (2.52), for a complete explanation of each.

Algebra and Arithmetic

(2.52)
$$a(b + c) = ab + ac$$
Example:
$$5(4 + 5) = 5(4) + 5(5)$$
$$= 20 + 25$$
$$= 45$$

(2.52)
$$(a + b)(c + d) = ac + ad + bc + bd$$
Example:
$$(2 + 3)(4 - 6) = (2)(4) + (2)(-6)$$
$$+ (3)(4) + (3)(-6)$$
$$= 8 - 12 + 12 - 18$$
$$= -10$$

(2.52)
$$(a + b)^2 = a^2 + 2ab + b^2$$

(2.52)
$$(a - b)^2 = a^2 - 2ab + b^2$$

(2.52; 2.6)
$$(a + b)(a - b) = a^2 - b^2$$

(2.52)
$$-(a - b) = b - a$$

(2.51)
$$a^2 = (a)(a)$$
Example: $2^2 = (2)(2) = 4$
$$a^3 = (a)(a)(a), \text{ etc.}$$

(2.51)
$$\frac{a^x}{a^y} = a^{x-y}$$
Examples:
$$\frac{a^3}{a^2} = a^{3-2} = a;$$
$$\frac{2^3}{2^2} = 2^{3-2} = 2$$

(2.51)
$$a^x a^y = a^{x+y}$$
Examples:
$$a^2 \times a^3 = a^5;$$
$$2^2 \times 2^3 = 2^5 = 32$$

(2.51)
$$a^0 = 1$$
$$10^0 = 1$$
$$10^1 = 10$$
$$10^2 = 100$$
$$10^3 = 1000, \text{ etc.}$$

Example:
$$8.6 \times 10^4 = 8.\underset{1\ 2\ 3\ 4}{6\,0\,0\,0}.0$$

(2.51)
$$(a^x)^y = a^{xy}$$
Examples:
$$(a^3)^5 = a^{15}; \quad (2^3)^5 = 2^{15}$$

(2.51)
$$(ab)^x = a^x b^x$$
Examples:
$$(2 \times 3)^3 = 2^3 \times 3^3; \quad (ab)^2 = a^2 b^2$$

(2.7)
If $y^2 = x$ then $y = \pm \sqrt{x}$
Example:
If $y^2 = 4$,
then $y = \pm \sqrt{4} = \pm 2$

(2.51)
$$a^{-y} = \frac{1}{a^y}$$
Example: $2^{-3} = \dfrac{1}{2^3} = \dfrac{1}{8}$

Percentage

$$x\% = \frac{x}{100}$$

Example:

$$5\% = \frac{5}{100}$$

(1.34)

Percentage Problems

Examples:

(1)   What percent of 5 is 2?

$$\frac{x}{100} \qquad \times 5 = 2$$

or

$$\left(\frac{x}{100}\right)(5) = 2$$

$$\frac{5x}{100} = 2$$

$$5x = 200$$

$$x = 40$$

Answer $= 40\%$

(1.36)

RULE: "What" becomes x

"Percent" becomes $\frac{1}{100}$

"of" becomes $\times$ (times)

"is" becomes $=$ (equals)

---

(2)   6   is what percent of 24?

$$6 = \frac{x}{100} \qquad \times 24$$

$$6 = \frac{24x}{100}$$

$$600 = 24x$$

$$100 = 4x \text{ (dividing both sides by 6)}$$

$$25 = x$$

Answer $= 25\%$

(1.36)

Equations

Example: $x^2 - 2x + 1 = 0$. Solve for x.
   Procedure:
   Factor: $(x - 1)(x - 1) = 0$ **(2.7)**
$$x - 1 = 0$$
$$x = 1$$

Example: $x + y = 1$; $x - y = 2$. Solve for x and y.
   Procedure:
   Add equations:

$$x + y = 1$$
$$\underline{x - y = 2}$$
$$2x + 0 = 3$$

Therefore $2x = 3$ and $x = \frac{3}{2}$

Substitute $x = \frac{3}{2}$ back into one of the equations:

$$x + y = 1$$
$$\frac{3}{2} + y = 1$$
$$y = -\frac{1}{2}$$

(2.3)

Equalities

$$
\begin{aligned}
a + b &= c \\
+ \quad\quad d &= d \\
\hline
a + b + d &= c + d
\end{aligned}
\qquad
\begin{aligned}
3 + 4 &= 7 \\
+ \quad\quad 2 &= 2 \\
\hline
3 + 4 + 2 &= 7 + 2
\end{aligned}
$$

(2.8)

Inequalities

$>$ means greater than, $<$ means less than, $\geqq$ means greater than or equal to, etc.

$$
\begin{aligned}
b &> c \\
d &> e \\
\hline
b + d &> c + e
\end{aligned}
\qquad
\begin{aligned}
4 &> 3 \\
7 &> 6 \\
\hline
11 &> 9
\end{aligned}
\qquad
\begin{aligned}
4 &> 3 \\
-6 &> -7 \\
\hline
-2 &> -4
\end{aligned}
$$

(2.8)

$$5 > 4$$
$$(6)5 > 4(6)$$
Thus
$$30 > 24$$

$$-5 < -4$$
$$-(-5) > -(-4) \quad \text{(reversing inequality)}$$
$$5 > 4$$

If $-2 < x < +2$ $a > b > 0$
then $+2 > -x > -2$ Thus $a^2 > b^2$

Geometry

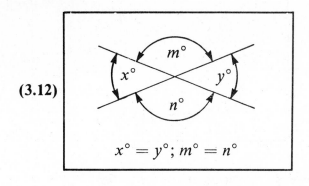

(3.12)

$$x° = y°; \ m° = n°$$

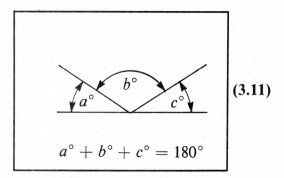

(3.11)

$$a° + b° + c° = 180°$$

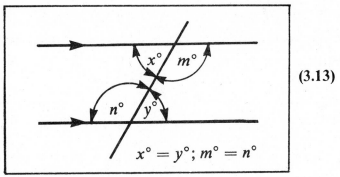

(3.13)

$$x° = y°; \ m° = n°$$

(3.21)

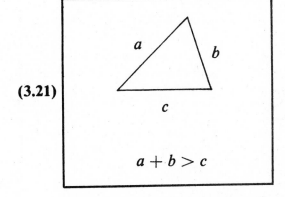

$$a + b > c$$

(3.21)

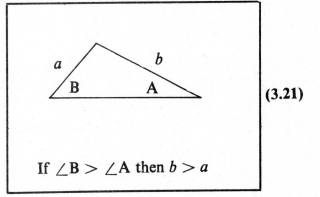

If $\angle B > \angle A$ then $b > a$

(3.21)

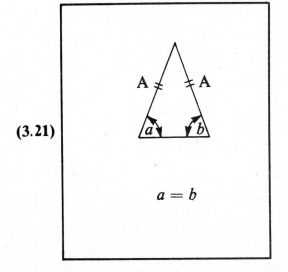

$$a = b$$

(3.21)

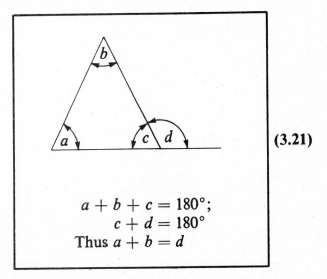

$$a + b + c = 180°;$$
$$c + d = 180°$$
Thus $a + b = d$

(3.21;
3.22)

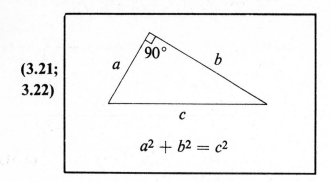

$a^2 + b^2 = c^2$

(3.22)

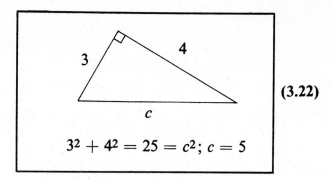

$3^2 + 4^2 = 25 = c^2; c = 5$

Here are some right triangles whose relationship of sides you should memorize:

(3.22)

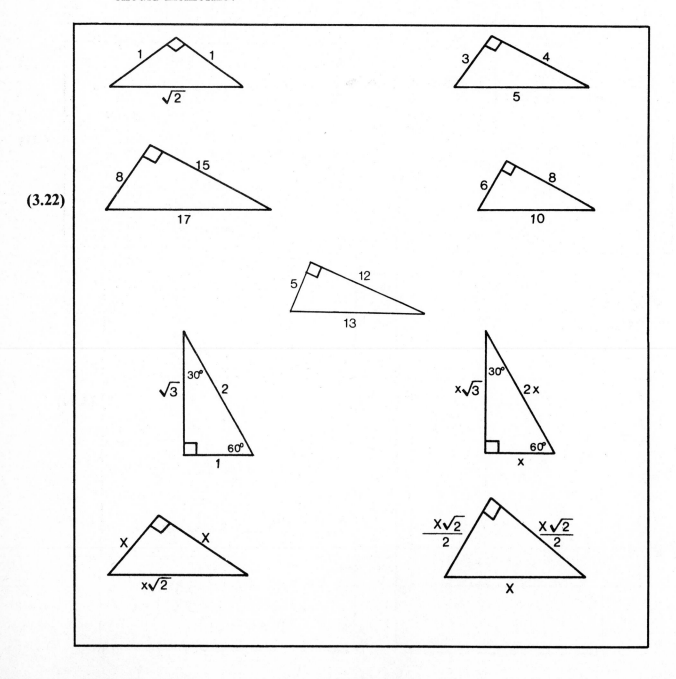

Areas & Perimeters

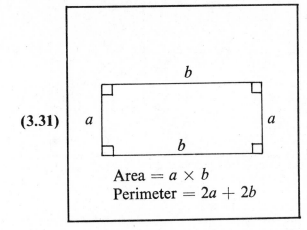

Area $= a \times b$
Perimeter $= 2a + 2b$

(3.31)

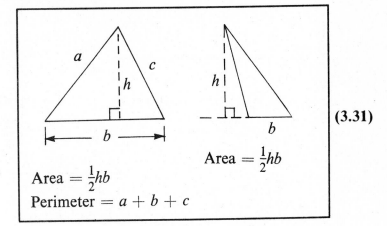

Area $= \frac{1}{2}hb$
Perimeter $= a + b + c$

Area $= \frac{1}{2}hb$

(3.31)

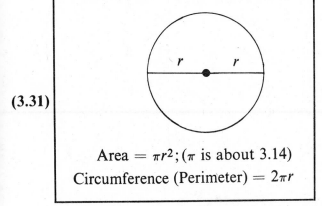

Area $= \pi r^2$; (π is about 3.14)
Circumference (Perimeter) $= 2\pi r$

(3.31)

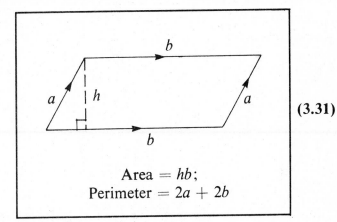

Area $= hb$;
Perimeter $= 2a + 2b$

(3.31)

More on Circles

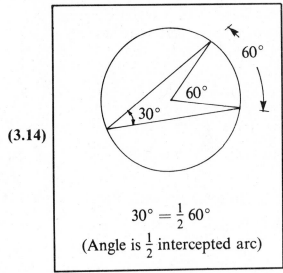

$30° = \frac{1}{2}60°$
(Angle is $\frac{1}{2}$ intercepted arc)

(3.14)

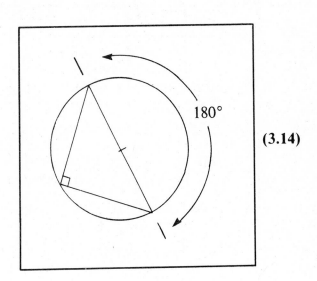

(3.14)

Coordinate Geometry

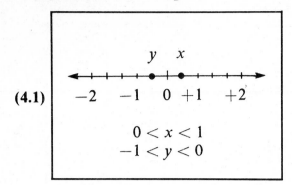

(4.1)

$0 < x < 1$
$-1 < y < 0$

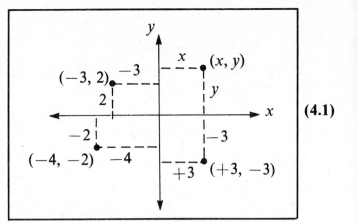

(4.1)

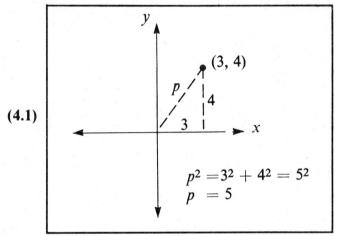

(4.1)

$p^2 = 3^2 + 4^2 = 5^2$
$p = 5$

WHAT THE SAT IS TESTING IN MATH AND HOW TO BE ONE STEP AHEAD

The SAT contains examples which test to see whether you can think in various ways, and whether you are able to use certain logical approaches in solving a problem. Here are the things that the SAT tests.

(1) Your ability to tell whether a problem can be solved from what is given and the knowledge you already have.

(2) Your ability to translate a verbal message into mathematical terms or equations.

(3) Your ability to use the simplest approach in solving the problem.

(4) Your ability to simplify a problem by drawing connecting lines in order to find the solution more quickly.

(5) Your ability to put problems or variables into a simpler and more apparent form.

(6) Your ability to understand the meaning of key words like "average" and "minimum."

Following are multiple choice simulated SAT math questions which test the six things outlined on the previous page.

(1) Your ability to tell whether a problem can be solved from what is given and the knowledge you already have.

Example 1:

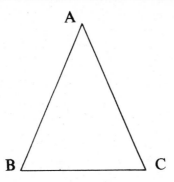

In the triangle above, AB = AC and ∠B = 70°

∠A is (A) 20° (B) 30° (C) 40° (D) 50° (E) 60°

In solving this problem, you should realize that if AB = AC, ∠B = ∠C. Therefore you should see that both ∠B and ∠C = 70°. Thus from what is given, you can find the base angles. Now you should remember that the sum of the angles of any triangle is 180°. That is something you should already know. At this point you should be aware that if you know the *two* base angles and you know the sum of *three* angles is 180°, you can find the third angle. Here's how to proceed: Call the third angle *x*. Then because the sum of the three angles is 180°,

$$70 + 70 + x = 180$$
$$140 + x = 180$$
$$x = 40$$

Thus, Choice C is correct.

Example 2:

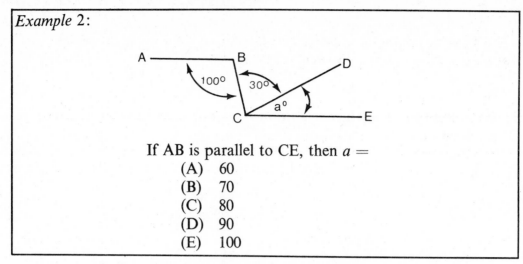

If AB is parallel to CE, then $a =$
    (A)   60
    (B)   70
    (C)   80
    (D)   90
    (E)   100

      You should first see that $\angle ABC = \angle BCE$ because AB and CE are parallel. Therefore, $\angle BCE = 100°$ since $\angle ABC = 100°$. You should realize now that the problem can be solved because $30° + a° = 100°$ and a can be solved for. Now we just have to actually solve for a, and that is fairly easy to do:

$$30 + a = 100$$
$$a = 100 - 30$$
$$a = 70$$

Thus Choice **B** is correct.

Example 3:

a	a	4
b	a	b
2	b	a

In the figure above, the sum of the numbers in each diagonal and the sum of the numbers in the *middle column* are equal. What is the value of b?
    (A)   3
    (B)   4
    (C)   5
    (D)   6
    (E)   cannot be determined

      You should see that by looking at the numbers in *both diagonals* you will get some type of equation involving only one variable "*a*." Thus you should certainly be able to solve for *a*. Now if you quickly look at the *middle column* you see that you have an *a* and a *b* in it. Since you already know that you can find the value of *a*, you should realize that you can also find the value of *b*. Let's actually proceed to solve the problem:

The sum of the numbers in one diagonal is

$$a + a + a = 3a$$

The sum of the numbers in the other diagonal is

$$2 + a + 4$$

Since this sum is given as equal we equate:

$$3a = 2 + a + 4$$
$$3a = 6 + a$$
$$2a = 6$$
$$a = 3$$

Now look at the *middle column*. The sum of the numbers in this column is

$$a + a + b$$

But since $a = 3$, the sum of the numbers is

$$3 + 3 + b = 6 + b$$

Since this sum is equal to the sum of the numbers in *any diagonal*, we can equate

$$3a = 6 + b$$

and since $a = 3$, we get,

$$9 = 6 + b$$
$$3 = b$$

Therefore, Choice A is correct.

---

(2) Your ability to translate a verbal message into mathematical terms or equations.

Example 1:

Mary is five years older than John. John is two years younger than Pete. Mary is how much older than Pete?

(A) 7 years (B) 6 years (C) 5 years (D) 4 years (E) 3 years

Here we have to translate what is said verbally into mathematics:

Let the age of Mary be represented by the letter M, the age of John be represented by the letter J, and the age of Pete be represented by the letter P.

Mary is five years older than John is translated mathematically into

M = 5 + J (Remember, "is" becomes " = ," "older" becomes " + .")

John is two years younger than Pete is translated to

J = P − 2 (Remember, "is" becomes " = ," "younger" becomes " − .")

What we want to do now is find how much older Mary is than Pete, or mathematically, we would like to find the relationship between M and P. We have two equations:

M = 5 + J
and
J = P − 2

In the equation M = 5 + J, substitute for J, J = P − 2 from the second equation. We do this to get rid of J since we just want to see the relation of M and P.

Thus
M = 5 + J = 5 + (P − 2)
So
M = 5 + P − 2 = 3 + P

Since M = 3 + P, this says that *Mary is 3 years older than Pete*, and thus Choice E is correct.

Example 2:
A rental company rents cars for x dollars a day and for y cents a mile. If a customer rents a car for z days and drives z miles, how many dollars would the customer be charged for the rental?

  (A) $xy + z$
  (B) $100xy + zx$

  (C) $\dfrac{z}{100}(100x + y)$

  (D) $\dfrac{zx + y}{100}$

  (E) $zx + y$

Notice here that the customer is charged not only by the day, but by the mile. If the customer is charged $\$x$ a day and the customer rents the car for z days, he or she will be charged $\$xz$. Since the customer is also charged y¢ a mile and drove the car z miles, the customer would be charged an additional yz¢. Now we add:

$$\$xz + yz\text{¢}$$

The question asks you to find the total charge in *dollars* so we must convert yz¢ to dollars. 1¢ $= \dfrac{1}{100}$ dollar, so

$$\$xz + yz\text{¢} = \$xz + \$\frac{yz}{100}$$

We notice in the choices that there is no answer

$$xz + \frac{yz}{100}$$

Don't panic! The answer is probably in a different but equivalent form. Notice above that we can factor out the z. That is:

$$xz + \frac{yz}{100} = z\left(x + \frac{y}{100}\right)$$

and this just corresponds to Choice C since

$$z\left(x + \frac{y}{100}\right) = \frac{z}{100}(100x + y)$$

Example 3:

Harry owes Sam \$30. Sam owes Phil \$20. Phil owes Harry \$50. To settle these debts
- (A)   Harry could give Phil \$30
- (B)   Sam could give Phil \$20 and Harry could give Sam \$40
- (C)   Harry could give Phil \$20 and Sam could give Phil \$10
- (D)·   Sam and Phil could give Harry \$50 total
- (E)   Phil could give Harry \$20 and could give Sam \$10

This is one of these SAT type questions that can give you a headache trying to solve. That is, if you do it with the wrong approach! Now there is a very clever way to attack this type of problem. You make a table of who's ahead and who's behind in money and then translate that table into mathematical terms. This is what we mean:

Harry owes Sam \$30. We can say then that Harry is +30 (since he hasn't paid Sam the \$30 yet and he is \$30 ahead), and Sam is −30 (since Sam hasn't received the \$30 yet and he is \$30 behind).

We start making a table:

Harry	Sam	Phil
+30	−30	

Now, Sam owes Phil \$20. So Sam is +20 and Phil is −20. Add this information to the table:

Harry	Sam	Phil
+30	−30	
	+20	−20

Finally, Phil owes Harry \$50. So Phil is +50 and Harry is −50. Now add this to the table:

Harry	Sam	Phil
+30	−30	
	+20	−20
−50		+50

Now add the numbers in each column:

Harry	Sam	Phil
+30	−30	
	+20	−20
−50	−10	+50
−20		+30

We see that we get

Harry as −20
Sam as −10
Phil as +30

Now this tells us that Phil is ahead by $30 and Harry is behind by $20 and Sam is behind by $10. In order for no one to be either ahead or behind, (that is, all debts are taken care of) Phil should give his $30 to Sam and Harry giving Sam $10 and Harry $20. Therefore Choice E is correct.

---

(3) Your ability to use the simplest approach in solving the problem.

Example 1:

If $x^2 + y^2 = 5$ and $xy = 2$, find the value of $x + y$:

(A) +3 only   (B) −3 only   (C) +3 or −3   (D) +7   (E) $\pm \sqrt{7}$

You may be tempted to solve for x, then solve for y, and then add x and y. That is *not* the simplest approach. What you should realize is something that you can do with $x^2 + y^2$ and with xy so that you can get $x + y$.

Procedure: Note that $x^2 + 2xy + y^2 = (x + y)^2$

Since $x^2 + y^2 = 5$ and $xy = 2$, we get

$(x + y)^2 = x^2 + 2xy + y^2 = 5 + 2(2) = 9$

Therefore,

$(x + y)^2 = 9$

and so

$x + y = \pm 3$

Choice C is correct.

Example 2:

If y ranges in value from 0.0002 to 0.002 and x ranges in value from 0.02 to 2.0, what is the smallest value of $\frac{y}{x}$?

    (A)   0.1
    (B)   0.01
    (C)   0.001
    (D)   0.0001
    (E)   0.00001

The worst thing you could do is to try substituting many values for x and y. You have to know that the smallest value of $\frac{y}{x}$ occurs when y *is smallest* and x *is largest*. Since y ranges from 0.0002 to 0.002, y is smallest when $y = 0.0002$. Since x ranges from 0.02 to 2.0, x is largest when $x = 2.0$. Therefore the *smallest value of* $\frac{y}{x}$ is

$$\frac{0.0002}{2.0}$$

Cancel the 2's and we get:

$$\frac{0.0001}{1.0}$$

This last quantity is equal to 0.0001 and thus Choice D is correct.

Example 3:

If $xyz = 0$, $xst = 0$ and $yts = 1$, which of the following must be true?

    (A) $x = 0$
    (B) $y = 0$
    (C) $z = 0$
    (D) $s = 0$
    (E) $t = 0$

You should see from the relation, $yts = 1$ that it is impossible that y, t, or s equal 0, because anything multiplied by 0 gives you 0 and not 1.

Now look at the relation $xst = 0$. Since we have found that s or t is not 0, the only way that the relation can be true is if $x = 0$. Therefore Choice A is correct. Note that if you worked with the relation $xyz = 0$, you wouldn't really be able to determine anything since you don't know here whether x or z is 0.

(4) Your ability to simplify a problem by drawing connecting lines in order to find the solution more quickly.

Example 1:

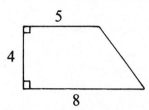

In the diagram above, the perimeter of the quadrilateral

(A) is 21   (B) is 22   (C) is 23   (D) is 24   (E) cannot be determined

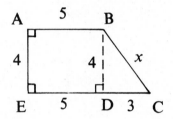

In order to find the perimeter we must find all the sides. Drop a perpendicular line from B to side EC, as shown above.

Notice that you have thus created a parallelogram ABDE.

Thus ED = AB = 5. Since EC = 8 (given), and ED = 5, *DC must be 3*. Now AE = BD (because ABDE is a parallelogram), so AE = *4 = BD*. Triangle BDC is a right triangle with sides 3 and 4. Call side BC = x.

Then
$3^2 + 4^2 = x^2$ (Pythagorean Theorem)
    $25 = x^2$
     $5 = x$

Thus the perimeter is

$4 + 5 + 8 + 5 = 22$

Choice **B** is correct.

Example 2:

The maximum distance between two points on or inside a square of side 3 is

  (A) $3\sqrt{2}$
  (B) 6
  (C) $3\sqrt{3}$
  (D) 9
  (E) 3.5

One should draw a diagram of the square:

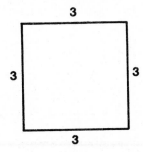

Now you should draw the diagonal:

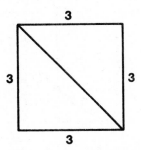

At this point you should be able to see that the maximum distance of two points is the length of the diagonal since the points at the ends of the diagonal are furthest from each other than any other points on or inside the square. The length of the diagonal is (by the Pythagorean Theorem) $\sqrt{3^2 + 3^2} = \sqrt{18} = 3\sqrt{2}$*. Thus Choice A is correct.

*You should memorize that the diagonal of a square with side x is $x\sqrt{2}$.

Example 3:

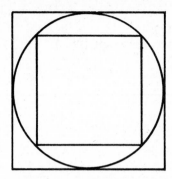

A square is inscribed in a circle above and the circle above is inscribed in a square. What is the ratio of the area of the larger square to that of the smaller?

(A) $\sqrt{2} : 1$
(B) $2 : 1$
(C) $\sqrt{3} : 1$
(D) $3 : 1$
(E) $4 : 1$

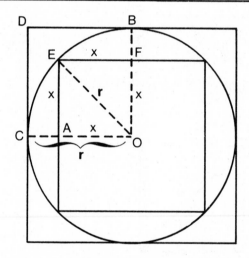

Draw from center of circle O, lines OC, OB and OE. You have created two squares (OAEF and OCDB) exactly one-quarter the size (area) of the respective smaller and larger squares of the original question. Thus the ratio of the areas of these "$\frac{1}{4}$" squares is the same ratio of areas of the original squares.

Now the *area of OCDB* is $r \times r = r^2$. (r is the radius of the circle). The *area of the square OAEF* is

$$x \times x = x^2$$

But we know by the Pythagorean Theorem (since OAE is a right triangle) that

$$x^2 + x^2 = r^2$$
$$2x^2 = r^2$$
$$x^2 = \frac{r^2}{2}$$

The ratio of the area of the large square to the small square is

$$\frac{r^2}{x^2}$$

and since $x^2 = \dfrac{r^2}{2}$, the ratio becomes

$$\frac{r^2}{\dfrac{r^2}{2}} = r^2 \times \frac{2}{r^2} = 2$$

Therefore Choice B is correct.

---

(5) Your ability to put problems or variables into a simpler and more apparent form.

Example 1:

If $\sqrt{2}$ is approximately 1.414, the closest value of

$$\frac{2}{\sqrt{2} - 2}$$

is (A) -3.414 (B) -3.828 (C) -3.415 (D) -3.413 (E) -3.416

It would be foolish of us to substitute $\sqrt{2} = 1.414$ into

$$\frac{2}{\sqrt{2} - 2}$$

and then evaluate. It is much better to "rationalize" the denominator. That is get all the square roots out of the denominator. We can do this as follows:

Multiply both numerator and denominator by

$\sqrt{2} + 2$

(Multiplying both the numerator and denominator by the same number does not change its value.)

We get

$$\frac{2}{\sqrt{2} - 2} \frac{(\sqrt{2} + 2)}{(\sqrt{2} + 2)} = \frac{2\sqrt{2} + 4}{2 - 4} = \frac{2\sqrt{2} + 4}{-2}$$

(Since $(\sqrt{2} - 2)(\sqrt{2} + 2) = \sqrt{2} \times \sqrt{2} - 2 \times 2 = 2 - 4$)

Dividing both numerator and denominator by 2 (to simplify) we get

$-(\sqrt{2} + 2)$

Now we can substitute $\sqrt{2} = 1.414$ and we get

$-(1.414 + 2) = -3.414$

Choice A is therefore correct.

Example 2:

If $(\frac{1}{y} + y)^2 = 36$, then $\frac{1}{y^2} + y^2 =$
    (A) 36
    (B) 6
    (C) 18
    (D) 38
    (E) 34

Put the problem in a more apparent form by multiplying out the $(\frac{1}{y} + y)^2$. We get

$$36 = (\tfrac{1}{y} + y)(\tfrac{1}{y} + y) = \tfrac{1}{y^2} + \tfrac{y}{y} + \tfrac{y}{y} + y^2$$
$$36 = \tfrac{1}{y^2} + 2 + y^2$$

Therefore, subtracting 2 from both sides of the above equation, we get

$$34 = \tfrac{1}{y^2} + y^2$$

Choice E is correct.

Example 3:

If $4y + 2x + 8 + xy = 0$ and $x + 4 = 9$, then $2 + y =$
    (A) -1
    (B) 0
    (C) $+1$
    (D) $+2$
    (E) $+3$

One may be first tempted to solve for x, plug the value of x into the first equation and then evaluate $2 + y$. However, there is a more insightful way to do this problem. Notice that if we multiply $(x + 4)$ with $(2 + y)$ we get

$$(x + 4)(2 + y) = 2x + 8 + xy + 4y$$

But $2x + 8 + xy + 4y = 0$ and $x + 4 = 9$ (given).
Thus $2 + y$ must be equal to 0, and Choice B is correct.

(6) Your ability to understand the meaning of key words like "average" and "minimum."

Example 1:

What is the average rate of a car traveling uphill at 40 miles per hour and downhill the same distance at 60 miles per hour?

(A) 50 mph   (B) 55 mph   (C) 48 mph   (D) 45 mph
(E) Cannot be determined.

You have to know what the word "average" means. Average is the sum of the entities divided by the number of entities. Since we know that rate = distance divided by time, "average rate" is *total distance* divided by *total time*. Thus we must find the *total distance* and the *total time* in order to find what the *average rate* is. If a car travels at 40 mph uphill and we'll call the uphill distance "d," the time (t_U) it takes to go uphill is given by

$$40 \times t_U = d$$

This is just using the formula rate × time = distance, calling the distance d, and the uphill time t_U.

The car travels 60 mph downhill the same distance d, so where t_D is the time it takes the car to go downhill,

$$60 \times t_D = d$$

Therefore we have two equations:

$$40 \times t_U = d$$
$$60 \times t_D = d$$

The *total time* is the uphill and the downhill time, which is

$$t_U + t_D$$

Since we can find that

$$t_U = \frac{d}{40}$$

and

$$t_D = \frac{d}{60}$$

we get

$$t_U + t_D = \frac{d}{40} + \frac{d}{60} = \frac{60d + 40d}{2400} = \frac{100d}{2400} = \frac{d}{24}$$

The *total distance* (uphill and downhill) is just

$$d + d = 2d$$

Therefore the average rate is

$$\frac{\text{Total distance}}{\text{Total time}} = \frac{2d}{t_U + t_D} = \frac{2d}{\dfrac{d}{24}}$$

$$= 2d \times \frac{24}{d} = 48$$

Notice that the *d*'s cancel and the answer is 48 mph.
Choice C is correct.

Example 2:

The difference between the greatest and smallest two-digit even integers which are exactly divisible by 4 is
(A)   82
(B)   84
(C)   96
(D)   88
(E)   80

You should know that examples of *two-digit even integers* are 12, 14, 16, etc. Examples of two-digit even integers *divisible by 4* are 12, 16, 20, etc. The *smallest* of these *two-digit integers which are exactly divisible* by 4 is the number *12*. The *greatest* of these *two-digit even integers which is exactly divisible by 4* is the number *96*. The *difference* between these numbers (96 and 12) is 84. Thus Choice B is correct.

Example 3:

A test was taken by 60 students and was scored from 0 to 100. Only 21 students scored higher than or equal to 80. What is the smallest possible average score of all 60 students?
(A)   25
(B)   34
(C)   36
(D)   70
(E)   28

You must know what the word *average* means, here. The average score of all the students is the *sum of the scores divided by the number of students*. Since we want to determine the *smallest* average score, we would try to have each student have the lowest score possible. Now of the *60* students, *21* must have gotten *at least 80*, and it is possible that all of the remaining $60 - 21 = 39$ students could have scored 0 (this is the lowest score they could have received.) The *lowest average score* would then be

$$\frac{\text{lowest total score}}{\text{number of students}} = \frac{\overset{(21\ times)}{80 + 80 + 80 + \ldots} + \overset{(39\ times)}{0 + 0 + 0 + \ldots}}{60}$$

$$= \frac{80 \times 21 + 0 \times 39}{60}$$

$$= \frac{80 \times 21}{60}$$

$$= \frac{\overset{4}{\cancel{80}} \times \overset{7}{\cancel{21}}}{\underset{20}{\cancel{60}}}$$

$$= 28$$

Thus Choice E is correct.

MATHEMATICAL SHORTCUTS YOU SHOULD KNOW

Adding Fractions

In many cases you do not have to look for a common denominator to add fractions:

Example:

Add: $\dfrac{2}{5} + \dfrac{7}{9}$

Procedure:

Multiply the 9 by the 2 and you get 18.
Multiply the 5 by the 7 and you get 35.
Add $18 + 35$ and you get 53. 53 is the *numerator* of the answer.
Multiply the 5 by the 9 and you get 45. 45 is the *denominator* of the answer.

The answer is thus $\dfrac{53}{45}$

Subtracting Fractions

Example:

Subtract: $\dfrac{2}{5} - \dfrac{7}{9}$

Procedure:

$$\dfrac{2}{5} \overset{\text{MULTIPLY}}{\underset{\text{MULTIPLY}}{\longleftarrow}} - \overset{\text{MULTIPLY}}{\longrightarrow} \dfrac{7}{9}$$

Multiply the 9 by the 2: $2 \times 9 = 18$.
Multiply the 5 by the 7: $5 \times 7 = 35$.
Subtract: $18 - 35 = -17$. This is the *numerator*.
Multiply 5 by 9: $5 \times 9 = 45$. This is the *denominator*.

The answer is thus $-\dfrac{17}{45}$

In general:

Add: $\dfrac{a}{b} + \dfrac{c}{d}$

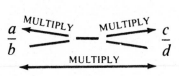

Answer: $\dfrac{ad + cb}{bd}$

Subtract: $\dfrac{a}{b} - \dfrac{c}{d}$

Answer: $\dfrac{ad - cb}{bd}$

Example:

Add: $\dfrac{3}{x} + \dfrac{3}{y}$

Answer: $\dfrac{3y + 3x}{xy}$

Comparing Fractions

Example: Which is greater, $\frac{3}{8}$ or $\frac{7}{18}$?

Procedure:

$$\frac{3}{8} \overset{\text{MULTIPLY \quad MULTIPLY}}{\times} \frac{7}{18}$$

Multiply the 18 by the 3. We get 54. Put the 54 on the *left* side.

54

Now *multiply* the 8 by the 7. We get 56. Put the 56 on the *right* side:

54   56

Since $56 > 54$ and 56 is on the *right* side, the fraction $\frac{7}{18}$ (which was also originally on the *right* side) is *greater* than the fraction $\frac{3}{8}$ (which was originally on the *left* side).

Example: If $y > x$, which is greater, $\frac{1}{x}$ or $\frac{1}{y}$? (x and y are positive numbers.)

Procedure:

$$\frac{1}{x} \overset{\text{MULTIPLY \quad MULTIPLY}}{\times} \frac{1}{y}$$

Multiply y by 1. We get y. Put y on the left:

y

Multiply x by 1. We get x. Put x on the right side.

y x

Since $y > x$ (given), $\frac{1}{x}$ (which was originally on the left) is greater than $\frac{1}{y}$ (which was originally on the right).

SHORTCUTS AND TECHNIQUES FOR ANSWERING THE QUANTITATIVE COMPARISON TYPE QUESTION

(1) Make sure that you memorize the directions for this type so you don't have to refer to them while working the problems.

(2) Remember that you are comparing the quantities in the two columns, Column A with Column B.

(3) Remember that you choose
   (A) if the quantity in Column A is *greater* than the quantity in Column B,
   (B) if the quantity in Column A is *less* that the quantity in Column B,
   (C) if the quantities are *equal,*
   (D) if you cannot make a determination as to the relative values of the quantities.

(4) You should be aware that any information in the middle of the columns refers to *both* columns.

(5) If the quantities in both columns are numbers such as $\frac{1}{2}$, $\frac{1}{4}$, etc. (in other words, *not* algebraic variables such as x, xy^2, etc.), answer choice D *cannot* be correct, since the quantities are determined and a comparison can always be made between numbers.

(6) If the quantities are algebraic variables such as x^2, x^3, xy, etc., you may use the following procedure: *If for one value of the variable, the quantities are equal, and for another value they are not equal, a definite comparison cannot be made and thus* answer choice D *is correct.* More on this method later.

Key Method for Solving Quantitative Comparison Type Questions

One of the best methods for solving quantitative comparison type questions is to *transform* or modify the columns so that they appear simpler. Here are some important rules to follow.

(1) You can *add* the *same* quantity to both columns and get the same relationship for the columns:

Example:

Column A	Column B
3	5

Note that Column B $>$ Column A.
Now add $+3$ to both columns:
We get:

Column A	Column B
$3 + 3$	$5 + 3$

Note that we still obtain Column B $>$ Column A.

(2) You can *subtract* the *same* quantity from both columns and still get the same relationship of the columns:

Example:

Column A	Column B
3	5

Note as before, Column B $>$ Column A.
Now subtract 3 from both columns:
We get:

Column A	Column B
$3 - 3$	$5 - 3$

Simplified, this becomes:

Column A	Column B
0	$+2$

We still therefore obtain Column B $>$ Column A.

(3) You can *multiply* both columns by the *same positive number* and still preserve the same relationship of the columns:

Example:

Column A	Column B
$\dfrac{3}{5}$	$\dfrac{4}{5}$

Note Column B $>$ Column A.
Let's multiply both columns by $+5$.
We get:

Column A	Column B
$\dfrac{3}{5} \times 5$	$\dfrac{4}{5} \times 5$

Simplified, this becomes:

Column A	Column B
3	4

And again we get Column B $>$ Column A.

(4) You can *divide* both columns by the *same positive number* and still preserve the relationship between the columns:

Example:

Column A	Column B
-3	-6

Note that Column A $>$ Column B.
Now divide both columns by 3:
We get:

Column A	Column B
$\dfrac{-3}{3}$	$\dfrac{-6}{3}$

Simplified, this becomes:

Column A	Column B
-1	-2

And we still find that Column A $>$ Column B.

As you will realize from upcoming examples, you will want to *transform* or modify the columns so that they look simpler. This technique provides a powerful shortcut that will save more time and be easier to work than actually calculating the two amounts being compared. So remember you may multiply, divide, subtract, or add the same quantity to both columns to make the columns simpler. For multiplication or division, multiply or divide *only* by positive numbers. Doing this does not change the relationship. Here are some examples:

Example 1:

Column A	Column B
$\frac{5}{6} - \frac{1}{2}$	$\frac{1}{2}$

Instead of calculating the quantity, $\frac{5}{6} - \frac{1}{2}$, let's *add $\frac{1}{2}$* to both columns:

We get:

Column A	Column B
$\frac{5}{6} - \frac{1}{2} + \frac{1}{2}$	$\frac{1}{2} + \frac{1}{2}$

Simplified, these columns become:

Column A	Column B
$\frac{5}{6}$	1

And since $1 > \frac{5}{6}$, Column B $>$ Column A and thus answer choice B is correct.

Example 2:

Column A		Column B
	$x > 0$	
	$y \neq 0$	
$\frac{x}{y}$		$\frac{x}{y^2}$

Since x is positive, divide both sides (both columns) by x:
We then obtain for the columns:

Column A	Column B
$\frac{1}{y}$	$\frac{1}{y^2}$

Now y can be *any* number (except 0). If $y = 1$, the columns are equal; if y is not 1, the columns are *not* equal and so a definite comparison cannot be made. Therefore, answer choice D would be correct.

What follows is a set of examples illustrating particular methods to solve quantitative comparison problems. *It is necessary for you to understand each method used since it has been shown that the method may be used for many of the questions of the Quantitative Comparison type on your SAT.*

Example 1: **Common quantities in each column.**

Column A	Column B
$\dfrac{1}{4} \times \dfrac{1}{3}$	$\dfrac{1}{5} \times \dfrac{1}{3}$

Because $\frac{1}{3}$ is positive, and is *common* to both columns, we cancel it. Thus we get

Column A	Column B
$\dfrac{1}{4}$	$\dfrac{1}{5}$

Since $\frac{1}{4} > \frac{1}{5}$ Choice A is correct.

Example 2: **Putting the relationship that is given in a form that relates to the quantities in the columns.**

Column A	$-3 < p < 3$	Column B
-3		$-p$

Put the relation on the top middle in a form that relates to the quantities in Columns A and B. We can do this by multiplying $-3 < p < 3$ by (-1). Remember that when multiplying an inequality by a negative number, we must *reverse* the inequality signs. Therefore

$$(-1)(-3) > (-1)(p) > (-1)(3)$$

so

$$3 > -p > -3$$

and so Choice B is correct.

Example 3:   **Modifying the quantities in the columns so that they look simpler.**

Column A	Column B
$\sqrt{17}$	4

Here we want to *modify the quantities in the columns so that they look simpler.* To do this we multiply $\sqrt{17}$ by itself. We get $\sqrt{17} \times \sqrt{17} = 17$. We must then multiply 4 by itself. We get $4 \times 4 = 16$. $17 > 16$ so the quantity in Column A is greater than the quantity in Column B.

Example 4:   **Showing that in one case the quantities in the columns are equal and in another case the quantities in the columns are not equal.**

Column A	Column B
$x^9 y^6$	$(xy)^{15}$

First see if for one value of x and y, the quantities are *equal.* Surely for $x = 0$ and $y = 0$, this is true. Then see if the quantities are *not equal* for one value of x and y. If $x = 1$, and y is negative, we can see that the quantities are not equal, the quantity in Column A being positive and the quantity in Column B being negative. *Thus in one case we have shown the quantities are equal and in another case we have shown that they are not equal. Thus a definite comparison cannot be made and Choice D is correct.*

Example 5:   **Noting the relationships of the numbers in the columns.**

Column A	Column B
35×65	34×66

Note the relationship of the numbers in the columns: Between 35 and 34 and 65 and 66. Whatever you do, *do not* multiply 35×65 and 34×66!

Divide 34 into the quantities in both columns and divide 65 into the quantities in both columns.
We get

Column A	Column B
$\dfrac{35 \times 65}{34 \times 65}$	$\dfrac{34 \times 66}{34 \times 65}$

Simplified, this becomes

Column A	Column B
$\dfrac{35}{34}$	$\dfrac{66}{65}$

Now $\frac{35}{34}$ is $1\frac{1}{34}$ and $\frac{66}{65}$ is $1\frac{1}{65}$. Since

$$\frac{1}{34} > \frac{1}{65}$$

the quantity in Column A is greater than the quantity in Column B and Choice A is correct.

Example 6: **Transforming the given to a form that is given in the columns.**

Column A	Column B
	$1 > p > 0$	
p^2	p

One may first be tempted to guess values for p. However a better way to approach this problem is as follows:

Write
$1 > p$ (given)

We now want to try to get a relationship between p and p^2 from the above inequality. We can see that if we multiplied both sides of the inequality by p, we would get

$$(1)\,(p) > (p)\,(p)$$

Since $p > 0$ (given) we don't have to worry about any reversing of the inequality signs.
The above says that $p > p^2$ and Choice B is therefore correct.

Example 7: **Putting the columns in the simplest forms.**

Column A	Column B
	$x > 1$	
$(x + 1)^3 - 2x$	$x^2 + 1$

In a case like this, *do not* multiply out $(x + 1)^3$. *Always try to put the columns in the simplest form.* That is, for the above case, add $2x$ to both columns:

We get:

Column A		Column B
	$x > 1$	
$(x + 1)^3 - 2x + 2x$		$x^2 + 1 + 2x$

Thus we get

Column A		Column B
	$x > 1$	
$(x + 1)^3$		$x^2 + 2x + 1$

Now you should realize that
$$x^2 + 2x + 1 = (x + 1)^2$$

Thus we get

Column A		Column B
	$x > 1$	
$(x + 1)^3$		$(x + 1)^2$

Since $x > 1$, surely, $(x + 1)^3 > (x + 1)^2$, and Choice A is correct.

Example 8: **Choosing small numbers or extreme values for the variables.**

Column A		Column B
	$x > 1$	
$x - 10$		$10 - x$

Here we choose *extreme values for x:* Let x be 1,000,000. Then $x - 10$ is very positive and $10 - x$ is very negative. For this case, the quantity in Column A is *greater* than the quantity in Column B. Now let x be just a little greater than 1, like 1.00001. The quantity in Column A (that is, $x - 10$) is negative and the quantity in Column B (that is, $10 - x$) is positive. Therefore, in this case the quantity in Column A is *less* than the quantity in Column B. Since in one case the quantity in Column A is greater than the quantity in Column B and in another case the quantity in Column A is less than the quantity in Column B, a definite comparison cannot be made. Thus Choice D is correct.

Here are eight more examples of quantitative comparison type questions. Try to see any similarity with the eight examples previously encountered. We hope you do since *each* of these examples is very much like examples you have just worked on.

For the next 8 examples, remember that you choose

(A) if the quantity in Column A > quantity in Column B
(B) if the quantity in Column A < quantity in Column B
(C) if the quantity in Column A = quantity in Column B
(D) if you cannot make a definite comparison of the quantities

(Quantities in the middle refer to both columns)

	Column A	Column B
1.	$a(b + a)$	$(c + b)a$

2.

$$2x + 3y = 16$$
$$3x - 3y = 7$$

	Column A	Column B
	x	y

	Column A	Column B
3.	$\left(\dfrac{12}{17}\right)^2$	$\sqrt{\dfrac{12}{17}}$

	Column A	Column B
4.	The average of a and b	$a - b$

	Column A	Column B
5.	69×71	70×70

6.

$$1 > p \qquad p \neq 0$$

	Column A	Column B
	p^2	p^3

7.

$$p > 0$$

	Column A	Column B
	3^{p-2}	$3^p - 3^{p-2}$

8.

$$a + b = 10$$

	Column A	Column B
	$\dfrac{1}{a} + \dfrac{1}{b}$	$\dfrac{1}{10}$

SOLUTIONS AND STRATEGIES:

1. **(D)**

    First multiply out Column A and Column B:

Column A	**Column B**
$ab + a^2$	$ca + ba$

    Now get rid of the quantities *common* to both columns. Get rid of the quantity ab. Thus we are left with

Column A	**Column B**
a^2	ca

    Since we do not know the value of c, that is, it may be greater than a or less than a, we cannot make a comparison of the columns. Thus Choice D is correct.

    NOTE THAT THIS EXAMPLE IS SIMILAR TO THE PREVIOUS *Example* 1, as far as strategic approach is concerned.

2. **(A)**

    This is a very tricky example. The key is in realizing that the *second equation* $(3x - 3y = 7)$ can be *put into a form which relates x and y directly*. Take this equation, $3x - 3y = 7$, and divide both sides by 3. We get

    $$x - y = \frac{7}{3}$$

    This really says that

    $$x - y > 0$$

    and thus

    $$x > y$$

    Choice A is now obviously correct.

    It's interesting that you didn't need to use the *first equation* to solve the problem.

    NOTE THAT THIS EXAMPLE IS SIMILAR TO THE PREVIOUS *Example* 2 as far as strategic approach is concerned.

3. **(B)**

    Modify the quantities so that they look simpler. In this case, get rid of the square root! So let's multiply the quantity in Column B by itself. Of course, we also have to multiply the quantity in Column A by itself to preserve the relationship of the quantities. We then get

Column A	**Column B**
$\left(\frac{12}{17}\right)^4$	$\frac{12}{17}$

    Now you should know that a fraction less than one, when multiplied by itself, is less than the original fraction. That is $\frac{12}{17} > \left(\frac{12}{17}\right)^2 > \left(\frac{12}{17}\right)^3$, etc. Thus $\left(\frac{12}{17}\right)^4 < \frac{12}{17}$, and Choice B is correct.

    NOTE THAT THE METHOD OF SOLUTION IS JUST LIKE THE METHOD USED IN THE PREVIOUS *Example* 3.

4.   (D)

The average of a and b is $\dfrac{a+b}{2}$. Thus we get for Column A and B,

Column A	Column B
$\dfrac{a+b}{2}$	$a-b$

First see if for values of a and b, the quantities are *equal*. Surely if $a=0$ and $b=0$, the quantities are both equal. Now see if we can get values for a and b, such that the quantities are *not equal*. If $b=0$ and $a=1$ the quantities are not equal. Thus we have shown that for one case ($a=0$, $b=0$) the quantities are equal and for another case ($a=1$, $b=0$) the quantities are not equal. Therefore, a definite comparison cannot be made and Choice D is correct. NOTE THAT THIS APPROACH IS JUST LIKE THE APPROACH USED IN THE PREVIOUS *Example* 4.

5.   (B)

Note a relationship of the numbers in the columns. Between 69 and 70 and between 71 and 70.
That is we write

$$69 = 70 - 1$$

and

$$71 = 70 + 1$$

We do this so that we can get a common ground for both columns. We then get

Column A	Column B
$(70-1)(70+1)$	$(70)(70)$

Now you should remember that for any a and b,

$$(a-b)(a+b) = a^2 - b^2$$

Doesn't Column A lend itself beautifully to that form? So,

$$(70-1)(70+1) = (70)(70) - (1)(1)$$
$$= (70)(70) - 1$$

Therefore, Column A is 1 less than Column B and thus Choice B is correct.

We could have, of course, multiplied the original 69 by 71 and 70 by 70, but this would have taken a much greater time. DO YOU SEE HOW THE STRATEGY OF THIS APPROACH FOR SOLUTION IS VERY MUCH LIKE THAT IN THE PREVIOUS *Example* 5?

6.   (A)

We want to get a relationship between p^2 and p^3 from what is given ($1 > p$ and $p \neq 0$).
Write

$$1 > p$$

Now we multiply both sides of this inequality by p^2. (We can do this without changing the direction of the inequality because $p^2 > 0$).

Therefore, since the direction of the inequality is the same we have

$$1 > p$$
$$(p^2)(1) > (p^2)(p)$$
$$p^2 > p^3$$

and thus Choice A is correct. NOTE HOW MUCH LIKE THIS STRATEGY IS LIKE THE ONE USED FOR *Example* 6 before.

7. **(B)**

Put the columns in the simplest form. We originally have

Column A		Column B
	$p > 0$	
3^{p-2}		$3^p - 3^{p-2}$

Add 3^{p-2}. to both columns. We get:

Column A		Column B
	$p > 0$	
$(2)(3^{p-2})$		3^p

Now you should know that

$$3^{p-2} = 3^p \times 3^{-2}$$

Substitute this in Column A:

Column A		Column B
	$p > 0$	
$(2)(3^p)(3^{-2})$		3^p

Since 3^p is not less than or equal to 0, we can *divide* both columns by 3^p without changing the relationship among the columns. We get

Column A		Column B
	$p > 0$	
$(2)(3^{-2})$		1

Now $3^{-2} = \frac{1}{3^2} = \frac{1}{9}$ so we get

Column A	Column B
$2(\frac{1}{9})$	1

Certainly the quantity in Column A is *less* than the quantity in Column B and thus Choice B is correct. NOTE THAT OUR ORIGINAL STRATEGY WAS VERY MUCH LIKE THE STRATEGY USED TO SOLVE THE QUESTION OF THE PREVIOUS *Example* 7.

8.   (D)

Choose extreme values for a or b. Let $a = 1000$. If $a = 1000$, since $a + b = 10$, then $b = -990$. *Column A becomes*

$$\frac{1}{a} + \frac{1}{b} = \frac{1}{1000} - \frac{1}{990} < 0.$$

Now choose $a = 1$. Since $a + b = 10$, b then is 9. *Column A* now becomes

$$\frac{1}{a} + \frac{1}{b} = \frac{1}{1} + \frac{1}{9} = 1\frac{1}{9}$$

For the first case *Column B* $\left(\frac{1}{10}\right)$ > *Column A* (less than 0) and for the second case *Column B* $\left(\frac{1}{10}\right)$ < *Column A* $\left(1\frac{1}{9}\right)$. Thus a definite comparison cannot be made and Choice D is correct. NOTICE HOW THE METHOD USED TO SOLVE THIS QUESTION IS VERY SIMILAR TO THE METHOD USED TO SOLVE THE QUESTION OF *Example* 8 seen previously.

GENERAL METHOD WHICH WORKS FOR MANY ALGEBRAIC QUANTITATIVE COMPARISON QUESTIONS

If you have a quantitative comparison question which involves variables like x, y, xy, xy^2, a, b, etc. choose a simple number for each variable, like $x = 0$ or $x = 1$. Usually the best numbers to choose are 0, -1, $+1$, -2 or $+2$. Now, if for one choice of the variable (variables) you find that there is a particular relationship of the columns (like Column A > Column B), and for another choice of the variable (variables) you find that there is a *different* relationship of the columns (like Column A < Column B or Column A = Column B) then you know that a definite comparison cannot be made and so Choice D is correct. Here's an example:

Column A	Column B
$5x^3 + 4x$	$x^2 + 6$

SOLUTION: Let $x = 0$. Then Column A becomes $5(0)^3 + 4(0) = 0$ and Column B becomes $0^2 + 6 = 6$. Thus for this case, that is, for $x = 0$, we have that *Column B (6) is greater than Column A (0)*.

Now let $x = 1$. Column A becomes $5(1)^3 + 4(1) = 9$ and Column B becomes $(1)^2 + 6 = 7$. We now have that *Column B is less than Column A*. Therefore, we cannot get a definite relationship between the columns (in one case Column A is greater than Column B and in another case Column A is less than Column B). Therefore, Choice D is correct.

For a more sophisticated version of this method, refer to the schematic on the following page, although it is not necessary for you to do this.

Following is a schematic chart which you may want to use when you encounter quantitative comparison type questions dealing with algebraic variables:

SCHEMATIC

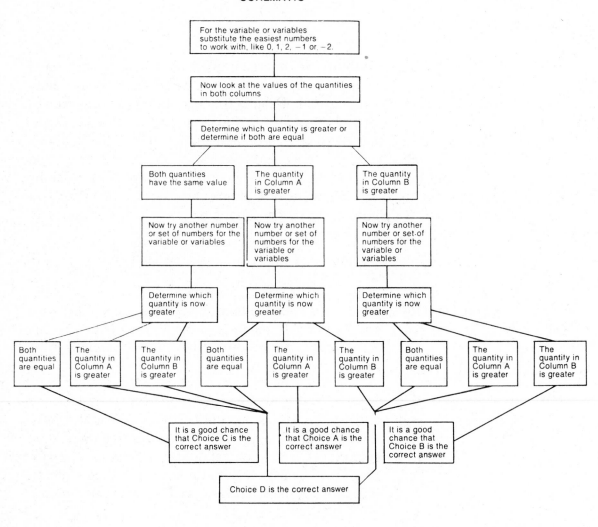

Example using the schematic:

Column A	**Column B**
$5x^3 + 4x$	$x^2 + 6$

Follow the schematic:
1. Substitute an easy number like $x = 0$ for the quantities in Columns A and B.
2. The value of the quantity in Column A becomes $5(0) + 4(0) = 0$ and the value of the quantity in Column B becomes $0 + 6 = 6$.
3. Determining which quantity is greater, we find that the quantity in Column B is greater because $6 > 0$.
4. Now, following the schematic, we try another number in place of x: Let's try $x = +1$. Column A becomes $5(1) + 4(1) = 9$ and Column B becomes $1 + 6 = 7$.
5. Again determining which quantity is greater, we find that the quantity in Column A is now greater than the quantity in Column B since $9 > 7$.
6. According to the schematic, the arrow indicates that Choice D is the correct answer.

part VII

80 ADDITIONAL QUANTITATIVE COMPARISON PRACTICE QUESTIONS

Tear out the answer sheet for this section at the end of the book.

80 QUANTITATIVE COMPARISON QUESTIONS

Directions: This section requires you to compare two quantities—the quantity in Column A and the quantity in Column B. After you have compared the two quantities, select

    (A) if the quantity in Column A is greater than the quantity in Column B;

    (B) if the quantity in Column B is greater than the quantity in Column A;

    (C) if the quantities in the two columns are equal;

    (D) if the information is not sufficient to make a valid comparison.

Any information that appears in a central position above the two quantities to be compared refers to both quantities.

Column A	**Column B**

$$x^2 + x = 6$$
$$y^2 + 16 = 8y$$

1. x y

---

2. The average number of hours worked per day by a man who, during one week, worked 2 hours and 20 minutes for the first 3 days, 2 hours and 30 minutes for the next 3 days, and 3 hours and 15 minutes for the last day $2\frac{1}{2}$ hours

---

$$19 = \sqrt{x} + 2$$

3. x 256

Questions 4–5 refer to this diagram.

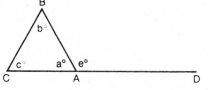

AB = BC

4. $180° - c° - b°$ $e°$

---

5. $180° - e°$ $c°$

> (A) if the quantity in Column A is greater than the quantity in Column B
> (B) if the quantity in Column B is greater than the quantity in Column A
> (C) if the quantities in the two columns are equal
> (D) if the information is not sufficient to make a valid comparison

6. $3^{-2} + 2^{-3}$ $4^{-2} + 2^{-4}$

$$\frac{a}{b} = \frac{c}{d}$$

7. $\dfrac{bc}{ad}$ $\dfrac{ad}{bc}$

Questions 8–10 refer to this graph.

WHO GROWS COTTON
1972 WORLD PRODUCTION—58.6 MILLION BALES

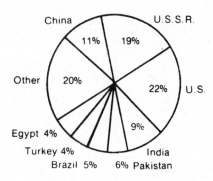

8. The difference in production between the two largest individual cotton producers | The difference in production between the third and fourth largest individual cotton producers

9. The smallest number of countries that add up to over half of the world production   4

> (A) if the quantity in Column A is greater than the quantity in Column B
> (B) if the quantity in Column B is greater than the quantity in Column A
> (C) if the quantities in the two columns are equal
> (D) if the information is not sufficient to make a valid comparison

10. The total number of bales of cotton produced by countries that are not individually listed   12 million

$$x < -1$$

11. $x^5 - x^3$ $x^4 - x^2$

12. $\dfrac{\frac{1}{2}}{\frac{3}{4}}$ $\dfrac{\frac{4}{3}}{\frac{2}{1}}$

Questions 13–14 refer to this diagram.

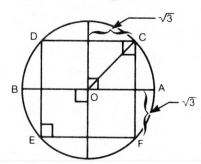

13.   Diameter of the circle $2\sqrt{5}$

14. Area of the large square CDEF   12 square units

15. $x^4 - 4$ $(x^2 + 2)\,(x + \sqrt{2})\,(x - \sqrt{2})$

$$6x - 3 \leq 4$$

16. x 1

17.   2% of 5% of 300   3% of 1

> (A) if the quantity in Column A is greater than the quantity in Column B
> (B) if the quantity in Column B is greater than the quantity in Column A
> (C) if the quantities in the two columns are equal
> (D) if the information is not sufficient to make a valid comparison

Column A	**Column B**

$$7x + 4y - 6 = 75$$
$$4x - y - 10 = 10$$

18. x y

19. $4\sqrt{13}$ $\sqrt{2^8}$

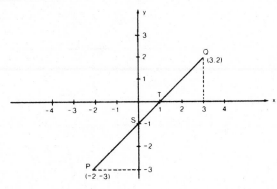

20. length of PQ $2\sqrt{8}$

n is an odd integer

21. $(-1)^n$ $(-1)^{n+1}$

22. $\dfrac{\sqrt[3]{8}}{2^{-3}}$ $\sqrt{256}$

23. $x^3 - 2x^2 - 5x + 6$ $(x - 1)(x + 2)(x - 3)$

$x > z > 1$

24. $x^2 - y^2 - z^2$ 0

$x \geqq 0$

25. $\dfrac{x}{2}$ $\dfrac{x}{3}$

(A) if the quantity in Column A is greater than the quantity in Column B
(B) if the quantity in Column B is greater than the quantity in Column A
(C) if the quantities in the two columns are equal
(D) if the information is not sufficient to make a valid comparison

Column A	Column B

$$x > 0$$

26. The average of
$x + 2, x + 9, x + 11$ $x + 7$

---

27. The least common denominator of $\dfrac{\sqrt{3}}{3}$ and $\dfrac{2\sqrt{2}}{5}$ The least common denominator of $\dfrac{\sqrt{2}}{4}$ and $\dfrac{1}{6}$

$$x \neq y$$

28. $\dfrac{x^6 - y^6}{y^3 - x^3}$ $0 - (x^3 + y^3)$

> (A) if the quantity in Column A is greater than the quantity in Column B
> (B) if the quantity in Column B is greater than the quantity in Column A
> (C) if the quantities in the two columns are equal
> (D) if the information is not sufficient to make a valid comparison

Questions 29–32 refer to this graph.

PARTICIPANTS IN FAVORITE AMERICAN PASTIMES

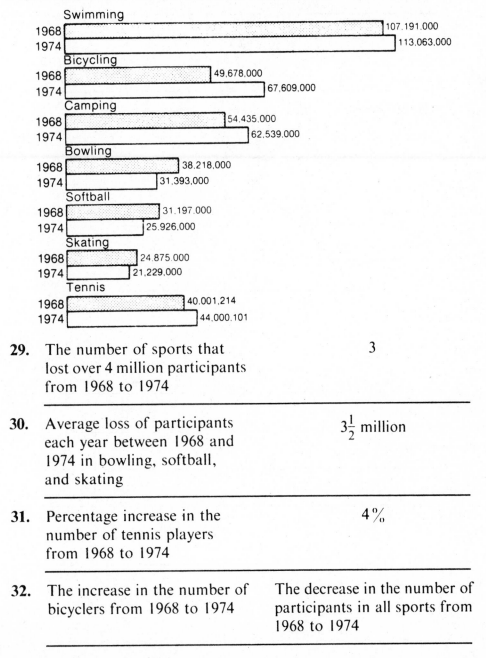

Swimming
1968   107,191,000
1974   113,063,000

Bicycling
1968   49,678,000
1974   67,609,000

Camping
1968   54,435,000
1974   62,539,000

Bowling
1968   38,218,000
1974   31,393,000

Softball
1968   31,197,000
1974   25,926,000

Skating
1968   24,875,000
1974   21,229,000

Tennis
1968   40,001,214
1974   44,000,101

29. The number of sports that lost over 4 million participants from 1968 to 1974   3

30. Average loss of participants each year between 1968 and 1974 in bowling, softball, and skating $3\frac{1}{2}$ million

31. Percentage increase in the number of tennis players from 1968 to 1974   4%

32. The increase in the number of bicyclers from 1968 to 1974   The decrease in the number of participants in all sports from 1968 to 1974

> (A) if the quantity in Column A is greater than the quantity in Column B
> (B) if the quantity in Column B is greater than the quantity in Column A
> (C) if the quantities in the two columns are equal
> (D) if the information is not sufficient to make a valid comparison

Column A	**Column B**

33. $2 - (x^n + x^{n+1})$ $2 - (x + 1)^{n+1}$

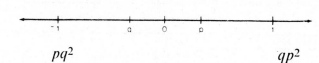

34. pq^2 qp^2

Questions 35–36 refer to this diagram.

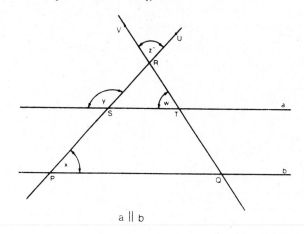

a ∥ b

35. $w^\circ + x^\circ + z^\circ$ 180°

36. $x^\circ - w^\circ$ 0°

37. $(x + y)(x - y) - 1$ $x^2 - y^2 + 1$

38. $7 - [6 - (-4)]$ $7 + [-6 - (-4)]$

39. $\dfrac{7}{x}$ $0 - x$

40.   The greatest integer smaller than $\dfrac{\sqrt{8}}{2}$ $\dfrac{2^4 \sqrt{256}}{256}$

(A) if the quantity in Column A is greater than the quantity in Column B
(B) if the quantity in Column B is greater than the quantity in Column A
(C) if the quantities in the two columns are equal
(D) if the information is not sufficient to make a valid comparison

Column A	Column B

$$x = 2$$

41. $\left((-x)^x + x\right)^x$ — $2(x^{2x}) + x^x$

42. $\dfrac{\sqrt{48}}{\sqrt{3}}$ — $4\sqrt{3}$

$$k^2 - 8k + 12 = 0$$
$$x^2 - 6x + 9 = 0$$

43. k — x

Questions 44–46 refer to the diagram below.

Equilateral triangle ABC is inscribed in a circle.
DC = 5, DB = 3

44. $\angle BDA$ — $\angle CDA$

45. 15 — Circumference of circle

46. AB — 6

$$b \neq 1$$

47. The average of $(b - 1)$, $(b - 2)$, and $(b + 6)$ — $\dfrac{b^2 - 1}{b - 1}$

48. $(81)^{\frac{1}{4}}$ — $(1/27)^{-\frac{1}{2}}$

(A) if the quantity in Column A is greater than the quantity in Column B
(B) if the quantity in Column B is greater than the quantity in Column A
(C) if the quantities in the two columns are equal
(D) if the information is not sufficient to make a valid comparison

$$\frac{18}{\sqrt{x}}(\sqrt{3}) = 20$$

49.   3 x

For all real numbers x,
$f(x) = 4x^2 - 6x + 3,$
and $g(x) = 4^x + 2x$

50. $f[g(-\frac{1}{2})]$ 8

Bag A has 3 green balls and 3 blue balls
Bag B has 4 red balls and 1 orange ball

51. The probability of picking 2 green balls from Bag A   The probability of picking an orange ball from Bag B

52. $a + 5$ $5 - a$

$y \neq x$

53. $\dfrac{x^2 - 2xy + y^2}{y - x}$ $y - x$

54. $(2a)^2 - 1$ $a^2 - 2$

(A) if the quantity in Column A is greater than the quantity in Column B
(B) if the quantity in Column B is greater than the quantity in Column A
(C) if the quantities in the two columns are equal
(D) if the information is not sufficient to make a valid comparison

Questions 55–57 refer to the chart below.

CALORIES AND MINERALS OF COMMON FRUITS

Fruit	Calories	Protein (gm.)	Calcium (mg.)	Iron (mg.)
Apple	70	—	8	.4
Banana	100	1	10	.8
Lemon	20	1	19	.4
Orange	65	1	54	.5
Peach	35	1	19	.5
Canteloupe (half)	60	1	27	.8
Grapefruit (half)	45	1	19	.5

55. The number of calories in 3 peaches, 2 oranges, and one apple

300

56. The calcium in one cantaloupe (entire melon)

The calcium in an orange

57. The difference in calories between the two fruits with the most calcium content

The difference in calories between the two fruits with the most iron content

58. The number of prime numbers between 80 and 100

The number of prime numbers between 10 and 20

(A) if the quantity in Column A is greater than the quantity in Column B
(B) if the quantity in Column B is greater than the quantity in Column A
(C) if the quantities in the two columns are equal
(D) if the information is not sufficient to make a valid comparison

All angles are right angles

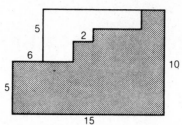

59.   50   Perimeter of shaded area

$$1 > a \geq b \geq -1; a \neq 0; b \neq 0$$

60.   1 $\dfrac{(ab)^2}{ab}$

The price of a bicycle has been raised 15% from the original list price so that it now costs $87

61. The original list price of the $80
bicycle

$$\frac{\text{Bob's salary}}{\text{Jim's salary}} = \frac{\text{Jim's salary}}{\text{Bill's salary}}$$

Bob earns $400 in a thirty-day month
Bill earns $30 a day

62. In a thirty-day month, the $640
average of Bob's, Jim's, and
Bill's salaries

(A) if the quantity in Column A is greater than the
     quantity in Column B
(B) if the quantity in Column B is greater than the
     quantity in Column A
(C) if the quantities in the two columns are equal
(D) if the information is not sufficient to make a
     valid comparison

Questions 63–64 refer to the diagram below.

AB is a diameter of Circle O
DC is a diameter of Circle P
AB = 12 = DC
Circle O is tangent to Circle P
Lines AD and BC are tangent to Circles O and P

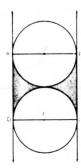

63.   Length of AC   17
_____

64.   36   Area of shaded area
_____

$$m = 8\sqrt{3}$$

$$n = 4\frac{\sqrt{3}}{3}$$

65. $\dfrac{n}{m}$ .16
_____

66. The amount of time it takes   7 seconds
        for a car traveling 50 mph to
        travel 1/10 of a mile
_____

$a - 4$, $b - 4$, and $c - 4$ are consecutive even integers
with $a - 4 > b - 4 > c - 4$ and $a - 4 < 2$

67.   3   The average of a, b, and c
_____

68. $\dfrac{3\sqrt{3} + 6}{2\sqrt{3} + 4}$ $\dfrac{3}{2}$
_____

(A) if the quantity in Column A is greater than the quantity in Column B
(B) if the quantity in Column B is greater than the quantity in Column A
(C) if the quantities in the two columns are equal
(D) if the information is not sufficient to make a valid comparison

$$a > 0$$

$$\frac{a^2 - b}{c} - d = e$$

69. a $(cd + b + ce)^{\frac{1}{2}}$

Line AB passes through the origin

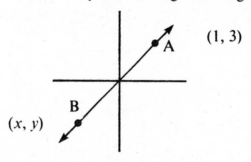

(1, 3)

(x, y)

70. x y

E, F, and G are midpoints of AB, BC, and AD, respectively. H has the coordinates (j, k) and is at the intersection of line segments AF and EG.

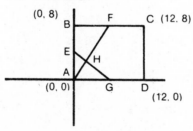

71. $j + k$ 5

72. The remainder when $5^{12} - 1$ is divided by 7   2

$$z = 0$$
$$10^y = x$$
$$10^z = y$$

73. x $(x - 10)^x$

(A) if the quantity in Column A is greater than the quantity in Column B
(B) if the quantity in Column B is greater than the quantity in Column A
(C) if the quantities in the two columns are equal
(D) if the information is not sufficient to make a valid comparison

---

Questions 74–77 refer to the graph below.

RETAIL SALES BY KIND OF BUSINESS GROUP

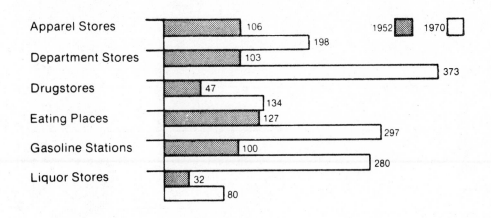

	Column A	Column B
74.	Percent increase in the group with the smallest increase in sales from 1952 to 1970	150%
75.	The average of the sales of Department Stores and Drug Stores in 1970	The average of the sales of Eating Places and Gasoline Stations in 1970
76.	2,500,000,000	The difference between the amount of sales of Apparel Stores in 1952 and the amount of sales of Liquor Stores in 1970
77.	The greatest increase of any group from 1952 to 1970	The least increase of any group from 1952 to 1970 × 6

(A) if the quantity in Column A is greater than the quantity in Column B
(B) if the quantity in Column B is greater than the quantity in Column A
(C) if the quantities in the two columns are equal
(D) if the information is not sufficient to make a valid comparison

Each number from 1 to 10 is represented by one and only one letter

$$
\begin{array}{r}
ab \\
\times\ c \\
\hline
dde
\end{array}
$$

$$c = 4;\ e = 6$$

78. a $\qquad$ 8

79. $a^2 - b^2$ $\qquad$ $(a - b)^2$

$$x = -2$$

80. $3x^3 - 6x^2 + 2x + 38$ $\qquad$ $\dfrac{\dfrac{\dfrac{8}{x} - 2}{x} + 13}{x} - 7$

EXPLANATORY ANSWERS

1. **(B)**
   $x^2 + x = 6$ can be written as
   $x^2 + x - 6 = 0$
   $x^2 + x - 6 = (x + 3)(x - 2) = 0$
   So, $x = -3$ or $x = 2$
   $y^2 + 16 = 8y$ can be rewritten as
   $y^2 + 16 - 8y = 0$
   $y^2 - 8y + 16 = (y - 4)(y - 4)$
   So, $y = 4$

2. **(A)**
   2 hours and 20 minutes $= 2\frac{1}{3}$ hours

   2 hours and 30 minutes $= 2\frac{1}{2}$ hours

   3 hours and 15 minutes $= 3\frac{1}{4}$ hours

   $\left(3 \times 2\frac{1}{3}\right) + \left(3 \times 2\frac{1}{2}\right) + 3\frac{1}{4} = 17\frac{3}{4}$

   Dividing $17\frac{3}{4}$ by 7, we get $2\frac{15}{28}$, which is greater than $2\frac{1}{2}$

3. **(A)**
   $19 = \sqrt{x} + 2$
   Therefore, $\sqrt{x} = 17$ and $x = 289$

4. **(B)**
   $c° + b° + a° = 180°$ since the sum of the angles of a triangle is $180°$.

   Therefore, $180° - c° - b° = a°$
   $a° < e°$

5. **(C)**
   Since this triangle is isosceles, $a° = c°$
   $180° - e° = a°$, so $180° - e° = c°$

6. **(A)**
   $3^{-2} + 2^{-3} = \dfrac{1}{3^2} + \dfrac{1}{2^3} = \dfrac{1}{9} + \dfrac{1}{8} = \dfrac{8}{72} + \dfrac{9}{72} = \dfrac{17}{72}$

   $4^{-2} + 2^{-4} = \dfrac{1}{4^2} + \dfrac{1}{2^4} = \dfrac{1}{16} + \dfrac{1}{16} = \dfrac{2}{16} = \dfrac{1}{8} = \dfrac{9}{72}$

7. **(C)**
    Since $bc = ad$, both are equal to 1 and to each other.

8. **(A)**
    The U.S. is the largest producer and the U.S.S.R. is second
    $22\% - 19\% = 3\%$

    Next largest are China and India
    $11\% - 9\% = 2\%$

9. **(B)**
    The U.S. produces 22%, the U.S.S.R. produces 19%, and China produces 11%. They total to 3 countries and 52%, which is over $\frac{1}{2}$.

10. **(B)**
    The countries not listed are indicated as "other." 20% of 58.6 million bales $= .2 \times 58.6 = 11.72$. This is less than 12.

'11. **(B)**
    x^5 and x^3 are both negative when $x < -1$. x^4 and x^2 are both positive and $x^4 > x^2$ when $x < -1$. So, $x^5 - x^3 < x^4 - x^2$ since $x^5 - x^3$ is negative and $x^4 - x^2$ is positive.

12. **(C)**
    $$\frac{\frac{1}{2}}{\frac{3}{4}} = \frac{4}{3} \cdot \frac{1}{2} = \frac{2}{3}$$

    $$\frac{\frac{4}{3}}{\frac{2}{1}} = \frac{1}{2} \cdot \frac{4}{3} = \frac{2}{3}$$

13. **(A)**
    The diameter is twice the length of line CO. By the Pythagorean Theorem, $CO^2 = \sqrt{3}^2 + \sqrt{3}^2 = 6$. Therefore, $CO = \sqrt{6}$. The diameter is equal to $2\sqrt{6}$, which is greater than $2\sqrt{5}$.

14. **(C)**
    The length of one side of the square is $2\sqrt{3}$. The area is $(2\sqrt{3})(2\sqrt{3}) = 4 \cdot 3 = 12$.

15. **(C)**
    $x^4 - 4 = (x^2 + 2)(x^2 - 2) = (x^2 + 2)(x + \sqrt{2})(x - \sqrt{2})$

16. **(D)**

If $x = \frac{7}{6}$, $6x - 3 \leq 4$ is satisfied. If $x = 1$, the relation $6x - 3 \leq 4$ is also satisfied. Thus, the relationship cannot be determined.

17. **(A)**

$.02 \times .05 \times 300 = .3$

$.03 \times 1 = .03$

18. **(B)**

$7x + 4y - 6 = 75$

$4x - y - 10 = 10$

$\qquad 4x - y = 20$

$\qquad 4x = 20 + y$

$\qquad x = \dfrac{20 + y}{4}$

Substituting into the first equation,

$7\left(\dfrac{20 + y}{4}\right) + 4y = 81$

So, $y = 8$

$x = \dfrac{20 + 8}{4} = 7$

19. **(B)**

$4\sqrt{13} = \sqrt{4^2 \cdot 13} = \sqrt{16 \cdot 13} = \sqrt{208}$

$\sqrt{2^8} = 2^4 = 16$

Since $16 = \sqrt{256}$, $16 > \sqrt{208}$

20. **(A)**

$PS = \sqrt{2^2 + 2^2} = \sqrt{8}$ by the Pythagorean Theorem, which states that for any right triangle, the length of the hypotenuse squared equals the sum of the legs of the triangle, each squared.

$ST = \sqrt{2}$

$QT = \sqrt{8}$

$PQ = 2\sqrt{8} + \sqrt{2}$

21. **(B)**

When -1 is raised to an odd power, it equals -1. When it is raised to an even power, it equals 1. n is odd and $n + 1$ is even.

22. (C)

$$\frac{\sqrt[3]{8}}{2^{-3}} = \frac{\frac{2}{1}}{\frac{1}{2^3}} = \frac{\frac{2}{1}}{\frac{1}{8}} = 16$$

$$\sqrt{256} = 16$$

23. (C)

$(x - 1)(x + 2)(x - 3) = (x^2 + x - 2)(x - 3) =$
$x^3 - 2x^2 - 5x + 6$

24. (D)

If $y^2 > x^2 - z^2$, then $x^2 - y^2 - z^2 < 0$
If $y^2 < x^2 - z^2$, then $x^2 - y^2 - z^2 > 0$
Thus, the relationship cannot be determined.

25. (D)

If $x = \frac{1}{2}$, $\frac{\frac{1}{2}}{2} = \frac{1}{4}$ and $\frac{\frac{1}{2}}{3} = \frac{1}{6}$

But if $x = 0$, $\frac{x}{2} = \frac{x}{3} = 0$

Thus, the relationship cannot be determined.

26. (A)

$$\frac{x + 2 + x + 9 + x + 11}{3} = \frac{3x + 22}{3} = x + \frac{22}{3}$$

$$x + \frac{22}{3} > x + \frac{21}{3}$$

27. (A)

The least common denominator of $\frac{\sqrt{3}}{3}$ and $\frac{2\sqrt{2}}{5}$ is the smallest number that is exactly divisible by both the denominators 3 and 5. This number is 15. The least common denominator of $\frac{\sqrt{2}}{4}$ and $\frac{1}{6}$ is the smallest number that is exactly divisible by both the denominators 4 and 6. This number is 12.

28. (C)

$$\frac{x^6 - y^6}{y^3 - x^3} = \frac{(x^3 + y^3)(x^3 - y^3)}{y^3 - x^3} = -x^3 - y^3$$

$$0 - (x^3 + y^3) = -x^3 - y^3$$

29. (B)
Only in bowling, softball, and skating did the number of participants decline from 1968 to 1974. In skating, the decline was only $3\frac{1}{2}$ million, approximately.

30. (B)
Here we can estimate. For bowling, 38 million − 31 million = 7 million. For softball, 31 million − 26 million = 5 million. For skating, 25 million − 21 million = 4 million.

$$\frac{7 + 5 + 4}{6} = \frac{16}{6} = 2\frac{2}{3} \text{ million}$$

31. (A)
The percentage increase is the increase in the number of participants expressed as a percentage of the number.

44 million − 40 million = 4 million

$$\frac{40 \text{ million}}{4 \text{ million}} = \frac{1}{10}$$

This means that the percentage increase is approximately 10%.

32. (A)
We can estimate. The increase in the number of bicyclers was about 18 million. The number of participants decreased only in softball, bowling, and skating. This total decrease was about $15\frac{1}{2}$ million.

33. (D)
If $n = 0$ and $x = 1$, then $2 - (x^n + x^{n+1}) = 0$ and $2 - (x + 1)^{n+1} = 0$
But if $n = 1$ and $x = 0$, then $2 - (x^n + x^{n+1}) = 2$ and $2 - (x + 1)^{n+1} = 1$
Therefore, the relationship cannot be determined.

34. (A)
Since any non-zero number squared is always positive, q^2 is positive as is p^2. Since p is positive, pq^2 is positive. Since q is negative, qp^2 is negative. Thus, $pq^2 > qp^2$.

35. (C)
$<$QPR $= <$TSR since corresponding angles are equal. $<$URV $= <$TRS since vertical angles are equal. So the sum of $w°$, $x°$ and $z°$ is the sum of the angles in this triangle, which is $180°$.

36. (D)
Since we have no way of knowing if $x° = w°$, we cannot determine this relationship.

37. (B)
Since $(x + y)(x - y) = x^2 - y^2$,
$(x + y)(x - y) - 1 < x^2 - y^2 + 1$

38. (B)
$7 - [6 - (-4)] = 7 - (6 + 4) = 7 - 10 = -3$
$7 + [-6 - (-4)] = 7 + (-6 + 4) =$
$7 + (-2) = 7 - 2 = 5$

39. (D)
If x is positive, $\dfrac{7}{x} > 0 - x$

But if x is negative, $\dfrac{7}{x} < 0 - x$

Thus, the relationship cannot be determined.

40. (C)
$\dfrac{\sqrt{8}}{2}$ is approximately equal to $\dfrac{2.8}{2}$, which is 1.4. The greatest integer smaller than 1.4 is 1.
$$\dfrac{2^4 \sqrt{256}}{256} = \dfrac{16 \cdot 16}{256} = \dfrac{256}{256} = 1$$

41. (C)
Substituting 2 for x in Column A, we get $(4 + 2)^2$, or 36. In Column B, we get $2(16) + 4$, or 36.

42. (B)
$$\dfrac{\sqrt{48}}{\sqrt{3}} = \dfrac{\sqrt{16}\sqrt{3}}{\sqrt{3}} = \dfrac{4\sqrt{3}}{\sqrt{3}} = 4$$
4 is less than $4\sqrt{3}$

43. (D)
$k^2 - 8k + 12 = (k - 6)(k - 2) = 0$
Therefore, $k = 6$ or 2
$x^2 - 6x + 9 = (x - 3)(x - 3) = 0$
Therefore, $x = (3)$

Consequently, it is impossible to tell whether k or x is greater.

44. (C)

Since angles ABC and ACB are congruent, then minor arcs AB and AC are also congruent. Therefore, angles BDA and CDA are congruent because they are inscribed angles that intercept congruent arcs.

45. (B)

If the diameter of the circle were 5, then the circumference of the circle would be 5π, or $15+$. But the diameter of the circle is greater than 5. Therefore, the circumference is greater than 15.

46. (A)

The law of cosines is used in triangle BDC. We get:

$(BC)^2 = 5^2 + 3^2 - 2(5)(3)(\cos 120°)$

$(BC)^2 = 34 - (30)(-.5)$

$(BC)^2 = 34 + 15 = 49$

$BC = 7$

47. (C)

$$\frac{(b-1) + (b-2) + (b+6)}{3} = \frac{3b+3}{3} = b+1$$

$$\frac{b^2-1}{b-1} = \frac{(b-1)(b+1)}{b-1} = b+1$$

48. (B)

$81^{\frac{1}{3}}$ is equal to $(27 \times 3)^{\frac{1}{3}}$, or $(3)3^{\frac{1}{3}}$. $(1/27)^{-\frac{1}{2}}$ is equal to $(27)^{\frac{1}{2}}$, or $3\sqrt{3}$. The square root of 3 is greater than the cube root of 3. Therefore, the value in Column B is greater than the value in Column A.

49. (A)

Solving for x, we get:

$18\sqrt{3} = 20\sqrt{x}$

When both sides are squared the result is:

$324(3) = 400x$

400 is divided into both sides, leaving $x = 2.43$.

50. (B)

$$g\left(-\frac{1}{2}\right) = 4^{-\frac{1}{2}} + 2\left(-\frac{1}{2}\right) = \frac{1}{2} - 1 = -\frac{1}{2}$$

$$f\left(-\frac{1}{2}\right) = 4\left(-\frac{1}{2}\right)^2 - 6\left(-\frac{1}{2}\right) + 3 = 4\left(\frac{1}{4}\right) + 3 + 3 = 7$$

51. (C)

The probability of choosing two green balls from Bag A is equal to the probability of picking the first green ball times the probability of picking the second green ball. In this case:

$$\frac{3}{6} \times \frac{2}{5} = \frac{1}{5}$$

The probability of picking the orange ball from Bag B is also $\frac{1}{5}$.

52. (D)

If a is positive,

$a + 5 > 5 - a$

But if a is negative,

$5 - a > a + 5$

Thus, the relationship cannot be determined.

53. (C)

The numerator of the fraction in Column A can be factored to $(x - y)(x - y)$. Then we multiply both the numerator and denominator of the fraction by -1. This gives us:

$$\frac{-1(x - y)(x - y)}{-1(y - x)} \text{ or } \frac{-1(x - y)(x - y)}{x - y}$$

This reduces to $-1(x - y)$, which is equal to $y - x$.

54. (A)

If $a \geq 1$ or $a \leq -1$, then $(2a)^2$ represents a greater value than a^2. The 2 subtracted from the a^2 only makes the difference between the greater value in Column A and the lesser value in Column B greater. If $-1 < a < 1$, then $(2a)^2$ is less than a^2. However, this difference is less than 1. When 1 is subtracted from $(2a)^2$ and 2 is subtracted from a^2, Column A is again greater than Column B.

55. (A)

$3(35) + 2(65) + 70 = 105 + 130 + 70 = 305$

56. (C)

One cantaloupe (entire melon) has 54 mg. of calcium. An orange has the same amount.

57. (B)

The two fruits with the most calcium are the orange and the cantaloupe (half). The difference in calories between them is 5.

    The banana and the cantaloupe (half) have the most iron content. The difference in calories between them is 40.

58. (B)
The only prime numbers between 80 and 100 are 83, 89, and 97. Between 10 and 20 there are four prime numbers—11, 13, 17, and 19.

59. (C)
All the lines going horizontally in the shaded figure add up to 30. Also, the lines going vertically add up to 20.

60. (D)
The value in Column B can be reduced to ab. This product can be equal to 1 if both a and b are -1. In all other cases, ab is less than 1. Therefore, it is impossible to tell which column has the greater value.

61. (B)
If we represent the original list price as x, we can set up the proportion:

$$\frac{115}{100} = \frac{87}{x}$$

Solving for x, the original list price of the bicycle is approximately $75.65.

62. (B)
Since Bob earns $400 in thirty days and Bill earns $900 in the same time period, it is possible, using the given proportion, to find out Jim's salary. Substituting the known values in the equation, we get:

$$\frac{\$400}{x} = \frac{x}{\$900}$$

Cross-multiplying, we now have the equation $360{,}000 = x^2$. When it is solved, $x = \$600$. The average of the three men's salaries is:

$$\frac{400 + 600 + 900}{3} \text{ or } \$633\tfrac{1}{3}$$

63. (B)
The length of AC can be found out because it is the hypotenuse of triangle ABC. Since OP equals the radius of Circle O plus the radius of Circle P and OP is congruent to BC, then BC $= 12$. Therefore:

$(AC)^2 = 12^2 + 12^2$
$(AC)^2 = 144 + 144$
$(AC)^2 = 288$
$AC = \sqrt{288}$

Since 17 equals $\sqrt{289}$, the value in Column B is greater.

64. **(A)**

Area of shaded area = Area of ABCD $- \frac{1}{2}$ area of Circle O $-$ $\frac{1}{2}$ area of Circle P.

$A = 144 - 18\pi - 18\pi$

If π were 3, then the area would be equal to 36. However, π is greater than 3 and the area is less than 36.

65. **(A)**

$$\frac{n}{m} = \frac{4\sqrt{3}}{3(8\sqrt{3})}$$

By reducing, we get $\dfrac{n}{m} = \dfrac{1}{6}$

$\dfrac{1}{6} = .166$

66. **(A)**

If a car is traveling 50 mph, it travels 5/6 of a mile in one minute. We can set up the following proportion:

$$\frac{5/6 \text{ mile}}{60 \text{ sec.}} = \frac{1/10 \text{ mile}}{x}$$

Cross-multiplying, we get

$(5/6)x = 6$ sec.

$x = 7.2$ sec.

67. **(A)**

Since $a - 4 < 2$, then $a < 6$. This means that the greatest possible values of a, b, and c are 4, 2, and 0, respectively. Therefore, the greatest average of a, b, and c is 2.

68. **(C)**

In Column A, multiply both the top and bottom of $2\sqrt{3} - 4$. We get:

$$\frac{6(3) - 24}{4(3) - 16} = \frac{18 - 24}{12 - 16} = \frac{-6}{-4} = \frac{3}{2}$$

69. **(C)**

Solving for a:

$a^2 - b - cd = ce$

$a^2 - b = cd + ce$

$a^2 = cd + ce + b$

$a = \sqrt{cd + ce + b}$

70. **(A)**
Point y is at a greater distance from the origin. However, since both x and y are negative, x is greater.

71. **(B)**
The coordinates of points E, F, and G are (0,4), (6,8), and (6,0), respectively. We can find out the numerical coordinates of point H because this point must fit on both AF and EG. The slope of AF is equal to:

$$\frac{8-0}{6-0} \text{ or } \frac{8}{6} \text{ or } \frac{4}{3}$$

The slope of EG is:

$$\frac{4-0}{0-6} \text{ or } \frac{4}{-6} \text{ or } -\frac{2}{3}$$

Therefore, we have these two equations

$$\frac{-2}{3} = \frac{4-k}{0-j} \text{ and } \frac{4}{3} = \frac{8-k}{6-j}$$

After solving simultaneously:

$$(j,k) = \left(2, \frac{8}{3}\right)$$

$$2 + \frac{8}{3} = \frac{14}{3} = 4\frac{2}{3}$$

72. **(B)**
$5^{12} - 1$ can be factored to
$(5^6 + 1)(5^3 + 1)(5^3 - 1)$

Now $5^3 + 1 = 126$ and 126 can be divided into evenly by 7. Because $5^3 + 1$ is a factor of $5^{12} - 1$, then $5^{12} - 1$ divided by 7 leaves no remainder.

73. **(A)**
Since z is equal to 0, then y is equal to 1. Similarly, since y equals 1, then x is equal to 10. In Column B, $(10 - 10)^{10} = 0$.

74. **(C)**
The group with the smallest increase in sales is the Liquor Stores. Their percent increase is 48/32, or 150%.

75. **(B)**
The average of the two groups in Column A is 253.5.

The average of the two groups in Column B is 288.5.

76. (B)
The difference in Column B is 106 — 80 hundred million dollars, or 2,600,000,000.

77. (B)
The greatest increase from 1952 to 1970 occurs in the Department Store group. The increase is $270 hundred million. The group with the least increase in the same time period is the Liquor Store group, which has an increase of $48 hundred million. Multiplied by 6, the product is $288 hundred million.

78. (B)
Since b times 4 has 6 as a units digit, b must either be 9 or 4. However, 4 is already represented by c, so b has to be 9. Multiplying, 9 times 4 is equal to 36, so 3 is the number carried in the multiplication of $a \times c$. Therefore, $4a + 3 = dd$. Then $dd - 3$ must be a multiple of 4. Consequently, $dd = 11$ and $a = 2$.

79. (D)
If $b > a$, then $a^2 - b^2 < 0$ and $(a - b)^2 > 0$
But if $b = 0$, $a^2 - b^2 = (a - b)^2$
Thus, the relationship cannot be determined.

80. (A)
Substituting in Column A, we get $3(-8) - 6(4) + 2(-2) + 38$
$= -24 - 24 - 4 + 38 = -52 + 38 = -14$

Substituting in Column B, we get

$$\frac{\frac{-4-2}{-2} + 13}{-2} - 7 = \frac{16}{-2} - 7 = -15$$

ANSWER SHEET FOR PRACTICE TEST 1

Note that 5 answer spaces are provided throughout this Answer Sheet. However, questions in some sections of the Practice Test will have only 4 possible answers (A or B or C or D).

SECTION 1:
Mathematics
Questions

1 Ⓐ Ⓑ Ⓒ Ⓓ Ⓔ
2 Ⓐ Ⓑ Ⓒ Ⓓ Ⓔ
3 Ⓐ Ⓑ Ⓒ Ⓓ Ⓔ
4 Ⓐ Ⓑ Ⓒ Ⓓ Ⓔ
5 Ⓐ Ⓑ Ⓒ Ⓓ Ⓔ
6 Ⓐ Ⓑ Ⓒ Ⓓ Ⓔ
7 Ⓐ Ⓑ Ⓒ Ⓓ Ⓔ
8 Ⓐ Ⓑ Ⓒ Ⓓ Ⓔ
9 Ⓐ Ⓑ Ⓒ Ⓓ Ⓔ
10 Ⓐ Ⓑ Ⓒ Ⓓ Ⓔ
11 Ⓐ Ⓑ Ⓒ Ⓓ Ⓔ
12 Ⓐ Ⓑ Ⓒ Ⓓ Ⓔ
13 Ⓐ Ⓑ Ⓒ Ⓓ Ⓔ
14 Ⓐ Ⓑ Ⓒ Ⓓ Ⓔ
15 Ⓐ Ⓑ Ⓒ Ⓓ Ⓔ
16 Ⓐ Ⓑ Ⓒ Ⓓ Ⓔ
17 Ⓐ Ⓑ Ⓒ Ⓓ Ⓔ
18 Ⓐ Ⓑ Ⓒ Ⓓ Ⓔ
19 Ⓐ Ⓑ Ⓒ Ⓓ Ⓔ
20 Ⓐ Ⓑ Ⓒ Ⓓ Ⓔ
21 Ⓐ Ⓑ Ⓒ Ⓓ Ⓔ
22 Ⓐ Ⓑ Ⓒ Ⓓ Ⓔ
23 Ⓐ Ⓑ Ⓒ Ⓓ Ⓔ
24 Ⓐ Ⓑ Ⓒ Ⓓ Ⓔ
25 Ⓐ Ⓑ Ⓒ Ⓓ Ⓔ

SECTION 2:
Verbal
Questions

1 Ⓐ Ⓑ Ⓒ Ⓓ Ⓔ
2 Ⓐ Ⓑ Ⓒ Ⓓ Ⓔ
3 Ⓐ Ⓑ Ⓒ Ⓓ Ⓔ
4 Ⓐ Ⓑ Ⓒ Ⓓ Ⓔ
5 Ⓐ Ⓑ Ⓒ Ⓓ Ⓔ
6 Ⓐ Ⓑ Ⓒ Ⓓ Ⓔ
7 Ⓐ Ⓑ Ⓒ Ⓓ Ⓔ
8 Ⓐ Ⓑ Ⓒ Ⓓ Ⓔ
9 Ⓐ Ⓑ Ⓒ Ⓓ Ⓔ
10 Ⓐ Ⓑ Ⓒ Ⓓ Ⓔ
11 Ⓐ Ⓑ Ⓒ Ⓓ Ⓔ
12 Ⓐ Ⓑ Ⓒ Ⓓ Ⓔ
13 Ⓐ Ⓑ Ⓒ Ⓓ Ⓔ
14 Ⓐ Ⓑ Ⓒ Ⓓ Ⓔ
15 Ⓐ Ⓑ Ⓒ Ⓓ Ⓔ
16 Ⓐ Ⓑ Ⓒ Ⓓ Ⓔ
17 Ⓐ Ⓑ Ⓒ Ⓓ Ⓔ
18 Ⓐ Ⓑ Ⓒ Ⓓ Ⓔ
19 Ⓐ Ⓑ Ⓒ Ⓓ Ⓔ
20 Ⓐ Ⓑ Ⓒ Ⓓ Ⓔ
21 Ⓐ Ⓑ Ⓒ Ⓓ Ⓔ
22 Ⓐ Ⓑ Ⓒ Ⓓ Ⓔ
23 Ⓐ Ⓑ Ⓒ Ⓓ Ⓔ
24 Ⓐ Ⓑ Ⓒ Ⓓ Ⓔ
25 Ⓐ Ⓑ Ⓒ Ⓓ Ⓔ
26 Ⓐ Ⓑ Ⓒ Ⓓ Ⓔ
27 Ⓐ Ⓑ Ⓒ Ⓓ Ⓔ
28 Ⓐ Ⓑ Ⓒ Ⓓ Ⓔ
29 Ⓐ Ⓑ Ⓒ Ⓓ Ⓔ
30 Ⓐ Ⓑ Ⓒ Ⓓ Ⓔ

31 Ⓐ Ⓑ Ⓒ Ⓓ Ⓔ
32 Ⓐ Ⓑ Ⓒ Ⓓ Ⓔ
33 Ⓐ Ⓑ Ⓒ Ⓓ Ⓔ
34 Ⓐ Ⓑ Ⓒ Ⓓ Ⓔ
35 Ⓐ Ⓑ Ⓒ Ⓓ Ⓔ
36 Ⓐ Ⓑ Ⓒ Ⓓ Ⓔ
37 Ⓐ Ⓑ Ⓒ Ⓓ Ⓔ
38 Ⓐ Ⓑ Ⓒ Ⓓ Ⓔ
39 Ⓐ Ⓑ Ⓒ Ⓓ Ⓔ
40 Ⓐ Ⓑ Ⓒ Ⓓ Ⓔ

SECTION 4:
Verbal
Questions

1 Ⓐ Ⓑ Ⓒ Ⓓ Ⓔ
2 Ⓐ Ⓑ Ⓒ Ⓓ Ⓔ
3 Ⓐ Ⓑ Ⓒ Ⓓ Ⓔ
4 Ⓐ Ⓑ Ⓒ Ⓓ Ⓔ
5 Ⓐ Ⓑ Ⓒ Ⓓ Ⓔ
6 Ⓐ Ⓑ Ⓒ Ⓓ Ⓔ
7 Ⓐ Ⓑ Ⓒ Ⓓ Ⓔ
8 Ⓐ Ⓑ Ⓒ Ⓓ Ⓔ
9 Ⓐ Ⓑ Ⓒ Ⓓ Ⓔ
10 Ⓐ Ⓑ Ⓒ Ⓓ Ⓔ
11 Ⓐ Ⓑ Ⓒ Ⓓ Ⓔ
12 Ⓐ Ⓑ Ⓒ Ⓓ Ⓔ
13 Ⓐ Ⓑ Ⓒ Ⓓ Ⓔ
14 Ⓐ Ⓑ Ⓒ Ⓓ Ⓔ
15 Ⓐ Ⓑ Ⓒ Ⓓ Ⓔ
16 Ⓐ Ⓑ Ⓒ Ⓓ Ⓔ
17 Ⓐ Ⓑ Ⓒ Ⓓ Ⓔ
18 Ⓐ Ⓑ Ⓒ Ⓓ Ⓔ
19 Ⓐ Ⓑ Ⓒ Ⓓ Ⓔ
20 Ⓐ Ⓑ Ⓒ Ⓓ Ⓔ
21 Ⓐ Ⓑ Ⓒ Ⓓ Ⓔ
22 Ⓐ Ⓑ Ⓒ Ⓓ Ⓔ
23 Ⓐ Ⓑ Ⓒ Ⓓ Ⓔ
24 Ⓐ Ⓑ Ⓒ Ⓓ Ⓔ
25 Ⓐ Ⓑ Ⓒ Ⓓ Ⓔ
26 Ⓐ Ⓑ Ⓒ Ⓓ Ⓔ
27 Ⓐ Ⓑ Ⓒ Ⓓ Ⓔ
28 Ⓐ Ⓑ Ⓒ Ⓓ Ⓔ
29 Ⓐ Ⓑ Ⓒ Ⓓ Ⓔ
30 Ⓐ Ⓑ Ⓒ Ⓓ Ⓔ

31 Ⓐ Ⓑ Ⓒ Ⓓ Ⓔ
32 Ⓐ Ⓑ Ⓒ Ⓓ Ⓔ
33 Ⓐ Ⓑ Ⓒ Ⓓ Ⓔ
34 Ⓐ Ⓑ Ⓒ Ⓓ Ⓔ
35 Ⓐ Ⓑ Ⓒ Ⓓ Ⓔ
36 Ⓐ Ⓑ Ⓒ Ⓓ Ⓔ
37 Ⓐ Ⓑ Ⓒ Ⓓ Ⓔ
38 Ⓐ Ⓑ Ⓒ Ⓓ Ⓔ
39 Ⓐ Ⓑ Ⓒ Ⓓ Ⓔ
40 Ⓐ Ⓑ Ⓒ Ⓓ Ⓔ
41 Ⓐ Ⓑ Ⓒ Ⓓ Ⓔ
42 Ⓐ Ⓑ Ⓒ Ⓓ Ⓔ
43 Ⓐ Ⓑ Ⓒ Ⓓ Ⓔ
44 Ⓐ Ⓑ Ⓒ Ⓓ Ⓔ
45 Ⓐ Ⓑ Ⓒ Ⓓ Ⓔ

(continued)

SECTION 5:
Mathematics
Questions

1 Ⓐ Ⓑ Ⓒ Ⓓ Ⓔ
2 Ⓐ Ⓑ Ⓒ Ⓓ Ⓔ
3 Ⓐ Ⓑ Ⓒ Ⓓ Ⓔ
4 Ⓐ Ⓑ Ⓒ Ⓓ Ⓔ
5 Ⓐ Ⓑ Ⓒ Ⓓ Ⓔ
6 Ⓐ Ⓑ Ⓒ Ⓓ Ⓔ
7 Ⓐ Ⓑ Ⓒ Ⓓ Ⓔ
8 Ⓐ Ⓑ Ⓒ Ⓓ Ⓔ
9 Ⓐ Ⓑ Ⓒ Ⓓ Ⓔ
10 Ⓐ Ⓑ Ⓒ Ⓓ Ⓔ
11 Ⓐ Ⓑ Ⓒ Ⓓ Ⓔ
12 Ⓐ Ⓑ Ⓒ Ⓓ Ⓔ
13 Ⓐ Ⓑ Ⓒ Ⓓ Ⓔ
14 Ⓐ Ⓑ Ⓒ Ⓓ Ⓔ
15 Ⓐ Ⓑ Ⓒ Ⓓ Ⓔ
16 Ⓐ Ⓑ Ⓒ Ⓓ Ⓔ
17 Ⓐ Ⓑ Ⓒ Ⓓ Ⓔ
18 Ⓐ Ⓑ Ⓒ Ⓓ Ⓔ
19 Ⓐ Ⓑ Ⓒ Ⓓ Ⓔ
20 Ⓐ Ⓑ Ⓒ Ⓓ Ⓔ
21 Ⓐ Ⓑ Ⓒ Ⓓ Ⓔ
22 Ⓐ Ⓑ Ⓒ Ⓓ Ⓔ
23 Ⓐ Ⓑ Ⓒ Ⓓ Ⓔ
24 Ⓐ Ⓑ Ⓒ Ⓓ Ⓔ
25 Ⓐ Ⓑ Ⓒ Ⓓ Ⓔ
26 Ⓐ Ⓑ Ⓒ Ⓓ Ⓔ
27 Ⓐ Ⓑ Ⓒ Ⓓ Ⓔ
28 Ⓐ Ⓑ Ⓒ Ⓓ Ⓔ
29 Ⓐ Ⓑ Ⓒ Ⓓ Ⓔ
30 Ⓐ Ⓑ Ⓒ Ⓓ Ⓔ
31 Ⓐ Ⓑ Ⓒ Ⓓ Ⓔ
32 Ⓐ Ⓑ Ⓒ Ⓓ Ⓔ
33 Ⓐ Ⓑ Ⓒ Ⓓ Ⓔ
34 Ⓐ Ⓑ Ⓒ Ⓓ Ⓔ
35 Ⓐ Ⓑ Ⓒ Ⓓ Ⓔ

SECTION 6:
Verbal
Questions

1 Ⓐ Ⓑ Ⓒ Ⓓ Ⓔ
2 Ⓐ Ⓑ Ⓒ Ⓓ Ⓔ
3 Ⓐ Ⓑ Ⓒ Ⓓ Ⓔ
4 Ⓐ Ⓑ Ⓒ Ⓓ Ⓔ
5 Ⓐ Ⓑ Ⓒ Ⓓ Ⓔ
6 Ⓐ Ⓑ Ⓒ Ⓓ Ⓔ
7 Ⓐ Ⓑ Ⓒ Ⓓ Ⓔ
8 Ⓐ Ⓑ Ⓒ Ⓓ Ⓔ
9 Ⓐ Ⓑ Ⓒ Ⓓ Ⓔ
10 Ⓐ Ⓑ Ⓒ Ⓓ Ⓔ
11 Ⓐ Ⓑ Ⓒ Ⓓ Ⓔ
12 Ⓐ Ⓑ Ⓒ Ⓓ Ⓔ
13 Ⓐ Ⓑ Ⓒ Ⓓ Ⓔ
14 Ⓐ Ⓑ Ⓒ Ⓓ Ⓔ
15 Ⓐ Ⓑ Ⓒ Ⓓ Ⓔ
16 Ⓐ Ⓑ Ⓒ Ⓓ Ⓔ
17 Ⓐ Ⓑ Ⓒ Ⓓ Ⓔ
18 Ⓐ Ⓑ Ⓒ Ⓓ Ⓔ
19 Ⓐ Ⓑ Ⓒ Ⓓ Ⓔ
20 Ⓐ Ⓑ Ⓒ Ⓓ Ⓔ
21 Ⓐ Ⓑ Ⓒ Ⓓ Ⓔ
22 Ⓐ Ⓑ Ⓒ Ⓓ Ⓔ
23 Ⓐ Ⓑ Ⓒ Ⓓ Ⓔ
24 Ⓐ Ⓑ Ⓒ Ⓓ Ⓔ
25 Ⓐ Ⓑ Ⓒ Ⓓ Ⓔ
26 Ⓐ Ⓑ Ⓒ Ⓓ Ⓔ
27 Ⓐ Ⓑ Ⓒ Ⓓ Ⓔ
28 Ⓐ Ⓑ Ⓒ Ⓓ Ⓔ
29 Ⓐ Ⓑ Ⓒ Ⓓ Ⓔ
30 Ⓐ Ⓑ Ⓒ Ⓓ Ⓔ
31 Ⓐ Ⓑ Ⓒ Ⓓ Ⓔ
32 Ⓐ Ⓑ Ⓒ Ⓓ Ⓔ
33 Ⓐ Ⓑ Ⓒ Ⓓ Ⓔ
34 Ⓐ Ⓑ Ⓒ Ⓓ Ⓔ
35 Ⓐ Ⓑ Ⓒ Ⓓ Ⓔ
36 Ⓐ Ⓑ Ⓒ Ⓓ Ⓔ
37 Ⓐ Ⓑ Ⓒ Ⓓ Ⓔ
38 Ⓐ Ⓑ Ⓒ Ⓓ Ⓔ
39 Ⓐ Ⓑ Ⓒ Ⓓ Ⓔ
40 Ⓐ Ⓑ Ⓒ Ⓓ Ⓔ

ANSWER SHEET FOR PRACTICE TEST 2

Note that 5 answer spaces are provided throughout this Answer Sheet. However, questions in some sections of the Practice Test will have only 4 possible answers (A or B or C or D).

SECTION 1: Verbal Questions

1 Ⓐ Ⓑ Ⓒ Ⓓ Ⓔ   36 Ⓐ Ⓑ Ⓒ Ⓓ Ⓔ
2 Ⓐ Ⓑ Ⓒ Ⓓ Ⓔ   37 Ⓐ Ⓑ Ⓒ Ⓓ Ⓔ
3 Ⓐ Ⓑ Ⓒ Ⓓ Ⓔ   38 Ⓐ Ⓑ Ⓒ Ⓓ Ⓔ
4 Ⓐ Ⓑ Ⓒ Ⓓ Ⓔ   39 Ⓐ Ⓑ Ⓒ Ⓓ Ⓔ
5 Ⓐ Ⓑ Ⓒ Ⓓ Ⓔ   40 Ⓐ Ⓑ Ⓒ Ⓓ Ⓔ
6 Ⓐ Ⓑ Ⓒ Ⓓ Ⓔ   41 Ⓐ Ⓑ Ⓒ Ⓓ Ⓔ
7 Ⓐ Ⓑ Ⓒ Ⓓ Ⓔ   42 Ⓐ Ⓑ Ⓒ Ⓓ Ⓔ
8 Ⓐ Ⓑ Ⓒ Ⓓ Ⓔ   43 Ⓐ Ⓑ Ⓒ Ⓓ Ⓔ
9 Ⓐ Ⓑ Ⓒ Ⓓ Ⓔ   44 Ⓐ Ⓑ Ⓒ Ⓓ Ⓔ
10 Ⓐ Ⓑ Ⓒ Ⓓ Ⓔ   45 Ⓐ Ⓑ Ⓒ Ⓓ Ⓔ
11 Ⓐ Ⓑ Ⓒ Ⓓ Ⓔ
12 Ⓐ Ⓑ Ⓒ Ⓓ Ⓔ
13 Ⓐ Ⓑ Ⓒ Ⓓ Ⓔ
14 Ⓐ Ⓑ Ⓒ Ⓓ Ⓔ
15 Ⓐ Ⓑ Ⓒ Ⓓ Ⓔ
16 Ⓐ Ⓑ Ⓒ Ⓓ Ⓔ
17 Ⓐ Ⓑ Ⓒ Ⓓ Ⓔ
18 Ⓐ Ⓑ Ⓒ Ⓓ Ⓔ
19 Ⓐ Ⓑ Ⓒ Ⓓ Ⓔ
20 Ⓐ Ⓑ Ⓒ Ⓓ Ⓔ
21 Ⓐ Ⓑ Ⓒ Ⓓ Ⓔ
22 Ⓐ Ⓑ Ⓒ Ⓓ Ⓔ
23 Ⓐ Ⓑ Ⓒ Ⓓ Ⓔ
24 Ⓐ Ⓑ Ⓒ Ⓓ Ⓔ
25 Ⓐ Ⓑ Ⓒ Ⓓ Ⓔ
26 Ⓐ Ⓑ Ⓒ Ⓓ Ⓔ
27 Ⓐ Ⓑ Ⓒ Ⓓ Ⓔ
28 Ⓐ Ⓑ Ⓒ Ⓓ Ⓔ
29 Ⓐ Ⓑ Ⓒ Ⓓ Ⓔ
30 Ⓐ Ⓑ Ⓒ Ⓓ Ⓔ
31 Ⓐ Ⓑ Ⓒ Ⓓ Ⓔ
32 Ⓐ Ⓑ Ⓒ Ⓓ Ⓔ
33 Ⓐ Ⓑ Ⓒ Ⓓ Ⓔ
34 Ⓐ Ⓑ Ⓒ Ⓓ Ⓔ
35 Ⓐ Ⓑ Ⓒ Ⓓ Ⓔ

SECTION 2: Mathematics Questions

1 Ⓐ Ⓑ Ⓒ Ⓓ Ⓔ
2 Ⓐ Ⓑ Ⓒ Ⓓ Ⓔ
3 Ⓐ Ⓑ Ⓒ Ⓓ Ⓔ
4 Ⓐ Ⓑ Ⓒ Ⓓ Ⓔ
5 Ⓐ Ⓑ Ⓒ Ⓓ Ⓔ
6 Ⓐ Ⓑ Ⓒ Ⓓ Ⓔ
7 Ⓐ Ⓑ Ⓒ Ⓓ Ⓔ
8 Ⓐ Ⓑ Ⓒ Ⓓ Ⓔ
9 Ⓐ Ⓑ Ⓒ Ⓓ Ⓔ
10 Ⓐ Ⓑ Ⓒ Ⓓ Ⓔ
11 Ⓐ Ⓑ Ⓒ Ⓓ Ⓔ
12 Ⓐ Ⓑ Ⓒ Ⓓ Ⓔ
13 Ⓐ Ⓑ Ⓒ Ⓓ Ⓔ
14 Ⓐ Ⓑ Ⓒ Ⓓ Ⓔ
15 Ⓐ Ⓑ Ⓒ Ⓓ Ⓔ
16 Ⓐ Ⓑ Ⓒ Ⓓ Ⓔ
17 Ⓐ Ⓑ Ⓒ Ⓓ Ⓔ
18 Ⓐ Ⓑ Ⓒ Ⓓ Ⓔ
19 Ⓐ Ⓑ Ⓒ Ⓓ Ⓔ
20 Ⓐ Ⓑ Ⓒ Ⓓ Ⓔ
21 Ⓐ Ⓑ Ⓒ Ⓓ Ⓔ
22 Ⓐ Ⓑ Ⓒ Ⓓ Ⓔ
23 Ⓐ Ⓑ Ⓒ Ⓓ Ⓔ
24 Ⓐ Ⓑ Ⓒ Ⓓ Ⓔ
25 Ⓐ Ⓑ Ⓒ Ⓓ Ⓔ

SECTION 3: Mathematics Questions

1 Ⓐ Ⓑ Ⓒ Ⓓ Ⓔ
2 Ⓐ Ⓑ Ⓒ Ⓓ Ⓔ
3 Ⓐ Ⓑ Ⓒ Ⓓ Ⓔ
4 Ⓐ Ⓑ Ⓒ Ⓓ Ⓔ
5 Ⓐ Ⓑ Ⓒ Ⓓ Ⓔ
6 Ⓐ Ⓑ Ⓒ Ⓓ Ⓔ
7 Ⓐ Ⓑ Ⓒ Ⓓ Ⓔ
8 Ⓐ Ⓑ Ⓒ Ⓓ Ⓔ
9 Ⓐ Ⓑ Ⓒ Ⓓ Ⓔ
10 Ⓐ Ⓑ Ⓒ Ⓓ Ⓔ
11 Ⓐ Ⓑ Ⓒ Ⓓ Ⓔ
12 Ⓐ Ⓑ Ⓒ Ⓓ Ⓔ
13 Ⓐ Ⓑ Ⓒ Ⓓ Ⓔ
14 Ⓐ Ⓑ Ⓒ Ⓓ Ⓔ
15 Ⓐ Ⓑ Ⓒ Ⓓ Ⓔ
16 Ⓐ Ⓑ Ⓒ Ⓓ Ⓔ
17 Ⓐ Ⓑ Ⓒ Ⓓ Ⓔ
18 Ⓐ Ⓑ Ⓒ Ⓓ Ⓔ
19 Ⓐ Ⓑ Ⓒ Ⓓ Ⓔ
20 Ⓐ Ⓑ Ⓒ Ⓓ Ⓔ
21 Ⓐ Ⓑ Ⓒ Ⓓ Ⓔ
22 Ⓐ Ⓑ Ⓒ Ⓓ Ⓔ
23 Ⓐ Ⓑ Ⓒ Ⓓ Ⓔ
24 Ⓐ Ⓑ Ⓒ Ⓓ Ⓔ
25 Ⓐ Ⓑ Ⓒ Ⓓ Ⓔ
26 Ⓐ Ⓑ Ⓒ Ⓓ Ⓔ
27 Ⓐ Ⓑ Ⓒ Ⓓ Ⓔ
28 Ⓐ Ⓑ Ⓒ Ⓓ Ⓔ
29 Ⓐ Ⓑ Ⓒ Ⓓ Ⓔ
30 Ⓐ Ⓑ Ⓒ Ⓓ Ⓔ
31 Ⓐ Ⓑ Ⓒ Ⓓ Ⓔ
32 Ⓐ Ⓑ Ⓒ Ⓓ Ⓔ
33 Ⓐ Ⓑ Ⓒ Ⓓ Ⓔ
34 Ⓐ Ⓑ Ⓒ Ⓓ Ⓔ
35 Ⓐ Ⓑ Ⓒ Ⓓ Ⓔ

(continued)

SECTION 5:
Verbal
Questions

1 Ⓐ Ⓑ Ⓒ Ⓓ Ⓔ	26 Ⓐ Ⓑ Ⓒ Ⓓ Ⓔ
2 Ⓐ Ⓑ Ⓒ Ⓓ Ⓔ	27 Ⓐ Ⓑ Ⓒ Ⓓ Ⓔ
3 Ⓐ Ⓑ Ⓒ Ⓓ Ⓔ	28 Ⓐ Ⓑ Ⓒ Ⓓ Ⓔ
4 Ⓐ Ⓑ Ⓒ Ⓓ Ⓔ	29 Ⓐ Ⓑ Ⓒ Ⓓ Ⓔ
5 Ⓐ Ⓑ Ⓒ Ⓓ Ⓔ	30 Ⓐ Ⓑ Ⓒ Ⓓ Ⓔ
6 Ⓐ Ⓑ Ⓒ Ⓓ Ⓔ	31 Ⓐ Ⓑ Ⓒ Ⓓ Ⓔ
7 Ⓐ Ⓑ Ⓒ Ⓓ Ⓔ	32 Ⓐ Ⓑ Ⓒ Ⓓ Ⓔ
8 Ⓐ Ⓑ Ⓒ Ⓓ Ⓔ	33 Ⓐ Ⓑ Ⓒ Ⓓ Ⓔ
9 Ⓐ Ⓑ Ⓒ Ⓓ Ⓔ	34 Ⓐ Ⓑ Ⓒ Ⓓ Ⓔ
10 Ⓐ Ⓑ Ⓒ Ⓓ Ⓔ	35 Ⓐ Ⓑ Ⓒ Ⓓ Ⓔ
11 Ⓐ Ⓑ Ⓒ Ⓓ Ⓔ	36 Ⓐ Ⓑ Ⓒ Ⓓ Ⓔ
12 Ⓐ Ⓑ Ⓒ Ⓓ Ⓔ	37 Ⓐ Ⓑ Ⓒ Ⓓ Ⓔ
13 Ⓐ Ⓑ Ⓒ Ⓓ Ⓔ	38 Ⓐ Ⓑ Ⓒ Ⓓ Ⓔ
14 Ⓐ Ⓑ Ⓒ Ⓓ Ⓔ	39 Ⓐ Ⓑ Ⓒ Ⓓ Ⓔ
15 Ⓐ Ⓑ Ⓒ Ⓓ Ⓔ	40 Ⓐ Ⓑ Ⓒ Ⓓ Ⓔ
16 Ⓐ Ⓑ Ⓒ Ⓓ Ⓔ	41 Ⓐ Ⓑ Ⓒ Ⓓ Ⓔ
17 Ⓐ Ⓑ Ⓒ Ⓓ Ⓔ	42 Ⓐ Ⓑ Ⓒ Ⓓ Ⓔ
18 Ⓐ Ⓑ Ⓒ Ⓓ Ⓔ	43 Ⓐ Ⓑ Ⓒ Ⓓ Ⓔ
19 Ⓐ Ⓑ Ⓒ Ⓓ Ⓔ	44 Ⓐ Ⓑ Ⓒ Ⓓ Ⓔ
20 Ⓐ Ⓑ Ⓒ Ⓓ Ⓔ	45 Ⓐ Ⓑ Ⓒ Ⓓ Ⓔ
21 Ⓐ Ⓑ Ⓒ Ⓓ Ⓔ	
22 Ⓐ Ⓑ Ⓒ Ⓓ Ⓔ	
23 Ⓐ Ⓑ Ⓒ Ⓓ Ⓔ	
24 Ⓐ Ⓑ Ⓒ Ⓓ Ⓔ	
25 Ⓐ Ⓑ Ⓒ Ⓓ Ⓔ	

SECTION 6:
Mathematics
Questions

1 Ⓐ Ⓑ Ⓒ Ⓓ Ⓔ
2 Ⓐ Ⓑ Ⓒ Ⓓ Ⓔ
3 Ⓐ Ⓑ Ⓒ Ⓓ Ⓔ
4 Ⓐ Ⓑ Ⓒ Ⓓ Ⓔ
5 Ⓐ Ⓑ Ⓒ Ⓓ Ⓔ
6 Ⓐ Ⓑ Ⓒ Ⓓ Ⓔ
7 Ⓐ Ⓑ Ⓒ Ⓓ Ⓔ
8 Ⓐ Ⓑ Ⓒ Ⓓ Ⓔ
9 Ⓐ Ⓑ Ⓒ Ⓓ Ⓔ
10 Ⓐ Ⓑ Ⓒ Ⓓ Ⓔ
11 Ⓐ Ⓑ Ⓒ Ⓓ Ⓔ
12 Ⓐ Ⓑ Ⓒ Ⓓ Ⓔ
13 Ⓐ Ⓑ Ⓒ Ⓓ Ⓔ
14 Ⓐ Ⓑ Ⓒ Ⓓ Ⓔ
15 Ⓐ Ⓑ Ⓒ Ⓓ Ⓔ
16 Ⓐ Ⓑ Ⓒ Ⓓ Ⓔ
17 Ⓐ Ⓑ Ⓒ Ⓓ Ⓔ
18 Ⓐ Ⓑ Ⓒ Ⓓ Ⓔ
19 Ⓐ Ⓑ Ⓒ Ⓓ Ⓔ
20 Ⓐ Ⓑ Ⓒ Ⓓ Ⓔ
21 Ⓐ Ⓑ Ⓒ Ⓓ Ⓔ
22 Ⓐ Ⓑ Ⓒ Ⓓ Ⓔ
23 Ⓐ Ⓑ Ⓒ Ⓓ Ⓔ
24 Ⓐ Ⓑ Ⓒ Ⓓ Ⓔ
25 Ⓐ Ⓑ Ⓒ Ⓓ Ⓔ

ANSWER SHEET FOR PRACTICE TEST 3

Note that 5 answer spaces are provided throughout this Answer Sheet. However, questions in some sections of the Practice Test will have only 4 possible answers (A or B or C or D).

SECTION 1: Mathematics Questions

1 Ⓐ Ⓑ Ⓒ Ⓓ Ⓔ
2 Ⓐ Ⓑ Ⓒ Ⓓ Ⓔ
3 Ⓐ Ⓑ Ⓒ Ⓓ Ⓔ
4 Ⓐ Ⓑ Ⓒ Ⓓ Ⓔ
5 Ⓐ Ⓑ Ⓒ Ⓓ Ⓔ
6 Ⓐ Ⓑ Ⓒ Ⓓ Ⓔ
7 Ⓐ Ⓑ Ⓒ Ⓓ Ⓔ
8 Ⓐ Ⓑ Ⓒ Ⓓ Ⓔ
9 Ⓐ Ⓑ Ⓒ Ⓓ Ⓔ
10 Ⓐ Ⓑ Ⓒ Ⓓ Ⓔ
11 Ⓐ Ⓑ Ⓒ Ⓓ Ⓔ
12 Ⓐ Ⓑ Ⓒ Ⓓ Ⓔ
13 Ⓐ Ⓑ Ⓒ Ⓓ Ⓔ
14 Ⓐ Ⓑ Ⓒ Ⓓ Ⓔ
15 Ⓐ Ⓑ Ⓒ Ⓓ Ⓔ
16 Ⓐ Ⓑ Ⓒ Ⓓ Ⓔ
17 Ⓐ Ⓑ Ⓒ Ⓓ Ⓔ
18 Ⓐ Ⓑ Ⓒ Ⓓ Ⓔ
19 Ⓐ Ⓑ Ⓒ Ⓓ Ⓔ
20 Ⓐ Ⓑ Ⓒ Ⓓ Ⓔ
21 Ⓐ Ⓑ Ⓒ Ⓓ Ⓔ
22 Ⓐ Ⓑ Ⓒ Ⓓ Ⓔ
23 Ⓐ Ⓑ Ⓒ Ⓓ Ⓔ
24 Ⓐ Ⓑ Ⓒ Ⓓ Ⓔ
25 Ⓐ Ⓑ Ⓒ Ⓓ Ⓔ

SECTION 2: Verbal Questions

1 Ⓐ Ⓑ Ⓒ Ⓓ Ⓔ
2 Ⓐ Ⓑ Ⓒ Ⓓ Ⓔ
3 Ⓐ Ⓑ Ⓒ Ⓓ Ⓔ
4 Ⓐ Ⓑ Ⓒ Ⓓ Ⓔ
5 Ⓐ Ⓑ Ⓒ Ⓓ Ⓔ
6 Ⓐ Ⓑ Ⓒ Ⓓ Ⓔ
7 Ⓐ Ⓑ Ⓒ Ⓓ Ⓔ
8 Ⓐ Ⓑ Ⓒ Ⓓ Ⓔ
9 Ⓐ Ⓑ Ⓒ Ⓓ Ⓔ
10 Ⓐ Ⓑ Ⓒ Ⓓ Ⓔ
11 Ⓐ Ⓑ Ⓒ Ⓓ Ⓔ
12 Ⓐ Ⓑ Ⓒ Ⓓ Ⓔ
13 Ⓐ Ⓑ Ⓒ Ⓓ Ⓔ
14 Ⓐ Ⓑ Ⓒ Ⓓ Ⓔ
15 Ⓐ Ⓑ Ⓒ Ⓓ Ⓔ
16 Ⓐ Ⓑ Ⓒ Ⓓ Ⓔ
17 Ⓐ Ⓑ Ⓒ Ⓓ Ⓔ
18 Ⓐ Ⓑ Ⓒ Ⓓ Ⓔ
19 Ⓐ Ⓑ Ⓒ Ⓓ Ⓔ
20 Ⓐ Ⓑ Ⓒ Ⓓ Ⓔ
21 Ⓐ Ⓑ Ⓒ Ⓓ Ⓔ
22 Ⓐ Ⓑ Ⓒ Ⓓ Ⓔ
23 Ⓐ Ⓑ Ⓒ Ⓓ Ⓔ
24 Ⓐ Ⓑ Ⓒ Ⓓ Ⓔ
25 Ⓐ Ⓑ Ⓒ Ⓓ Ⓔ

26 Ⓐ Ⓑ Ⓒ Ⓓ Ⓔ
27 Ⓐ Ⓑ Ⓒ Ⓓ Ⓔ
28 Ⓐ Ⓑ Ⓒ Ⓓ Ⓔ
29 Ⓐ Ⓑ Ⓒ Ⓓ Ⓔ
30 Ⓐ Ⓑ Ⓒ Ⓓ Ⓔ
31 Ⓐ Ⓑ Ⓒ Ⓓ Ⓔ
32 Ⓐ Ⓑ Ⓒ Ⓓ Ⓔ
33 Ⓐ Ⓑ Ⓒ Ⓓ Ⓔ
34 Ⓐ Ⓑ Ⓒ Ⓓ Ⓔ
35 Ⓐ Ⓑ Ⓒ Ⓓ Ⓔ
36 Ⓐ Ⓑ Ⓒ Ⓓ Ⓔ
37 Ⓐ Ⓑ Ⓒ Ⓓ Ⓔ
38 Ⓐ Ⓑ Ⓒ Ⓓ Ⓔ
39 Ⓐ Ⓑ Ⓒ Ⓓ Ⓔ
40 Ⓐ Ⓑ Ⓒ Ⓓ Ⓔ
41 Ⓐ Ⓑ Ⓒ Ⓓ Ⓔ
42 Ⓐ Ⓑ Ⓒ Ⓓ Ⓔ
43 Ⓐ Ⓑ Ⓒ Ⓓ Ⓔ
44 Ⓐ Ⓑ Ⓒ Ⓓ Ⓔ
45 Ⓐ Ⓑ Ⓒ Ⓓ Ⓔ

SECTION 3: Mathematics Questions

1 Ⓐ Ⓑ Ⓒ Ⓓ Ⓔ
2 Ⓐ Ⓑ Ⓒ Ⓓ Ⓔ
3 Ⓐ Ⓑ Ⓒ Ⓓ Ⓔ
4 Ⓐ Ⓑ Ⓒ Ⓓ Ⓔ
5 Ⓐ Ⓑ Ⓒ Ⓓ Ⓔ
6 Ⓐ Ⓑ Ⓒ Ⓓ Ⓔ
7 Ⓐ Ⓑ Ⓒ Ⓓ Ⓔ
8 Ⓐ Ⓑ Ⓒ Ⓓ Ⓔ
9 Ⓐ Ⓑ Ⓒ Ⓓ Ⓔ
10 Ⓐ Ⓑ Ⓒ Ⓓ Ⓔ
11 Ⓐ Ⓑ Ⓒ Ⓓ Ⓔ
12 Ⓐ Ⓑ Ⓒ Ⓓ Ⓔ
13 Ⓐ Ⓑ Ⓒ Ⓓ Ⓔ
14 Ⓐ Ⓑ Ⓒ Ⓓ Ⓔ
15 Ⓐ Ⓑ Ⓒ Ⓓ Ⓔ
16 Ⓐ Ⓑ Ⓒ Ⓓ Ⓔ
17 Ⓐ Ⓑ Ⓒ Ⓓ Ⓔ
18 Ⓐ Ⓑ Ⓒ Ⓓ Ⓔ
19 Ⓐ Ⓑ Ⓒ Ⓓ Ⓔ
20 Ⓐ Ⓑ Ⓒ Ⓓ Ⓔ
21 Ⓐ Ⓑ Ⓒ Ⓓ Ⓔ
22 Ⓐ Ⓑ Ⓒ Ⓓ Ⓔ
23 Ⓐ Ⓑ Ⓒ Ⓓ Ⓔ
24 Ⓐ Ⓑ Ⓒ Ⓓ Ⓔ
25 Ⓐ Ⓑ Ⓒ Ⓓ Ⓔ
26 Ⓐ Ⓑ Ⓒ Ⓓ Ⓔ
27 Ⓐ Ⓑ Ⓒ Ⓓ Ⓔ
28 Ⓐ Ⓑ Ⓒ Ⓓ Ⓔ
29 Ⓐ Ⓑ Ⓒ Ⓓ Ⓔ
30 Ⓐ Ⓑ Ⓒ Ⓓ Ⓔ

(continued)

SECTION 4:
Verbal
Questions

1 Ⓐ Ⓑ Ⓒ Ⓓ Ⓔ
2 Ⓐ Ⓑ Ⓒ Ⓓ Ⓔ
3 Ⓐ Ⓑ Ⓒ Ⓓ Ⓔ
4 Ⓐ Ⓑ Ⓒ Ⓓ Ⓔ
5 Ⓐ Ⓑ Ⓒ Ⓓ Ⓔ
6 Ⓐ Ⓑ Ⓒ Ⓓ Ⓔ
7 Ⓐ Ⓑ Ⓒ Ⓓ Ⓔ
8 Ⓐ Ⓑ Ⓒ Ⓓ Ⓔ
9 Ⓐ Ⓑ Ⓒ Ⓓ Ⓔ
10 Ⓐ Ⓑ Ⓒ Ⓓ Ⓔ
11 Ⓐ Ⓑ Ⓒ Ⓓ Ⓔ
12 Ⓐ Ⓑ Ⓒ Ⓓ Ⓔ
13 Ⓐ Ⓑ Ⓒ Ⓓ Ⓔ
14 Ⓐ Ⓑ Ⓒ Ⓓ Ⓔ
15 Ⓐ Ⓑ Ⓒ Ⓓ Ⓔ
16 Ⓐ Ⓑ Ⓒ Ⓓ Ⓔ
17 Ⓐ Ⓑ Ⓒ Ⓓ Ⓔ
18 Ⓐ Ⓑ Ⓒ Ⓓ Ⓔ
19 Ⓐ Ⓑ Ⓒ Ⓓ Ⓔ
20 Ⓐ Ⓑ Ⓒ Ⓓ Ⓔ
21 Ⓐ Ⓑ Ⓒ Ⓓ Ⓔ
22 Ⓐ Ⓑ Ⓒ Ⓓ Ⓔ
23 Ⓐ Ⓑ Ⓒ Ⓓ Ⓔ
24 Ⓐ Ⓑ Ⓒ Ⓓ Ⓔ
25 Ⓐ Ⓑ Ⓒ Ⓓ Ⓔ
26 Ⓐ Ⓑ Ⓒ Ⓓ Ⓔ
27 Ⓐ Ⓑ Ⓒ Ⓓ Ⓔ
28 Ⓐ Ⓑ Ⓒ Ⓓ Ⓔ
29 Ⓐ Ⓑ Ⓒ Ⓓ Ⓔ
30 Ⓐ Ⓑ Ⓒ Ⓓ Ⓔ

31 Ⓐ Ⓑ Ⓒ Ⓓ Ⓔ
32 Ⓐ Ⓑ Ⓒ Ⓓ Ⓔ
33 Ⓐ Ⓑ Ⓒ Ⓓ Ⓔ
34 Ⓐ Ⓑ Ⓒ Ⓓ Ⓔ
35 Ⓐ Ⓑ Ⓒ Ⓓ Ⓔ
36 Ⓐ Ⓑ Ⓒ Ⓓ Ⓔ
37 Ⓐ Ⓑ Ⓒ Ⓓ Ⓔ
38 Ⓐ Ⓑ Ⓒ Ⓓ Ⓔ
39 Ⓐ Ⓑ Ⓒ Ⓓ Ⓔ
40 Ⓐ Ⓑ Ⓒ Ⓓ Ⓔ

SECTION 5:
Mathematics
Questions

1 Ⓐ Ⓑ Ⓒ Ⓓ Ⓔ
2 Ⓐ Ⓑ Ⓒ Ⓓ Ⓔ
3 Ⓐ Ⓑ Ⓒ Ⓓ Ⓔ
4 Ⓐ Ⓑ Ⓒ Ⓓ Ⓔ
5 Ⓐ Ⓑ Ⓒ Ⓓ Ⓔ
6 Ⓐ Ⓑ Ⓒ Ⓓ Ⓔ
7 Ⓐ Ⓑ Ⓒ Ⓓ Ⓔ
8 Ⓐ Ⓑ Ⓒ Ⓓ Ⓔ
9 Ⓐ Ⓑ Ⓒ Ⓓ Ⓔ
10 Ⓐ Ⓑ Ⓒ Ⓓ Ⓔ
11 Ⓐ Ⓑ Ⓒ Ⓓ Ⓔ
12 Ⓐ Ⓑ Ⓒ Ⓓ Ⓔ
13 Ⓐ Ⓑ Ⓒ Ⓓ Ⓔ
14 Ⓐ Ⓑ Ⓒ Ⓓ Ⓔ
15 Ⓐ Ⓑ Ⓒ Ⓓ Ⓔ
16 Ⓐ Ⓑ Ⓒ Ⓓ Ⓔ
17 Ⓐ Ⓑ Ⓒ Ⓓ Ⓔ
18 Ⓐ Ⓑ Ⓒ Ⓓ Ⓔ
19 Ⓐ Ⓑ Ⓒ Ⓓ Ⓔ
20 Ⓐ Ⓑ Ⓒ Ⓓ Ⓔ
21 Ⓐ Ⓑ Ⓒ Ⓓ Ⓔ
22 Ⓐ Ⓑ Ⓒ Ⓓ Ⓔ
23 Ⓐ Ⓑ Ⓒ Ⓓ Ⓔ
24 Ⓐ Ⓑ Ⓒ Ⓓ Ⓔ
25 Ⓐ Ⓑ Ⓒ Ⓓ Ⓔ
26 Ⓐ Ⓑ Ⓒ Ⓓ Ⓔ
27 Ⓐ Ⓑ Ⓒ Ⓓ Ⓔ
28 Ⓐ Ⓑ Ⓒ Ⓓ Ⓔ
29 Ⓐ Ⓑ Ⓒ Ⓓ Ⓔ
30 Ⓐ Ⓑ Ⓒ Ⓓ Ⓔ
31 Ⓐ Ⓑ Ⓒ Ⓓ Ⓔ
32 Ⓐ Ⓑ Ⓒ Ⓓ Ⓔ
33 Ⓐ Ⓑ Ⓒ Ⓓ Ⓔ
34 Ⓐ Ⓑ Ⓒ Ⓓ Ⓔ
35 Ⓐ Ⓑ Ⓒ Ⓓ Ⓔ

ANSWER SHEET FOR PRACTICE TEST 4

Note that 5 answer spaces are provided throughout this Answer Sheet. However, questions in some sections of the Practice Test will have only 4 possible answers (A or B or C or D).

SECTION 1:
Verbal
Questions

1 Ⓐ Ⓑ Ⓒ Ⓓ Ⓔ	31 Ⓐ Ⓑ Ⓒ Ⓓ Ⓔ
2 Ⓐ Ⓑ Ⓒ Ⓓ Ⓔ	32 Ⓐ Ⓑ Ⓒ Ⓓ Ⓔ
3 Ⓐ Ⓑ Ⓒ Ⓓ Ⓔ	33 Ⓐ Ⓑ Ⓒ Ⓓ Ⓔ
4 Ⓐ Ⓑ Ⓒ Ⓓ Ⓔ	34 Ⓐ Ⓑ Ⓒ Ⓓ Ⓔ
5 Ⓐ Ⓑ Ⓒ Ⓓ Ⓔ	35 Ⓐ Ⓑ Ⓒ Ⓓ Ⓔ
6 Ⓐ Ⓑ Ⓒ Ⓓ Ⓔ	36 Ⓐ Ⓑ Ⓒ Ⓓ Ⓔ
7 Ⓐ Ⓑ Ⓒ Ⓓ Ⓔ	37 Ⓐ Ⓑ Ⓒ Ⓓ Ⓔ
8 Ⓐ Ⓑ Ⓒ Ⓓ Ⓔ	38 Ⓐ Ⓑ Ⓒ Ⓓ Ⓔ
9 Ⓐ Ⓑ Ⓒ Ⓓ Ⓔ	39 Ⓐ Ⓑ Ⓒ Ⓓ Ⓔ
10 Ⓐ Ⓑ Ⓒ Ⓓ Ⓔ	40 Ⓐ Ⓑ Ⓒ Ⓓ Ⓔ
11 Ⓐ Ⓑ Ⓒ Ⓓ Ⓔ	
12 Ⓐ Ⓑ Ⓒ Ⓓ Ⓔ	
13 Ⓐ Ⓑ Ⓒ Ⓓ Ⓔ	
14 Ⓐ Ⓑ Ⓒ Ⓓ Ⓔ	
15 Ⓐ Ⓑ Ⓒ Ⓓ Ⓔ	
16 Ⓐ Ⓑ Ⓒ Ⓓ Ⓔ	
17 Ⓐ Ⓑ Ⓒ Ⓓ Ⓔ	
18 Ⓐ Ⓑ Ⓒ Ⓓ Ⓔ	
19 Ⓐ Ⓑ Ⓒ Ⓓ Ⓔ	
20 Ⓐ Ⓑ Ⓒ Ⓓ Ⓔ	
21 Ⓐ Ⓑ Ⓒ Ⓓ Ⓔ	
22 Ⓐ Ⓑ Ⓒ Ⓓ Ⓔ	
23 Ⓐ Ⓑ Ⓒ Ⓓ Ⓔ	
24 Ⓐ Ⓑ Ⓒ Ⓓ Ⓔ	
25 Ⓐ Ⓑ Ⓒ Ⓓ Ⓔ	
26 Ⓐ Ⓑ Ⓒ Ⓓ Ⓔ	
27 Ⓐ Ⓑ Ⓒ Ⓓ Ⓔ	
28 Ⓐ Ⓑ Ⓒ Ⓓ Ⓔ	
29 Ⓐ Ⓑ Ⓒ Ⓓ Ⓔ	
30 Ⓐ Ⓑ Ⓒ Ⓓ Ⓔ	

SECTION 2:
Mathematics
Questions

1 Ⓐ Ⓑ Ⓒ Ⓓ Ⓔ
2 Ⓐ Ⓑ Ⓒ Ⓓ Ⓔ
3 Ⓐ Ⓑ Ⓒ Ⓓ Ⓔ
4 Ⓐ Ⓑ Ⓒ Ⓓ Ⓔ
5 Ⓐ Ⓑ Ⓒ Ⓓ Ⓔ
6 Ⓐ Ⓑ Ⓒ Ⓓ Ⓔ
7 Ⓐ Ⓑ Ⓒ Ⓓ Ⓔ
8 Ⓐ Ⓑ Ⓒ Ⓓ Ⓔ
9 Ⓐ Ⓑ Ⓒ Ⓓ Ⓔ
10 Ⓐ Ⓑ Ⓒ Ⓓ Ⓔ
11 Ⓐ Ⓑ Ⓒ Ⓓ Ⓔ
12 Ⓐ Ⓑ Ⓒ Ⓓ Ⓔ
13 Ⓐ Ⓑ Ⓒ Ⓓ Ⓔ
14 Ⓐ Ⓑ Ⓒ Ⓓ Ⓔ
15 Ⓐ Ⓑ Ⓒ Ⓓ Ⓔ
16 Ⓐ Ⓑ Ⓒ Ⓓ Ⓔ
17 Ⓐ Ⓑ Ⓒ Ⓓ Ⓔ
18 Ⓐ Ⓑ Ⓒ Ⓓ Ⓔ
19 Ⓐ Ⓑ Ⓒ Ⓓ Ⓔ
20 Ⓐ Ⓑ Ⓒ Ⓓ Ⓔ
21 Ⓐ Ⓑ Ⓒ Ⓓ Ⓔ
22 Ⓐ Ⓑ Ⓒ Ⓓ Ⓔ
23 Ⓐ Ⓑ Ⓒ Ⓓ Ⓔ
24 Ⓐ Ⓑ Ⓒ Ⓓ Ⓔ
25 Ⓐ Ⓑ Ⓒ Ⓓ Ⓔ

SECTION 3:
Verbal
Questions

1 Ⓐ Ⓑ Ⓒ Ⓓ Ⓔ	31 Ⓐ Ⓑ Ⓒ Ⓓ Ⓔ
2 Ⓐ Ⓑ Ⓒ Ⓓ Ⓔ	32 Ⓐ Ⓑ Ⓒ Ⓓ Ⓔ
3 Ⓐ Ⓑ Ⓒ Ⓓ Ⓔ	33 Ⓐ Ⓑ Ⓒ Ⓓ Ⓔ
4 Ⓐ Ⓑ Ⓒ Ⓓ Ⓔ	34 Ⓐ Ⓑ Ⓒ Ⓓ Ⓔ
5 Ⓐ Ⓑ Ⓒ Ⓓ Ⓔ	35 Ⓐ Ⓑ Ⓒ Ⓓ Ⓔ
6 Ⓐ Ⓑ Ⓒ Ⓓ Ⓔ	36 Ⓐ Ⓑ Ⓒ Ⓓ Ⓔ
7 Ⓐ Ⓑ Ⓒ Ⓓ Ⓔ	37 Ⓐ Ⓑ Ⓒ Ⓓ Ⓔ
8 Ⓐ Ⓑ Ⓒ Ⓓ Ⓔ	38 Ⓐ Ⓑ Ⓒ Ⓓ Ⓔ
9 Ⓐ Ⓑ Ⓒ Ⓓ Ⓔ	39 Ⓐ Ⓑ Ⓒ Ⓓ Ⓔ
10 Ⓐ Ⓑ Ⓒ Ⓓ Ⓔ	40 Ⓐ Ⓑ Ⓒ Ⓓ Ⓔ
11 Ⓐ Ⓑ Ⓒ Ⓓ Ⓔ	
12 Ⓐ Ⓑ Ⓒ Ⓓ Ⓔ	
13 Ⓐ Ⓑ Ⓒ Ⓓ Ⓔ	
14 Ⓐ Ⓑ Ⓒ Ⓓ Ⓔ	
15 Ⓐ Ⓑ Ⓒ Ⓓ Ⓔ	
16 Ⓐ Ⓑ Ⓒ Ⓓ Ⓔ	
17 Ⓐ Ⓑ Ⓒ Ⓓ Ⓔ	
18 Ⓐ Ⓑ Ⓒ Ⓓ Ⓔ	
19 Ⓐ Ⓑ Ⓒ Ⓓ Ⓔ	
20 Ⓐ Ⓑ Ⓒ Ⓓ Ⓔ	
21 Ⓐ Ⓑ Ⓒ Ⓓ Ⓔ	
22 Ⓐ Ⓑ Ⓒ Ⓓ Ⓔ	
23 Ⓐ Ⓑ Ⓒ Ⓓ Ⓔ	
24 Ⓐ Ⓑ Ⓒ Ⓓ Ⓔ	
25 Ⓐ Ⓑ Ⓒ Ⓓ Ⓔ	
26 Ⓐ Ⓑ Ⓒ Ⓓ Ⓔ	
27 Ⓐ Ⓑ Ⓒ Ⓓ Ⓔ	
28 Ⓐ Ⓑ Ⓒ Ⓓ Ⓔ	
29 Ⓐ Ⓑ Ⓒ Ⓓ Ⓔ	
30 Ⓐ Ⓑ Ⓒ Ⓓ Ⓔ	

(continued)

SECTION 5: Mathematics Questions

1 Ⓐ Ⓑ Ⓒ Ⓓ Ⓔ
2 Ⓐ Ⓑ Ⓒ Ⓓ Ⓔ
3 Ⓐ Ⓑ Ⓒ Ⓓ Ⓔ
4 Ⓐ Ⓑ Ⓒ Ⓓ Ⓔ
5 Ⓐ Ⓑ Ⓒ Ⓓ Ⓔ
6 Ⓐ Ⓑ Ⓒ Ⓓ Ⓔ
7 Ⓐ Ⓑ Ⓒ Ⓓ Ⓔ
8 Ⓐ Ⓑ Ⓒ Ⓓ Ⓔ
9 Ⓐ Ⓑ Ⓒ Ⓓ Ⓔ
10 Ⓐ Ⓑ Ⓒ Ⓓ Ⓔ
11 Ⓐ Ⓑ Ⓒ Ⓓ Ⓔ
12 Ⓐ Ⓑ Ⓒ Ⓓ Ⓔ
13 Ⓐ Ⓑ Ⓒ Ⓓ Ⓔ
14 Ⓐ Ⓑ Ⓒ Ⓓ Ⓔ
15 Ⓐ Ⓑ Ⓒ Ⓓ Ⓔ
16 Ⓐ Ⓑ Ⓒ Ⓓ Ⓔ
17 Ⓐ Ⓑ Ⓒ Ⓓ Ⓔ
18 Ⓐ Ⓑ Ⓒ Ⓓ Ⓔ
19 Ⓐ Ⓑ Ⓒ Ⓓ Ⓔ
20 Ⓐ Ⓑ Ⓒ Ⓓ Ⓔ
21 Ⓐ Ⓑ Ⓒ Ⓓ Ⓔ
22 Ⓐ Ⓑ Ⓒ Ⓓ Ⓔ
23 Ⓐ Ⓑ Ⓒ Ⓓ Ⓔ
24 Ⓐ Ⓑ Ⓒ Ⓓ Ⓔ
25 Ⓐ Ⓑ Ⓒ Ⓓ Ⓔ
26 Ⓐ Ⓑ Ⓒ Ⓓ Ⓔ
27 Ⓐ Ⓑ Ⓒ Ⓓ Ⓔ
28 Ⓐ Ⓑ Ⓒ Ⓓ Ⓔ
29 Ⓐ Ⓑ Ⓒ Ⓓ Ⓔ
30 Ⓐ Ⓑ Ⓒ Ⓓ Ⓔ
31 Ⓐ Ⓑ Ⓒ Ⓓ Ⓔ
32 Ⓐ Ⓑ Ⓒ Ⓓ Ⓔ
33 Ⓐ Ⓑ Ⓒ Ⓓ Ⓔ
34 Ⓐ Ⓑ Ⓒ Ⓓ Ⓔ
35 Ⓐ Ⓑ Ⓒ Ⓓ Ⓔ

SECTION 6: Verbal Questions

1 Ⓐ Ⓑ Ⓒ Ⓓ Ⓔ
2 Ⓐ Ⓑ Ⓒ Ⓓ Ⓔ
3 Ⓐ Ⓑ Ⓒ Ⓓ Ⓔ
4 Ⓐ Ⓑ Ⓒ Ⓓ Ⓔ
5 Ⓐ Ⓑ Ⓒ Ⓓ Ⓔ
6 Ⓐ Ⓑ Ⓒ Ⓓ Ⓔ
7 Ⓐ Ⓑ Ⓒ Ⓓ Ⓔ
8 Ⓐ Ⓑ Ⓒ Ⓓ Ⓔ
9 Ⓐ Ⓑ Ⓒ Ⓓ Ⓔ
10 Ⓐ Ⓑ Ⓒ Ⓓ Ⓔ
11 Ⓐ Ⓑ Ⓒ Ⓓ Ⓔ
12 Ⓐ Ⓑ Ⓒ Ⓓ Ⓔ
13 Ⓐ Ⓑ Ⓒ Ⓓ Ⓔ
14 Ⓐ Ⓑ Ⓒ Ⓓ Ⓔ
15 Ⓐ Ⓑ Ⓒ Ⓓ Ⓔ
16 Ⓐ Ⓑ Ⓒ Ⓓ Ⓔ
17 Ⓐ Ⓑ Ⓒ Ⓓ Ⓔ
18 Ⓐ Ⓑ Ⓒ Ⓓ Ⓔ
19 Ⓐ Ⓑ Ⓒ Ⓓ Ⓔ
20 Ⓐ Ⓑ Ⓒ Ⓓ Ⓔ
21 Ⓐ Ⓑ Ⓒ Ⓓ Ⓔ
22 Ⓐ Ⓑ Ⓒ Ⓓ Ⓔ
23 Ⓐ Ⓑ Ⓒ Ⓓ Ⓔ
24 Ⓐ Ⓑ Ⓒ Ⓓ Ⓔ
25 Ⓐ Ⓑ Ⓒ Ⓓ Ⓔ
26 Ⓐ Ⓑ Ⓒ Ⓓ Ⓔ
27 Ⓐ Ⓑ Ⓒ Ⓓ Ⓔ
28 Ⓐ Ⓑ Ⓒ Ⓓ Ⓔ
29 Ⓐ Ⓑ Ⓒ Ⓓ Ⓔ
30 Ⓐ Ⓑ Ⓒ Ⓓ Ⓔ

31 Ⓐ Ⓑ Ⓒ Ⓓ Ⓔ
32 Ⓐ Ⓑ Ⓒ Ⓓ Ⓔ
33 Ⓐ Ⓑ Ⓒ Ⓓ Ⓔ
34 Ⓐ Ⓑ Ⓒ Ⓓ Ⓔ
35 Ⓐ Ⓑ Ⓒ Ⓓ Ⓔ
36 Ⓐ Ⓑ Ⓒ Ⓓ Ⓔ
37 Ⓐ Ⓑ Ⓒ Ⓓ Ⓔ
38 Ⓐ Ⓑ Ⓒ Ⓓ Ⓔ
39 Ⓐ Ⓑ Ⓒ Ⓓ Ⓔ
40 Ⓐ Ⓑ Ⓒ Ⓓ Ⓔ
41 Ⓐ Ⓑ Ⓒ Ⓓ Ⓔ
42 Ⓐ Ⓑ Ⓒ Ⓓ Ⓔ
43 Ⓐ Ⓑ Ⓒ Ⓓ Ⓔ
44 Ⓐ Ⓑ Ⓒ Ⓓ Ⓔ
45 Ⓐ Ⓑ Ⓒ Ⓓ Ⓔ

QUANTITATIVE COMPARISON

1 Ⓐ Ⓑ Ⓒ Ⓓ Ⓔ	21 Ⓐ Ⓑ Ⓒ Ⓓ Ⓔ	41 Ⓐ Ⓑ Ⓒ Ⓓ Ⓔ	61 Ⓐ Ⓑ Ⓒ Ⓓ Ⓔ
2 Ⓐ Ⓑ Ⓒ Ⓓ Ⓔ	22 Ⓐ Ⓑ Ⓒ Ⓓ Ⓔ	42 Ⓐ Ⓑ Ⓒ Ⓓ Ⓔ	62 Ⓐ Ⓑ Ⓒ Ⓓ Ⓔ
3 Ⓐ Ⓑ Ⓒ Ⓓ Ⓔ	23 Ⓐ Ⓑ Ⓒ Ⓓ Ⓔ	43 Ⓐ Ⓑ Ⓒ Ⓓ Ⓔ	63 Ⓐ Ⓑ Ⓒ Ⓓ Ⓔ
4 Ⓐ Ⓑ Ⓒ Ⓓ Ⓔ	24 Ⓐ Ⓑ Ⓒ Ⓓ Ⓔ	44 Ⓐ Ⓑ Ⓒ Ⓓ Ⓔ	64 Ⓐ Ⓑ Ⓒ Ⓓ Ⓔ
5 Ⓐ Ⓑ Ⓒ Ⓓ Ⓔ	25 Ⓐ Ⓑ Ⓒ Ⓓ Ⓔ	45 Ⓐ Ⓑ Ⓒ Ⓓ Ⓔ	65 Ⓐ Ⓑ Ⓒ Ⓓ Ⓔ
6 Ⓐ Ⓑ Ⓒ Ⓓ Ⓔ	26 Ⓐ Ⓑ Ⓒ Ⓓ Ⓔ	46 Ⓐ Ⓑ Ⓒ Ⓓ Ⓔ	66 Ⓐ Ⓑ Ⓒ Ⓓ Ⓔ
7 Ⓐ Ⓑ Ⓒ Ⓓ Ⓔ	27 Ⓐ Ⓑ Ⓒ Ⓓ Ⓔ	47 Ⓐ Ⓑ Ⓒ Ⓓ Ⓔ	67 Ⓐ Ⓑ Ⓒ Ⓓ Ⓔ
8 Ⓐ Ⓑ Ⓒ Ⓓ Ⓔ	28 Ⓐ Ⓑ Ⓒ Ⓓ Ⓔ	48 Ⓐ Ⓑ Ⓒ Ⓓ Ⓔ	68 Ⓐ Ⓑ Ⓒ Ⓓ Ⓔ
9 Ⓐ Ⓑ Ⓒ Ⓓ Ⓔ	29 Ⓐ Ⓑ Ⓒ Ⓓ Ⓔ	49 Ⓐ Ⓑ Ⓒ Ⓓ Ⓔ	69 Ⓐ Ⓑ Ⓒ Ⓓ Ⓔ
10 Ⓐ Ⓑ Ⓒ Ⓓ Ⓔ	30 Ⓐ Ⓑ Ⓒ Ⓓ Ⓔ	50 Ⓐ Ⓑ Ⓒ Ⓓ Ⓔ	70 Ⓐ Ⓑ Ⓒ Ⓓ Ⓔ
11 Ⓐ Ⓑ Ⓒ Ⓓ Ⓔ	31 Ⓐ Ⓑ Ⓒ Ⓓ Ⓔ	51 Ⓐ Ⓑ Ⓒ Ⓓ Ⓔ	71 Ⓐ Ⓑ Ⓒ Ⓓ Ⓔ
12 Ⓐ Ⓑ Ⓒ Ⓓ Ⓔ	32 Ⓐ Ⓑ Ⓒ Ⓓ Ⓔ	52 Ⓐ Ⓑ Ⓒ Ⓓ Ⓔ	72 Ⓐ Ⓑ Ⓒ Ⓓ Ⓔ
13 Ⓐ Ⓑ Ⓒ Ⓓ Ⓔ	33 Ⓐ Ⓑ Ⓒ Ⓓ Ⓔ	53 Ⓐ Ⓑ Ⓒ Ⓓ Ⓔ	73 Ⓐ Ⓑ Ⓒ Ⓓ Ⓔ
14 Ⓐ Ⓑ Ⓒ Ⓓ Ⓔ	34 Ⓐ Ⓑ Ⓒ Ⓓ Ⓔ	54 Ⓐ Ⓑ Ⓒ Ⓓ Ⓔ	74 Ⓐ Ⓑ Ⓒ Ⓓ Ⓔ
15 Ⓐ Ⓑ Ⓒ Ⓓ Ⓔ	35 Ⓐ Ⓑ Ⓒ Ⓓ Ⓔ	55 Ⓐ Ⓑ Ⓒ Ⓓ Ⓔ	75 Ⓐ Ⓑ Ⓒ Ⓓ Ⓔ
16 Ⓐ Ⓑ Ⓒ Ⓓ Ⓔ	36 Ⓐ Ⓑ Ⓒ Ⓓ Ⓔ	56 Ⓐ Ⓑ Ⓒ Ⓓ Ⓔ	76 Ⓐ Ⓑ Ⓒ Ⓓ Ⓔ
17 Ⓐ Ⓑ Ⓒ Ⓓ Ⓔ	37 Ⓐ Ⓑ Ⓒ Ⓓ Ⓔ	57 Ⓐ Ⓑ Ⓒ Ⓓ Ⓔ	77 Ⓐ Ⓑ Ⓒ Ⓓ Ⓔ
18 Ⓐ Ⓑ Ⓒ Ⓓ Ⓔ	38 Ⓐ Ⓑ Ⓒ Ⓓ Ⓔ	58 Ⓐ Ⓑ Ⓒ Ⓓ Ⓔ	78 Ⓐ Ⓑ Ⓒ Ⓓ Ⓔ
19 Ⓐ Ⓑ Ⓒ Ⓓ Ⓔ	39 Ⓐ Ⓑ Ⓒ Ⓓ Ⓔ	59 Ⓐ Ⓑ Ⓒ Ⓓ Ⓔ	79 Ⓐ Ⓑ Ⓒ Ⓓ Ⓔ
20 Ⓐ Ⓑ Ⓒ Ⓓ Ⓔ	40 Ⓐ Ⓑ Ⓒ Ⓓ Ⓔ	60 Ⓐ Ⓑ Ⓒ Ⓓ Ⓔ	80 Ⓐ Ⓑ Ⓒ Ⓓ Ⓔ

ANSWER SHEET FOR PRACTICE TEST 1

Note that 5 answer spaces are provided throughout this Answer Sheet. However, questions in some sections of the Practice Test will have only 4 possible answers (A or B or C or D).

SECTION 1:
Mathematics
Questions

1 Ⓐ Ⓑ Ⓒ Ⓓ Ⓔ
2 Ⓐ Ⓑ Ⓒ Ⓓ Ⓔ
3 Ⓐ Ⓑ Ⓒ Ⓓ Ⓔ
4 Ⓐ Ⓑ Ⓒ Ⓓ Ⓔ
5 Ⓐ Ⓑ Ⓒ Ⓓ Ⓔ
6 Ⓐ Ⓑ Ⓒ Ⓓ Ⓔ
7 Ⓐ Ⓑ Ⓒ Ⓓ Ⓔ
8 Ⓐ Ⓑ Ⓒ Ⓓ Ⓔ
9 Ⓐ Ⓑ Ⓒ Ⓓ Ⓔ
10 Ⓐ Ⓑ Ⓒ Ⓓ Ⓔ
11 Ⓐ Ⓑ Ⓒ Ⓓ Ⓔ
12 Ⓐ Ⓑ Ⓒ Ⓓ Ⓔ
13 Ⓐ Ⓑ Ⓒ Ⓓ Ⓔ
14 Ⓐ Ⓑ Ⓒ Ⓓ Ⓔ
15 Ⓐ Ⓑ Ⓒ Ⓓ Ⓔ
16 Ⓐ Ⓑ Ⓒ Ⓓ Ⓔ
17 Ⓐ Ⓑ Ⓒ Ⓓ Ⓔ
18 Ⓐ Ⓑ Ⓒ Ⓓ Ⓔ
19 Ⓐ Ⓑ Ⓒ Ⓓ Ⓔ
20 Ⓐ Ⓑ Ⓒ Ⓓ Ⓔ
21 Ⓐ Ⓑ Ⓒ Ⓓ Ⓔ
22 Ⓐ Ⓑ Ⓒ Ⓓ Ⓔ
23 Ⓐ Ⓑ Ⓒ Ⓓ Ⓔ
24 Ⓐ Ⓑ Ⓒ Ⓓ Ⓔ
25 Ⓐ Ⓑ Ⓒ Ⓓ Ⓔ

SECTION 2:
Verbal
Questions

1 Ⓐ Ⓑ Ⓒ Ⓓ Ⓔ
2 Ⓐ Ⓑ Ⓒ Ⓓ Ⓔ
3 Ⓐ Ⓑ Ⓒ Ⓓ Ⓔ
4 Ⓐ Ⓑ Ⓒ Ⓓ Ⓔ
5 Ⓐ Ⓑ Ⓒ Ⓓ Ⓔ
6 Ⓐ Ⓑ Ⓒ Ⓓ Ⓔ
7 Ⓐ Ⓑ Ⓒ Ⓓ Ⓔ
8 Ⓐ Ⓑ Ⓒ Ⓓ Ⓔ
9 Ⓐ Ⓑ Ⓒ Ⓓ Ⓔ
10 Ⓐ Ⓑ Ⓒ Ⓓ Ⓔ
11 Ⓐ Ⓑ Ⓒ Ⓓ Ⓔ
12 Ⓐ Ⓑ Ⓒ Ⓓ Ⓔ
13 Ⓐ Ⓑ Ⓒ Ⓓ Ⓔ
14 Ⓐ Ⓑ Ⓒ Ⓓ Ⓔ
15 Ⓐ Ⓑ Ⓒ Ⓓ Ⓔ
16 Ⓐ Ⓑ Ⓒ Ⓓ Ⓔ
17 Ⓐ Ⓑ Ⓒ Ⓓ Ⓔ
18 Ⓐ Ⓑ Ⓒ Ⓓ Ⓔ
19 Ⓐ Ⓑ Ⓒ Ⓓ Ⓔ
20 Ⓐ Ⓑ Ⓒ Ⓓ Ⓔ
21 Ⓐ Ⓑ Ⓒ Ⓓ Ⓔ
22 Ⓐ Ⓑ Ⓒ Ⓓ Ⓔ
23 Ⓐ Ⓑ Ⓒ Ⓓ Ⓔ
24 Ⓐ Ⓑ Ⓒ Ⓓ Ⓔ
25 Ⓐ Ⓑ Ⓒ Ⓓ Ⓔ
26 Ⓐ Ⓑ Ⓒ Ⓓ Ⓔ
27 Ⓐ Ⓑ Ⓒ Ⓓ Ⓔ
28 Ⓐ Ⓑ Ⓒ Ⓓ Ⓔ
29 Ⓐ Ⓑ Ⓒ Ⓓ Ⓔ
30 Ⓐ Ⓑ Ⓒ Ⓓ Ⓔ

31 Ⓐ Ⓑ Ⓒ Ⓓ Ⓔ
32 Ⓐ Ⓑ Ⓒ Ⓓ Ⓔ
33 Ⓐ Ⓑ Ⓒ Ⓓ Ⓔ
34 Ⓐ Ⓑ Ⓒ Ⓓ Ⓔ
35 Ⓐ Ⓑ Ⓒ Ⓓ Ⓔ
36 Ⓐ Ⓑ Ⓒ Ⓓ Ⓔ
37 Ⓐ Ⓑ Ⓒ Ⓓ Ⓔ
38 Ⓐ Ⓑ Ⓒ Ⓓ Ⓔ
39 Ⓐ Ⓑ Ⓒ Ⓓ Ⓔ
40 Ⓐ Ⓑ Ⓒ Ⓓ Ⓔ

SECTION 4:
Verbal
Questions

1 Ⓐ Ⓑ Ⓒ Ⓓ Ⓔ
2 Ⓐ Ⓑ Ⓒ Ⓓ Ⓔ
3 Ⓐ Ⓑ Ⓒ Ⓓ Ⓔ
4 Ⓐ Ⓑ Ⓒ Ⓓ Ⓔ
5 Ⓐ Ⓑ Ⓒ Ⓓ Ⓔ
6 Ⓐ Ⓑ Ⓒ Ⓓ Ⓔ
7 Ⓐ Ⓑ Ⓒ Ⓓ Ⓔ
8 Ⓐ Ⓑ Ⓒ Ⓓ Ⓔ
9 Ⓐ Ⓑ Ⓒ Ⓓ Ⓔ
10 Ⓐ Ⓑ Ⓒ Ⓓ Ⓔ
11 Ⓐ Ⓑ Ⓒ Ⓓ Ⓔ
12 Ⓐ Ⓑ Ⓒ Ⓓ Ⓔ
13 Ⓐ Ⓑ Ⓒ Ⓓ Ⓔ
14 Ⓐ Ⓑ Ⓒ Ⓓ Ⓔ
15 Ⓐ Ⓑ Ⓒ Ⓓ Ⓔ
16 Ⓐ Ⓑ Ⓒ Ⓓ Ⓔ
17 Ⓐ Ⓑ Ⓒ Ⓓ Ⓔ
18 Ⓐ Ⓑ Ⓒ Ⓓ Ⓔ
19 Ⓐ Ⓑ Ⓒ Ⓓ Ⓔ
20 Ⓐ Ⓑ Ⓒ Ⓓ Ⓔ
21 Ⓐ Ⓑ Ⓒ Ⓓ Ⓔ
22 Ⓐ Ⓑ Ⓒ Ⓓ Ⓔ
23 Ⓐ Ⓑ Ⓒ Ⓓ Ⓔ
24 Ⓐ Ⓑ Ⓒ Ⓓ Ⓔ
25 Ⓐ Ⓑ Ⓒ Ⓓ Ⓔ
26 Ⓐ Ⓑ Ⓒ Ⓓ Ⓔ
27 Ⓐ Ⓑ Ⓒ Ⓓ Ⓔ
28 Ⓐ Ⓑ Ⓒ Ⓓ Ⓔ
29 Ⓐ Ⓑ Ⓒ Ⓓ Ⓔ
30 Ⓐ Ⓑ Ⓒ Ⓓ Ⓔ

31 Ⓐ Ⓑ Ⓒ Ⓓ Ⓔ
32 Ⓐ Ⓑ Ⓒ Ⓓ Ⓔ
33 Ⓐ Ⓑ Ⓒ Ⓓ Ⓔ
34 Ⓐ Ⓑ Ⓒ Ⓓ Ⓔ
35 Ⓐ Ⓑ Ⓒ Ⓓ Ⓔ
36 Ⓐ Ⓑ Ⓒ Ⓓ Ⓔ
37 Ⓐ Ⓑ Ⓒ Ⓓ Ⓔ
38 Ⓐ Ⓑ Ⓒ Ⓓ Ⓔ
39 Ⓐ Ⓑ Ⓒ Ⓓ Ⓔ
40 Ⓐ Ⓑ Ⓒ Ⓓ Ⓔ
41 Ⓐ Ⓑ Ⓒ Ⓓ Ⓔ
42 Ⓐ Ⓑ Ⓒ Ⓓ Ⓔ
43 Ⓐ Ⓑ Ⓒ Ⓓ Ⓔ
44 Ⓐ Ⓑ Ⓒ Ⓓ Ⓔ
45 Ⓐ Ⓑ Ⓒ Ⓓ Ⓔ

(continued)

SECTION 5:
Mathematics
Questions

1 Ⓐ Ⓑ Ⓒ Ⓓ Ⓔ
2 Ⓐ Ⓑ Ⓒ Ⓓ Ⓔ
3 Ⓐ Ⓑ Ⓒ Ⓓ Ⓔ
4 Ⓐ Ⓑ Ⓒ Ⓓ Ⓔ
5 Ⓐ Ⓑ Ⓒ Ⓓ Ⓔ
6 Ⓐ Ⓑ Ⓒ Ⓓ Ⓔ
7 Ⓐ Ⓑ Ⓒ Ⓓ Ⓔ
8 Ⓐ Ⓑ Ⓒ Ⓓ Ⓔ
9 Ⓐ Ⓑ Ⓒ Ⓓ Ⓔ
10 Ⓐ Ⓑ Ⓒ Ⓓ Ⓔ
11 Ⓐ Ⓑ Ⓒ Ⓓ Ⓔ
12 Ⓐ Ⓑ Ⓒ Ⓓ Ⓔ
13 Ⓐ Ⓑ Ⓒ Ⓓ Ⓔ
14 Ⓐ Ⓑ Ⓒ Ⓓ Ⓔ
15 Ⓐ Ⓑ Ⓒ Ⓓ Ⓔ
16 Ⓐ Ⓑ Ⓒ Ⓓ Ⓔ
17 Ⓐ Ⓑ Ⓒ Ⓓ Ⓔ
18 Ⓐ Ⓑ Ⓒ Ⓓ Ⓔ
19 Ⓐ Ⓑ Ⓒ Ⓓ Ⓔ
20 Ⓐ Ⓑ Ⓒ Ⓓ Ⓔ
21 Ⓐ Ⓑ Ⓒ Ⓓ Ⓔ
22 Ⓐ Ⓑ Ⓒ Ⓓ Ⓔ
23 Ⓐ Ⓑ Ⓒ Ⓓ Ⓔ
24 Ⓐ Ⓑ Ⓒ Ⓓ Ⓔ
25 Ⓐ Ⓑ Ⓒ Ⓓ Ⓔ
26 Ⓐ Ⓑ Ⓒ Ⓓ Ⓔ
27 Ⓐ Ⓑ Ⓒ Ⓓ Ⓔ
28 Ⓐ Ⓑ Ⓒ Ⓓ Ⓔ
29 Ⓐ Ⓑ Ⓒ Ⓓ Ⓔ
30 Ⓐ Ⓑ Ⓒ Ⓓ Ⓔ
31 Ⓐ Ⓑ Ⓒ Ⓓ Ⓔ
32 Ⓐ Ⓑ Ⓒ Ⓓ Ⓔ
33 Ⓐ Ⓑ Ⓒ Ⓓ Ⓔ
34 Ⓐ Ⓑ Ⓒ Ⓓ Ⓔ
35 Ⓐ Ⓑ Ⓒ Ⓓ Ⓔ

SECTION 6:
Verbal
Questions

1 Ⓐ Ⓑ Ⓒ Ⓓ Ⓔ
2 Ⓐ Ⓑ Ⓒ Ⓓ Ⓔ
3 Ⓐ Ⓑ Ⓒ Ⓓ Ⓔ
4 Ⓐ Ⓑ Ⓒ Ⓓ Ⓔ
5 Ⓐ Ⓑ Ⓒ Ⓓ Ⓔ
6 Ⓐ Ⓑ Ⓒ Ⓓ Ⓔ
7 Ⓐ Ⓑ Ⓒ Ⓓ Ⓔ
8 Ⓐ Ⓑ Ⓒ Ⓓ Ⓔ
9 Ⓐ Ⓑ Ⓒ Ⓓ Ⓔ
10 Ⓐ Ⓑ Ⓒ Ⓓ Ⓔ
11 Ⓐ Ⓑ Ⓒ Ⓓ Ⓔ
12 Ⓐ Ⓑ Ⓒ Ⓓ Ⓔ
13 Ⓐ Ⓑ Ⓒ Ⓓ Ⓔ
14 Ⓐ Ⓑ Ⓒ Ⓓ Ⓔ
15 Ⓐ Ⓑ Ⓒ Ⓓ Ⓔ
16 Ⓐ Ⓑ Ⓒ Ⓓ Ⓔ
17 Ⓐ Ⓑ Ⓒ Ⓓ Ⓔ
18 Ⓐ Ⓑ Ⓒ Ⓓ Ⓔ
19 Ⓐ Ⓑ Ⓒ Ⓓ Ⓔ
20 Ⓐ Ⓑ Ⓒ Ⓓ Ⓔ
21 Ⓐ Ⓑ Ⓒ Ⓓ Ⓔ
22 Ⓐ Ⓑ Ⓒ Ⓓ Ⓔ
23 Ⓐ Ⓑ Ⓒ Ⓓ Ⓔ
24 Ⓐ Ⓑ Ⓒ Ⓓ Ⓔ
25 Ⓐ Ⓑ Ⓒ Ⓓ Ⓔ
26 Ⓐ Ⓑ Ⓒ Ⓓ Ⓔ
27 Ⓐ Ⓑ Ⓒ Ⓓ Ⓔ
28 Ⓐ Ⓑ Ⓒ Ⓓ Ⓔ
29 Ⓐ Ⓑ Ⓒ Ⓓ Ⓔ
30 Ⓐ Ⓑ Ⓒ Ⓓ Ⓔ
31 Ⓐ Ⓑ Ⓒ Ⓓ Ⓔ
32 Ⓐ Ⓑ Ⓒ Ⓓ Ⓔ
33 Ⓐ Ⓑ Ⓒ Ⓓ Ⓔ
34 Ⓐ Ⓑ Ⓒ Ⓓ Ⓔ
35 Ⓐ Ⓑ Ⓒ Ⓓ Ⓔ
36 Ⓐ Ⓑ Ⓒ Ⓓ Ⓔ
37 Ⓐ Ⓑ Ⓒ Ⓓ Ⓔ
38 Ⓐ Ⓑ Ⓒ Ⓓ Ⓔ
39 Ⓐ Ⓑ Ⓒ Ⓓ Ⓔ
40 Ⓐ Ⓑ Ⓒ Ⓓ Ⓔ

ANSWER SHEET FOR PRACTICE TEST 2

Note that 5 answer spaces are provided throughout this Answer Sheet. However, questions in some sections of the Practice Test will have only 4 possible answers (A or B or C or D).

SECTION 1:
Verbal
Questions

1 Ⓐ Ⓑ Ⓒ Ⓓ Ⓔ   36 Ⓐ Ⓑ Ⓒ Ⓓ Ⓔ
2 Ⓐ Ⓑ Ⓒ Ⓓ Ⓔ   37 Ⓐ Ⓑ Ⓒ Ⓓ Ⓔ
3 Ⓐ Ⓑ Ⓒ Ⓓ Ⓔ   38 Ⓐ Ⓑ Ⓒ Ⓓ Ⓔ
4 Ⓐ Ⓑ Ⓒ Ⓓ Ⓔ   39 Ⓐ Ⓑ Ⓒ Ⓓ Ⓔ
5 Ⓐ Ⓑ Ⓒ Ⓓ Ⓔ   40 Ⓐ Ⓑ Ⓒ Ⓓ Ⓔ
6 Ⓐ Ⓑ Ⓒ Ⓓ Ⓔ   41 Ⓐ Ⓑ Ⓒ Ⓓ Ⓔ
7 Ⓐ Ⓑ Ⓒ Ⓓ Ⓔ   42 Ⓐ Ⓑ Ⓒ Ⓓ Ⓔ
8 Ⓐ Ⓑ Ⓒ Ⓓ Ⓔ   43 Ⓐ Ⓑ Ⓒ Ⓓ Ⓔ
9 Ⓐ Ⓑ Ⓒ Ⓓ Ⓔ   44 Ⓐ Ⓑ Ⓒ Ⓓ Ⓔ
10 Ⓐ Ⓑ Ⓒ Ⓓ Ⓔ   45 Ⓐ Ⓑ Ⓒ Ⓓ Ⓔ
11 Ⓐ Ⓑ Ⓒ Ⓓ Ⓔ
12 Ⓐ Ⓑ Ⓒ Ⓓ Ⓔ
13 Ⓐ Ⓑ Ⓒ Ⓓ Ⓔ
14 Ⓐ Ⓑ Ⓒ Ⓓ Ⓔ
15 Ⓐ Ⓑ Ⓒ Ⓓ Ⓔ
16 Ⓐ Ⓑ Ⓒ Ⓓ Ⓔ
17 Ⓐ Ⓑ Ⓒ Ⓓ Ⓔ
18 Ⓐ Ⓑ Ⓒ Ⓓ Ⓔ
19 Ⓐ Ⓑ Ⓒ Ⓓ Ⓔ
20 Ⓐ Ⓑ Ⓒ Ⓓ Ⓔ
21 Ⓐ Ⓑ Ⓒ Ⓓ Ⓔ
22 Ⓐ Ⓑ Ⓒ Ⓓ Ⓔ
23 Ⓐ Ⓑ Ⓒ Ⓓ Ⓔ
24 Ⓐ Ⓑ Ⓒ Ⓓ Ⓔ
25 Ⓐ Ⓑ Ⓒ Ⓓ Ⓔ
26 Ⓐ Ⓑ Ⓒ Ⓓ Ⓔ
27 Ⓐ Ⓑ Ⓒ Ⓓ Ⓔ
28 Ⓐ Ⓑ Ⓒ Ⓓ Ⓔ
29 Ⓐ Ⓑ Ⓒ Ⓓ Ⓔ
30 Ⓐ Ⓑ Ⓒ Ⓓ Ⓔ
31 Ⓐ Ⓑ Ⓒ Ⓓ Ⓔ
32 Ⓐ Ⓑ Ⓒ Ⓓ Ⓔ
33 Ⓐ Ⓑ Ⓒ Ⓓ Ⓔ
34 Ⓐ Ⓑ Ⓒ Ⓓ Ⓔ
35 Ⓐ Ⓑ Ⓒ Ⓓ Ⓔ

SECTION 2:
Mathematics
Questions

1 Ⓐ Ⓑ Ⓒ Ⓓ Ⓔ
2 Ⓐ Ⓑ Ⓒ Ⓓ Ⓔ
3 Ⓐ Ⓑ Ⓒ Ⓓ Ⓔ
4 Ⓐ Ⓑ Ⓒ Ⓓ Ⓔ
5 Ⓐ Ⓑ Ⓒ Ⓓ Ⓔ
6 Ⓐ Ⓑ Ⓒ Ⓓ Ⓔ
7 Ⓐ Ⓑ Ⓒ Ⓓ Ⓔ
8 Ⓐ Ⓑ Ⓒ Ⓓ Ⓔ
9 Ⓐ Ⓑ Ⓒ Ⓓ Ⓔ
10 Ⓐ Ⓑ Ⓒ Ⓓ Ⓔ
11 Ⓐ Ⓑ Ⓒ Ⓓ Ⓔ
12 Ⓐ Ⓑ Ⓒ Ⓓ Ⓔ
13 Ⓐ Ⓑ Ⓒ Ⓓ Ⓔ
14 Ⓐ Ⓑ Ⓒ Ⓓ Ⓔ
15 Ⓐ Ⓑ Ⓒ Ⓓ Ⓔ
16 Ⓐ Ⓑ Ⓒ Ⓓ Ⓔ
17 Ⓐ Ⓑ Ⓒ Ⓓ Ⓔ
18 Ⓐ Ⓑ Ⓒ Ⓓ Ⓔ
19 Ⓐ Ⓑ Ⓒ Ⓓ Ⓔ
20 Ⓐ Ⓑ Ⓒ Ⓓ Ⓔ
21 Ⓐ Ⓑ Ⓒ Ⓓ Ⓔ
22 Ⓐ Ⓑ Ⓒ Ⓓ Ⓔ
23 Ⓐ Ⓑ Ⓒ Ⓓ Ⓔ
24 Ⓐ Ⓑ Ⓒ Ⓓ Ⓔ
25 Ⓐ Ⓑ Ⓒ Ⓓ Ⓔ

SECTION 3:
Mathematics
Questions

1 Ⓐ Ⓑ Ⓒ Ⓓ Ⓔ
2 Ⓐ Ⓑ Ⓒ Ⓓ Ⓔ
3 Ⓐ Ⓑ Ⓒ Ⓓ Ⓔ
4 Ⓐ Ⓑ Ⓒ Ⓓ Ⓔ
5 Ⓐ Ⓑ Ⓒ Ⓓ Ⓔ
6 Ⓐ Ⓑ Ⓒ Ⓓ Ⓔ
7 Ⓐ Ⓑ Ⓒ Ⓓ Ⓔ
8 Ⓐ Ⓑ Ⓒ Ⓓ Ⓔ
9 Ⓐ Ⓑ Ⓒ Ⓓ Ⓔ
10 Ⓐ Ⓑ Ⓒ Ⓓ Ⓔ
11 Ⓐ Ⓑ Ⓒ Ⓓ Ⓔ
12 Ⓐ Ⓑ Ⓒ Ⓓ Ⓔ
13 Ⓐ Ⓑ Ⓒ Ⓓ Ⓔ
14 Ⓐ Ⓑ Ⓒ Ⓓ Ⓔ
15 Ⓐ Ⓑ Ⓒ Ⓓ Ⓔ
16 Ⓐ Ⓑ Ⓒ Ⓓ Ⓔ
17 Ⓐ Ⓑ Ⓒ Ⓓ Ⓔ
18 Ⓐ Ⓑ Ⓒ Ⓓ Ⓔ
19 Ⓐ Ⓑ Ⓒ Ⓓ Ⓔ
20 Ⓐ Ⓑ Ⓒ Ⓓ Ⓔ
21 Ⓐ Ⓑ Ⓒ Ⓓ Ⓔ
22 Ⓐ Ⓑ Ⓒ Ⓓ Ⓔ
23 Ⓐ Ⓑ Ⓒ Ⓓ Ⓔ
24 Ⓐ Ⓑ Ⓒ Ⓓ Ⓔ
25 Ⓐ Ⓑ Ⓒ Ⓓ Ⓔ
26 Ⓐ Ⓑ Ⓒ Ⓓ Ⓔ
27 Ⓐ Ⓑ Ⓒ Ⓓ Ⓔ
28 Ⓐ Ⓑ Ⓒ Ⓓ Ⓔ
29 Ⓐ Ⓑ Ⓒ Ⓓ Ⓔ
30 Ⓐ Ⓑ Ⓒ Ⓓ Ⓔ
31 Ⓐ Ⓑ Ⓒ Ⓓ Ⓔ
32 Ⓐ Ⓑ Ⓒ Ⓓ Ⓔ
33 Ⓐ Ⓑ Ⓒ Ⓓ Ⓔ
34 Ⓐ Ⓑ Ⓒ Ⓓ Ⓔ
35 Ⓐ Ⓑ Ⓒ Ⓓ Ⓔ

(continued)

SECTION 5:
Verbal Questions

1 Ⓐ Ⓑ Ⓒ Ⓓ Ⓔ	26 Ⓐ Ⓑ Ⓒ Ⓓ Ⓔ	
2 Ⓐ Ⓑ Ⓒ Ⓓ Ⓔ	27 Ⓐ Ⓑ Ⓒ Ⓓ Ⓔ	
3 Ⓐ Ⓑ Ⓒ Ⓓ Ⓔ	28 Ⓐ Ⓑ Ⓒ Ⓓ Ⓔ	
4 Ⓐ Ⓑ Ⓒ Ⓓ Ⓔ	29 Ⓐ Ⓑ Ⓒ Ⓓ Ⓔ	
5 Ⓐ Ⓑ Ⓒ Ⓓ Ⓔ	30 Ⓐ Ⓑ Ⓒ Ⓓ Ⓔ	
6 Ⓐ Ⓑ Ⓒ Ⓓ Ⓔ	31 Ⓐ Ⓑ Ⓒ Ⓓ Ⓔ	
7 Ⓐ Ⓑ Ⓒ Ⓓ Ⓔ	32 Ⓐ Ⓑ Ⓒ Ⓓ Ⓔ	
8 Ⓐ Ⓑ Ⓒ Ⓓ Ⓔ	33 Ⓐ Ⓑ Ⓒ Ⓓ Ⓔ	
9 Ⓐ Ⓑ Ⓒ Ⓓ Ⓔ	34 Ⓐ Ⓑ Ⓒ Ⓓ Ⓔ	
10 Ⓐ Ⓑ Ⓒ Ⓓ Ⓔ	35 Ⓐ Ⓑ Ⓒ Ⓓ Ⓔ	
11 Ⓐ Ⓑ Ⓒ Ⓓ Ⓔ	36 Ⓐ Ⓑ Ⓒ Ⓓ Ⓔ	
12 Ⓐ Ⓑ Ⓒ Ⓓ Ⓔ	37 Ⓐ Ⓑ Ⓒ Ⓓ Ⓔ	
13 Ⓐ Ⓑ Ⓒ Ⓓ Ⓔ	38 Ⓐ Ⓑ Ⓒ Ⓓ Ⓔ	
14 Ⓐ Ⓑ Ⓒ Ⓓ Ⓔ	39 Ⓐ Ⓑ Ⓒ Ⓓ Ⓔ	
15 Ⓐ Ⓑ Ⓒ Ⓓ Ⓔ	40 Ⓐ Ⓑ Ⓒ Ⓓ Ⓔ	
16 Ⓐ Ⓑ Ⓒ Ⓓ Ⓔ	41 Ⓐ Ⓑ Ⓒ Ⓓ Ⓔ	
17 Ⓐ Ⓑ Ⓒ Ⓓ Ⓔ	42 Ⓐ Ⓑ Ⓒ Ⓓ Ⓔ	
18 Ⓐ Ⓑ Ⓒ Ⓓ Ⓔ	43 Ⓐ Ⓑ Ⓒ Ⓓ Ⓔ	
19 Ⓐ Ⓑ Ⓒ Ⓓ Ⓔ	44 Ⓐ Ⓑ Ⓒ Ⓓ Ⓔ	
20 Ⓐ Ⓑ Ⓒ Ⓓ Ⓔ	45 Ⓐ Ⓑ Ⓒ Ⓓ Ⓔ	
21 Ⓐ Ⓑ Ⓒ Ⓓ Ⓔ		
22 Ⓐ Ⓑ Ⓒ Ⓓ Ⓔ		
23 Ⓐ Ⓑ Ⓒ Ⓓ Ⓔ		
24 Ⓐ Ⓑ Ⓒ Ⓓ Ⓔ		
25 Ⓐ Ⓑ Ⓒ Ⓓ Ⓔ		

SECTION 6:
Mathematics Questions

1 Ⓐ Ⓑ Ⓒ Ⓓ Ⓔ
2 Ⓐ Ⓑ Ⓒ Ⓓ Ⓔ
3 Ⓐ Ⓑ Ⓒ Ⓓ Ⓔ
4 Ⓐ Ⓑ Ⓒ Ⓓ Ⓔ
5 Ⓐ Ⓑ Ⓒ Ⓓ Ⓔ
6 Ⓐ Ⓑ Ⓒ Ⓓ Ⓔ
7 Ⓐ Ⓑ Ⓒ Ⓓ Ⓔ
8 Ⓐ Ⓑ Ⓒ Ⓓ Ⓔ
9 Ⓐ Ⓑ Ⓒ Ⓓ Ⓔ
10 Ⓐ Ⓑ Ⓒ Ⓓ Ⓔ
11 Ⓐ Ⓑ Ⓒ Ⓓ Ⓔ
12 Ⓐ Ⓑ Ⓒ Ⓓ Ⓔ
13 Ⓐ Ⓑ Ⓒ Ⓓ Ⓔ
14 Ⓐ Ⓑ Ⓒ Ⓓ Ⓔ
15 Ⓐ Ⓑ Ⓒ Ⓓ Ⓔ
16 Ⓐ Ⓑ Ⓒ Ⓓ Ⓔ
17 Ⓐ Ⓑ Ⓒ Ⓓ Ⓔ
18 Ⓐ Ⓑ Ⓒ Ⓓ Ⓔ
19 Ⓐ Ⓑ Ⓒ Ⓓ Ⓔ
20 Ⓐ Ⓑ Ⓒ Ⓓ Ⓔ
21 Ⓐ Ⓑ Ⓒ Ⓓ Ⓔ
22 Ⓐ Ⓑ Ⓒ Ⓓ Ⓔ
23 Ⓐ Ⓑ Ⓒ Ⓓ Ⓔ
24 Ⓐ Ⓑ Ⓒ Ⓓ Ⓔ
25 Ⓐ Ⓑ Ⓒ Ⓓ Ⓔ

ANSWER SHEET FOR PRACTICE TEST 3

Note that 5 answer spaces are provided throughout this Answer Sheet. However, questions in some sections of the Practice Test will have only 4 possible answers (A or B or C or D).

SECTION 1:
Mathematics
Questions

1 Ⓐ Ⓑ Ⓒ Ⓓ Ⓔ
2 Ⓐ Ⓑ Ⓒ Ⓓ Ⓔ
3 Ⓐ Ⓑ Ⓒ Ⓓ Ⓔ
4 Ⓐ Ⓑ Ⓒ Ⓓ Ⓔ
5 Ⓐ Ⓑ Ⓒ Ⓓ Ⓔ
6 Ⓐ Ⓑ Ⓒ Ⓓ Ⓔ
7 Ⓐ Ⓑ Ⓒ Ⓓ Ⓔ
8 Ⓐ Ⓑ Ⓒ Ⓓ Ⓔ
9 Ⓐ Ⓑ Ⓒ Ⓓ Ⓔ
10 Ⓐ Ⓑ Ⓒ Ⓓ Ⓔ
11 Ⓐ Ⓑ Ⓒ Ⓓ Ⓔ
12 Ⓐ Ⓑ Ⓒ Ⓓ Ⓔ
13 Ⓐ Ⓑ Ⓒ Ⓓ Ⓔ
14 Ⓐ Ⓑ Ⓒ Ⓓ Ⓔ
15 Ⓐ Ⓑ Ⓒ Ⓓ Ⓔ
16 Ⓐ Ⓑ Ⓒ Ⓓ Ⓔ
17 Ⓐ Ⓑ Ⓒ Ⓓ Ⓔ
18 Ⓐ Ⓑ Ⓒ Ⓓ Ⓔ
19 Ⓐ Ⓑ Ⓒ Ⓓ Ⓔ
20 Ⓐ Ⓑ Ⓒ Ⓓ Ⓔ
21 Ⓐ Ⓑ Ⓒ Ⓓ Ⓔ
22 Ⓐ Ⓑ Ⓒ Ⓓ Ⓔ
23 Ⓐ Ⓑ Ⓒ Ⓓ Ⓔ
24 Ⓐ Ⓑ Ⓒ Ⓓ Ⓔ
25 Ⓐ Ⓑ Ⓒ Ⓓ Ⓔ

SECTION 2:
Verbal
Questions

1 Ⓐ Ⓑ Ⓒ Ⓓ Ⓔ
2 Ⓐ Ⓑ Ⓒ Ⓓ Ⓔ
3 Ⓐ Ⓑ Ⓒ Ⓓ Ⓔ
4 Ⓐ Ⓑ Ⓒ Ⓓ Ⓔ
5 Ⓐ Ⓑ Ⓒ Ⓓ Ⓔ
6 Ⓐ Ⓑ Ⓒ Ⓓ Ⓔ
7 Ⓐ Ⓑ Ⓒ Ⓓ Ⓔ
8 Ⓐ Ⓑ Ⓒ Ⓓ Ⓔ
9 Ⓐ Ⓑ Ⓒ Ⓓ Ⓔ
10 Ⓐ Ⓑ Ⓒ Ⓓ Ⓔ
11 Ⓐ Ⓑ Ⓒ Ⓓ Ⓔ
12 Ⓐ Ⓑ Ⓒ Ⓓ Ⓔ
13 Ⓐ Ⓑ Ⓒ Ⓓ Ⓔ
14 Ⓐ Ⓑ Ⓒ Ⓓ Ⓔ
15 Ⓐ Ⓑ Ⓒ Ⓓ Ⓔ
16 Ⓐ Ⓑ Ⓒ Ⓓ Ⓔ
17 Ⓐ Ⓑ Ⓒ Ⓓ Ⓔ
18 Ⓐ Ⓑ Ⓒ Ⓓ Ⓔ
19 Ⓐ Ⓑ Ⓒ Ⓓ Ⓔ
20 Ⓐ Ⓑ Ⓒ Ⓓ Ⓔ
21 Ⓐ Ⓑ Ⓒ Ⓓ Ⓔ
22 Ⓐ Ⓑ Ⓒ Ⓓ Ⓔ
23 Ⓐ Ⓑ Ⓒ Ⓓ Ⓔ
24 Ⓐ Ⓑ Ⓒ Ⓓ Ⓔ
25 Ⓐ Ⓑ Ⓒ Ⓓ Ⓔ

26 Ⓐ Ⓑ Ⓒ Ⓓ Ⓔ
27 Ⓐ Ⓑ Ⓒ Ⓓ Ⓔ
28 Ⓐ Ⓑ Ⓒ Ⓓ Ⓔ
29 Ⓐ Ⓑ Ⓒ Ⓓ Ⓔ
30 Ⓐ Ⓑ Ⓒ Ⓓ Ⓔ
31 Ⓐ Ⓑ Ⓒ Ⓓ Ⓔ
32 Ⓐ Ⓑ Ⓒ Ⓓ Ⓔ
33 Ⓐ Ⓑ Ⓒ Ⓓ Ⓔ
34 Ⓐ Ⓑ Ⓒ Ⓓ Ⓔ
35 Ⓐ Ⓑ Ⓒ Ⓓ Ⓔ
36 Ⓐ Ⓑ Ⓒ Ⓓ Ⓔ
37 Ⓐ Ⓑ Ⓒ Ⓓ Ⓔ
38 Ⓐ Ⓑ Ⓒ Ⓓ Ⓔ
39 Ⓐ Ⓑ Ⓒ Ⓓ Ⓔ
40 Ⓐ Ⓑ Ⓒ Ⓓ Ⓔ
41 Ⓐ Ⓑ Ⓒ Ⓓ Ⓔ
42 Ⓐ Ⓑ Ⓒ Ⓓ Ⓔ
43 Ⓐ Ⓑ Ⓒ Ⓓ Ⓔ
44 Ⓐ Ⓑ Ⓒ Ⓓ Ⓔ
45 Ⓐ Ⓑ Ⓒ Ⓓ Ⓔ

SECTION 3:
Mathematics
Questions

1 Ⓐ Ⓑ Ⓒ Ⓓ Ⓔ
2 Ⓐ Ⓑ Ⓒ Ⓓ Ⓔ
3 Ⓐ Ⓑ Ⓒ Ⓓ Ⓔ
4 Ⓐ Ⓑ Ⓒ Ⓓ Ⓔ
5 Ⓐ Ⓑ Ⓒ Ⓓ Ⓔ
6 Ⓐ Ⓑ Ⓒ Ⓓ Ⓔ
7 Ⓐ Ⓑ Ⓒ Ⓓ Ⓔ
8 Ⓐ Ⓑ Ⓒ Ⓓ Ⓔ
9 Ⓐ Ⓑ Ⓒ Ⓓ Ⓔ
10 Ⓐ Ⓑ Ⓒ Ⓓ Ⓔ
11 Ⓐ Ⓑ Ⓒ Ⓓ Ⓔ
12 Ⓐ Ⓑ Ⓒ Ⓓ Ⓔ
13 Ⓐ Ⓑ Ⓒ Ⓓ Ⓔ
14 Ⓐ Ⓑ Ⓒ Ⓓ Ⓔ
15 Ⓐ Ⓑ Ⓒ Ⓓ Ⓔ
16 Ⓐ Ⓑ Ⓒ Ⓓ Ⓔ
17 Ⓐ Ⓑ Ⓒ Ⓓ Ⓔ
18 Ⓐ Ⓑ Ⓒ Ⓓ Ⓔ
19 Ⓐ Ⓑ Ⓒ Ⓓ Ⓔ
20 Ⓐ Ⓑ Ⓒ Ⓓ Ⓔ
21 Ⓐ Ⓑ Ⓒ Ⓓ Ⓔ
22 Ⓐ Ⓑ Ⓒ Ⓓ Ⓔ
23 Ⓐ Ⓑ Ⓒ Ⓓ Ⓔ
24 Ⓐ Ⓑ Ⓒ Ⓓ Ⓔ
25 Ⓐ Ⓑ Ⓒ Ⓓ Ⓔ
26 Ⓐ Ⓑ Ⓒ Ⓓ Ⓔ
27 Ⓐ Ⓑ Ⓒ Ⓓ Ⓔ
28 Ⓐ Ⓑ Ⓒ Ⓓ Ⓔ
29 Ⓐ Ⓑ Ⓒ Ⓓ Ⓔ
30 Ⓐ Ⓑ Ⓒ Ⓓ Ⓔ

(continued)

SECTION 4:
Verbal
Questions

1 Ⓐ Ⓑ Ⓒ Ⓓ Ⓔ	31 Ⓐ Ⓑ Ⓒ Ⓓ Ⓔ
2 Ⓐ Ⓑ Ⓒ Ⓓ Ⓔ	32 Ⓐ Ⓑ Ⓒ Ⓓ Ⓔ
3 Ⓐ Ⓑ Ⓒ Ⓓ Ⓔ	33 Ⓐ Ⓑ Ⓒ Ⓓ Ⓔ
4 Ⓐ Ⓑ Ⓒ Ⓓ Ⓔ	34 Ⓐ Ⓑ Ⓒ Ⓓ Ⓔ
5 Ⓐ Ⓑ Ⓒ Ⓓ Ⓔ	35 Ⓐ Ⓑ Ⓒ Ⓓ Ⓔ
6 Ⓐ Ⓑ Ⓒ Ⓓ Ⓔ	36 Ⓐ Ⓑ Ⓒ Ⓓ Ⓔ
7 Ⓐ Ⓑ Ⓒ Ⓓ Ⓔ	37 Ⓐ Ⓑ Ⓒ Ⓓ Ⓔ
8 Ⓐ Ⓑ Ⓒ Ⓓ Ⓔ	38 Ⓐ Ⓑ Ⓒ Ⓓ Ⓔ
9 Ⓐ Ⓑ Ⓒ Ⓓ Ⓔ	39 Ⓐ Ⓑ Ⓒ Ⓓ Ⓔ
10 Ⓐ Ⓑ Ⓒ Ⓓ Ⓔ	40 Ⓐ Ⓑ Ⓒ Ⓓ Ⓔ
11 Ⓐ Ⓑ Ⓒ Ⓓ Ⓔ	
12 Ⓐ Ⓑ Ⓒ Ⓓ Ⓔ	
13 Ⓐ Ⓑ Ⓒ Ⓓ Ⓔ	
14 Ⓐ Ⓑ Ⓒ Ⓓ Ⓔ	
15 Ⓐ Ⓑ Ⓒ Ⓓ Ⓔ	
16 Ⓐ Ⓑ Ⓒ Ⓓ Ⓔ	
17 Ⓐ Ⓑ Ⓒ Ⓓ Ⓔ	
18 Ⓐ Ⓑ Ⓒ Ⓓ Ⓔ	
19 Ⓐ Ⓑ Ⓒ Ⓓ Ⓔ	
20 Ⓐ Ⓑ Ⓒ Ⓓ Ⓔ	
21 Ⓐ Ⓑ Ⓒ Ⓓ Ⓔ	
22 Ⓐ Ⓑ Ⓒ Ⓓ Ⓔ	
23 Ⓐ Ⓑ Ⓒ Ⓓ Ⓔ	
24 Ⓐ Ⓑ Ⓒ Ⓓ Ⓔ	
25 Ⓐ Ⓑ Ⓒ Ⓓ Ⓔ	
26 Ⓐ Ⓑ Ⓒ Ⓓ Ⓔ	
27 Ⓐ Ⓑ Ⓒ Ⓓ Ⓔ	
28 Ⓐ Ⓑ Ⓒ Ⓓ Ⓔ	
29 Ⓐ Ⓑ Ⓒ Ⓓ Ⓔ	
30 Ⓐ Ⓑ Ⓒ Ⓓ Ⓔ	

SECTION 5:
Mathematics
Questions

1 Ⓐ Ⓑ Ⓒ Ⓓ Ⓔ
2 Ⓐ Ⓑ Ⓒ Ⓓ Ⓔ
3 Ⓐ Ⓑ Ⓒ Ⓓ Ⓔ
4 Ⓐ Ⓑ Ⓒ Ⓓ Ⓔ
5 Ⓐ Ⓑ Ⓒ Ⓓ Ⓔ
6 Ⓐ Ⓑ Ⓒ Ⓓ Ⓔ
7 Ⓐ Ⓑ Ⓒ Ⓓ Ⓔ
8 Ⓐ Ⓑ Ⓒ Ⓓ Ⓔ
9 Ⓐ Ⓑ Ⓒ Ⓓ Ⓔ
10 Ⓐ Ⓑ Ⓒ Ⓓ Ⓔ
11 Ⓐ Ⓑ Ⓒ Ⓓ Ⓔ
12 Ⓐ Ⓑ Ⓒ Ⓓ Ⓔ
13 Ⓐ Ⓑ Ⓒ Ⓓ Ⓔ
14 Ⓐ Ⓑ Ⓒ Ⓓ Ⓔ
15 Ⓐ Ⓑ Ⓒ Ⓓ Ⓔ
16 Ⓐ Ⓑ Ⓒ Ⓓ Ⓔ
17 Ⓐ Ⓑ Ⓒ Ⓓ Ⓔ
18 Ⓐ Ⓑ Ⓒ Ⓓ Ⓔ
19 Ⓐ Ⓑ Ⓒ Ⓓ Ⓔ
20 Ⓐ Ⓑ Ⓒ Ⓓ Ⓔ
21 Ⓐ Ⓑ Ⓒ Ⓓ Ⓔ
22 Ⓐ Ⓑ Ⓒ Ⓓ Ⓔ
23 Ⓐ Ⓑ Ⓒ Ⓓ Ⓔ
24 Ⓐ Ⓑ Ⓒ Ⓓ Ⓔ
25 Ⓐ Ⓑ Ⓒ Ⓓ Ⓔ
26 Ⓐ Ⓑ Ⓒ Ⓓ Ⓔ
27 Ⓐ Ⓑ Ⓒ Ⓓ Ⓔ
28 Ⓐ Ⓑ Ⓒ Ⓓ Ⓔ
29 Ⓐ Ⓑ Ⓒ Ⓓ Ⓔ
30 Ⓐ Ⓑ Ⓒ Ⓓ Ⓔ
31 Ⓐ Ⓑ Ⓒ Ⓓ Ⓔ
32 Ⓐ Ⓑ Ⓒ Ⓓ Ⓔ
33 Ⓐ Ⓑ Ⓒ Ⓓ Ⓔ
34 Ⓐ Ⓑ Ⓒ Ⓓ Ⓔ
35 Ⓐ Ⓑ Ⓒ Ⓓ Ⓔ

ANSWER SHEET FOR PRACTICE TEST 4

Note that 5 answer spaces are provided throughout this Answer Sheet. However, questions in some sections of the Practice Test will have only 4 possible answers (A or B or C or D).

SECTION 1:
Verbal
Questions

1 Ⓐ Ⓑ Ⓒ Ⓓ Ⓔ	31 Ⓐ Ⓑ Ⓒ Ⓓ Ⓔ
2 Ⓐ Ⓑ Ⓒ Ⓓ Ⓔ	32 Ⓐ Ⓑ Ⓒ Ⓓ Ⓔ
3 Ⓐ Ⓑ Ⓒ Ⓓ Ⓔ	33 Ⓐ Ⓑ Ⓒ Ⓓ Ⓔ
4 Ⓐ Ⓑ Ⓒ Ⓓ Ⓔ	34 Ⓐ Ⓑ Ⓒ Ⓓ Ⓔ
5 Ⓐ Ⓑ Ⓒ Ⓓ Ⓔ	35 Ⓐ Ⓑ Ⓒ Ⓓ Ⓔ
6 Ⓐ Ⓑ Ⓒ Ⓓ Ⓔ	36 Ⓐ Ⓑ Ⓒ Ⓓ Ⓔ
7 Ⓐ Ⓑ Ⓒ Ⓓ Ⓔ	37 Ⓐ Ⓑ Ⓒ Ⓓ Ⓔ
8 Ⓐ Ⓑ Ⓒ Ⓓ Ⓔ	38 Ⓐ Ⓑ Ⓒ Ⓓ Ⓔ
9 Ⓐ Ⓑ Ⓒ Ⓓ Ⓔ	39 Ⓐ Ⓑ Ⓒ Ⓓ Ⓔ
10 Ⓐ Ⓑ Ⓒ Ⓓ Ⓔ	40 Ⓐ Ⓑ Ⓒ Ⓓ Ⓔ
11 Ⓐ Ⓑ Ⓒ Ⓓ Ⓔ	
12 Ⓐ Ⓑ Ⓒ Ⓓ Ⓔ	
13 Ⓐ Ⓑ Ⓒ Ⓓ Ⓔ	
14 Ⓐ Ⓑ Ⓒ Ⓓ Ⓔ	
15 Ⓐ Ⓑ Ⓒ Ⓓ Ⓔ	
16 Ⓐ Ⓑ Ⓒ Ⓓ Ⓔ	
17 Ⓐ Ⓑ Ⓒ Ⓓ Ⓔ	
18 Ⓐ Ⓑ Ⓒ Ⓓ Ⓔ	
19 Ⓐ Ⓑ Ⓒ Ⓓ Ⓔ	
20 Ⓐ Ⓑ Ⓒ Ⓓ Ⓔ	
21 Ⓐ Ⓑ Ⓒ Ⓓ Ⓔ	
22 Ⓐ Ⓑ Ⓒ Ⓓ Ⓔ	
23 Ⓐ Ⓑ Ⓒ Ⓓ Ⓔ	
24 Ⓐ Ⓑ Ⓒ Ⓓ Ⓔ	
25 Ⓐ Ⓑ Ⓒ Ⓓ Ⓔ	
26 Ⓐ Ⓑ Ⓒ Ⓓ Ⓔ	
27 Ⓐ Ⓑ Ⓒ Ⓓ Ⓔ	
28 Ⓐ Ⓑ Ⓒ Ⓓ Ⓔ	
29 Ⓐ Ⓑ Ⓒ Ⓓ Ⓔ	
30 Ⓐ Ⓑ Ⓒ Ⓓ Ⓔ	

SECTION 2:
Mathematics
Questions

1 Ⓐ Ⓑ Ⓒ Ⓓ Ⓔ
2 Ⓐ Ⓑ Ⓒ Ⓓ Ⓔ
3 Ⓐ Ⓑ Ⓒ Ⓓ Ⓔ
4 Ⓐ Ⓑ Ⓒ Ⓓ Ⓔ
5 Ⓐ Ⓑ Ⓒ Ⓓ Ⓔ
6 Ⓐ Ⓑ Ⓒ Ⓓ Ⓔ
7 Ⓐ Ⓑ Ⓒ Ⓓ Ⓔ
8 Ⓐ Ⓑ Ⓒ Ⓓ Ⓔ
9 Ⓐ Ⓑ Ⓒ Ⓓ Ⓔ
10 Ⓐ Ⓑ Ⓒ Ⓓ Ⓔ
11 Ⓐ Ⓑ Ⓒ Ⓓ Ⓔ
12 Ⓐ Ⓑ Ⓒ Ⓓ Ⓔ
13 Ⓐ Ⓑ Ⓒ Ⓓ Ⓔ
14 Ⓐ Ⓑ Ⓒ Ⓓ Ⓔ
15 Ⓐ Ⓑ Ⓒ Ⓓ Ⓔ
16 Ⓐ Ⓑ Ⓒ Ⓓ Ⓔ
17 Ⓐ Ⓑ Ⓒ Ⓓ Ⓔ
18 Ⓐ Ⓑ Ⓒ Ⓓ Ⓔ
19 Ⓐ Ⓑ Ⓒ Ⓓ Ⓔ
20 Ⓐ Ⓑ Ⓒ Ⓓ Ⓔ
21 Ⓐ Ⓑ Ⓒ Ⓓ Ⓔ
22 Ⓐ Ⓑ Ⓒ Ⓓ Ⓔ
23 Ⓐ Ⓑ Ⓒ Ⓓ Ⓔ
24 Ⓐ Ⓑ Ⓒ Ⓓ Ⓔ
25 Ⓐ Ⓑ Ⓒ Ⓓ Ⓔ

SECTION 3:
Verbal
Questions

1 Ⓐ Ⓑ Ⓒ Ⓓ Ⓔ	31 Ⓐ Ⓑ Ⓒ Ⓓ Ⓔ
2 Ⓐ Ⓑ Ⓒ Ⓓ Ⓔ	32 Ⓐ Ⓑ Ⓒ Ⓓ Ⓔ
3 Ⓐ Ⓑ Ⓒ Ⓓ Ⓔ	33 Ⓐ Ⓑ Ⓒ Ⓓ Ⓔ
4 Ⓐ Ⓑ Ⓒ Ⓓ Ⓔ	34 Ⓐ Ⓑ Ⓒ Ⓓ Ⓔ
5 Ⓐ Ⓑ Ⓒ Ⓓ Ⓔ	35 Ⓐ Ⓑ Ⓒ Ⓓ Ⓔ
6 Ⓐ Ⓑ Ⓒ Ⓓ Ⓔ	36 Ⓐ Ⓑ Ⓒ Ⓓ Ⓔ
7 Ⓐ Ⓑ Ⓒ Ⓓ Ⓔ	37 Ⓐ Ⓑ Ⓒ Ⓓ Ⓔ
8 Ⓐ Ⓑ Ⓒ Ⓓ Ⓔ	38 Ⓐ Ⓑ Ⓒ Ⓓ Ⓔ
9 Ⓐ Ⓑ Ⓒ Ⓓ Ⓔ	39 Ⓐ Ⓑ Ⓒ Ⓓ Ⓔ
10 Ⓐ Ⓑ Ⓒ Ⓓ Ⓔ	40 Ⓐ Ⓑ Ⓒ Ⓓ Ⓔ
11 Ⓐ Ⓑ Ⓒ Ⓓ Ⓔ	
12 Ⓐ Ⓑ Ⓒ Ⓓ Ⓔ	
13 Ⓐ Ⓑ Ⓒ Ⓓ Ⓔ	
14 Ⓐ Ⓑ Ⓒ Ⓓ Ⓔ	
15 Ⓐ Ⓑ Ⓒ Ⓓ Ⓔ	
16 Ⓐ Ⓑ Ⓒ Ⓓ Ⓔ	
17 Ⓐ Ⓑ Ⓒ Ⓓ Ⓔ	
18 Ⓐ Ⓑ Ⓒ Ⓓ Ⓔ	
19 Ⓐ Ⓑ Ⓒ Ⓓ Ⓔ	
20 Ⓐ Ⓑ Ⓒ Ⓓ Ⓔ	
21 Ⓐ Ⓑ Ⓒ Ⓓ Ⓔ	
22 Ⓐ Ⓑ Ⓒ Ⓓ Ⓔ	
23 Ⓐ Ⓑ Ⓒ Ⓓ Ⓔ	
24 Ⓐ Ⓑ Ⓒ Ⓓ Ⓔ	
25 Ⓐ Ⓑ Ⓒ Ⓓ Ⓔ	
26 Ⓐ Ⓑ Ⓒ Ⓓ Ⓔ	
27 Ⓐ Ⓑ Ⓒ Ⓓ Ⓔ	
28 Ⓐ Ⓑ Ⓒ Ⓓ Ⓔ	
29 Ⓐ Ⓑ Ⓒ Ⓓ Ⓔ	
30 Ⓐ Ⓑ Ⓒ Ⓓ Ⓔ	

(continued)

SECTION 5:
Mathematics
Questions

1 Ⓐ Ⓑ Ⓒ Ⓓ Ⓔ
2 Ⓐ Ⓑ Ⓒ Ⓓ Ⓔ
3 Ⓐ Ⓑ Ⓒ Ⓓ Ⓔ
4 Ⓐ Ⓑ Ⓒ Ⓓ Ⓔ
5 Ⓐ Ⓑ Ⓒ Ⓓ Ⓔ
6 Ⓐ Ⓑ Ⓒ Ⓓ Ⓔ
7 Ⓐ Ⓑ Ⓒ Ⓓ Ⓔ
8 Ⓐ Ⓑ Ⓒ Ⓓ Ⓔ
9 Ⓐ Ⓑ Ⓒ Ⓓ Ⓔ
10 Ⓐ Ⓑ Ⓒ Ⓓ Ⓔ
11 Ⓐ Ⓑ Ⓒ Ⓓ Ⓔ
12 Ⓐ Ⓑ Ⓒ Ⓓ Ⓔ
13 Ⓐ Ⓑ Ⓒ Ⓓ Ⓔ
14 Ⓐ Ⓑ Ⓒ Ⓓ Ⓔ
15 Ⓐ Ⓑ Ⓒ Ⓓ Ⓔ
16 Ⓐ Ⓑ Ⓒ Ⓓ Ⓔ
17 Ⓐ Ⓑ Ⓒ Ⓓ Ⓔ
18 Ⓐ Ⓑ Ⓒ Ⓓ Ⓔ
19 Ⓐ Ⓑ Ⓒ Ⓓ Ⓔ
20 Ⓐ Ⓑ Ⓒ Ⓓ Ⓔ
21 Ⓐ Ⓑ Ⓒ Ⓓ Ⓔ
22 Ⓐ Ⓑ Ⓒ Ⓓ Ⓔ
23 Ⓐ Ⓑ Ⓒ Ⓓ Ⓔ
24 Ⓐ Ⓑ Ⓒ Ⓓ Ⓔ
25 Ⓐ Ⓑ Ⓒ Ⓓ Ⓔ
26 Ⓐ Ⓑ Ⓒ Ⓓ Ⓔ
27 Ⓐ Ⓑ Ⓒ Ⓓ Ⓔ
28 Ⓐ Ⓑ Ⓒ Ⓓ Ⓔ
29 Ⓐ Ⓑ Ⓒ Ⓓ Ⓔ
30 Ⓐ Ⓑ Ⓒ Ⓓ Ⓔ
31 Ⓐ Ⓑ Ⓒ Ⓓ Ⓔ
32 Ⓐ Ⓑ Ⓒ Ⓓ Ⓔ
33 Ⓐ Ⓑ Ⓒ Ⓓ Ⓔ
34 Ⓐ Ⓑ Ⓒ Ⓓ Ⓔ
35 Ⓐ Ⓑ Ⓒ Ⓓ Ⓔ

SECTION 6:
Verbal
Questions

1 Ⓐ Ⓑ Ⓒ Ⓓ Ⓔ
2 Ⓐ Ⓑ Ⓒ Ⓓ Ⓔ
3 Ⓐ Ⓑ Ⓒ Ⓓ Ⓔ
4 Ⓐ Ⓑ Ⓒ Ⓓ Ⓔ
5 Ⓐ Ⓑ Ⓒ Ⓓ Ⓔ
6 Ⓐ Ⓑ Ⓒ Ⓓ Ⓔ
7 Ⓐ Ⓑ Ⓒ Ⓓ Ⓔ
8 Ⓐ Ⓑ Ⓒ Ⓓ Ⓔ
9 Ⓐ Ⓑ Ⓒ Ⓓ Ⓔ
10 Ⓐ Ⓑ Ⓒ Ⓓ Ⓔ
11 Ⓐ Ⓑ Ⓒ Ⓓ Ⓔ
12 Ⓐ Ⓑ Ⓒ Ⓓ Ⓔ
13 Ⓐ Ⓑ Ⓒ Ⓓ Ⓔ
14 Ⓐ Ⓑ Ⓒ Ⓓ Ⓔ
15 Ⓐ Ⓑ Ⓒ Ⓓ Ⓔ
16 Ⓐ Ⓑ Ⓒ Ⓓ Ⓔ
17 Ⓐ Ⓑ Ⓒ Ⓓ Ⓔ
18 Ⓐ Ⓑ Ⓒ Ⓓ Ⓔ
19 Ⓐ Ⓑ Ⓒ Ⓓ Ⓔ
20 Ⓐ Ⓑ Ⓒ Ⓓ Ⓔ
21 Ⓐ Ⓑ Ⓒ Ⓓ Ⓔ
22 Ⓐ Ⓑ Ⓒ Ⓓ Ⓔ
23 Ⓐ Ⓑ Ⓒ Ⓓ Ⓔ
24 Ⓐ Ⓑ Ⓒ Ⓓ Ⓔ
25 Ⓐ Ⓑ Ⓒ Ⓓ Ⓔ
26 Ⓐ Ⓑ Ⓒ Ⓓ Ⓔ
27 Ⓐ Ⓑ Ⓒ Ⓓ Ⓔ
28 Ⓐ Ⓑ Ⓒ Ⓓ Ⓔ
29 Ⓐ Ⓑ Ⓒ Ⓓ Ⓔ
30 Ⓐ Ⓑ Ⓒ Ⓓ Ⓔ

31 Ⓐ Ⓑ Ⓒ Ⓓ Ⓔ
32 Ⓐ Ⓑ Ⓒ Ⓓ Ⓔ
33 Ⓐ Ⓑ Ⓒ Ⓓ Ⓔ
34 Ⓐ Ⓑ Ⓒ Ⓓ Ⓔ
35 Ⓐ Ⓑ Ⓒ Ⓓ Ⓔ
36 Ⓐ Ⓑ Ⓒ Ⓓ Ⓔ
37 Ⓐ Ⓑ Ⓒ Ⓓ Ⓔ
38 Ⓐ Ⓑ Ⓒ Ⓓ Ⓔ
39 Ⓐ Ⓑ Ⓒ Ⓓ Ⓔ
40 Ⓐ Ⓑ Ⓒ Ⓓ Ⓔ
41 Ⓐ Ⓑ Ⓒ Ⓓ Ⓔ
42 Ⓐ Ⓑ Ⓒ Ⓓ Ⓔ
43 Ⓐ Ⓑ Ⓒ Ⓓ Ⓔ
44 Ⓐ Ⓑ Ⓒ Ⓓ Ⓔ
45 Ⓐ Ⓑ Ⓒ Ⓓ Ⓔ

QUANTITATIVE COMPARISON

1 Ⓐ Ⓑ Ⓒ Ⓓ Ⓔ	21 Ⓐ Ⓑ Ⓒ Ⓓ Ⓔ	41 Ⓐ Ⓑ Ⓒ Ⓓ Ⓔ	61 Ⓐ Ⓑ Ⓒ Ⓓ Ⓔ
2 Ⓐ Ⓑ Ⓒ Ⓓ Ⓔ	22 Ⓐ Ⓑ Ⓒ Ⓓ Ⓔ	42 Ⓐ Ⓑ Ⓒ Ⓓ Ⓔ	62 Ⓐ Ⓑ Ⓒ Ⓓ Ⓔ
3 Ⓐ Ⓑ Ⓒ Ⓓ Ⓔ	23 Ⓐ Ⓑ Ⓒ Ⓓ Ⓔ	43 Ⓐ Ⓑ Ⓒ Ⓓ Ⓔ	63 Ⓐ Ⓑ Ⓒ Ⓓ Ⓔ
4 Ⓐ Ⓑ Ⓒ Ⓓ Ⓔ	24 Ⓐ Ⓑ Ⓒ Ⓓ Ⓔ	44 Ⓐ Ⓑ Ⓒ Ⓓ Ⓔ	64 Ⓐ Ⓑ Ⓒ Ⓓ Ⓔ
5 Ⓐ Ⓑ Ⓒ Ⓓ Ⓔ	25 Ⓐ Ⓑ Ⓒ Ⓓ Ⓔ	45 Ⓐ Ⓑ Ⓒ Ⓓ Ⓔ	65 Ⓐ Ⓑ Ⓒ Ⓓ Ⓔ
6 Ⓐ Ⓑ Ⓒ Ⓓ Ⓔ	26 Ⓐ Ⓑ Ⓒ Ⓓ Ⓔ	46 Ⓐ Ⓑ Ⓒ Ⓓ Ⓔ	66 Ⓐ Ⓑ Ⓒ Ⓓ Ⓔ
7 Ⓐ Ⓑ Ⓒ Ⓓ Ⓔ	27 Ⓐ Ⓑ Ⓒ Ⓓ Ⓔ	47 Ⓐ Ⓑ Ⓒ Ⓓ Ⓔ	67 Ⓐ Ⓑ Ⓒ Ⓓ Ⓔ
8 Ⓐ Ⓑ Ⓒ Ⓓ Ⓔ	28 Ⓐ Ⓑ Ⓒ Ⓓ Ⓔ	48 Ⓐ Ⓑ Ⓒ Ⓓ Ⓔ	68 Ⓐ Ⓑ Ⓒ Ⓓ Ⓔ
9 Ⓐ Ⓑ Ⓒ Ⓓ Ⓔ	29 Ⓐ Ⓑ Ⓒ Ⓓ Ⓔ	49 Ⓐ Ⓑ Ⓒ Ⓓ Ⓔ	69 Ⓐ Ⓑ Ⓒ Ⓓ Ⓔ
10 Ⓐ Ⓑ Ⓒ Ⓓ Ⓔ	30 Ⓐ Ⓑ Ⓒ Ⓓ Ⓔ	50 Ⓐ Ⓑ Ⓒ Ⓓ Ⓔ	70 Ⓐ Ⓑ Ⓒ Ⓓ Ⓔ
11 Ⓐ Ⓑ Ⓒ Ⓓ Ⓔ	31 Ⓐ Ⓑ Ⓒ Ⓓ Ⓔ	51 Ⓐ Ⓑ Ⓒ Ⓓ Ⓔ	71 Ⓐ Ⓑ Ⓒ Ⓓ Ⓔ
12 Ⓐ Ⓑ Ⓒ Ⓓ Ⓔ	32 Ⓐ Ⓑ Ⓒ Ⓓ Ⓔ	52 Ⓐ Ⓑ Ⓒ Ⓓ Ⓔ	72 Ⓐ Ⓑ Ⓒ Ⓓ Ⓔ
13 Ⓐ Ⓑ Ⓒ Ⓓ Ⓔ	33 Ⓐ Ⓑ Ⓒ Ⓓ Ⓔ	53 Ⓐ Ⓑ Ⓒ Ⓓ Ⓔ	73 Ⓐ Ⓑ Ⓒ Ⓓ Ⓔ
14 Ⓐ Ⓑ Ⓒ Ⓓ Ⓔ	34 Ⓐ Ⓑ Ⓒ Ⓓ Ⓔ	54 Ⓐ Ⓑ Ⓒ Ⓓ Ⓔ	74 Ⓐ Ⓑ Ⓒ Ⓓ Ⓔ
15 Ⓐ Ⓑ Ⓒ Ⓓ Ⓔ	35 Ⓐ Ⓑ Ⓒ Ⓓ Ⓔ	55 Ⓐ Ⓑ Ⓒ Ⓓ Ⓔ	75 Ⓐ Ⓑ Ⓒ Ⓓ Ⓔ
16 Ⓐ Ⓑ Ⓒ Ⓓ Ⓔ	36 Ⓐ Ⓑ Ⓒ Ⓓ Ⓔ	56 Ⓐ Ⓑ Ⓒ Ⓓ Ⓔ	76 Ⓐ Ⓑ Ⓒ Ⓓ Ⓔ
17 Ⓐ Ⓑ Ⓒ Ⓓ Ⓔ	37 Ⓐ Ⓑ Ⓒ Ⓓ Ⓔ	57 Ⓐ Ⓑ Ⓒ Ⓓ Ⓔ	77 Ⓐ Ⓑ Ⓒ Ⓓ Ⓔ
18 Ⓐ Ⓑ Ⓒ Ⓓ Ⓔ	38 Ⓐ Ⓑ Ⓒ Ⓓ Ⓔ	58 Ⓐ Ⓑ Ⓒ Ⓓ Ⓔ	78 Ⓐ Ⓑ Ⓒ Ⓓ Ⓔ
19 Ⓐ Ⓑ Ⓒ Ⓓ Ⓔ	39 Ⓐ Ⓑ Ⓒ Ⓓ Ⓔ	59 Ⓐ Ⓑ Ⓒ Ⓓ Ⓔ	79 Ⓐ Ⓑ Ⓒ Ⓓ Ⓔ
20 Ⓐ Ⓑ Ⓒ Ⓓ Ⓔ	40 Ⓐ Ⓑ Ⓒ Ⓓ Ⓔ	60 Ⓐ Ⓑ Ⓒ Ⓓ Ⓔ	80 Ⓐ Ⓑ Ⓒ Ⓓ Ⓔ